THE GREEN GUIDE
Canada

Dog sledding, Charlevoix, Quebec © Patrice Halley/Quebec Tourism

MICHELIN

THEGREENGUIDE **CANADA**

Editorial Director	Cynthia Clayton Ochterbeck
Editor	Sophie Friedman
Principal Writer	Gregory B. Gallagher
Production Manager	Natasha George
Cartography	Peter Wrenn
Photo Editor	Yoshimi Kanazawa
Interior Design	Chris Bell
Layout	Natasha George
Cover Design	Chris Bell, Christelle Le Déan

Contact Us	Michelin Travel and Lifestyle North America
	One Parkway South
	Greenville, SC 29615
	USA
	travel.lifestyle@us.michelin.com
	Michelin Travel Partner
	Hannay House
	39 Clarendon Road
	Watford, Herts WD17 1JA
	UK
	✆01923 205240
	travelpubsales@uk.michelin.com
	www.ViaMichelin.com
Special Sales	For information regarding bulk sales, customized editions and premium sales, please contact us at: travel.lifestyle@us.michelin.com

HOW TO USE THIS GUIDE

PLANNING YOUR TRIP

The blue-tabbed PLANNING YOUR TRIP section at the front of the guide gives you **ideas for your trip** and **practical information** to help you organize it. You'll find tours, practical information, a host of outdoor activities, a calendar of events, information on shopping, sightseeing, kids' activities and more.

INTRODUCTION

The orange-tabbed INTRODUCTION section explores Canada's **Nature** and geology. The **History** section travels from Prehistory through colonialism up to today. The **Art and Culture** section covers architecture, art, literature and music, while the **Country Today** delves into modern Canadian life.

DISCOVERING

The green-tabbed DISCOVERING section features Principal Sights by region, featuring the most interesting local **Sights**, **Walking Tours**, nearby **Excursions**, and detailed **Driving Tours**. Admission prices shown are normally for a single adult.

ADDRESSES

We've selected the best hotels, restaurants, cafes shops, nightlife and entertainment to fit all budgets. See the Legend on the cover flap for an explanation of the price categories. See the back of the guide for an index of hotels and restaurants.

Sidebars

Throughout the guide you will find blue, peach and green-colored text boxes with lively anecdotes, detailed history and background information.

🙂 A Bit of Advice 🙂

Green advice boxes found in this guide contain practical tips and handy information relevant to your visit or to a sight in the Discovering section.

STAR RATINGS★★★

Michelin has given star ratings for more than 100 years. If you're pressed for time, we recommend you visit the ★★★, or ★★ sights first:

★★★	**Highly recommended**
★★	**Recommended**
★	**Interesting**

MAPS

🙂 National Driving Tours map, Places to Stay map and Sights map.
🙂 Region maps.
🙂 Maps for major cities and villages.
🙂 Local tour maps.

All maps in this guide are oriented north, unless otherwise indicated by a directional arrow. The term "Local Map" refers to a map within the chapter or Tourism Region. A complete list of the maps found in the guide appears at the back of this book.

© All Canada photo/hemis.fr

INTRODUCTION TO CANADA

PLANNING YOUR TRIP

DISCOVERING CANADA

CONTENTS

Welcome to Canada

Welcome to the second largest country on the planet, and one of the youngest at only 150 years as a nation (2017). A captivating land of salty-aired seaports, dusty cattle towns, snow-bitten mountain peaks, hip urban centres, and isolated coastal ports. It's a spacious terrain of giant glaciers, frozen tundra, mighty rivers, vast forests, productive fields and close-knit communities stretching from the Pacific Ocean east to the Atlantic and from the US border to the Arctic Ocean, Baffin Island and the North Pole.

BRITISH COLOMBIA, ROCKIES, YUKON *(pp70–165)*

Edging the Pacific Ocean, British Columbia is the westernmost of Canada's provinces. The Coast Mountains parallel its western portion; the snow-capped Rocky Mountains, with their National Parks and grand railway hotels, monopolize the eastern boundary. Vancouver Island, off the southwestern extremity, holds the provincial capital of Victoria, famed for its Butchart Gardens. North of the island, Haida Gwaii (formerly the Queen Charlotte Islands) are a reserve of Haida First Nations Peoples. In the southwest corner of the mainland, Vancouver is one of the country's largest cities, offering cultural and recreational amenities in abundance. In the interior, the Cariboo Region embodies Western living, with stockyards, dude ranches and rodeos, plus remote coastal inlets, dry grasslands, and a rainforest. The Okanagan Valley is known for its wineries and fruit orchards. The Fraser and Thompson canyons boast lengthy rivers and the Hat Creek Ranch. North of British Columbia, the Yukon Territory is a sparsely populated frontier of dramatic scenery dominated by the mighty Yukon River.

PRAIRIE PROVINCES *(pp166–213)*

A vast, flat landscape of endless prairie farmland and infinite blue sky, the provinces of Alberta, Saskatchewan and Manitoba are Canada's heartland and breadbasket to the world. Their varied topography is seen

False Creek and Yaletown from Granville Island, Vancouver, BC

© Pietro Canali/Sime/Photononstop

in the sculpted buttes of Alberta's badlands—home to dinosaur fossils and the Royal Tyrrell Museum—and the 10,000ft-plus peaks of the Rocky Mountains to the rolling Cypress Hills of southern Saskatchewan and the snow-covered tundra of Manitoba's Churchill. Major cities are the Westernized Calgary, famed for its Stampede, Alberta's capital of Edmonton with the world's largest shopping mall, Manitoba's Winnipeg, a capital with surprising options, and Regina, Saskatchewan's high quality of life capital, surging with growth.

ONTARIO *(pp214–299)*

Canada's most populous province is a land of lakes and rivers. Its southern city of Toronto rose on the north shore of Lake Ontario to become the nation's largest metropolis, and a financial and cultural hub. Toronto's CN Tower, Royal Ontario Museum, Toronto Zoo and Science Centre should not be missed. Another must-see, the world-famous Niagara Falls form midway in the Niagara River's course from

Lake Erie to Lake Ontario. Sitting on the Ottawa River, Ontario's seat of national government is home to fine museums and the superb National Art Gallery. Ottawa also attracts visitors to its Parliament buildings and historic Rideau Canal, a boaters' haven in summer and winter wonderland for skaters. Just east, Upper Canada Village, a living museum with 500 buildings, preserves Ontario's rural life of the 1860s.

QUEBEC (pp300–355)

This large province encompasses the treeless tundra of the forbidding north, the Laurentian Mountain Range, and forests to the south that cover much of its land. North America's bastion of French-Canadian culture, the province retains remnants of France's 17C continental empire, best seen in Quebec City's quaint Upper Town and Lower Town. In contrast, Montreal is a modern city, known for its international jazz festival, gastronomy, and boutiques; the Olympic Park, cobblestone streets of Old Montreal, and legacy of nightlife are also highlights. Be sure to also see the Charlevoix Coast, the Saguenay Fjord, and Gatineau's Canadian Museum of History.

ATLANTIC PROVINCES
(pp356–437)

The Maritime Provinces of New Brunswick, Nova Scotia and Prince Edward Island occupy the Atlantic Ocean side of Canada. Their northeast neighbour, Newfoundland and Labrador, lies in the country's eastern extreme. These seacoast provinces evidence their Scottish-English heritage in the major cities of Halifax, St. John's, Saint John and Charlottetown. Newfoundland's L'Anse aux Meadows traces the presence of Vikings, and Nova Scotia's Fortress of Louisbourg captures the French-English stuggle for the

New World. Caraquet and Chéticamp are colourful Acadian villages.

NORTHWEST TERRITORIES
(pp438–451)

This immense northwestern outpost, sparsely settled except for its capital of Yellowknife, has two UNESCO World Heritage Sites: Wood Buffalo and Nahanni. National Park Reserve. Its spectacular terrain and indigenous cultures are major attractions as well.

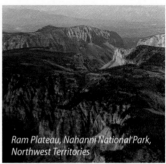

Ram Plateau, Nahanni National Park, Northwest Territories

© Robert Postma/Design Pics/Photononstop

NUNAVUT (pp452–465)

Canada's rooftop territory, stretching north from Manitoba's border, takes up a fifth of the country's landmass. This land of ice and snow is the ancestral home of the Inuit, whose carvings and crafts are magnets for collectors. Though tourism facilities are evolving, Nunavut's national parks, heritage rivers, Arctic ranges, native communities, and wildlife (caribou, whales, musk ox, walrus, and polar bears) attract adventure travellers.

Cape Bonavista coastline, Newfoundland

© Barrett & MacKay/age fotostock

Killer whales off Northern Vancouver Island, BC

Michelin Driving Tours

Driving allows travellers to appreciate the vastness of this country, where distances between cities and towns can be great. The varied topography of the land is experienced from the perspective of the road.

The following fast-paced tours, two- to three-weeks in duration, are intended as planning tools, not as fixed routes, taking in much of each province.

1 BRITISH COLUMBIA AND THE ROCKIES

Round-trip of 3,309km/2,056mi (not including ferries) from Vancouver. Time: 18 days. This tour combines the beauty of British Columbia's coast with its mountainous interior culminating in the Rockies. The cities of Vancouver

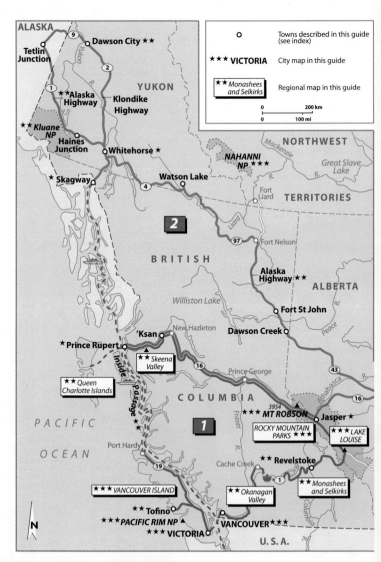

o	Towns described in this guide (see index)
★★★ VICTORIA	City map in this guide
★★ Monashees and Selkirks	Regional map in this guide

0   200 km
0   100 mi

and Victoria are highlights as is the Skeena Valley with its native villages.

DAYS/ ITINERARY/ SIGHTS

1–3 **Vancouver**★★★
4 **Vancouver – Cache Creek** (335km/208mi); Fraser Canyon★★ via Hope and Lytton
5 **Cache Creek – Revelstoke** (286km/178mi); Thompson Canyon★ via Shuswap Lake, Monashees and Selkirks★★, Eagle Pass★, Revelstoke★★
6 **Revelstoke – Lake Louise** (228km/142mi); Rogers Pass★★, Rocky Mountain Parks★★★, Emerald Lake★★★, Yoho Valley★★, Kicking Horse Pass
7 **Lake Louise excursions** (81km/50mi); Lake Louise★★★, Mt. Whitehorn★, Moraine Lake★★★
8 **Lake Louise – Jasper** (233km/145mi); Rocky Mountain Parks★★★, Icefields Parkway★★★
9 **Jasper excursions** (167km/104mi); Jasper National Park★★★, Mt. Edith Cavell★★, Maligne Valley★★★
10 **Jasper – Prince George** (376km/234mi); Yellowhead Highway★★, Mt. Robson Provincial Park★★, Mt. Robson★★★
11 **Prince George – New Hazelton** (446km/277mi); 'Ksan
12 **New Hazelton – Prince Rupert**★ (295km/183mi, *described in opposite direction*); Skeena Valley★★

13 **Prince Rupert – Port Hardy** by ferry; Inside Passage★★
14 **Port Hardy – Tofino** (from 542km/337mi); Vancouver Island★★★, Parksville to Pacific Coast
15 **Tofino – Victoria** (320km/198mi); Pacific Rim National Park Reserve★★★
16–17 **Victoria**★★★
18 **Victoria – Vancouver** by ferry; Butchart Gardens★★★

2 NORTHERN BRITISH COLUMBIA AND THE YUKON

Round-trip of 5,185km/ 3,222mi (not including ferry) from Edmonton. Time: 17 days. This tour combines the wild beauty of the Yukon with the adventure of driving the Alaska Highway, and the misty and romantic Inside Passage cruise down the West Coast.

DAYS/ ITINERARY/ SIGHTS

1–2 **Edmonton** ★★
3 **Edmonton – Fort St. John** (665km/413mi); Alaska Highway★★
4 **Fort St. John – Fort Nelson** (416km/258mi); Alaska Highway★★
5 **Fort Nelson – Watson Lake** (546km/339mi); Alaska Highway★★

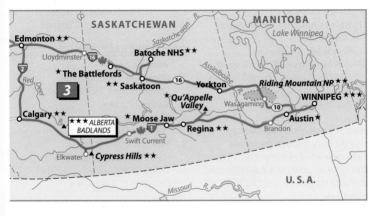

Distances between major cities

Seattle to **Vancouver**
270 km/168 mi

Vancouver to **Calgary**
953 km/591 mi

Calgary to **Edmonton**
304 km/188 mi

Calgary to **Regina**
744 km/461 mi

Saskatoon to **Regina**
251 km/156 mi

Regina to **Winnipeg**
573 km/355 mi

Winnipeg to **Sault Ste. Marie**
1395 km/865 mi

Sault Ste. Marie to **Toronto**
715 km/443 mi

Toronto to **Ottawa**
398 km/247 mi

Toronto to **Detroit**
378 km/234 mi

Ottawa to **Montreal**
185 km/115 mi

Montreal to **Quebec**
262 km/162 mi

Montreal to **New York**
631 km/391 mi

Quebec to **Fredericton**
521 km/323 mi

Fredericton to **Halifax**
480 km/298 mi

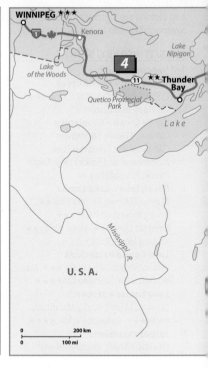

6   **Watson Lake – Whitehorse**
(455km/283mi);
Alaska Highway★★
7   **Whitehorse★**
8   **Whitehorse – Dawson City**
(540km/336mi); Yukon Circuit★★,
Klondike Highway
9   **Dawson City★★**
10 **Dawson City – Haines Junction**
(744km/462mi); Yukon Circuit★★,
Top of the World Highway★★,
Alaska Highway★★,
Kluane Lake★★
11 **Haines Junction – Whitehorse**
(161km/100mi);
Kluane National Park★★
12–13 **Whitehorse – Prince Rupert**
(180km/112mi and ferry); Klondike
Highway to Skagway★, Inside
Passage★★ (US)

From Prince Rupert, travellers can
take the ferry through the **Inside
Passage★★** to Bellingham, arriving
Day 15, or an optional 3-day excursion
to **Haida Gawaii** (Queen Charlotte
Islands)★★.

14–16 **Prince Rupert – Jasper**
(☕ see Days 12, 11, 10 of Tour 1)
17 **Jasper – Edmonton**
(361km/224mi)

③ THE PRAIRIES

Round-trip of 3,371km/2,095mi from
Winnipeg. Time: 17 days. This tour
enables visitors to discover some of
the fascination of the Prairies—grand
vistas, wheat fields, ranches and
cowboys. The oil-rich Alberta cities of
Calgary and Edmonton are visited as
well as the central city of Winnipeg.

DAYS/ ITINERARY/ SIGHTS

1–2 **Winnipeg★★★**
3   **Winnipeg – Wasagaming**
(265km/165mi); Riding Mountain
National Park★★
4   **Wasagaming – Yorkton**
(230km/143mi); Yorkton
5   **Yorkton – Saskatoon**
(331km/205mi); Saskatoon★
6   176km/109mi;
Excursion to Batoche★★

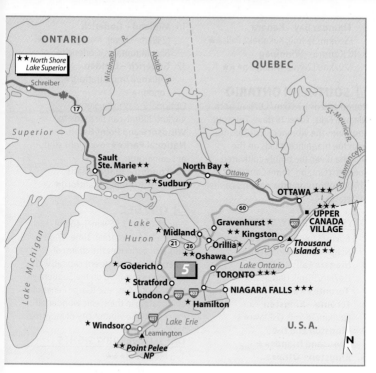

ONTARIO

QUEBEC

★★ *North Shore Lake Superior*

Schreiber

Superior

Sault Ste. Marie ★★

North Bay ★

★★ Sudbury

OTTAWA ★★★

★★★ UPPER CANADA VILLAGE

Lake Huron

Gravenhurst ★

★★ Kingston

Midland

Orillia ★

Thousand Islands ★★

★★ Oshawa

Lake Ontario

Goderich

TORONTO ★★★

Stratford

★ London

NIAGARA FALLS ★★★

Hamilton

Lake Michigan

Lake Erie

U.S.A.

★ Windsor

Leamington

★★ Point Pelee NP

N

7 **Saskatoon – Lloydminster**
(276km/171mi); The Battlefords
8–9 **Lloydminster – Edmonton**
(248km/154mi); Edmonton★★

Optional 5-day excursion of 1,034km/642mi can be made to the Rockies as follows:

Edmonton–Jasper 339km/210mi; Jasper–Lake Louise 🄲 *see Days 9, 8, 7 of Tour 1*; Lake Louise–Calgary 214km/133mi.

10–11 **Edmonton – Calgary**
(297km/185mi); Calgary★★
12 **Calgary – Elkwater**
(432km/268mi); Alberta Badlands★★★
13 **Elkwater – Swift Current**
(227km/141mi); Cypress Hills★★
14 **Swift Current – Regina**
(243km/151mi); Moose Jaw★
15 **Regina**★★
16 **Regina – Brandon**
(423km/263mi);
Qu' Appelle Valley★

17 **Brandon – Winnipeg**
(211km/131mi); Austin★

④ NORTHERN ONTARIO

Trip of 2,271km/1,411mi from Ottawa to Winnipeg. Time: 10 days. On this tour visitors can experience the wild, untouched beauty of the Canadian Shield topography with its rocks, trees and lovely lakes. Driving Lake Superior's "lakehead" is not to be missed.

DAYS/ ITINERARY/ SIGHTS

1–2 **Ottawa**★★★
3 **Ottawa – North Bay**
(363km/226mi); North Bay
4 **North Bay – Sault Ste Marie**
(427km/265mi); Sudbury★★
5 Sault Ste. Marie★★
6 **Sault Ste Marie – Thunder Bay**
(705km/438mi); Lake Superior Drive★★, North Shore Lake Superior★★, (described in other direction)
7 **Thunder Bay**★★

8   **Thunder Bay – Kenora**
(569km/353mi); Kakabeka Falls★★
9–10 **Kenora – Winnipeg**
(207km/129mi); Winnipeg★★★

5 SOUTHERN ONTARIO

Round-trip of 1,737km/1,079mi from
Niagara Falls. Time: 18 days. This tour
combines the vibrant city of Toronto
with the magnificent falls on the
Niagara River, the highly cultivated
southern Ontario, some Canadian
Shield country and the nation's capital
of Ottawa.

DAYS/ ITINERARY/ SIGHTS

1–2 60km/37mi; **Niagara Falls★★★**,
Niagara Parkway (North)★★
3   **Niagara Falls – Toronto**
(147km/91mi); Hamilton★
4–7 **Toronto★★★**
8   **Toronto – Kingston**
(269km/167mi); Oshawa★★
9   **Kingston and the
Thousand Islands★★**
10 **Kingston – Ottawa**
(201km/125mi); Upper Canada
Village★★★
11–12 **Ottawa★★★**
13 **Ottawa – Gravenhurst**
(406km/252mi); Gravenhurst★
14 **Gravenhurst – Midland** (56km/
35mi); Orillia★, Ste.-Marie among
the Hurons★★, Midland★
15 **Penetanguishene★**,
Georgian Bay★★

16 **Midland – Goderich**
(249km/155mi); Wasaga Beach★,
Blue Mountains, Goderich★
17 **Goderich – London**
(140km/87mi); Stratford★,
London★
Optional 2-day excursion,
482km/300mi, can be made to
Windsor★ and **Point Pelee
National Park★★**; overnight stop
at Leamington.
18 **London – Niagara Falls**
(209km/130mi); Brantford★

6 QUEBEC

Round-trip of 2,359km/1,466ml (excl.
ferries) from Montreal. Time: 17 days.
This tour combines the charm of
Quebec City, the ancient capital, with
the impressive fjord on the Saguenay;
the beautiful Gaspésie (Gaspé Peninsula)
culminating in the scenic wonder of
Percé; and the vibrant city of Montreal.

DAYS/ ITINERARY/ SIGHTS

1–3 **Montreal★★★**
4   **Montreal – Quebec City**
(277km/172mi); Trois-Rivières★★
5–6 **Quebec City★★★**
7   **Quebec City – Île aux Coudres**
(107km/67mi and ferry); Côte
de Beaupré ★★, Côte de
Charlevoix★★★, Île aux Coudres★★
8   **Île aux Coudres – Tadoussac**
(104km/65mi and ferry); Cote de
Charlevoix★★★, Tadoussac★★

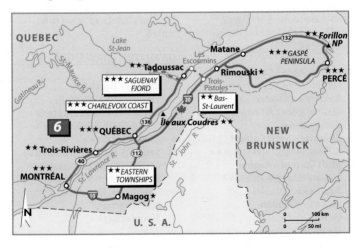

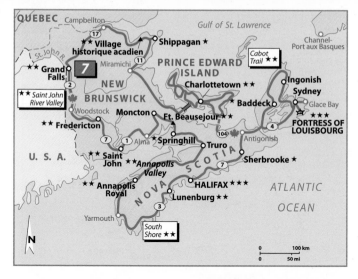

9 Whale-Watching Cruise★★ or Cruise on fjord du Saguenay★★★

10 **Tadoussac – Matane** (204km/127mi, ferry Les Escoumins – Trois-Pistoles); Gaspésie★★★, Jardins (gardens) de Métis★★, Matane

11 **Matane – Percé** (404km/251mi); Parc national Forillon★★, Gaspé★

12–13 Percé★★★

14 **Percé – Rimouski** (466km/290mi); Gaspésie★★★, Côte Sud (South Coast), Rimouski

15 **Rimouski – Quebec City** (312km/194mi); Bas-Saint-Laurent★★, (described in opposite direction)

16 **Quebec City – Magog** (275km/171mi); Cantons de l'Est★★, Magog★

17 **Magog – Montreal** (210km/130mi); Vallée du Richelieu★★

7 MARITIME PROVINCES

Round-trip of 4,235km/2,632mi (excl. ferries) from Halifax. Time: 22 days. This tour of the three Maritime Provinces is a tantalizing blend of seascapes, rocky headlands, sandy beaches and the high tides of the Bay of Fundy with historical highlights such as the French fortress of Louisbourg, Halifax and its citadel, the original Acadian settlement and the dynamic fishing port of Saint John.

DAYS/ ITINERARY/ SIGHTS

1–2 Halifax★

3 **Halifax – Antigonish** (261km/162mi); Sherbrooke★

4 **Antigonish – Sydney** (212km/132mi); Louisbourg Fortress★★★

5 **Sydney – Ingonish** (127km/79mi); Glace Bay (Miners' Museum★★), Cabot Trail★★ (described in opposite direction), Ingonish

6 **Ingonish – Baddeck** (233km/145mi); Cabot Trail★★, Cape Breton Highlands National Park★★, Chéticamp, Baddeck★

7 **Baddeck – Charlottetown** (263km/163mi and ferry); Prince Edward Island, Charlottetown★★

8–9–10 800km/500mi (maximum) Prince Edward Island Scenic Drives

11 **Charlottetown – Miramichi** (259km/161mi and ferry)

12 **Miramichi – Campbellton** (301km/187mi); Shippagan★, Village Historique Acadien

13 **Campbellton – Woodstock** (311km/193mi); Saint John River Valley★★ (described in opposite direction), Grand Falls★★, Hartland★

14 **Woodstock – Fredericton** (101km/63mi); Kings Landing★★

15 **Fredericton – Saint John** (109km/68mi); Fredericton★★

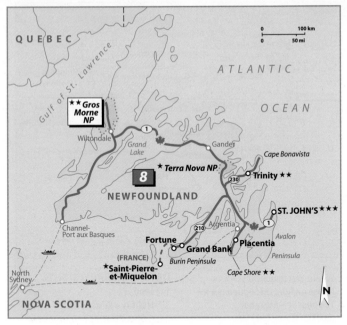

16 Saint John★

17 **Saint John – Alma** (143km/89mi);
Fundy National Park★★

18 **Alma – Truro** (254km/158mi);
Hopewell Cape★★, Moncton, Fort
Beausejour★★, Springhill

19 **Truro – Annapolis Royal**
(243km/151mi); Truro, Annapolis
Valley★★ (described in other
direction)

20 **Annapolis Royal – Yarmouth**
(131km/81mi); Annapolis Royal★★,
Port Royal Habitation★★

21 **Yarmouth – Lunenburg**
(311km/193mi); South Shore★★
(described in opposite direction),
Liverpool, Ovens Natural Park★,
Lunenburg★★

22 **Lunenburg – Halifax★★★**
(176km/109mi); South Shore★★,
Peggy's Cove★★

8 NEWFOUNDLAND

Round-trip of 2,073km/1,288mi (not
including ferries) from North Sydney,
Nova Scotia. Time: 12 days. This tour
of the island part of Canada's most
easterly province enables visitors to
discover the scenic wonders of Gros
Morne, St.-Pierre-et-Miquelon islands

(protectorate of France), and the old
port city of St. John's.

DAYS/ ITINERARY/ SIGHTS

1 **North Sydney – Port aux
Basques by ferry**
(🚢 it is advisable to spend the
previous night in Sydney)

2 **Port aux Basques – Wiltondale**
(305km/190mi)

3 191mi/119mi; Gros Morne National
Park★★

4 **Wiltondale – Gander**
(356km/221mi)

5–6 **Gander – Trinity** (182km/113mi);
Terra Nova National Park★, Cape
Bonavista, Trinity

7 **Trinity – Grand Bank**
(333km/206mi); Burin Peninsula,
Grand Bank

8 **Grand Bank – St.-Pierre-et-
Miquelon** (Fortune ferry); St.-
Pierre★

9–10 **St.-Pierre – St. John's**
(362km/224mi); St. John's★★

11 **St. John's – Cape Shore**
(175km/109mi); Placentia
(Castle Hill★), Cape St. Mary's★

12 **Cape Shore – North Sydney**
(by ferry from Argentia)

When and Where to Go

WHEN TO GO
CLIMATE

Climatic conditions vary greatly in Canada *(for climate information ☝see regional introductions)*.

Daily weather reports by Environment Canada are available via television, radio, newspapers, and online at www.weatheroffice.gc.ca.

For weather for specific cities covered in this guide, visit the websites, if available, listed within the Principal Sights in the *Discovering Canada* section.

SEASONS

Canada's main **tourist season** extends from the last weekend in May (Victoria Day) to the first weekend in September (Labour Day).

Many attractions lengthen the season to the Thanksgiving weekend (second Monday in October), during which the fall colours are ablaze across the nation. In mid-size to large cities, sights are usually open year-round. From mid-March to mid-May, visitors can enjoy comfortable daytime temperatures but chilly nights in **spring**; in some areas, spring skiing is still possible. Ontario, Quebec and New Brunswick celebrate the harvest of maple syrup with sugaring-off parties.

Most visitors go to Canada during the **summer** season, extending from the last weekend in May to early September. July and August are considered peak season and are ideal for outdoor activities such as sailing, kayaking, canoeing or hiking. Hot and often humid days with temperatures ranging from 22°-35°C/70°-95°F can be enjoyed in most provinces. May and September are pleasant months with warm days but cool evenings. However, many attractions have curtailed visiting hours, so phone ahead. The southern regions along the Canada/US border offer spectacular displays of fall colours from mid-September until the end of October.

For the sports enthusiast, the Canadian winter, generally from mid-November to mid-March, offers excellent opportunities to enjoy numerous **winter** activities such as downhill skiing, cross-country skiing, snowmobiling and outdoor hockey. Most provinces experience heavy snowfall. Main highways are snowploughed, but vehicles should be winterized and snow tires are recommended.

Note:

Extreme northern regions of Canada are accessible during July and August since the temperature rises above 0°C/32°F for only a few months each year. As climate change increases hot summers in Nunavut can be common.

WHAT TO PACK

Year-round, it is advisable to have a raincoat or hooded coat, and umbrella, in view of the range of weather across this vast country. Warmer wear, including a hat, neck scarf and gloves, is necessary in early spring, late autumn and, of course, winter, when heavy top coats and layers of clothing are essential. In summer it can be cool in the evenings in many places, so taking some warmer clothes is recommended. As there will be numerous times when walking is the ideal means of transport in both the cities and the countryside, comfortable footwear is essential, especially for sightseeing. Ladies should be especially careful to refrain from wearing high heels on the cobblestone streets of Montreal and Quebec Cty. If you are an outdoor enthusiast, pack your hiking boots. It's a good idea to take along an extra tote bag for shopping at outdoor markets, carrying a picnic, and bringing your purchases home.

THEMED TOURS

☝*See Special Excursions in the Practical Information section within each province.*

Know Before You Go

USEFUL WEBSITES

Canadian Tourism
www.canada.travel
(The official site of the Canadian Tourism Commission)

Government of Canada:
www.canada.gc.ca
(links to all government departments)

Canadian Government Publishing:
http://publications.gc.ca

The Canadian Encyclopedia online:
www.thecanadianencyclopedia.com

Current information:
www.canoe.ca
www.canada.com
www.cbc.ca

TOURIST OFFICES

Also see Visitor Information in the Practical Information section within each province.
Official government tourist offices operated by provincial, municipal and regional agencies distribute road maps and brochures that provide information on points of interest, seasonal events, accommodations and recreational activities. All publications are available free of charge (*see regional introductions*). Local tourist offices (telephone numbers and websites listed under each entry heading in this guide) provide additional information about accommodations, shopping, entertainment, festivals and recreation. On the maps in this guide, information centres are indicated by the symbol. A website that may be useful in planning your trip is *www. travelcanada.ca*.

INTERNATIONAL VISITORS

In addition to tourism offices, visitors from outside Canada may obtain information from the nearest Canadian embassy or consulate in their country of residence. Embassies of other countries are located in Canada's capital, Ottawa. Most foreign countries maintain consulates in Canada's provincial capitals. For further information on all Canadian embassies and consulates abroad, contact the website of **Foreign Affairs and International Trade Canada:** *www.international.gc.ca*.

SELECTED CANADIAN CONSULATES AND EMBASSIES

United States
◆ 1175 Peachtree St. NE, 100 Colony Square, Suite 1700, Atlanta, GA 30361-6205,
℘404-532-2000.
www.atlanta.gc.ca
◆ 1251 Avenue of the Americas, New York, NY 10020-1175,
℘212-596-1628.
www.newyork.gc.ca
◆ 550 South Hope St., Los Angeles, CA 90071-2627,
℘213-346-2700.
www.losangeles.gc.ca

Australia
◆ High Commission of Canada in Canberra, Commonwealth Ave., Canberra ACT 2600.
℘(02) 6270 4000.
www.international.gc.ca/australia

Germany
◆ Leipziger Platz 17, 10117 Berlin,
℘30-203120. www.berlin.gc.ca

United Kingdom
◆ Canada House, Trafalgar Square, London, SW1Y 5BJ
℘0207 004 6000
www.london.gc.ca

ENTRY REQUIREMENTS

Citizens of the US need a valid **passport** to visit Canada and return to the US by air. Canadian and US citizens must present a passport, or both a government-issued photo ID (such as a driver's license) and a birth certificate, to cross the Canada/

US border by land or sea. Parents bringing children into Canada must present a birth certificate for their children under age 18. To bring children into Canada, a single parent must bring a notarized permission letter from the other parent. All other visitors to Canada must have a valid **passport** and, in some cases, a visa (*see list of countries at www.cic.gc.ca/ english/visit/visas.asp*).

No vaccinations are necessary. For entry into Canada via the US, all persons other than US citizens or legal residents are required to present a valid passport. Check with the Canadian embassy or consulate in your home country about entry regulations and proper travel documents.

CUSTOMS REGULATIONS

Non-residents may import personal baggage temporarily without payment of duties. Persons of legal age as prescribed by the province or territory *(see regional introductions)* may bring into Canada duty-free 200 cigarettes, 50 cigars and some other forms of **tobacco**. **Alcohol** is limited to 1.14 litres (40 imperial ounces) of wine or spirits, or 24 bottles or cans (up to 8.5 litres total) of beer or ale. All **prescription drugs** should be clearly labelled and for personal use only; it is recommended that visitors carry a copy of the prescription. For more information, call **Border Information Service** *800 461-9999 (within Canada) or 204-983-3500;* or visit **Canada Border Services Agency**: *www.cbsa.gc.ca.*

Canada has stringent legislation on firearms. A firearm cannot be brought into the country for personal protection while travelling. Only long guns may be imported by visitors 18 years or older for hunting or sporting purposes. Certain **firearms** are prohibited entry; restricted firearms, which include handguns, may only be imported with a permit by a person attending an approved shooting competition. For further information on entry of firearms, contact the

Canada Firearms Centre (*800-731-4000 or 506-624-6626 outside Canada or the U.S.); www.cbsa.gc.ca).*

Most animals, except domesticated dogs and cats, must be issued a Canadian import permit prior to entry into Canada. **Pets** must be accompanied by an official certificate of vaccination against rabies from the country of origin. Payment of an inspection fee may be necessary. For details, contact **Canadian Food Inspection Agency** (*613-773-2342 or 800-442-2342; www.inspection.gc.ca).*

CURRENCY EXCHANGE

See Money in Basic Information.

HEALTH

Before travelling, visitors should check with their health care insurance to determine if doctor's visits, medication and hospitalization in Canada are covered; otherwise supplementary insurance may be necessary. Manulife Financial offers reimbursement for expenses as a result of emergencies under their Visitors to Canada Plan. The plan must be purchased before arrival, or within five days of arrival, in Canada. For details contact **Manulife Financial** (*877-268-3763; www.coverme.com).*

ACCESSIBILITY

Full wheelchair access to sights described in this guide is indicated in admission information by the symbol . Most public buildings and many attractions, restaurants and hotels provide wheelchair access. Disabled parking is provided and the law is strictly enforced. For details contact the provincial tourist office (*see regional introductions).* Many national and provincial parks have facilities for the disabled (such as wheelchair-accessible nature trails or tour buses). For details about a specific park, call *888-773-8888 or* visit *www.pc.gc.ca.* Additional information is available from **Easter Seals Canada** (*416-932-*

8382 or 877-376-6362; www.easterseals. ca). Passengers who need assistance should give 24-48hrs advance notice; also contact the following to request their informative literature for riders with disabilities:

Via Rail
📞888-842-7245. *Special Needs Services:* 📞800-268-9503 (TTY). www.viarail.ca.

Greyhound Canada
📞800-661-8747 (Canada)
📞800-397-7870 (TTY)
www.greyhound.ca

Reservations for hand-controlled cars at rental companies should be made well in advance.

Getting There and Getting Around

BY PLANE
♿*See also the Practical Information section for each province.*
American carriers offer **air** service to Canada's major airports. **Air Canada** *(📞888-247-2262 Canada/US; www. aircanada.com)* flies from larger US cities. Amtrak offers daily **rail** service to Montreal from Washington DC and New York City, as well as from New York City to Toronto. Aside from these direct routes, connections are offered from many major US cities. For schedules in the US *📞800-872-7245, TDD/TTY 800-523-6590* or *www.amtrak.com*. **Bus** travel from the US is offered by Greyhound. For information and schedules *www. greyhound.ca* or call the local US bus terminal. It is advisable to book well in advance when travelling during peak season.
Air Canada offers service to and from all major European cities, the Caribbean, Asia, South America and the Pacific. Vancouver is the western gateway city, offering connections to Australia, New Zealand and the Far East. Domestic air service is offered by Canada's national airline Air Canada *(📞888-247-2262 or 800-361-8071 TTY)* as well as its affiliated regional airlines and by Calgary-based WestJet *(📞888-937-8538 or 877-952-0100 TTY; www. westjet.com).*

Air service to remote areas is provided by many charter companies.
For specifics, contact the provincial tourist office (♿*see regional introductions).*

Major airports in Canada serviced by international airlines are:
- **Vancouver, BC (YVR)**
  Vancouver International Airport
  14km/9mi south of downtown
  📞604-207-7077
  www.yvr.ca
- **Calgary, AB (YYC)**
  Calgary International Airport
  17km/11mi northeast of downtown
  📞403-735-1200
  www.calgaryairport.com
- **Edmonton, AB (YEG)**
  Edmonton International Airport
  20km/14mi south of downtown
  📞780-890-8382 or 800-268-7134
  www.flyeia.com
- **Winnipeg, MB (YWG)**
  Winnipeg International Airport
  8km/5mi west of downtown
  📞204-987-9402.
  www.waa.ca
- **Toronto, ON (YYZ)**
  Lester B. Pearson
  International Airport
  27km/17mi northwest of downtown
  📞866-207-1690
  www.torontopearson.com
- **Montreal, QC (YUL)**
  Pierre Elliott Trudeau International
  Airport *22km/14mi west of downtown*
  📞514-394-7377 or 800-465-1213
  www.admtl.com

♦ **Ottawa, ON (YOW)**
Ottawa International Airport
18km/11mi south of downtown
📞613-248-2125
www.ottawa-airport.ca

♦ **St. John's, NL (YYT)**
St. John's International Airport
10km/6mi northwest of downtown
📞709-758-8500 or 866-758-8581
www.stjohnsairport.com

Note: Upon departure from some Canadian cities, travellers should be prepared to pay a $25 or higher Airport Improvement Fee before boarding the aircraft.
Many smaller regional airlines serve the provinces and territories. Air service to remote areas is provided by several charter companies. Check with the regional tourist offices regarding your specific destination.

BY SHIP
Canada maintains an extensive ferry-boat system. Contact the regional tourist offices for information and schedules (*see regional introductions for details; for Vancouver Island, see Entry Heading*).

BY TRAIN
VIA Rail, Canada's national passenger rail network, traverses the country with 19 major routes from coast to coast. First-class, coach and sleep-ing accommodations are available on transcontinental, regional and intercity trains. Amenities offered are dome cars, dining cars, lounges, WiFi, baggage handling (including bicycles), reservation of medical equipment, wheelchairs and preboarding aid with 24hr minimum notice. Unlimited train travel for 60 days is available system-wide through **CANRAILPASS** *for $1299, and VIA 6-Pak prices for students (ex. any of 6 stops between Montreal-London for $681)* with an ISIC card, plus discounts for youth and senior citizens.

Reservations should be made well in advance, especially during summer months and on popular routes like Edmonton to Vancouver. Canada's legendary cross-country train, The Canadian, travels the almost 4,424km/2,700mi from Toronto to Vancouver in four days *(one-way from $448, advance purchase, plus sleeping accommodation surcharge and taxes).* For information and schedules in Canada contact the nearest VIA Rail office or call 📞888-842-7245 (US & Canada); www.viarail.ca. The Plan Your Trip section of the Via Rail website lists overseas agents and a Google Transit interface.

BY COACH/BUS
Long-distance buses reach almost every corner of Canada. **Greyhound** Canada Transportation Corp., *(1111*

Ferry to Dartmouth in Halifax Harbour, Nova Scotia

©Bruce Bishop/Michelin

International Blvd., Ste. 700, Burlington, Ontario L7L6W1) operates the only trans-Canadian service. Peak season rates range from $376 to $750 *(reduced rates available in off-season and for senior citizens)*. For fares and schedules, call Greyhound: *℘800-661-8747 (Canada), ℘800-231-2222 (US); www.greyhound.ca.* Greyhound Express offers many new routes, reserved seats, WiFi, and discounted rates in select areas across Canada. Other regional companies supplement Canada's extensive motorcoach service *(see the yellow pages of local telephone directories)*.

BY CAR

See also the Practical Information section for each province.
Given Canada's enormous size, it is impossible to cover all of the country during one visit. *See Driving Tours for suggested two- to three-week itineraries.*
Canada has an extensive system of well-maintained major roads. In the northern regions and off main arteries, however, many roads are gravel or even dirt. Extreme caution should be taken when travelling these roads.

DOCUMENTS

Foreign **driver's licenses** are valid for varying time periods depending on the province. Drivers must carry vehicle **registration** information and/or rental contract at all times. Vehicle **insurance** is compulsory in all provinces (minimum liability coverage). US visitors should obtain a Canadian Non-Resident Inter-Province Motor Vehicle Insurance Liability Card **(Yellow Card)**, available from US insurance companies.
For additional information contact the Insurance Bureau of Canada, *(777 Bay St., Suite 2400, Toronto, ON M5G 2C8; ℘844-227-5422; www.ibc.ca).*

GASOLINE/PETROL

Gasoline is sold by the litre (1 gallon = 3.78 litres); prices vary from province to province. All distances and speed limits are posted in kilometres (1 mile = 1.6 kilometres). During winter it is advisable to check road conditions before setting out. **Snow tires** and an **emergency kit** are imperative. Studded tires are allowed in winter in some provinces; for seasonal limitations, contact the regional Ministry of Transportation *(check the blue pages in the local telephone directories or check the ministry website)*.

ROAD REGULATIONS

Unless otherwise posted, the speed limit on rural highways is 100km/h (60mph) and in urban areas 50km/h (30mph). Service stations that are open 24 hours can be found in large cities and along major highways.
The use of **seat belts** is mandatory for all drivers and passengers. Most provinces prohibit **radar detection devices** in vehicles. Traffic in both directions must stop (except on divided roads) for a yellow school bus when signals are flashing. In all provinces *except* some cities in Quebec (such as Montreal), **right turns on red** are allowed after coming to a complete stop. Information on highway conditions in each province can be obtained by contacting the regional Ministry of Transportation *(check the blue pages in the local telephone directories or the ministry website)*.

IN CASE OF ACCIDENT

If you are involved in an accident resulting in property damage and/or personal injury, you must notify the local police and remain at the scene until dismissed by investigating officers. For assistance contact the local Government Insurance Corporation. First-aid stations are clearly designated along highways.

CANADIAN AUTOMOBILE ASSOCIATION (CAA)

This national member-based organization *(℘800-267-2847; www.caa.ca)* offers, through its offices across Canada, services such as travel information, maps and tour books, accommodation reservations, insurance, technical and legal advice, and emergency roadside assistance. These benefits are extended to members of other internationally affiliated clubs (proof of membership is required).

The CAA maintains for its members a **24hr emergency road service** ℰ**800-222-HELP (4357)** (*see regional introductions for CAA listings) Also dial 222 on any cellphone for help.*

CAR RENTAL

Most major rental car agencies have offices at airports and in large cities in Canada. Minimum age for rental is usually 25. To avoid a large cash deposit, payment by credit card is recommended. More favourable rates can sometimes be obtained by making a reservation before arriving in Canada, but be aware of drop-off charges.

Avis: ℰ800-879-2847
Hertz: ℰ800-654-3131
Budget: ℰ800-268-8900
National: ℰ800-227-7368

Where to Stay and Eat

Hotel & Restaurant listings fall within the Addresses sections of each province. For price ranges, see the Legend on the cover flap.

WHERE TO STAY

*For a selection of accommodations, see the sections titled **Addresses** within the major cities and areas described in the guide. Lodgings in this guide can also be found in the Index under the heading **Where to Stay**.*

Canada offers accommodations suited to every taste and pocketbook. Luxury **hotels** generally are found in major cities, while **motels** normally are clustered on the outskirts of towns. **Bed-and-breakfast inns** (B&Bs) are found in residential areas of cities and towns, as well as in more secluded natural areas. Many properties offer special packages and weekend rates that may not be extended during peak summer months *(late May–late Aug)* and during winter holiday seasons, especially near ski resorts. Most resort properties include outdoor recreational facilities such as golf courses, tennis courts, swimming pools and fitness centres. Activities—hiking, mountain biking and horseback riding—often can

be arranged by contacting the hotel staff. Many cities and communities levy a **hotel occupancy tax** that is not reflected in hotel rates. Provincial and regional tourist offices offer free publications listing accommodations by location and type (*see regional introductions for addresses*). Government tourist offices supply listings *(free)* that give locations, phone numbers, types of service, amenities, prices and other details (*see regional introductions for addresses*). Canada is a vast country, and in less populated regions it may be difficult to find accommodations at the end of a long day's drive. Advance reservations are recommended, especially during the tourist season *(Victoria Day to Labour Day)*. During the off-season, establishments outside urban centres may be closed; it is therefore advisable to telephone ahead. Guaranteeing reservations with a credit card is recommended.

HOTELS

Rates for hotels vary greatly on season and location. Expect to pay higher rates during holiday and peak seasons. For deluxe hotels, plan to pay at least $450-$850/night per standard room, based on double occupancy in peak season. Moderate hotels usually will charge $150-$250/night.

When making a reservation, ask about packages including meals, longstay rates if appropriate, passes to local attractions, etc.. Typical amenities at hotels include televisions, alarm clocks, in-room phones, smoking/non-smoking rooms, restaurants and swimming pools. Suites and in-room efficiency kitchens are available at some hotels. Always advise the reservations clerk of late arrival; unless confirmed with a credit card, rooms may not be held after 6pm.

MOTELS

Along major highways or close to urban areas motels such as Comfort Inn, Quality Inn and Choice Hotels &877-424-6423, Travelodge &800-578-7878 and Days Inn &800-329-7466 offer accommodations at moderate prices ($80–$150), depending upon the location. Amenities include in-room television, alarm clock and telephone. Smoking and non-smoking rooms, restaurants and swimming pools are often available on-site. Some in-room efficiency kitchens may be available, sometimes for longstay periods. Family-owned establishments and small, independent guest houses that offer basic comfort can be found all across Canada.

BED AND BREAKFASTS AND COUNTRY INNS

Most B&Bs and country inns are privately owned; some are located in historic structures in residential sections of cities or small towns. In rural areas lodgings can be a rustic cabin or a farmhouse. At B&Bs the room rate includes complimentary breakfast ranging from continental fare to a gourmet repast; some offer afternoon tea and evening sherry or light snacks. Private baths are not always available, and often there is no phone in individual rooms. Guests are invited to use the sitting room and garden spots. Country inns are larger establishments, usually with more than 15 rooms and with full-service dining facilities. Smoking indoors may

not be permitted. Reservations should be made well in advance, especially during peak seasons and holidays. Ask about minimum stay requirements, and cancellation and refund policies. Most establishments accept major credit cards, but some B&Bs may not. Rates vary seasonally ($85-$200) for a double room per night. Rates may be higher when amenities such as hot tubs, private entrances and scenic views are offered.

RESERVATIONS SERVICES

Numerous organizations offer reservation services for B&Bs and country inns. Many services tend to be regional, but the **Professional Association of Innkeepers International** (&856-310-1102 or 800-468-7244; www.paii.org) and **BedandBreakfast.com** include properties for Canada as a whole. The **Independent Innkeepers' Association** publishes an annual register that includes Canadian B&Bs and country inns; &269-789-0393 or 800-344-5244 or book online: www.selectregistry.com. For a complete listing, search the Internet using the keyword "bed and breakfast" or ask your travel agent.

HOSTELS

Hostelling International Canada, affiliated with the International Youth Hostel Federation, offers a network of budget accommodations from coast to coast. A simple, no-frills alternative to hotels and inns, hostels are inexpensive dormitory-style accommodations (blankets and pillows are provided) with separate quarters for males and females. Many have private family/couples rooms that may be reserved in advance. Amenities include fully equipped self-service kitchens, dining areas, common rooms and laundry facilities. Rates average $28–$60 per night for members (higher for non-members). Hostels often organize special programs and activities for guests. Advance booking is advisable during peak travel times, but walk-ins are welcome. Membership is $35/year or $175 lifetime, but non-members are also admitted. When booking, ask for available discounts at area attractions, rental car companies and restaurants. For information and a free directory, contact **Hostelling International Canada** *(301-20 James Street, Ottawa, K2P 0T6;* ✆*613-237-7884 or 800-663-5777; www.hihostels.ca).*

UNIVERSITIES AND COLLEGES

Most universities make their dormitory space available to travellers during summer vacation *(May–Aug)*. Rooms are sparse; linens are provided.

Bathrooms are communal and there are no in-room telephones. Rates average $30–$60/day per person. Reservations are accepted. When booking, ask about on-campus parking and food service. For more information contact the local tourist office or the university directly.

FARM AND RANCH VACATIONS

Farm and ranch lodgings are rustic and especially suited for families with children. Visitors are paying guests on a working grain or livestock farm or a cattle/horse ranch, and participation in daily chores depends on the host's

Ice Hotel, Quebec City

© Xavier Dachez/Canadian Tourism Commission

Off-Beat Stays

In British Columbia's Fraser Canyon, the **houseboat** industry thrives in summertime. Many vacationers rent houseboats in the town of Sicamous to drift along on Shuswap Lake. The Saint John River in New Brunswick is also a popular houseboating spot. Near Yoho National Park in the Rockies, patrons of Beaverfoot Lodge can choose to sleep in **wagon train** bunks (✆*604-629-5741; www.beaverfootlodge.com).* Along the BC coast, travellers often book a berth on a cruise ship, or even on a ferry: on the Alaska Marine Highway route, passengers are permitted to camp overnight outside on the deck. Farther west, in the Prairies, campers can gaze at the stars before bedding down in a **teepee** (or tipi) at the foot of remote Head-Smashed-In Buffalo Jump (✆*403-553-2731);* Quaaout Lodge in Salmon Arm, BC, also offers teepee stays. Near Churchill, Manitoba, polar bear-watching patrons find haven in a **tundra buggy** train.

On Cape Breton Island in Nova Scotia, a whisky **distillery** beckons tired travellers to its adjoining inn *(Glenora Inn & Distillery, Rte. 19 near Inverness* ✆*800-839-0491; www.glenoradistillery.com).* Also in Nova Scotia, an inn within a former train station puts guests up in **cabooses** *(Train Station Inn* ✆*888-RAILBED; www.trainstation.ca).* On Prince Edward Island, folks can book a room in a working **lighthouse,** complete with ocean views. And way up north in Nunavut, visitors can stay overnight in an **igloo,** while in Quebec City, accommodations are possible in an **ice hotel,** appointed with standard amenities. *For details on the above accommodations, contact provincial tourist offices (*❧ *see regional introductions).*

Camping by Crimson Lake Provincial Park, Alberta

© Sabrina Hill/Travel Alberta

preference. Guests might be asked to gather eggs, feed animals or perhaps milk a cow. Wagon and sleigh rides, hiking through pasture, canoeing or fishing at an on-site pond, even berry picking, may be available activities. Breakfast is included. Other meals can often be requested and may be taken with the host family.

Rates begin at $60-$90 for double occupancy. Inquire about deposit and refund policies and minimum stay requirements. Credit cards may not always be accepted.

GUEST RANCHES

Primarily located in the mountain regions of British Columbia or the rolling hills of the Prairie Provinces, guest ranches offer a vacation that can be enjoyed by singles, couples or families. Comfortable accommodations may be a room in a main lodge or in a cabin. Home-cooked meals are usually served family-style; in addition, scenic trail rides, overnight camp-outs, hiking, guided fishing trips, swimming, rafting, country dancing and campfire gatherings are often available. All equipment is provided and some ranches offer supervised youth programs. Many are working cattle and horse ranches and guests are encouraged to pitch in. Rates average $670–$1,750/week per person; some ranches may require a minimum stay.

Ask about deposit and refund policies when booking a reservation.
For a selection of BC guest ranches, see Entry Heading Cariboo.
For more information on ranch vacations in British Columbia, contact the **Dude Ranchers' Assn.** (*866-399-2339; www.duderanch.org*) or the **BC Guest Ranchers' Assn.** (*877-278-2922); www.bcguestranches.com*).

CAMPING AND RV PARKS

Canada has excellent campgrounds that are operated privately or by the federal and provincial governments. Government sites are located in the many national and provincial parks. Fees are nominal. These campgrounds are well equipped and fill up quickly. Most park **campgrounds** are open mid-May through Labour Day, and usually operate on a first-come, first-served basis. Dates are subject to change: visitors should check with park visitor centres for rates and maximum length of stay. Some parks offer reservation services; some offer winter camping.

Campsites often include a level tent pad, picnic table, fireplace or fire grill with firewood, and parking space near a potable water source. Most have toilet buildings and kitchen shelters. Some campgrounds are for tents only; others allow recreational vehicles; most do not have trailer hook-ups, although many have sewage disposal stations. Many accommodate persons with disabilities. Rustic campgrounds, located near hiking trails in the backcountry, can be reached only on foot. Some parks offer hut-to-hut cross-country skiing with primitive overnight accommodations or winter tent sites.

For a list of campgrounds contact the provincial tourist office (& *see regional introductions for addresses).* Advance reservations are recommended, especially during summer and holidays. In most parks and forests, campgrounds are made available on a first-come, first-served basis.

NATIONAL AND PROVINCIAL PARKS

Campgrounds are relatively inexpensive but fill rapidly, especially during school holidays. Facilities range from simple tent sites to full RV hook-ups *(reserve 60 days in advance),* rustic cabins or yurts (& *reserve one year in advance).* Fees vary according to season and available facilities (picnic tables, water/electric hook-ups, used-water disposal, recreational equipment, restrooms, showers): camping & RV sites $10–$35/day; cabins $30–$110/day.

For all Canadian National Park reservations, contact the park you are visiting or **Parks Canada** (&*888-773-8888; www.pc.gc.ca).*

For **Provincial Parks**, contact the provincial or local tourism office for information (& *see Provincial Parks in the index).* As well as National Parks, there are some 1,000 **Provincial Parks**, more than 750 **National Historic Sites,** and 18 **UNESCO World Heritage Sites** in Canada.

Designed for daytime visits, most sites are open from Victoria Day to Labour Day, with reduced hours in the early spring and fall. Most charge a nominal admission fee and at many, interpretation centres and costumed guides provide insight into Canada's history and cultural heritage.

For more information, contact Parks Canada (& *see above).*

PRIVATE CAMPGROUNDS

Commercial campgrounds offer facilities ranging from simple tent sites to full RV hook-ups. They are slightly more expensive *($15–$60/day for tent sites, $30–$50/day for RVs)* but offer amenities such as laundry facilities, hot showers, convenience stores, children's playgrounds, pools, air-conditioned cabins and outdoor recreational facilities. Most accept daily, weekly or monthly occupancy. During the winter months *(Nov–Apr),* campgrounds in northern regions may be closed. Advance reservations for these campgrounds are strongly recommended, especially for longer stays and in popular resort areas.

Sonora Lodge, Sonora Island, northeast of Campbell River, British Columbia

©Eric P. Lucas/Michelin

FISHING CAMPS, FLY-IN LODGES AND WILDERNESS CAMPS

Individual lodges are described in coloured boxes throughout the BC/Rockies/Yukon section of this guide.
Canada offers the experienced angler or the outdoor enthusiast a variety of fishing lodges and camps, some of which are so remote they can be reached only on foot or by private boat or float plane. Cabins, backcountry huts, main lodge and dormitory-style buildings are typical accommodations. Summer tent camping may also be offered. Outfitters offer packages that include transportation, accommodations, meals, supplies, equipment and expeditions led by experienced guides. Activities can include trail riding, lake and stream fishing, boating and climbing. Some camps have hot tubs or saunas.

Wilderness camps located in Canada's northern regions offer all-inclusive hunting packages. Non-residents must be accompanied by licensed guides. Permits can be obtained through the outfitter, who can also assist with game registration (*required by law*). These packages are costly and the number of spaces is usually limited. It is advisable to make reservations well in advance.

For information on fishing and hunting regulations and license fees, as well as listings of outfitters, contact the provincial tourist office (*see regional introductions*).

WHERE TO EAT

*For a selection of restaurants, see **Addresses** in the major cities in the guide. Also see the Index.*
From Quebec's *tourtière* (meat pie) to Alberta's beef, Canada's regional cuisines encompass traditional comfort foods as well as novel creations. Originally, foods that were hunted and gathered (moose, salmon, goose, whale blubber, berries, and wild rice, for example) formed aboriginal and early Europeans' diets. Since then, Canada's traditional dishes, supplemented by those of its diverse ethnic population, have resulted in a richly varied cuisine. In-season and not-to-be-missed culinary experiences include Quebec's sugaring-off season, where sugar shacks serve freshly made maple syrup with pancakes, beans and sausages; or Atlantic Canada's choice seafood (lobster, scallops, mussels, oysters and cod). Quebec's artisanal cheeses are renowned, with excellent selections found in Montreal's Atwater Market. Today Canadian wines, icewines and ice-apple ciders win international awards.

© Tourism PEI/Yvonne Duivenvoorden

Prince Edward Island's oysters, mussels and clams

What to See and Do

OUTDOOR FUN

♿ *See Recreation in the Practical Information section of each province.*

CANOEING AND KAYAKING

From circuit canoe trips (Bowron Lakes, BC; Killarney and Quetico parks, Ontario), sea kayaking (Broken Islands, BC; Malpeque Bay, PEI), white-water rafting (Ottawa River, Ontario) and numerous accessible routes in Ontario's Algonquin Park to lodge-based paddles of tranquil lakes (Kenauk, Quebec), Canada is a paddler's heaven. Lifejackets are mandatory in Canada and it's illegal to drink and boat.

For trip planning and information about the sports in Canada, visit www.paddlingcanada.com, www.canoekayak.ca and for leaving no trace travel, go to https://lnt.org/.

FISHING AND HUNTING

Licenses are required for **fishing** and can be obtained from National and Provincial Park offices, designated sporting goods stores or other retail businesses. Some parks offer boat and canoe rentals. **Hunting** is not permitted within the National Parks.

HIKING

Hiking in Canada is primarily enjoyed in National and Provincial Parks. Hikers should ask park officials about trail conditions, weather forecasts and safety precautions. Overnight **hikers** in backcountry areas are required to register at the park office before setting out and to deregister upon completion of the trip.

Trail distances are given from trailhead to destination, not round-trip, unless otherwise posted. Topographic maps and a compass are indispensable for backcountry hiking; Gem Trek Publishing (*☏ 778-402-4216 or 877-921-6277; www.gemtrek.com*) and World of Maps (*☏ 613-724-6776 or 800-214-8524; www.worldofmaps.com*) are two sources for obtaining detailed topographic maps.

RIDING

Horseback riding opportunities in Canada range from hour-long trail rides to one week-or-longer expeditions, dude ranch experiences where you can round up cattle, and workshops where you learn from experts, with or without your own animal.

Also check the Royal Canadian Mounted Police Musical Ride for summer demonstrations or visit their stables in Ottawa, Ontario.

For Canadian equestrian events, contact Equestrian Canada (*☏ 866-282-8395; www.equestrian.ca*).

SKIING AND BOARDING

Canadian skiing and snowboarding opportunities are as varied as the country is vast. Enjoy spectacular mountain conditions for alpine as well as Nordic (cross-country) skiing and boarding (British Columbia, Alberta, Quebec) and Nordic skiing with some alpine in other provinces and territories.

Check *www.skicanada.org* for packages, resorts, ski and snowboard organizations across Canada; for snowboarding: www.canadasnowboard.ca.

WILDLIFE WATCHING

Canada is renowned for its wildlife, whether it's viewing grizzly or polar bears, gazing at beluga whales, or observing birds such as bald eagles, ganetts, snow geese or woodpeckers. For information about Canadian wildlife, visit the Canadian Wildlife Federation's website: www.cwf-fcf.org. Wildlife is best observed in Canada's Provincial and National Park systems, which include Marine Protected Reserves such as Saguenay-St. Lawrence Marine Park for whale observation. When watching or photographing wildlife, respectful distance is crucial.

☺ Precautions ☺

♦ Although Canada experiences severe winters, many regions are afflicted by hordes of biting insects in the summer. Late May to June is black-fly season, and in July the mosquitoes arrive. For outdoor activities, insect repellent is a must.

♦ Sturdy footwear with nonslip soles is recommended for hiking.

♦ To protect against surprise storms or cool mountain evenings, carry raingear and warm clothing.

Stiff fines are given in parks for feeding and otherwise habituating wildlife; so never feed, pet or disturb wild creatures of any kind.

SPAS

Wellness and spas go hand in hand, particularly when married to idyllic, spectacular nature. In Canada, you can be pampered with a massage beside the Pacific Ocean, soak in a hot tub overlooking the Rocky Mountains, or enjoy treatments at a heritage estate. Day spas, destination spas (which serve gourmet cuisine and offer lifestyle improvement), resort spas, mineral and medical spas are thriving. Browse *www.leadingspasofcanada. com* to see what Canada has to offer.

ACTIVITIES FOR KIDS ♟♞

In this guide, sights of particular interest to children are indicated with a ♟♞ symbol. Many of these attractions offer discounted admission to visitors under 12 years of age as well as special children's programs designed for all ages. Canada's National Parks usually offer discount fees for children. In addition, many hotels and resorts feature special family discount packages, and most restaurants offer children's menus.

CALENDAR OF EVENTS

Canada has a wide variety of fairs, festivals and celebrations throughout the year and in most parts of the country, many based on historic events. *⏱See Principal Festivals in the Practical Information section of each province.*

SHOPPING
BUSINESS HOURS

Business hours in Canada are, for the most part, Monday to Friday 9am-5pm. In general, retail stores are open Monday to Friday 9am-6pm (until 9pm Thursday and Friday), Saturday 9am-5pm. In most cities, shops are usually open on Sunday afternoon; many small convenience stores in gas stations may be open much longer hours. *⏱For banking hours, see Money in the Basic Information chapter.*

GENERAL MERCHANDISE

Downtown areas provide opportunities for shopping at department stores, national chains, specialty stores, art galleries and antiques shops.

Major department stores in Canada include Hudson's Bay Co. (known locally as "The Bay"), Eaton's, Simon's, Walmart and Ogilvy's.

Revitalized historic districts, such as the Old Port in Montreal or the Exchange District in Winnipeg, house boutiques, art galleries, cinemas and restaurants. Large **shopping malls**—or mammoth ones like West Edmonton Mall on the outskirts of Edmonton—are generally located outside downtown areas.

Bargain hunters will want to look for **outlet malls** that offer savings of up to 70% at brand-name factory stores. Recreational **outerwear** companies, such as Mountain Equipment Co-op enable visitors to equip themselves from head to toe before setting out on hiking, hunting or fishing trips.

As for fashionable, but probably pricey **ski clothes**, try Whistler, Banff, Mont-Tremblant and even Quebec City. Searching for a cowboy hat or colourful neckerchief? The latest in **Western gear** is available at stores in Calgary, Edmonton, Regina and Whitehorse.

How about a full-length silver fox coat with matching hat? **Furriers** are plentiful, particularly in Montreal, Ottawa, Toronto and Winnipeg, the latter being the site of the Fur Exchange, with its vast selection.

ARTS AND CRAFTS

Hooked rugs, mats and other **Acadian crafts** can be found at the gift shops at the Acadian Museum in Cabot Trail's Chéticamp and at Grand-Pré National Historic Site east of Wolfville. Tartans, kilts and other **Scottish attire** are for sale in Nova Scotia, particularly along the Cabot Trail. Bordering the Chaudière River, the Beauce and Rigaud regions of Quebec are famed for **maple syrup products** like taffy, maple syrup ice cream and liqueurs. In the outports of Newfoundland, handknit items such as mittens, scarves and hats can be purchased at local historical museums. In many parts of the country, native arts and crafts are plentiful; museums, and cultural centres on tribal lands, exhibit and sell baskets, carvings, jewellery and other handiwork. To visit Haida artists' on Haida Gwaii (Queen Charlotte Islands), inquire at the local band office. The museum shops at Victoria's Royal BC Museum and Vancouver's UBC Museum of Anthropology are filled with First Nations art, as are the gift shops at Wanuskewin in Saskatoon, and Head-Smashed-In Buffalo Jump UNESCO site near Fort Macleod in Alberta. The Alcheringa Gallery in Victoria has a fine selection of First Nations art, with emphasis on the Northwest Coast region. Inuit arts, especially stone sculpture, are highly prized works among collectors and connoisseurs. A number of sales outlets, including artists' studios, are located in Nunavut, Canada's newest territory, particularly on Baffin Island.

FARMERS' MARKETS

Prince Edward Island is known for its potato harvests, and Quebec's southern regions, especially the Montreal and St. Lawrence Valley areas produce fruit and vegetables, beef and dairy products. Alberta beef is world renowned and the Maritimes are famed for oysters, mussels, clams and other fruits of the sea. A number of towns and cities across Canada hold seasonal and year-round markets. In Ontario, **Kitchener's** indoor market is held throughout the year.

St. Lawrence Market (open year-round) in **Toronto** sells fresh produce, seafood, baked goods, flowers, souvenirs and crafts. Nearby Hamilton boasts one of Ontario's largest indoor markets, open throughout the year. A festival atmosphere prevails at **Ottawa's** year-round ByWard Market, stretching over several blocks (indoors in winter), while **Montreal's** Jean-Talon Market occupies the Little Italy neighborhood, offering indoor parking, organic fresh fruits, veggies, and artisan foods galore.

Charlottetown's lively farmers' market gives islander craft and food vendors a place to display their wares. During harvest time, many farmers sell produce at roadside stands as well as at farmers' markets. Visitors can pick their own fruits and vegetables (for a small fee) at farms that are open to the public.

Annapolis Valley in Nova Scotia is a large apple-growing area; fruit stands can be seen here along the roads in autumn. Producers invite visitors to try the many varieties that grow in the **Niagara Peninsula**, one of Canada's chief fruit-growing regions. In British Columbia, the **Okanagan Valley's** climate fosters a variety of crops that include apples, peaches and apricots.

WINERIES

A wine-making industry thrives in the **Niagara Peninsula** on the shores of Lake Ontario.

The **Okanagan Valley** in British Columbia produces some of the finest pinot noir, chardonnay and riesling wines, and Okanagan's pricey icewines are growing in popularity as dessert drinks. Most wineries welcome visitors with guided tours that include free wine tastings. Many wineries will sell their vintages to the public. During the fall harvest season, check with area visitor centres to find out about festivals and special events.

For a list of specific wineries, see OKANAGAN VALLEY.

SIGHTSEEING
NATIONAL PARKS AND RESERVES

Since the creation of North America's first National Park in Banff in 1885, the amount of protected land managed by Parks Canada has grown to 244,540sq km/ 94,392sq mi. The 43 National Parks and National Reserves (including two marine parks) offer the visitor spectacular scenery, a wealth of wildlife and fauna, as well as unlimited recreational opportunities. Some 14 million people visit the parks yearly. Canada's newest park is the legendary

---

☺ A Word of Caution ☺

Bears and other large animals are present in many of Canada's National Parks. Human encounters with them may result in serious injury. Visitors are asked to respect wildlife and observe park rules: don't hike alone; do not take along a dog; stay in open areas wherever possible; never go near a bear or bear cub; keep campsites clean; and store food away from tents or in the trunk of your car. Visitors should keep a safe distance from bears, moose, elk and other large animals and practice safe camping rules. Consult local authorities for current warnings. Detailed information is available at all visitor centres and park offices. Avoid hypothermia. Beware of wind, dampness and exhaustion in regions where weather changes rapidly; carry weatherproof clothing, plastic sheeting and nylon twine for emergency shelter; and eat high-calorie foods.

Sable Island National Park, off the coast of Nova Scotia, and home to a large family of wild horses. Contact Adventure Canada for small cruise. www.adventurecanada.com

General Information

Most points of interest are in the southern National Parks, accessible by car. Most backcountry hiking trails are well-marked. Parks are open year-round, but some roads may be closed in the winter. Daily entry or use fees range from $6 to $12. Discounts are offered at some parks to senior citizens (25%) and children (50%). Additional fees are charged for camping, fishing and guided programs. **Visitor Centres** (*open daily late May–Labour Day; reduced hours the rest of the year*) are usually located at park entrances. Staff are available to help visitors plan activities. Trail maps and literature on park facilities are available on-site free of charge. Interpretive programs, guided hikes and exhibits introduce the visitor to each park's history, geology and habitats.

For in-park activities, see specific parks within each province. A good reference is **Canada's National Parks** (Canopy 2010).

DISCOUNTS
For Students and Youths

Student discounts are frequently available for travel, entertainment and admissions. Age eligibility varies: children's rates usually apply for up to 12 years old; youth rates from 12–17 years of age. With a valid student card, any student 12 years and older can obtain an International Student Identity Card for discounts on rail travel and more (available at many ViaRail stations, or online from www.isic.org).

For Senior Citizens

Many attractions, hotels, restaurants, entertainment venues and public transportation systems offer discounts to visitors age 62 or older (proof of age may be required). Canada's

National Parks usually offer discount fees for seniors. Canada's national organization for retirees or citizens over 50 is called CARP (www.carp.ca or 800-363-9736), so visiting seniors should feel free to ask them about discounts, health issues, etc.

BOOKS

The Group of Seven and Tom Thomson. David P. Silcox. (2006). Nearly 400 colour reproductions illustrate how Canada's best known artists interpreted their deeply personal views of their surroundings.

Canada's Century: An Illustrated History of the People and Events that Shaped Our Identity. Carl Mollins. (2001). Selected articles from 2,500 issues published by *Maclean's* magazine since its inception in 1905 provide historical perspective through tidbits of news and commentary.

Canadians are Not Americans: Myths and Literary Traditions. Katherine L. Morrison. (2003). Examines both countries' national views of history, home, humour, law, religion, race and class to provide insights as to why Canadians differ from Americans.

Canadians: A portrait of a country and its people. Roy MacGregor. (2007). Entertaining insight into what makes a Canadian: anecdotes and reflective writing about recent historical topics from the perspective of an accomplished journalist.

Notes from the Century Before: A Journal from British Columbia. Edward Hoagland. (2002). The author's exploration of northwestern BC blends his observations of the land and people with those of the current inhabitants.

Plant Technology of the First Peoples of British Columbia. Nancy Turner. (2001). Explains how First Peoples used plant materials for the necessities of life—clothing, transportation, shelter—and for insect repellents, and recreational activities.

Nitsitapiisinni: The Story of the Blackfoot People. Glenbow Museum (2001). Produced by The Blackfoot Gallery Committee of Calgary's Glenbow Museum, this book chronicles Blackfoot life and history.

Roughing It in the Bush. Susanna Moodie. (1852, 1997). Land agents eager to attract immigrants painted Canada as a promised land; this still very readable account by the wife of a military officer describes the harsh reality of daily pioneer life.

FILMS

The Red Violin (1998) This epic tells of lives touched by a mysterious violin over three centuries.

Last Night (1998) Residents in a Canadian city come to terms with news that the world will come to an end at midnight.

The World Before Her" (2012; English) India-born, Toronto-bred Director Nisha Pahuja creates a lively, provocative portrait of India at a critical transitional moment.

Stardom (2000) Young female hockey player evolves to celebrity status and scandal as a fashion model.

The Apprenticeship of Duddy Kravtiz (1974, English) A poor young Jewish boy grows up in Montreal obsessed with power and money.

(Atanarjuat (The Fast Runner) (2001) Canada's first feature-length film in an aboriginal language (English and French subtitles) depicts the disruptive impact of long-standing hatred between two Inuit families.

Men with Brooms (2002) Four old curling buddies reunite to realize their late coach's dream of winning a big trophy.

Stories We Tell (2012) Sarah Polley's poignant documentary about her family.

Useful Words and Phrases

French Words

	Translated
Anse	Cove, Bay
Autoroute	Highway
Baie	Bay
Belvédère	Lookout
Cap	Cape
Centre d'accueil	Welcome Centre
Interpretation Centre d'interprétation	Centre
Chute	Waterfall
Côte	Shore, Coast
Croisière	Cruise, Boat Trip
Est	East
Église	Church
Gare	Train Station
Hôtel de Ville	City Hall
Île	Island
Jardin	Garden
Lac	Lake
Maison	House
Manoir	Manor
Métro	Subway
Monastère	Monastery
Mont	Mount
Montagne	Mountain
Moulin	Mill
Musée	Museum
Nord	North
Ouest	West
Palais de Justice	Courthouse
Parc	Park
Phare	Lighthouse
Place	Square
Plage	Beach
Pont	Bridge
Rapides	Rapids
Réserve Faunique	Wildlife Conservation Area
Rivière	River
Rocher	Rock
Rue	Street
Stationnement	Parking
Sud	South
Téléphérique	Gondola
Traversier	Ferry Boat
Vallée	Valley
Ville	City, Town

USEFUL PHRASES

Do you speak English?
Parlez-vous anglais?
I don't understand
Je ne comprends pas
Talk slowly Parlez lentement
Where's...? Où est...?
When does the ... leave?
A quelle heure part...?
When does the ... arrive?
A quelle heure arrive...?
When does the museum open?..
A quelle heure ouvre le musée?
When is the show?
A quelle heure est la
spectacle?
When is breakfast served?
A quelle heure sert-on le
petit-déjeuner?
What does it cost? Alt: How many?
Combien?
**Where can I buy a newspaper
in English?** Où puis-je acheter
un journal en anglais?
**Where is the nearest petrol/
gas station?** Où se trouve la station
essence la plus proche?
**Where can I change traveller's
cheques?** Où puis-je échanger des
cheques pour les voyageurs?
Where are the toilets?
Où sont les toilettes?
Do you accept credit cards?
Acceptez-vous les cartes
de crédit?

WHERE FRENCH IS SPOKEN

The official language of the Province of Quebec is French, spoken by 80% of the population. The second language is English. Visitors can expect residents in urban areas and in southern Quebec to be bilingual. In much of the rest of the province, however, don't expect everyone to understand basic English. Except in Montreal and some border areas, all road signs are in French. Tourist information is generally available in both languages.
New Brunswick is bilingual; about 35 percent of the population speaks French. All road signs are in English and French in the province.

Basic Information

ELECTRICITY

120 volts, 60 cycles.
Most small American appliances can be used. European appliances require an electrical transformer, available at electric supply stores.

EMERGENCIES

Most Canadian cities and many rural areas have 911 telephone service for emergency response. When 911 is dialled from any telephone in a served area, a central dispatch office sees the dialling location and can redirect the call to the appropriate emergency response agency—fire department, police or ambulance. Much of rural Canada is not within range of cellular telephone service, and although coverage extends along most major highways, service can be unreliable in mountainous regions. Public Safety Canada maintains extensive links and services on public safety: 1-800-830-3118, www.safecanada.ca.

MAIL/POST

Post offices across Canada are generally open Monday to Friday 8am–5.30pm; extended hours are available in some locations. Sample rates for first-class mail (letter or postcard; up to 30 grams): within Canada, $1 dollar; to the US, $1.20; international mail, $2.50. Mail service for all but local deliveries is by air. Visitors can receive mail c/o "General Delivery" addressed to Main Post Office, City, Province and Postal Code. Mail will be held for 15 days and has to be picked up by the addressee.
Some post offices have fax services, and all post offices offer international courier service. Postal facilities are located at selected Canadian retailers throughout the country.
For information regarding postal codes or locations of facilities call ℘800-267-1177; www.canadapost.ca.

METRIC SYSTEM

Canada has adopted the International System of Units popularly known as the metric system. Weather temperatures are given in Celsius (C°), milk and wine are sold by millilitres and litres, and grocery items are measured in grams. All distances and speed limits are posted in kilometres (to obtain the equivalent in miles, multiply by 0.6). Some examples of metric conversions are:

♦ 1 kilometre (km) = 0.62 miles
♦ 1 metre (m) = 3.28 feet
♦ 1 kilogram (kg) = 2.2 pounds
♦ 1 litre (L) = 33.8 fluid ounces = 0.26 gallons (1 US quart = 32 fluid ounces)

MONEY

Canadian currency is based on the decimal system (100 cents to the dollar). Bills are issued in $5, $10, $20, $50, $100, $500 and $1,000 denominations; coins are minted in 5 cents, 10 cents, 25 cents, $1 and $2. Exchange money at banking institutions for the most favourable exchange rate.
You don't need to carry much cash while visiting Canada: ATM machines are widely available, and most merchants accept debit or credit cards. Self-serve gas, parking lots and even store check-outs are common. Do carry a few "loonies" or "toonies" —the $1 and $2 coins— for parking meters, tips and snacks. Most public telephones accept calling cards at no charge, but local calls cost 50¢ (two quarters). Most ATMs dispense cash in increments of $20.

BANKS

Banking institutions are generally open Monday to Friday 9am–5pm. Many banks are now open on Saturdays and some even on Sundays. Banks at large airports have foreign exchange counters and extended hours. Some institutions may charge a small fee for cashing traveller's cheques. Most principal bank cards are honoured at affiliated Canadian banks.
Ⓢ Use bank branded ATM machines

to avoid the higher fees charged by private operators.

CREDIT CARDS AND TRAVELLER'S CHEQUES

The following major credit cards are accepted in Canada: American Express, Carte Blanche, Discover, Diners Club, MasterCard/Eurocard and Visa. Most banks will cash traveller's cheques and process cash advances on major credit cards with proper personal identification.

CURRENCY EXCHANGE

The most favourable exchange rate can usually be obtained at branch offices of a national bank. Some banks charge a small fee for this transaction. Private exchange companies generally charge higher fees. Airports and visitor centres in large cities may have exchange outlets as do some hotels. The Canadian dollar fluctuates with the international exchange rate. Exchange facilities tend to be limited in rural and remote areas. If arriving in Canada late in the day or on a weekend, visitors may wish to exchange some funds prior to arrival (some banks are open on Saturdays and Sundays in major cities).

☺ You can use ATMs to withdraw Canadian currency from your home account, but check with your bank first to see if it has reciprocal arrangements with a Canadian bank for a lower fee.

TAXES

Canada levies a 5% Goods and Services Tax (GST) on most goods and services. Provinces (except Alberta) levy additional taxes of 7% to 10% on some goods and services. The Maritime Provinces and Quebec have the highest rates, but refund programs for visitors are available in some places, such as Quebec. Ask merchants for the form.

PUBLIC HOLIDAYS

For provincial holidays, see regional introductions.
The abovementioned holidays are observed throughout Canada. Most

PUBLIC HOLIDAYS	
New Year's Day	January 1
Good Friday	Friday before Easter Sunday
Easter Monday	Monday after Easter Sunday
Victoria Day	Monday on or before May 24
Canada Day	July 1
Labour Day	1st Monday in September
Thanksgiving	2nd Monday in October
Remembrance Day	2nd Wednesday in November
Christmas Day	December 25
Boxing Day	December 26

banks, government offices and schools are closed.

SMOKING

All Canadian provinces and territories have enacted comprehensive smoke-free legislation, and municipal bylaws are commonplace. Smoking has been banned from aircraft, buses, trains and most offices for some time, but restrictions for other public spaces vary: for example, Quebec's 2006 legislation banned smoking in bars, restaurants, taverns, casinos, on school grounds and within nine metres of any exterior door of a health, social services or educational institution—yet smoking is still allowed on outdoor patios.
if you want to smoke in Canada, it's best to ask before you light up.

TELEPHONES

For long distance within Canada and to the U.S., dial 1+ area code + number. For overseas calls, refer to the country codes listed in most phone directories, or dial "0" for operator assistance. All operators speak English and French. Collect calls and credit card calls can be made from public pay phones. For local directory assistance, check the white pages of

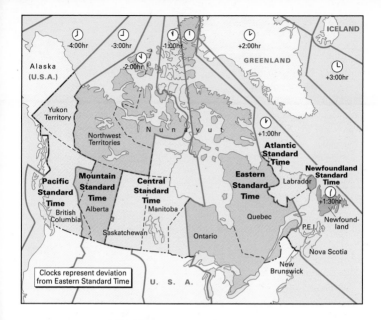

Clocks represent deviation from Eastern Standard Time

a phone directory or dial 411; outside the local area code dial 1+ area code + 555-1212. Telephone numbers that start with **800, 855, 844, 866, 877** or **888** are toll-free. A local call costs 50 cents. Be aware that many hotels place a surcharge on all calls.

EMERGENCY NUMBERS

911 service is operative in major cities; otherwise dial "0" for the operator and ask for police. If you see your name in the newspaper or hear it on the radio, contact the nearest RCMP office immediately.

TIME

🔊 See map above

Canada spans six time zones, but the coast-to-coast time difference is only 4hrs 30min because in Newfoundland and a coastal portion of Labrador, the time is 30min in advance of the rest of Labrador and the Maritime provinces, which are on Atlantic Time.

Except for some areas in Alberta, Daylight Saving Time (clocks are advanced 1 hour) is in effect from the second Sunday in March to the first Sunday in November (🔊 see regional introductions for details).

TIPS

Tips or service charges are not normally added to a bill in Canada. However, it is customary in Canada to leave a tip (an expression of appreciation) for services received from food servers, porters, hotel maids and taxi drivers. In restaurants and for taxi drivers, it is customary to tip 15–20 per cent of the total amount of the bill. At hotels, porters should be tipped $2–3 per bag, and maids $2–5 per night, depending on the size of your accommodation.

WIRELESS AND INTERNET

The Internet and in particular, wireless access, is becoming more widely available in Canada, especially in urban areas, at major airports, hotels, Wi-Fi hot spots and Internet cafes. Most of the major hotels, especially those owned by international hoteliers, provide in-room wireless access (some charge a nominal fee); others have a business centre with access provided on a fee basis. Some libraries in the major cities, such as Toronto's Reference Library, provide access to the Internet, often at no charge.

37

INTRODUCTION TO CANADA

Hoodoos at Drumheller, Badlands, Alberta
© All Canada photo/hemis.fr

Canada Today

Since the mid-1990s, fiscal management and rising prices for natural resources—particularly fossil fuels—have buoyed the country's economy. Canada traditionally ranks high among the world's wealthiest nations.
See also the introduction for each province.

POPULATION

Population figures in this guide are based on the 2011 census. The next Canadian census are to be released in 2017.

This immense country is inhabited by a relatively small number of people: 36 million in 2016, compared to more than 323 million in the US.

Overall, the population density is only 3.5 persons per sq km compared to 246 per sq km in the United Kingdom. Canada's inhabitants are largely concentrated in a band about 160km/100mi wide immediately north of the Canadian/US border. *The illustrations opposite show traditional costumes still worn today.*

The regional distribution is approximately as follows: British Columbia, Rockies, Yukon 13 percent; the Prairie provinces 17 percent; Ontario 38 percent; Quebec 24 percent; the Atlantic provinces 8 percent; Northwest Territories 0.2 percent. Although 62 percent of the population lives in Ontario and Quebec, mainly between Quebec City and Windsor, Canada is strongly characterized by regional distinctions.

THE ECONOMY

The following is a very general account of economic activity in Canada. Additional information can be found in the regional introductions. Statistics Canada provides detailed information online at www.statcan.gc.ca.
The Canadian Government's website http://canada.gc.ca provides links to all government publications.

Canada's great strength lies in its wealth of natural resources: forests, minerals and energy fuels that contribute much to its economy. Mining and agriculture are part of the country's highly diversified economy, whereas energy is among the top-performing sectors, along with transportation and telecommunications. With nearly 70 percent of Canadians living within 300km/186mi of the US border, it is not surprising that the US is Canada's largest trading partner. Increased trade contributed to a gross domestic product (GDP) growth rate of 4.3 percent by 2000—the highest of the major industrialized countries. Steady growth and strong fiscal management enabled the federal government to apply budget surpluses to reduce Canada's large public-sector debt, but given the current global recession, the GDP is contracting.

Rue Saint-Paul, Vieux-Montréal, Montreal

© Philippe Renault/hemis.fr

Scottish Bagpiper   *Inuit Hunter*   *Acadian Woman*

Ukrainian Woman   *Aboriginal Canadian*

R. Corbel/MICHELIN

Per Statistics Canada, real GDP declined almost 1.5 percent in the first quarter 2009, the largest quarterly decrease in 18 years, and it continues to roller coaster despite new Prime Minister Justin Trudeau's legacy of efforts.

LAND OF FORESTS

Forests are of prime importance to Canada; trees in one form or another are among the country's most valuable assets. Over half the total land area is forested, and the forest-products industry exists in every province. Although no longer dominant in British Columbia, which is best known for its sawed lumber, the industry is still important there, and Quebec is a major producer of **newsprint**. Canada is the world's largest exporter of the latter commodity, supplying nearly a third of total world consumption.

TRADITIONAL OCCUPATIONS

Despite Canada's tough climate and terrain, **agriculture** occupies an important position in the economy, making up 2.3 percent of the country's GDP. Wheat has long been the leader in agricultural exports from the Prairie provinces, challenged in more recent years by canola, a relatively new oilseed crop. Beef cattle are also raised in the Prairie provinces, whereas dairy products, poultry and hogs are more important in British Columbia, Ontario and Quebec. Potatoes, which have been a mainstay of the Maritime provinces, are of growing significance in the prairie lands. Apples, grapes and several hardy small fruits are harvested in the southernmost areas of the country, especially in Ontario and British Columbia.

Fishing and **trapping** were for centuries Canada's primary industries. Today, Canada is still a leading exporter of fish in the world, although the country's east and west coasts have seen declines in fish stocks in recent years.

The Atlantic Coast supplies the vast majority of this resource, while 15 percent of the value is provided by the Pacific salmon fishery. Canada remains one of the largest suppliers of animal pelts in the world. The country's total exports have increased significantly in recent years; new and emerging markets for Canada's fur products include China and Greece.

RICHES BENEATH THE SOIL

Although in decline in some parts of the country, mining has played an important economic role in every region of Canada; it is a particularly active industry in the Northwest Territories and the Yukon. The country is a leading international producer of metals including nickel (Ontario, Manitoba), zinc (New Brunswick, Northwest Territories, Quebec, Ontario), molybdenum (British Columbia), uranium (Saskatchewan, Ontario), gold (Ontario, Quebec, Northwest Territories, Yukon) and lead (New Brunswick, British Columbia, Northwest Territories). Leading non-metals are potash (Saskatchewan, New Brunswick) and asbestos (Quebec). Iron ore is produced in the Labrador Trough (Quebec and Newfoundland) and in Ontario.

The leading province for **fossil fuels** is Alberta, which possesses immense reserves awaiting exploitation in its Athabasca oil sands, and shares substantial coal reserves with British Columbia. Although fossil fuel production is almost entirely restricted to western Canada at present, offshore oil development such as the Hibernia project on the continental shelf off Newfoundland, is changing this imbalance.

Container ship in Halifax Port, Nova Scotia

©Mike Clarke/iStockphoto.com

Daniel Johnson Dam at Manic-5, Côte-Nord, Quebec

©Hydro-Québec

TRANSPORTATION

Because of Canada's size, transportation has always been of prime importance. Until about 1850, waterways commanded the country's economic growth. Since then, wheat farming, mining, and pulp and paper industries have grown largely dependent on rail transport.

Even in these industries, movement of goods by water is not insignificant.

The network of locks and canals known as the **St. Lawrence Seaway** significantly boosted Canada's economy: in particular, the country became an exporter of iron ore after the seaway facilitated exploitation of Labrador and Quebec's huge deposits. The road network has expanded since World War II with the completion of the Trans-Canada Highway and the opening of the great northern roads—the Alaska and the Dempster highways. Aviation plays an important role, especially in the North.

HYDROELECTRIC GIANT

The abundance and power of Canada's water sources offer exceptional opportunities for generation of hydroelectricity. Almost two-thirds of the country's electricity comes from this source. Generating stations operate in every province except Prince Edward Island, and Quebec's massive **James Bay Hydroelectric Project,** with a capacity of more than 12,000 megawatts, is one of the largest hydroelectric engineering projects in the world. In Labrador a huge generating station is located on the Churchill River.

Other examples are in British Columbia on the Peace and Columbia rivers, in Quebec on the Manicouagan and Outardes rivers, in both Ontario and Quebec on the St. Lawrence, in Saskatchewan on the South Saskatchewan, and in Manitoba on the Nelson.

Electricity produced by such projects powers industries engaged in natural

Gross Domestic Product

Formerly known as the GNP (gross national product), the GDP is a measurement (traditionally an annual one) of the monetary value of goods and services produced in Canada. Closely linked to such variables as productivity and the unemployment rate, the GDP is the most commonly used, and widely considered the best, indicator of the country's economic performance. Calculated by deducting imports from total spending, the GDP actually presents an estimate of the value of goods and services.

Source: *Statistics Canada*

resource utilization such as smelting businesses and pulp mills.

Plentiful and inexpensive hydroelectricity has attracted other industries, such as the aluminum industry to British Columbia and Quebec. Canada's energy is transported via high-voltage power lines to southern Canada and surplus electricity is exported to the US.

MANUFACTURING AND THE NEW ECONOMY

Canada's manufacturing industry, traditionally based on resource-processing (forest products, minerals, food and beverages, for example), has largely shifted into secondary manufacturing. A significant petrochemical industry exists in Alberta, Manitoba, Ontario and Quebec. Automobile and auto parts manufacturing and electrical and electronics industries are based mainly in Ontario and Quebec.

British Columbia's Vancouver and Ontario's Toronto are centres for telecommunications, pharmaceuticals and biotechnology as well as film and video production. In Atlantic Canada commercial medicine, environmental industries and information technologies (the latter most notably in New Brunswick) complement traditional industries.

INFORMATION AND COMMUNICATIONS TECHNOLOGIES

On a per capita basis, Canada is next only to the United States in the number of personal computers, with 699 per 1,000 inhabitants in 2005. Long considered one of the best-wired countries, Canada boasts comprehensive and inexpensive **telecommunications services**—no doubt a contributing factor to the nation's top ranking in worldwide Internet use per capita. Canada's long-distance telephone services were deregulated in 1992. Deregulation of the local telephone market in 1998 resulted in alternative carriers and resellers entering the market with new competitive services, although downturns in the worldwide telecommunications industry in 2001 led to consolidation and layoffs within Canada. Several Canadian companies are world leaders in the telecommunications equipment market.

INVESTMENT AND BANKING

In the past decade, Canada's economy has sustained steady growth. By 2007 inflation was at 2.2 percent and the unemployment rate was at 6.1 percent. The S&P/TSX Composite Index , which accounts for 95 percent of all equity trading in Canada, reached record levels in mid-2000, but fell back sharply in 2001. Until the 2008-2009 global downturn, steady growth in energy and manufacturing stocks had pushed the well past the 2000 levels.

Consumers have been quick to adopt new technologies and services introduced by Canadian financial institutions. In 2004 Canada ranked first in debit card usage, with 88.2 transactions per inhabitant. Use of the Internet for banking continues to grow: while only 8 percent of Canadians used it in 1999, while 69 percent used it for banking by 2014.

GOVERNMENT

Canada is a **federal state** with 10 provinces and three territories. Each province has its own elected legislature controlling regional affairs. Canada's three territories—the Yukon, the Northwest Territories (which is only one territory despite its name) and newly created Nunavut (1999)—have elected legislative assemblies to govern their respective territories. Nunavut, in addition, has a number of joint resource-management bodies composed of Inuit, federal and territorial government appointees who play important decision-making roles. The central government in **Ottawa,** the federal capital, assumes responsibility for such matters as defence, foreign affairs, transportation, trade, commerce, money and banking, and criminal law.

Though officially part of the Commonwealth, Canada functions in actuality as an independent nation. The Canadian head of state is the **British Monarch.**

Her authority is exercised by the **Governor General,** who was at one time appointed by the monarch but today is chosen by the elected representatives of the Canadian people. However, the Governor General is little more than a figurehead as actual power lies in the hands of the Canadian **Prime Minister,** the leader of the majority party in Canadian **Parliament.** This latter institution consists of an elected legislature called the **House of Commons** and an appointed **Senate**, members of which are chosen by the governing party. The Prime Minister rules through a cabinet drawn from elected representatives (and sometimes from members of the Senate), and must submit his or her government for re-election after a maximum of five years, or if he or she is defeated in the House of Commons.

INTERNATIONAL RELATIONS

After World War II Canada was catapulted to global leadership as a founding country in the United Nations and as a member of the North Atlantic Treaty Organization (NATO). The country retains diplomatic missions in over 150 countries and has earned respect as an international peacekeeper. In addition, Canada is a regular participant in international conferences, including the yearly economic summit of the eight major industrialized democracies, known as the G8. In 1994 Canada, Mexico and the US implemented the **North American Free Trade Agreement** (NAFTA), a pact designed to increase trade and investment among the three countries largely by eliminating tariffs and other barriers, and the TPP or Trans-Pacific Partnership was also signed in 2016 between the twelve Pacific Rim nations, promising an extensive menu of benefits for all.

FOOD AND DRINK

Food in Canada has many regional specialties. Staples of the Plains First Nations, such as **buffalo stew** with bannock (bread), still provide sustenance for Canada's First Nations people today.

British Columbia is famous for its **seafood,** especially king crab and salmon. The country produces a variety of fruit, such as apples, peaches, cherries, and its own wine in the Okanagan Valley in British Columbia and from Niagara in Ontario to Quebec's Eastern Townships. In the Prairies, especially in the Province of Alberta, the **beef** is excellent, along with fresh lake fish in the north, wild rice, berries of all types, and the heritage of immigrant cultures—cabbage rolls, pierogies (dumplings) and borscht, for example.

Quebec's French heritage provides it with a fine culinary tradition, and many restaurants serve traditional French-Canadian cuisine—pork dishes, meat pie (tourtière), soups, thick stews (ragout) and a generous quantity of maple syrup. Quebec's Beauce region is well known for its maple products: sugar pie, maple syrup, ice cream and taffy.

The Atlantic provinces are a great **seafood** region. Lobster is the most valuable catch for the Maritime provinces. Nova Scotia is known for its Digby scallops, Prince Edward Island for its mussels and Malpeque oysters. Bluefin tuna are caught off the shores of all three provinces. In Newfoundland **squid burgers** are an island peculiarity. **Screech,** a heady dark rum, or one of the country's fine **beers**, is a common beverage. Newfoundland's traditional **jigg's dinners** are a hearty meat and potatoes plate piled high with carrots, cabbage and peas pudding. Fruits of the region include partridgeberries and yellow **bakeapples**, the latter raspberry-like in appearance but with a distinctive taste. **Figgy duff** (steamed pudding à la 16C) is a popular dessert. New Brunswick is famous for **fiddleheads,** the new shoots of ferns (May–Jun), and for **dulse,** an edible seaweed.

Moose meat and fresh lake fish are available in the Northwest Territories, as is **Arctic char,** a delicacy similar to trout and salmon in taste.

History

Immigration and exploration have shaped Canada's history, with archaeological evidence of people in the northwest of the country some 15,000 years ago. Vikings settled briefly in Newfoundland 1,000 years ago, and Europeans established temporary settlements as they fished the rich Gulf of Saint Lawrence some 500 years ago. Reports of abundant natural resources from French and English explorers led to colonization and brought European conflicts to the New World, with aboriginal peoples forming alliances on both sides. The fur trade pushed exploration westward, and by the late 1800s, completion of a transcontinental railroad enabled the Dominion of Canada to extend to the Pacific Ocean.

&See also the introduction for each province or territory.

PREHISTORY TO PRESENT
PREHISTORIC AND NATIVE PEOPLES

Man is not indigenous to North America. According to recent archaeological findings, prehistoric tribes from the mountains of Mongolia and the steppes of Siberia came to the continent some 15,000 to 26,000 years ago by a land bridge that once existed over the **Bering Strait**. They gradually moved south across the whole continent and into South America. Their descendants are the aboriginal and Inuit peoples of Canada today, and they can be divided into six groups.

The **Northwest Coast tribes** constituted a highly developed civilization, well known for its totem poles and other carved objects. Principal tribal groups are the Bella Coola, Coast Salish, Haida, Kwakiutl, Nootka (along the West Coast), Tlingit and Tsimshian (including the Gitxsan). Also known as the Plateau culture (named after the Columbian Plateau region), the **Cordillers Indians** eked out an existence in the British Columbia interior as hunters and fishermen. The Athapaskan, Salishan and Kutenai language families are indigenous to this native culture. The **Plains Indians**— the Assiniboine, Stoney, Blackfoot, Plains Cree, Plains Ojibwa and Sarcee tribes—were nomadic buffalo hunters who lived in teepees and wore decorative clothing made of animal skins. The Beothuk, Cree, Dene, Montagnais and other **subarctic Indians** lived a nomadic existence hunting caribou and other animals. The Algonquin and the Iroquoian peoples formed the **Eastern Woodlands** culture of bellicose farmers who lived in fortified villages, growing corn and squash. Nomadic inhabitants of the most northerly regions, the **Inuit** traditionally lived in ice houses in winter, and in tents and sod houses during the summer. Using their highly developed navigational skills, they hunted seals and whales off the coast, and caribou and waterfowl in the interior.

FIRST CONTACT

Long after the migrations of Asiatic peoples from the west, Europeans arrived on the shores of present-day Canada and proceeded to conquer the land and impose their own civilization. The Norse explored the coast of Labrador in the 10C and are believed to have founded the earliest known European settlement in North America around AD 1000. English and Basque fishermen knew of the rich resources of the Grand Banks as early as the 15C.

However, the first permanent settlements began in the 17C. Within seven years of each other (1603-10), Frenchman **Samuel de Champlain** and Englishmen Henry Hudson (who, in 1610, discovered the huge waterway that bears his name) and John Guy claimed the riches of the continent for their respective kings. Their claims led to nearly two centuries of war among the empires of France and England and the indigenous peoples for hegemony. The rivalry in North America revolved mainly around the lucrative fur trade. In 1713 the **Treaty of Utrecht** secured a temporary peace that lasted until the **Seven Years' War** (1756-63),

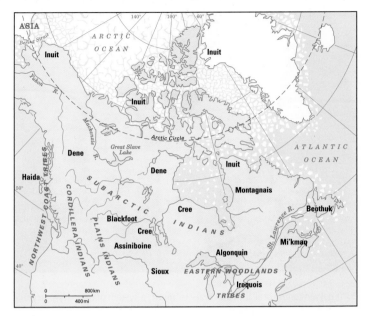

in which France, Spain, Austria and Russia opposed Britain and Prussia. Before their final defeat by the British on the **Plains of Abraham** in 1759, the French not only established enduring settlements in the St. Lawrence Valley, but also explored half the continent, founding an empire known as **New France**, which, at its greatest extent, stretched from Hudson Bay to New Orleans (Louisiana) and from Newfoundland nearly to the Rockies. This empire thrived on the fur trade. However, England's **Hudson's Bay Company (HBC)**, founded in

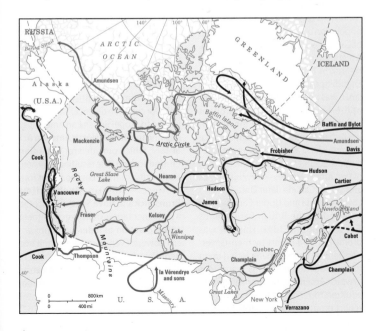

Arrival of Champlain (1608) by George Agnew Reid

Library and Archives Canada (C-11015)

1670, gained control of all the lands draining into the great bay and exercised a monopoly over that area, challenged only by Scottish merchants who established themselves in Montreal after the British conquest of France and formed the **North West Company** in 1783.

TOWARD CONFEDERATION

In 1763, when the fall of New France was confirmed by the **Treaty of Paris**, the population of the future confederation of Canada was overwhelmingly French. A few settlements in Newfoundland and Halifax in Nova Scotia were the only English-speaking exceptions. This imbalance was not to endure. The aftermath of the American Revolution brought thousands of **Loyalists** to the remaining British colonies (Nova Scotia, Prince Edward Island and Lower Canada, later named Quebec) and led to the creation of two more colonies—New Brunswick and Upper Canada (later Ontario).

Lower Canada and Upper Canada were reunited by the British Parliament's **Act of Union** in 1841. This law was prompted by a report by then-Governor General Lord Durham, based upon his investigation of the 1837 rebellions in which Americans had participated. In addition to recommending union, the report proposed **responsible govern-ment,** a system of majority-party rule in the assembly (the British government did not formally implement this system until 1847), partly in the hope of reducing American influence.

Threats and incursions by Americans during the War of 1812, the Rebellions of 1837, the American Civil War and the Fenian Raids of 1866-70 convinced the British government that more settlers were needed if their colonies were to survive. The policy of offering free land to potential settlers played a significant role in the development of Canada during the 19C and early 20C.

Fear of American takeover encouraged the small groups of British colonists to unite for common defence. Their actions helped to propel British Parliament into ratifying the **British North America Act** of 1867, which provided for **Canadian Confederation**. The resulting new political entity, initially composed of four provinces—**Ontario, Quebec, New Brunswick** and **Nova Scotia**—adopted a parliamentary system of government and separation of federal and provincial powers. Even as confederation was negotiated, chief proponents John A. Macdonald and George-Étienne Cartier envisaged a dominion stretching from coast to coast.

Between the eastern provinces and the small colony of British Columbia on the West Coast lay the immense, empty domain of the Hudson's Bay Company. Pressured by the British Government, the company finally agreed to relinquish its lands to the new Confederation for a cash settlement and rights to its posts and some land. As the new Dominion of Canada took possession, the Métis rebellion in the Red River Valley led to the creation of the fifth province, **Manitoba**, in 1870. Meanwhile, **British Columbia** began negotiations to become the sixth province, prompted by fear of an American takeover, and **Prince Edward Island** joined its sister Maritime Provinces in Confederation in 1873. The Yukon Territory was created in 1898 and entered Confederation in the same year.

"Canada has been created because there has existed within the hearts of its people a determination to build for themselves an enduring home."

A.R.M. Lower, *Colony to Nation*, 1946

THE TRANSCONTINENTAL RAILWAY

To encourage British Columbia to join Confederation in 1871, the province was promised a transcontinental rail link. After a few false starts, construction of the **Canadian Pacific Railway** finally got under way in 1881. It was an immense and difficult project, the western mountain ranges alone posing a formidable barrier. Building the line over the steep grades of **Kicking Horse Pass**, for example, was one of the great achievements of railroad engineering. **Rogers Pass** and **Fraser Canyon** were only slightly lesser obstacles.

Serious problems beset the laying of track in the Canadian Shield country north of Lake Superior, where, at one moment, tonnes of granite had to be blasted out and, at the next, track lines would sink into the muskeg.

In the Prairies, however, all records for tracklaying were broken: in one day, a total of 10km/6mi were laid, a record never surpassed by manual labour. This progress was achieved under the dynamic management of **William Van Horne** an American who later became president of the Canadian Pacific Railway Co. In only four years, the line was completed.

THE 20TH CENTURY

Canada's purchase of land controlled by the HBC opened the way for settlement of the West; the building of the transcontinental rail line provided the means. Thousands of immigrants poured into the region, necessitating the creation of two provinces in 1905: **Saskatchewan** and **Alberta**. By 1912 the remaining parts of the Northwest Territories south of the 60th parallel had been redistributed to Manitoba, Ontario and Quebec.

Canada played a substantial role in both world wars, and finally achieved complete control of its external affairs in 1931 by the **Statute of Westminster**, a British law that clarified Canada's parliamentary powers. After World War II Canada's tenth province was added when the citizens of **Newfoundland** voted to join Confederation in 1949. In the postwar years Canada found itself becoming a major industrial country, with an influx of immigrants who provided the skills and labour vital to economic growth.

The 1960s saw the beginnings of Quebec's **separatist movement**, resulting from cumulative grievances of French Canadians. The federal government accelerated efforts to accommodate Quebeckers' demands, including broader educational funding and official recognition of the French language. In 1969 institutional bilingualism was established at the federal level by the Official Languages Act. Separatists were defeated at the provincial polls in 1973, but were victorious in 1976. In 1980 the Quebec electorate rejected a move toward independence, but the controversy continued.

In 1982 the British North American Act (1867) was renamed the Constitution Act, which repatriated the constitution from London. Quebec refused to sign the constitution, mainly because the agreement did not provide for transfer of legislative powers between federal and provincial governments. In 1987 the **Meech Lake Accord** called for special status for Quebec. Federal and provincial ratification was not forthcoming by 1990, however. In 1992 a national referendum that would have granted special constitutional status to Quebec was defeated, but the movement toward independence gained support within Quebec. Secession from Canada was narrowly defeated in the fall of 1995 by voters in the province by a margin of just over 1 percent. In 1998 Canada's Supreme Court declared that, under constitutional law, Quebec has no legal right of unilateral secession.

Canada's aboriginal population continues to press for autonomy and land settlements. A goal of the **Assembly of First Nations** (AFN), representing some 500,000 of the country's nearly one-million-strong aboriginal population, is constitutionally guaranteed rights of First Nations Peoples. The defeated 1992 referendum included a provision for self-governing powers for First Nations. In a plebiscite earlier that year, however, Northwest Territories voters approved proposed boundaries of a new territory to be formed in the eastern part of the region. A large majority (84.7 percent) of the region's voters ratified terms of the Land Claim Agreement in November as the final step in dividing the Northwest Territories. After a seven-year transitional period, the self-administered Inuit homeland called Nunavut became Canada's third territory, in April 1999.

THE NEW MILLENNIUM

Many of the same issues of the past century face Canadians as the new millennium begins. The **Nisga's Treaty** signed in April 2000 is considered by some Canadians to be a contentious model for self-governance for other First Nations Peoples. In addition to providing law-making powers for British Columbia's Nisga'a over their lands, assets, language and culture, the treaty includes cash payments and control over natural resources. Critics fear that overall costs of treaties based on this model will be too high and that clear definitions of territory claimed by other First Nations groups will be difficult to achieve.

In June 2000 Canada's political landscape changed with the emergence of the Canadian Alliance Party. An initiative of the western-based Reform Party, this new entity challenged the domain of the Progressive Conservatives, one of the country's two founding political parties. The parties agreed to merge in 2003, forming the new Conservative Party of Canada. Despite their hopes this move would unite the right, the new party was unable to unseat the governing Liberals in the 2004 general election. However, political scandals and party discord weakened the Liberals, and the January 2006 election resulted in a minority Conservative government.

Sovereignist politicians in Quebec have vowed to try yet again for a mandate to separate the province from Canada, however the younger Gen-Xers have a more global view than their fathers. The issue shows no sign of disappearing, but has lost most of its real threat.

Multiculturalism is nothing new to Canada, a nation of great ethnic and racial diversity. It remains to be seen, however, if the current socio-political upheaval and continuing introspection will fracture national unity or restore it. For the time being, Canada remains an ideal for many other nations.

TIME LINE
PRE-COLONIAL PERIOD

20,000-15,000BC	Estimated earliest human crossings of the land bridge across the Bering Strait from Mongolia to present-day Alaska.
c. AD 1000	Norse reach Newfoundland.
1492	Christopher Columbus lands on San Salvador.
1497	John Cabot explores east coast of Canada.

NEW FRANCE

1534	**Jacques Cartier** claims Canada for France.

1565	St. Augustine, Florida, the oldest city in the US, is founded by Spaniards.
1583	Sir Humphrey Gilbert claims Newfoundland for England.
1605	Samuel de **Champlain** establishes **Port Royal**.
1610	**Henry Hudson** enters Hudson Bay.
1620	Pilgrims found Plymouth, Massachusetts.
1670	**Hudson's Bay Company** is formed.
1713	Treaty of Utrecht is signed. France cedes Acadia to Britain.
1722	**Six Nations Iroquois Confederacy** is formed.
1730s-40s	La Vérendrye family explores Canadian West.
1755	Acadian Deportation from Nova Scotia begins.
1756-63	Seven Years' War.
1759	British defeat the French in Quebec City.
1763	**Treaty of Paris** is signed. France cedes New France to Britain.

BRITISH REGIME

1775	War of Independence begins in American colonies.

1778	James Cook explores coast of British Columbia.
1783	American colonies gain independence from Britain. Loyalists migrate to Canada.
1791	**Constitutional Act** creates Upper Canada (Ontario) and Lower Canada (Quebec).
1793	Alexander Mackenzie crosses British Columbia to the West Coast.
1812-14	War of 1812.
1837	Rebellions in Upper and Lower Canada.
1841	**Act of Union** creates the United Province of Canada.
1847	**Responsible government** system is implemented in Canada.
1848	California Gold Rush begins.
1858-61	British Columbia's gold rushes.
1861-65	American Civil War.

CANADIAN CONFEDERATION

1867	British North America Act establishes Canadian Confederation.
1869-70	Riel Rebellion occurs in Red River Valley.
1870	Canadian Confederation buys Hudson's Bay Company land; Manitoba is created.

Klondike gold fields in c. 1901

Yukon Archives, Adams & Larkin fonds #9151

1872	**Dominion Lands Act** is passed.
1873	North West Mounted Police established.
1881-85	Canadian Pacific Railway is constructed.
1885	Northwest Rebellion occurs. Canada's **first National Park** is created.
1896	Gold is discovered in the Klondike.
1914-18	World War I.
1931	**Statute of Westminster** grants Canada control of external affairs.
1939-45	World War II. Canada receives large numbers of European immigrants.
1942	Alaska Highway is completed.

CONTEMPORARY CANADA

1959	**St. Lawrence Seaway** is opened.
1962	Trans-Canada Highway is completed.
1968	Québécois Party is founded.
1982	**Constitution Act** is passed. Quebec refuses to sign the new constitution.
1987	**Meech Lake Accord** calls for special status for Quebec.
1990	Manitoba and Newfoundland refuse to sign Meech Lake Accord. Quebec refuses to sign 1982 constitution. **Oka**, Quebec, is site of armed conflict between Mohawks and Canadian government over native land claims.
1992	A national referendum to grant Quebec special status is defeated. Voters in Northwest Territories ratify land claim agreements, a key step to Nunavut's establishment.
1993	Negotiation of **North American Free Trade Agreement** (NAFTA) among Canada, Mexico and the US.

1994	Approved by Canada, Mexico and the US, NAFTA takes effect Jan 1.
1995	Quebecers vote by a narrow margin (50.6 percent to 49.4 percent) not to grant the provincial government the mandate to negotiate secession from the rest of Canada.
1998	Canada experiences its worst ice storm in the country's history. Some 3.5 million people are without power.
1999	Self-administration for the new territory of **Nunavut** officially begins. In business for 130 years, Eaton's (a department store chain) files for bankruptcy.

THE NEW MILLENNIUM

2000	Landmark federal treaty with British Columbia's **Nisga'a** First Nations People grants self-governance.
2001	Official name of the province is changed to Newfoundland and Labrador.
2002	Canadian troops join international peacekeeping mission in Afghanistan.
2004	The Liberal party forms the first minority government in 25 years.
2005	Haitian-born broadcaster **Michaëlle Jean** becomes 27th Governor General.
2006	The national **census** shows that more than 80 percent of all 31.6 million Canadians live in urban areas.
2008	Governor General grants Prime Minister Stephen Harper's request to suspend Parliament until late January.
2015	Former PM Pierre Elliott Trudeau's son Justin is elected Prime Minister for the Liberals, ending Stephen Harper's reign.

Art and Culture

Canadian culture is rooted in a blend of British, French, and Aboriginal traditions, and influenced by successive waves of First Nations Peoples. American media and entertainment dominate, but various federal government programs and laws attempt to support Canadian cultural initiatives. The federally funded Canadian Broadcasting Corporation (CBC) provides country-wide television and radio coverage; the National Film Board provides funding and distribution support for film; and other federally funded programs support art, music and dance.

ART
FIRST NATIONS EXPRESSIONS

Over centuries, Canada's First Nations Peoples have developed diverse modes of artistic expression that bear witness to their distinctive lifestyles and beliefs. Since the First Nations Peoples were generally nomadic, little remains of their prehistoric art. However, petroglyphs, or carvings on rock, found in various sites in British Columbia and Ontario are as much as 5,000 years old. The remains of totem poles and stone and bone carvings discovered in sites along the West Coast date back to 500BC. Decorated with representations of animals and geometric designs, Iroquoian pottery dating from 900-1600AD has been unearthed in Ontario and Quebec.

Traditional Art

Most Algonquian-speaking aboriginals (notably Abenaki, Algonquin, Cree, Mi'kmaq, Montagnais and Naskapi) are descended from First Nations Peoples, who excelled in the art of beadwork (shell, bone, rock or seed) and embroideries (porcupine quills and moose or caribou hair). Caribou-hide vests and moccasins and various birchbark objects were often adorned with geometric incisions and drawings. Elaborate belts of **wampum** (beads made from shells) feature motifs illustrating significant events in native history. Wampum was exchanged at peace ceremonies and during the signing of treaties. The smaller, quasi-sedentary, Iroquoian-speaking groups included Hurons, Mohawks, Onondagas and Senecas. As agricultural societies, they formed semipermanent villages and constructed multifamily dwellings known as longhouses; out of their sedentary lifestyle evolved an artistic repertoire free from the constraints of nomadism. Among their most beautiful works are exquisite moosehair embroideries that gradually began incorporating floral motifs under European influence. Wooden masks known as **false faces** represented mythological figures associated with traditional healing practices. The First Nations of the Plains, such as the Assiniboine, Blackfoot and Cree, painted their teepees, robes of bison and rawhide containers with everyday motifs; the horse quickly became an important icon in their decoration.

The art of the Northwest Coast cultures is unlike any other in North America. Having leisure time, they developed a creative expression unequalled on the continent north of Mexico. Tall tree trunks were chiselled with designs of birds, animals, humans and mythological creatures and raised as **totem poles**. Their purpose varied: sometimes they were functional, serving as house corner posts; sometimes decorative, serving as the entrance to a house (a hole was made at the bottom of the pole); other times they were memorials to deceased relatives. The golden age of carving was 1850 to 1900, after the introduction of metal tools by Europeans. Haida carvers often worked in **argillite,** a shiny, black slatelike rock, creating miniature figures of animals and humans, totem poles and pipes.

Contemporary Works

First Nations art has undergone a profound transformation in recent years. Whereas artists traditionally relied on the use of natural materials such as hide and bark, today they are experimenting with canvas, acrylics, charcoal and other new media; consequently, innovative techniques have emerged, although

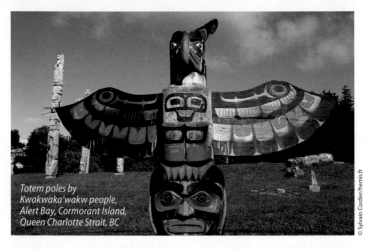

Totem poles by
Kwakwaka'wakw people,
Alert Bay, Cormorant Island,
Queen Charlotte Strait, BC

© Sylvain Cordier/hemis.fr

inspiration is still drawn from social and cultural traditions. The result is a fresh, contemporary vision of aboriginal art that keeps alive the First Nations Peoples of the past. Three major schools prevail in contemporary First Nations art: Woodlands, West Coast and Inuit. Woodland artists in eastern Canada have been influenced by the iconographic style of Ojibwa **Norval Morrisseau** in the 1970s, in particular his renderings of mythological creatures. His contemporaries Odawa artist **Daphne Odjig** and Cree artist **Carl Ray** (1943-78) further evolved Morrisseau's style through personal interpretation. Hailed as the country's first aboriginal modernist, **Alex Janvier,** also a Morrisseau contemporary, forged a unique style. The elegant but spare representations of birds and animals by Benjamin Chee Chee (1944-77) are widely imitated.

On the West Coast, a resurgence of Haida art was begun in the late 1950s under the leadership of famed artist **Bill Reid** (1920-98). Reid achieved worldwide recognition as the popularizer of his ancestral Haida artistic style, to which he brought modern design sensibilities and savvy.

Raven and the First Men, a large carving in yellow cedar, is considered his masterpiece. The Haida style has been continued in the works of master carver **Robert Davidson** and his brother **Reg Davidson**.

INUIT ART

Art forms developed over centuries have brought no small renown to the inhabitants of North America's Arctic regions.

Origins

The earliest known artifacts produced by the Inuit are small stone projectile points attributed to the Pre-Dorset and Dorset cultures in the first millennium BC. Petroglyphs attributed to these cultures have been found in the steatite (soapstone) hills of Kangiqsujuaq in Nunavik. The Thule people, generally considered to be the ancestors of the present-day Inuit, crafted small objects including combs and figurines; these early artifacts were generally associated with religious beliefs.

Beginning in the 19C, many miniature sculptures made of stone, ivory (walrus and narwhal tusks) and whalebone were traded for staples such as salt and firearms, provided by Europeans. With the decline of traditional lifestyles resulting from increased contact with nonindigenous peoples, sculpture and other forms of arts and crafts gradually lost their magic or religious significance and provided a new source of income to the Inuit population.

Inuit Art Today

The term "Inuit Art" evokes images of **stone carvings.** Abundant in the northern regions, soapstone is a soft rock ranging from greyish green to brown. Other harder rocks commonly used include green serpentine, argillite, dolomite and quartz. Modern Inuit sculptures, which can reach impressive dimensions, represent local fauna, life in the great northern regions and other arctic themes. Printmaking, sculpted caribou antlers, rock engravings and tapestries are other common art forms in the Arctic.

The most renowned centres for Inuit sculpture are the villages of Povungnituk, Inukjuak, Salluit and Ivujivik in the Nunavik region of Quebec, and **Cape Dorset,** Iqaluit and Pangnirtung in the territory of Nunavut. Three artists had a profound effect on the development of Inuit sculpture are Nunavik's **Joe Talirunili** (1893-1976), **Davidialuk** (1910-76) and **Charlie Sivuarapik** (1911-68). Among the foremost sculptors of the current generation are Joanassie and Peter Ittukalak from Povungnituk, and Eli Elijassiapik, Lukassie Echaluk and Abraham Pov of Inukjuak. Nunavut's best-known carvers include **Osoetuk Ipeelie,** Kiawak Ashoona and **Pauta Saila,** all from Cape Dorset.

Inuit prints, in general, illustrate the animals, legends and traditions of the North in a highly decorative, two-dimensional style. Cape Dorset artists **Kenojuak Ashevak** and Lucy Qinnuayuak are well known, especially for their depiction of birds. Printmakers from Baker Lake exhibit highly individualistic styles and include artists William Noah and Simon Toookoome.

PAINTING AND SCULPTURE

17C-18C

The arrival of French and British colonists in the early 17C introduced European aesthetics and forms to the artistic landscape. Religion dominated life in what was then New France; thus, church decoration was the focus of early Canadian art. Paintings and statuary were first imported from France, but craftsmen were soon trained locally. Decorative arts for use in the liturgy flourished; prominent sculptors of the time included brothers **Noël Levasseur** and **Pierre-Noël Levasseur,** who were commissioned to decorate ships of the French navy, as well as churches. In Quebec three generations of the **Baillairgé family** were widely recognized for their exquisite wood sculptures and church decoration in general. After the British victory on the Plains of Abraham (1759), religious art declined and nonreligious painting gained prominence. Artists, primarily European-trained, began producing works that focused on such popular subjects as **landscapes** and, above all, **portraits,** commissioned by an emerging and wealthy bourgeoisie. The best known among these artists is **Antoine Plamondon** (1802-1895), who also painted religious themes (Portrait of Sister Saint-Alphonse, 1841).

Art was the means of depicting topography. British army officers were sent to Quebec to paint topographic views of the colony for military purposes. Some of these works, inspired by the romantic ideals of late 18C England, are best exemplified by the carefully executed watercolours of officer Thomas Davies (1737-1812).

19C

Secular art blossomed in the early 19C with such works as **William Berczy's** (1744-1813) Neoclassical painting The Woolsey Family and his portrait of Mohawk Chief Joseph Brant. The expanding middle class wanted portraits of themselves. their pets and horses—as well as their pastimes and business ventures. Robert Clow Todd (1809-1866) was commissioned by the Gilmour family to paint its shipyards (Wolfe's Cove, Québec, 1840), for example. Throughout the 19C, the arrival of European artists had a decisive impact on Canadian painting. **Paul Kane** (1810-71), born in Ireland, came to Canada as a child. He travelled the country extensively; his detailed portraits of native peoples (The Death of Omoxesisixany c.1856) are of significant historical interest today. Dutch-born **Cornelius Kreighoff** (1815-72) captured colourful French Canadian rural life in unprecedented detail in *The Habitant Farm* (1856) and other paintings. He is known for his superb landscapes and scenes of daily life in the Montreal region.

By the mid-19C Montreal had evolved into a sophisticated city, prosperous and interested in the arts. The oldest art gallery in Quebec, the **Art Association of Montreal,** was founded in 1860, the forerunner of Montreal's Museum of Fine Arts (Musée des Beaux-Arts). In Ottawa, Governor General the Marquess of Lorne created the **Royal Canadian Academy of Arts** in 1880, which eventually became the National Gallery of Canada. At this time, however, most artists trained in Paris (then the art capital of the world), though the subject matter of both their paintings and sculpted works was largely Canadian.

Early 20C

At the onset of the 20C, the influence of the so-called Paris School was visible in Canadian art, particularly in the works of Quebec artist Wyatt Eaton (1849-1896) and Montreal art professor **William Brymner** (1855-1925), one of the first Canadians to study abroad; his painting *A Wreath of Flowers* (1884) is an embodiment of French techniques. Their followers include Impressionist-style painters **Marc-Aurèle de Foy Suzor-Côté** (1869-1937), **Clarence Gagnon** (1881-1942) and **James Wilson Morrice** (1865-1924). **Robert Harris** (1849-1919) left Prince Edward Island to train in Paris, but returned to execute perhaps the most prestigious commission in Canada, *The Fathers of Confederation* (1883); thereafter, Harris became one of Canada's eminent portraitists. Hailing from London, Ontario, **Paul Peel** (1860-92) studied and lived abroad, though he exhibited in Canada. His works, several of which were controversial (*A Venetian Bather and After the Bath*), gained him international attention.

Sculpture

The turn of the 20C was the era of great commemorative monuments. Among the most notable sculptors in Quebec were artist-architect Napoléon Bourassa (1827-1916) and the celebrated **Louis-Philippe Hébert** (1850-1917). **Alfred Laliberté** (1878-1953) fashioned sculptures along the fluid lines of the Art-Nouveau style while maintaining an academic approach. Suzor-Côté, a close friend of Laliberté, used the same Art-Nouveau techniques to create a series of bronze works. In the 1930s the Art-Deco style influenced several Canadian sculptors, including Torontonian **Elizabeth Wyn Wood** (*Passing Rain*).

Cubism, constructivism and other European styles did not surface in Canadian sculpture until the early 1950s, when they were evident in the works of **Anne Kahane** and **Louis Archambault.** Following World War II, Canadian sculpture was invigorated by the availability of many new materials, which fostered experimentation in techniques and shapes. A movement known as Structurism developed in the 1950s, particularly in the Prairie Provinces, under the guidance of Eli Bornstein. In the 1960s talented painters **Michael Snow** and Les Levine established reputations based largely on their sculpted works: Snow's stainless steel forms and Levine's plastic modules. Yves Trudeau and Gerald Gladstone experimented with welded-steel constructions. Otto Rogers in Saskatoon and John Nugent in Regina also worked with steel. **Sorel Etrog** is recognized for his signature knotted-bronze works, which suggest the influence of cubism, and **Robert Murray** is internationally known for his large, colourful metal structures. Ed Aelenak and Walter Redinger turned to fibreglass for their constructions, while Michael Hayden created his kinetic works from neon tubing.

Budding Nationalism

World War I profoundly affected artists who regarded Canada as a proud young nation to be accepted on its own terms: why look to Europe, they felt. Trained in commercial design, **Tom Thomson** (1877-1917), an expert outdoorsman, painted Algonquin Park and other parts of Ontario in a bold new way. Thomson's vibrant colors and intense brushwork infused his paintings of the rugged terrain with a vitality that leaps from the canvas. *The West Wind* and *The Jack Pine* are among his best-known works. Like-minded artist-friends based in Toronto formed the **Group of Seven** in 1920, the first truly Canadian school, which included Lawren Harris (1885-1970), J.E.H. MacDonald (1873-1932) and A.Y. Jackson (1892-1974). Harris' austere depictions of the Canadian landscape, in particular *North Shore, Lake Superior* (1926), inspired the country's new modernists. Influenced by members of the Group of Seven, Carl Schaefer, painting in the 1930s, imbued psychological and sociological symbolism into his renderings of the Canadian landscape (*Ontario Farmhouse*, 1934). Another painter profoundly attached to the Canadian landscape, particularly that of British Columbia, was Victoria-born **Emily Carr** (1871-1945), Canada's first prominent female artist; her reverence for native art and culture, as well as nature, manifested itself in her unique style. Ontario-born **David Milne** (1882-1953) emphasized form and brush technique over subject matter; his paintings exhibited a wide variety of subjects, from cityscapes and rural scenes to still life (*Water Lilies and the Sunday Paper*, 1929).

In the 1930s Montreal artists began to rebel against the "wild landscape nationalism" of the Group of Seven. A staunch critic of the group, **John Lyman** (1886-1967) attempted to redirect Canadian art according to the precepts of the Paris school of thought. In 1939 he created the Contemporary Arts Society and organized a group known as the Modernists. Its members included **Marc-Aurèle Fortin** (1888-1970), Goodridge Roberts (1904-74), and Paul-Émile Borduas (1905-60).

THE POST-WAR ERA

World War II marked a turning point in the evolution of Canadian art. In 1940 **Alfred Pellan** (1906-88) returned to Quebec from France to exhibit paintings influenced by Picasso and other proponents of Cubism. **Paul-Émile Borduas** and several fellow artists, including **Jean-Paul Riopelle** (1923-2002), founded the **Automatist** group, whose paintings reflected Surrealism's goal of transferring the creative impulses of the psyche to the canvas. As a response to the spontaneity of the Automatists, **Guido Molinari** and **Claude Tousignant** founded the **Plasticist** group (1955) with the intent of freeing painting from the Surrealist idiom through the use of an abstract geometric vocabulary; form and color were key elements of their work.

After World War II, however, no single school of thought prevailed over the inspirational and creative effervescence of contemporary art, although several Montreal painters, **Yves Gaucher** and Ulysse Comtois among them, and sculptors Armand Vaillancourt, Charles Daudelin and Robert Roussil, exhibited intensely individual modes of expression. Throughout Canada, artists strove to develop their own highly personal styles, like the representational art (*To Prince Edward Island*, 1965) of Atlantic artist **Alex Colville** (b.1920) or William Kurulek's (1927-77) personal reminiscences of Ukrainian prairie life.

THE CONTEMPORARY SCENE

In recent years, Canadian Art has evolved alongside major international currents; it has distanced itself from traditional painting while emphasizing more diversified forms and techniques, including "installation," a primarily sculptural idiom that also includes other art forms, such as photography and painting, plus transmedia productions, crossing over numerous mediums in one concept. Among proponents of Installation Art are **Betty Goodwin,** Barbara Steinman, Geneviève Cadieux, Jocelyne Alloucherie and Dominique Blain. Art becomes "performance," having little intrinsic worth, in the mixed-media installations of such artists as Toronto-based A.A. Bronson, Felix Partz and Jorge Zontal. As new technologies emerge (lasers, computers, holograms), Canadian artists continue to express themselves in different genres and contexts. Contemporary movements aside, the precise realism of the paintings by **Robert Bateman,** who depicts animals in their natural habitats, remains popular with an international as well as a domestic buying public.

LITERATURE AND LANGUAGE
LITERATURE

In large measure, Canadian literature resonates with a rich sense of place. Whether in the explorers' journals of the early 17-18C, the diaries and novels of 19C immigrant settlers, or the poems and literary works of the 20C and 21C, writers grapple with what it means to be Canadian.

Early Works

Throughout the era of exploration and colonization, the literature of New France was limited to travel memoirs (Cartier, Champlain), stories, descriptive writings (Sagard, Charlevoix) and the famous historical missives known as the **Relations,** written by Jesuit missionaries, who recorded their lives and work in the New World. In 1837 Philippe Aubert de Gaspé published the first French-Canadian novel *L'influence d'un livre,* based primarily on legends. The first fiction novels were influenced mainly by rural traditions, as evidenced in *The Canadians of Old (Les Anciens Canadiens),* written in 1863 by **Philippe Aubert de Gaspé** senior. Historical novels, inspired by **François-Xavier Garneau's** *History of Canada (Histoire du Canada)* published in the 1840s, became very popular in the mid-1800s, as did the romantic poetry of Octave Crémazie (1827-79) and Louis-Honoré Fréchette (1839-1908). English settlers, such as **Susanna Moodie,** described the challenges of making a home in the Canadian wilderness (*Roughing It in the Bush,* 1852).

The Emergence of Canadian Literature

Canadian Confederation, in 1867, engendered confidence: Canada became a nation and its writers found their voice. "Confederation Poets" **Duncan Campbell Scott** and **Archibald Lampman** celebrated the realities of the Canadian landscape; Scott particularly admired Québécois and aboriginal culture. Meanwhile, anthropomorphization of wild animals, à la Beatrix Potter, characterized books by **Charles G.D. Roberts,** while his contemporary Ernest Thompson Seton wrote from a more scientific point of view. Children's literature blossomed at the end of the 19C with Margaret Marshall Saunders' *Beautiful Joe* and, in 1908, when **Lucy Maud Montgomery** began her enduring *Anne of Green Gables* series. The early 20C brought the humorous poems of **Robert Service,** the poet of the Yukon, who has also been dubbed "Canada's Kipling."

Quebec's early-20C writing was dominated by the nationalist works of writer and historian **Lionel Groulx** (1878-1967), leader of the "Action française," and by the poet Émile Nelligan (1879-1941). In 1916 French-born **Louis Hémon's** novel *Maria Chapdelaine,* depicting life in rural Quebec, was published posthumously, and is now translated into eight languages. In 1933 **Claude-Henri Grignon** wrote his celebrated novel *The Woman and the Miser (Un homme et son péché).* The story of survival, this time in the parched prairies, resurfaced in the first novel of Sinclair Ross, *As for Me and My House* (1941); and later, Northern Manitoba's wilderness was the setting for Gabrielle Roy's *Where Nests the Water Hen* (1951).

Post-War Perplexities

Urbanization and the trauma of World War II resulted in greater introspection among Canadian writers as they questioned the established order. Novelist Robert Charbonneau abandoned his tales of rural life for psychological novels. The McGill Group of poets (F.R. Scott and A.J.M. Smith, among others) paralleled the Group of Seven's avant-garde approach to painting. Meanwhile, feminist authors **Madge Macbeth** and others examined how urbanization and post-war reality affected women in society. Other writers grappled with racism, immigration and social upheaval. **Frederick Philip Grove,** who described Swedish immigrants taming the prairies in his novel *Settlers of the Marsh,* is credited with introducing realism into Canadian literature. Mazo de la Roche penned the *Jalna* series, chronicling how generations of a Southern Ontario family adapted to life there between the years 1927-60. Farther west, in Victoria, BC, artist Emily Carr's autobiographies introduced the world to West Coast First Nations art and sensibilities.

In the 1950s Montreal modernists **Irving Layton**, Milton Acorn and Al Purdy changed the face of Canadian poetry; they influenced future generations of poets, including Gwendolyn MacEwen (*The Shadow-Maker*, 1969), with an earthy, streetwise style, freed from the taboos of subject matter and language. Poets **Gaston Miron** (1928-96), Gatien Lapointe and Fernand Ouellette instilled energy into Quebec literature during the Quiet Revolution of the 1960s. New novelists rose to prominence, and already well-known writers became associated with the finest of Quebec letters, among them **Anne Hébert** (*Kamouraska,* 1973) and Yves Thériault (*Agaguk*). Nova Scotia-born novelist **Hugh MacLennan** (1907-90), a professor at Montreal's McGill University, focused on contemporary life, and became the first major English-speaking writer to forge a national character for the country. His best-selling novel *Two Solitudes* (1945) confronted the issue of Quebec's relationship to the rest of Canada. Well-known anglophone Quebec novelist **Mordecai Richler** (1931–2001) (*The Apprenticeship of Duddy Kravitz*) has won numerous literary prizes, including the prestigious Prix du Gouverneur Général. Poet-singer-novelist **Leonard Cohen** wrote in the 1960s and 70s of the sexual revolution and resistance to the Vietnam War. The times were characterized by a broad diversity of styles, most notably the psychological novel. Prominent writers from this extremely prolific period of literature include Louis Hamelin (*La rage*) and Monique Larue (*True Copies/Copies conformes*). In chronicling the building of Canada's transcontinental railroad (*The National Dream: The Great Railway 1871-1881*), Pierre Berton infused Canadian historical writing with a compelling new style and gained immediate commercial success. Best-selling author **Farley Mowat** (*Never Cry Wolf, Sea of Slaughter*) remains Canada's champion of the environment with his compelling recountings of humanity's destructive impact.

Contemporary Currents

Beginning with the late 1960s and continuing into the 21C, the fertile years of Canadian writing have produced a harvest of talented authors who probe the Canadian consciousness and explore the nation's cultural mosaic: **Margaret Atwood** (*The Handmaid's Tale*), Margaret Laurence (*The Stone Angel, The Diviners*), Timothy Findley (*The Wars*), **Robertson Davies** (*The Deptford Trilogy*), Joy Kogawa (*Obasan*) and Rudy Wiebe (*The Temptations of Big Bear*), among others. Atwood's book *Survival* elevated the internationally acclaimed author to guru status, to the point where her questioning of Canadianness became a yardstick of Canadian culture. It is fitting that, in the year 2000, Atwood should win Britain's most coveted literary prize, The Booker. Along with other world writers working in a multitude of genres, Canadian authors, such as **Michael Ondaatje** (*The English Patient, Anil's Ghost*), Alice Munro (*Lives of Girls and Women, Runaway*) and New Brunswick's Antonine Maillet have won international honours.

LANGUAGE

Canada is a land of immigrants. A population of 5 million in 1900 grew to 12 million by the end of World War II and to more than 36 million in 2016, thanks largely to immigration. Considered to be the **"founding" nations,** the British and the French are the largest populations (37 and 32 percent respectively). To reflect this composition, Canada is officially bilingual. The largest concentration of French-speaking people is in Quebec, but francophones are found in every province. The federal government tries to provide services in both languages nationwide. There are significant numbers of Germans, Italians, Ukrainians, Dutch and Poles, especially in the Prairie Provinces, and of First Nations Peoples, resulting in an interesting mosaic of cultures across the country.

"Canada could have enjoyed:
English government, French culture, and American know-how.
Instead it ended up with:
English know-how, French government, and American culture."

John Robert Colombo,
Oh Canada, 1965

Canada practises institutional bilingualism: English and French are the official languages for all federal and judicial bodies, federally mandated administrative agencies and Crown corporations. The practice has spread to provincial governments and some parts of the private sector. However, in the Province of Quebec, the official language is French. In Nunavut, official languages are Inuktitut and English; since the territory is part of Canada, all federal communications are also in French.

MUSIC AND DANCE
CANADA'S MUSIC

From throat singing to classical music and rock, Canada's multifarious musical genres hum with creativity. Every region boasts its form of **traditional music**, whether the Celtic rhythms of Cape Breton Island; the Irish, Scottish and French fiddle music found in Quebec and Eastern Ontario; or the Inuit throat singing heard in Nunavut. Today, singers **Susan Aglukark** and the duo named Tudjaat continue to popularize Inuit songs. Montreal is known for its international **jazz** festival. Canadian jazz artists include the late **Oscar Peterson** (1925-2007), and trumpeter Maynard Ferguson, the late be-bopper Moe Koffman, drummer Claude Ranger and saxophonist, clarinetists & flutist Jim Galloway. Quebec's widely-acclaimed **Cirque du Soleil** delights audiences around the world with its innovative and enchanting blend of traditional music, circus entertainment, theatre and dance. Canada's **classical music** tradition was under way in colonial times, with concert announcements appearing in newspapers as early as 1751. Quebec City had a concert hall by 1764 and Halifax audiences were delighted by performances of the music of Handel, Bach and Mozart. The 1840s exposed Canadians to international touring performers such as singer Jenny Lind. Local and regional musical societies—the precursors of today's philharmonic orchestras—sprang up around the country. The years between the world wars saw Canada's first musician to achieve national stature (and the only Canadian musician ever knighted): noted conductor Sir **Ernest Macmillan** (1893-1973). He founded one of Canada's first string quartets, and his composition *Two Sketches for Strings* became a Canadian classic. Other Canadians of renown included singer Rodolphe Plamondon, pianist Léo-Pol Morin and violinist Kathleen Parlow. It was conductor **Wilfrid Pelletier** (1896-1982) who launched Montreal's dynamic music scene, while Claude Champagne (1891-1965), composer of the *Symphonie gaspésienne,* opened the way for numerous other composers. Internationally renowned Canadian pianist **Glenn Gould** (1932-82) retired from concert tours in 1964, concentrating on studio recordings; he is noted in particular for his recordings of Bach's *Goldberg Variations.* Yet another classical genre was internationally popularized by guitarist Liona Boyd (b.1950), who branched into New Age music via her 1986 recording *Persona.*

Several outstanding Canadian voices—contralto **Maureen Forrester** and father and son baritones Louis and Gino Quilico among them—are heard on the **opera** stages of Milan, New York, Paris and London, as well as in home-town concert halls in Vancouver, Toronto and Montreal. Composer **R. Murray Schafer's** *Ra* premiered in 1983 and at 11 hours in length remains Canada's most experimental theatrical-music experience. The country sustains the

Canadian Opera Company in Toronto, Opera du Québec, Opera du Montréal, and companies in Vancouver, Calgary, Edmonton. Opera Lyra performs in Ottawa.

Canada's **folk music** boasts a varied tapestry of prominent singer-songwriters: balladeers Ian Tyson (Ian and Sylvia), **Anne Murray,** Stan Rogers (1949-83) and **Gordon Lightfoot** (his *Canadian Railroad Trilogy* became a classic); Alberta-born folk-jazz singer **Joni Mitchell;** Celtic songster Loreena McKennitt; and Quebec "chansonneur" **Gilles Vigneault,** whose song *Mon Pays (Gens de mon pays)* became the separatist movement's anthem in the late 1960s. French-Canadians Adolphe-Basile Routhier (1839-1920) and Calixa Lavallée (1842-91) originated the national anthem, *O Canada*.

The **rock music** of Robert Charlebois reflected a more critical social outlook typical of the 1960s. At that time, large-scale shows and a recording industry heavily influenced by American culture were adding a whole new dimension to Canada's music scene. The California counterculture was echoed in the music of groups such as Harmonium and Beau Dommage. In the early 1970s, bands like the **Guess Who** burst on the scene with their now-classic *American Woman,* whose lyrics became the anthem for the anti-Vietnam War movement.

The Quebec rock group Offenbach also rose to prominence in the 1970s and Ginette Reno is considered one of the province's most acclaimed pop singers. In 1987 lead singer Robbie Robertson of The Band established his solo career as a rock singer-songwriter of world note. The 1990s witnessed the phenomenal rise of Quebec's diva **Céline Dion,** whose acclaim today extends worldwide.

Canada's contemporary rock bands include **Bare Naked Ladies,** Nickelback and the Maritime's Great Big Sea. Contemporary single artists include long-time folk-rocker **Neil Young**, Avril Lavigne, k.d. lang, Nelly Furtado, country-western singer **Shania Twain** and jazz crooners **Diana Krall** and **Michael Bublé.**

DANCE

Early European explorers, such as John Cabot, chronicled the traditional dances of the aboriginal peoples. Later, in the early 19C, Edmond Curtis photographed remarkable footage of West Coast First Nations Peoples dancing in their war canoes. It was not until the early 20C, when Anna Pavlova toured the country several times, that **ballet** truly arrived in Canada. The country's first professional company was the renowned **Royal Winnipeg Ballet**, founded in 1949. British dancer Celia Franca established the National Ballet of Canada in 1951 in Toronto. Montreal's Les Grandes Ballets Canadiens followed in 1958. All of these companies continue to stage splendid performances throughout Canada and abroad. Canadian ballerinas **Karen Kain** and Evelyn Hart are dear to their fellow countrymen, and choreographers Brian Macdonald and James Kudelka have gained wide recognition.

Modern dance in Canada owes its existence to European and Americans who established schools and troupes in the country. The **Toronto Dance Theatre** (1968) was established by Patricia Beatty, Peter Randazzo and David Earle, who trained in the techniques of American dance pioneer Martha Graham. In the early 1970s, former member of the Winnipeg Ballet Rachel Browne founded the dance company **Winnipeg's Contemporary Dancers** (WCD). Also in the 1970s, Montreal became a centre for the genre, following the opening of the experimental troupe La Groupe de la Place Royale. Vancouver-based Karen Jamieson and choreographer Conrad Alexandrowicz explored new forms of expression. Canadian modern dance continues to evolve, becoming less dependent upon external influences.

CINEMA

Although most films shown in Canada are imported from the US, Canadians factor significantly in a number of major films—as actors, directors, animators and producers. Canadian locations are frequently chosen for their lower production costs and visual similarity to the

James McAvoy on red carpet with fans, Toronto International Film Festival

US. Vancouver and Toronto have thriving production companies and employ many actors as extras in international films. Quebec has long had a vibrant film industry, with both a local and international market for French-language films. Founded in 1939, the National Film Board of Canada (NFB), a federal institution, has acquired an international reputation for animated films, such as *Crac!* in 1982 by two-time Oscar-winner Frédéric Back (*The Man Who Planted Trees*, 1988). In 1999 the NFB's *When the Day Breaks* (by Wendy Tilby) won the Palme d'or prize for Best Short Film at Cannes. The NFB is also known for its documentary tradition, which evolved into a new genre known as "cinéma-vérité," a widely recognized trend in Quebec's film industry, best seen in the works of **Pierre Perrault** (*The Moontrap*, 1963; *Wake up, mes bons amis!*, 1970) and Michel Brault (*Les Ordres*, 1974). The Ottawa International Animation Festival has become North America's largest showcase for the genre since its founding in 1976.

Canada produces about 40 feature films a year, almost 40 percent of financing for English-language features and 80 percent of funding for French-language features being provided by government. Noted Canadian **directors** include **Claude Jutra,** who won international fame for *Mon Oncle Antoine* (1971) and *Kamouraska* (1973), based on Anne Hébert's novel; **Denys Arcand** reached European and American audiences with his films *The Decline of the American Empire* (1986) and *Jesus of Montreal* (1989), the latter receiving nominations at Cannes and Hollywood. Once reviled in Canadian Parliament as a public menace, director **David Cronenberg** has unnerved film-goers with his gripping treatment of dark subjects—from his first commercial breakthrough, *Scanners* (1981) to *The Fly* (1986), then *Crash* (1996), *A History of Violence* (2005) and *Eastern Promises* (2007). The films of Toronto-based director **Atom Egoyan** are more works of art than traditional movies; with *The Sweet Hereafter* (1997), he became a player in American commercial cinema. His latest film, *Adoration,* which premiered at the Cannes Film Festival in 2008, takes on weighty contemporary issues. **Norman Jewison** is known for Oscar-winning *Fiddler On The Roof* (1971) and *Moonstruck* (1987). The director of *Titanic* (1997), **James Cameron** also wrote and directed *The Terminator* (1984) and science-fiction action films like *Aliens* (1986) and *Terminator 2: Judgment Day* (1991). Paul Gross' directorial debut, *Men with Brooms* (2002), became the top-grossing English-Canadian film of the last 20 years. Numerous awards for Western-Canadian director Gary Burns' *waydowntown* (2002) followed the critical success of his *Kitchen Party* (1998).

Nature

Covering nearly 10 million sq km/3.9 million sq mi, Canada is the second largest country in the world in terms of physical size. It is exceeded only by Russia, whose landmass totals some 17 million sq km/6.6 million sq mi. Having shores on three oceans (Atlantic, Pacific and Arctic), Canada occupies most of the northern part of the North American continent. Yet its inhabitants, largely concentrated along the Canadian/US border, number only about 36 million. The country is divided into 10 provinces and three territories. Spanning six time zones, the country stretches from latitude 41°47′N at **Pelee Island** in Lake Erie (the same latitude as Rome, Italy) to 83°07′N at **Cape Columbia** on Ellesmere Island, a mere 800km/500mi from the North Pole. This north-south extension of about 4,600km/2,900mi is countered only by its width. Canada covers more than 5,500km/3,400mi from **Cape Spear** in Newfoundland (longitude 52°37′W) to the **Yukon/Alaska** border (141°W).

One of the most remarkable features is the immense bite cut out of the coastline by **Hudson Bay,** named for famed British explorer Henry Hudson. This enormous gulf or inland sea (637,000sq km/245,946sq mi) could be considered part of either the Atlantic Ocean or the Arctic Ocean. In common with the US, Canada shares another noteworthy feature—the **Great Lakes,** which together form the largest body of fresh water in the world. Finally, the country is characterized by its extremely mountainous western rim, the most famous peaks of which are the 3,000m/10,000ft Canadian Rockies.

☙See also the introduction for each province or territory.

GEOLOGIC PAST
THE GREAT ICE AGES

The physiographic regions described below have been extensively modified in more recent geological times by the advance and retreat of glacial ice. Four times during the past million years, the North American climate has become progressively colder. Snowfall became increasingly heavy in the north and was gradually compressed into ice. This ice began to flow south, reaching as far as the Ohio and Missouri river valleys in the US before retreating. At peak coverage, 97 percent of Canada was submerged under ice up to 3km/2mi deep at the centre and 1.6km/1mi deep at the edges. Only the Cypress Hills and the Klondike region of the Yukon escaped this cover. The last Ice Age receded more than 10,000 years ago.

A sheet of ice of such thickness exerts a great deal of pressure on the earth below. As the ice from each glacial advance retreated, hollows were scoured out of the land and filled with water, and mountain ranges were worn away and sculptured. Today about 2 percent of Canada is covered by glacial ice, mainly in the Arctic islands, but glaciers are found in the western mountains (Columbia Icefield and St. Elias Mountains).

MAJOR NATURAL REGIONS

Physiographically, Canada has at its centre a massive upland known as the Canadian Shield, which forms the geological platform for the whole country. This upland is partially surrounded by areas of lowland. That lowland is, in turn, rimmed by mountain ranges on three of Canada's four sides; to the south the country lies open to the US. Only in parts of the north do these mountain rims flatten out to form a coastal plain. Seven major physiographic regions can be distinguished.

THE CANADIAN SHIELD

This massive horseshoe-shaped region surrounding Hudson Bay encompasses nearly half of Canada's area. The terrain is formed of ancient, hard rocks of the

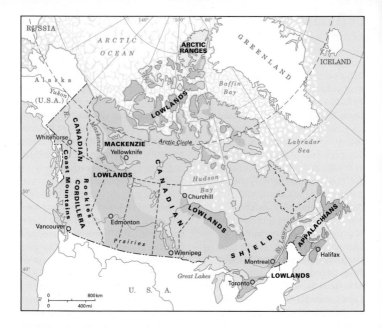

Precambrian era (over 500 million years old) known for their great rigidity and strength. This strength and the region's shape are the origin of the name "Shield." The region is characterized by its innumerable lakes and rivers (Canada possesses as much as a quarter of the world's total supply of fresh water, largely concentrated in the Shield), by its rugged nature (a combination of rock and bog that makes much of the area inaccessible) and by its lack of agricultural soil. However, the region is also the source of much of the country's extensive mineral, forest and hydroelectric wealth.

GREAT LAKES/ ST. LAWRENCE LOWLANDS

Despite their comparatively small size, these lowlands, which extend south into one of the great industrial and agricultural belts of the continent, are home to over 50 percent of the country's inhabitants.

They were created in **Palaeozoic** times (200 million–500 million years ago) when great stretches of the region were flooded by the sea for long periods. During this flooding thousands of feet of sedimentary rock accumulated on top of the Canadian Shield, providing fertile soil that has made the region important for agriculture today. This factor, combined with a favourable climate and proximity to the US, has made these lowlands Canada's richest and most industrialized area as well as its most populous.

PRAIRIES AND MACKENZIE LOWLANDS

The geologic history of these lowlands is similar to those of the Great Lakes/St. Lawrence region. Material eroded from the Shield and the marginal mountains (in particular, the Rockies) was first deposited in shallow seas. Subsequently swept by glaciers, the flat plains in the south consist of fertile soils ideal for wheat and general farming. The Mackenzie Lowlands begin north of a low divide between the Saskatchewan and Athabasca rivers, and support little agriculture because of their northerly latitude. In places where the Mackenzie Plain joins the Shield, a series of large natural basins form great lakes—Winnipeg, Athabasca, Great Slave, Great Bear and others.

HUDSON BAY AND ARCTIC ARCHIPELAGO LOWLANDS

The northern counterpart of the Great Lakes/St. Lawrence region, these lowlands are widely scattered portions of a partially drowned plain of Palaeozoic rock that once covered the northern part of the Shield. They slope gently away from the Shield with little relief. Owing to its northerly latitude, severe climate and frozen soil, this area supports little except a vegetation of moss, lichens and small hardy shrubs in sheltered areas.

APPALACHIAN MOUNTAINS

About 200 million years ago, these mountains, which stretch from Alabama in the US to Newfoundland, were the first to be folded on the edges of the continent. Since then, extensive erosion by ice, rivers and sea has reduced them to mere stumps of their former heights. Today the region is a series of generally flat to rounded uplands, with few sharp peaks rising to no more than 1,280m/4,200ft. Prince Edward Island, and the Annapolis, Ristigouche and Saint John River valleys are notable areas of plains where ancient glacial lakes have left fertile soil.

CANADIAN CORDILLERA

The Canadian Cordillera consists of five major parts (from east to west): the Rocky Mountains, the interior basins and plateaus, the Coast Mountains, the Inside Passage along the coast and, finally, the outer system of islands. Covering the western quarter of the country, this great sweep of mountains is part of North America's long mountain system known as the **Western Cordillera.**

The Canadian Cordillera is a relatively recent geological development. About 70 million years ago, enormous earth forces thrust these mountains up with a great deal of faulting, folding and volcanic activity. Since then, erosion and uplifting by glaciers, and partial drowning by sea have produced a deeply indented coast.

ARCTIC RANGES

These mountains in the extreme north of the country probably rose after the Appalachians. They consist of two fairly distinct parts: the rounded hills of the Parry Islands and the folded peaks of Ellesmere Island.

GEOGRAPHICAL FEATURES
VEGETATION

The flora of Canada consists of roughly 4,200 species, about 30 percent of which have been introduced. The tree line crosses Canada in a rough diagonal from the Mackenzie Delta to Hudson Bay and the Atlantic. The **tundra** lies north of this line, a land of lichens, sedges and stunted shrubs. Because the growing season is too short to allow vegetation to germinate and produce seed, most flowering plants are small perennials, sprouting large flowers to attract insect pollinators. Farther north, ice and bare rock dominate, yet some hardy species flourish here, growing as dense mats wherever moisture, heat and nutrients create favourable microhabitats.

South of the tree line, the **boreal forest** of spruce, tamarack and other conifers gradually begins, interspersed with innumerable bogs, marshes and other wetlands. Farther south, broadleaf trees such as birch, aspen and poplar appear, and some wetlands support commercial cranberry and blueberry farms. More deciduous trees are found until **mixed forest** predominates.

In the east, forestry, agriculture and urbanization have left only isolated pockets of old-growth forest. Hardwoods such as maple, birch and beech compete for well-drained soils with commercial stands of conifers like spruce and pine, while stands of cedar and alder occupy wetter areas. Only in Southern Ontario are the conifers of the north completely left behind and a true **deciduous forest** exists. The remaining wetlands support cattails, water lilies, sedges and ferns, as well as successful alien species like purple loosestrife, which came from Europe some 200 years ago as seeds in cattle fodder.

In the west, conifers give way to vast groves of aspen and poplar as one travels south from the tree line, until trees almost completely disappear once again, replaced by rolling prairie **grasslands.** The region is now highly cultivated, producing much of Canada's grain crops, so that only scattered remnants of the natural grasses remain in their native state. The mountain region of the West also has its own vegetation pattern, the trees thinning out as they approach the alpine tree line in the same way as they do in the North.

Along the Pacific Coast, temperate rain forests with the highest biomass per hectare on earth flourish due to a combination of year-round mild temperatures and very heavy rainfall. As clouds move eastward, they deposit most of their moisture on western slopes, leaving pockets of the interior mountain region dry and dominated by sparse grasses, sagebrush and cactus.

WILDLIFE

Canada's varied landscape hosts several species of animals typical of regional fauna. Vast forests provide habitat for **white-tailed deer, black-tailed deer** and **mule deer,** while **wapiti,** also known as the American elk, populate mountainous terrain and prairieland. Largest of the deer family

Caribou in Western Newfoundland

© Go Western Newfoundland/Aiden Mahoney/Canadian Tourism Commission

is a distinctively Canadian animal, the **moose,** which inhabits the forests of Newfoundland west to British Columbia, as do **woodland caribou,** another member of the deer family. Also distinct is the Canada **lynx,** previously located throughout the country but now surviving in the northern mainland and in Newfoundland.

Rare in Canada is the **wolverine** (of the weasel family), found in sparse populations in the western and northern part of the country. The **grizzly bear** and particularly the **black bear** are common denizens of Canada's coniferous and deciduous forests. Trapped nearly to extinction, **beavers** once again thrive across Canada, occupying the streams and ponds of forested regions. Once common to forest, prairies and tundra, **wolves** reside primarily in the northern wilderness.

Populating Arctic coasts and islands are **polar bears** that feed on Canada's varied **seal** population, such as the grey, harp and hooded seals. Over 30 species of **whales** ply Canada's coastal waters, including the humpback and fin (off Newfoundland); the orca and the grey (off British Columbia); and the beluga, blue, fin and minke (St. Lawrence estuary). The Arctic tundra supports **musk-oxen,** lemmings, foxes and wolves as well as barren-ground caribou.

Wildlife of the prairies includes the **gopher, jackrabbit** and **grouse** in addition to **pronghorns** and **bison** (cattle family), known more commonly in North America as buffalo. Once numbering in the millions, bison were nearly extinct by 1885, hunted for their hides and meat. Wood Buffalo National Park protects a large population today.

Roaming the mountains of western Canada are **mountain goats** and mountain sheep. Thinhorn or **Dall sheep** are found along Canada's Alaska Highway, while **bighorn sheep** frequent British Columbia's south-central ranges and the Canadian Rocky Mountains.

Canada's bird population ranges from waterfowl such as the Canada goose, Atlantic puffin and piping plover to the interior's peregrine falcon and rare whooping crane. The **bald eagle** breeds in parts of northern and eastern Canada, but is most commonly seen along the British Columbia coast. Although most species are migratory, over 400 species of birds have been documented as breeding in Canada.

CLIMATE

Canada's climate is as varied and extreme as its geography. In a large area of the country, winter lasts longer than summer, yet the latter, when it comes, can be very hot. In the north, long hours of daylight in the summer cause prolific plant growth. The central provinces of Canada receive the most snow, far more than the Arctic, which in fact receives the least precipitation of any region.

One major factor influencing climate is proximity to large bodies of water: chiefly, the Pacific and Atlantic oceans, Hudson Bay and the Great Lakes. Such expanses tend to make winters warmer and summers cooler. Regions distant to them are inclined, therefore, to have much colder winters and hotter summers. But terrain is also a factor. In the West the high Coast Mountains shield the interior of British Columbia and the Yukon from the mild and moist Pacific

Pitcher Plant, Newfoundland and Labrador's provincial flower

Newfoundland and Labrador Tourism

air, making their climate more extreme than their location would indicate. The Rockies intensify this trend, leaving the prairies vulnerable to both Arctic winds and hot southern breezes.

Each regional introduction has a summary of climatic conditions with average summer temperatures and precipitation.

Floral Emblems of the Canadian Provinces and Territories

Traditionally, the flora selected to represent a territory or province in Canada must be fairly prevalent within that province or territory. Tree branches or leaves, as well as flowers, may serve as emblems. Floral emblems typically appear on provincial or territorial flags, coats of arms or other official seals.

- ◆ **Canada**   sugar maple
- ◆ **Alberta**   wild (or prickly) rose
- ◆ **British Columbia**   Pacific dogwood
- ◆ **Manitoba**   prairie crocus (or crocus anemone)
- ◆ **New Brunswick**   purple violet
- ◆ **Newfoundland and Labrador   purple** pitcher plant
- ◆ **Northwest Territories**   mountain avens
- ◆ **Nova Scotia**   mayflower
- ◆ **Nunavut**   Purple saxifrage
- ◆ **Ontario**   white trillium
- ◆ **Prince Edward Island**   pink lady's slipper
- ◆ **Quebec**   Blue flag iris
- ◆ **Saskatchewan**   western red (or prairie) lily
- ◆ **Yukon**   fireweed

Toronto skyline from Centre Island
© Peter Mintz/age fotostock

B.C., ROCKIES AND YUKON

Known as the **Canadian Cordillera**, this region consists of the Province of British Columbia, part of the Province of Alberta, and the Yukon Territory. Covering the extreme west, it stretches from the Pacific Ocean to the Rockies and from the Canadian/US border to the Beaufort Sea. The high snowcapped peaks, massive glaciers, rugged ranges, mighty rivers, wild streams and tranquil lakes of this land of beauty attract millions of tourists every year.

- ⊛ **Don't Miss:** Vancouver, Victoria, and at least one of the Canadian Rockies parks.
- 🕒 **Timing:** If you plan to drive, allow plenty of time to cover the long distances and the many stops you'll want to make. *See the Regional Driving Tours at the front of the guide for itinerary ideas.*
- 👥 **Kids:** The Aquarium and Science World in Vancouver.

Geography

Mountainous Terrain – From the west, the **Coast Mountains** rise steeply out of the deeply indented and heavily forested Pacific Coast to over 4,000m/13,123ft. North of this chain in the Yukon are the St. Elias Mountains, which peak with **Mount Logan** at 5,959m/19,551ft, the highest point in Canada.

To the east of the coastal ranges, an immense **plateau** nearly 300km/200mi wide contains the Cariboo ranch lands and the irrigated Okanagan fruit-growing belt. The **Columbia Mountains** define the plateau's eastern edge. In the north, it changes to an area of rugged mountains—the Skeena and Cassiar ranges—before spreading out into the vast Yukon Plateau, a basinlike area of rolling uplands, encircled by high mountains and drained by the Yukon River and its tributaries.

East of this interior plateau and the Rocky Mountain Trench, the Canadian **Rockies** stretch north from the 49th parallel. Rugged, with numerous peaks over 3,954m/12,972ft, the Rockies' front ranges rise abruptly above the foothills and prairie lands of Alberta. At the Yukon/British Columbia boundary, the **Liard River**, a tributary of the Mackenzie River, carves a channel between the Rockies and the **Mackenzie Mountains**. North of the Mackenzies, the Richardson and British mountains stretch almost to the Beaufort Sea.

Forest in Haida Gwaii, BC

© Canadian Tourism Commission

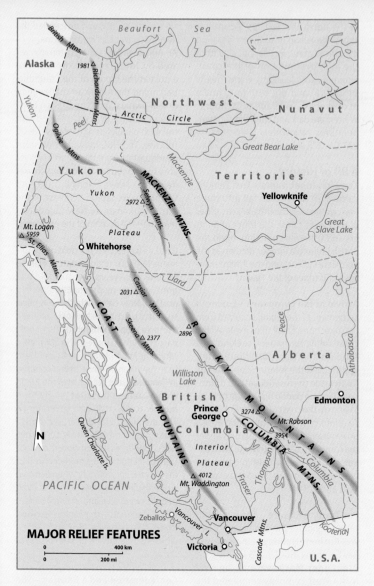

MAJOR RELIEF FEATURES

0	400 km
0	200 mi

N

Beaufort Sea

Alaska

British Mtns.
1981

Richardson Mtns.

Ogilvie Mtns.

Yukon

Peel

Arctic Circle

Northwest

Nunavut

Great Bear Lake

Territories

Yellowknife

Yukon

Plateau

MACKENZIE MTNS.
2972 Selwyn Mtns.

Mackenzie

Mt. Logan
5959
St. Elias Mtns.

Whitehorse

Liard

Great Slave Lake

COAST

Cassiar Mtns.
2031

Skeena Mtns. 2377

2896

R O C K Y

Peace

Alberta

Athabasca

Williston Lake

British

MOUNTAINS

Prince George
3274
Mt. Robson
3954

COLUMBIA

M O U N T A I N S

Edmonton

Queen Charlotte Is.

Columbia

Interior

Plateau

4012
Mt. Waddington

Fraser

Thompson

Columbia

Columbia MTNS.

PACIFIC OCEAN

Zeballos

Vancouver I.

Vancouver

Victoria

Cascade Mtns.

Kootenay

U.S.A.

Climate – Tremendous variation marks the climate of this region, which extends from latitude 49° to north of the Arctic Circle and has coasts on two oceans: the cool Pacific and the icy Arctic.

The climate of coastal British Columbia is influenced by the temperate waters of the Pacific, the prevailing westerly winds and the high Coast Mountains. Winters are mild (0°–5°C/30°–40°F) and summers warm, though not hot (15°–24°C/60°–75°F). Rainfall can be low in protected areas, but among the heaviest in the world in locations exposed to the moisture-laden winds off the Pacific. Greater extremes of temperature and lower rainfall are found to the east, with winters averaging –5°C/23°F and summers 22°C/72°F. Irrigation is needed in the Okanagan Valley to allow cultivation of its famous wine-making fruit.

In the north the St. Elias Mountains shield the Yukon from the moderating influences of the Pacific, but also from the high precipitation of the coast. Summers are pleasantly warm (nearly 21°C/70°F) and dry with long hours of daylight (an average of 20 hours). Winters are dark and cold, though temperatures vary widely (Dawson City −27°C/−16°F, Whitehorse −15°C/−5°F).

A Bit of History

The First Inhabitants – First Nations cultures of this region fall into three basic groups: the wealthy, artistic tribes of the Pacific Coast; the tribes of hunters and fishermen who inhabited the British Columbia interior (known as the Cordillera Indians); and the Athapaskan-speaking tribes of the Yukon.

Arrival of the Europeans – European settlement of the region occurred from two directions. Small ships explored the coast, while fur traders, seeking new supplies and transportation routes, approached the interior. Capt. **James Cook** made the first documented European landing during his voyage of 1778, sailing up the coast of British Columbia. To reinforce its land claims, the British government sent an expedition under the command of Capt. **George Vancouver**, who had been a midshipman on the Cook voyage, to map the coast between 1792 and 1794.

Fur-Trading Empire – The first European to glimpse the Canadian Rockies was **Anthony Henday** of the Hudson's Bay Company (HBC) in 1754.
Alexander Mackenzie of the rival North West Company completed the first crossing of the continent north of Mexico in 1793.
Other "Nor'westers" sought alternative routes through the Rockies to the rich fur area west of the mountains. By following the Columbia and Kootenay rivers, **David Thompson** explored the Howse and Athabasca passes, the southeast corner of British Columbia and northern Washington state between 1804 and 1811. **Simon Fraser** retraced Macken-zie's route in 1808 and descended the river that now bears Fraser's name.
An American fur-trading company created by **John Jacob Astor** founded a post at the mouth of the Columbia, beginning the American challenge to British ownership of the Oregon territory. In 1846 the rivalry was settled with the 49th parallel designated as the US frontier. The HBC moved its western headquarters from the Columbia River area to **Vancouver Island**, which was declared a crown colony in 1849 with Victoria as its capital. The rest of the territory (known as New Caledonia) remained the domain of the company.

Gold – The discovery of gold in California in 1848 attracted people seeking a fortune. Nine years later the gold was gone, and many prospectors moved north to New Caledonia. In 1858 news spread of gold in the lower Fraser River. **Victoria** (pop. 400) saw 20,000 people pass through en route to the goldfields. Afraid the influx of Americans would lead to an American takeover (as had occurred in California), the governor of the island colony, **James Douglas**, stepped in quickly to assert British sovereignty. The mainland was declared a British colony and named British Columbia, with Douglas as its first governor. Poor transportation routes made control of the new territory difficult. When rich gold strikes in the Cariboo brought even more people, Douglas planned construction of a wagon road—the famous **Cariboo Road**, built between 1862 and 1865—which helped ensure British control of the area.

Confederation and a Railway – The two western colonies united in 1866 as British colonies in the east were discussing confederation (which became a reality in 1867). The US purchase of Alaska in 1867 raised new fears of an American takeover and prompted negotiations to become part of the new Canada, located 3,200km/2,000mi away.
British Columbia entered Confederation in 1871 on the condition that a railway be built to connect the province with the

east within 10 years. The birth pains of the project nearly led to British Columbia's withdrawal; but initiated in 1881, it was completed within only four years. The railway brought tourists, settlers and capital to the impoverished region, and encouraged the search for mineral wealth.

"Ho for the Klondike" – When the Cariboo goldfields were exhausted, prospectors again moved north. Gold was found in the Omineca and Cassiar Mountains. Then prospectors entered the Yukon. The long-hoped-for big strike was made in 1896 on a small creek renamed "Bonanza," which drained into the Klondike River, a tributary of the Yukon River. As news spread, thousands of men and women set off from all parts of the globe for the Klondike. In eight years $100 million worth of gold was shipped out, providing an enormous stimulus for this western frontier.

Population – The population of **British Columbia** increased from just over 50,000 at the dawn of the 20C to 4.4 million by the 21C (2011), 13 percent of Canada's total. The great majority of these inhabitants live in the southwest corner of the province, nearly half in the Vancouver metropolitan area.

Today, the population of 33,897 in the **Yukon** is just slightly greater than in 1900. Two-thirds of the residents live in the territorial capital of Whitehorse.

The Economy

British Columbia – The turn of the 19C brought on the resource-extraction economy that dominated British Columbia for most of the 1900s. A second national rail line reached the lower mainland, and the decline of timber supplies elsewhere made the province's huge reserves more valuable. Construction of the **Panama Canal**, opened in 1915, stimulated exploitation and export of the province's minerals by providing a cheap means of transport to Europe. The Great Depression and World War II slowed economic growth, but the postwar boom across North America brought renewed demand for BC's forest products. The second half of the 20C garnered increased trade with Asia and a huge influx of new residents, whose arrival created new economic growth.

Timber – Once paramount, the forest-products industry remains crucial but not dominant. Virtually all the wood cut is softwood, with lodgepole pine, spruce, hemlock and Douglas fir the leading species. Mills convert about 20 percent of this wood into pulp and paper products; the vast majority is exported to the rest of Canada, the US and overseas.

Trade – Vancouver is by far Canada's most active port, shipping huge exports of forest products, grain and mine ores, and handling significant imports of cars,

Gold miners on W.M. West's claim #126 Spruce Creek in 1899

Yukon Archives, Anton Vogee fonds, #171

73

electronic goods and other finished products. The port handles about 102 million metric tons of cargo a year; most of which is in bulk commodities such as wheat (from the Prairie provinces), ore and timber products.

Mining – Although gold is still mined in British Columbia, the focus long ago shifted to lesser-value commodities. The overall value of mineral production is more than $9.2 billion; coal, natural gas, and copper all exceed gold in revenues.

Agriculture – Despite only 3 percent of land available to British Columbia farmers, the province leads Canada in production of apples, peaches, pears, grapes and numerous other fruits; the greenhouses of the Fraser Delta ship tomatoes and other produce throughout North America.

The great interior plateau is cattle-raising country; and the Peace River country east of the Rockies is British Columbia's chief grain-growing area. Agriculture constitutes a $2.75 billion industry in British Columbia.

Fisheries contribute another $709 million to the provincial economy, with more than 80 species of fish, shellfish and marine plants harvested.

Film and Tourism Industries – Cheaper production costs and tax breaks for foreign-film investors are factors in Vancouver's popularity as a filmmaking capital.

Both the film and tourism industries benefit from the province's scenery and diversity. Vancouver's and Victoria's attractions and British Columbia's islands, coast, mountains and wildlife draw more than 22 million visitors each year, who pour almost $8 billion into the provincial economy. Ecotourism and outdoor adventure are key activities in British Columbia, which boasts some of the world's best fishing, camping, hiking, canoeing and kayaking opportunities.

Serving almost 18 million passengers a year, Vancouver International Airport ranks as the West Coast's second busiest (after Los Angeles, California). And the port of Vancouver is a major debarkation point for cruise ships, with nearly 840,000 passengers utilizing British Columbia docks annually.

BC Today – Fueled by growth in trade and population, Vancouver is booming and Victoria thrives on tourism and government. Elsewhere, the decline in mining, logging and fishing has led to more than 20 percent unemployment in some isolated areas, though growth in tourism is beginning to help.

The Rockies – The Canadian Rockies remain major tourist magnets, drawing some 6 million sightseers a year. The Rockies attract hordes of outdoor adventurers and sports enthusiasts. The proper balance between mankind and nature continues to be elusive.

Filming of Stargate on the beach in Whiterock, BC

© Creative BC

The Yukon – The golden years of the Klondike Stampede were followed by years of economic stagnation. Construction of the Alaska Highway during World War II led to increased exploitation of the Territory's mineral wealth. Mining entered a steep decline in the 1990s, though, with only gold still a significant resource. Today, tourism and energy development are the brightest stars in the Yukon's future.

PRACTICAL INFORMATION
GETTING THERE

BY AIR– International and domestic flights to Vancouver International Airport (*15km/9mi south of downtown;* ℘*604-207-7077; www.yvr.ca*) via Air Canada (℘*888-247-2262; www.aircanada.com*), WestJet (℘*888-937-8538; www.westjet.com*) and other major carriers. Taxi to downtown Vancouver (*approx. 25min; $35 flat rate*). Canada Line is the new rapid transit rail connecting YVR airport to downtown Vancouver (*approx.26 min; $5*). Airport limo (LimoJet Limousine Service) ℘*604-273-1331 (one-way $75 + $20 Meet & Greet + 15% GST tax*). Major car rental agencies also at the airport.

BY BUS AND TRAIN – Greyhound **bus** service to BC and the Yukon: ℘*800-661-8747; www.greyhound.ca*. **VIA Rail** Canada operates the Skeena route from Jasper to Prince Rupert, connects Victoria to Courtenay and links Vancouver to Toronto ℘*888-842-7245. www.viarail.ca*.

BY BOAT – **BC Ferries** operates year-round scheduled ferries linking Vancouver Island, the mainland, and many of the islands. BC Ferries ℘*888-223-3779*, or outside North America ℘*250-386-3431*, www.bcferries.com. For ferries from the US to British Columbia *see VANCOUVER ISLAND*.

GENERAL INFORMATION

Accommodations and Visitor Information – Government tourist offices produce annually updated guides on accommodations, camping, fishing, skiing and vacations. The *BC Vacation Planner* suggests driving tours and gives general travel tips, and the *Accommodations Guide* is a comprehensive catalog of hotels, inns, B&Bs and campgrounds. All publications and a map are available free of charge from: **Tourism British Columbia** (*Parliament Buildings, Victoria, BC, V8V 1X4;* ℘*800-435-5622; www.hellobc.com*).

The *Yukon Vacation Guide*, updated annually, provides details about facilities and attractions, entertainment, adventure travel, outdoor activities and gives travel tips. This publication and a road map are available free of charge from **Tourism Yukon** (*Box 2703, Whitehorse, YT, Y1A 2C6;* ℘*800-661-0494; www.yukonwild.com.com*). Both British Columbia and the Yukon maintain extensive networks of provincial and territorial **campgrounds** containing more than 10,000 campsites along major highways. BC campgrounds are booked well in advance during summer holidays and weekends. Fees range from $5 per night, and reservations are advisable; contact Discover BC Reservations: ℘*800-689-9025 (Apr 1-Sept 15); www.discovercamping.ca*. In the Yukon, the nightly fee for campgrounds is $12; travellers must stop at visitor centres to purchase camping permits.

Road Regulations – BC, Alberta and the Yukon have good paved roads. Although there are few freeways, major roads are built to high-speed standards and passing lanes are common. Secondary roads vary in quality; it's a good idea to ask locally about road conditions before leaving the main highway. Throughout the north in BC and the

Yukon, summer brings considerable road repair and construction; be alert and patient. Unless otherwise posted, speed limits are: in British Columbia it is 120km/h (72mph) and the Yukon 100km/h (60mph) on provincial highways and 50km/h (30mph) in cities; in Alberta 110km/h (66mph) on provincial highways and 50km/h (30mph) in cities. For road conditions in British Columbia ✆800-550-4997 or *www.drivebc.ca*. For road conditions in the Yukon ✆867-667-5811 or *www.511yukon.ca*. **Seat belt** use is mandatory. Not mandatory, but practically universal, is courtesy—horn-honking is almost never heard in Vancouver.

Time Zones – Alberta and the BC Rockies region are on Mountain Standard Time. The rest of BC and the Yukon are on Pacific Standard Time. Daylight Saving Time is observed from the second Sunday in March to the first Sunday in November. The northeast corner of BC is on Mountain Standard Time year-round.

Taxes – In addition to the national 5% GST national sales tax, BC levies a 7 per cent provincial sales tax.

Liquor Laws – The legal drinking age is 19. Liquor is sold in government stores.

Provincial/Territorial Holidays – **BC Day**: 1st Monday in August. **Discovery Day, Yukon**: 3rd Monday in August.

Recreation – **Outdoor Activities** – The rivers, mountains and many parks of this vast and sparsely populated region offer outdoor enthusiasts a variety of recreational activities: hiking, horseback riding, fishing, river rafting, canoeing and kayaking. Many **fishing** lodges arrange fly-in packages to remote lakes that attract anglers from around the world. Separate licenses are required for saltwater and freshwater fishing, and can be obtained locally. For more information, contact the BC Fishing Resorts & Outfitters Assn. ✆866-374-

6836 or *www.bcfroa.ca*.

The many navigable waterways, especially in the Shuswap Lake District, offer a host of water sports as well as houseboating. Marine adventures and **cruises** that include nature observation are popular along the coastline. Whistler, north of Vancouver, is one of the world's top ski resorts, with first-class accommodations and facilities, including glacier skiing from June through October. The three ski resorts in the Rockies offer a variety of **winter activities**. For information on recreation, contact Tourism British Columbia (*above*) or www.hellobc.com/ski.

Special Excursions – The **Rocky Mountaineer** journeys through some of the most spectacular mountain scenery in North America during a two-day rail trip from Vancouver to Jasper or Banff. The train travels in the daylight hours only; passengers spend the night in Kamloops. Eastbound, westbound and round-trip travel is possible *(departs from Vancouver Apr–Oct Sun, Tue & Thu 7:30am; one-way $1,741–$2,356/person, double occupancy; cost of lodgings in Kamloops, all meals + drinks included; reservations required;* ✗✆🅿*; Rocky Mountaineer Vacations* ✆*604-606-7245 or 877-460-3200; www.rockymountaineer.com)*.

Pack trips and trail ride excursions are offered *(1-10 days)* for all levels of riding ability. Warner Guiding and Outfitting (✆*800-661-8352; www.horseback.com*) leads rides *(1-7 hrs)* from Banff into the surrounding wilderness. Tonquin Valley Adventures (✆*780-852-1188; www.tonquinadventures.com)* guides small groups to a remote lake within the Jasper backcountry, overnighting *(2-6 nights)* in a rustic lodge, or for day trips. Don't miss the Glacier Skywalk in Jasper National Park. Departs from the Columbia Icefield Glacier Discovery Centre (✆*866-606-6700. www.explorerockies.com)*.

PRINCIPAL FESTIVALS
BRITISH COLUMBIA, YUKON

FEB	**Sourdough Rendezvous,** *Whitehorse, YT*
	Yukon Quest Sled Dog Race, *Whitehorse, YT*
MAY	**Swiftsure Yacht Race Weekend,** *Victoria, BC*
JUN–JUL	**Stampede,** *Williams Lake, BC*
JUN–AUG	**Summer Arts Festival,** *Banff, AB*
AUG	**Loggers' Sports Day,** *Squamish, BC*
	Peach Festival, *Penticton, BC*
	Discovery Day, *Dawson City, YT*
AUG–SEPT	**Pacific National Exhibition,** *Vancouver, BC*
AUG	**Classic Boat Festival** *Victoria, BC*
SEPT–OCT	**International Film Festival** *Vancouver, BC*
OCT	**Okanagan Wine Festival** *Penticton, BC*

Alaska Highway★★

British Columbia, Yukon, Alaska

This great road to the North passes through a land of mountains and lakes of rare beauty, largely untouched by mankind except for a scattering of small communities. Beginning at Dawson Creek in British Columbia, the highway parallels the Rocky Mountains, enters the Yukon along the valley of the Liard River, touches the Cassiar and the Coast Mountains of British Columbia, and follows the St. Elias Mountains to enter Alaska, finally terminating in Fairbanks.

A BIT OF HISTORY

When the Japanese bombed Pearl Harbor in 1941 and landed in the Aleutian Islands, Americans feared an imminent invasion of mainland Alaska.

After a joint agreement between Canada and the US, a land route was pushed through muskeg swamps, over rivers and mountain ranges from Dawson Creek to Alaska in only nine months during 1942.

The 2,232km/1,387mi highway has become a legend in the annals of road construction. Upgraded after World War II and opened to civilian traffic, it now transports the region's resources and the tourists who travel its length.

Info: *The Milepost* is an annually updated directory of natural and historic sights, eating establishments and overnight accommodations mile by mile. Available at bookstores or directly from ☎800-726-4707 (Canada/US) or www.themilepost.com.

Location: The Alaska Highway starts in Dawson Creek—a nine hour drive from Edmonton or an 18-hour drive from Vancouver—and requires some 28 hours to drive to the border between the Yukon and Alaska.

Don't Miss: Liard Hot Springs

Timing: The parks at Muncho Lake and Liard River Hot Springs are good halfway stopping points for the 22 hour drive between Dawson Creek and Whitehorse.

FROM DAWSON CREEK TO FORT NELSON
483km/300mi

The Alaska Highway begins at **Dawson Creek**, BC, in the most northerly corner of the Great Plains that stretch all the way south into Mexico. The descent into

Alaska Highway along Muncho Lake

JF Bergeron/Enviro Foto/Northern BC Tourism

the Peace River valley is lengthy and somewhat winding, crossing the river at **Taylor**, in the midst of a vast natural gas and oil field. Gas processing plants can be seen along the highway, and oil pipelines run beneath fields of crops all the way to **Fort St. John**.

After the junction with Highway 29, the Alaska Highway passes through flat and heavily wooded country, dominated by spruce muskeg and threaded by gas pipelines, that gradually becomes more mountainous until the road reaches **Fort Nelson**. This busy lumber centre and base for oil and gas exploration is also the junction of the Liard Highway to Fort Simpson (Northwest Territories), and access to spectacular Nahanni National Park Reserve.

FROM FORT NELSON TO WHITEHORSE★★

991km/616mi (not including excursion)
After leaving Fort Nelson, the highway turns west into aspen parkland and boreal forest as it climbs into the Rocky Mountains. The countryside is very open, affording many sweeping views of largely flat-topped mountains.

Muncho Lake Provincial Park★★

KM 681/mi 408. Open May–mid-Sept. 250-776-3311. www.bcparks.ca.
This park is one of the most beautiful and geologically interesting parts of the drive. From the wide rocky valley of the Toad River, the vista widens and

more mountains come into view, many of them snow-capped. Stone sheep can often be seen licking salt from the roadbed. Held in a high valley between two towering ranges, **Muncho Lake★★** mirrors the surrounding folded mountains as the road traverses the many alluvial fans of eroded material washed down from the peaks. This provincial park has two good campgrounds and several lodges.

Liard River Hot Springs Provincial Park★

KM 765/mi 478. Exit highway right to the parking area; follow the boardwalk. Open year-round daily; $5. 250-776-7000. www.bcparks.ca.
This small park consists of large, hot sulphur pools (temperature averages 42°C/107°F) in bucolic, forested surroundings. One pool is deep enough for swimming; the lower, hotter pool draws the largest crowds. Both have been developed with boardwalks and changing rooms. The park is one of the most popular overnight stops on the Alaska Highway; during summer months the campground fills up in early afternoon (*reservations are highly advisable*).
About 10km/6mi past the hot springs, the highway enters a massive burn area. The 1982 fire burned 182,725 hectares, the second-largest conflagration in BC history; the landscape is now being reclaimed by aspen, willow and fireweed, the pioneering species that typically follow a fire.

PRACTICAL INFORMATION
DRIVING THE HIGHWAY

The Alaska Highway is paved over its entire length, and navigable year round. Snowfall is inevitable in fall, winter and spring and possible even in May and August. Driving conditions can also be difficult during spring thaw, and road repair is endemic in summer; however, highway advisories are broadcast promptly. Vehicles should be in good mechanical condition before starting out, but service stations are situated at regular intervals. The speed limit varies from 80km/h (50mph) to 100km/h (60mph); watch posted signs. Headlights should be kept on at all times. For the latest road conditions in BC, *800-550-4997 or www.drivebc.ca*. In the Yukon, *867-456-7623 or www.511yukon.ca*.

DISTANCES

Alaska Highway distances were derived from a destination's mileage from Dawson Creek in British Columbia—the official starting point of the highway. Canada's conversion to the metric system and constant highway improvement have complicated the distance measurements, although many businesses still use the original mileage indicators of their location. Along the Canadian portion of the highway, distances are now marked by kilometre posts from Dawson Creek; on the US side, distances are given in miles.

ACCOMMODATIONS AND VISITOR INFORMATION

Overnight accommodations and visitor information are provided in *The Milepost* (*see Information, above*). Most travellers divide the journey from Dawson Creek to Whitehorse with a stop halfway at Muncho Lake Provincial Park or Liard River Hot Springs, where there are camp-grounds and small inns and motels. Reservations are strongly advised for provincial park campsites in BC *800-689-9025*.

The **Liard River** [lee-ARD] is crossed at km 788/mi 490. This wild and turbulent river flows south from the Yukon before turning north near here to join the Mackenzie River. Its valley marks the northern limit of the Rocky Mountains.

At km 947/mi 588 the highway crosses the 60th parallel, entering the Yukon Territory.

The exit from British Columbia is not yet final, however, as the highway crosses and recrosses the boundary several

Liard River Hot Springs Provincial Park

©Eric P. Lucas/Michelin

times. Travellers along this road are rewarded with fine views of the **Cassiar Mountains**.

Watson Lake
KM 1,025/mi 636.5.

This transportation and communications centre for southern Yukon is famous for its collection of **signposts**. In 1942 a homesick soldier, employed in the highway's construction, erected a sign with the name of his hometown and its direction. Tourists have kept up the tradition. Today over 30,000 signs from all over the continent and abroad are stacked on posts in a wide field in the middle of town near the visitor centre. From the south the **Stewart-Cassiar Highway** (Route 37) joins the Alaska Highway at KM 1,044/mi 649. Winding 800km/500mi through western British Columbia, this road provides an alternate route to the Yukon. After this junction the Alaska Highway begins to cross the Cassiar Mountains, with views of snowy peaks on both sides of the road.

At KM 1,162/mi 722 a rise of land is traversed that marks the divide between two great river systems, the Mackenzie and the Yukon, which empty into the Beaufort and Bering seas respectively.

Teslin Lake
KM 1,286/mi 804.

The name of this stretch of water means "long lake" in local native dialect. The highway crosses Nisutlin Bay and hugs the shore for about 48km/30mi. Clusters of the Yukon's adopted emblem, the pinkish flower called **fireweed**, border the lake. The climate here is dry (less than 305mm/12in of precipitation) and warm in summer.

At the head of the lake, the road crosses the Teslin River by a high bridge.

Atlin★
Excursion: 196km/122mi round-trip from Jake's Corner at KM 1,392/mi 865; take road south. An isolated drive on unpaved road. Visitor Centre (in the Atlin Museum, 3rd & Trainor Sts.) ⊙open mid-May–mid-Sept daily 10am–6pm; ℘250-651-7522.

An old gold-mining centre, this small community in British Columbia has a pretty **site** overlooking beautiful Atlin Lake, backed by majestic snow-covered peaks. The excursion boat *MV Trahane* is beached in town, a remnant of Atlin's more prosperous days, and the local historical society occasionally offers tours in summer. From Warm Bay Road, Llewellyn Glacier can be seen beyond the lake on a clear day. The town is a set-off point for adventures in the spectacular wilderness of Atlin Provincial Park.

Marsh Lake★★
KM 1,428/mi 887.

Surrounded by mountains, this lake is an arm of the much larger **Tagish Lake** to the south. At the end of the lake, the road crosses the Yukon River at a dam. At KM 1,445/mi 898 there is a **view**★ from above the steep, white cliffs and clear green water of the fabled **Yukon River**, which rises only 24km/15mi from the Pacific Ocean and meanders nearly 3,200km/2,000mi, crossing the Arctic Circle before reaching the Bering Sea.

Whitehorse★
KM 1,474/mi 918.
⌚See entry heading.

ADDRESSES

⌂ STAY
Accommodations along the Alaska Highway are mostly quite rudimentary, on the order of vintage roadside motels. Two nice inns are located about halfway between Dawson and Whitehorse.

$$ Northern Rockies Lodge (*℘250-776-3481 or 800-663-5269; www.northern rockieslodge.com; 45 rooms*) is a lakeshore, spruce-log structure within Muncho Lake Provincial Park, with tidy rooms, modern conveniences and efficient staff.

Across the road from the hot springs park is **$ Liard Hotsprings Lodge** (*℘250-776-7349; 12 rooms, 1 cabin*). One cabin and a dozen wood-panelled rooms at this roadside accommodation feature upscale rustic furnishings. The hot springs are a convenient 10-minute walk from the lodge.

The Cariboo★

British Columbia

The Cariboo is the name given to the region centred in the valley of the Fraser River north of the Thompson River. Part of the central plateau of British Columbia, this region is a vast rolling upland of low arid hills, lakes, sagebrush, and lodgepole and fir forests bounded to the east by the Cariboo Mountains—from which the area gets its name—and to the west by the Coast Mountains.

A BIT OF HISTORY

The Cariboo Gold Rush – Opened by fur traders, the Cariboo first reached prominence with the gold rush of 1861, which led to the building of the Cariboo Road. Gold was first found in this area in 1859 by prospectors who had made their way from California to the lower Fraser and then north, following the gold trail. Large quantities were being extracted from the upper part of Williams Creek by 1862, when **Billy Barker**, a Cornish sailor who had jumped ship at Victoria to try his luck, hit pay dirt in its lower reaches. Within 48 hours he had extracted $1,000 worth of gold. The area boomed and towns such as Barkerville (named for Billy), Camerontown and Richfield sprang up.

Within 10 years, the easily-accessible gold was gone, and the towns of the Cariboo were almost deserted. Barkerville was uninhabited until 1958, when

Info: ℘250-392-2226 or 800-663-5885. www.land withoutlimits.com.

Location: Williams Lake, the centre of the region, is an eight-hour drive north of Vancouver through the scenic Fraser Canyon.

Timing: The most interesting places to visit require excursions from Highway 97, and may require backtracking to return to the main highway. Plan to spend a night near Barkerville so you can enjoy a full day exploring it (℘ see Addresses).

Kids: Barkerville Historic Town.

the provincial government transformed the site into a museum-town, carefully restoring it to its former splendour.

Cattle Country – After the boom of the gold rush, the rail and road links that had been built for mining brought wood and ranch products to market in Vancouver, and today the main economic activities are timber harvesting and cattle raising (some of the largest ranches in Canada are found in this region). The annual stampede held in **Williams Lake** during the first week of July is considered the premier rodeo of the province, with cowboys from all over North America

---

Saddle sore

Often thought of as ghosts of the past, **cattle drives** still take place in Western Canada, where ranchers send herds into the high country to graze in spring and bring them down in the fall. An annual summer event in the Cariboo replicates the more amiable aspects of a drive for riders of all types. All you need is moderate riding experience; horses and tack can be rented. Based in cattle capital Williams Lake, the **Great Cariboo Ride** is no-frills and bovine-free (no cows) but traverses spectacular countryside and includes high-country hiking, swimming and fishing (℘250-395-2400; www.greatcaribooride.org). The schedule, route and costs for the trip vary from year to year. Several guest ranches in central BC offer experienced riders an opportunity to come along on roundups. *For more information, contact the BC Guest Ranchers' Assn.* ℘877-278-2922; www.bcguestranches.com.

vying for trophies. A popular tourist area, the region is known for its sports fishing, game hunting, dude ranches and other traditional features of "Western" living, and for the restored gold rush town of **Barkerville**.

The Cariboo Road – To facilitate transportation to the boomtowns of the gold rush, the Government of British Columbia built a wagon road to Barkerville from the lower Fraser River near Yale, some 650km/403mi away. Following the wild rocky canyon of the Fraser, the road, opened in 1864, was a remarkable engineering achievement. The old road has been transformed into the Trans-Canada Highway, the Cariboo Highway (97) and Highway 26.

Highway 97 from Cache Creek first climbs out of the Thompson Canyon desert into the Cariboo uplands—a scenic, rolling plateau of aspen, fir and spruce forest interspersed with broad meadows. The rest stop at **108 Mile Ranch** in the heart of this region incorporates a half-dozen historic buildings from a century-old roadhouse. A two-storey 1908 **log barn★** built for the Clydesdales that once trod the highway is the largest wood barn in Canada, and functions today as a community dance hall. After passing through **Williams Lake**, the highway continues north to Quesnel, a timber-mill centre. The **drive★** from Quesnel to Barkerville (Hwy. 26) penetrates the Cariboo Mountains, passing **Cottonwood House★** (&. Ⓞ open mid-May–Sept daily 10am–5pm; ☞$5.; ✗ ℰ250-992-2071; www.cottonwoodhouse.ca). One of

the few remaining roadhouses (lunch is served) on the old wagon road, the house was constructed in 1865 of cottonwood logs. The mining community of **Wells** neighbors Barkerville. Several small inns in the area, such as the Wells Hotel, or the St. George Inn in Barkerville, offer overnight accommodations to modern travellers (contact the district Chamber of Commerce: ℰ877-451-9355; www. wellsbc.com).

BARKERVILLE HISTORIC TOWN★★

♟♦ 90km/56mi east of Quesnel by Hwy. 26. &.Ⓞ Open year-round daily 8am–8pm. ☞$14.50 (child $4.75) for the 2-Day Pass. ✗ ℰ250-994-3332 or 888-994-3332. www.barkerville.ca.

The old gold-mining centre has a fine **site★** surrounded by mountains in the valley of Williams Creek. The restored buildings of Barkerville include the stores, hotels, saloons and assay office of a mining community. In the **Visitor Centre** the video shows and displays on the town, the Gold Rush and methods of mining are a good introduction. Note the rather unusually shaped **St. Saviour's Anglican Church**, a structure of whipsawed timber and square nails. At the far end of the street is the Chinese section, with its **Chinese Freemasons' Hall** (the Chinese followed the other gold rushers north from California but tended to stay within their own community). **Billy Barker's claim** is marked, and the **Theatre Royal** stages typical Gold Rush-era shows (&.open mid-May–end of September, call for hours; ☞$12.95; reservations suggested; ✗). Visitors can also pan for gold Eldorado Mine (fee).

WELLS GRAY PROVINCIAL PARK★★

204km/127mi east of Williams Lake to Clearwater by Hwy. 97 South, Hwy. 24 West and Hwy. 5 North. At Clearwater, proceed 35km/22mi north to the park entrance. Hiking, canoeing, swimming, fishing and horseback riding. Ⓞ Park open year-round. Visitor centre open May–Oct daily 9am–5:30pm. ⚠

St. Saviour's Anglican Church

R. Corbel/MICHELIN

250-674-3334 ext.102. www.wellsgray.ca. Maps available at Visitor Centre. Spread across a spectacular mountain canyon and the western flanks of the southern Cariboo range, this park is a million-acre scenic and recreational treasure, with hiking through its forests and extensive backcountry, as well as water sports in its four main lakes. Its best-known attraction is **Helmcken Falls** (*accessible via Clearwater Rd.*), where the Murtle River plunges 137m/452ft over a wide basalt cliff. **Clearwater Lake** is the site of a popular campground, and the departure point for daylong or weeklong wilderness canoe treks. **Murtle Lake**, sheltered in a mountain bowl on the park's southeast fringe, is the largest lake in North America reserved for nonmotorized boat travel.

ADDRESSES

🏨 STAY

BC GUEST RANCHES

Below is a selection of the best-known ranches. For more information, contact them individually or the BC Guest Ranchers' Assn. (*877-278-2922; www.bcguestranches.com*).

$$$ Big Bar Ranch – *250-459-2333 or www.bigbarranch.com.* This down-home family-style guest ranch offers economical lodging, riding and fishing in the Marble Mountain uplands near Clinton. Accommodations are available in the main ranch house, log cabins or the teepee.

$$$$ Douglas Lake Ranch – *250-350-3344 or 800-663-4838. www.douglaslake.com.* Canada's largest working cattle ranch embraces half-million acres of bunchgrass-prairie upland. Lodges, camp sites, remote cabins and yurts, plus horseback riding and fishing.

$$$$ Echo Valley Ranch – *250-459-2386 or 800-253-8831. www.evranch.com.* Founded in 1994 by a high-tech entrepreneur, Echo Valley features spruce-log lodges and cabins, a full-service spa, indoor pool, gourmet meals, and guided rides along the Fraser Canyon rimrock.

$$ Wells Gray Ranch – *250-674-2792 or 866-467-4346. www.wellsgrayranch.com. Open May–mid-Oct & mid-Dec–Mar.* This wilderness compound has 10 log cabins, bunkhouses, and room to pitch tents for the more economy-minded. Trail rides take in the rim of Clearwater Canyon. The ranch's saloon is a popular nightspot.

$$ Helmcken Falls Lodge – *250-674-3657; www.helmckenfalls.com.* This historic lodge (1948) and guest ranch near Wells Gray Park overlooks Trophy Mountain. Guests have 33 total rooms in 8 log cabins, 11 double units in chalets or twin cottage units. This soft-adventure lodge offers guided hiking, canoeing and riding tours.

$$$$ Elkin Creek Ranch – *250-394-5175 or 877-346-9378. www.adventurewestresorts.com.* Set in a pristine valley in the far Chilcotin Region, Elkin Creek is spectacular. Handsome log cabins are set in an aspen grove, and fishing in nearby lakes is usually superb.

$$$ Flying U Ranch – *250-456-7717. www.flyingu.com.* The Flying U is Canada's oldest guest ranch, in operation since the 1920s. Famed for its laissez-faire ambience, guests here saddle their own horses and set off by themselves through peaceful aspen/fir forests. Lodgings are comfortably funky.

$$ Spruce Hill Resort– *250-791-5225 or 250-395-0695. www.sprucehillresort.com.* Devoted equally to fitness and riding, the Hills offers excellent spa cuisine and wonderful riding through verdant Cariboo hay meadows. Family-style chalets, and 16 Spa rooms with Rosehip oil treatments, indoor pool and Jacuzzi.

$$$ Sundance Guest Ranch – *250-453-2422 or 800-553-3533. www.sundanceguestranch.com.* Just four hours from Vancouver, Sundance offers amenities Club-Med style. Perched on a bend above Thompson Canyon near Ashcroft, the resort has guided horseback rides, tennis courts, a billiards room, a heated pool and other amenities appealing to singles.

Dawson City★★

Yukon Territory

Set on a dramatic site on the east bank of the wide Yukon at its confluence with the Klondike, this historic frontier town—the heart of the gold rush—is truly a delight. Remarkably like a Western movie set, the former destination of thousands of fortune seekers now hosts thousands of tourists, yet retains its unpaved streets, pedestrian boardwalks and false façades, which enhance the feeling of a bygone era. Several Dawson City buildings compose the Dawson Historical Complex, a National Historic Site of Canada.

▶ **Population:** 1,319

Info: Tourist Office ✆867-993-5575 or www.dawsoncity.ca.

Location: Klondike National Historic Sites of Canada (*Front & King Sts.*) for a map and tour times. Take the 1hr guided tour (*see Visiting box*).

Don't Miss: The floor show at Diamond Tooth Gertie's (*see Downtown*).

Timing: Allow an hour for Downtown Dawson City. The Robert Service cabin and Jack London Centre will need 2hrs. Allow one day for the Excursions.

A BIT OF HISTORY

The Great Stampede – On August 16, 1896, **George Carmack** and his Indian brothers-in-law, Skookum Jim and Tagish Charlie, found gold on **Bonanza Creek**, a tiny stream emptying into the bigger **Klondike River**, itself a tributary of the mighty Yukon. When news of their find reached the outside world, an estimated 100,000 people left their homes from as far away as Australia to begin the long, arduous trek to Dawson City, the town that sprang up at the mouth of the Klondike. Stories of their travels and travails are legion. Many never made it; of those who did, few made a fortune.

The Routes of '98 – Of several routes to Dawson City during the gold rush, the longest, yet easiest, was by sea to the mouth of the Yukon and then by riverboat the 2,092km/1,300mi upstream. But this passage was only for the rich. A few people tried an overland course from Edmonton through almost impassable muskeg and bush, following more or less the present-day Alaska Highway route. The majority, however, sailed up the Pacific Coast via the Inside Passage to Skagway or Dyea, tiny way stations on the Alaska Panhandle, and trudged into the Yukon across the Coast Mountains.

Home of the Klondike – Soon after the discovery, the whole area near Bonanza Creek was staked by prospectors. Instead of making a claim, a trader named **Joe Ladue** laid out a townsite on the level swampland at the mouth of the Klondike, amassing a fortune from his foresight. Lots were soon selling for as much as $5,000 a front foot on the main street. The heyday of Dawson was under way. Prices were sky-high: eggs $1 each, nails $8 a pound; but everything was available, from the latest Paris fashions to the best wines and foods. At the many saloons, drinks were normally paid for in gold dust.

Dawson had a unique feature: despite being the biggest and richest of all the mining boomtowns, it was the most law-abiding. The North West Mounted Police maintained tight control. Everything was closed down on Sundays. No one carried a gun except the police. Offenders were given a "blue ticket" (i.e., run out of town).

Decline and Revival – The heyday was short-lived. By 1904 the rich **placer** fields were exhausted: $100 million in gold had been shipped out. Complicated machinery was needed to exploit any gold that remained.

Dawson City's Downtown

©Oksanaphoto/Dreamstime

People left; the glamor departed. Once the largest Canadian city (pop. 30,000) west of Winnipeg, Dawson City maintained its preeminence until World War II, when Whitehorse—connected to the outside world by road (Alaska Highway), rail and air—took over, growing as Dawson shrank. In 1953 Whitehorse was made the capital of the Yukon. With this blow and the end of commercial gold mining in 1966, Dawson might have become a ghost town were it not for the tourist boom reviving the city. People still make a living mining the creeks, but little gold is found in comparison to the $66 million discovered in 1898.

The year-round population of just over 2,000 swells in summertime with the arrival of tourists and seasonal residents. Situated less than 300km/200mi south of the Arctic Circle on fertile soil untouched by the last Ice Age, Dawson enjoys hot summers with nearly 24 hours of daylight. Vegetables are cultivated in gardens, and flowers sprout through cracks along the streets. Many old buildings tell the story of a grandeur and wealth seen nowhere else so far north. Some lean sideways, however, because of permafrost. A Canadian government restoration project is returning the town to some of its former splendour.

Festivities – On June 21, the midnight sun barely dips down behind the Ogilvie Mountains, and the third weekend in August, the anniversary of **Discovery Day** is celebrated.

DOWNTOWN★★

Laid out in a grid pattern, the town lies in the shadow of the huge hill known as the Midnight Dome. On its face is **Moosehide Slide**, a natural landslide thought to be the result of an underground spring.

On **Front Street** (also called 1st Avenue) stands the **SS Keno**, a stern-wheeler

Visiting Dawson City

Dawson's sights and tourist activities are numerous, so stop first at the Parks Canada Visitor Centre *(Front & King Sts.; ♿ 🕐 open Jun–mid-Sept daily 8am–8pm; ☎ 867-993-7200; www.pc.gc.ca)* for a schedule of events and guided tours as well as a map. Informative audiovisuals and displays are also in the centre. Sights that can be visited by one-hour guided tour only *(Jun–mid-Sept daily; 💲 $6.30)* are indicated below by "*(guided tour).*" Historic buildings that are not open to the public usually have a window display depicting the structure's history.

Additional information can be obtained from the Klondike Visitors Association *(☎ 867-993-5575; www.dawsoncity.ca).*

once used to transport silver, lead and zinc on the Stewart River from the mines in the Mayo district. Built in Whitehorse in 1922, the steamer also made trips to Dawson. After its last voyage in 1960, it was permanently dry-docked there. The extensive damage caused by the flood of 1979 led to the building of a dike along the riverbank where the steamers once docked. Next to the *Keno* is the former **Canadian Imperial Bank of Commerce**, a stately building with a pressed-tin façade made to imitate stone. The plaque on the exterior refers to its famous teller Robert Service.

The former **British North American Bank** (guided tour), with its handsome polished-wood teller enclosure, occupies the corner of Queen Street and 2nd Avenue. South on 2nd Avenue is **Ruby's Place** (*window display*), formerly a brothel, and now one of several restored town buildings.

At Princess Street and 3rd, the renovated **Harrington's Store** (open mid-May–mid-Sept daily), built in 1900, contains the comprehensive photo exhibit, "Dawson As They Saw It." Across the street is **Billy Bigg's** blacksmith shop (*window display*) and north on 3rd, note the **KTM Building** (*window display*), which served as a warehouse for the Klondike Thawing Machine Co. in 1912.

Formerly a Carnegie Library, the Neoclassical **Masonic Temple** corners 4th and Queen, while diagonally across the street is **Diamond Tooth Gertie's Gambling Hall**, a non-profit business. Named for a notorious female resident, this establishment boasts a legalized casino (open May–Sept Sun–Wed 7pm–2am, Fri–Sat 2pm–2am; floor shows nightly; $6; 867-993-5525).

Back on 3rd Avenue are the **Dawson Daily News** (1898-1953), and **Madame Tremblay's Store**, restored to its 1913 appearance (*both window displays*). Opposite, a clapboard building with a squat tower houses the original 1900 **Post Office** (open Jun–mid-Sept daily), designed by **Thomas W. Fuller**, who served as Canada's chief architect for 15 years. He also designed the Government House and the Old Territorial Administration Building. Across King Street stands a replica of the **Palace Grand Theatre**★ (guided tour), a distinctive pinewood structure with an elaborate false front. Built in 1899, the theatre offered everything from opera to Wild West shows. Draped with Old Glory and Union Jacks, the colorful two-tiered, U-shaped interior seats audiences in rows of padded "kitchen chairs." One street over is aptly named Church Street, site of the clapboard **St. Paul's Anglican Church**, built in 1902 with money collected from miners in the creeks.

Southward, double-porticoed **Commissioner's Residence**, where the Yukon's commissioner, or governor, lived in the

---

Bards of the North

Jack London and **Robert Service** were the two writers who helped make the Klondike Gold Rush an enduring part of the history of adventure. Both men had residences in or near Dawson City. London, a young Californian, arrived in the Yukon in 1897 to seek his fortune. Back in California, he discovered a more valuable Yukon treasure when he sold, in 1903, *Call of the Wild*, the tale of a Northland sled dog who returns to the wilderness. London became the most famous and best-paid American author of his time. Robert Service arrived in the Yukon in 1904. *Songs of a Sourdough*, his first success (1907), was a popular collection of his Yukon tales set to verse, including the famous "The Shooting of Dan McGrew."

"Back of the bar, in a solo game,
sat Dangerous Dan McGrew,
And watching his luck was his light-o'-love,
the lady that's known as Lou."

early 1900s, overlooks Front Street. The original residence had a more ornate exterior than the present structure, a replacement after a house fire in 1906. The house and grounds, abundant with flowers, were the centre of Dawson's social life—host to afternoon teas, dinner receptions and summer garden parties (*open Jun–mid-Sept daily; $6.30*). To the rear are the remains of **Fort Herchmer** (*grounds open to the public*), a former North West Mounted Police barracks complete with married quarters, stables, jail and commanding officer's residence. The renovated St. Andrews **Presbyterian Manse** stands behind **St. Andrews Church**, at 4th Avenue.

ADDITIONAL SIGHTS
Dawson City Museum★
595 Fifth Ave. Open mid-May–mid-Sept daily 10am–6pm. Rest of the year by appointment. $9. 867-993-5291.
Dominating the upper section of 5th Avenue, the impressive Neoclassical styled Old Territorial Administration Building (1901, T.W. Fuller) houses the museum. The South Gallery has exhibits and re-creations of Dawson's gold rush; the North Gallery features early 20C city life in Dawson City. Locomotives of the short-lived Klondike Mines Railway are on display in an outdoor shelter.

Robert Service Cabin
8th Ave. at Hanson St.
Overlooking the town from the southeast is a two-room log cabin with moose antlers over the door—the residence from 1909 to 1912 of the "Poet of the Yukon" (1874-1958). Here he wrote his only novel, *The Trail of Ninety-Eight*, and his last Yukon verses, *Songs of a Rolling Stone*. Though he arrived in Dawson shortly after the Gold Rush, his poetry—*Songs of a Sourdough* in particular—vividly re-creates the atmosphere of the times. Outdoor **recitals** (*1hr*) of his poems are presented on the grounds (*open Jun–mid-Sept daily 9am–5pm; $6.30*).

Jack London Interpretive Centre
8th Ave. at Firth St.
The cabin of another writer who spent time in Dawson City during its heyday, American author **Jack London** (1876-1916), has been reconstructed on the property. His stories of the North, *Call of the Wild* and *White Fang* are among his best-known works. The adjacent centre (*open mid-May–mid-Sept daily 11am–6pm; $5; half-price with Gertie's Pass; 867-993-5575*) houses a photo exhibit of London's life in the Klondike. There are also **readings** (*30min*) of his works (*twice daily*).

EXCURSIONS
Midnight Dome
9km/5mi by Dome Rd., a steep, winding road.
So named because of the midnight sun visible here on June 21, this mountain rises 884m/2,900ft behind the townsite. From the summit the **view★★** is splendid day or night. Below lies Dawson at the junction of the Yukon and Klondike rivers—and Bonanza Creek can be seen entering the Klondike. The devastation of the whole area caused by the dredges is evident. There are mountains in all directions; to the north, the Ogilvie Mountains are particularly impressive.

Bonanza Creek★★
4km/2.5mi by Klondike Hwy. from town to Bonanza Creek Rd.
The unpaved road (*maintained for 16km/10mi*) along Bonanza Creek winds through huge piles of **tailings**, or washed gravel refuse, left by mining dredges. The largest remnant of earlier mining equipment is **No. 4 dredge** (*open Jun–mid-Sept; $6.30; tickets available from visitor centre*) on Claim 17BD.
Signs designate a claim provided by the Klondike Visitors Assn. for those who wish to **pan for gold** (*867-993-5575*). A simple plaque marks the place where the Klondike Stampede began: **Discovery Claim** itself (*14.5km/9mi from junction with Klondike Hwy.*).

ADDRESSES

🏠 STAY

$$$ Bombay Peggy's – *2nd & Princess St.* *☎867-993-6969. www.bombaypeggys.com. 9 rooms.* Named for a legendary Dawson madam of the 1950s, this property was a largely abandoned, but still handsome 3-storey Victorian house (1900), until two enterprising Dawson residents bought it in 1998, moved it downtown and transformed it into an opulent inn. The current owners have refurbished it with burgundy wallpaper and period furnishings like claw-foot tubs and canopy beds.

Three of the guests rooms have shared bathrooms. There's even a player piano in the sitting room. The inn's lounge proffers appetizers and alcoholic beverages to guests and the public.

Fort St.James★

British Columbia

In a lovely setting beside Stuart Lake, this town, 154km/96mi northwest of Prince George, is one of the oldest settlements in western Canada. Simon Fraser founded a trading post here that became the chief Hudson's Bay Company post in New Caledonia after 1821. It remained in operation until 1971. Since the site is still fairly remote today, it's easy to imagine how isolated early traders posted here must have felt.

A BIT OF HISTORY

Today a National Historic Site of Canada, Fort St. James, restored to the year 1896, is a testament to life in a fur-trading post. Canada's fur trade at the beginning of the 19C was largely in the hands of the Hudson's Bay Company and its rival, the North West Company. In 1806 Simon Fraser, a member of the North West Company, established a trading post at Stuart Lake as an administrative hub for the fur trade west of the Rockies. Upon the merger of the two companies in 1821, the post, by then named Fort St. James, fell under the supervision of the "new" Hudson's Bay Company.

A harsh climate, limited diet, separation from loved ones and daily routine plagued company employees stationed at Fort St. James.

▸ **Population:** 4,500.
▹ **Location:** Fort St. James sits at the end of Highway 27, an hour's drive north of Vanderhoof.
🕐 **Timing:** The fort and its grounds can be explored in 3–4 hours.
There is a picnic ground at the fort and there are campgrounds nearby.

VISIT

Beside the lake in town. ♿🕐*Open June–Sept daily 9am–5pm.* 💳*7.80.* ✗ *☎250-996-7191. www.pc.gc.ca.*

The National Historic Site contains several restored Hudson's Bay Company buildings that date from 1884 to 1889, as well as an exciting new Interpretive Centre called Strangers and Swan's Down . The **men's house** and officer's dwelling with their meticulously restored furnishings can be visited, as can a reconstruction of the original trading store.

Built off the ground, the **fish cache** holds displays of dried fish and pork, and the log **general warehouse** contains a priceless **collection** of furs. Throughout the site, costumed interpreters offer knowledgeable tales about 19C wilderness life and perform chores common to fort life.

In the visitor centre, displays and artifacts are on view and an excellent film (*9min*) about the fort's history is shown.

Fraser Canyon Country★★

British Columbia

Between the city of Vancouver and Shuswap Lake, the Trans-Canada Highway (Highway 1) follows deep valleys, cut by two of the most powerful rivers in the province, through the rocky Coast Mountains and the dry, hilly scrubland of central British Columbia: the Fraser River and the Thompson River.

A BIT OF HISTORY

The first European to see the Fraser River was **Alexander Mackenzie** on his epic journey to the Pacific in 1793. His partner in the North West Company, **Simon Fraser**, descended and reascended the river's entire length in 1808. Fraser gave the river's major tributary the name of his fellow North Westerner, geographer **David Thompson**, who returned the favour by naming the Fraser. Too wild for a fur-trading route, the Fraser was little used until gold was discovered at **Hill's Bar** near Yale in 1858. The canyons were selected in the 19C for the Canadian Pacific Railway's route, now traversed by a second railway and the Trans-Canada Highway.

① FRASER CANYON★★ – FROM HOPE TO LYTTON

109km/68mi (not including excursion)

Hope★

The mountains close in around this community as the valley narrows and swings northward. The wildness and unpredictability of the region were well demonstrated by the **Hope Slide★** of 1965. One January day an immense amount of rock from Johnson Peak (*18km/11mi east by Rte. 3*) slid into the valley, filling a lake and forcing its waters up the other side. Route 3 had to be rebuilt more than 45m/148ft above its original level.

Manning Provincial Park

Excursion: 136km/84mi round-trip from Hope by Rte. 3 East.

◔ **Michelin Map:** pp100-101.

▯ **Info:** British Columbia Tourism; 919 Water Ave., Hope. 604-869-2021 or www.hellobc.com or Thompson Okanagan Tourism (✆800-567-2275; www.totabc.com).

⊛ **Don't Miss:** Hell's Gate.

◔ **Timing:** Shuswap Lake is an 8hr drive from Vancouver, so stay overnight at a campground or motel between Lytton and Kamloops.

▲▲ **Kids:** Hat Creek Ranch.

After entering the park (◔*open year-round; hiking, horseback riding, bicycling, cross-country skiing;* △), Route 3 traverses an area called **Rhododendron Flats★**, where these wild plants flower in profusion in mid-June. This park is one of only two places in Canada where visitors can drive to extensive subalpine meadows (*the other is Mt. Revelstoke*).

After Hope, mountains close in abruptly. Surrounded by impressive cliffs, the tiny hamlet of Yale was a town of 20,000 during the Gold Rush when it was the terminus of river navigation and the beginning of the Cariboo Road. To the north the cliffs are sheer, the valley is narrow, tunnels are frequent and the river below seethes along, around and over rocks. Just after Spuzzum, the road crosses the river and continues on the east side.

Hell's Gate★★

The canyon here is 180m/600ft deep, but the river, rushing past at 8m/25ft per second, is only 36m/120ft wide. The river was once wider, but during construction of the Canadian National Railway in 1914, a rockslide occurred, narrowing the gap. Thereafter, upstream passage was almost impossible for the salmon, their spawning grounds being the lakes and streams throughout British Columbia's interior. A sharp decline

Pacific Salmon

Every summer and autumn British Columbia's five salmon species—sockeye, pink, coho, chinook and chum—leave the ocean and swim far inland up the province's rivers and streams to spawn. In none are their numbers greater than in the Fraser River—which contains 10 million or more salmon in good years—where they travel as far as 48km/30mi a day. Spawning grounds lie as far north as Stuart Lake, near Fort St. James. Soon after spawning, they die. Their offspring remain in fresh water for about two years before heading to the ocean, where they mature in two to five years. Then the epic return journey to their spawning grounds occurs.

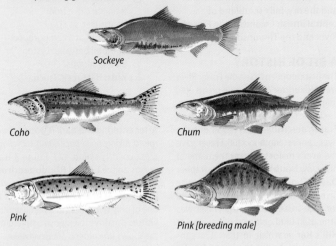

Sockeye

Coho

Chum

Pink

Pink [breeding male]

R. Corbel/MICHELIN

in the Pacific salmon fishing industry occurred until "fishways" were constructed during the 1940s to enable the salmon to bypass the turbulent water. **Airtram★★** (&⏲open mid-May–Labour Day daily 10am–5pm; mid-Apr–early May and rest of Sept–mid-Oct daily 10am–4pm; ⌨$22; ✆604-867-9277; www.hellsgateairtram.com) descends 150m/500ft to river level, where the canyon and the incredible speed of the water can be appreciated. There are displays on the salmon and the fishways as well as a film (20min), and the paranormal exhibition. Visitors can also hike down a steep road (.5km) just south of the airtram parking lot to take a look at the narrow defile. After Hell's Gate, the canyon becomes less dark and formidable, and there are fewer trees on its rocky slopes. From **Jackass Mountain** there is a fine **view★** of the canyon from high above the river.

Lytton

This community regularly registers the highest temperatures in Canada; its record, shared with the town of Lillooet farther north, is 44°C/112°F. At this point the clear blue waters of the Thompson River surge into the muddy brown Fraser, making a streak visible for a short distance downstream.

② THOMPSON CANYON★★ – FROM LYTTON TO SHUSWAP LAKE

230km/143mi (not including excursion)
The Trans-Canada Highway and the two railways leave the valley of the Fraser and turn east along the Thompson, passing through a dry, treeless and steep-sided canyon. The road winds and weaves along, making sharp bends. At Spences Bridge, where the road crosses the river, the river **valley★** gradually widens into a semidesert area, where

scrub vegetation and sagebrush predominate.

👥 Hat Creek Ranch★★

Excursion: 22km/14mi round-trip from Cache Creek via Rte. 97. 🕐*Open May, Jun daily 9am–5pm (Jul–Aug til 6pm), Sept 9am–5pm.* 👁️*$9 (child $6).* 📞*800-782-0922; www.hatcreekranch.com.*
Once a way station along the Cariboo Road, this provincial heritage site offers an impressive collection of restored 19C buildings. The **Hat Creek House** is a handsome Victorian, once a hotel; the **Freight Horse Barn** is still floored with well-worn original timbers. Visitors enjoy wagon rides, drawn by draft horses, around the pretty site. Just upstream, a local First Nations band demonstrates a traditional **summer encampment**.

Just before Savona the Thompson expands to form **Kamloops Lake**. From the Trans-Canada Highway there are some pleasant **views★** of this blue lake set in rocky arid hills. The highway bypasses the rapidly growing commercial and government centre city of **Kamloops★**, which hosts one of Western Canada's best native heritage sites.

Secwepemc Museum and Native Heritage Park★★

355 Yellowhead Hwy. (Rte. 5), in Kamloops. ♿🕐*Open year-round daily 8am–4pm.* 🕐*Closed Sun & major holidays.* 👁️*$10.* 🍴🅿️📞*250-828-9749. www.secwepemcmuseum.com.*
The museum shows how the native Shuswap people lived; the ethnobotanical gardens indicate how they used the plants of this region.
The Trans-Canada Highway follows the south branch of the Thompson River to its headwaters in **Shuswap Lake**. Here the country changes from dry barrenness to verdant green. The stretch of water extending north from the lake is home to one of the world's largest salmon runs *(Oct)*, as many as 2 million. At **Roderick Haig-Brown Provincial Park** *(7km/4mi north of Hwy. 1)*, visitors can watch the salmon spawn and learn about their life cycle. The lake's warm

summer waters draw thousands of vacationers, many of whom rent **houseboats** to ply the lake's unpopulated back channels (called "arms").
For houseboat rental information, contact Twin Anchors 📞*800-663-4026; www.twinanchors.com.*

ADDRESSES

🏨STAY

$$ Quaaout Lodge & Spa at Talking Rock– N*orth shore of Little Shuswap Lake, across Squilax Bridge at Hwy. 1.* 📞*250-679-3090 or 800-663-4303. www.quaaoutlodge.com. 70 rooms and 2 suites.* This peaceful, native-owned resort is set amid ponderosa pines along the best beach on Little Shuswap Lake. Quaaout's massive carved fir doors are works of art in themselves. Sleep in a room with a lake view or a suite with a Jacuzzi. Guests may access the sweat lodge and indoor pool with Jacuzzi.

MARKET

Horsting's Farm Market – *2km/1mi north of Cache Creek on Rte. 97.* 📞*250-457-6546; www.horstingsfarm.com.* Freshly made bread goes into the oven early every morning at Horsting's, followed by fresh fruit pies. All are done in time for lunch, a bountiful selection of thick-sliced sandwiches, hearty soups and homemade pies. Virtually all the produce is grown on the farm. Many travellers stock up here for their journeys north.

TOUR

Gort's Gouda Cheese – *Salmon River Rd., just west of Salmon Arm.* 📞*250-832-4274. www.gortsgoudacheese.bc.ca.* Nestled in a pastoral valley beneath the Monashee Mountains, Arie Gort's Gouda cheese factory uses locally produced organic milk to make Gouda, Swiss and other European cheeses, including savory well-aged wheels that will serve the average family for an entire month. Tours to explain the cheese-making process are available *(Jul–Aug)*.

Inside Passage★★

British Columbia

This protected inland waterway, the result of past glaciation, cuts between the wildly indented northwest coast and the myriad islands that stretch 1,696km/1,060 mi from Puget Sound in Washington state to Skagway, Alaska. The Inside Passage route extends 507km/314mi from Port Hardy on the northern tip of Vancouver Island to Prince Rupert on the northwest coast of British Columbia, ushering visitors into a world of lush, tranquil beauty.

CRUISE

Departs Port Hardy mid-May–Sept every other day 7.30am, arrives Prince Rupert 11.30pm (odd-numbered days Jun, Jul & Sept; even-numbered days May & Aug). Reservations required 🕮. Check for seasonal rates. Check-in 1hr before sailing. ✕ ♿ 🅿 *BC Ferries* 📞250-386-3431 or 📞888-223-3779. bcferries.com.

From Port Hardy the ferry crosses the open sea at Queen Charlotte Strait, then enters the sheltered waters of Fitz Hugh Sound. The remainder of this voyage through the narrow, spectacular Inside Passage offers close-up **views★★**, weather permitting, of islands to the west and BC's fjord-slashed coast to the east. The densely forested, mountainous

▷ **Location:** The Inside Passage route starts at Port Hardy, a 6 hour drive north of Nanaimo on Vancouver island, or from Prince Rupert, 1,500km/925mi by road from Vancouver.

🕐 **Timing:** By using the ferries, you can make a loop from Vancouver to Vancouver Island, then north to take the Inside Passage to Prince Rupert. From there, return to Vancouver via the scenic Cariboo and Fraser Canyon regions. Since the Inside Passage ferry leaves from Port Hardy early in the morning, plan to arrive there the night before.

terrain drops steeply into the sea. Several abandoned cannery communities are passed during the cruise.

Eagles and seabirds, as well as such marine mammals as seals, dolphins, orca and humpback whales, may be sighted during spring and fall migration. The highlight of the voyage comes near its northern end as the ferry enters the 40km/25mi **Grenville Channel★★**. At its narrowest the channel measures only 549m/1,800ft across, with a maximum depth of 377m/1,236ft.

The Spirit Bear

Although it is technically just a rare colour variation of Canada's ubiquitous black bear, the **Kermode bear** of British Columbia's central coast has long been considered spiritually significant by the area's First Nations inhabitants.

Found only in the coastal rain-forest islands and valleys south of Prince Rupert, these bears are rare—there may be just 60 to 100 such creatures left in the world. Ranging in colour from pale white to light cinnamon, the "Spirit Bears," as they are known to the aboriginal peoples, are most often glimpsed in the early autumn near coastal salmon streams. Conservationists are pressing the Government of British Columbia to preserve the bears' homeland, forestalling massive logging proposed for the central coast. First Nations guided tour: www.spiritbear.com

ADDRESSES

🛏 STAY

$$$$$ King Pacific Lodge – *Barnard Harbour, BC. ☎604-987-5452 or 888-592-5464. www.kingpacificlodge.com. 17 rooms.* This luxurious floating retreat, voted "Best Resort in Canada" by Condé Nast readers four years running, is moored on Princess Royal Island, reached only by float plane. Guests enjoy spectacular scenery, wildlife viewing and outdoor adventure along BC's famed Inside Passage. The three-storey wood lodge has amenities ranging from a communal sauna and steam room to soaking tubs and floor-to-ceiling windows in each of the 17 spacious guest rooms and Royal Suite. Gourmet chefs prepare all meals, which highlight local seafood. Fishing, kayaking, canoeing and watching for whales, sea lions, bears and wolves occupy daylight hours. Helicopters and motorboats provide access to the island's breathtaking scenery of deep fjords, soaring granite mountains and remote inland lakes.

The Kootenay Rockies★

British Columbia

Rising in the Rockies, the Kootenay River winds throught the southeast corner of British Columbia, joining the Columbia River at Castlegar. Kootenay Lake, 104km/65mi long, is surrounded on all sides by towering glacier-clad peaks in the Purcell and Selkirk ranges. At the south end of the lake, the valley around **Creston** holds grainfields and orchards. The **Elk Valley** area has some of the largest soft-coal deposits in North America. Farther west, copper, lead, zinc and silver are mined and processed in the huge smelter at **Trail**. Kootenay National Park, on the Alberta border, is one of the four Rocky Mountain Parks.

A BIT OF HISTORY

Gold brought the first settlers to the valley of the Wild Horse River in 1864. When land disputes with the Kootenay Indians erupted, a detachment of the North West Mounted Police under the famed Mountie **Sam Steele** (1849-1919) restored peace, and the settlement took the name Fort Steele.

SIGHTS
👪 Fort Steele Heritage Town★
16km/10mi northeast of Cranbrook by Rte. 95. ◷*Open May–mid-June, Oct*

- 🛈 **Info:** Kootenay Rockies Tourism, 1905 Warren Ave., Kimberley. ☎250-427-4838. www.kootenay rockies.com.
- ▶ **Location:** The Kootenay Rockies stretch from the British Columbia-Alberta border, north of Montana, westwards to Kootenay Lake, north of Idaho.
- ⊛ **Don't Miss:** The *SS Moyie* in Kaslo is a wonderfully restored paddle wheeler.
- ◷ **Timing:** The Kootenay area encompasses several provincial and national parks that offer spectacular scenery as well as recreation.
- 👪 **Kids:** At Fort Steele you can ride a steam locomotive and attend the rip-roaring Wildhorse Theatre.

daily 9.30am–5pm; mid-June -Sept 9.30am–6pm, rest of the year daily 10am–4pm (shops and attractions closed). ⬠*$12 (child $5), (mid-Oct–Apr contribution requested).* ☎*250-417-6000. www.fortsteele.ca.*
Fort Steele, a fine **site** at the foot of the Rockies, flourished in the early 1890s until the railway over Crowsnest Pass bypassed it. The provincial government began restoration in 1961.

SS Moyie National Historic Site

© Andrew Penner/www.KootenayRockies.com

The **museum** sits in a redux hotel. Live shows in the **Wildhorse Theatre** *(Jul–Labour Day daily 2pm;* ⊛*$10;* ✆*250-417-6000)*. An old steam locomotive offers rides *(Jul–Aug; 20min;* ⊛*$10)*. Costumed staff portray townspeople, while shops and cafes offer artisan goods and food.

Kimberley

43km/27mi west of Fort Steele via Rtes. 95 & 95A. www.tourismkimberley.com
A former mining centre 30 min from Ft. Steele, Kimberley offers golf courses, nature park, ski centre and summer festivals. **Kimberley Alpine Resort** *(www.skikimberley.com)* has 80 runs, 5 lifts and dependable snow.

Nelson

234km/145mi west of Kimberley via Rtes. 95 South, 3 West & 6 North. www.nelsonkootenay.com.
This former mining centre has some 350 lovingly restored buildings and houses, many in granite. The town's historic charm featured in *Roxanne* in 1984.

Kaslo

66km/41mi north of Nelson via Rtes. 3A & 31. www.kaslo.com.
This small lake town prospered a century ago as a shipping centre for Kootenay silver ore. Today it offers tree-lined streets, well-preserved buildings and an incomparable lakeside site, as well as the popular annual Kaslo Jazz Festival *(kaslojazzfest.com)*.

SS Moyie National Historic Site

Front St. on lake ⏲*Open mid-May/mid-Oct daily 10am–5pm.* ⊛*$8.50.* ✆*250-353-2525. www.klhs.bc.ca.*
This vessel is the world's oldest intact passenger sternwheeler. In its heyday it carried passengers, supplies and silver ore in velvet comfort downlake to the railhead at Creston.

The Gentleman Bandit

Billy Miner (c.1847-1913), an American, gained notoriety when, in September 1904, he robbed the Canadian Pacific Railway's Transcontinental Express. During a later holdup near Kamloops, Miner and his cohorts were apprehended by the North West Mounted Police. He escaped and fled back to the US, where he died in a Georgia prison after robbing banks as well as more trains. Known for his courtesy, he is believed to have originated the command, "Hands up!" The award-winning 1983 film, The Grey Fox, starring Richard Farnsworth, is an affectionate tribute.

Monashees and Selkirks★★

British Columbia

The Trans-Canada Highway crosses the the the Monashee and Selkirk ranges by an often spectacular route through Eagle and Rogers passes.

FROM SICAMOUS TO GOLDEN

219km/136mi by Trans-Can Hwy.
From the small town of **Sicamous**, the Trans-Canada begins to climb the valley of the Eagle River. After 26km/16mi the highway reaches **Craigellachie** where, on November 7, 1885, the last spike of the Canadian Pacific Railway, linking east and west, was driven (*note the plaque off the road on the right*).

The valley narrows before the road reaches **Three Valley Gap★** *(47km/29mi)*, occupying a lovely **site★** beside Three Valley Lake, edged with sheer cliffs. Soon afterward the road arrives at the top of Eagle Pass (55km/34mi) and then begins a steep descent to the Columbia River in the valley of Tonakwatla Creek.

Eagle Pass★

71km/44mi Sicamous to Revelstoke.
According to legend, this pass through the Monashee Mountains was discovered in 1865 when **Walter Moberly** fired his gun at an eagle's nest and saw the birds fly up a valley pass, which eventually became the route of the Canadian Pacific Railway as well as the Trans-Canada Highway.

Revelstoke★★

📖 ✆*800-487-1493.*
www.seerevelstoke.com.
Set on the east bank of the Columbia River at its junction with the Illecillewaet, this small community has a picturesque **site★**.It has become a summer-winter sports centre because of its proximity to 100 year-old (2014) **Mount Revelstoke National Park** (*hiking, fishing, skiing, cross-country skiing, kids*

- ⚓ **Michelin Map:** p96
- 🏛 **Info:** Glacier National Park ✆250-837-7500; Mount Revelstoke National Park ✆250-837-7500. www.pc.gc.ca.
- ◗ **Location:** The Monashee and Selkirk ranges are located in southeastern British Columbia between the central plateau and the Rockies.
- ◎ **Don't Miss:** Meadows-in-the-Sky Parkway, in Revelstoke National Park, has spectacular views.
- 🕐 **Timing:** Abundant snowfalls can block roads; check conditions before making plans.

Xplorers program; 🕐*open daily year-round;* ✆*250-837-7500; www.pc.gc.ca).*
Revelstoke Mountain Resort, known for helicopter, snowcat and back-country skiing, opened a gondola and high-speed lift in 2007 that claims to have North America's longest skiable vertical at 1,713m/5, 620ft.

Just to the north, the **Revelstoke Dam** can be seen rising 175m/574ft above the Columbia River. A Visitor Centre (*4km/2.5mi north by Rte. 23 (*♿🕐*open Jun–mid-Oct daily 10am–5pm; $6;* ✆*250-814-6697)* features displays of Columbia River power projects.

Meadows-in-the-Sky Parkway★★

27km/16mi of paved road, unsuitable for trailers. Begins on Trans-Can Hwy. 1.6km/1mi east of Revelstoke turnoff. 45min ascent (visitors must board free park shuttle for last 1.5km/.9mi). 🕐*Open daylight hours in snowfree season only. Shuttle runs Jul–Sept 10am–5.30pm.*
◎ *Be sure to check that the road is open.*
This road ascends Mt. Revelstoke in a series of switchbacks, with a **viewpoint★** of the town of Revelstoke. At the summit the **view★★** extends to the Columbia

Rogers Pass

www.KootenayRockies.com

valley and the Clachnacudainn Range. Paths at the summit descend into the **alpine meadows**. Farther up Highway 1, some 20km/12mi east of Revelstoke, the park's **Giant Cedars Trail** is a short (.5km) boardwalk among ancient Western red cedars.

Rogers Pass★★

148km/92mi from Revelstoke to Golden. In 1881 a determined surveyor, **Albert Rogers**, followed the Illecillewaet River and discovered the pass through the Selkirk, through which the railroad was routed.

From Rogers Pass to Golden★★

May be temporarily closed when avalanche control is under way. Winter travellers must follow instructions by park wardens.

The Trans-Canada Highway follows the high-walled valley of the Illecillewaet River into the Selkirks and soon passes through snowsheds that provide winter protection for the road. After 48km/30mi the highway enters **Glacier National Park** (& ⊙ *open daily year-round;* ⊜*$7.80/day;* ☎*250-837-7500; www.pc.gc.ca).* Ahead, the four

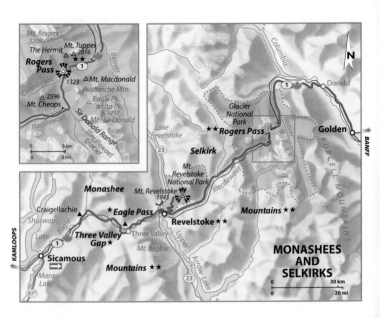

RECREATION

Waterborne adventures in the Golden area range from running rapids on the famed Kicking Horse River to watching wildlife while floating on the Columbia wetlands. Outfitters and guides as well as lodges are listed on www.tourismgolden.com. Here's a sampling: **Kicking Horse Mountain Resort** – 13km/8mi west of Golden. ✆250-439-5424 or 800-754-5425. www.kickinghorseresort.com. This four-season recreational haven is accessible by an 8-person gondola that transports visitors high above the valley floor. Watch out for viewing resident grizzly bear "Boo" in his favorite pond below. Eagle's Eye Restaurant is Canada's highest dining experience, featuring inspired local cuisine. Summer hiking trails offer spectacular views. Mountain bike trails, and rentals. Skiing and snowboarding in winter. Area accommodations.

The Alpine Rafting Company – ✆888-599-5299. www.alpinerafting.com. Rafting guides will take you down the Kicking Horse River. Kootenay River Runners – ✆800-599-4399. www.raftingtherockies.com. Contact these guides for expert local advice and trips on the fast area rivers. Whitewater Kayaking Association of British Columbia has information at www.canoekayakbc.ca.

Columbia River Safaris – ✆877-494-5322. www.riversafaris.com. Wetland eco-tours with naturalist-guides on rafts, boats, or jeeps.

peaks of the **Sir Donald Range** are visible (left to right): Avalanche Mountain, Eagle Peak, Uto Peak and Mt. Sir Donald itself. To the north, the steep pyramidal form of **Mount Cheops** can be seen. The road swings around the Napoleon Spur of Mt. Cheops to reach the summit of the pass (72km/45mi).

The **Rogers Pass Discovery Centre★** has displays, models and films that explain the history of the pass and the annual battle against avalanches (&. ⏱ open summer daily 8am–7pm, spring and fall 7am–4pm, winter 7am–4pm; ⏱ closed Christmas Day & Tue–Wed; 16 Oct–22 Nov; ✆250-837-7500; www.pc.gc.ca). The **view★** includes the slide-scarred peaks of **Mount Tupper** and **The Hermit**. The road descends under the looming form of **Mount Macdonald**. Passing through reinforced concrete snowsheds, it swings into the valley of the Beaver River, then leaves the park, crosses the Columbia at Donald and follows the river south to **Golden**.

Golden

🄸 ✆800-622-4653. www.golden.ca. www.tourismgolden.com.

This rail centre in the heart of the upper Columbia Valley is renowned for its many river rafting, hiking, skiing, mountain climbing and wildlife-watching outfitters.

The ski gondola at the **Kicking Horse Resort** rises to 7,705ft/2,350m, and features Canada's highest elevated dining experience. Many inns and lodges offer accommodation.

ADDRESSES

🏨STAY

$$$ Alpine Meadows Lodge – 6km/4mi west of Golden. ✆250-344-5863. Twenty-nine architecturally designed log chalets, plus camping & RV sites. Situated on slopes above the Columbia River.

🍴EAT

$$$ Eagle's Eye Restaurant – ✆250-439-5413. The restaurant, at 2,347m/7,700ft (access by gondola), is part of the Kicking Horse Mountain Resort (&see contact information in Recreation, above).

Okanagan Valley★★

British Columbia

Constant microclimate sunshine and intensive use of lake water for irrigation have established vineyards as well as apple, peach, plum, grape, cherry, apricot and pear growing possible in this area of low rainfall, arid hills and sagebrush. Beautiful lakes, sandy beaches, warm summers and golf courses have made the valley a popular resort, especially for wine lovers and outdoor fans.

OSOYOOS TO VERNON
177km/110mi by Rte. 97

Osoyoos

🚩 *Town of Osoyoos, 8707 Main St. 📞250-495-6515 or 888-495-6515. www.osoyoos.ca.*
The arid hills around **Osoyoos Lake** contrast sharply with the green orchards on the lakeshore. **Anarchist Mountain** *(6km/4mi east by Rte. 3)* provides a fine **view★★** of the area.

The **Desert Centre★** *(4km/2.5mi north off Rte. 97; ○late April–mid-May 10am–2pm; May 16–Sept 15 daily 9:30am–4:30pm, reduced hours rest of the year; ▪▪▪1hr guided tours May–mid-Sept daily 10am, noon & 2pm; ▪▪$7; 📞250-495-2470 or 877-899-0897; www.desert.org)* offers tours along a boardwalk through the desert-like foothills.

Similkameen River Valley

Excursion: 138km/86mi round-trip from Osoyoos by Rte. 3 W.
The drive from Osoyoos to **Keremeos** *(www.keremeos.com)* climbs up to a low pass and descends into the verdant Similkameen River Valley, between the ramparts of the Cathedral Mountains. The area around Cawston *(36km/22mi northwest of Osoyoos)* is particularly dense with fruit stands. Near Keremeos sits an 1877 **gristmill★** *(about 3km/1.5mi northeast of Keremeos off Rte. 3A; follow signs to Upper Branch Rd.; 📞250-356-1432)*. Southwest of Keremeos *(22km/14mi)*, along a mostly gravel road, lies **Cathedral Provincial Park★**, a premier hiking area explorable only by foot *(○open May–Oct daily dawn–dusk; www.oldgristmill.ca)*.
Cathedral Lakes Lodge provides jeep transport from its property on the Ashnola River to its resort near the Quiniscoe Lake campground *($100 adults, $75 youth, $50 kids, return, including tax; book 48hrs in advance)*; day trips are possible. The heart of the park is a high alpine basin containing the five Cathedral Lakes. There are campgrounds by three of the lakes.

Route 97 to Penticton★★

Through orchards, Route 97 follows the Okanagan River from Osoyoos to Oliver. As the road approaches **Vaseux Lake★**, huge rocks and barren slopes appear. Watch for bighorn sheep, while the lakeshore is a waterfowl preserve. In contrast, the sandy hills surrounding lovely blue **Skaha Lake★** are covered with sagebrush.

⚬ **Michelin Map:** pp100-101.
🚩 **Info:** Individual towns have tourist offices, given below. For general information go to www.hellobc.com.
▶ **Location:** This valley in southcentral British Columbia extends 200km/125mi north from Washington state in the US, taking in Lake Okanagan, several smaller lakes and the Okanagan River.
✦ **Don't Miss:** There are some 60 wineries in the area, and nearly all offer tours.
🕐 **Timing:** This area of British Columbia is relatively compact and well-served by roads open reliably all year round.
👪 **Kids:** The O'Keefe Ranch near Vernon offers a glimpse of ranch life.

Touring the Wineries

Home to Mission Hill Estate Family Winery, 2013 Best Pinot Noir winner from Decanter World Wine Awards, the best way to see a selection of the Okanagan Valley's 120 wineries is to use Kelowna or Penticton as a base and devote an early autumn day to touring and tasting. (In summer, tour buses sometimes overwhelm the major wineries.) You can find lists of area wineries, maps and wine country tours on local websites (www.penticton.ca, www.osoyoos.ca, www.tourismkelowna.com). Tourism offices can also help plan a travel itinerary and provide maps but highway signs indicate major wineries. Almost all wineries offer tastings and special-purchase bargains; many also serve food. Children can visit as well, but those under 19 cannot taste wine. Nearly all wineries have websites, or you can telephone for information.

Among the most notable Kelowna area wineries are Quail's Gate, Mission Hill, Summerhill, Gray Monk, St. Hubertus, Cedar Creek, Hainle Vineyards and Calona. Penticton highlights include Sumac Ridge, Stag's Hollow, Jackson Triggs, Tinhorn Creek, Gehringer Brothers, Hester Creek and Inniskillan.

Okanagan late-harvest ice wine (the grapes are picked frozen) is a well-regarded dessert wine.

Penticton

🛈 *Wine Country Visitor Centre, 553 Vees Dr. 𝒫250-276-2170 or 800-663-5052. www.tourismpenticton.com.*

Set on a pleasant **site★** on narrows between Okanagan Lake and Skaha Lake, Penticton is a tourist resort. Beside Okanagan Lake lies the **SS Sicamous**, a stern-wheeler once used on the lake (◷*open mid-May–mid-Sept; daily 9am–5pm; rest of the year Tue–Sat 10am–4pm; ⊚$6.50; 𝒫250-492-0403 or 866-492-0403; www.sssicamous.com).*

Route 97 to Kelowna★★

Leaving Penticton, Route 97 follows **Okanagan Lake★★**, offering lovely views. According to local Indian legend, the monster **Ogopogo** lives beneath the cliffs. Like his name, Ogopogo is said to look the same viewed from either end; a popular statue in Kelowna's City Park purports to represent the creature.

Summerhill Pyramid Winery, Kelowna

© Canadian Tourism Commission

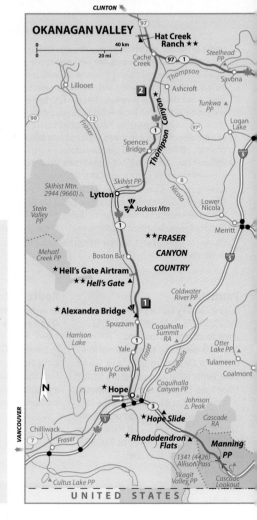

Kettle Valley Railway★

🕐*Mid-May–early Oct Thur–Mon 10:30am & 1:30pm (Jul–Aug Thur–Sat).* ✆*$22.* 📞*877-494-8424. www.kettlevalley rail.org.* Run by railroad enthusiasts, the **Kettle Valley Steam Railway** makes regular trips over the remaining 16km/10mi of track on a 1912 steam locomotive, the "3716," out of the Prairie Valley Station in Summerland. The train traverses the spectacular Trout Creek Trestle Bridge.

Kelowna★

🚩 *Visitor Centre, 544 Harvey Ave. 📞800-663-4345. www.tourism kelowna.com.*

Route 97 crosses the narrows of Lake Okanagan by a floating bridge. In 1859, **Father Pandosy**, an Oblate priest established a **mission★**, which still stands at Benvoulin and Casorso roads in south Kelowna. Okanagan **Wine & Orchard Museums** (*1304 Ellis St.; 📞778-478-0325 or 250-763-2417; www.kelownamuseums. ca*) hold compact exhibits about these signature local industries.

Route 97 to Vernon

After Kelowna the road skirts Wood Lake and winds along the eastern edge of **Kalamalka Lake★★**.

Vernon★

🚩 *Vernon Tourism, 3004 39th Ave. 📞250-542-1415 or 800-665-0795. www.vernontourism.com.*

Along Highway 97 the town's central **Polson Park** stretches along Vernon Creek.

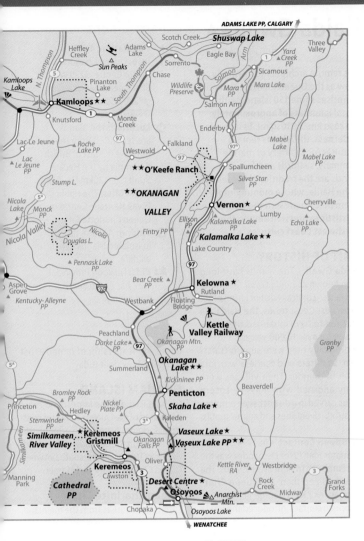

👥 O'Keefe Ranch★★

In Spallumcheen,12km/7.5mi northwest of Vernon on Rte. 97; turn toward Kamloops, continue 4km/2.5mi.
🕐 Open May–Oct daily 10am–5pm (early Aug til 6pm). 🎟$13.50 (youth$10).
✕ 🖉250-542-7868.
www.okeeferanch.ca.

Founded in 1867 by Cornelius O'Keefe, the ranch remained in the family until 1977. The summer **Cowboy Festival** showcases riding and roping contests.

🏨STAY

$$$ Cathedral Lakes Lodge – 🖉250-469-9454 (Jun–Oct) or 888-255-4453 (US/Canada). www.cathedral-lakes-lodge.com. 10 rooms, 7 cabins. Rates include meals, boats & transport. Minimum 2-night stay. Closed mid-Oct–May. Situated on Quiniscoe Lake, across from Cathedral Park's campground, the resort welcomes park visitors, especially hikers, for whom it serves as a base camp. It is accessible only by foot or via the resort's four-wheel-drive shuttle (1hr), which also transports campers. Hearty meals fortify guests for a day's exersions. The resort's isolation—and lack of TV and radio—provide total peace.

Haida Gwaii★★

British Columbia

This remote archipelago, formerly know as the Queen Charlotte islands, comprises some 150 islands with a total landmass of approximately 10,126sq km/3,910sq mi. Essentially wilderness, the islands remain a habitat for a variety of marine mammals, seabirds and fish. The islands are the traditional homeland of the Haida, whose monumental totem poles represent the height of artistic expression among the Northwest Coast cultures.

A BIT OF HISTORY

Haida Gwaii – The islands have long been known as *Haida Gwaii*, "Island of the Haida." Ethnically distinct from other Northwest Coast tribes, the Haida are believed to have inhabited this archipelago for over 10,000 years.

Traditionally they were superb craftsmen, seafarers and fearless warriors given to plunder. Their villages were richly adorned with massive **totem poles** carved in a distinct style employing strong ovoid lines and animal motifs.

European Contact – In 1774 Spanish navigator Juan Perez Hernandez was the first European to sight these islands. The British named them for **Queen Charlotte**, wife of King George III.

European contact introduced the Haida to iron tools that facilitated their wood carving. By the end of the 19C, however, diseases had decimated the population and by the early 20C the Haida had relocated to Graham Island.

The Islands Today – Though located only 55km/34mi south of the Alaska panhandle, the islands enjoy a temperate climate, thanks to the warm Kuroshio Current. High annual rainfall and fertile soil support forests of Sitka spruce, hemlock and cedar. The southern third of the archipelago is a national park reserve that contains a World Heritage Site. A resurgence of Haida art and traditions, begun in the late 1950s

▶ **Population:** 4,761.

Info: Queen Charlotte Visitor Centre, 3220 Wharf St., Queen Charlotte City. ℘250-559-8316. www.qcinfo.ca.

Location: The islands are separated from the northwest coast of British Columbia by the Hecate Strait (50–130km/31–81mi).

Don't Miss: The Haida Gwaii Heritage Centre in Queen Charlotte City.

Timing: A cruise takes in isolated islands rich in wildlife.

Kids: Naikoon Provincial Park has Agate Beach and hiking.

under the leadership of famed artist **Bill Reid**, is evident today.

GRAHAM ISLAND

Graham Island is the largest and most populated of the Queen Charlottes, with small logging, fishing and administrative towns on the east side of the island. Highway 16 runs north–south between Queen Charlotte City and Masset.

Queen Charlotte City

Catering to tourists from the mainland, many of whom arrive by ferry at nearby **Skidegate** [SKID-eh-get] **Landing**, the town's centre offers hostelries, restaurants, and shops along Skidegate Inlet.

Haida Heritage Centre★★

At Kaay Llnagaay, 1km/.6mi north of the ferry landing. &○*Open Sep-May 10am-5pm, Jul/Aug 10am-6pm.* ○*Closed Dec 25–Jan 5.* ⊚*$15.* ℘*250-559-7885. www.haidaheritagecentre.com.*

This complex of 10 longhouses has exhibits, shops and the **Haida Gwaii Museum★★**, and offers meals and tours. The Bill Reid Teaching Centre and Canoe House holds the **Loo Taas★★**, an ornate, 15m/50ft hand-crafted dugout canoe

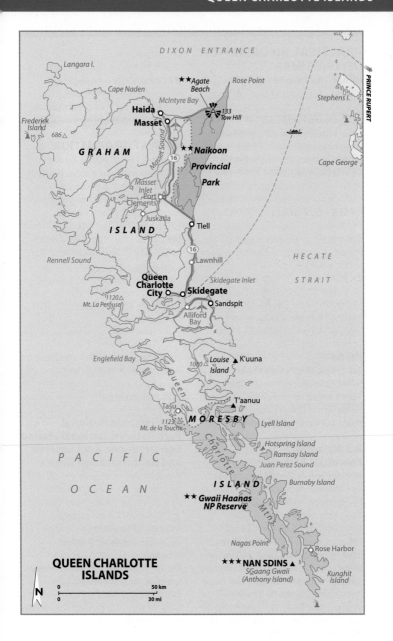

produced in traditional Haida style for Expo '86 in Vancouver.

Skidegate

1.5km/.9mi from ferry.

Facing Rooney Bay, this is the seat of the Haida Skidegate Band Council; the elaborate **totem pole**★★ in front of the Council's cedar longhouse was carved by the renowned Haida artist Bill Reid.

Masset

Located on Masset Sound, near its entrance to the open waters of McIntyre Bay, the town attracts sports anglers and beachcombers.

PRACTICAL INFORMATION

GETTING THERE

BY AIR – **Air Canada Jazz** (📞888-247-2262; www.flyjazz.ca) provides daily flights from Vancouver to Sandspit while **Ocean Pacific Air** (📞 250-624-5879; http://oceanpacificair.ca) offers floatplane service from Prince Rupert to Masset and to Sandspit. **Pacific Coastal Airline** (📞604-273-8666 or 800-663-2872; www.pacific-coastal.com) flies from Vancouver to Masset.

BY SEA – **BC Ferries** (📞250-386-3431 or 888-223-3779; www.bcferries.bc.ca) offers year-round service from Prince Rupert to Skidegate-Alliford Bay; book well in advance.

BY BOAT – You can also arrive in your own boat, docking at Sandspit, Queen Charlotte City or Masset. Arriving from the south, contact the Gwaii Haanas National Park (📞250-559-8818; www.pc.gc.ca).

BY CAR AND RV – Available in Sandspit, Queen Charlotte City and Masset. For a list of companies, contact the Queen Charlotte Visitor Centre.

TOURIST INFORMATION

To visit sites inaccessible by road, including the Gwaii Haanas National Park, it is advisable to use an outfitter. Lists of licensed outfitters are provided by Parks Canada (📞250-559-8818; www.pc.gc.ca) or the Queen Charlotte Visitor Centre (📞250-559-8316; www.qcinfo.com).

Visitors must reserve and take an orientation session (📞800-435-5622 in North America; 250-387-1642 from elsewhere; 604-435-5622 from the Vancouver area).

Haida

Adjacent to Masset, Haida boasts several totem poles, notably one in front of St. John's Anglican Church by acclaimed Haida artist Robert Davidson. Craft shops sell works of Haida artists.

👥 Naikoon Provincial Park

9km/6mi east of Masset. Unpaved, but well-maintained beach access road. 🕐*Open year-round.* 📞*250-557-4390. Park visitor centre in Tlell. Hiking, fishing, beachcombing, camping.*
This park, with a 110km/62.5mi beachfront, encompasses the low-lying northeast corner of Graham Island. The two campgrounds operate on a first come, first served basis; **Agate Beach★★** is the most popular. **Tow Hill**, a forested basalt outcropping, rises 133m/436ft above the beach. An easy trail (🚶1hr round-trip) to the summit affords **views★** of the beach and, weather permitting, Alaska across the Dixon Entrance.

MORESBY ISLAND

Abundant rainfall in the Queen Charlotte Mountains has nourished impressive **rain forests★★** of towering spruce and cedar, luxuriant ferns and mosses, where wildlife is abundant. The only town, Sandspit, is a 20-minute ferry ride from Graham Island.

Gwaii Haanas National Park Reserve, National Marine Conservationa Area Reserve and Haida Heritage Site★★

Access by sea or chartered aircraft only. 🕐*Open daily May–Sept.* 🎫*$19.60 daily access fee. Reservations required.* 📞*250-559-8818. www.pc.gc.ca. Touring with an outfitter is strongly recommended;* 🕯*see Practical Information.*
Though many villages have reverted to forest, at some sites Haida totem poles still stand and ruins are clearly discernible. At several important sites, **Haida Gwaii Watchmen** serve as caretakers.

Nan Sdins★★★

Added to the UNESCO World Heritage list in 1981, SGaang Gwaii (or Anthony Island), accessible by boat, occupies a spectacular site at the edge of the Pacific. Occupied for 1,500 years, Nan Sdins gives the visitor a rare taste of 19C Haida culture.

Rocky Mountain Parks★★★

Alberta, British Columbia

Internationally known for spectacular mountain scenery, this chain of four national parks with their diverse topography, vegetation and wildlife, is the jewel of western Canada. Modern parkways dissect the region's wide river valleys, and hiking trails crisscross the backcountry, allowing access to an awesome landscape of soaring peaks, alpine lakes, waterfalls and glaciers. The major parks in the Canadian Rockies are Banff, Jasper, Yoho and Kootenay National Parks and Mount Robson Provincial Park. They form one of the largest mountain parklands in the world, covering over 22,274sq km/8,600sq mi.

GEOGRAPHY

Canada's Rooftop – Frequently rising over 3,000m/10,000ft, the Canadian Rockies stretch roughly 1,550km/900mi from the US border through western Alberta and eastern British Columbia. To the north the range is bounded by the broad plain of the Liard River; to the east by the Interior Plains; and to the west by the **Rocky Mountain Trench**, one of the longest continuous valleys in the world. The spine of the Rockies forms part of the **Continental Divide**.

Fauna and Flora – Still largely wilderness, the Rockies are inhabited by a variety of animal and plant life. Even along roadways black bear, coyote, elk, moose, mule deer, mountain sheep are often seen. Mountain goats and bighorn sheep may be sighted, and in more remote areas, grizzly bears and mountain lions roam. Plant life varies greatly due to drastic changes in elevation. Wildflowers follow the snowmelt up the mountainsides *(late Jun– early Aug)*. Stands of Douglas fir, lodgepole pine, white spruce and

- **Michelin Maps:** pp 107, 109, 113 and 115.
- **Info:** Each park has a Visitor Centre. Parks Canada: www. pc.gc.ca.
  For transportation, **lodging** and **restaurants**, see the end of this chapter.
- **Location:** The parks are connected by excellent roadways. Highway 93, starting at Radium Hot Springs, BC, stretches north to link the Kootenay, Banff and Jasper parks. East-west, Highway 1, the Trans-Canada Highway, links Calgary to Banff, then turns north to Lake Louise, where it again turns west, crossing Yoho park to emerge at Golden, BC. In the north, Route 16, the Yellowhead Highway, also runs east-west, linking Edmonton to Jasper, crossing the park and emerging at Tête Jaune Cache, BC.
- **Parking:** When hiking or skiing, park only in designated lots: police ticket cars parked on the roadside. Never get out of your car to photograph or feed wildlife, a potentially ticketable offence.
- **Don't Miss:** Icefields Parkway between Lake Louise and Jasper offers spectacular views; you can stand astride the Continental Divide. the Vermillion Pass in Kootenay National Park.

trembling aspen in the valleys gradually give way to alpine fir, Lyall's larch and Engelmann spruce on the higher slopes. Just below the tree line lies a band of krummholz vegetation—trees dwarfed by the severe conditions. Above the tree line (normally 2,200m/7,200ft on south-

Canmore

This former coal-mining town just off Highway 1, a half hour east of Banff (*22km/13mi*), was propelled into tourism by the 1988 Alberta Olympics, when it was the venue for Nordic events. Accommodation is modern and varied. Outdoor activities include golf, hiking, biking, soaring, climbing, kayaking and river rafting. Nearby are five alpine ski centres, as well as facilities for Nordic skiing and snow-shoeing. Set in a wide vale in the Bow River Valley, Canmore is also a gateway to Kananaskis Country, the popular Alberta recreation and wilderness reserve. Good for strolling and less hectic than Banff, downtown Canmore is a tidy district of shops, cafes and small inns.

🄸 Tourism Canmore, *907-7th Ave., Canmore, AB, T1W 2V3. ℘403-678-1295, 866-226-6673 or www.tourismcanmore.com.*

facing slopes, lower on north facing), only the mosses, lichens, wildflowers and grasses of the alpine tundra survive.

A BIT OF HISTORY

Archaeological evidence indicates nomads traversed this region 10,000 years ago. First Nations living here were overwhelmed, prior to European contact, by the **Stoney Nation**, who moved into the Rockies in the early 1700s. During the 18C, the **fur trade** burgeoned in the Rockies, and by the mid-19C, mountaineers and explorers had arrived.

By 1885 the **Canadian Pacific Railway** (CPR) line had reached the West Coast. Recognizing the mountains' tourist potential, the CPR convinced the government to establish "preserves"– the origin of the parks.

During the late 18C and early 19C, the railway company built fine mountain chalets and hotels, a number of which are still in operation. By the 1920s all four Rocky Mountain national parks had been established. In 1984 the combined four parks were designated a UNESCO World Heritage Site.

1️⃣ BANFF NATIONAL PARK★★★

Canada's first and most famous national park, was only the world's third. Banff encompasses impressive peaks, scenic river valleys and popular resort towns of Banff and Lake Louise. In the 1880s construction of the transcontinental railroad and discovery of natural hot springs on Sulphur Mountain elevated Banff to international prominence. The mineral springs were first noted by Sir **James Hector** in 1858, the first European to cross Kicking Horse Pass, which became the rail route through the Rockies.

Moraine Lake and the valley of the Ten Peaks, Banff National Park

© Jon Arnold / hemis.fr

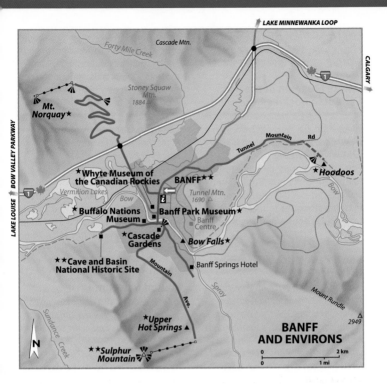

LAKE MINNEWANKA LOOP

CALGARY

Cascade Mtn.

Forty Mile Creek

Stoney Squaw
Mtn.
1884

★ Mt.
Norquay ★

Tunnel Mountain Rd

LAKE LOUISE ▶ BOW VALLEY PARKWAY

★ Whyte Museum of
the Canadian Rockies

Vermilion Lakes

Bow

★ Buffalo Nations
Museum

BANFF ★★

★ Hoodoos

Tunnel Mtn.
1690

Banff Park Museum ★

Banff
Centre

★ Cascade
Gardens

▲ Bow Falls ★

★★ Cave and Basin
National Historic Site

Mountain

Banff Springs Hotel

Spray

Mount Rundle

★ Upper
Hot Springs ▲

△
2949

N

★★ Sulphur
Mountain ★

Sundance Creek

**BANFF
AND ENVIRONS**

0   2 km
0   1 mi

In 1883 Siding 29 was constructed near the springs. Canadian Pacific president **George Stephen** called the springs Banff after his native Banffshire, Scotland. The Banff Hot Springs Reserve was established in 1885 around Cave and Basin Hot Springs. In 1888 the CPR opened what was then the world's largest hotel, the **Banff Springs Hotel.**

TOWN OF BANFF AND ENVIRONS★★

403-762-0270. www.banff.ca. www.banfflakelouise.com.
This well-known resort town on the Bow River sits at an elevation of 1,380m/4,534ft amid breathtaking mountains. Though bustling with visitors, the community maintains the charm of a small alpine town. June through August, it hosts the **Banff Arts Festival**.
Operated by Parks Canada, the **Banff Visitor Centre** (*224 Banff Ave.*) provides information on park activities and services. *Open Jan 1–mid-May 9am–5pm; May 15–Jun 19 9am–6pm; (Jul–Sept*

9am–7pm). Rest of the year daily 9am–5pm. Closed Dec 25. 403-762-8421. www.pc.gc.ca.
Next door, you'll find Friends of Banff National Park (*403-760-5331; www. friendsofbanff.com*), where topographic

Float Your Own Boat

Summertime crowds in downtown Banff can be daunting, but a remarkably serene interlude lies the corner of Bow Ave. and Wolf St. **Rocky Mountain Raft Tours** (*403-762-3632; www.banffrafttours. com*) offers tours on oar-powered rafts down the Bow River, led by a guide. $50 for one hour, $85 for 2.5 hours wildlife tour; children half price. Rent a canoe and take a quiet trip up the valley along Echo Creek to the three Vermilion Lakes and back, amid hushed forests. You are likely to see elk, deer, bears and eagles.

maps, books and gifts are sold. Both places offer 🐾free guided nature walks.

Whyte Museum of the Canadian Rockies★ *(map p107)*

111 Bear St. ♿🕐*Open year-round daily 10am–5pm.* 🕐*Closed Jan 1, Dec 25.* 💶*$10 Donations accepted.* ✆*403-762-2291. www.whyte.org.*

This contemporary building displays historical items and Stoney Indian artifacts, art exhibits and archives. The museum also gives tours of seven historical local houses and offers regular lectures.

Banff Park Museum National Historic Site★ *(map p107).*

91 Banff Ave. 🕐*Open mid-May–Jun 30 Wed–Sun 10am–5pm; Jul–Sept daily 10am–5pm; Sept 3–Oct 12 Wed–Sun 10am–5pm.* 🐾*Tours in summer daily 3pm; rest of year Sat-Sun 2.30pm.* 💶*$4. (in 2017 the $9.80 Annual Pass is good for two full years.* ✆*403-762-1558. www.pc.gc.ca.*

Constructed in the "railway pagoda" style in 1903, this national historic site displays minerals and stuffed animals of the Rocky Mountains. Among the collections is a series of prints by renowned artist **Robert Bateman**.

Cascade Gardens★ *(map p107)*

At the south end of Banff Ave., across Bow River Bridge. 🕐*Open Jun–Sept daily. Free admission.*

These terraced gardens provide an excellent **view★** of **Cascade Mountain**, the 2,999m/9,840ft peak that towers above the north end of Banff Avenue. The stone 1935 Gothic Revival building houses the park administration offices.

👥 Buffalo Nations Luxton Museum★

♿*On the south bank of the Bow River. 1 Birch Ave.* 🕐*Open May–early Oct daily 11am–6pm. Rest of the year daily 11am–5pm.* 💶*$10.* ✆*403-762-2388. www.buffalonationsmuseum.com.*

Newly renovated (2014) replica of a log fur-trading fort, this museum displays

---

Grand Railway Hotels

The Canadian Pacific Railroad (CPR) opened up the scenic wonders of the Rockies to eastern travellers, but there were no sophisticated hotels for them. CPR president William Van Horne solved the problem in typically grandiose fashion: his **Banff Springs Hotel** was the world's largest (250 rooms) and grandest when it opened in 1888. Although it no longer taps the mountain's hot springs, now the Fairmont Banff Springs Hotel's Willow Stream Spa has a mineral pool reminiscent of nearby Cave springs.

Chateau Lake Louise followed in 1890 and launched the Canadian mountain-guiding tradition. Its spectacular lakeside setting is one of the most photographed in North America. Built by the Grand Trunk Pacific Railway in 1922, **Jasper Park Lodge** opened as the world's largest single-storey log structure. With its 18-hole golf course, designed by Canada's master golf-course architect Stanley Thompson, the lodge was hugely popular with Bing Crosby, Marilyn Monroe and other Hollywood celebrities in the 1950s. It served as the setting for films such as *River of No Return.*

Over the years, all three properties—now owned by Fairmont—have been damaged by fire, rebuilt and vastly expanded. The interior of each hotel is unique, with significant art collections, expansive lobbies and even shopping arcades. Aware of their historic status, all three hotels welcome tourists to most of their public spaces. A free heritage tour of the Banff Springs Hotel is worthwhile, as is hiring a guide from Fairmont's Mountain Heritage Guide Program. $60 half-day; $75 full-day.

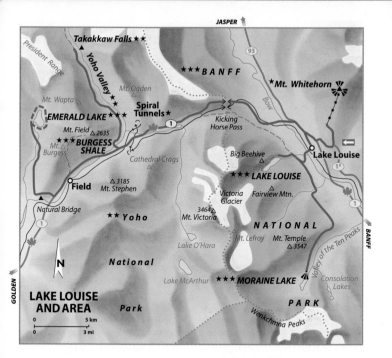

LAKE LOUISE AND AREA

0 ___ 5 km
0 ___ 3 mi

native artifacts and life-size dioramas depicting aspects of Plains Indian life.

Bow Falls★

At the foot of the Fairmont Banff Springs Hotel, the Bow River tumbles over a wide, low lip, just before its confluence with the Spray River.

Cave and Basin National Historic Site★★

♿⏱*Open mid-May–Jun 30 Tue–Sun 10am–5pm; Jul–Sept daily 10am–5pm; Sep 8–Oct 12 Tue–Sun 10am–5pm; Oct 13–May Wed–Sun 10am–5pm.* ⏱*Closed Jan 1, Dec 25-26.* 📷*Tours in summer 11am & 2:30pm, Campfire Singalong Sat at 3:30 & 4:30pm.* ☞*No charge w/admission.* 📞*403-762-1566. www.pc.gc.ca.*

1914 stone building surrounds an open-air swimming pool (*not open for swimming*) of hot springs water (average temperatures 30–35°C/86–95°F), and features an interpretive media centre.

Sulphur Mountain★★

3.5km/2.2mi from downtown. ♿⏱*Access by gondola (8min ascent) year-round daily. Hours vary.* ☞*$49.* 📞*403-762-2523. www.banffgondola.com.*

The 2,285m/7,500ft summit allows a splendid 360-degree **panorama★★★** of the Bow Valley and surroundings.

👥 Upper Hot Springs★

♿*3.5km/2.2mi from downtown; follow Mountain Ave.* ⏱*Open mid-May–mid-Oct daily 9am–11pm. Rest of the year Sun–Thu 10am–10pm, Fri–Sat 10am–11pm.* ☞*$7.30.* 📞*403-762-1515 or 800-767-1611. www.hotsprings.ca.*

Discovered a year after the Cave and Basin hot springs, the mineral waters (average temperature 38°C/100°F) now feed a large public pool perched on the mountainside overlooking Bow Valley.

Hoodoos★

These naturally sculpted pillars of cemented rock and gravel can be viewed from a scenic nature trail above Bow River (*1km/.6mi; trailhead off Tunnel Mountain Rd.*).

Paddling on Lake Louise

©Leslie Forsberg/Michelin

Lake Minnewanka Loop★

Begins 4km/2.4mi from downtown.
Along this 16km/10mi drive are three lakes known for water sports: Johnson, Two Jack and Minnewanka, a reservoir. Tour boats offer cruises *(90min)* down to Devil's Gap *(early May–early Oct, sailings daily 10am, noon, 2pm, 4pm and 6pm; ◎$60; Minnewanka Tours ♪403-762-3479; www.explorerockies.com.com)*. The road passes **Bankhead**, an abandoned early-20C coal-mining operation. An interpretive trail explains the the site.

BOW VALLEY PARKWAY TO LAKE LOUISE (HIGHWAY 1A)★

48km/30mi. Begins 5.5km/3.5mi west of town.
Running along the north bank of the Bow River parallel to the Trans-Canada Highway, this scenic parkway was the original 1920s road connecting Banff and Lake Louise. The route offers **views**★ of the Sawback Range to the northeast—in particular, crenellated Castle Mountain—and of the Great Divide peaks to

the southwest. At **Johnston Canyon**★★ *(17km/11mi)* a paved pathway over the narrow limestone canyon leads to the **lower falls**★★ *(about 1km/.6mi)* and the **upper falls**★★ *(about 1.6km/1mi)*. The Inkpots, a collection of cold springs, are beyond the upper falls *(6km/4mi)*.

▶ At Castle Junction, Hwy. 93 leads west from Bow Valley Parkway to Kootenay National Park.

LAKE LOUISE AND AREA★★★

Smaller and less congested than Banff, this township and the park's west-central section encompass massive, glaciated peaks and pristine lakes, notably Lake Louise, named for Queen Victoria's daughter, Princess Louise, wife of a Governor-General. By the early 1900s a road had been built to the lake, a large chalet had been constructed and guests were flocking there. In 1925 the CPR completed the **Château Lake Louise**.

Laggan's Mountain Bakery & Delicatessen

Samson Mall, 101 Village Road, Lake Louise. ♪403-522-2017. http://laggans. pagecloud.com. Tucked away in Lake Louise's only shopping centre, this bakery provides an inexpensive option. Glass-fronted cabinets display breakfast croissants, pastries, muffins and cakes. Order sandwiches from the blackboard menu. Coffee is self-serve. If all tables are full, enjoy your meal beside the Pipestone River, behind the adjacent alleyway.

Lake Louise Village

The resort is located just off the Trans-Canada Highway. A park **Visitor Centre** (*open late Jun–Labour Day daily 9am–7pm; rest of the year hours vary; closed Dec 25; 403-522-3833; www.banfflakelouise.com* features excellent **displays** on the natural history of the area, including the Burgess Shale.

Lake Louise★★★

4km/2.5mi from village.
Set in a hanging valley backdropped by the majestic mountains of the Continental Divide, this beautiful glacier-fed lake remains one of the most iconic sites in the Canadian Rockies.
Fed by glacial meltwater, the lake (maximum temperature 4°C/40°F) changes color with light conditions and as the summer progresses. Known as glacial flour, fine powdery silt suspended in the water refracts the green rays of the spectrum and emits hues ranging from bluish-green to emerald.
The far end of the lake is dominated by **Mount Victoria** (3,464m/11,362ft) and **Victoria Glacier**. To the left of Victoria stands **Fairview Mountain** (2,744m/9,000ft), and to the right rises **Big Beehive**. A 2km/1.2mi trail leads along the lake's north shore. Two popular day hikes lead to teahouses: one at Lake Agnes (*3.5km/2.2mi from the lake*) and another at the Plain of Six Glaciers (*5.5km/3.3mi from the lake*).

Moraine Lake★★★

13km/8mi from village.
Smaller and less visited than Lake Louise, Moraine Lake occupies a splendid **site** below the sheer walls of the Wenkchemna peaks.
Moraine Lake Road climbs above the Bow Valley, affording an impressive **view★★** of ice-capped **Mount Temple** (3,547m/11,644ft) and of the glaciated **Wenkchemna** or **Ten Peaks**. A short walk leads up the rock pile damming the north end of the lake, providing the best **view★** of the surroundings. Other trails lead to the end of the lake and to nearby back-country lakes and valleys.

Mount Whitehorn★

Access by gondola (15min ascent) mid-Jun–early Sept daily 9am–5pm (last ride 4:30pm). Restaurant at base, and FREE shuttle from the village. $25. 403-522-3555. 877-956-8473 www.lakelouisegondola.com.
From the top of the Friendly Giant gondola, a **panorama★★** of Bow Valley spreads out: the Wenkchemna peaks and Mt. Temple, with Lake Louise to the west below the Victoria Glacier.

YOHO NATIONAL PARK★★

Smallest and most compact of the parks, Yoho (a native word meaning "awe") is a place of raging rivers and waterfalls and the site of the Burgess Shale, one of the most important fossil beds ever discovered.
The Trans-Canada Highway cuts across the park, passing over **Kicking Horse Pass** (1,625m/5,330ft), a point on the Great Divide which is also the boundary between Alberta and British Columbia and between Banff and Yoho National Parks. Here, geologist **James Hector** of the Palliser Expedition (1857-60) was kicked by his horse, fell unconscious and, mistaken for dead, was almost buried by his men.

The **Visitor Centre** in the small town of **Field** features displays on the Burgess Shale and other park attractions, and check our Google Maps street view. (*open May 1–Jun 20 daily 9am–5pm; Jun 21–Sep 2nd 8.30am–7pm; rest of Sep & Oct 9am–4pm; $9.80 park fee; 250-343-6783; www.pc.gc.ca).*

Spiral Tunnels★

In the shape of an elongated figure eight, these tunnels allowed trains to make the treacherously steep, 4.5 percent descent down "the big hill" leading into the valley of the Kicking Horse River.

Yoho Valley★★

Access road of 13km/8mi with switchbacks; no trailers allowed.
Situated between Mt. Field and Mt. Ogden, lovely Yoho Valley is accessed by a climbing road that includes a lookout above the confluence of Yoho and

Kicking Horse rivers. Near the road's end Yoho Peak and Glacier can be seen straight ahead, with Takakkaw Falls to the right.

Takakkaw Falls★★

One of the highest waterfalls on the continent, this torrent of meltwater from the Daly Glacier cascades in two stages for a combined total of 254m/833ft to join the Yoho River. A short paved walk leads to the base of the falls.

Burgess Shale★★

Visit by guided hike only, the website has a virtual tour. 6km/3.6mi round-trip to Mt. Stephen's fossil beds; 20km/12mi round-trip to Burgess Shale. Both are strenuous all-day hikes on steep trails. Reservations required. Contact Burgess Shale Geoscience Foundation between Mon–Fri 9am–3pm. ℘800-343-3006. Start at Yoho Trading Post. www.burgess-shale.bc.ca.

Located on **Mount Field** (2,635m /8,643ft), the Burgess Shale, considered the richest Cambrian site in the world, contains evidence of multicellular life in the oceans 515 million years ago. The challenging trail to the Burgess Shale offers excellent **views★★** of Emerald Lake and the President Range.

Emerald Lake★★★

Accessible via 8km/5mi road off Trans-Can Hwy. ✕Food and lodging available.

This beautiful lake at the foot of the President Range is fed by glacial runoff that colours the water a striking green.

The road to the lake offers views, from a parking area, of a **natural bridge** of limestone cut by the Kicking Horse River. The **site** is lovely, with Mt. Stephen rising to the northeast and mountains of the Van Horne Range visible downstream. At the southeastern end of the lake, Emerald Lake Lodge traces its beginnings to a 1902 CPR chalet. Mt. Wapta lies to the northeast and the peaks of the President Range to the west. A pleasant **trail** (5km/3mi) circles the lake.

After the turnoff to Emerald Lake, the Trans-Canada Highway follows the scenic **lower gorge** of the Kicking Horse

River to its junction with the Columbia River and the town of Golden.

ICEFIELDS PARKWAY★★★

233km/145mi (Trans-Canada Hwy. junction to Jasper).

Designed expressly to dramatize the incredible landscape, this unequalled parkway (Highway 93) runs below the highest mountains in the Canadian Rockies. Following the valleys of five rivers, the road angles northwesterly along the eastern flank of the Continental Divide, connecting Banff and Jasper parks. Glaciers, lakes and waterfalls are abundant along the route.

For many travelers, this is an absolutely spectacular zone in which to witness the remaining North American wilderness at its finest.

This is **grizzly bear** country, so consult with park officials for safety advice before venturing in. Protected areas are home to a wide list of wild animals, including the grizzly and black bears, **Canada lynx**, mountain lion, cougar, wolf, red fox, mountain goat, bighorn sheep, elk, caribou, white-tailed deer, porcupine, striped skunk, peregrine falcon, eagle, snowy owl and others.

Hector Lake★

16km/10mi.

The lake is set below the Waputik Range (south), Mt. Hector (east) and Bow Peak (north).

Crowfoot Glacier★★

33km/20mi.

After rounding Bow Peak the parkway reaches a viewpoint from which this glacier spreads across the lower rock plateaus of Crowfoot Mountain.

Bow Lake★★

37km/23mi.

Directly by the road, this lovely lake is best seen from the lookout leading to historic, red-roofed Num-Ti-Jah Lodge (see Addresses). The Bow Glacier hangs above the lake between Portal and St. Nicholas peaks.

Passing through a green meadowland of birch and willow, the parkway reaches Bow Summit (2,069m/6,786ft), the highest pass on the route.

Peyto Lake ★★★

40km/25mi to spur road. 🅿️ *Park in the lower lot; a short trail leads to a viewpoint.*

The striking turquoise waters of this lake are fed by Peyto Glacier. **Mistaya Mountain** rises sheerly from the opposite side of the lake, with Peyto Peak on its left. The road descends to the valley and passes a series of lakes. At **Lower Waterfowl Lake** lookout (*56km/35mi*), there is a fine **view★** of the Great Divide peaks, especially towering Howse Peak (3,290m/10,791ft) and pyramidal Mt. Chephren (3,307m/10,847ft).

Mistaya Canyon ★

72km/45mi to spur road for parking; follow trail into valley for 400m/.3mi.

This narrow gorge, cut by the Mistaya River, has sculpted limestone walls.

Continuing northward, the parkway passes Mt. Murchison (3,337m/10,945ft), which rises to the east, and the steep cliffs of Mt. Wilson (3,261m/10,696ft), looming above the road. After the road descends into the valley of the North Saskatchewan River, a lookout (*76km/47mi; trail through trees*) affords a **view** of the Howse River Valley.

After the junction with Highway 11, the parkway runs below the massive cliffs of Mt. Wilson (to the east), with views of Survey Peak and Mt. Erasmus to the west and then the facade of **Mt. Amery**.

The road hugs the base of Cirrus Mountain, whose sheer cliffs are known as the

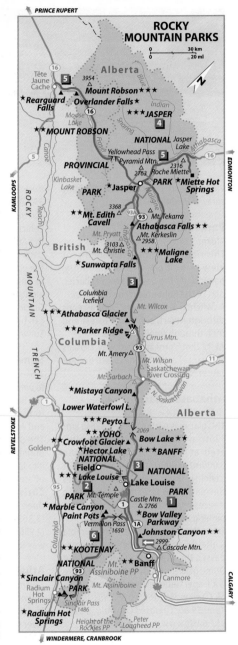

Weeping Wall because streams cascade down them. The parkway rounds "the big bend" and climbs quickly above the valley to a lookout with a spectacular **view★★** of the North Saskatchewan

Athabasca Glacier

© Douglas Peebles/age fotostock

Valley. A second lookout faces the filmy spray of **Bridal Veil Falls**.

Parker Ridge★★
118km/73mi.
This ridgetop affords a magnificent **view★★★** of glaciated backcountry, particularly the Saskatchewan Glacier, part of the Columbia Icefield *(below)*. A switchback trail *(2.4km/1.5mi)* ascends through dwarf, subalpine forest and then through treeless tundra.
At 122km/76mi the parkway crosses Sunwapta Pass (2,035m/6,675ft) to enter Jasper National Park.

Athabasca Glacier★★★
127km/79mi.
This glacier is part of the vast 325sq km/126sq mi **Columbia Icefield**, situated at an altitude of more than 3,000m/10,000ft, the largest subpolar icefield in the Rockies. In recent decades the glacier has retreated dramatically. It recession is marked on signs on the parking lot's road.
From the parking lot of the Columbia Icefield Centre, a **view★★★** encompasses the Athabasca, Kitchener and Dome glaciers. Inside the Icefield Centre is a Jasper National Park **Visitor Centre** (&🕙*open May 16–Sep 28 daily 10am–4pm; $9.80;* 🕙*closed Oct–Apr;* ☎*780-852-6288; www.pc.gc.ca).*

Ice Explorer Tours on the Glacier★★
Expect long lines in Jul & Aug, but tours leave every 15 minutes weather permitting 10am–4pm. &🕙*Tours (duration 90min) depart from Icefield Centre* ☞*$85 (Now includes Glacier Skywalk).*

Brewster Tours ☎*403-762-6700 or 888-350-7433; www.explorerockies.com/columbia-icefield.* These ultra-terrain vehicles travel a short distance onto the Athabasca Glacier and allow passengers to get off to briefly walk on the glacial surface. The perfect ending to this tour has members strolling along the cliff-edged walkway of the Glacier Skywalk, where giant glaciers can be seen above, and awesome Sunwapta Valley and wildlife below.

Sunwapta Falls★
176km/109mi; 400m/.3mi spur road to parking.
The Sunwapta River plunges over a cliff, turns around an ancient glacial moraine and enters a deep limestone canyon. The parkway enters the valley of the mighty **Athabasca River** and follows it to Jasper. On the west is the distinctive off-centre pyramidal shape of **Mount Christie** (3,103m/10,180ft) and the three pinnacles of the Mt. Fryatt massif (3,361m/11,024ft). **Mount Kerkeslin** (2,956m/9,696ft) towers over the parkway to the east.

Athabasca Falls★★
199km/123mi, turn left on Rte 93A for 400m/.3mi.
The silt-laden waters of the Athabasca River roar down a canyon smoothed by the force of the rushing waters. Backdropping the cataract is Mt. Kerkeslin. As the parkway approaches Jasper, the Whistlers can be seen to the west. Straight ahead rises Pyramid Mountain and to the east, the pinnacled peak of **Mount Tekarra**.

JASPER NATIONAL PARK★★★

The largest and northernmost of the four Rocky Mountain parks, Jasper National Park covers 10,878sq km/4,200sq mi, most of which is remote wilderness.

TOWN OF JASPER AND ENVIRONS★

This pleasant town sits in the valley of the Athabasca River near its confluence with the Miette River, surrounded by small and very beautiful lakes: **Pyramid, Patricia, Annette, Edith** and **Beauvert**. The peak of Mt. Edith Cavell is visible to the south and rugged **Pyramid Mountain** (2,763m/9,063ft) to the north.

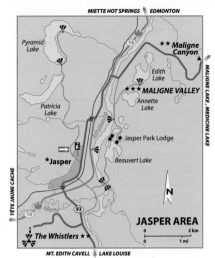

Jasper, which grew from a Grand Trunk Pacific Railway construction camp set up in 1911, is the site of the park **Visitor Centre** (*500 Connaught Dr.; open Mar 1–late-May daily 9am–5pm; late-May–mid-Sept 9am–7pm; Labour Day daily 8.30am–7pm; rest of the year hours vary; closed Nov 1–Dec 4; 780-852-6176; www.pc.gc.ca*).

The Whistlers★★

Access by tramway (7min ascent) late Jun–mid-Aug daily 9am–8pm; call for hrs. for other months mid-May-mid-Oct. $39.95; (at the top). 866-850-8726. www.jaspertramway.com.
The tramway ascends more than 900m/3,000ft to the terminal perched on the ridge. The **panorama★★★** takes in the townsite, the lake-dotted Athabasca Valley and the Colin Range to the northeast, and Mt. Yellowhead and the Victoria Cross Ranges to the northwest.

Mount Edith Cavell★★

24km/15mi from townsite. Access via Icefields Pkwy. to junction with 93A, then Mt. Edith Cavell Rd.
This massif (3,368m/11,047ft) was named for an English nurse executed by the Germans in World War I.
The narrow, twisting access road climbs steeply into the high country, paralleling the dramatic Astoria River Valley. A short walk to **Cavell Lake** from the parking area for the Tonquin Valley Trail (*26km/17mi*) leads to a **view** of

Pyramid Mountain, Jasper National Park

© All Canada photo/hemis.fr

115

Peaks of the Parks

Numerous mountains of the Canadian Rockies approach or exceed the 3,000m/10,000ft mark. Here are some of the high risers, in order of elevation, mentioned in this guide:

Mount Kerkeslin: 2,956m/9,696ft
Cascade Mountain: 2,999m/9,840ft
Mount Christie: 3,103m/10,180ft
Mount Stephen: 3,185m/10,447ft
Mount Charlton: 3,260m/10,693ft
Mount Wilson: 3,261m/10,696ft
Howse Peak: 3,290m/10,791ft
Mount Unwin: 3,300m/10,824ft
Mount Chephren: 3,307m/10,847ft
Mount Murchison: 3,337m/10,945ft
Mount Fryatt: 3,361m/11,024ft
Mount Edith Cavell:
3,368m/11,047ft
Mount Victoria: 3,464m/11,362ft
Mount Temple: 3,549m/11,644ft
Mount Robson: 3,954m/12,972ft
(highest peak in the Canadian Rockies)

the mountain. The lake's bright-green waters feed from **Angel Glacier**. At the end of the road (*2km/1.2mi drive*), is the trailhead for the Path of the Glacier Trail, which follows the toe of this ice river.

MALIGNE VALLEY★★★

96km/60mi round-trip by Hwy. 16 and Maligne Lake Rd.
This valley cradles a magnificent lake and canyon, both also named Maligne [Ma-LEEN], or "mean-spirited" in French.

Maligne Canyon★★

7km/4mi from Hwy. 16 junction.
This spectacular gorge reaches depths of 50m/164ft, while spanning widths of less than 3m/10ft in some places. A paved trail follows the the canyon rim.

Medicine Lake★

22km/14mi.
The Colin Range to the north and the Maligne Range to the south hem in this lovely lake. After the snowmelt of early summer, the lake gradually shrinks,

sometimes becoming only mud flats. The road follows the lake for 8km/5mi.

Maligne Lake★★★

For boat rentals, hiking trips or whitewater rafting, contact Maligne Tours in Jasper. ☎780-852-3370 or 866-625-4463. www.malignelake.com.
At 23km/14mi long, Maligne is the largest natural lake in the Rockies and one of the most spectacular. From the road, the twin peaks of **Mounts Unwin** (3,300m/10,824ft) and **Charlton** (3,260m/10,693ft) loom prominently.

Boat Trip★★★

Departs chalet at Maligne Lake early Jun until ice forms in the fall, daily 10am–4pm hourly. 90min. ☜$65. *Maligne Tours* ☽*see Maligne Lake above.*
While cruising note the water color changes from green to turquoise due to suspended glacial silt. Passengers can disembark near tiny **Spirit Island** to enjoy the **view★★★** of the peaks at the south end of the lake.

5 THE YELLOWHEAD HIGHWAY★★

This major thoroughfare, Highway 16, runs east-west through Jasper and Mt. Robson parks and continues westward to the Pacific at Prince Rupert.

FROM JASPER TO MIETTE HOT SPRINGS★★

60km/37mi
East of Jasper the highway enters the broad valley of the Athabasca River, offering breathtaking **views★★★**. The road passes between **Talbot Lake** (east) and **Jasper Lake**, backdropped by the **De Smet Range**. At the Disaster Point **animal lick**, small pools on the east side of the road attract mountain sheep and sometimes mountain goats. The drive holds fine views of **Roche Miette**.

Miette Hot Springs★

42km/26mi to Miette Hot Springs Rd.
♿⌚*Open mid-May–mid-Oct 10.30am –9pm; high season 8.30am–10.30pm.* ☜ *$6.05.* ☎780-866-3939 or 800-767-1611.

Canoeing by Spirit Island, Maligne Lake

© Katie Goldie/Travel Alberta

These springs are rich in natural minerals and are the hottest in the Canadian Rockies (maximum temperature 54°C/129°F). The mountainous **setting**★ makes this *the* location of all park bathhouses.

FROM JASPER TO REARGUARD FALLS★
100km/62mi

At **Yellowhead Pass**, the road leaves Jasper National Park (*24km/15mi*) and enters Mt. Robson Provincial Park.

Mount Robson Provincial Park★★

East boundary at 24km/15mi. ⓧOpen year-round. ℰ250-566-9174. Campground reservation ℰ800-689-9025. This 224,866ha/555,650 acre park is named for its greatest attraction: 3,954m/12,972ft **Mount Robson**★★★, the highest peak in the Canadian Rockies. Just beyond **Overlander Falls**★ (*88km/55mi; accessible by trail*) sits the park Visitor Centre (♿ⓧ*open early-May–mid-Oct daily 8am–5pm; www.env.gov.bc.ca*).

Rearguard Falls★

🚶3.2km/2mi walk.

Chinook salmon leap upstream during August spawning season, having made a 1,200km/744mi journey inland from the Fraser outlet on the Pacific.

⑥ KOOTENAY NATIONAL PARK★★

Kootenay National Park Visitor Centre is located in Radium Hot Springs

(*7556 Main St. East; ℰ250-347-9505; ⓧopen mid-May–early Oct 9am–5pm, Jul–Aug til 6pm*). In off-season, contact Yoho National Park Visitor Centre ℰ250-343-6783.

FROM CASTLE JUNCTION TO RADIUM HOT SPRINGS
105km/65mi by Rte. 93

This picturesque **route**★★ through the park leaves the highway at Castle Junction and climbs to the summit of **Vermilion Pass** marking the Great Divide.

Marble Canyon★
17km/11mi from junction.

The rushing waters of Tokumm Creek charge through this narrow limestone gorge on their way to meet the Vermilion River. The **visitor centre** (♿ⓧ*for hours, see above; ℰ403-762-9196 or 250-347-9615/winter*) for the park's north entrance is located here. Interpretive signs explain the geology of white-dolomite outcroppings, a natural bridge and other features along the trail (*1.6km/1mi*) through the canyon.

Paint Pots
20km/12mi from junction; trail of 1.2km/.7mi.

This area contains pools of ochre clay used as body paint and dyes by Indians and later mined by Europeans. Native tribes considered the three cold **mineral springs**★ places of spiritual power.

At 89km/55mi a lookout provides a sweeping **view**★ of the wide, wooded **Kootenay Valley** and the **Mitchell Range** flanking its west side. After topping Sinclair Pass (1,486m/4,874ft), the road follows Sinclair Creek's tumbling descent through **Sinclair Valley★**.

🚶 Radium Hot Springs★

103km/64mi. ♿🕐Open mid-May–early Oct daily 9am–11pm. Rest of the year Sun–Thu noon–9pm, Fri–Sat noon–10pm. 🎫$6.30 ($5.40 children 3-17). 📞250-347-9485 or 800-767-1611. www.hotsprings.ca.

The waters of these springs (average temperature 47°C/117°F) feed the swimming pools in the park complex. A park **information centre** sits at the corner of Main Street East and Redstreak Campground Road (*📞250-347-9505 or 250-347-9615/winter; www.pc.gc.ca*). After the hot springs, the highway passes through **Sinclair Canyon★** before reaching the park's southern entrance gate.

PRACTICAL INFORMATION
GETTING THERE

BY AIR – Canadian, US and international air carriers serve Calgary International Airport *(17km/11mi from downtown Calgary)*, and Edmonton International Airport (30km/19mi from downtown Edmonton) . Banff is 128km/79mi west of Calgary via the Trans-Canada Highway and Jasper is 366km/227mi west of Edmonton via Hwy. 16. Scheduled van and bus services connect Banff and Lake Louise to the Calgary airport, with frequent departures daily, as do chartered shuttle and bus services. Buses also connect the Calgary airport with Jasper, while regular bus service by Greyhound and Sun Dog Tour Company connects Edmonton with Jasper (👜*see below*). Air Jasper offers charter service out of Jasper Hinton Airport (*📞780-865-3616; www.airjasper.com*).

CAR RENTAL – Major car-rental agencies serve the Calgary and Edmonton airports, as well as Banff and Jasper. Since Banff and Jasper, as well as Field, BC (Yoho), are within national parks, you will need to pay entry fees at the gate: $9.80 per person per day, or $19.80 per day for a car with 2–7 passengers.

🚐 Yoho and Kootenay parks are less well served by public transport.

BY BUS – Greyhound provides **bus** service between Calgary and the Banff/Lake Louise area and between Edmonton and Jasper; it provides Canada's most extensive inter-city bus service (*📞800-661-8747,*

www.greyhound.ca). Sun Dog Tour Company provides bus connections among Calgary, Banff, Lake Louise and Jasper as well as sight-seeing tours (*📞780-852-4056 or 888-786-3641, www.sundogtours.com*).

BY TRAIN – VIA Rail (*📞888-842-7245, www.viarail.ca*) runs the Skeena between Jasper and Prince Rupert, with an overnight stop in Prince George, year-round. The Canadian, runs between Toronto and Vancouver, stopping in Winnipeg, Regina, Edmonton and Jasper, or the Snow Train, taking skiers to Jasper from Edmonton, Vancouver or Toronto, and points along the way. There is no passenger rail service to Banff. Rocky Mountaineer Vacations offers spectacular train rides on three routes that take in Vancouver, Whistler, BC; Banff; Jasper; and Calgary (*📞877-460-3200 or international toll-free 1-604-606-7245, www.rockymountaineer.com*).

GENERAL INFORMATION

WHEN TO GO – The Rocky Mountain parks are open year-round. The **summer season** is June to mid-September, peak season being July and August, when daylight extends to 10pm. Visitors should be prepared for cold weather even in summer, since snowfall in August and September is not unusual. Throughout the **winter**, most park roads remain open. Parkways are regularly cleared, but snow tires are strongly recommended from November to April.

VISITOR INFORMATION

Each national park has a visitor centre, operated by Parks Canada, where schedules, pamphlets, maps and permits are available. Go to the Parks Canada website, www.pc.gc.ca and select the specific website you wish to access. A park pass (*$9.80 per person per day, valid until 4pm the next day*) is interchangeable among national parks (multiday passes available) and can be obtained from park visitor centres, entrance gates or campground kiosks. For specific information about each park, consult the white pages in this chapter.

ACCOMMODATIONS

The Canadian Rockies are known for their **back-country lodges**, sometimes accessible only by hiking, skiing or helicopter. These wilderness hostelries range from rustic cabins to comfortable alpine chalets with fine food. Primitive cabins that rent for $25 per night per person, or $50 per family, can be reserved in both national and provincial parks through The Alpine Club of Canada *(Indian Flats Rd., Canmore, AB; ℘403-678-3200; www.alpineclubofcanada.ca)*. Campgrounds are located throughout the national parks. At least one campground in each park offers powered sites and showers. All sites are offered on a first-come, first-served basis. Hotels, resorts, motels, B&Bs, chalets and condominiums abound in the area. For lodging information, contact the Banff/Lake Louise Tourism Bureau (*℘403-762-8421; www.banfflakelouise.com*) or the Jasper Chamber of Commerce (*℘780.852.4621; www.jasper.travel*).

RECREATION

All four national parks, as well as many provincial parks, offer **hiking, backpacking, bicycling, horseback riding, canoeing, fishing, swimming** (except Yoho) and **winter sports**. Banff and Jasper have facilities for **tennis** and **golf**; Banff has bowling; boat tours and canoe rentals are also available. For details contact Parks Canada (◖see *above*).

Fairmont Banff Springs, Fairmont Lake Louise and Fairmont Jasper Lodge hotels offer 👣 **guided hikes/snowshoe/ski excursions.** Skilled naturalist guides explain the history, ecology, and legends of the mountains. Available for everyone, not only hotel guests. Reservations can be made with the hotel concierge: Fairmont Banff Springs ℘403-762-2211; The Fairmont Chateau Lake Louise ℘403-522-3511; Jasper Park Lodge ℘780-852-3301.

The Fairmont Banff Springs and the Jasper Park Lodge have renowned golf courses, while Kananaskis Country Golf Course has two 18-hole courses (℘403-591-7272 or 877-591-2525). Other popular golf courses are located at Canmore, AB, and Radium Hot Springs, BC.

Outfitters specializing in **wilderness excursions** provide equipment, guides and transportation. Flightseeing is not permitted within the national parks. Canmore-based Alpine Helicopters Ltd. offers sightseeing and heli-hiking (℘403-678-4802; www.alpinehelicopter.com). For more info, contact the Banff/Lake Louise Tourism Bureau (℘403-762-8421; www.banfflakelouise.com) or the Jasper Chamber of Commerce (℘780-852-4621, www.jaspercanadianrockies.com).

The Canadian Rockies offer **winter sports** from mid-November to mid-May including downhill skiing, snowboarding, ice-skating, dogsledding and cross-country. Three major ski resorts are located near Banff: Lake Louise (℘403-522-3555 or 877-956-8473; www.skilouise.com); Sunshine Village (℘403-277-7669 or 877-542-2633; www.sunshinemountainlodge.com); Ski Banff @ Norquay (℘403-762-4421; www.banffnorquay.com). Marmot Basin lies near Jasper (℘780-852-3816 or 866-952-3816; www.skimarmot.com). Amenities include restaurants, ski rentals, ski schools and day-care services. An adult lift ticket at these resorts runs $90 a day, but there are many packages. The multi-day Tri-Area pass at Banff includes free transport between your hotel and the slopes. Buses shuttle skiers from lodgings to the slopes for $7 one-way. For Nordic skiers, there are 80km of trails around Banff, while the parks, notably Kananaskis, have vast networks.

The **Canmore Nordic Centre Provincial Park** (*403-678-2400; www.kananaskis-country.ca*) on the site of the 1988 Olympic Nordic events, has 70km/43mi of trails for the intermediate and advanced cross-country skier. Facilities include ski rentals, lessons and a day lodge.

USEFUL NUMBERS

Area Codes: Banff 403, Jasper 780, Yoho and Kootenay 250.
RCMP (Police): 403-762-2228
Park Weather Forecasts: 1-900-565-5555 (charge of $2.99/minute) or 888-292-2222 (from cell or pay phones, credit card required (charge of $2.99/minute) or www.weatheroffice.gc.ca.
Trail Conditions: Banff: 403-762-1550; Jasper 780-852-6177. Look on Parks Canada website, www.pc.gc.ca.
Avalanche Hazard: Parks Canada, www.pc.gc.ca, or www.avalanche.ca.

ADDRESSES

🛏️ STAY

🛏️ *Almost all hotels in the parks area offer access to outdoor activities, guides and outfitters. The Fairmont hotels also offer Mountain Heritage Guide programs.*

$ HI-Lake Louise Alpine Centre – *203 Village Rd., Lake Louise, AB. *403-522-2201 or 866-762-4122. www.hihostels.ca. 46 rooms, including family rooms, 164 beds.* ⚓🅿️. This hostel's stylish wood-framed appearance and high standards make budget travel a pleasant experience. Dorm-style rooms are spotless and come with two to six beds. Private rooms are also available. Guests have access to a kitchen, a reading room, laundry facilities, a café and wireless Internet. Other Hostelling International facilities in the region are located in Banff, Jasper and Yoho parks, Golden, BC, and along the Icefields Parkway.

$$ Blue Mountain Lodge – *137 Muskrat St., Banff, AB.* 🅿️ ☕ *403-762-5134. www.bluemtnlodge.com. 10 rooms.* Minimum 2-night stay. Built in 1908, this small bed-and-breakfast offers affordable rooms, all with a private bath, cable TV and wireless Internet. The rate includes an ample cold breakfast buffet. Guests also have use of a communal kitchen and a ski-storage area.

$$ Spruce Grove Inn – *545 Banff Ave., Banff, AB.* *403-762-3301 or 800-879-1991. www.banffvoyagerinn.com. 120 rooms.* ⚓🅿️. Built in 2003, this lodging is spanking new by the venerable standards of many park hotels. It is on a strip of motels that leads into downtown Banff from the Trans-Canada Highway. Although the inn keeps rates relatively low by offering fewer amenities, its rooms are spacious and comfortable. Ski storage and heated underground parking are included in the rate. Many restaurants lie within a 10-minute walk

$$$ Brewster's Mountain Lodge – *208 Caribou St., Banff, AB.* *403-762-2900 or 888-762-2900. www.brewstermountainlodge.com. 60 rooms, 17 suites.* ⚓🅿️☕. This western-style hotel, with its distinctive peeled-log exterior,is just one block from downtown Banff. A timber stairway leads upstairs to spacious, updated bedrooms. Bountiful breakfasts in an inviting downstairs dining room.

$$$ Num-Ti-Jah Lodge – *40km/25mi north of Lake Louise on Hwy. 93 North, Lake Louise, AB.* *403-522-2167. www.sntj.ca. 16 rooms.* ⚓🅿️✗. The original lodge was built some 80 years ago by Jimmy Simpson, a mountain guide. Refurbished and expanded, the timber-frame inn overlooks Bow Glacier and Bow lake, in a splendid setting. The **Elkhorn Dining Room ($$$)** offers a table d'hôte. Comfortable lounge and library. No TV or phone, although a satellite phone is available.

$$$ Paradise Lodge & Bungalows – *105 Lake Louise Dr., Lake Louise, AB. Closed Oct–May.* ⚓🅿️ *403-522-3595. www.paradiselodge.com. 45 cabins and suites.*

The undeniable charm of this heritage property, located between the valley floor and Lake Louise, attracts the same guests year after year. Well-tended gardens surround the tidy cabins, built in the 1930s, some of which feature vaulted ceilings and claw-foot tubs. Larger than the cabins, the suites contain fireplaces and offer the best views; some have kitchens, equipped with basic amenities. No pets.

$$$ Tekarra Lodge – *1.6km/1mi south of Jasper. Hwy 93A South, Jasper, AB. 780-852-3058 or 877-532-5862. www. tekarralodge.com. 52 cabins*. Closed Nov–Apr. ♿️🄿✕. After 1913, when motor vehicles were permitted in the Rocky Mountain parks, "bungalow camps" such as this one sprang up. Tekarra dots the open forest above the Athabasca River with rustic cabins featuring comfortable beds, cooking facilities and wood-burning fireplaces. There is a telephone at the front desk, but no TV. The **Tekarra Restaurant** ($$) serves a varied menu, on the hearty side.

$$$$ Baker Creek Chalets – *Bow Valley Pkwy., Lake Louise, AB. 403-522-3761. www.bakercreek.com. 33 cabins and suites.* ♿️🄿✕. Situated between Lake Louise and Banff on the Bow Valley Parkway, Baker Creek's cozy log chalets provide well-priced accommodations. The chalets all have balconies and kitchenettes. Suites in a newer building are done up in warm, earthy tones. Plan to eat at the **Baker Creek Bistro** ($$$), an unpretentious dining room that serves up hearty Canadian-style meals.

$$$$ Buffalo Mountain Lodge – *Tunnel Mountain Rd., Banff, AB. 403-410-7417 or 800-661-1367. 108 rooms.* ♿️🄿✕. This sprawling lodge offers a peaceful retreat from the bustle of Banff, just a short walk away. The sizable bedrooms include a fireplace, and a balcony or patio. Some bathrooms feature claw-foot bathtubs and heated floors. The renowned **Sleeping Buffalo Restaurant** ($$$$) specializes in local produce and game raised on a ranch nearby. As well as the customary strenuous activities, the hotel offers the Cilantro Mountain Café for pizza, pasta, mussels and more.

$$$$$ Emerald Lake Lodge – *In Yoho National Park. Field, BC. 403-410-7417 or 800-663-6336. www.crmr.com. 85 rooms in 24 chalets, including a limited number of pet friendly rooms.* ♿️🄿✕. Set among towering evergreens, this quintessential mountain getaway overlooks one of the region's most picturesque lakes. Large comfortable rooms with fieldstone fireplaces, pine furnishings and private entrances, promote a restful stay. Take your meals at the Mount Burgess Dining Room, or at the casual lakeside cafe Cilantro on the Lake. A wide range of summer and winter activities, and a free shuttle connects to the Lake Louise ski resort.

$$$$$ Fairmont Banff Springs – *405 Spray Ave., Banff, AB. 403-762-2211 or 866-540-4406. www.fairmont.com. 778 rooms.* ♿️🄿✕ Spa. This turreted château overlooking the Bow River is one of the world's best-known mountain playgrounds. First opened in 1888, "The Springs" has since been thoroughly modernized. Rooms are smartly decorated, although on the smallish side. The real attractions are the opulent ambience and an abundance of facilities, including its luxurious Willow Stream Spa, a 27-hole golf course designed by Stanley Thompson and riding stables. No less than 11 restaurants range from an intimate wine bar to the top-drawer **1888 Chophouse ($$$$),** specializing in roasted Alberta lamb and beef, bison carpaccio, venison and other Canadian classics. Visitors are welcome at all hotel eateries. Ski shuttle $15 return.

$$$$$ Fairmont Chateau Lake Louise *111 Lake Louise Dr., Lake Louise, AB. 403-522-3511 or 866-540-4413. www. fairmont.com. 489 rooms.* ♿️🄿✕ Spa. This famous mountain resort's stunning view of turquoise-blue Lake Louise is perhaps the most renowned in the Canadian Rockies. Restaurants include the **Fairview Room ($$$)**, offering fine contemporary fare accompanied by dramatic views. Outside, colourful gardens lead to a paved walkway bordering the lakeshore. Activites offered range from rock-climbing to barn dancing.

$$$$$ Fairmont Jasper Park Lodge – *Old Lodge Rd., Jasper, AB. 780-852-3301 or 866-540-4454. www.fairmont.com. 446 rooms in a complex of cabins and lodges.* ♿️🄿✕ Spa. Sprawling along turquoise-colored Beauvert Lake, this historic property boasts its own championship golf course as well as extensive sports facilities. Accommodations range from chalet-style cottages to log cabins that have hosted royalty, including Queen Elizabeth II. Dining spots include the illustrious **Orso Trattoria ($$$$)**, with a menu of Canadian game and seafood.

$$$$$ Lake O'Hara Lodge – *In Yoho National Park. Lake Louise, AB.* ℰ*250-343-6418, 403-678-4110 (off-season). www. lakeohara.com. 23 cabins and rooms.* ✕ *Minimum 2-night stay. Rates include all meals and shuttle to the lodge.* Closed Oct–Jan, early-Apr–mid-Jun. Originally built by the Canadian Pacific as a backcountry lodge, this site on Lake O'Hara is one of the most splendid in Canada. The main lodge holds a restaurant and eight standard guest rooms (double beds), but the lakeside cabins are more coveted (queen beds). Access to the property is by shuttle; no private cars are allowed on the site (*parking is 15km/9mi east of Field*). In the winter season (early-Feb–early-Apr), guests ski or snowshoe 12km/7.5mi to the lodge. No TV, radio or internet connections. /Parks Canada and the Alpine Club of Canada (Tsee above) have far less pricey sites on Lake O'Hara.

$$$$$ Post Hotel and Spa – *200 Pipestone Rd., Lake Louise, AB.* ℰ*403-522-3989 or 800-661-1586. www.posthotel.com. 94 rooms.* 🅿✕🆂🅿🅰 A short walk from the village, this stylish retreat, part of the French Relais & Châteaux group, is set along the tumbling waters of the Pipestone River. Spacious guestrooms feature polished logwork, luxurious bathrooms, and balconies; many rooms have a hot tub and fireplace. The **Outpost ($$)** offers a cozy pub atmosphere alternative to the main dining room.

ℙ/EAT

$ Grizzly Paw Brewing Company – *622 8th (Main) St., Canmore, AB.* ℰ*403-678-9983. www.thegrizzlypaw.com.* **Canadian**. Billed as the only brewing company in the Rockies, Grizzly Paw serves up burgers, nachos, quesadillas, chicken wings and other favourites. The beer selection is large and especially welcome on a sunny day on the patio. The "Paw" crafts its own soda pop using less sugar than commercial products.

$$ Becker's Gourmet Restaurant – *Hwy. 93 S, Jasper, AB.* ℰ*780-852-3779. www.beckerschalets.com. Open May–Oct*

for breakfast & dinner. **Canadian**. Diners can look across the Athabasca River to distant mountains while enjoying cuisine prepared from fresh Alberta beef, lamb, bison, venison and rainbow trout. On colder evenings, a fire crackles in the riverstone fireplace. Repeat customers ask for a bowl of housemade ice-cream.

$$ Bumpers Beef House – *In The Rundlestone Lodge, 537 Banff Ave., Banff, AB.* ℰ*403-762-2201 or 800-661-8630. www.rundlestone.com.* Breakfast from 6.30am and dinner from 5pm. **Canadian**. Located away from the town centre, this eatery serves hearty breakfast plates, plus famous AAA Alberta beef. Knowledgeable wait staff and a good representation of Canadian wines (try a glass of British Columbia ice wine with your dessert) round out a pleasant dining experience.

$$ The Station Restaurant and Heritage Railway Station – *200 Sentinel Rd., Lake Louise, AB. www.lakelouisestation.com.* ℰ*403-522-2600. Lunch & dinner.* **Contemporary**. This former Canadian Pacific Railway station, built in 1910 and renovated in 1994, is furnished with Arts and Crafts furniture, offers a contemporary burger menu with some serious meat eater classics at dinner. For authenticity, CPR freight trains still rumble past. Gift shop.

$$ Melissa's Missteak – *218 Lynx St., Banff, AB.* ℰ*403-762-5511. www.melissas missteak.com.* **Steakhouse**. This perennial favourite serves breakfast until 4pm, plus burgers, charbroiled steaks, seafood classics, and BYOB for dinner. Families are welcome at this long-running eatery.

$$$ Maple Leaf Grill & Lounge – *137 Banff Ave., Banff, AB.* ℰ*403-760-7680 or 866-760-7680. www.banffmapleleaf.com.* **Canadian**. This popular dining room, faced in cedar and presided over by a moose head, offers imaginative Canadian cuisine.Lunch begins at 11am featuring their famous pizzas, soup of the day, and early bird poutine. Dinner from 5pm offers onion soup, regional game platters, elk, bison, Arctic char, BBQ salmon, AAA Alberta beef and vegetarian option. Desserts here are especially tempting. Request an upstairs table for the best views and a quieter dining experience.

Skeena Valley★★

British Columbia

This verdant river valley holds the second-largest river in the province. Rising in the Skeena Mountains of the interior, the 565km/350mi "river of mists" flows south to the town of New Hazelton, then southwest to the Hecate Strait, following a massive channel cut by Ice Age glaciers. The valley is noted for its rich Tsimshian culture of the Gitxsan tribe, which still inhabits the riverbanks. The river itself is famed worldwide for its steelhead trout; fishing lodges are situated along its banks.

Info: Northern British Columbia Tourist Association. ℘250-561-0432 or 800-663-8843. www.nbctourism.com.

Location: The western portion of Route 16 between Prince George and Prince Rupert takes you through the Skeena Valley, lying between New Hazelton and Kitwanga.

Don't Miss: The totem poles and reconstructed K'san village near New Hazelton; the Cow Bay waterfront area in Prince Rupert.

Kids: Museum of Northern British Columbia.

A BIT OF HISTORY

Ancestral Home – The Skeena River and its tributaries have been the territory of the Gitxsan First Nations People for close to 10,000 years. The Gitxsan subsisted on salmon, berries and western red cedar, which was used for their longhouses, canoes, clothing and elaborate totem poles. Pole-raisings and important occasions were accompanied by great feasts called **potlatches**.

European Contact – In the 19C European fur-trading posts, dominated by the Hudson's Bay Company, were established along the river. In the 1880s stern-wheelers came to the Skeena. In 1912 the Grand Trunk Pacific Railway was completed. Today the Yellowhead Highway follows the Skeena from east of Prince Rupert to New Hazelton.

First Nations Decline & Renewal – The Gitxsan First Nations were greatly affected by the arrival of Europeans. Old patterns of hunting and gathering were curtailed in favor of supplying furs to the new immigrants; missionary zeal and European misapprehensions about the potlatch led to its ban between 1884 and 1951; totem poles were destroyed; and the introduction of diseases such as smallpox significantly reduced the native population. In the 1970s a renaissance of First Nations culture began. Today their language, Tsimshian, is taught in reserve schools, and traditional art and crafts has been revived. Silk-screening, introduced in the past few decades, has allowed artists to develop innovative approaches to classic designs.

PRINCE RUPERT

Served by BC Ferries (℅ see Inside Passage). Atlin Terminal, 100-215 Cow Bay Rd. ℘250-624-8687, or 800-667-1994. www.visitprincerupert.com.
Situated on Kaien Island near the mouth of the Skeena, this maritime city faces a deepwater harbor dotted with islands. Located just south of the Alaska Panhandle, Prince Rupert was established in 1906 as the terminus of the Grand Trunk Pacific. With its ice-free harbor, the city today is a fishing and fish-processing centre as well as a port. Prince Rupert receives an annual rainfall of 2,564mm/100in. Reproductions of Tsimshian and Haida **totem poles★** are scattered throughout the city.
The **Cow Bay** area has a dockside, with cafes, small inns and shops. A Grand Trunk Pacific station removed to the waterfront, the small **Kwinitsa Railway Station Museum★** has displays of railroading artifacts and old photographs

123

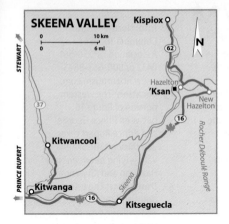

SKEENA VALLEY

(◔Open Jun–Aug daily 9am–noon, 1pm–5pm; ⬭contribution requested; ✆250-624-3207).

👤👤 Museum of Northern British Columbia★★

100 First Ave. W. and Hwy. 16. ♿◔Open Jun–Aug daily 9am–5pm. Rest of the year Tue–Sat 9am–5pm. ⬭$6 (child $2). ✆250-624-3207. www.museumof northernbc.com.

The museum is known for native Northwest basketry, argillite and wood carvings. The Tsimshian **mortuary frog** is the only remaining item of its kind. The **museum building** 👤👤 is constructed of massive red cedar posts and beams. At the carving shed visitors can watch First Nations craftspeople at work.

FROM PRINCE RUPERT★★ TO 'KSAN

307km/184mi by Hwy. 16

North Pacific Historic Fishing Village★★

22km/14mi east of Prince Rupert, 6km/3mi southeast of Port Edward. 1889 Skeena Dr., Prince Edward, BC. ♿◔Open Jul & Aug daily 9.30am–5pm, May–Jun & early–late Sept Tue–Sun 10am–4pm. ⬭$12. ✆250-628-3538. www.northpacificcannery.ca.

Built in 1889 on an arm of the Skeena, the complex is the oldest surviving cannery village on the north coast. Fishing and canning methods are explained

on guided tours. There is a bed-and-breakfast inn, a restaurant specializing in seafood and a cafe offering light meals.

East of Port Edward Highway 16 meets the Skeena River, following it through its magnificent valley. The entire route provides lovely views of the broad, turbulent river and of the cloud-shrouded, snowy Coast Mountains rising to 2,000m/6,000ft. In the town of **Terrace**, the **Heritage Park**, a collection of eight old log buildings moved here from outlying areas, depicts pioneer life in the region. The river waters around the town and around nearby Kitimat to the south (*52km/31mi*) provide excellent sportfishing for trout and salmon.

After Terrace, where the valley widens briefly, the road winds through the Hazelton Mountains. East of Terrace (*12km/7mi*) at the village of **Usk**, a small cable ferry crosses the treacherous waters of the Skeena.

TOUR OF THE TOTEMS★★

Begin this self-guided driving tour in New Hazelton. 🛈 New Hazelton Visitor Centre, corner Hwy. 16 and Hwy. 62. ♿◔Open May17–Sept daily. ✆250-842-6071. www.newhazelton.ca.

Today the Gitxsan still inhabit five ancient villages along the Skeena and its tributaries. Four of these villages have impressive stands of **totem poles** ★★★ that date from the late 19C. The weathered poles, devoid of paint, range in height from 5m/15ft to 9m/30ft.

▷ Drive to junction of Hwy. 16 and Hwy. 37 North, after crossing the Skeena River; then turn right on Bridge St.

Kitwanga

Situated beside the Skeena River, a fine stand of about a dozen 19C totem poles graces a flat, grass-covered field against a backdrop of the impressive **Seven Sisters** Mountains (2,755m/9,039ft).

Totem Poles and houses at 'Ksan
Historical Village and Museum

JF Bergeron/Enviro Foto/Northern BC Tourism

Kitwancool

Hwy. 37, 18km/11mi north of Kitwanga.
This village has the oldest existing stand
of Gitxsan totem poles, though several
of its most venerable ones are now stored in a shed at the rear of the totem
field for preservation.

▶ Return to Hwy. 16 and
continue east.

Kitseguecla

*Hwy. 16, 19km/12mi east of junction
with Hwy. 37.*
The original totem poles in this village
were destroyed by fire (1872) and by
flood. New poles, however, now stand
throughout.

▶ Continue east to New Hazelton
and turn left on Hwy. 62.

'Ksan★★

*Hwy. 62, 7km/4mi northwest of New
Hazelton.* ◷*Open daily 10am–5pm.*
👣*Guided tours $15. Museum & gift
shop also open daily 10am–5pm.* 👓*$8
grounds & museum.* ☏*250-842-5544 or
877-842-5518. www.ksan.org.*
A complex of totem poles and longhouses re-created in the traditional
style, this historical village museum provides an insight into the Gitxsan culture.
'Ksan, the Gitxsan name for the Skeena,

consists of seven major buildings, including a carving house and a silk-screen
workshop as well as a museum and
gift shop. An extensive **collection★★**
of native artifacts is used to explain
the culture and lifestyle of these First
Nations people. The traditional Gitxsan
salmon recipes are available inside the
Eagle House, along with other treats.

Kispiox

*19km/12mi north of 'Ksan on
Kispiox Valley Rd.*
Situated near the confluence of the
Skeena and Kispiox rivers, this large vil-
lage boasts a dozen totems in a field by
the waters of the Kispiox.

ADDRESSES

🍴EAT

$$$ Cow Bay Café – *205 Cow Bay Rd.,
Prince Rupert, BC.* ☏*250-627-1212.
Closed Sun and Mon.* This small waterfront
cafe offers creative fresh cuisine and
an exceptional site overlooking Prince
Rupert's harbour. Five days a week
it serves up fresh local seafood and
especially delicious crab cakes (*in season*),
along with housemade desserts and
a good selection of wines and Vegan
choices. *Reservations advised.*

Vancouver★★★

British Columbia

Canada's third-largest metropolis, Vancouver has a magnificent **site** on a peninsula protruding into the Strait of Georgia. To the north the Coast Mountains rise steeply; to the west across the Strait of Georgia stand the mountains of Vancouver Island and to the southeast rises the Cascade Range. A protected deep-sea port, accessibility to the Pacific Ocean, and a virtually snow-free climate have contributed to this West Coast city's rapid growth, attracting a multi-ethnic population. The cultural diversity and liveliness here are matched by few cities elsewhere. In 2010 the city hosted the Winter Olympics and Paralympics, and 2014 marked the city's first TED Conference.

A BIT OF HISTORY

Early History – The shores of the Strait of Georgia were the preserve of the Coast Salish Indians until 1791, when Spanish captain José Maria Narvaez entered its waters. (English explorer Francis Drake had likely visited two centuries earlier.) A year later, British Capt. **George Vancouver** explored Burrard Inlet, and in 1808 Simon Fraser saw the area from the land side. In the 1860s entrepreneurs built a brickyard, sawmills to process the area's rich timber and a saloon. The village known as Gastown became Granville in 1869, when government surveyors laid out a townsite.

The Coming of the Railway – When it was finally decided to route the Canadian Pacific Railway (CPR) down the Fraser Valley to Burrard Inlet, land prices skyrocketed, prompting **William Van Horne**, president of the railway, in 1884 to extend the line farther down the inlet to Granville, which he renamed Vancouver. Despite a destructive fire in in 1886, the community was rebuilt sufficiently to welcome the first trans-Canadian passenger train In 1887.

▶ **Population:** 2,476,145 (metro.)

Michelin Maps: pp128-129, pp134-135, p138.

Information: Tourist Info Centre, Plaza level, 200 Burrard St. ℘604-682-2222. www.tourism vancouver.com.

▶ **Location:** Downtown Vancouver sits on a peninsula, with Stanley Park on the northwest end. To the southwest, walking and cycle paths connect the beaches of English Bay. To the south, Yaletown and new residential towers are rapidly filling the space along the False Creek waterfront. To the east, BC Place Stadium and Chinatown are separated from the shops of Gastown by the seedy East Hastings area (*best avoided*).

P **Parking:** Garage and metered street parking are available downtown, but elusive during working hours. Consider walking, cycling or taking public transit.

Don't Miss: Stanley Park's trails and seawalks; the Aquarium; University of British Columbia's Museum of Anthropology.

Timing: A good way to start your visit is to take the elevator to the Observation Deck atop the Harbour Centre Tower, from which the city spreads out clearly below.

Kids: Kids will love the Aquarium, especially the beluga performances, as well as Science World. There are also many free outdoor activities.

False Creek and Downtown Vancouver

© Alamy/hemis.fr

Vancouver Today – The financial, commercial and industrial centre of British Columbia, Vancouver is also Canada's **largest port**, trading some $43 billion in goods annually, chiefly with Japan and other Pacific Rim countries. It is a centre for forest products and fishing as well, although technology is now a bigger employer; areas of strong growth are biotechnology, environmental businesses, software, new media and telecom/wireless firms. Tourism is still a major employer. Vancouver is also a film industry centre, often called Hollywood North, as foreign productions are attracted by scenic locations, excellent production facilities and a highly qualified workforce.

At the conclusion of its centennial world exposition, **Expo '86**, the city sold the site to Concord Pacific Group, which invested $3 billion in a condo project, with 61ha/150 acres reserved for parks and a seawall walkway.

2010 Winter Olympics
Vancouver hosted the Winter Olympic Games in 2010. The venues stretched over a 120km/75mi zone from Richmond, south of Vancouver, through the city centre and up into the mountain resort of Whistler. Some 5,500 athletes from 80 countries participated; and shortly after, the Paralympic Games brought another 1,350 participants. Organizers' standards for environmental impact and social responsibility were notably high.

STANLEY PARK★★★

This 405ha/1,000 acre park is the third largest in North America, and has a magnificent **site** at the end of a peninsula that almost closes Burrard Inlet at **First Narrows**. The park contains several fine restaurants and family attractions.

Visiting the Park

✗⚐🕓*Open daily year-round.* ✆*604-257-8400. www.stanleyparkinfo.ca. It is illegal to feed Stanley Park's wild animals.* To access the park by car, stay in the far right lane of Georgia Street and follow the overhead sign. Coin-operated parking metres (*summer rates: $1–6 per hour*) are located throughout the park but the city encourages visitors to cycle, roller-blade or take the bus (*No.19*) to the park, or to park their car and use the **free shuttle** (🕓*mid-Jun–mid-Sept 10am–6.30pm; passes every 12–15min*) that circles the park. Numerous walking trails crisscross the forested interior, and a path known as the **seawall** rims the shoreline. Facilities include cricket grounds, tennis and shuffleboard courts, picnic areas, children's playgrounds, and a swimming pool at Second Beach. Horse-drawn **carriage tours** (*1hr*) depart from Coal Harbour parking lot near the Georgia Street entrance (⚐🕓*open Mar–Oct, schedule*

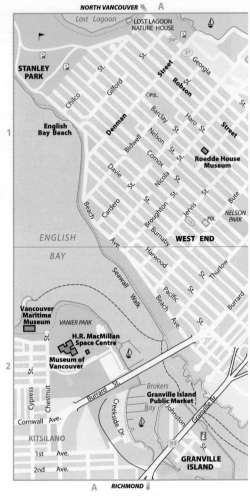

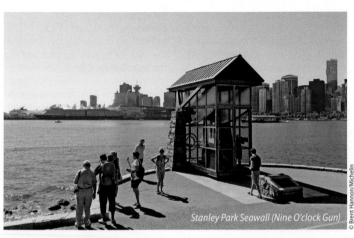

Stanley Park Seawall (Nine O'clock Gun)

© Brent Hannon/Michelin

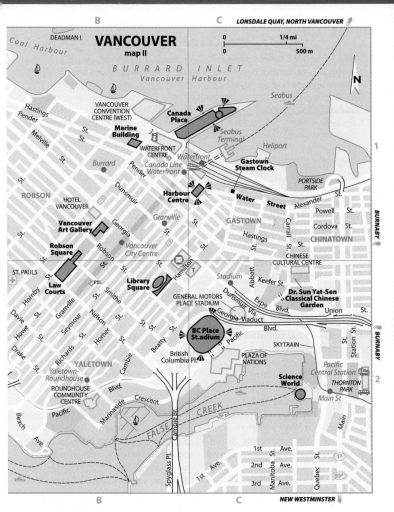

Vancouver map II

varies; ⊷ $39.99; Stanley Park Horse-Drawn Tours Ltd; ℘604-681-5115. www.stanleypark.com).

Scenic Drive★

10km/6mi.

Circling the park in a counterclockwise direction, the drive begins and ends at Georgia Street. The route follows the edge of Coal Harbour, offering views of the yacht clubs, port and city as far as **Brockton Point**. Just before the point note the display of brightly painted **totem poles★★★**, the work of the Northwest Coast Indians.

The road continues to **Prospect Point★** where ships pass through First Narrows.

Then the road turns inland, but paths lead to the seawall near **Siwash Rock★**. From **Ferguson Point** there are **views** of **Third Beach★**, Point Grey Peninsula, where the University of British Columbia sits, and the mountains. **Cardero's ($$$** ℘604-669-7666; www.vancouverdine. com) at Ferguson Point features fresh local cuisine and fine vistas. The road continues past Second Beach, various sports facilities and Lost Lagoon.

The Park on Foot

Circumnavigating Stanley Park by the 9km/5.5mi **seawall★★** takes about two hours, but allow extra time for attractions along the way, such as the

West Coast Seafood

Vancouver's location along the north Pacific Ocean provides for superlative seafood. Oysters, clams, Dungeness crabs, halibut and a half-dozen kinds of salmon are grown and/or harvested in British Columbia, along with the more exotic prawns, sea cucumber, squid and octopus. Traditional recipes are simple: salmon grilled over maple-wood, clams steamed in big pots, halibut roasted in the oven. Modern chefs add Asian and European influences—curried salmon filets, for example, or seafood cioppino, cooked with tomatoes, wine, herbs and spices. Note that lobster, which many visitors expect to find, must be shipped clear across Canada from the Maritime provinces—there is no Northwest species.

The major species of native Northwest salmon include chinook, coho, sockeye, pink, chum and steelhead (actually a sea-running form of rainbow trout). Farm-grown salmon is usually Atlantic salmon; the "farms" are pens in protected inland waters along the central British Columbia coast and Vancouver Island. Wild chinook (or king) salmon is widely considered the top choice, but many connoisseurs prefer sockeye or coho, which have higher natural oils, greater colour and stronger flavour. Halibut is moist and mild, cod smoky and oily. Whatever you order, if it's fresh, of Northwest origin and properly prepared, it's certain to be memorable.

totem poles, the aquarium and Siwash Rock. The pleasant forest trails should not be travelled after dark.

Vancouver Aquarium★★

✕ ♿ P ⏰ Open daily 10am–5pm (until 6pm seasonally). $36 adult (child $21). 604-659-3474. www.vanaqua.org.
Calling this excellent aquarium home are myriad marine mammals, including dolphins, **beluga whales, and sea otters**. A highlight is the walk-in **Graham Amazon Gallery**, where crocodiles, anacondas, turtles, lizards and two-toed sloths live in a jungle environment with brightly coloured birds and butterflies. Daily programs for children under 8 offer parents a welcome break and kids the chance to sing, craft and watch puppet shows. Near the aquarium is the **Children's Farmyard & Miniature Railway** (2099 Beach Ave; ♿ ⏰ open Jun–Labour Day daily, train Mon–Thu 11am–4pm; Fri–Sun until 5pm; 604-257-8531; $7, child $3.50, for each attraction). The petting

Sea otters, Vancouver Aquarium

© Vancouver Aquarium

zoo features domestic animals, and First Nations Spirit Catcher train replicas provide an unforgettable experience.

DOWNTOWN★★

Granville Street, the commercial centre, is closed to all traffic except trolley cars for a six-block pedestrian thoroughfare known as The Mall. The major department stores and extensive underground shopping areas called the Pacific and Vancouver Centres are located here. The Granville Entertainment District is the city's adult evening destination for bars, clubs, and live entertainment. At the northern end is Granville Square, a plaza with views of port activities on the wharves below.

Steps lead to the rail station from which the SeaBus crosses Burrard Inlet to Londsdale Quay in North Vancouver (*see Practical Information*), offering good **views** of the harbour and city.

Canada Place★★

Designed by architect Eberhard Zeidler as the Canada Pavilion for Expo '86, the complex consists of a hotel, office tower and convention centre. Exhibition halls are enclosed by the "sails" of fibreglass yarn coated with Teflon, tensioned to appear as though they are catching the ocean winds.

Marine Building★

355 Burrard St.
Open during business hours.
Opened in 1930, this 21-storey landmark is one of the finest Art Deco buildings in the world. The decorative terra-cotta work depicts marine scenes to honour Vancouver's ties to the sea.

Vancouver Lookout★

Atop the Harbour Centre Complex, 555 West Hastings St. Observation deck open May–mid-Oct daily 8:30am– 10:30pm. Rest of the year daily 9am– 9pm. $16.25. 604-689-0421. www.vancouverlookout.com.
Visitors ascend this distinctive office building via exterior elevators to arrive at the circular observation deck, 167m/553ft above ground, with its mag-

nificent **view★★★** of the city, mountains and ocean.

Vancouver Art Gallery★★

750 Hornby St. Open daily 10am–5pm (Tue, Thu til 9pm). $24. 604-662-4719 (24-hr info line) www.vanartgallery.bc.ca.
Five international architectural firms were chosen in 2014 to bid on the new gallery construction plans, possibly moving the entire operation to Cambie Street.
Designed in 1907 by Francis Rattenbury, the current Neoclassical building served as the city courthouse for 70 years. It was converted by Canadian architect Arthur Erickson so galleries open off the central rotunda with its glass-topped dome.
A highlight are the paintings and drawings by British Columbian **Emily Carr**, whose West Coast themes are striking. Works on display include *Big Raven* (c.1931) and *Scorned as Timber, Beloved of the Sky* (c.1936).
The art gallery's north-side lawn and south-side steps are often ground zero for political protests in Vancouver.

Robson Square★

Stretching from Nelson Street almost to Georgia Street, this complex was also designed by Arthur Erickson. Now housing the provincial **law courts**, the seven-storey building with a spectacular slanted-glass roof complements a series of terraced gardens with waterfalls and plants on top of offices (*between Smithe and Robson Sts.*). A plaza under Robson Street contains outdoor cafes, a skating rink and a conference centre.

Library Square★★

350 W. Georgia St. Open Mon–Thu 10am–9pm, Fri–Sat 10am– 6pm, Sun noon–5pm. Closed public holidays. 604-331-3603. www.vpl.ca.
Moshe Safdie's breathtaking 1995 building, with its nine-storey office tower, houses the main branch of the Vancouver Public Library. Punctuated with small shops and cafes, the atrium courtyard is a popular gathering place. Built over a two-year period at a cost of $156 million,

the 36,270sq m/390,000sq ft library is the largest publicly funded project in Vancouver history.

BC Place Stadium★

Main entrance Robson & Beatty Sts. 777 Pacific Blvd. ♿ 🅿 🚻 *Guided tours (1hr 30min) mid-Jun–Labour Day Tue 11am & 1pm, event schedule permitting.* ✆$20 All Access Tour. ✆604-669-2300. www.bcplacestadium.com.

Resembling an enormous quilted marshmallow, this stadium is the largest air-supported domed amphitheatre in the world. Designed by Phillips Barrett, it opened in 1983 and hosts football games (the BC Lions), soccer matches, trade shows, concerts and the B.C. Sports Hall of Fame. A glass-enclosed concourse on the upper level offers a city **panorama**.

The stadium was the site for ceremonies for the 2010 Winter Olympics.

Chinatown★

Pender St. between Carrall St. and Gore Ave.

This colourful quarter is the centre of Vancouver's large Chinese community. Many restaurants and shops sell Asian foods and wares. The neighbourhood is a wonderful place for a daytime stroll.

Dr. Sun Yat-Sen Classical Chinese Garden★

578 Carrall St. Behind the Chinese Cultural Centre on Pender St. ♿🕐*Open mid-Jun–Aug daily 9:30am–7pm. Rest of the year daily 10am–6pm (Oct–Apr daily 10am–4.30pm).* 🕐*Closed Mon Nov–Apr; Jan 1 & Dec 25.*🚻*Guided tours daily included in ticket price.* ✆$12. ✆604-662-3207. www.vancouverchinesegarden.com. Site plan available in box at entrance.*

Modelled after classical gardens of the Ming dynasty (14-17C), this Chinese garden is the first full-scale classical garden constructed outside China, opening in 1986. Among other features are a jade water pavilion and scholar's courtyard. Its name honours the first president of the Republic of China.

Next door to the garden is the equally serene **Dr. Sun Yat-Sen Park**, a public park graced by a large, placid pond.

Gastown★

This attractive area between Carrall and Richards streets combines restored late 19C buildings with modern structures constructed to blend with their surroundings. The area was named for a garrulous English saloonkeeper, Gassy Jack, whose statue stands on Maple Tree Square. A **steam clock** anchors the corner of Cambie Street.

NEARBY ATTRACTIONS
Museum of Vancouver★★

In Vanier Park. 1100 Chestnut St. ♿🅿🕐*Open year-round daily 10am–5pm (Thu 8pm, Fri & Sat 9pm)* 🕐*Closed Mon Sept–Jun & Dec 25.* ✆$15. ✆604-736-4431. www.museumofvancouver.ca.*

This museum specializes in the history of Vancouver and of the First Nations of the Pacific Northwest Coast. It also has a fine collection of Asian artifacts as well as items from around the world.

From the parking area there is an excellent **view**★★ of the city and North Shore mountains.

H.R. MacMillan Space Centre★

In Vanier Park. 1100 Chestnut St. ♿🅿🕐*Open Jul–Labour Day daily 10am–3pm, weekends 10am–5pm. Rest of the year Tue–Sun 10am–5pm.* 🕐*Closed Dec 25.* ✆$18 (child $13). ✆604-738-7827. www.spacecentre.ca.*

To the left of the Vancouver Museum rises the distinctive conical dome of the **MacMillan Planetarium**, part of the Space Center, which houses a space station, flight simulator and other interactive displays on space research.

👥 Maritime Museum★★

In Vanier Park. 1905 Ogden Ave. 🅿🕐*Open daily 10am–5pm, Sun noon–5pm.* 🕐*Closed Mon & Dec 25.* ✆$11 (youth $8.50). ✆604-257-8300. www.vancouvermaritimemuseum.com.*

The highlights are the **St. Roch**, a Royal Canadian Mounted Police patrol ship, the first ship to navigate the Northwest

Passage in both directions, 1940-45, and the **North Star of Herschel**, last of the sailing Arctic cargo vessels. Among other activities, visitors can pilot a tug and learn about the famous Franklin shipwreck discovery in Canada's Arctic waters.

👥 Granville Island★

Accessible by car from Granville St. Bridge & West 4th Ave. (follow signs; pass under the bridge), or by ferry from Vancouver Aquatic Centre on Beach Ave. or from the Maritime Museum. ✕👤🅿️ *📞604-666-6655. www.granvilleisland. com. Shops directory available from dispensers.*

This onetime industrial area under Granville Bridge has been renovated to house art galleries and studios, boutiques, restaurants, theatres and a hotel. The island's highlight is the **public market** (🕐*open daily 9am–7pm*), where stalls of fresh produce vie with products of Vancouver's many ethnic groups. Vancouver Foodie Tours offers 2-hr market tasting tours, all food & drink included. (🕐*10:30am-12:30pm daily;* 👛*$50 weekdays-$54 weekends; book ahead on website;* 📞*604-295-8844 or 877-804-9220 (www.foodietours.ca).*

👥 Telus World of Science★

1455 Quebec St. ✕👤🅿️🕐*Open Mon–Fri 10am–5pm (Sat–Sun & holidays til 6pm)* 🕐*Closed Labour Day & Dec 25.* 👛*$22.50 (child $15.25).* 📞*604-443-7440. www.scienceworld.ca.*

Situated on the Expo '86 site overlooking False Creek, this complex features interactive exhibits and includes an Omnimax theatre and **Wee Explorers** for young children 3–5 years of age. Our World investigates a sustainable planet and children will want to check out the **BC Green Games Project** to learn about the environment and win prizes.

👥 West End

Downtown northwest of Broughton St.

City fathers proudly advertise the West End as the most densely populated urban neighbourhood in North America, with its towering apartment and condo-

Granville Island Public Market

©Leslie Forsberg/Michelin

minium complexes overlooking Stanley Park, False Creek and the North Shore. **Denman Street**, a hive of small stores and cafes, is worth a stroll. At **English Bay Beach★★** (*Beach Ave. and Denman St.*) parks officials maintain a series of palm gardens as testimony to Vancouver's balmy climate. Along the promenade that connects to Stanley Park's seawall, artists set up shop on sunny days.

Roedde House Museum

1415 Barclay St. 👁*Visit by guided tour (45min) only, Tue–Fri 10am–4pm, Sat noon-5pm, Sun 1pm–4pm.* 🕐*Closed Mon, Sat & public holidays.* 👛*$5 ($8 Sun, incl tea & tour).* 📞*604-684-7040. www.roeddehouse.org.*

This Queen Anne-style house with its characteristic polygonal tower was built in 1893 for Vancouver bookbinder Gustav Roedde. Its design is attributed to Francis Rattenbury, architect of the Vancouver Art Gallery and Victoria's famed Empress Hotel.

Furnished to the period, nine rooms on the ground and second floors of the three-storey dwelling can be visited. A Victorian garden with a gazebo graces one side of the house; Barclay Heritage Square park borders the other side. Jazz concerts are popular every second Thursday of the month at 7pm, and every second Sunday for classical.

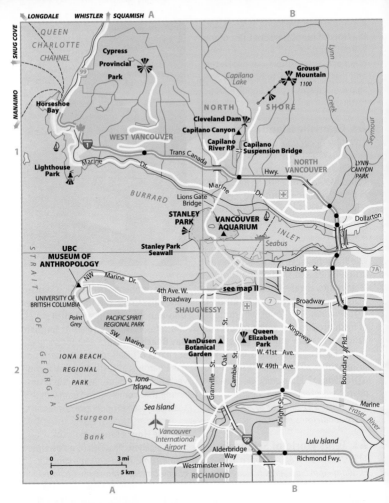

LONGDALE WHISTLER SQUAMISH A

SNUG COVE

NANAIMO

QUEEN CHARLOTTE CHANNEL

Cypress Provincial Park

Capilano Lake

Grouse Mountain
1100

Horseshoe Bay

NORTH SHORE

99

Cleveland Dam
Capilano Canyon

WEST VANCOUVER

Capilano River RP

Capilano Suspension Bridge

NORTH VANCOUVER

Lighthouse Park

Marine Dr.

Trans Canada

Hwy.

LYNN CANYON PARK

Seymour

BURRARD

Marine Dr.

Lions Gate Bridge

Dollarton

STANLEY PARK

VANCOUVER AQUARIUM

INLET

Seabus

UBC MUSEUM OF ANTHROPOLOGY

Stanley Park Seawall

Hastings St.

(7A)

STRAIT

UNIVERSITY OF BRITISH COLUMBIA

NW Marine Dr.

4th Ave. W.

Broadway

see map II

Broadway

7

Point Grey

PACIFIC SPIRIT REGIONAL PARK

SHAUGNESSY

Kingsway

Boundary Rd.

OF

SW Marine Dr.

Queen Elizabeth Park

VanDusen Botanical Garden

W. 41st Ave.

W. 49th Ave.

GEORGIA

IONA BEACH REGIONAL PARK

Iona Island

Granville St.

Oak St.

Cambie St.

Knight St.

Marine

Fraser River

Sturgeon Bank

Sea Island

Vancouver International Airport

99

Lulu Island

Alderbridge Way

Richmond Fwy.

0   3 mi
0   5 km

Westminster Hwy.

RICHMOND

A   B

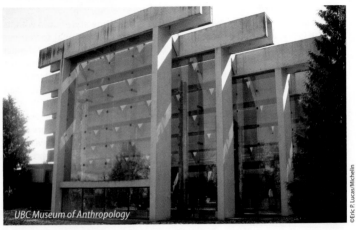

UBC Museum of Anthropology

©Eric P. Lucas/Michelin

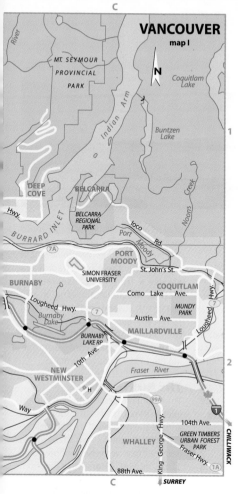

VANCOUVER
map I

OUTSIDE DOWNTOWN

UBC Museum of Anthropology★★★

6393 N.W. Marine Dr.

✕&🅿🕐*Open mid-May–early Oct 10am–5pm, (Thu til 9pm).* 🕐*Closed Mon, & Dec 25–26.* ⊛*$18.* 𝄞*604-822-5087. www.moa.ubc.ca. The museum is open during a major renovation project, expected to be completed in early 2010.*

The University of British Columbia campus overlooks the Strait of Georgia and Vancouver Island. The university is known for its collection of BC First Nations art, considered among the finest in the world. Opened in 1976, the **museum building**—the work of Arthur Erickson—is a glass and concrete structure that lets in light. The translucent walls of the **Great Hall** rise 14m/45ft around the magnificent collection of Haida and Kwakwaka'wakw **totem poles**, many dating to the 19C. Highlights of the collection include the largest collection in the world of works by Haida artist **Bill Reid**: to be found in the Bill Reid Rotunda, including a bear statue and his masterpiece, *Raven and the First Men★★★*, a massive work in yellow-cedar depicting the Haida creation story.

Multiversity Galleries (Ways of Knowing) galleries are home to a vast collection of objects from the Museum's worldwide research collections. MOA labours with communities whose ancestors made pieces on display. On the grounds a reproduction of a **First Nations village** includes a big house.

Howe Sound

©Nina Ignatova/Dreamstime.com

VanDusen Botanical Garden★★

5251 Oak St.
✕♿🅿🕐*Open Jun–Aug daily 9am–8:30pm. Rest of the year hours vary.* 🕐*Closed Dec 25.* ✆*$8.25.* ✆*604-257-8335 24-hr info. www.vandusengarden.org.*

This rolling 22ha/55-acre expanse holds 7,500 kinds of plants, in arrangements ensuring that something is in bloom every month. Vancouver's largest garden showcases everything from traditional perennial beds to heritage gardens depicting pioneer herb beds.

Queen Elizabeth Park★

West 33rd Ave. and Cambie St.
Lovely **quarry gardens** offer winding pathways and waterfalls. The entrance road climbs to the **Bloedel Floral Conservatory**, a geodesic-domed structure of glass and aluminum (✕♿🅿🕐*open daily 6am-10pm* 🕐*closed Dec 25;* ✆*$4.80;* ✆*604-800-9050; http://vancouver.ca*). In clear weather there are extraordinary **views★★** from the conservatory's plaza of the mountains. The on-site restaurant, **Seasons in the Park ($$$)** (✆*604-874-8008; www.vancouverdine. com*), hosted US President Bill Clinton and Russian President Boris Yeltsin during the 1993 Vancouver summit.

THE NORTH SHORE

The mountains descend toward Burrard Inlet on its north side, cut by deep fjords and the steep valleys of several small rivers. Scenic Highway 1 (which becomes Route 99) follows the North Shore slope, 12km/7mi west to **Horseshoe Bay**, from where BC Ferries depart for Vancouver Island, Bowen Island and the Sunshine Coast, north of Howe Sound.

Lighthouse Park★★

10km/6mi west of downtown West Vancouver along Marine Dr, take bus #250 from downtown. ✆*604-925-7200. www.westvancouver.net.*

Situated on a headland protruding into Howe Sound, this park offers excellent hikes 🚶 through the finest old-growth forest in the metropolitan area. Today ancient **Douglas-firs** rise hundreds of feet overhead. Rocky headlands provide spectacular **views★★★** across the Strait of Georgia and of Stanley Park, the Vancouver skyline and Mt. Baker in the distance. Trails lead down to the lighthouse

Lighthouse Park

©Lijuan Guo/Dreamstime.com

(1912), the best place to watch sunsets over Georgia Strait..

Cypress Provincial Park★

12km/7mi from downtown by Lions Gate Bridge and Hwy. 1/Rte. 99.
&♿🅿️🕐*Open year-round (gates* 🕐*Closed 11pm–7am).* ☎*604-926-5612. www.env.gov.bc.ca.*
This 3,000ha/7,400-acre park includes Cypress Mountain (☎*604-926-5612. www.cypressmountain.com*), a popular ski area which hosted freestyle skiing and snowboarding at the 2010 Winter Olympics. The access road leads to Highview Lookout, which permits a breathtaking **view★★★** of the Vancouver area.

Capilano Canyon★

9km/6mi from downtown by Lions Gate Bridge at 3735 Capilano Rd.
This deep canyon can be crossed by a narrow pedestrian **suspension bridge** 70m/230ft above the Capilano River (🅿️🕐*open mid-May–Labour Day daily 8:30am–8pm; rest of the year, hours vary;* 🕐*closed Dec 25;* ☜*$39.95;* ☎*604-985-7474; www.capbridge.com*). Built in 1889, the bridge is 137m/450ft long and sways as visitors walk across it. .
Farther along Capilano Road, **Capilano River Regional Park** offers pleasant walks and views of the canyon. At the northern end of the park (*access from Nancy Greene Way*) are Cleveland Dam and Capilano Lake. Across the lake is a **view★** of the twin peaks of The Lions.

Grouse Mountain★

3km/8mi from downtown by Lions Gate Bridge, Capilano Rd. and Nancy Greene Way.
✕&🅿️🕐*Tram operates year-round daily 9am–10pm.* ☜*$43.95.* ☎*604-980-9311 (snow info* ☎*604-986-6262). www.grousemountain.com.*
The aerial tram rises to an elevation of 1,100m/3,700ft, offering, as it ascends, a splendid **view★★** of the city. At the top are a resort and recreation area. The **Peak Chalet** offers a restaurant, ATM, café, Spirit Gallery Gift Shop and much more.

EXCURSIONS
Sea to Sky Highway★★

Route 99 is the 102km/63mi highway that stretches from **Horseshoe Bay**, a picturesque ferry port west of Vancouver, past Squamish to just beyond Whistler. Running from sea level into the mountains, the road takes in a remarkable coast-to-range **panorama★★★**.
The highway hugs a narrow shelf along **Howe Sound**, a deep 48km/30mi-long fjord, then casts upward into the Coast Range peaks, offering campgrounds, bed and breakfasts, hostels, motels, resorts, eateries, activities for the kids and much more. This is one of the most beautoful drives in North America, not to be missed.

Britannia Mine Museum★★

In Britannia Beach, 38km/24mi north of Horseshoe Bay.
🕐*Open daily 10am–4pm.* 👣*Tours (1hr30min) at various times, check website for seasonal details.* ☜*$29.* ☎*604-896-2233 or 800-896-4044. www.bcmuseumofmining.org.*
The Britannia mine was once the largest copper producer in the British empire. From here, copper was shipped around the world from 1904–74. The historic mining town went through a huge environmental overhaul as of 2004 which continues today. Mining equipment on display includes the 235-ton "Super" haul truck. Visitors can watch underground demonstrations, ride heritage rail cars, and pan for gold.

Shannon Falls★

45km/28mi.
These impressive falls cascade 335m/1,100ft over a cliff. Near **Squamish**, popular with hikers, bikers, climbers, sailboarders and kayakers, **Stawamus Chief★**, a 700m/2,296ft granite monolith, comes into view.

Whistler★★★

🛈 *Visitor Centre, 4230 Gateway Dr.* ☎*604-935-3357. Activity Centre, 4010 Whistler Way.* ☎*604-935-3357 or 877-991-9988. www.whistler.com.*

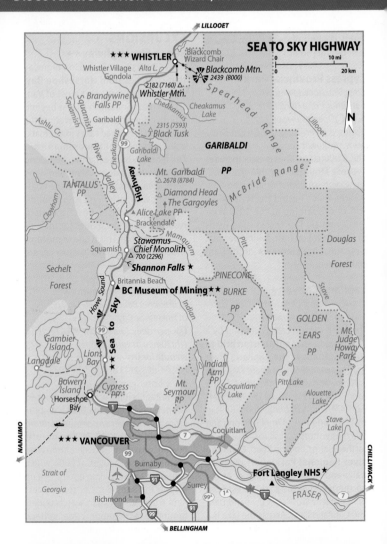

SEA TO SKY HIGHWAY

LILLOOET

★★★ **WHISTLER**
Blackcomb
Wizard Chair
Whistler Village
Gondola
Alta L.
Blackcomb Mtn.
2439 (8000)
2182 (7160) △
Whistler Mtn.
Spearhead Range
Brandywine
Falls PP
Chedkamus
Cheakamus
Lake
Squamish
Garibaldi
Ashlu Cr.
2315 (7593)
Black Tusk
GARIBALDI
Squamish River
Garibaldi
Lake
99
PP
Valley
Cheakamus
Highway
Mt. Garibaldi
△ 2678 (8784)
McBride Range
TANTALUS
PP
Diamond Head
The Gargoyles
Clowhom
Alice Lake PP
Brackendale
Douglas
Mamquam
Stawamus
Chief Monolith
△ 700 (2296)
Squamish
Sechelt
Forest
Shannon Falls ★
Pitt
PINECONE
Forest
Britannia Beach
BC Museum of Mining ★★
BURKE
Howe Sound
Indian
PP
Stave
Gambier
Island
99
Sea to Sky
GOLDEN
Lions
Bay
★★
EARS
Mt.
Judge
Howay
Park
Langdale
Indian
Arm
PP
PP
Bowen
Island
Cypress
PP
Mt.
Seymour
PP
Coquitlam
Lake
Pitt Lake
Alouette
Lake
Horseshoe
Bay
1
NANAIMO
★★★ **VANCOUVER**
Coquitlam
Stave
Lake
99
7
Burnaby
Fort Langley NHS ★
CHILLIWACK
Strait of
Georgia
91
Surrey
1A
1
FRASER
7
Richmond
99A
91
99
BELLINGHAM

0   10 mi
0   20 km

N

Skiiing in Whistler

Whistler, among the world's top ski resorts, has grown to international prominence in its 40 years. It was the venue for alpine, nordic, ski-jumping and sliding events of the 2010 Winter Olympics. All Paralympic were also held here. The three alpine hamlets (Whistler Village, Village North and Upper Village) are dominated by **Blackcomb Mountain** (2,439m/8,000ft) and **Whistler Mountain** (2,182m/7,160ft).

Warm-weather recreation is plentiful, and the resort village offers fine shops, nightclubs, restaurants. The **Whistler Museum and Archives** (*4333 Main St.;* ⏱*open daily 11am–5pm;* ⊶*$7.50;* ☎*604-932-2019; www.whistlermuseum.org*) depicts the area's early history as a logging and fishing camp, and its astounding growth as a ski resort.

Nearby **Garibaldi Provincial Park**, 🚶 a hike-in only park, offers trails and campsites. ⏱*Open year-round; parking area accessible by paved road from Whistler Village. BC Parks.* ☎*604-898-3678. www.env.gov.bc.ca.*

👥 Fort Langley National Historic Site★

56km/35mi southeast of Vancouver by Trans-Can Hwy. 23433 Mavis Ave., Fort Langley. ♿🅿⏱*Open Jul–Aug daily 9am–8pm. Rest of the year daily 10am–5pm.* ⏱*Closed Jan 1 & Dec 25–26.* ⊶*$7.80 (child $3.90).* ☎*604-513-4777. www.pc.gc.ca.*

The fort was one of a network established by the Hudson's Bay Company in the early 19C. The storehouse, the only structure original to the site, has a fine **collection** of furs and trading goods. In the Big House, quarters of the HBC officials can be seen. Costumed staff demonstrate blacksmithing, yarn spinning and other mid-19C skills.

PRACTICAL INFORMATION
GETTING AROUND
BY PUBLIC TRANSPORTATION – Vancouver Regional Transit System operates an integrated network of rapid transit, ferries (*below*) and buses. Hours of operation vary among the services. **SkyTrain**, the city's rapid transit, serves Downtown, Burnaby, New Westminster and Surrey (*daily 5:08am–1:15am; every 2–4 min*); a new line runs between the airport and downtown. **Fares** are based on zones travelled, with discounts evening and weekends. Buses require exact fare; SkyTrain accepts coins, bills, debit and credit cards. Keep your ticket: you may be asked to show it to an agent. DayPass (*$9.75*) are available from ticket machines and outlets. Transfers are free for 90min of unlimited travel. **Bus service** connects SkyTrain and SeaBus at all stations. Buses operate 7 days/wk. *Transit* maps are conveniently available online, or paper maps at convenience stores throughout the city. ♿The entire system is accessible. For route information and schedules: ☎604-953-3333; www.translink.ca.

BY CAR – Use of public transportation or walking is strongly encouraged within the city as roads are often congested, and street parking may be difficult to find. Metered and garage parking available.

BY BOAT – SeaBus, passenger harbour ferries, operates between two Vancouver terminals (downtown & Lonsdale Quay) and the North Shore (*leaves every 15 minutes during daylight & every 30 minutes evenings*). Adult fare is $2.75; exact fare required. Bus service connects SkyTrain and SeaBus at all stations: ☎604-953-3333; www.translink.ca.

A **harbour tour** by paddle wheeler takes in Vancouver's busy port. *Departs from Vancouver Harbour Flight Centre April 26–Sep 30 daily 11am, 12:15pm, 1:30pm & 2:45pm; Round-trip 1hr. $34.95.* ☎*604-688-7246 or 800-663-1500. www.boatcruises.com).*

BY TAXI – Black Top & Checker Cabs ℰ604-731-1111; Yellow Cab ℰ604-258-4700. **North Shore: North Shore Taxi Ltd.** ℰ604-987-7171; Sunshine Cabs ℰ604-922-3333.

ON FOOT – Vancouver is an excellent city to tour on foot, as most major sights are within 15-20 minutes' walk of virtually all the downtown hotels (many hotels offer shuttle service to Stanley Park and Granville Island).
ⓧ *Visitors should avoid the stretch of Hastings Street between Cambie and Main, a dangerous drug-dealing district. To reach Chinatown, follow Pender Street.*

GENERAL INFORMATION
ACCOMMODATIONS AND VISITOR INFORMATION
For **hotels/motels**, contact **Tourism Vancouver**, *200 Burrard St.* ℰ604-682-2222. *www.tourismvancouver.com.* Visitor Centre located on Plaza Level 604-683-2000. Reservation services: British Columbia B&Bs www.bbcanada.com. Advance reservations strongly recommended Jun–Aug and May and Sept.

LOCAL PRESS – Daily: *The Vancouver Sun* and *The Province.* Weekly: *The Georgia Strait* and *The Westender.*

ENTERTAINMENT – *The Georgia Straight* and the *Westender* have entertainment listings, as does *West Coast Life,* in the Thursday issue of the *Vancouver Sun.* Online, go to *Where.ca/vancouver.* Ticketmaster ℰ604-280-4444. www. ticketmaster.ca (major credit cards accepted). For last-minute and half-price tickets, go to www.ticketstonight.ca;

ticket booth at Plaza level, 200 Burrard St., daily 8:30am–6pm, ℰ877-840-0457. The Alliance for Arts and Culture is an arts clearinghouse, with info on events (*100-938 Howe St.; ℰ604-681-3535. www.allianceforarts.com*).

SPORTS – **BC Lions Football Club**: home games at BC Place Stadium. Season Jun–Nov; ticket office ℰ604-589-7627 or www.bclions.com.

Vancouver Canadians (baseball): home games at Nat Bailey Stadium. Season Jun–Sept. ℰ604-872-5232 or www. canadiansbaseball.com. **Vancouver Canucks** (ice hockey): home games at General Motors Place. Season Oct–Apr. Info line ℰ604-899-4610 or http:// canucks.nhl.com. Tickets also from Ticketmaster ℰ604-280-4444. www. ticketmaster.ca (major credit cards accepted).

USEFUL NUMBERS – ℰCallers must dial all 10 digits (area code plus the phone number) when making local calls.
Area Codes: 604, 778, 250 and 236.
Police: 911 (emergency) or 604-717-3535.
VIA Rail *1150 Station St.(Pacific Central Station)*: 888-842-7245 Amtrack Pacific Central Station: 800-872-7245
BC Ferries 888-223-3779 **Greyhound Lines of Canada** (bus): 604-661-0328 or 800-661-8747 **Vancouver International Airport**: general inquiries: 604-207-7077
Canadian Automobile Assn. *999 W. Broadway*: 604-268-5600
CAA Emergency Road Service (24hr): 604-293-2222, cell users *222
Shoppers Drug Mart (24hr pharmacy), *1125 Davie St.*: 604-669-2424. 885 W. Broadway: 604-708-1135
Road Conditions: 800-550-4997
Weather (24hr) : 604-664-9010

ADDRESSES

🏠STAY

$ Hostelling International Vancouver –*1114 Burnaby St.* ℰ778-328. 2220 or 866. 762.4122. www.hihostels.ca. 222 beds. ▱ This clean, economical lodging may be the best choice for budget travellers in downtown Vancouver; its West End location is convenient to Stanley Park and Granville Island. The hostel lies just off busy Davie Street district with its shops and cafes.

$$ Sylvia Hotel – *1154 Gilford St.* ℰ604-681-9321. www.sylviahotel.com. 120 rooms. ✕&. This ivy-covered, 1912 brick and terra-cotta landmark borders English Bay. Many rooms here have kitchenettes; the larger units are an exceptional value for families, who can prepare all their meals in-room, and enjoy Stanley Park two blocks away.

$$$ Hotel Le Soleil – *567 Hornby St.* ℰ604-632-3000 or 877-662-3030. www. lesoleilhotel.com. 119 rooms. ✕&▣. This inconspicuous downtown building won the Travelers Award from Tripadvisor and sports a sumptuous decor; royal hues of burgundy and gold dominate the colour scheme. Service is savvy, discreet & pet-friendly. Amenities; bathrobes, Internet access & large desks.

$$$$ Rosewood Hotel Georgia-801 W.Georgia St. *604-682-5566, www. rosewoodhotels.com.* Originally opened in 1927, this legendary edifice was once the toast of the town. Completely renovated in 2011, the grandeur and elegance of her bygone fame has returned in 156 plush rooms and suites. Led by Les Clefs D'Or concierge service and 24-hr dining in-room, amenities incluse a 56' salwater pool, Rose Buds program for kids, and even a complimentary Bentley for in-town errands upon availability.

$$$ Residences on Georgia and The Palisades – *1200 & 1288 W. Georgia St. *604-891-6181. www.vancouverex-tendedstay.com. 100 units.* Popular with the film industry, these sophisticated high-tech twin towers are just the thing for extended stays (there's even an on-site screening room). Units are smartly furnished with compact kitchens, small offices and breakfast nooks. Penthouse units boast views of mountains and harbour.

$$$ Thistledown House – *3910 Capilano Rd. *604-986-7173 or 888-633-7173. www.thistle-down.com. 6 rooms.* Set amid gardens in North Vancouver, the superbly renovated 1920 Craftsman-style mansion offers elegant, quiet rooms near Grouse Mountain and Capilano Canyon. Multicourse breakfasts feature such entrées as alder-smoked-salmon omelettes and crepe primavera in chantilly sauce.

$$$$ Listel Vancouver – *1300 Robson St. *604-684-8461 or 800-663-5491. www. thelistelhotel.com. 129 rooms.* Close to West End and Stanley Park, yet within walking distance of the financial hub, "Van's most artful hotel" attracts business travellers, tourists, and artists alike. The Museum Floors showcase Northwest Coast-inspired decor and art; the Gallery Floors feature artworks from nearby Buschlen Mowatt Galleries; Chris Whittaker's two dining creations; Timber and Forage supply classic farm-to-table nourishment options daily.

$$$$ Loden Hotel – *1177 Melville St. *604-669-5060. www.lodenvancouver.com. 77 rooms.* Tucked into a quiet street near Coal Harbour, three blocks from Robson Street shopping, the Loden is a hip, high-tech lodging that maintains a personal touch. With wood trim and caramel-toned decor, the rooms are warm and welcoming; amenities include floor-to-ceiling windows that open to let in the harbour breeze, electronic privacy signs, broad spectrum technology access in the rooms, a fitness studio (open 24/7) and a small spa. Complimentary downtown London-style cab on availability.

$$$$ Metropolitan Hotel – *645 Howe St. *604-687-1122 or 800-667-2300. www. metropolitan.com. 197 rooms.* This high-style, small hotel caters to business travellers with an exceptional health club featuring a heated indoor pool, steam room and squash court. Angular but spacious rooms include Italian linens, down duvets, marble baths and deep soaking tubs. The hotel's location (near Howe & W.Georgia St.) provides convenient access to Canada Place and theatre district. A favourite pre-theatre stop, **Diva at the Met ($$$)** is renowned for its West Coast cuisine amid a glitzy decor serving breakfast. lunch & dinner.

$$$$ Opus Hotel – *322 Davie St. *604-642-6787 or 866-642-6787. www.opushotel.com. 96 rooms.* Popular with film industry and high-tech types, this Yaletown hotel came in 4th from CondeNast Traveler Readers 2016. The lobby features dozens of votive candles. Rooms are decorated with lots of black and brushed metal; and bathrooms have large picture windows overlooking the street. Adjacent to seawall.

$$$$ Sutton Place Hotel – *845 Burrard St. *604-682-5511 or 866-378-8866. www. suttonplace.com. 396 rooms.* A pink-sided modern high rise a half-block off Robson Street, Sutton Place is favoured by members of the film industry, whose limousines are constantly pulling up to the porticoed entrance. Service is expert and discreet. **Boulevard Kitchen & Oyster Bar ($$$)** is expansive and features the culinary seafood inventions of Executive Chef Alex Chen. Next door, **La Grande Résidence** offers 164 suites for those staying a week or more.

$$$$ Wedgewood Hotel & Spa – *845 Hornby St. *604-689-7777 or 800-663-0666. www.wedgewoodhotel.com. 83 rooms.* Comfortable and

Dim Sum

Among Vancouver's best-known dim sum palaces are the **Imperial Chinese Seafood Restaurant** (355 Burrard St. &604-688-8191. www.imperialrest.com), which melds superb food with a matchless location in the Marine Building; **Sun Sui Wah Seafood Restaurant** (3888 Main St. &604-872-8822 or 866-872-8822. www.sunsuiwah.com), which earns consistent raves from food critics; and **Pink Pearl Chinese Restaurant** (1132 E. Hastings St. &604-253-4316. www.pinkpearl.com), a venerable 700-seat hall, especially popular with government officials.

spacious guest quarters, distinctively designed by owner Eleni Skalbania with antiques and original artwork, characterize this Relais & Châteaux hotel, constructed in 1984 on Robson Square. The on-site spa offers a full list of treatments. Mediterranean accents spice up the French cuisine at **Bacchus ($$$)**; the lounge is a popular after-work spot, with piano music nightly.

$$$$$ Fairmont Hotel Vancouver – 900 W. Georgia St. &604-684-3131 or 866-540-4452. www.fairmont.ca. 555 rooms. ✕⚕⛾🅿🆂🅿🅰⛲. This copper-roofed landmark château welcomed King George VI and Queen Elizabeth after it opened in 1939. Renovated in the mid-1990s, the Hotel Vancouver now boasts a sleek Art Déco-style lobby and quiet rooms with period reproduction furnishings. The popular **Roof Restaurant & Bar** returns to delight visitors on the 15th foor. In the evening, **Notch8 Restaurant & Bar ($$$$)** serves up celebrated martinis and live music Wed-Sat, as well as prime or Angus beef and fresh seafood.

$$$$$ Fairmont Waterfront – 900 Canada Place Way. &604-691-1991 or 866-540-4509. www.fairmont.ca. 489 rooms. ✕⚕⛾🅿⛲🆂🅿🅰. A classy, modern business hotel, the Fairmont Waterfront is linked by a covered walkway to Canada Place and the Cruise Ship Terminal. Rooms are tastefully decorated, most of them in warm pastels and light-coloured woods; more than half the rooms overlook Vancouver Harbour. An aviary, herb garden, and recycling policy keep this hotel a leader.

🍽 EAT

$ TAPShack – 1199 W. Cordova St. &604-687-6455. www.tapshack.ca. **Pubfood+**. ⛾. Located along Coal Harbour promenade, this hospitality collective serves up pub charcuterie featuring Two Rivers meats from North Van, fresh eggs from the Fraser Valley, Pacific seafoods, wood fired pizzas, and brunch. Features largest patio in Vancouver with 20 rotating beer taps, while looking across the marina to Stanley Park.

$ Stepho's Souvlakia – 1124 Davie St. &604-683-2555. **Greek**. ⛾. Locals love this West End restaurant for its dependable food and good value—lines often wind out the door and down the street. The fare is standard, but portions are generous and the atmosphere friendly.

$ Sawasdee – 4250 Main St. &604-876-4030. www.sawasdeethairestaurant.com. No lunch Sat-Sun. **Thai**. ⛾. Vancouver's first Thai restaurant has been called its best, with highly flavoured curries and soups, and exotic desserts such as banana fritters. The pad thai is excellent, and the green curry chicken is a standout. The basic dinner platter heaps up lamb, rice, potatoes, salad and rolls—main dishes for less than $15.

$$ The Sandbar – 1535 Johnston St., Creekhouse #102, Granville Island. &604-669-9030. www.vancouverdine.com/sandbar/home.html. **Seafood**. ⛾. Tucked under the Granville Street Bridge, this cavernous 300-seat eatery offers views of False Creek, the skyline and the mountains while you dine on fresh fish, much of which is caught locally. Seafood offerings are extensive and prepared to your liking in the bustling open kitchen. Lobsters and crabs are plucked from the restaurant's on-site shellfish tank. Try the cedar plank West Coast salmon, a Sandbar specialty. Open daily at 11:30am, with live music weekends.

$$$ Blue Water Cafe – 1095 Hamilton St., Yaletown. &604-688-8078. www.bluewatercafe.net. **Seafood**. ⛾. This glamorous seafood shrine has been the centrepiece of Vancouver's gentrified warehouse district since 2000. Warm woods and soft lighting enhance its selective menu of seafood, meat and fowl. Entrées focus on regional offerings: Arctic char with yellow foot chanterelles, broccolini and kohlrabi; Kobe style beef short ribs; white sturgeon with red beet panna cotta.

$$$ Lift – *333 Menchions Mews.* ℰ604-689-5438. www.liftbarandgrill.com. **Contemporary**. ♿. Overlooking Coal Harbour, this sleek restaurant offers interior and outside dining with great views of the marina and the Coast Mountains. Diners feast on the likes of roasted venison loin and Barbary duck, scallops or sablefish, partnered with a glass of Okanagan Valley wine.

$$$$ Bishop's – *2183 W. 4th Ave. Kitsilano.* ℰ604-738-2025. www.bishopsonline.com. *Dinner only.* **West Coast**. Impeccable service and an intimate atmosphere mark this high-end Vancouver institution. Owner John Bishop was one of the originators of West Coast cuisine, which, in Bishop's case, is based on organic regional ingredients. Artfully presented dishes on the weekly changing menu incorporate such local bounty as Dungeness crab, Haida Gwaii halibut and Qualicum Bay scallops.

$$$$ Ancora Waterfront Dining & Patio – *2-1600 Howe St., on False Creek.* ℰ604-681-1164. www.crestaurant.com. **Seafood**. ♿. Inside this striking industrial-chic dining space with floor-to-ceiling windows overlooking False Creek, creative and sustainable Northwest foods reign. Fishnet-inspired chandeliers accentuate a menu featuring Hada Gawaii pan-seared halibut with "Forbidden" rice paella, or South America grilled steak with yucca fries, but save room for the rum panna cotta, or spiced picarones.

$$$$$ Hawksworth Restaurant – *801 West Georgia St.*, 604-673-7000, www. hawsworthrestaurant.com. Contemporary Canadian. Priding their menu on the marriage of fresh local ingredients with original presentation and pairings, this find dining eatery inside the Rosewood Hotel Georgia beckons all who seek to create culinary memories while visiting Vancouver. Breakfast, lunch or dinner available. Try their Tasting Menu.

🏨 STAY AND 🍴 EAT

WHISTLER

$$$$ First Tracks Lodge – *2202 Gondola Way.* ℰ604-296-5241or 866-385-0614. www.firsttrackslodge.com. 84 rooms. ✕♿🅿️Spa☃. Sitting steps away from the Creekside Gondola at Whistler Mountain, this stylish lodge offers superb comfort in studios and suites with full

kitchens. Its quiet location makes it one of Whistler's few genuine ski-in, ski-out accommodations; the lodge's hot tub, steam and sauna facilities are exceptional.

$$$$ Nita Lake Lodge – *2131 Lake Placid Rd.* ℰ604-966-5700 or 888-755-6482. www.nitalakelodge.com. 77 rooms. ✕♿🅿️. Recalling Canada famed rail lodges of a century ago, this 2008 property in Creekside Village houses the station for the Whistler Mountaineer train. The hotel looks out on its namesake lake; the gabled entry and massive beams reflect the mountains visible on every side. Rooms sport dark earth tones, and include soaking tubs and fireplaces.

$$$$$ Fairmont Chateau Whistler – *4599 Chateau Blvd.* ℰ604-606-8244. www.fairmont.ca. 550 rooms.✕♿🅿️Spa☃ Located next to the ski lifts at the foot of Blackcomb Mountain, the grande dame of Whistler full-scale hotels envelops guests in upscale elegance with country-style furnishings and large bathrooms. Most rooms include sleeper-sofas and window seats for the great views of Whistler Valley. **The Wildflower ($$$$)** dining room serves innovative West Coast cuisine.

$$$ Grill & Vine – *In the Westin hotel, 4090 Whistler Way.* ℰ604-905-5000. www.westinwhistler.com. **Contemporary West Coast**. ♿. Calling on producers in southern BC for many of his ingredients, the chef here serves savoury dishes like Fraser Valley Duck Breast, Beef Flat Iron & Veal Cheek, Neopolitan-style stone baked pizza, and pasta plates with sea scallops, wild mushrooms or sausage. The restaurant's towering ceiling and glass windows add to the experience.

$$Wizard Grill – *4553 Blackcomb Way,* 604-938-7700. **Burgers**. Located inside the Blackcomb Day Lodge, this family eatery offers inexpensive breakfasts and lunches, as well as Snack Packs to go. Full service capachino bar, with muffins, juices and lactose sensitive options as well.

SHOPPING

Sikora's Classical Records
432 West Hastings St., Vancouver BC. Closed Sun am. ℰ604-685-0625. www. sikorasclassical.com. An inconspicuos storefront at the edge of the Gastown district conceals a treasure trove of recordings, mostly classical music.

Vancouver Island★★★

British Columbia

Covering an area of more than 32,000sq km/12,000sq mi, Vancouver Island is the largest island off the Pacific Coast of North America. Mountains rise to over 2,100m/7,000ft in the centre. The west coast is deeply indented by inlets or fjords, while the east coast slopes gradually, with wide beaches in the south and mountains farther north. The climate is temperate. Rainfall varies greatly: Victoria in the southeast receives 680mm/27in annually; Zeballos on the west coast receives 6,480mm/255in. With rainfall supporting dense forests, the island's major industry is logging. Most people live in Victoria and along the Strait of Georgia.

Victoria★★★
See Entry Heading.

FROM PARKSVILLE TO PACIFIC RIM★★
154km/95mi by Rte. 4

This winding route traverses the mountain backbone of the island through lovely scenery. Some parts are wild and untouched; others are bustling, particularly with logging activity.

From Parksville, take Rte. 4 and continue through Port Alberni, spectacular Cathedral Grove, Kennedy Lake to Pacific Rim National Park, Ucluluet and Tofino (200km/120mi.)

Englishman River Falls★
This river tumbles over two sets of falls. The upper ones are narrow and deep, dropping into a gorge. A path bridges the river, leading to the lower falls through a dense forest. The lower falls drop around a rock into a deep pool. Route 4 enters the mountains.

Michelin Map: pp146-147.

Info: Tourism Vancouver Island, 501-65 Front Street, Nanaimo. 250-754-3500. www.tourismvi.ca.

Location: Trans-Canada Hwy runs along the east of the island from Victoria in the south to Port Hardy in the north. Pacific Rim Hwy west at Nanaimo to Tofino & Long Beach.

Don't Miss: Victoria's downtown; Butchart Gardens; the Pacific Rim beaches near Tofino.

Timing: If you arrive by ferry in the south, consider driving north and returning to the mainland from Nanaimo (central) or from Port Hardy (far north) to either Bella Coola or Prince Rupert.

Kids: Pacific Rim beaches invite, but the very cold water keeps kids from venturing in too far.

Little Qualicum Falls★
26km/16mi from Parksville; turn right to parking area.

The Little Qualicum River descends over two sets of falls connected by a gorge. The lower falls are small, but the walk through forest to the upper falls is pleasant, providing views of the canyon. The **upper falls** are on two levels, with a pool between them.

Route 4 follows the south side of **Cameron Lake**, glimpsed through the trees.

Cathedral Grove★★
35km/22mi from Parksville, part of MacMillan Provincial Park. www.env.gov. bc.ca/bcparks. Park beside highway.

Containing some of the island's original tall trees, Cathedral Grove was preserved by the MacMillan Bloedel Paper Company and donated to the province.

Many of these Douglas-firs rise past 60m/200ft, and the largest trees are 800 years old. A viewing platform affords an elevated look.

Route 4 descends to the coast and bypasses Port Alberni, an important lumber and boating centre at the head of Alberni Inlet. It is the departure point for the *MV Lady Rose*, a small freighter that has served Port Alberni Inlet and Barkley Sound more than 50 years (◐✕*departs from Argyle St. dock in Alberni Jun–late Sept Mon–Sat 8am, additional departure Jul–Labour Day Sun 8am; rest of the year Tue, Thu & Sat 8am; round-trip 8–10hrs. reservations required;* ⊜*$56–78 round trip; Alberni Marine Transportation* 𝒫*250-723-8313, or 800-663-7192 (Apr–Sept); www. ladyrosemarine.com).* The *Lady Rose* ferries visitors to the Broken Group Islands (*below*) or Bamfield.

After leaving Port Alberni, Route 4 follows Sproat Lake with good views of glacier-clad Klitsa Mountain and Mt. Gibson. Logging activity is evident along the road, from cut areas to huge logging trucks. After leaving the lake, Route 4 begins to climb Klitsa Mountain along the valley of the Taylor River.

After crossing a low pass, the road begins its winding descent to the Pacific along the Kennedy River, offering **views★** of snow-capped peaks. The river widens into **Kennedy Lake**, the largest stretch of fresh water on the island. The road follows the lake, rising above it and dipping to water level. Pacific Rim National Park Reserve is reached near the junction with the Tofino-to-Ucluelet road. The park's Long Beach Unit Visitor Centre is located here.

PACIFIC RIM NATIONAL PARK RESERVE★★★

◔*Open year-round. Hiking, canoeing, kayaking, sailing, cycling, swimming, camping.* ⊜*$7.80. Park office open year-round, call for hours.* 𝒫*250-726-3500. www.pc.gc.ca. iPark information at Pacific Rim Visitor Centre, 2175 Pacific Rim Hwy., just before junction of Hwy.4 & Ucluelet Rd.*

ACCESS

The Island is served by these ferries:

Washington State Ferries – Anacortes WA to Sidney BC (Victoria). 𝒫206-464-6400. www.wsdot.wa.gov/ferries

Black Ball Transport – Port Angeles WA to Victoria BC. 𝒫360-457-4491(Port Angeles). 250-386-2202 (Victoria). www.cohoferry.com

BC Ferries – British Columbia mainland to Vancouver Island. 𝒫250-386-3431 or 888-223-3779. www.bcferries.ca

Clipper Navigation, Inc.– Seattle WA to Victoria BC. 𝒫206-448-5000 or 800-888-2535. www.victoriaclipper.com

This reserve is a long, narrow strip of rocky islands and headlands, stretching intermittently for about 130km/80mi between Port Renfrew and Tofino.

For most of the park's annual one million visitors, this area is the only place in Canada where they can experience the sights, sounds and smells of this rugged coastline. The park consists of the notoriously difficult 75km/47mi **West Coast Trail** 🚶 for expert wilderness backpackers between Port Renfrew and Bamfield *(each end is accessible by road; orientation session required; hiking/camping fees $127.50 per person, reservation fees $24.50, ferries $15 each);*

Pacific Whale Watching

Whale watching is one of the Pacific Northwest's top visitor activities, but marine biologists now suspect excess attention may adversely affect the whales, especially orcas. Visitors who patronize whale-watching services can help by demanding that tour operators maintain a healthy distance from whales (at least 100 yards), and refrain from chasing or harassing any marine species. For information, contact The Whale Centre in Tofino, 411 Campbell Street, Tofino, t250-725-2132. Open 8am-8pm. www.tofinowhalecentre.com.

🚶 Juan Fuca Trail

You don't have to brave the notorious West Coast Trail to enjoy the Pacific Coast of Vancouver. The Juan de Fuca Trail is designed for moderate to easy day hikes or strenuous two- to five-day treks. China Beach, a half-hour west of Sooke, and several other points along Route 14, the trail offers wide breezy beaches, rocky headlands, tidepools, and lots of wildlife-watching opportunities. 📞 250-474-1336. www.gocampingbc.com

about 100 islands and rocky islets in Barkley Sound known as the **Broken Group Islands**, beloved for sea kayaking; and the famous **Long Beach unit,** reachable by road.

Long Beach★★

😊 *Visitors can surf and swim. However the water is cold (10°C/50°F) and can be extremely dangerous due to tides and currents. For details contact the park office.*

Pounded by the surf, this 11km/7mi curve of sand and rock is backed by a dense rain forest and mountains rising to 1,200m/4,000ft. Offshore, sea lions bask on the rocks, and Pacific gray whales are often spotted.

🚶 There are several points of access to Long Beach. The **Schooner Cove Trail** (*2km/1mi*) 🚶 takes hikers through old-growth forest and down to an isolated beach. The **Spruce Fringe Trail** (*2km/1mi*) 🚶 guides visitors through the shoreline forest that's shaped by the area's wind and rain. **The Wickaninnish Trail** (*3km/1.5mi*) 🚶 leads through spruce forest to Florencia Bay. From Combers Beach **sea lion rocks** can be seen offshore (*binoculars advised*).

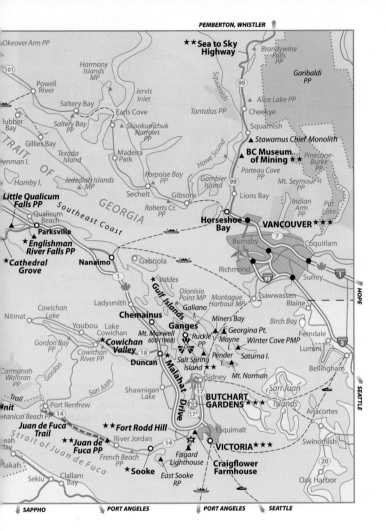

Radar Hill★★

22km/14mi from Ucluelet junction.
🥾 *Take the road to left, climbing 1.6km/1mi to a viewpoint.*

From this point above the forest, a splendid **panorama★★** *(telescope available)* opens of mountains, as well as the wild and rocky coastline.

Tofino★

ℹ *Tourism Tofino.* 𝒫 *250-725-3414. www.tourismtofino.com.*

Quiet and low-key in the winter, Tofino is a busy staging area the rest of the year for exploring Pacific Rim National Park

Reserve, charter fishing, sailing, surfing, kayaking and hiking.

The **Raincoast Interpretive Centre** *(1084 Pacific Rim Hwy.;* 𝒫*250-725-2560; www.raincoasteducation.org)* has info on Clayoquot Sound and its ecology.

Tofino is also the departure point for **whale-watching** and sightseeing cruises into Clayoquot Sound, including day trips to the waterside bathing pools at **Hot Springs Cove**. One popular tour operator is Jamie's Whaling Station *(606 Campbell St.;* 𝒫*250-725-3919 or 800-667-9913; www. jamies.com).*

Tofino harbour

©Eric P. Lucas/Michelin

ADDRESSES

STAY

$$$$ Tigh-na-Mara Resort & Spa – *1155 Resort Dr., Parksville. ℘250-248-2072 or 800-663-7373. www.tigh-na-mara.com. 192 rooms.* ✕♿P Spa ♒. This vacation retreat centres on its huge spa, including a water grotto with soaking pool and waterfalls. Guest rooms range from waterfront hotel-style rooms to cabins tucked into the woods. Several dining options onsite.

$$$$$ Clayoquot Wilderness Resorts – *Tofino. ℘250-726-8235 or 888-333-5405. www.wildretreat.com. Closed Oct–Apr. 20 tents.* ✕ Spa. Guests stay in tent cabins on wooden decks at the Outpost on Bedwell River, within 8km/5mi of Tofino, or 30min by boat. Horseback riding and hiking complement various marine activites. The cuisine is West Coast gourmet.

$$$$$ Eagle Nook Ocean Wilderness Resort – Brentwood Bay, *Barkley Sound. ℘604-357-3361 or 800-760-2777. www.eaglenook.com. Closed Oct–May. 17 rooms & 2 cabins.* ✕ Spa. This luxury hotel occupies a spectacular setting in Jane Bay. Guests kayak, beachcomb, fish and swim, and enjoy hearty meals of local seafood. Rooms are spacious and quiet. You can take a seaplane from Seattle or Vancouver, or a water taxi from Tofino/Ucluelet.

$$$$$ Wickaninnish Inn – *500 Osprey Lane at Chesterman Beach. ℘250-725-3100 or 800-333-4604. www.wickinn.com. 75 rooms.* ✕ P Spa. While summer is lovely along Long Beach, Nov–Mar offers spectacular **storm-watching** at this luxurious lodge built on a rocky headland facing the Pacific. Airy, wood-panelled rooms offer ocean views, and guests can watch whales from Mar–Jun. Cuisine based on fresh seafood and regional produce. **Ancient Cedars Spa** services make leaving difficult.

EAT

$ Common Loaf Bake Shop – *180 1st St., Tofino. ℘250-725-3915.* **Bakery.** The bulletin board here is news central for residents, drawn also by homemade muffins, pastries, breads, and strong coffee. In summer, there are pizzas and East Indian dishes. Soups, sandwiches and daily specials for lunch.

$$$ Shelter Restaurant – *601 Campbell Street. t250.725.3353. www.shelterrestaurant.com.* West Coast Contemporary. Fare is harvested from local sources, such as hormone-free, grass-fed beef, salmon, halibut, & prawns caught by Tofino fishermen, and herbs are grown onsite.

$$$$$ Sooke Harbour House – *1528 Whiffen Spit Rd., Sooke. ℘250-642-3421 or 800-889-9688. www.sookeharbourhouse.com. Reservations essential.* **Contemporary.** This 28-room inn is a 45min-drive west of Victoria. Gardens provide much of the provender; the rest comes from island farms and ranches and nearby waters. Menus change daily. Seafood includes octopus in aspic, sea cucumbers or grilled goat loin. Local art throughout.

Victoria★★★

British Columbia

Facing the **Juan de Fuca Strait** and the **Olympic** and **Cascade Mountains** of Washington state, the capital of British Columbia is famous for its mild climate, spectacular views, beautiful gardens and British traditions. Today's visitors treasure the city for its cosmopolitan culture, shopping and outdoor lifestyle.

A BIT OF HISTORY

The Hudson's Bay Company built a trading post in 1843 on the site of present-day Victoria, naming it after the Queen of England. Gold rushes brought prosperity, and eventually the settlement became capital of British Columbia. Other than the Canadian Forces' Pacific base in nearby **Esquimalt**, major employers for the Victoria area are the government and the tourism industry. The city's pleasant climate has attracted a large retirement population.

DOWNTOWN★★

The city centre is situated along **Government Street**, the main shopping area, and around the James Bay section of the harbour, where ferries from Port Angeles and Seattle dock. On the north edge of the Inner Harbour sits the **Visitor Centre** *(812 Wharf St.)*, topped by an Art Deco tower. Shops, restaurants

▶ **Population:** 344,615.

Information: Visitor Centre, 812 Wharf St. ℘250-953-2033 or 800-663-3883. www.tourismvictoria.com.

▷ **Location:** From the Art Déco tower of the Visitor Centre on Wharf Street, you can get a good view of central Victoria.

🅿 **Parking:** Meters are enforced Mon–Sat 9am–6pm, and both indoor and outdoor lots are available in the downtown area.

⊛ **Don't Miss:** The scenic Marine Drive takes you through old neighbourhoods and offers views across the Straits of Juan de Fuca. You may even see whales.

🕐 **Timing:** The downtown area is quite compact, and walking is the best way to explore it.

👥 **Kids:** Royal BC Museum is a favourite destination for school groups for many years.

and cafes line intriguing little squares and alleys such as **Bastion Square** and Trounce Alley. Just north, vibrant

Parliament Buildings

© bluejayphoto/iStockphoto.com

149

Market Square, a collection of older renovated buildings, has shops around courtyard gardens. Fort Street is an extensive antiques district. To the south, off Belleville Street, is Heritage Court, which houses the Royal BC Museum. The narrow columns and arches on the ground floor of these striking modern buildings add a distinct Islamic flavor. The **Netherlands Carillon Tower**, an open-sided 27m/88ft campanile containing 62 bells, was given to the province by Canadians of Dutch origin (*concerts seasonally*).

Parliament Buildings★

501 Belleville St. ◐*Open daily 9am–5pm.* ☛*Free guided tours (30-60min) 9am–4pm.* ◐*Closed major holidays.* ☏*250-387-3046 or 800-663-7867 (BC only). www.leg.bc.ca.*

On the south side of James Bay stands a long, squat stone building with a central dome, topped by a gilt statue of Capt. George Vancouver.

Designed by **Francis Rattenbury** (1867-1935) and completed in 1898, "the buildings" house the British Columbia Legislative Assembly and government offices. In front is a bronze statue of **Queen Victoria**. A high decorated arch beneath the dome marks the entrance. At dusk thousands of small lights outline the buildings' exterior, adding a romantic flair.

♟♟ Royal BC Museum★★★

675 Belleville St. ✕⚙◐*Open year-round daily 9 or 10am–5pm.* ◐*Closed Jan 1, Dec 25.* ⊜*$24.* ☏*250-356-7226 or 888-447-7977. www.royalbcmuseum.bc.ca.*

One of the top museums in the world, this institution focuses on the natural and human history of the province.

At the north end of the entrance hall, the **Glass House** contains totem poles from all over the province.

On the second floor British Columbia's **natural history** is featured in a series of spectacular **dioramas** of the coastal forest and seashore regions. 100 Objects of Interest features the highlights from 6 million artifacts in the museum, chosen by curators and scientists. **Ocean Station** focuses on the marine world; its Victorian-era submarine-like setting is a favourite with young visitors. The third floor **First Peoples Gallery** displays native art, arranged in striking dioramas.

The reconstructed **big house** and re-created **pit house** are highlights, as are the ceremonial **masks** in a nearby gallery. Bordering the museum, small **Thunderbird Park** has a fine collection of original and replica totem poles.

Next to Thunderbird Park stands an 1852 clapboard dwelling, **Helmcken House★** (◐*contact Royal BC Museum;* ☏*250-356-7226*), the home of Dr. John Helmcken,

Kwakwaka'wakw House, First Peoples Gallery, Royal BC Museum

© Royal BC Museum

physician to the Hudson's Bay Company.

Empress Hotel★

&See Fairmont Empress in the Addresses.

👥 Miniature World

&🕐Open early May–Labour Day daily 9am–9pm. Rest of the year daily, closing hrs vary. 🕐Closed Dec 25. 🎫$15 (child $10). 📞250-385-9731. www.miniatureworld.com. Located in the Empress Hotel complex, on the Humboldt Street side, **Miniature World** showcases small-size re-creations ranging from the Battle of Waterloo to the Canadian Pacific Railway. Check out their online Isle of Minutiae 3D world.

👥 Victoria Bug Zoo★

631 Courtney St. &🕐Open year-round Mon–Fri 11am–4:30pm, Sat/Sun 11am–5pm. 🕐Closed Jan 1 & Dec 25. 🎫$12 (child $8. 📞250-384-2847. www.bugzoo.bc.ca. Residents here include giant walking-sticks, tarantulas, scorpions and millipedes, some of which may be touched by braver visitors.

Maritime Museum of British Columbia★

634 Humboldt St. &🕐Open year-round daily 10:00am–5:00pm. 🕐Closed Dec 25. 🎫$12. 📞250-385-4222. www.mmbc.bc.ca. Inside the building are model ships, marine paraphernalia, and displays on Northwest Coast explorers. Of special interest are the *Tilikum*, a converted Indian dugout canoe that sailed from Victoria to England in the early 1900s; and the *Trekka*, a 6m/20ft sailing boat built in Victoria that sailed around the world from 1955 to 1959.

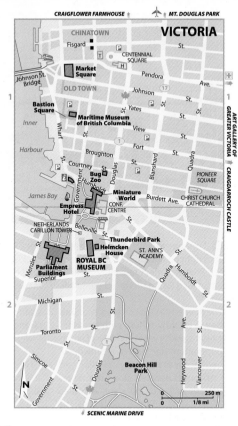

SCENIC MARINE DRIVE★★

13km/8mi
This beautiful marine drive enables visitors to appreciate Victoria's grand site and lovely gardens.

▶ Leave from Thunderbird Park and take Douglas St.

Skirting the large, flower-filled **Beacon Hill Park**, the road passes a plaque marking the initial kilometre of the nearly 8,000km/5,000mi **Trans-Canada Highway**, which stretches to St. John's, Newfoundland.

▶ Turn left on Dallas Rd.

From Finlayson and Clover points, there are fine **views★★** of the Olympic Mountains.

Inner Harbour, with the Fairmont Empress Hotel

©Leslie Forsberg/Michelin

▶ Continue to Hollywood Crescent. Turn right on Ross St. (at Robertson St.); Ross becomes Crescent Rd. Bear left at King George Terrace; ascend hill.

The drive enters the community of **Oak Bay**, a wealthy suburb with beautiful gardens, pretty views and a very English population. Harling Point provides a good **view** of the rocky coastline and the houses perched along the shore. Directly below on the right, Gonzales Bay is visible, and the Trial Islands can be seen offshore to the left.

▶ Take Beach Dr.

The drive continues around McNeill Bay. Bisected by the road, the Victoria Golf Course on Gonzales Point has **views★★** of the sea *(weather permitting)*, the San Juan Islands and the snow-clad peaks of the Cascades, dominated by Mt. Baker. This is the oldest golf club in Canada. The drive then passes through **Uplands Park**, a pleasant section of Oak Bay. **Cattle Point** offers views of the coast.

▶ Go south on Beach Dr. Turn right onto Bowker Ave., left onto Cadboro Bay Rd. and then Fort St. to downtown.

ADDITIONAL SIGHTS
Craigdarroch Castle★
1050 Joan Crescent. ◷*Open mid-Jun– Labour Day daily 9am–7pm. Rest of year daily 10am–4:30pm.* ◷*Closed Jan 1, &*

Dec 25–26. ◉*$13.95.* 🅿 ✆*250-592- 5323. www.craigdarrochcastle.com.*
Built by Robert Dunsmuir, a Scot who made a fortune from coal, the huge 1880s stone mansion has dozens of stained-glass windows that create rainbows of light. From the top of the tower there is a good view of Victoria.

Art Gallery of Greater Victoria★
1040 Moss St. ♿🅿◉*Open mid-May– Aug Mon–Sat 10am–5pm (Thu til 9pm), Sun & holidays noon–5pm. Rest of year closed Mon.* ◷*Closed Good Friday & Dec 25.* ◉*$13.* ✆*250-384-4171, www.aggv.ca.*
Housed in a Victorian mansion (1889), the gallery offers an eclectic mix of East and West, as well as paintings by Emily Carr. A highlight of the Asian art is the Japanese garden's Shinto Shrine.

Fort Rodd Hill★★
14km/9mi west by Hwys. 1, 1A and Ocean Blvd. 🅿◉*Open mid-Feb–Oct daily 10am–5:30pm. Rest of the year daily 9am–4:30pm.* ◷*Closed Dec 25.* ◉*$3.90.* ✆*250-478-5849. www.pc.gc.ca.*
Set on 18ha/44 acres of land at the southwest corner of Esquimalt's harbour, the fort contains the remains of three coastal artillery-gun batteries which, until 1956, protected the approaches to the naval base at Esquimalt.
From beside **Fisgard Lighthouse**, there are **views★** of Juan de Fuca Strait, the

Sanctuary and Solitude

👥👤 **Swan Lake Christmas Hill Nature Sanctuary** (*3873 Swan Lake Rd.; ✆250-479-0211; www.swanlake.bc.ca*). This peaceful 45ha/110-acre preserve includes wetlands, fields forest and a lily pad-filled lake that provides refuge for waterfowl and nesting birds. Nature House features displays and activities for children. The trail (*2.5km/1.5mi*) up Christmas Hill crosses residential streets, but the summit reveals a panorama of Victoria and its environs, including Elk Lake to the north, Blankinsop to the east.

Olympic Mountains and the naval base. Both the lighthouse and fort are National Historic Sites.

Robert Batemen Centre

470 Belleville St., in the Steamship Terminal Building. 🅿🕐*Open daily 10am–5pm.* ⬤*$8.50.* ✆*250-940-3630. www.batemancentre.org*

This centre displays the largest exhibition of original artworks by one of the world's great wildlife artist. From the smallest drawings to massive wall paintings, the magnitude and splendour of this presentation is surely one of a kind in the world of art. Bateman's creations span the geographic world, from his B.C. home on Salt Spring Island, to the African savannah and many points in between. Watch Bateman work live too.

EXCURSIONS
Butchart Gardens★★★

800 Benvento Ave. in Brentwood Bay, 21km/13mi north by Rte. 17 and Keating X Rd. or by Rte. 17A.

🍴♿🅿🕐*Open year-round daily 9am (Dec 25 til 1pm). Closings vary.* ⬤*$32.10 mid-Jun–Sept ($17.75-29.90 other).* ✆*250-652-5256 or 866-652-4422. www.butchartgardens.com.*

Now 20ha/50acres in size, these internationally famous gardens were started in 1904 by Jennie Butchart to beautify the quarry pit resulting from her husband's cement business. The grounds are maintained year-round by a small army of gardeners.

The floral showpiece is the **sunken garden** with its green lawns, trees and exquisite flower arrangements. Set in a huge pit with ivy-covered sides, the garden is best viewed from above or from the rock island at its centre. Paths weave down through a rockery.

The other gardens include the **Ross Fountain**, with its changing water displays; the **Rose Garden**, with rose-covered arbors full of blooms (*Jun-Sept*); the secluded **Japanese Garden**; and the formal **Italian Garden**, with statues and a star-shaped lily pond.

Butchart Gardens
© Gwen Cannon/MICHELIN

Malahat Drive★

▶ Take Douglas St. north to Hwy. 1 (Trans-Can Hwy.). The drive begins about 18km/11mi north of Victoria.

This attractive stretch of road (*some 19km/12mi between Goldstream Provincial Park and Mill Bay Rd.*) crosses Malahat Ridge with good **views★** of Finlayson Arm, Saanich Inlet, the Gulf Islands, and the mainland. On a clear day Mt. Baker is visible through the trees.

Quw'utsun' Cultural and Conference Centre

200 Cowichan Way, in Duncan, about 60km/37mi north by Hwy. 1.
&⊙*Open Jun–Sept Tue–Sat 10am–3pm.* ✕⊚*$15.* ℘*250-746-8119 or 877-746-8119. www.quwutsun.ca.*
Operated by the Quw'utsun' tribes, the wooden buildings from Expo '86 in Vancouver were bought here. At the large **carving shed**, native craftsmen transform logs into totems and war canoes. The on-site **Riverwalk Café ($)** serves native dishes.

BC Forest Discovery Centre★

2892 Drinkwater Rd., north of Duncan.
&⊙*Open daily Jun–Labour Day daily 10am–5pm. Rest of the year, hours vary.*
⊚*$12-16.* ℘*250-715-1113.*
http://bcforestdiscoverycentre.com.
Visitors walk through forest of Douglas-fir trees, visit a logging museum, see a reconstructed logging camp and ride narrow-gauge steam railway (*April–early Oct, & holidays*).

Chemainus Festival of Murals

78km/48mi north by Hwy. 1.
Visitor centre at 9796 Willow St.
℘*250-246-3944. www.muraltown.com.*
Waterfront town is famous for 40 **murals**. Note especially *Native Heritage*, symbolizing the three tribes of the Coast Salish Nation, and *Arrival of the 'Reindeer' in Horseshoe Bay*, featuring a native woman in a colourful robe watching a ship enter the bay.

ADDRESSES

🛏 STAY

$$ Bedford Regency – *1140 Government St.* ℘*250-384-6835 or 800-665-6500. www.bedfordregency.com. 40 rooms.* ✕
This five-storey boutique hotel is located a short walk from the Inner Harbour and Government Street shops. Guest rooms have large cushy chairs and goose-down duvets. Some rooms feature fireplaces, Jacuzzis and views of James Bay. Pub fare is served in the English-style **Garrick's Head ($) and The Churchill.**

$$ English Inn and Resort – *429 Lampson St., Esquimalt.* P ℘*250-388-4353 or 866-388-4353. www.englishinn.ca. 28 suites.* This inn sits within 5 acres of gardens that hold a replica of Anne Hathaway's thatched-roof cottage. Guest rooms follow the Old English theme with antique furnishings and canopy beds; some have fireplaces and kitchenettes. The on-site **Rosemeade Dining Room & Lounge ($$)** serves dinner and drinks.

$$ Fairholme Manor – *638 Rockland Pl.* P Spa ℘*250-598-3240 or 877-511-3322. www.fairholmemanor.com. 5 suites.* Built in 1885, the Italianate mansion occupies a bucolic hilltop in Victoria's Rockland district. Annex apartments are done in light woods, while the suites have fireplaces, bay windows and expansive baths; some have decks and Jacuzzis. Breakfast features fresh bakery goods.

$$$ Haterleigh Heritage Inn – *243 Kingston St.* ℘*250-384-9995 or 866-234-2244. www.haterleigh.com. 6 rooms.* P
Light pours through huge stained-glass windows in this elegant 1901 home near Victoria's Inner Harbour and downtown. All rooms have private baths and are furnished with antiques; most have Jacuzzi tubs. Afternoon tea and evening sherry.

$$$$ Laurel Point Resort – *680 Montreal St.* ℘*250-386-8721 or 800-663-7667. www.laurelpoint.com. 200 rooms.* ✕
This glitzy glass-and-steel complex occupies a small peninsula at the entrance to Victoria's Inner Harbour, giving it expansive bay views. Spacious, bright rooms feature balconies and cozy down comforters. Exercise and leisure facilities include a pool, saunas and hot tubs. Outside, guests can relax in the

Japanese garden, graced with a reflecting pond and waterfall. Dining at Aura's waterfront restaurant & pub.

$$$$$ Westin Bear Mountain Golf Resort & Spa – *1999 Country Club Way. 250-391-7160. www.bearmountain.ca.*
Set on the foothills of Mount Finlayson & overlooks Victoria Harbour, this luxurious resort offers the best of many worlds. Site of Canada's only Jack and Steve Nicklaus-designed 36-hole golf course, Bear Mountain Resort is a rugged and lush mountainside landscape with vistas of the Olympic Mountain Range and Strait of Juan de Fuca. Bella Montagna and Masters Lounge cater with dining and drinks onsite.

$$$$$ Fairmont Empress – *721 Government St. 250-384-8111 or 866-540-4429. www.fairmont.ca. 476 rooms.*
✕ P ⚑ Spa. The Empress has welcomed distinguished guests from Rudyard Kipling to Queen Elizabeth II since it opened in 1908. The public areas—Palm Court, the Crystal Ballroom, the Empress Dining Room—are splendid. Guest rooms are richly appointed, and their famous afternoon tea (**$$$**) is served daily from noon; reservations (*250-389-2727*) and appropriate attire are required. The Willow Stream Spa offers services fit for a queen.

🍽/EAT

$ Blue Fox Café– *919 Fort St. 250-380-1683. Open daily 7:30am–4pm, Sat/Sun 8am–3pm.* **Canadian**. Crowds line up to get into this antiques-district bistro, which offers breakfast all day. Huge platters of "very fat French toast," huevos rancheros and three-egg omelettes. Expansive sandwiches, burgers and wraps round out the simple menu.

$ Murchie's – *1110 Government St. 250-383-3112. www.murchies.com.* **Canadian**. Known as purveyors of fine teas and coffees since 1894, the Murchie family presents a smorgasbord of delectables for breakfast and lunch. Enjoy afternoon tea, then browse the adjacent shop for specialty teas, coffee and all the accoutrements (down to the tea cozy).

$$ Spinnaker's Gastro Brewpub – *308 Catherine St. 250-386-2739 or 877-838-2739. www.spinnakers.com.* **Pub Fare.** This brew pub occupies a Tudor-style building on the Inner Harbour, and several commercial outlets for their homemade vinegars and bakedgoods, including at the airport. High-class pub fare such as pork tenderloin with yam fritters, or local seafood with herbs and local vegetables. Guesthouse rooms.

$$$ Café Brio – *944 Fort St. Dinner only from 5pm. 250-383-0009 or 866-270-5461. www.cafe-brio.com. Reservations recommended.* **West Coast/Italian.**
The decor in this sunny yellow building along antiques row is discreet; wood floors and fine art line the stucco dining room walls. Tuscan-inspired dishes include butter-poached pheasant breast, and *cacciucco* (fish stew).

SHOPPING

Alcheringa Gallery – *621 Fort St. 250-383-8224. www.alcheringa-gallery.com.*
The gallery focuses on aboriginal art from the entire Pacific Rim as well as the Northwest. Note the striking similarities among New Zealand, New Guinea and British Columbia coastal works. Most works are modern, evidencing a resurgence of traditional art along the Pacific Rim.

Munro's Books – *1108 Government St. 250-382-2464 or 888-243-2464. www.munrobooks.com.* Housed in a Neoclassical stone building, this bookshop has more than 50,000 titles, with a strong focus on Canadian authors and topics. A must-see.

Rogers Chocolates – *913 Government St. 250-384-7021. www.rogerschocolates. com.* This 1903 heritage building houses a fine chocolate shop, which dates to 1885. Many visitors refuse to leave Victoria without a box of Rogers Chocolates.

Silk Road –*1624 Government St. 250-704-2688. www.silkroadteastore.com.* Aromatic teas, oils, candles and other sensory delights. Herbal preparations supplement traditional black teas.

Waterton Lakes National Park★★

Alberta

This Rocky Mountain preserve "where the prairies meet the mountains," forms an International Peace Park with Glacier National Park in Montana. The mountains have been sculptured by erosion and glaciation into sharp peaks, narrow ridges and interlocked U-shaped valleys. The three Waterton Lakes lie in a deep glacial trough. Formerly a Blackfoot Indian stronghold, the area was explored by the Palliser Expedition in 1858; the lakes were named for 18C English naturalist **Charles Waterton**. The area was designated a national park in 1895.

VISIT

◔*Park open year-round, but very few facilities open late fall–early spring. Hiking, camping, horseback riding, fishing, boating, golf, winter sports.* ✆*$7.80. day use fee. www.pc.gc.ca.*

Waterton Townsite

The town has a lovely **site★★** near the point where Upper Lake narrows into the Bosporus Strait, which separates it from Middle Lake. Just south behind

Info: Visitor Information Centre: Park Entrance Rd. ✆403-859-5133. www.pc.gc.ca. Open early Apr–mid-Oct.

Location: Waterton Lakes lies in southwest Alberta, near B.C. Take Highway #2 from Calgary to Lethbridge.

Don't Miss: A cruise on the Waterton lakes.

Timing: The Waterton townsite, located at the centre of the park, has extensive tourist facilities. https://mywaterton.ca.

Kids: The Buffalo Paddock is near the park entrance.

the townsite, **Mount Richards** can be distinguished. Beside it stands **Mount Bertha**, marked by pale green streaks caused by snowslides that swept trees down the mountainside. Across the lake rise **Vimy Peak** and **Vimy Ridge**.

Upper Lake stretches south into Montana, separating the mountains of the Lewis and Clark Range. In summer **boat tours★★** head down the lake to the US ranger station at the southern end (◔*depart from Waterton Marina late May–mid-Oct 10am, 1pm & 4pm, also 7pm late Jun–Aug; rest of May & rest of*

Waterton Lakes with Prince of Wales Hotel on left

© Katie Goldie/Travel Alberta

Bison Paddock, Waterton Lakes National Park

© Randall Wiebe/Travel Alberta

Sept–early Oct 10am & 1pm; round-trip 2hrs 15min; commentary; ☞$47; Waterton Inter-Nation Shoreline Cruise Co. Ltd.; ☏403-859-2362; www.waterton cruise.com). Behind the townsite, **Cameron Falls** can be seen dropping over a layered cliff.

Cameron Lake★★

17km/11mi from townsite by Akamina Hwy.

The jewel-toned lake, circuited by gentle hiking trails but with access to more challenging ones, is set immediately below the Continental Divide and like Upper Waterton, spans the international border. Dominating the view across the lake are, left to right, **Mount Custer** and **Forum Peak**. A scenic trail *(1.6km/1mi)* traces the western shore of the lake.

Red Rock Canyon★

*19km/12mi from townsite,
turn left at Blakiston Creek.*

The drive to this small canyon offers good **views★** of the surrounding mountains. A **nature trail** 🚶 *(2km/1.2mi)* follows the narrow canyon.

👥 Buffalo Paddock★

*400m/.2mi from park entrance.
Auto circuit 3km/2mi. For safety, stay in your vehicle.*

A small herd of buffalo occupies a large enclosure on a fine site backed by Bellevue Mountain and Mount Galway.

Bison or Buffalo?

While most people use the words interchangeably, purists will opt for the term bison when referring to the North American animal. Early settlers in the US called bison buffalo, since they saw a similarity to the buffalo of Asia and Europe. In fact, the ancestors of modern bison are thought to have migrated from Asia to North America across the Bering Strait thousands of years ago when the two continents were united by a land bridge. Some 200 years ago Plains bison inhabited the grasslands of the prairies. The larger wood bison, fewer in number, made the forested fringes of the northwestern prairie their home. Bison are wild bovids, members of the same family as cattle and sheep. An adult male can weigh as much as 2,200 pounds but can charge at a speed of 40mph. Calves weigh up to 70 pounds when born and can walk within 20 minutes of birth. Mature at three years, a bison can live as many as 30 years.

Source: Parks Canada

Whitehorse★

Yukon Territory

Situated on the Yukon River, Whitehorse is the capital of the Yukon Territory. Today the city is a centre for tourism. Proud of its part in the Klondike Gold Rush Stampede, the community stages a celebration called the **Sourdough Rendezvous** every February, when people dress in the costumes of 1898 and race dog teams on the frozen Yukon River. This time of year is also the height of Northern Lights (*Aurora Borealis*) viewing season, an event that draws thousands of visitors, from Japan especially.

A BIT OF HISTORY

The city owes it existence to the difficulty encountered by the Dawson City-bound **Klondike Stampeders** negotiating Miles Canyon. The **White Pass and Yukon Route Railway,** a unique narrow-gauge train, changed area transport; its decision to end its line at Whitehorse made the site a bustling centre for transferring goods to riverboats or overland stages bound onward to Dawson City. In 1953 the territorial capital was moved here.

SIGHTS

Whitehorse retains some historic structures, notably: the old **log church** on Elliott at Third Avenue, built in 1900; the "**skyscrapers**" on Lambert between Second and Third avenues, built after World War II; and the log **railway station** on First Avenue at Main. In contrast is the modern steel and aluminum Yukon government **Administration Building** on Second Avenue, opened in 1976. The Yukon Permanent Art Collection installed here consists of contemporary as well as traditional native art. The **Philipsen Law Centre★** at Second and Jarvis houses a significant collection of contemporary regional art.

MacBride Museum★

1124 Front Street ○*Open mid-May–Labour Day daily 9:30am–5pm. Rest of the year Tue–Sat 10am–4pm.*
&*$10.* ℘*867-667-2709.*
www.macbridemuseum.com
Situated in a log building (1967) with a sod roof, this museum features gold-rush memorabilia, Indian cultural objects and a splendid collection of old **photographs** of the Yukon. Outside are relics of Yukon transport, early machinery, the cabin of legendary Sam McGee (immortalized by Robert Service) and a government telegraph office c.1900. Prince William and Kate visited here in 2016, echoing Queen Elizabeth's visit in 1958.

SS Klondike★★

6 Robert Service Way. &○*Open Victoria Day (May 19) to Labour Day (varies) daily 9:30am–5pm.* &*$3 for brochure, admission is free.* ℘*800-661-0486 or 867-667-4511. www.pc.gc.ca.*
Upper decks not wheelchair accessible.
One of some 200 stern-wheelers that once plied the Yukon between Whitehorse and Dawson City, this 1937 craft, now a Parks Canada National Historic Site, is the only steamboat open to the public in the Territory.

▶ **Population:** 28,000.

🄸 **Info:** Tourist Office, 100 Hanson St., ℘867-667-3084. www.travelyukon.com.

◖ **Location:** Whitehorse lies in southwestern Yukon; to the west stretches the Alaskan panhandle.

🅿 **Parking:** For road conditions, call ℘867-456-7623 or toll-free within the Yukon 877-456-7623. www.gov.yk.ca.

🙪 **Don't Miss:** The Frantic Follies revue is locally produced, and great fun.

🕐 **Timing:** Besides a day or 2 visiting the town, you'll want to devote multiple days to excursions.

Yukon Cancans

Although it's unlikely gold-rush miners ever saw shows quite like these, the separately operated dance-hall extravaganzas in Whitehorse and Dawson City (☝ *see Dawson City entry*) are among the Yukon's most popular attractions.

In Dawson City, **Diamond Tooth Gertie's Gambling Hall**, Canada's oldest legal casino, presents nightly shows including a boisterous cancan performed in colourful costumes. The midnight show is the liveliest. ♿🕐*Open May–Sept daily. Shows at 8:30pm, 10:00pm & 12:00am.* ✕ ☜*$12.* ☏*867-993-5525. www.dawsoncity.ca.*

Whitehorse's **Frantic Follies Vaudeville Revue,** which has toured Canada and the US, is a more sophisticated production staged in a local hotel. A lively cancan performance is also included. 🕐*Performances Jun 1–Aug 31 nightly 8:30pm.* ☜*$24.* ☏*867-668-2042. www.franticfollies.com. Westmark Whitehorse Hotel.*

Cross the river via Robert Campbell Bridge and stop to see the **fish ladder** at **Whitehorse Dam**, built to enable the chinook salmon to circumnavigate the dam and reach their spawning grounds upriver (*usually Aug*). The dam is best viewed from the observation deck.

Miles Canyon★

9km/6mi south of Whitehorse via Canyon Rd.

Following the edge of Schwatka Lake, **Canyon Road** passes the MV *Schwatka* dock (☝*below*) and climbs above the canyon (☝sharp curves and steep grades), where there is a **view★** from the lookout. Near the parking lot above Miles Canyon is another **view★**.

Canyon **cruises** afford good **views★** of the green waters of the Yukon and the steep canyon walls. ♿🕐 *MV Schwatka departs late May–early Sept daily 2pm; mid-Jun–mid-Aug 2pm & 4pm. Round-trip 2hrs. Reservations required.* ☜*$30. Yukon River Cruises Ltd.* ☏*867-668-4716. www. yukonadventures.com. To access boat landing, take South Access Rd. toward centre of Whitehorse and turn right onto unpaved road just past railroad tracks. Tune your ears to the call of the wild and join the legacy of famous writer Jack London and his legendary gold rush stampeders.*

SS Klondike

©Vera Bogaerts/iStockphoto.com

Chilkoot Pass

Starting in Dyea, this route climbs at an angle of 35° in places. Raw rock in summer, the pass became slick ice and snow in winter, with temperatures of minus 50°C/minus 58°F, it was a nightmare to climb. Yet over the winter of 1897-98, some 22,000 people scaled it, not just once but 30 to 40 times! The North West Mounted Police at the Canadian border insisted that anyone entering Canada have a year's supply of food and equipment. To carry this "ton" of goods over the pass, stampeders had to make numerous trips. Today the **Chilkoot Trail** (*53km/33mi*) starts for hikers at the abandoned site of Skagway's former rival, **Dyea** (*15km/9mi north of Skagway by dirt road*) and ends at Bennett Lake. The 54km/33mi trek can take up to five days (*contact Parks Canada 867-667-3910*).

Beringia Interpretive Centre★

Next to Transportation Museum at Kilometer #1423 Alaska Hwy. &⊙*Open May–Sept daily 9am–6pm. Rest of year 12pm–5pm, or by appointment.* ⊛*$6.* &*867-667-8855. www.beringia.com.*
The centre offers a scientific look at the region's prehistoric past. Beringia is the name given the Siberia/Alaska/Canada North 15,000 years ago when the Bering Strait land bridge was open.

Yukon Transportation Museum

30 Electra Crescent, near the airport via Alaska Hwy. &⊙*Open mid-May–Aug daily 10am–6pm, Tue until 9pm.* ⊛*$10.* &*867-668-4792. www.goytm.ca.*
There is a replica of the 1920s mail plane, **Queen of the Yukon**, as well as dog-sleds, early cars and trucks. The building of the Alaska Highway is showcased.

Yukon Arts Centre

300 College Dr., northwest end of Whitehorse. ⊙*Open year-round Mon–Fri 10am–3pm, Sat/Sun noon–5pm and for performances.* &*867-667-8575. www.yukonartscentre.org.*
This modern performing arts facility includes a 424-seat theatre and a public art gallery that displays the work of professional Yukon artists in a minimum of 10 changing exhibits a year. Live music concerts take place in the Old Fire Hall covering many styles.

EXCURSION TO SKAGWAY★★

Note: Skagway is in Alaska. Canadian citizens need passports to enter the US. Visitors from some countries also need US visas, available from any US consulate, but not in Whitehorse.

An impressive trip in the Yukon is the traverse of the Coast Mountains to Skagway—terminus of the Klondike Highway—on the Alaska Panhandle. Most gold seekers en route to Dawson City sailed up the Pacific Coast to Skagway or **Dyea** (&*see Chilkoot Pass sidebar*) and trudged into the Yukon across the Coast Mountains. From Skagway the trail followed the **White Pass**, a climb of 888m/2,914ft. When this route was

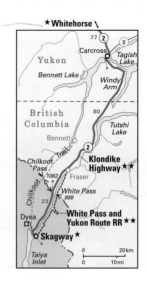

© Rocky Grimes/iStockphoto.com

White Pass and Yukon Route Railroad

closed in 1897, stampeders turned to the more difficult **Chilkoot Pass** (&see sidebar above).

Klondike Highway to Skagway★★

180km/112mi by Alaska Hwy. and Klondike Hwy. (Rte. 2). ◐*US border open year-round daily 24hrs. Canada Customs in Fraser open Apr–Oct daily 24hrs. Nov 1–Mar 31 daily 8am–midnight.* ✆*800-461-9999 (Canada Customs) or 907-983-2325 (US Customs).*
Adjoining the Alaska Highway south of Whitehorse, the Klondike Highway passes through forest and gradually enters the mountains. At **Carcross**— where the final rail was laid for the White Pass and Yukon Route—the road follows the shores of **Tagish Lake**, **Windy Arm** and **Tutshi** [TOO-shy] **Lake**. After leaving Tutshi Lake, the road begins the traverse of the desolate White Pass. The steep descent to Skagway offers views of the **Taiya Inlet** of the Lynn Canal far below.

Skagway★

The wide Pacific lying at its door, this "Gateway to the Klondike" is a small busy port and the northern terminus of the southeast ferry system. A port of call on the Inside Passage, this tiny, historic town, with its frontier flavour, attracts scores of visitors annually. The Klondike Highway from Skagway to Carcross was laid in 1978, and the railway restored in 1988.

The Town

🚹 *Skagway Convention & Visitor Bureau, 245 Broadway.* ✆*907-983-2854. www.skagway.com.*
The Park Service **Visitor Centre** (*2nd & Broadway;* &◐*open early May–late Sept daily 8:30am–5:30pm;* ◕*45min town tours daily 9am, 10am, 11am, 2pm & 3pm;* ✆*907-983-9200; www.nps.gov/klgo).*

White Pass and Yukon Route Railroad★★ &◐*White Pass Summit Excursion departs from 2nd & Spring Sts. early May–late Sept daily 8:15am & 12:45pm (additional departure mid-May early Sept daily 4:30pm). Round-trip 3hrs.* ◉*US$103 (+ tax).* ✆*800-343-7373. www.wpyr.com. Reservations essential.*
This narrow-gauge railroad originally linked Skagway to Whitehorse. The refurbished railroad cars climb to an elevation of 873m/2,865ft, providing spectacular **views★** of Skagway and the rugged peaks dominating the town. The train concludes its thrilling 45km/28mi run at the Canadian station in Fraser, British Columbia. This trip is highly recommended.

ADDRESSES

⌂ STAY

$$$$$ Tincup Wilderness Lodge – *On Tincup Lake. ✆604-484-4418. www.tincup-lodge.com. Open mid-Jun–mid-Sept. 4 cabins.* Guests are flown into this wilderness site on Tincup Lake *(the pickup is usually in Whitehorse.)* Trout fishing, hiking and berry picking during the day precede splendid evening meals of fresh fish or Canadian beef, after which guests can relax in the wood-heated sauna or hot tub. Guests can even take cooking classes during their stay. The four comfortable red-roofed cedar cabins are deluxe by wilderness standards, with showers and wood stoves. The main lodge contains the dining room, a lounge and large deck.

♈/EAT

$ The Chocolate Claim – *305 Strickland St. ✆867-667-2202. www.chocolateclaim. com.* This spacious coffee house sells scrumptious pastries and chocolates, light lunches and coffee roasted by a Whitehorse company, Bean North.

Yukon Circuit★★

Yukon Territory, Alaska

This scenic journey through the Yukon rewards travellers willing to traverse a relatively isolated frontier to witness nature's grandeur and mankind's diversions. Covering a 483,450sq km/186,660sq mi triangle in Canada's northwest corner, the legendary Yukon conjures up images of snow-clad mountains and the midnight sun. The majestic Yukon River, a silent but ever-present companion, dominates half the circuit.

A BIT OF HISTORY

During the gold rush, thousands of stampeders travelling from Skagway ended their winter trek through Chilkoot Pass at **Bennett Lake**.

There, in the spring, they constructed boats to complete the journey via the Yukon and its tributaries to Dawson City (♍*see entry*), a distance of some 800km/500mi.

Miles Canyon and other hazards on the voyage seemed minor after traversing the treacherous pass, but were harrowing in their own right.

Today thousands of people follow the route alongside the river to discover the wild northland.

- ⌚ **Michelin Map:** p 163
- ▣ **Info:** Dept of Tourism and Culture, Government of Yukon. 800-661-0494. www.travelyukon.com.
- ▶ **Location:** The Yukon Territory covers a 483,450sqkm/186,660sq mi triangle in Canada's northwest corner.
- ▣ **Parking:** Check out road conditions at ✆867-456-7623 or toll-free within the Yukon 877-456-7623. www.gov.yk.ca
- ⌾ **Don't Miss:** Museums in Mayo and Keno City offer a poignant look at bygone boom times and at native culture.
- ⌚ **Timing:** Those in a hurry can arrange air transport at Haines Junction.

🚗 DRIVING TOUR

About 1,500km/930mi from Whitehorse via Klondike, Top of the World, Taylor and Alaska Hwys. Lengthy drive over stretches of gravel road. Several roads in the Yukon, notably Silver Trail and Top of the World Highway, contain lengthy stretches of oiled gravel, which can be quite slick when wet. It is advisable to check road conditions in advance. In

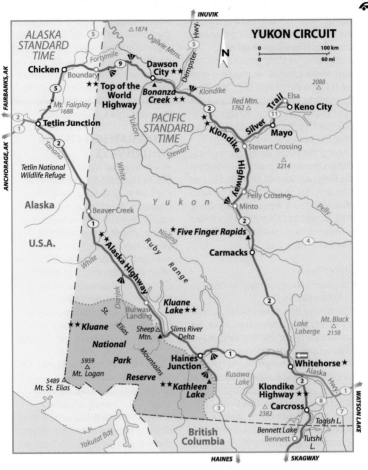

YUKON CIRCUIT

INUVIK

ALASKA STANDARD TIME

Chicken

Boundary

★★ Top of the World Highway

Mt. Fairplay 1688

Tetlin Junction

Tetlin National Wildlife Refuge

Alaska

Beaver Creek

U.S.A.

★★ Alaska Highway

Burwash Landing

★★ Kluane

National

5959 △ Mt. Logan

5489 △ Mt. St. Elias

Park

Reserve

★★ Kathleen Lake

Yakutat Bay

British Columbia

HAINES

FAIRBANKS, AK

ANCHORAGE, AK

Tanana

White

Dawson City ★★

Bonanza Creek ★★

Klondike

Red Mtn. 1762 △

PACIFIC STANDARD TIME

★ Klondike

Stewart

Stewart Crossing

2088 △

Elsa

Silver Trail

Keno City

11

Mayo

2214 △

Klondike Highway

Pelly Crossing

Minto

2

Pelly

Y u k o n

Nisling

Ruby Range

★ Five Finger Rapids

Carmacks

Donjek

St. Elias Mountains

Kluane Lake ★★

Sheep Mtn.

Slims River Delta

Haines Junction

Kusawa Lake

Lake Laberge

Mt. Black 2158

1

Whitehorse ★

Alaska Hwy.

Klondike Highway ★★

Carcross

2382 △

3

Bennett Lake

Bennett

Tagish L.

Tutshi L.

SKAGWAY

WATSON LAKE

0   100 km
0   60 mi

N

△ 1874

Ogilvie Mtns.

Dempster Hwy.

Fortymile

5

9

5

2

1

2

2

1

1

2

2

4

8

7

some sections, service facilities are few and infrequent. Prepare for emergencies with food, warm clothing and vehicle supplies. Know how to protect yourself from bad weather and wild animals.

FROM WHITEHORSE TO DAWSON CITY★

540km/335mi by Klondike Hwy. (Rte. 2), not including excursion.

Whitehorse★

See WHITEHORSE.

The **Klondike Highway** skirts Lake Laberge (*barely visible from the road*), through which the Yukon River runs. At the end of the unpaved access road to the campground, there is a lovely **view** of this lake and the mountains

The Mighty Yukon

One of the longest rivers in North America, this giant of the remote North—its Loucheux Indian name *Yu-kun-ah* means "great river"—traverses 3,185km/1,975mi of rugged territory. Originating in Tagish Lake on the Yukon/British Columbia boundary, the greenish-blue river flows northward through the Yukon Territory and Alaska to empty into the Bering Sea.

beyond. The highway rejoins the river at **Carmacks** (*178km/110mi*), named for the discoverer of Klondike gold. After 196km/122mi, just beyond a bend in the

Yukon, small rock islands have divided the river into five fast-flowing channels, known as **Five Finger Rapids★**.

In the vicinity of Minto, about 2km/1.4mi past Minto Resorts, an unpaved road leads to the riverside (*1.6km/1mi*). Here a sign marks the Overland Trail, a wagon road built in 1902 from Whitehorse to Dawson City. The **view★** of the Yukon from the bank is grand.

Leaving the Yukon Valley, the highway crosses the central plateau and bridges the Pelly and Stewart rivers. At Stewart Crossing, Route 11 (*unpaved between Mayo and Keno*), designated the Silver Trail, begins its 112km/69mi northeast traverse through the villages of Mayo and Elsa to Keno City.

Silver Trail

Excursion: 224km/138mi round-trip from Klondike Hwy.

This byway into Yukon mining country offers landscapes typical of the subarctic interior. The first stop, **Mayo** (*53km/33mi*), experiences extreme climates. Summer temperatures have hit 36°C/98°F (a Yukon record), while winter lows have dropped to −62°C/−79°F. The **Binet House Interpretive Centre** presents an explanation of permafrost, and photos of First Nations life (*Center St. & Second Ave.;* ○*open May 20–Sep 19 daily 10am–6pm;* ℘*867-996-2926, seasonal*).

Keno City (*112km/69mi*) was a thriving town until the last mine closed in 1989. **Keno City Mining Museum** (*end of the Silver Trail);* ○*open late May–early Sept daily 10am–6pm;* ℘*867-995-2792, seasonal; www.yukonmuseums.ca*) has a collection of 1950s-era **photographs★** by a miner and photographer.

From the designated lookout about 61km/38mi south of Dawson City, a **view** of the vast **Tintina Trench,** vivid evidence of plate tectonics, unfolds. There is a **viewpoint**, after 483km/300mi, of the valley of the Klondike River from above, with the Ogilvie Mountains to the northeast. The road then follows the Klondike.

At 494km/307mi note that the **Dempster Highway** heads northward to Inuvik in the Mackenzie Delta across the Ogilvie and Richardson Mountains. (○*open all year except spring breakup and fall freeze-up when the Peel and Mackenzie river ferries do not operate*). The Klondike Highway crosses the Klondike River after 538km/334mi and enters **Dawson City★★** (℘*See DAWSON CITY*).

FROM DAWSON CITY TO WHITEHORSE

945km/586mi by Top of the World (Rte. 9), Taylor (US 5) (both highways ○*closed in winter) and Alaska Hwys. Caution: Reduced speeds necessary, usually 40–64km/h/25–40mph on winding and often unpaved road (Alaska Hwy. is paved). Drive with headlights on. Canada and US Customs offices at border crossing for Rtes. 9 & 5.* ○*open mid-May–mid-Sept daily 9am–9pm (8am–8pm Alaska time). Alaska Hwy. border open year-round daily 24hrs.* ℘*867-862-7230 (Canada Customs).* ℘*907-774-2252 (US Customs).*

Top of the World Highway★★

108km/67mi to Alaska border.
○*Road closed in winter. Entry only when US Customs open (above).*

Route 9 is called Top of the World Highway because most of its length is above the tree line, allowing magnificent **views★★★**. It leaves Dawson by the ferry across the Yukon (*continuous 24hr service May–Sept*). For about 5km/3mi, the road climbs to a **viewpoint** at a bend in the road. After 14km/9mi there is another **viewpoint** of the Ogilvie Mountains, the Yukon Valley and, visible to the north, the Tintina Trench. The road then follows the ridgetops for 90km/50mi.

The Route in Alaska

306km/190mi. ○ *At Alaska border, set watches back 1hr.*

Route 9 joins the Taylor Highway (US 5) after 23km/14mi (*services available at Boundary, Alaska*) and heads south along the valley of the Fortymile River. Tiny **Chicken**, Alaska (*food and fuel; www.chickenalaska.com*), offers frontier history. Wanting to name their camp "ptarmigan," miners settled on "chicken," it is said, because they could spell it! The Chicken Creek Cafe *(Airport Rd.)* serves up burgers and other fare. At **Tetlin Junction** take the Alaska Highway south to the Canadian border (⏰*set watches forward 1hr).*

Alaska Highway★★

491km/305mi from Alaska border to Whitehorse. Highway posts indicate the distance from Dawson Creek, BC, where the highway begins. Kilometres/miles shown here are in descending order to conform with these post readings.

North of the Canadian/US border, near Northway, Alaska, is the **Tetlin National Wildlife Refuge**, a 384,620ha/730,000-acre preserve of boreal forest, wetlands, lakes and glacial rivers *(Visitor Centre, milepost 1229, Alaska Hwy.;* ♿ ⏰*open mid-May–mid Sept daily 8am–4:30pm;* ☎*907-883-5312; http://tetlin.fws.gov).*
After crossing the Canada/US border *(KM1969/mi 1221),* the highway (⏰*caution: intermittent bumps)* passes through flat muskeg country and crosses the White and then the Donjek rivers. From the latter *(KM1810/mi 1125),* there is a **view** of the **St. Elias Mountains**.

Kluane Lake★★

Just before Burwash Landing *(KM1759/mi 1093),* the road approaches this vast lake, paralleling it 64km/40mi and offering fine **views★★**. Kluane [kloo-ON-ee] is fed by glaciers, the factor in its colour. To the south and west lie the **Kluane Ranges**, to the north and east the **Ruby Range**. In Burwash Landing, the **Kluane Museum of Natural History** is housed in a six-sided log building. **Dioramas★** of native wildlife line the interior (♿ ⏰*open mid-May–mid-Sept daily 9am–6:30pm;* ☜*$3.95;* ☎ *867-841-5561; www.yukon museums.ca).*

Kluane National Park Reserve★★

♿⏰*Park open year-round. Hiking, camping, rafting, fishing, cross-country skiing.* ☜*$15.70 for camping, park entry is free. Park office and Visitor Centre in Haines Junction; Visitor Centre also* near Sheep Mountain. ☎*877-852-3100. www.pc.gc.ca.* ⏰*Open mid-May–early-Sept daily 9am–5pm and by appointment rest of year. Limited 4-wheel-drive vehicle access to park's interior (streams must be forded). Arrangements to visit interior must be made in advance with park authorities. Sifton Air offers charters and tours year-round.* ☎*867-634-2916 or 888-634-2916, www.kluaneglacierairtours.com. TransNorth Helicopter offers heli-tours and charters year-round,* ☎*867-634-2177. www.tntaheli.com.*
From the Alaska Highway the Kluane Ranges (as high as 2,500m/8,000ft) can be seen. Behind them are the **Icefield Ranges**, which contain peaks exceeding 4,500m/15,000ft. Best known are **Mount St. Elias** (5,489m/18,008ft) and **Mount Logan** (5,959m/19,550ft), second in height only to Mount McKinley (6,194m/20,320ft) in Alaska, the highest point on the continent.
At KM 1707/mi 1061 the Alaska Highway passes **Tachal Dhal (Sheep Mountain)**, a rocky and barren peak so named for the white Dall sheep on its slopes. The Alaska Highway crosses the large **Slims River Delta** *(KM 1707–2/mi 1061–58).*

Haines Junction

KM 1635/mi1016.
At the junction of the Alaska and Haines (Route 3) highways, this community sits at the foot of the Auriol Range.
Haines Highway crosses the Chilkat Pass before entering Alaska. About 20km/12mi south of Haines Junction via Route 3, there is a **view★★** of **Kathleen Lake★★**. Returning to Haines Junction, drivers can continue to Whitehorse *(KM 1474/mi 916)* on the Alaska Highway.

Towards Haines Junction from Kluane National Park

© Gwen Cannon/MICHELIN

PRAIRIE PROVINCES

Alberta, Saskatchewan and Manitoba, known collectively as the Prairie Provinces, are often thought of as flat and monotonous. But there is something awe-inspiring about the wide open spaces, extensively cultivated, yet sparsely populated (just under 6 million people). In places, rivers have cut deep valleys into the soft soil of the prairie and in Alberta and Saskatchewan have formed the sculpted buttes of **badlands**. The countryside is a patchwork of colours: massive rectangles of wheat, green in the spring, turn gold before harvest. Flax has a small blue or white flower, canola a yellow one. Tall brightly painted **grain elevators**—the "cathedrals of the plains"—rise beside railway tracks. Above extends an infinite blue sky, dotted with puffy white clouds, sometimes black as a thunderstorm approaches.

🛈 **Info:** Each prairie province has a tourist office Travel Alberta, Tourism Saskatchewan, Travel Manitoba. 🖫 *See Practical Information section.*

▶ **Location:** The three Prairie Provinces cover a vast region of 1,963,00sq km/758,000sq mi (larger than Alaska), in the centre of Canada.

👁 **Don't Miss:** Try to take in at least one agricultural fair or stampede.

🕐 **Timing:** Allow a minimum one week to 10 days for a visit.

👥 **Kids:** The Royal Tyrrell Museum and the Calgary Zoo.

Geography

Diverse Region –The French word *prairie* was given to the large area of grassland in the interior of the North American continent where the bison, roaming in huge herds, were hunted by Plains Indians. In Canada the term "Prairies" now applies to all three provinces.

Semiarid Southwest – The southernmost part of Alberta and Saskatchewan is a relatively dry land of short grass. Widespread use of irrigation has brought much of the region into cultivation today. The native grasses provide pasture for cattle and this region, especially the vicinity of Cypress Hills.

Grain-Growing Crescent – To the north of the arid lands lies a crescent-shaped region of fertile soil, graced with more abundant rainfall. This is the grain belt, the prairie of many people's imagination. Prim farm buildings dot the enormous fields of wheat, barley,

Canola fields, Alberta

© Canadian Tourism Commission

canola and flax. The old grain elevators, easily visible for miles, serve as town landmarks.

Aspen Parkland – North of the wheat belt is another roughly crescent-shaped region, where trees grow in good soil and mixed farming flourishes. This is a region of rolling parkland, a transitional zone between the prairie and the forest of the north. Most inhabitants of the three provinces live in this region.

Boreal Forest and Tundra – The northern halves of the three provinces lie directly on the Precambrian rock of the Canadian Shield. This expanse is a pristine land of countless lakes, trees and rock outcroppings, dotted by small towns and First Nations communities.

Prairie "Steps" – Apart from deep valleys cut by rivers, the Prairies rise gradually in three main levels; sea level at Hudson Bay to nearly 1,200m/4,000ft west of the Rockies. The first step ends with the **Manitoba Escarpment**, which rises to 831m/2,726ft. Encompassing the flattest lands, the second step ends with the **Missouri Coteau** at 879m/2,883ft. The third step borders the Rockies. The Prairies are also broken by numerous ranges of small hills in the north and by the Cypress Hills and the Pembina Valley in the south.

Climate – The Prairies experience a climate of extremes; winter is generally long and cold; summer is short and hot. Precipitation is low (380-500mm/15-20in a year), sometimes arriving in the form of blizzards in winter and violent thunderstorms in summer. July is the driest and hottest month (mean maximum for Calgary is 24°C/76°F, Regina 27°C/81°F, Winnipeg 27°C/80°F). In the southwest winter is alleviated by the chinook winds, which blow warm air from the Pacific through the Rockies. In a few hours temperatures can rise as much as 28°C/82°F.

A Bit of History

First Nations of the Plains – The Assiniboine, Blackfoot, Cree, Gros Ventre and Sarcee First Nations Peoples lived almost exclusively on bison, which were driven over cliffs or stampeded into pounds. Their meat was often dried and made into **pemmican**—a nutritious mixture of pounded meat, animal fat and sometimes saskatoon berries—which could be preserved for up to a year. Bison hides were used to make moccasins, clothing and winter robes. Home was a **teepee**, a conical structure of poles (some almost 12m/40ft tall) covered with buffalo hides.The use of guns by First Nations and incoming homesteaders resulted in the gradual extinction of the great herds. By the 1880s European settlers had arrived and fenced the once-open prairie.

Fur Traders – Eager to reduce the long journey by canoe between present-day Montreal and Lake Superior, two traders, **Radisson** and **Groseilliers,** proposed quicker ways to transport furs to Europe via Hudson Bay. France showed little interest in the scheme, but Charles II of England granted a royal charter. The **Hudson's Bay Company** (HBC), as it became known, held sole right to trade in the vast watershed that drains into the bay. Forts and factories were established on its shores .

The Métis and the Creation of Manitoba – A consequence of the fur trade was the creation of a new ethnic group, the Métis—offspring of the First Nations women and French coureurs des bois (and later of Scots and English traders). Though mainly French-speaking Roman Catholics, the Métis preserved the traditional lifestyle of their native forebears. The first real threat to them came with the arrival of settlers along the Red River in 1812. In 1870 the situation escalated when the new Dominion of Canada decided to take over the vast lands of the Hudson's Bay Company. The Métis saw their traditional life disappearing with the arrival of more settlers. The Métis turned to 25-year-old **Louis Riel**, who set up his own provisional government to recognise Métis rights. Riel gained no sympathy from English Métis and other settlers. After foiling a plot to assassinate him, Riel executed an adventurer from Ontario, **Thomas Scott,** an act that he was long to regret.

PRACTICAL INFORMATION
GETTING THERE

BY AIR – Major airlines such as **Air Canada** (℘*514-393-3333 or 888-247-2262; www.aircanada.com*) service Calgary, Edmonton, Regina, Saskatoon and Winnipeg. Regional carriers include Westjet Airlines (℘*888-937-8538, Canada/US; www.westjet.com*).

BY TRAIN – VIA **Rail Canada** has regularly scheduled service to all three provinces (℘*514-989-2626 or 888-842-7245, Canada/US; www.viarail.ca*).

BY BUS – **Greyhound** services communities across the Prairies: ℘*800-661-8747 (Canada),* ℘*800-231-2222 (US). www.greyhound.ca.*

GENERAL INFORMATION
ACCOMMODATIONS AND VISITOR INFORMATION

The government tourist offices produce annually updated guides listing approved accommodations. **Travel Alberta** (*Edmonton;* ℘*780-427-4321 or 800-252-3782, Canada/US; www.travelalberta.com*).

Travel Manitoba (*21 Forks Market Rod., Winnipeg;* ℘*204-927-7800 or 800-665-0040, Canada/US; www.travelmanitoba.com*).

Tourism Saskatchewan (*#189-1621 Albert St., Regina;* ℘*306-787-9600 or 877-237-2273, Canada/US; www. tourismsaskatchewan.com*).

Most major hotel chains have facilities in these provinces. Independent hotels and B&B lodgings can be found along major routes. **Farm vacations** are offered in all three provinces. Alberta in particular boasts many **guest ranches**.

ROAD REGULATIONS – Unless otherwise posted, speed limits on provincial highways are: Alberta 100km/h (60mph), or 90km/h (55mph) in parks; Manitoba 100km/h (60mph); Saskatchewan from 90-110km/h (55-70mph). Use of **seat belts** is compulsory.

TIME ZONES – Alberta: Mountain Standard Time. Manitoba: Central Standard Time. Both observe Daylight Saving Time from the 2nd Sun in March to 1st Sun in November. Most of Saskatchewan remains on Central Standard Time all year. Some border communities keep the same time as the neighboring province all year.

TAXES – In addition to the national 5% GST, Manitoba levies a 8% and Saskatchewan a 5% retail sales tax on all items. In Alberta there is a 4% hotel tax, the 5% GST, but no provincial sales or restaurant tax.

LIQUOR LAWS – The legal drinking age is 18 in Manitoba and Alberta, 19 in Saskatchewan. In Manitoba and Saskatchewan, liquor and wine can be purchased only in government liquor stores and approved retail outlets. In Alberta liquor can be bought in privately owned liquor stores. In isolated parts of the North where no government stores exist, grocery stores are licensed.

PROVINCIAL HOLIDAYS

Family Day (Alberta only) –
3rd Monday in February
Louis Riel Day (Manitoba only)
3rd Monday in February
Saskatchewan Day (Sask. only)
3rd Monday in February

RECREATION
OUTDOOR ACTIVITIES

Water sports are popular because of the many lakes and river systems. Saskatchewan offers **white-water rafting,** especially along the Clearwater River, and Alberta offers rafting trips. The region has many national and provincial parks, offering hiking, biking, horse trails and campsites in summer, and downhill and cross-country skiing, snowshoeing and snowmobiling in winter. Wildlife viewing includes whooping cranes in Saskatchewan, polar bears in Manitoba and bighorn sheep in Alberta.Northern Manitoba and Saskatchewan are famous for their fly-in fishing lodges. Lac la Ronge in Saskatchewan is well known for sportfishing. Anglers and hunters must have a valid license, obtainable in most sporting-goods stores. Fishing and hunting guidebooks are available free from provincial tourist offices.

SPECIAL EXCURSIONS

Birding trips *(May–Jun)* and **beluga-whale** *(Jul–Aug)* and **polar-bear** *(Oct–Nov)* watching in Churchill, MB, are offered by such companies as **Natural Habitat Adventures** *(℘303-449-3711 or 800-543-8917; www.nathab.com)*, or **Sea North Tours** *(℘204-675-2195; www.seanorthtours.com)*. Contact Travel Manitoba *(℅p168)* for a complete list of adventure tour operators. Paddling trips on Saskatchewan's historic **Churchill River** are popular *(℘877-511-2726; www.churchillrivercanoe.com)*. Trail rides and horse-pack trips are exciting options. Contact **Travel Alberta** *(℅p168)* for specifics.

PRINCIPAL FESTIVALS

Feb	**Northern Manitoba Trappers' Festival**, *The Pas MB*
	Festival du Voyageur, *Saint-Boniface MB*
	Winter Festival, *Prince Albert SK*
Jun	**Manitoba Summer Fair**, *Brandon MB*
	Western Canada Farm Progress Show, *Regina SK*
	Red River Exhibition, *Winnipeg MB*
Jul	**Folk Festival**, *Winnipeg MB*
	Manitoba Threshermen's Reunion, *Austin MB*
	Calgary Exhibition and Stampede, *Calgary AB*
	Klondike Days, *Edmonton AB*
	Craven Country Jamboree, *Craven SK*
Aug	**Saskatoon Exhibition**, *Saskatoon SK*
	Manitoba Highland Gathering, *Selkirk MB*
	National Ukrainian Festival, *Dauphin MB*
	Pioneer Days, *Steinbach MB*
	Buffalo Days, *Regina SK*
	Whoop-up Days and Rodeo, *Lethbridge AB*
	Icelandic Fest., *Gimli MB*
	Corn and Apple Festival, *Morden MB*
	Folklorama, *Winnipeg MB*
	Folkfest, *Saskatoon SK*
Nov	**Canadian Western Agribition**, *Regina SK*

Watching beluga whales near Churchill

Nevertheless his plea on behalf of his people was heard. In July 1870 the new province of Manitoba was created.

A Human Mosaic – Treaties negotiated with the residents of the region proved unsuccessful, as the Northwest Rebellion of 1885 showed. Some means of enforcing law and order was needed. In 1873 the **North West Mounted Police** force was created. Additionally, land had to be distributed. The **Dominion Lands Act** of 1872 allowed prospective homesteaders to register for a quarter section (65ha/160 acres). When construction of the **Canadian Pacific Railway** was completed in 1885, the population of the Prairies was about 150,000; by 1914 it had reached 1.5 million.

The prospect of free land attracted inhabitants of an overcrowded Europe and religious refugees. The Canadian Government under Prime Minister **Sir Wilfrid Laurier** advertised the Prairies all over the world. Millions indeed came. The provinces of **Alberta** and **Saskatchewan** were created in 1905.

The population of the provinces today, as measured by the 2016 Statscan estimate, is nearly 6.4 million (Alberta 4,233,933; Manitoba 1,318,128; and Saskatchewan 1,115,632).

ECONOMY

Agriculture – Between 1876 and 1915, the land where the fur trade once reigned supreme suddenly developed a wheat economy. In 1842 David Fife of Ontario developed a strain of wheat that later proved ideal for cultivation on the prairies. Called **Red Fife** for its rich colour, it is the ancestor of all the strains used today.

Today about 80 percent of Canada's agricultural land is in Alberta, Manitoba and Saskatchewan. Wheat, canola and flax are major crops. Mixed farming—including beef farming—and poultry, egg and pork production are also important.

Cattle Country – Although grain is the major economic staple of the Prairies, ranching is a secondary industry. With so much open land, Alberta boasts nearly 6 million head of cattle, or 40 percent of Canada's total. Beef is that province's number one agri-food export. Southern Alberta and Saskatchewan are "cowboy country," and rodeos abound, including the internationally renowned Calgary Stampede.

Manufacturing – Although agriculture is Saskatchewan's top industry, it is second to manufacturing in Manitoba and third after petrochemical production and mining in Alberta. Manitoba has a broad-based manufacturing sector, which includes food processing, equipment, printing, clothing and furniture. Alberta's petrochemical production is surpassed by Quebec and Ontario.

Riches Below the Earth – Alberta produces most of Canada's oil and **natural gas**. Its **Athabasca Tar Sands** are said to be the largest known hydrocarbon accumulation in the world. Canada's fastest growing community in 2014 was Fort McMurray in northern Alberta, opening a completely new airport terminal in the same year to handle 1.5 million passengers. After the huge forest fires of 2016, the town is now in permanent rebuild mode.

Saskatchewan is the largest producer of **potash**—used for fertilizer— in the world. Oil and **sodium sulphate** are found in Lloydminster, Swift Current and Estevan.

The giant **zinc, cadmium** and **copper** field at Flin Flon, Manitoba, was established in 1915. Copper was discovered near Lynn Lake, Manitoba, and **gold** in the Lake Athabasca area of Saskatchewan. **Uranium** was found in the late 1940s in Saskatchewan, and in the 1960s the giant **nickel** field of Thompson, Manitoba, came into production.

Alberta Badlands★★★

Alberta

The meltwaters of the last continental glacier eroded a deep valley across Southern Alberta, through which the Red Deer River now flows, and exposed rocks formed during the Cretaceous period (64 million-140 million years ago). This area is the Alberta Badlands, a striking panorama of steep bluffs and fluted gullies. In Cretaceous times, the area was a subtropical lowland inhabited by dinosaurs; it now holds one of the world's richest deposits of fossils. Several hundred complete skeletons have been unearthed since the first discovery in 1884.

DINOSAUR TRAIL

51km/32mi circular drive. See map.
Connecting the sights of the Drumheller area, this loop on the plain above Red Deer River offers good views of the badlands.

Drumheller★

Visitor centre 60 1st Ave. W. ⊙Open Jul–Aug daily 9am–9pm; rest of the year daily 10am–5:30pm. ℘866-823-8100. www.traveldrumheller.com.
Dominating the entrance to the visitor centre is a 25m/86ft-high fiber-

▪ **Info:** Information Centre, 60 1st Ave. W., Drumheller. ℘866-823-8100. www.traveldrumheller.com and www.canadian badlands.com.

◑ **Location:** Drumheller is 138km/86mi northeast of Calgary. The Dinosaur Trail extends northwest along both sides of the Red Deer River.

P **Parking:** All of the attractions along the Dinosaur Trail have parking areas.

⊘ **Don't Miss:** The Royal Tyrrell Museum and the Hoodoos.

◔ **Timing:** Give yourself a half day to tour the Dinosaur Trail and visit the Royal Tyrell Museum. Then drive southeast along the Red Deer River to see the Hoodoos and Dinosaur Provincial Park.

▲▴ **Kids:** The Royal Tyrrell Museum is a must for children, and the Dinosaur Trail offers weird rock formations holding fossil remains.

Red Deer River Valley, Badlands

© Don Johnston/age fotostock

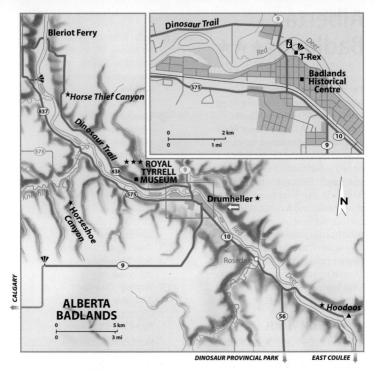

glass replica of a *Tyrannosaurus rex* that contains a stairwell leading to a viewing platform (☜$3.*Same hours as visitor centre*). The **view★** of the river valley is worth the climb *(106 steps)*.

The centre serves as the departure point for bus tours of Dinosaur Provincial Park (☝*see below*).

Royal Tyrrell Museum

© Canadian Tourism Commission/Travel Alberta

Badlands Historical Centre
335 1st St. E. ♿🕐*Open Jun–Sept daily 10am–6pm. Rest of the year by appointment.* ☜$4.
☎403-823-2593.

The centre features exhibits, interactive displays and a **collection** of dinosaur fossils, Indian artifacts and oddities.

👥 Royal Tyrrell Museum★★★
6km/4mi northwest of Drumheller by Hwy. 838 (North Dinosaur Trail). 🍴♿
🕐*Open mid-May–Aug daily 9am–9pm. Rest of the year Tue–Sun 10am–5pm.*
🕐*Closed Jan 1, Dec 24-25.* ☜$18 *(child $10).* ☎403-823-7707 or 888-440-4240.
www.tyrrellmuseum.com.

This splendid museum, opened in 1985 and operated by the Alberta government, is one of the largest in the world devoted to the study of life-forms from past geological periods.

Highlight are the enormous **Dinosaur Halls 1 and 2**, where the huge *Tyrannosaurus rex*, *Albertosaurus*, the armored *Stegosaurus* and smaller birdlike dinosaurs can be seen. The **Devonian Reef**

Hunting Fossils

Look for fossils where sedimentary rocks are exposed such as in quarries, along road cuts, cliffs and seashores. **Always get permission** from local authorities or landowners before you begin your search.

Be aware of legal restrictions: in Alberta, it is illegal to remove fossils from provincial and federal parks or to sell or take fossils out of the province without a government certificate. Check with the Royal Tyrrell Museum regarding excavation permits. Whether surface collecting or excavating, you need a map, compass, magnifying glass, notebook, small paintbrush, knife, trowel and geological hammer. Safety gear includes gloves, goggles and a hard hat. Take paper towels or newspaper to wrap the fossil and plastic bags for carrying it. Give the specimen a number and handle it properly to maintain the scientific information held within. Record the location and date of your find in your notebook. Also describe the colour and texture of the rocks in which the fossil was found (e.g., hard limestone block). In Drumheller, you can buy fossils and related materials at the **Badlands Historical Centre** or **The Fossil Shop** *(61 Bridge St. ; ℘403-823-6774; www.thefossilshop.com)* or the **Museum Shop** in the Tyrrell Museum. The Tyrrell offers day-long and week-long field research courses *(You must be age 18 or older; contact the museum for details).*

takes visitors back more than 3.90 billion years to the dawn of life on earth. The **Ice Ages and Time Tunnel** shows a time when sheets of ice a mile thick covered Canada. The recently found **Eotricerotops xerinsuleris** is on display. Check out their online community offerings as well.

Dinosaur Trail provides a view of the badlands from **Horse Thief Canyon★**, with its rounded, almost barren hills stretching to the river. The trail crosses the river by the **Bleriot cable ferry** and climbs to a fine **view★** of the valley.

ADDITIONAL SIGHTS
Horseshoe Canyon★
18km/11mi southwest of Drumheller by Rte. 9.
Paths leading through the hillocks to the river provide some of the best **views** of the badlands in the area.

Hoodoos★
17km/10mi southeast of Drumheller by Rte. 10.
These strange rock formations illustrate the work of erosion in the valley.

Dinosaur Provincial Park★★★
174km/108mi southeast of Drumheller by Rte. 56 & Trans-Can Hwy. east to Brooks. Take Hwy. 873 for 10km/6mi, then turn right on Hwy. 544, and left on Hwy. 551. Open daily year-round. Visitor Centre open mid-May–Labour Day daily 9am–4pm, Fri & Sat til 7pm. Rest of year hours vary. ℘403-378-4342 ext.235. http://tpr.alberta.ca.

Set in the most spectacular part of Red Deer River Valley and the richest fossil area, which UNESCO placed on the World Heritage list in 1979. Immediately upon entrance to the park, an excellent **viewpoint★★★** overlooks nearly 3,000ha/7,000 acres of badlands cut by the Red Deer River. The road then descends to the valley.

A **circular drive** *(5km/3mi)* takes the visitor through this wild and desolate landscape. At several points, short walks lead to dinosaur bones preserved where they were found. Most of the park, however, is accessible only by a special **bus tour★** *(2hr; departs from Drumheller Visitor Centre mid-May–Labour Day daily 9am–noon & 1pm–4pm; 1-day advance reservations required; ⬿$14; ℘403-378-4344)* or by **conducted hikes** *(reservations ℘403-378-4344).* ♿*Wheelchair access to bus by arrangement and on some trails; ask ahead of time.*

Austin★

Manitoba

Set in the centre of a rich agricultural region, this pleasant rural community is renowned for its collection of operating vintage farm machinery and an annual reunion celebration.

SIGHT
👥 Manitoba Agricultural Museum★
On Hwy. 34, 3km/2mi south of Trans-Can Hwy (Austin Corner).
♿🕐*Open May–Sept daily 9am–5pm.*
👓*$15 (child $8).* 📞*204-637-2354.*
www.ag-museum.mb.ca.

This museum has a splendid collection of "prairie giants"—steam tractors, threshing machines and the cumbersome gasoline machines that replaced them in the early 20C. Every July these machines are paraded and demonstrated at the Manitoba **Threshermen's Reunion**, held on the grounds of the museum. The festival has threshing contests, square dancing, races and children's rides. Depicting life in the late 1800s, the homesteaders' village includes log houses, churches and a school, each staffed with a costumed guide.

ℹ️ **Info:** Manitoba Agricultural Museum, 📞204-637-2354. www.ag-museum.mb.ca
🧭 **Location:** Austin lies 123km/76mi west of Winnipeg on Hwy 1.
🅿️ **Parking:** Museum parking lot.
👁️ **Don't Miss:** The Threshermen's Reunion, if possible; the Homesteaders Village.
🕐 **Timing:** Nearby Brandon, MB is a good-sized town (pop 46,016) with accommodations and restaurants.

The Battlefords★

Saskatchewan

Surrounded by rolling country, the twin communities of **Battleford** and **North Battleford** face each other across the valley of the North Saskatchewan River. North Battleford has a fine **site** overlooking the river.

A BIT OF HISTORY

Fur traders established posts on the Battleford (south) side of the river in the 18C, but it was not until 1874 that the first settlers arrived. A North West Mounted Police post was established in 1876, and the settlement was chosen as the home of the government of the Northwest Territories. Then the Canadian Pacific Railway Co. routed its line to the south, and in 1883 Battleford lost its status as territorial capital when government offices were moved from

▶ **Population:** 18,405.
ℹ️ **Info:** 📞306-445-2000 or 800-243-0394. www.battlefordstourism.com.
🧭 **Location:** The Battlefords lie along the Yellowhead Highway (Hwy. 16), 153km/96mi northwest of Saskatoon.
🅿️ **Parking:** The attractions provide ample parking.
👁️ **Don't Miss:** Fort Battleford and the heritage village at the Western Development Museum.
🕐 **Timing:** Fort Battleford will take 2-3hrs to visit, especially with children.
👥 **Kids:** At Fort Battleford, children can dress up and take part in mock police drills.

Curling: Canada's Other Ice Sport

More than a million Canadians enjoy this winter activity, which became an Olympic sport at Calgary in 1988, and both the men's and women's teams won gold medals at Sochi in 2014. Here's how the game works:

During 8 to 10 rounds ("ends"), two four-person teams (wearing rubber-soled shoes, not ice skates) take turns "throwing" their 20kg/42lb granite stones along the ice toward a **bull's-eye** at the opposite end of a 42m/138ft by 4.3m/14ft rink. "Sweepers" use brooms to alter the ice in front of a teammate's stone in order to increase its speed or help determine its path. The captains signal their players to knock the opponent's stones away from the target area. A point is awarded for each stone resting closer to the centre mark than the nearest of the opponent's stones. Curling probably developed in the 16C in **Scotland**, and was introduced to Canada in the 18C by Scottish troops. Clubs were established by 1807, and the Canadian Curling Association was formed in 1935. **Manitoba** is Canada's curling centre. Many clubs have a visitors' viewing gallery, and important matches are televised. 🖽 *Canadian Curling Assn. www.curling.ca.*

Battleford to Pile O'Bones Creek (later Regina). During the Northwest Rebellion of 1885, Battleford was looted and burned by Poundmaker Crees. The death knell sounded in 1903 when the Canadian Northern Railway was built along the opposite side of the river, creating North Battleford, which grew as Battleford shrank.

Today the Battlefords, convenient to several highways, including the Yellowhead Highway, are important service and distribution centres.

SIGHTS
👥 Fort Battleford★

Central Ave., Battleford.
♿🕐*Open mid-May–Labour Day daily 10am–5pm.* ⊛ *$3.90 (child $1.90).*
📞*306-937-2621. www.pc.gc.ca.*
This North West Mounted Police post, attacked during the Northwest Rebellion, was abandoned in 1924. Today restored, this Parks Canada National Historic Site provides insight into police life in the late 19C.

The **commanding officers' residence**, the **officers' quarters** and guardhouse have been renovated to reflect their 1880s appearance. The **interpretation centre** provides an account of the rebellion.

Children should ask about Club Parka and membership benefits.

Western Development Museum★

Highway 16 & 40, North Battleford.
♿🕐*Open Apr–Dec daily 9am–5pm. Rest of the year Tue-Sun 10am–5pm (closed Mon Jan–Mar).* ⊛ *$10.*
📞 *306-445-8033. www.wdm.ca.*
This branch of the Western Development Museum—one of four in the province (the others are in Moose Jaw, Saskatoon and Yorkton)—displays agricultural machinery and domestic artifacts from the 1920s.

Outside, a **heritage farm and village** of 1925 is set out with houses and churches reflecting the diverse origins of the peoples who settled this province. Closed mid-Oct-May.

ALLEN SAPP GALLERY

1 Railway Ave. E., North Battleford.
📞*306-445-1760. www.allensapp.com.*
Images of the Northern Plains Cree painted by Cree artist **Allen Sapp** (1928-2015) are on view in a large building located just off Highway 16 (Yellowhead Highway).

A descendant of Chief Poundmaker, Sapp was born on an Indian reserve south of the city. His paintings vividly record Cree traditions and the rugged frontier life. Limited and open editions of his prints are on sale in the gift shop.

Calgary★★

Alberta

Calgary is Canada's fastest-growing metropolis, its prosperity due largely to Alberta's vast oil wealth, favourable business climate (no sales tax) and importance as a transportation hub. Blessed with a pleasant climate (moderate rainfall, low humidity, lots of sunshine and a moderately cold winter, tempered by warm chinook winds), this tourist mecca is renowned for its Stampede and remembered fondly as host of the 1988 Winter Olympic Games.

A BIT OF HISTORY

Origins – In 1875 a North West Mounted Police post was built on this site and named Fort Calgary by Col. James Macleod, police commander in the Northwest, for his home in Scotland. Then, in the 1880s, the Canadian Pacific Railway Co. routed its railway through Calgary, bringing a huge influx of settlers to the lush grazing lands of the region. The Dominion Lands Act encouraged the movement of cattle herds northward from the US. Well-to-do Englishmen arrived to establish ranches. **"Black Gold"** – The discovery of oil in 1914 at Turner Valley, southwest of Calgary, marked the birth of western Canada's petroleum industry. Then in 1947 a great discovery was made at Leduc, launching Calgary on its phenomenal growth. As well, Calgary has become a financial centre, second only to Toronto in attracting corporate head offices.

DOWNTOWN *See map.*

Attractive, glass-fronted high rises such as the Calgary Tower as well as the brown marble headquarters of **Petro-Canada** dominate Calgary's glittering skyline; a **pedestrian mall** stretches along 8th Avenue. Most of downtown lies along a network of sky bridges that allow pedestrians to escape winter's cold.

The easterly stretch of the 8th Avenue mall, known locally as the Stephen Avenue Walk, is filled with early-1900s

▶ **Population:** 1,235,171.

ℹ **Info:** Tourist Office 200-238 11 Ave SE. ☎403-263-8510 or 800-661-1678. www.tourismcalgary.com.

▶ **Location:** Calgary is set in the foothills of the Canadian Rockies, at the confluence of the Bow and Elbow rivers. The Trans-Canada Highway passes here.

🅿 **Parking:** Parking meters operate from 6am–5pm daily; rates range from $1 to $3.50 per hour. The Light Rail Transit (LRT) is free in downtown Calgary.

👁 **Don't Miss:** The Glenbow Museum and the Calgary Zoo.

🕐 **Timing:** To attend the Stampede, book up to a year ahead.

👫 **Kids:** Heritage Park and the Bar-U Ranch are surefire winners.

Alberta sandstone buildings now converted to small shops and cafes. At 7th Avenue and Macleod Trail SE stands the 1907 Romanesque Revival city hall building. The tiered, blue reflecting-glass structure east of city hall is Calgary's **Municipal Building,** around a 12-storey atrium. Across 2nd Street SE lies the **Arts Commons centre for the performing arts**.

The CORE Shopping Centre features the only indoor city park, an indoor greenhouse called the **Devonian Gardens★**, with fountains, sculptures and 20,000 tropical plants (♿🕐*open daily check for times; ☎403-441-4940).*

Glenbow Museum★★

130 9th Ave. SE, in the TELUS Convention Centre. ✕♿🕐 *Open daily 9am–5pm.* 🕐*Closed Mon & Dec 25.* 💳 *$16.* ☎*403-268-4100. www.glenbow.org.* This 8-storey building houses western Canada's largest museum, opened in

Chuckwagon racing

© Shane Kuhn/Calgary Stampede/Travel Alberta

The Calgary Stampede

Hailed as "the Greatest Outdoor Show on Earth," the **Calgary Stampede** is a grand 10-day event held in early July that attracts hundreds of thousands of spectators and competitors every year *(reservations recommended)*. Almost the entire population of Calgary dons western garb (boots, jeans and hats) and joins the festivities. There are flapjack breakfasts, street dances, and a huge parade in the city. Livestock shows and the famous **rodeo** and **chuckwagon races** are held in Stampede Park, where a lengthy midway features rides, games, live musical entertainment and food galore. Invented in Calgary, the chuckwagon races recall the wagon races held by cowboys after a roundup and are an exciting part of the stampede. Near the South Gate, the Indian Village showcases several colourful teepees and offers native arts and crafts for sale. *℘403-261-0101 or 800-661-1260 (Canada/US). www.calgarystampede.com.*

1976. Galleries on three floors contain displays that encompass the human history of Alberta. A highlight is the **Nitsitapiisinni Gallery** *(third floor)*, which reflects the colourful history of the Blackfoot First Nations tribe. Exhibits focus on the fur trade, the North West Mounted Police, missionaries, the Canadian Pacific Railway, farming and ranching, Métis life, and the discovery of oil. The newest exhibit, **Mavericks: An Incorrigible History of Alberta,** looks at the past 100 years in the Calgary area.

Calgary Tower★★
In Palliser Square, 101 9th Ave. SW. ♿⏱*Open daily 9am–9pm.* ⏱*Closed Dec 25.* ✕🅿 ⚬$18. ℘403-266-7171. *www.calgarytower.com.*
The observation deck at this 190m/626ft high tower provides a great **view★★** of the city and its site. To the west the snowy peaks of the Rockies rise above

rolling, arid foothills. The slowly evolving Sky 360 Restaurant *(top floor)* offers a panorama of the city.

ADDITIONAL SIGHTS
Crescent Road Viewpoint
Rising above the Bow River and Prince's Island Park, this road offers a fine view of downtown and the snow-clad Rockies.

Fort Calgary
806 9th Ave. SE. ♿⏱*Open daily 9am–5pm.* ⏱*Closed Jan 1, Good Friday, Dec 24–26 & 31.* ✕🅿 ⚬$12. ℘403-290-1875. *www.fortcalgary.com.*
An **interpretation centre** on the site of the original North West Mounted Police post recounts the history of the city. The adjacent **Deane House** (⚅*see Addresses*), former home of the NWMP superintendent, is now a restaurant. A pedestrian bridge allows access to St. George's Island and the zoo.

Watching an otter, Calgary Zoo

© Kelly Hofer Studios/Tourism Calgary/Travel Alberta

👥 Calgary Zoo ★★

1300 Zoo Rd. NE. ♿🕐*Open year-round daily 9am–5pm.* 🕐*Closed Dec 25.* ✕🅿️👓*$23 (child $15)* 📞*403-232-9300, or 800-588-9993. www.calgaryzoo.com.*
Located partly on an island in the Bow River, this fine zoo houses animals and a tropical greenhouse. The **prehistoric park** re-creates western Canada as it looked when dinosaurs roamed. **Canadian Wilds**, adjacent to the park, reproduces habitats of western Canada. Jungle, savannah and other terrain make up habitats in **African Savannah.**

Grain Academy ★

In the BMO Centre, Stampede Park. 20 Roundup Way. 🅿️ *($10/vehicle)* ♿🕐*Open year-round Mon–Fri 10am–4pm.* 🕐*Closed major holidays.* 📞*403-263-4594. www.grainacademymuseum.com.*
This museum presents a working model of a prairie grain elevator, a model railway and a film *(12min)* about grain. It sits near the 20,240-seat **Scotiabank-Saddledome ★**, constructed in 1983 *(555 Saddledome Rise;* 🕐*open year-round;* 🐾*free tours on non-event days with reservations* 📞*403-777-4646;* 📞*403-777-1375; www.scotiabanksaddledome.com).*

👥 Heritage Park ★

16km/10mi southwest of downtown. Take Macleod Trail SW. 1900 Heritage Dr. SW. ✕🅿️🕐*Open mid-May–mid-Oct daily 9:30am–5pm.* 👓*$26.25 (child $13.50) (rides $4 extra).* 📞*403-268-8500. www.heritagepark.ca.*
Occupying a pleasant site overlooking Glenmore Reservoir, this 26ha/64-acre park re-creates prairie life of a bygone

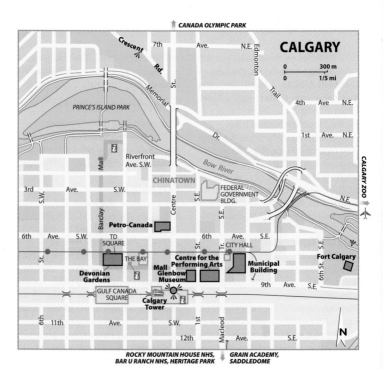

🏔 CANADA OLYMPIC PARK

CALGARY

0   300 m
0   1/5 mi

PRINCE'S ISLAND PARK

Crescent Rd.
7th   Ave.   N.E.
Memorial   Dr.
Edmonton Trail
4th   Ave.   N.E.
1st   Ave.   N.E.

Riverfront Ave. S.W.

Bow River

CHINATOWN

FEDERAL GOVERNMENT BLDG.

Mall

3rd   Ave.   S.W.   S.W.

Barclay   Centre

Petro-Canada

6th   Ave.   S.W.   6th   Ave.   S.E.   CALGARY ZOO

TD SQUARE   CITY HALL

THE BAY   Centre for the Performing Arts   Municipal Building   Fort Calgary

Devonian Gardens   Mall   Glenbow Museum   9th   Ave.   S.E.

GULF CANADA SQUARE   Calgary Tower

6th   11th   Ave.   S.W.

Macleod

12th   Ave.   S.E.

N

ROCKY MOUNTAIN HOUSE NHS, BAR U RANCH NHS, HERITAGE PARK   GRAIN ACADEMY, SADDLEDOME

Heritage Park

© JTB Photo Communications, Inc./age fotostock

era with a pioneer community and a reconstructed Hudson's Bay Company post. The turn-of-the-19C town includes a church, general store, bakery, post office and other buildings.

A **steam train** gives tours, a replica **paddle wheeler** sails on the reservoir *(every 35mi)*, and the antique **midway** has fun rides. New attractions are an 1893 railway station and Gasoline Alley, complete with vintage cars and a heritage garage.

Canada Olympic Park

12km/7mi west by Trans-Can Hwy. 88 Canada Olympic Rd. SW. ✕ & 🅿 🕐 *Open daily & times vary.* 🕐 *Closed Dec 25.* 🕮 *Prices vary (park passport $25).* ✆ *403-247-5452. www.winsport.ca.*

This large hub facility for **WinSport's Winter Sports Institute** training and competition was developed to host ski-jumping, luge, bobsled and free-style-skiing events during the 1988 Winter Olympic Games. In summer, a chair lift provides access to the 90-meter ski-jump tower; one ride simulates a ski jump. The park is home to the **Canada Sports Hall of Fame Museum** ($12).

EXCURSIONS
👥 Bar U Ranch National Historic Site★★

92km/57mi south of Calgary via Rtes. 2 South (Macleod Trail), 22X West and 22 South. & 🕐 *Open mid-May–late Sept daily 9am–5pm.* ✕ 🕮 *$7.80 (child $3.90).*

Bar U Café closed Tue/Wed. ✆ *403-395-2212 or 888-773-8888 (Canada/US). www.pc.gc.ca.*

In operation from 1882 to 1950, this working ranch was once the epitome of Alberta ranching. The Parks Canada National Historic Site preserves early 20C ranch buildings, including an ice house, large barns and the ranch post office. Visitors can ride in buckboard wagons and watch demonstrations of ranchhand activities. Check Google Street View to see ranch up close. Highway 541, which intersects Route 22 north of the ranch, offers a spectacular 210km/130mi loop **drive★★** to the west to return to Calgary. Climbing into the Rockies, the road becomes Route 40, and traverses Kananaskis Country, a spectacular reserve.

Rocky Mountain House National Historic Site★

6 km west of Rocky Mountain House on Highway 11A. (7km/4mi). & 🕐 *Open mid-May–Labour Day daily 10am–5pm. Rest of Sept–early Oct Mon–Fri 10am–5pm.* 🕮 *$3.90.* ✆ *403-845-2412. www.pc.gc.ca.*

On the banks of the North Saskatchewan River, this post, founded in 1799, was David Thompson's headquarters for exploring western Canada. Only two chimneys remain, but trails interpret the life of a fur trader. A reconstructed **York boat** shows how furs were floated downriver. The **visitor centre** exhibits artifacts excavated on the site.

ADDRESSES

🛏 STAY

$ Westways B&B – *216 25th Ave. SW.* 📞*403-229-1758 or 866-846-7038. www.westways.ab.ca. 5 rooms.* 🅿️ ☕. Built in 1912 in the Arts and Crafts style, this pleasant inn is a 20min walk from downtown. All rooms come with a private bath and high-speed Internet connection. For couples, either of the two largest rooms—each with a king bed and gas fireplace—is more than adequate. Copious breakfast included.

$$ Inglewood B&B – *1006-8th Ave. SE.,* 📞*403-262-6570. www.inglewoodbreakfast.com. 3 rooms.* 🅿️ ☕. A pleasant backyard along the Bow River and simply furnished rooms with private baths make this bed-and-breakfast lodging a good choice for travellers looking for a simple alternative to a regular hotel. The property is within easy walking distance of Stampede Park and other major attractions.

$$$ Hotel Arts – *119 12th Ave. SW.* 📞*403-266-4611 or 800-661-9378. www.hotelarts.ca. 185* pet-friendly *rooms and suites.* 🍴♿🅿️☕. Rooms in this renovated chic, high-rise hotel are decorated by local artists and designers and equipped with sleek furnishings and flat-screen TVs. The remodeled Raw Bar is an example of Vietmodern, a hip spot for sushi and martinis. A fitness centre and an outdoor pool complete the amenities.

$$$$ Fairmont Palliser – *133-9th Ave. SW.* 📞*403-262-1234 or 866-540-4477. www.fairmont.com. 405 rooms.* 🍴♿🅿️☕. Although not as conspicuous as its famous sister properties in the Canadian Rockies, this historic, 15-storey hotel is an elegant oasis amid Calgary's urban bustle. The Alberta sandstone landmark (1914) sits close to the financial district, attracting business travellers as well as vacationers. Many rooms are on the small side, but each comes with plush duvets and bathrobes, as well as modern conveniences such as high-speed Internet access.

$$$$ Kensington Riverside Inn – *1126 Memorial Dr. NW.* 📞*403-228-4442 or 877-313-3733. www.kensingtonriversideinn.com. 19 rooms.* 🍴♿🅿️ ☕. Situated in the Kensington district across from downtown, this somewhat tired boutique hotel offers perks such as Egyptian cotton sheets, heated towel bars and polar fleece bathrobes. Rooms feature high ceilings and some have private balconies, garden patios or gas fireplaces. Rates include evening hors d'oeuvres, free local calls, wireless Internet, a daily newspaper and a gourmet breakfast in the AAA 4-Diamond rated Chef's Table, with patio & Fireside Room. Interior parking.

🍴 EAT

$ Diner Deluxe – *804 Edmonton Trail NE.* ♿📞*403-276-5499. www.deluxediner.com.* **Canadian.** Piled-high, all-day breakfasts (opens at 7:30am), fun decoration and friendly staff are the reasons for long lines outside the door. Just north of downtown, the family-run diner offers comfort food from omelettes and organic chicken sausages at brunch to white-cheddar baked macaroni and cheese at dinner. Try their Breakfast Poutine.

$$ Bottle Screw Bill's Pub/Buzzards Restaurant & Bar – *140-10th Ave. SW.* ♿📞*403-263-7900. www.bottlescrewbill.com.* **Pub Food**. A rustic interior decorated with authentic ranching relics and a contemporary menu of western specialties make this eatery a popular spot. Whether dining on Angus beef, Malay pork curry, or Bill's Nachos, this pub/resto is memorable.

$$ Deane House – *806 9th Ave. SE. Lunch, dinner & Weekend Brunch.* ♿📞*403-290-1875. www.fortcalgary.ab.ca.* **Contemporary**. Built in 1906 for the commanding officer of the North West Mounted Police, this two-storey wooden house is perfect for a light lunch after visiting adjacent Fort Calgary or the zoo. Following a renovation completed in 2014, their innovative wood-fired grilled Albacore, Okanagan Dent Corn Polenta, and Tasting Menu, are even sweeter than ever.

$$ Thai Sa-On – *351 10th Ave. SW.* 📞*403-264-3526. www.thai-sa-on.com.* **Thai.** The diversity and complexity of Thai cuisine make for an extensive menu, but everything at this unpretentious, family-run restaurant is authentically fresh and flavourful. Hearty eaters love the whole snapper, spiced and served with savory vegetables and coconut rice. Vegetarians can choose from the likes of pad paq tua, a peanut-based curry.

$$$ The Ranche – *15979 Bow Bottom Trail SE.* ♿ ✆*403-476-1310. www.bvrrestaurant. com.* **Canadian.** At this beautifully restored 1896 ranch house, set in Fish Creek Provincial Park, the imaginative menu is based on local products. Fresh and smoked game (buffalo, elk, caribou), Alberta beef, lamb and pork and a variety of seafood are creatively partnered with berries, organic vegetables, and herbs grown onsite. For example, medaillions of caribou are served with blueberry sourdough bread. Sunday brunch on the veranda is a real treat.

$$$ River Café – *25 Prince's Island Park.* ♿ ✆*403-261-7670. www.river-cafe.com. Closed Jan.* **Canadian.** With the ambience of a rustic fishing lodge, this restaurant, set on an island in central Calgary along the Bow River, offers seasonal cuisine focusing on Canadian ingredients such as buffalo, Alberta beef, maple syrup, cranberries, salmon and prairie grains. Dine inside around the fieldstone fireplace or outdoors on a wide patio overlooking the river.

SHOPPING

Callebaut Chocolate – *1313 1st St. SE.* ✆*403-266-4300 or 800-661-8367. www.bernardcallebaut.com.* Bernard Callebaut came to Calgary from Belgium 25 years ago and set about creating the best chocolates in Canada, using fresh Alberta dairy products. Now, Callebaut confections are available in 28 retail outlets in Canada, two in the US and through catalog sales. Specialties include nut clusters, truffles and nougats. Daily factory tours *(call ahead)* and, best of all, free samples.

Calgary Farmers' Market –*510 77th Ave SE.* 🅿 ✆*403-240-9113. www.calgary farmersmarket.ca.* You'll find plenty to keep you busy just off Blackfoot Trail & Heritage Drive. This year-round market *(Thu-Sun 9am-5pm)* overflows with farm produce, organic foods, handmade sausages, baked goods and other food items. The emphasis here is always on supporting Alberta and British Columbia vendors. A food court offers every cuisine and vendors often put out free samples (don't miss local favourite Simple Simon Pies).

Alberta Boot – *#50-50th Ave. SE.,* ✆*403-263-4623. www.albertaboot.com.* This store specializes in fine handmade Western boots (the Mounties' footwear of choice). With hundreds of pairs, the selection is vast and prices range from economical to astronomical.

Lammle's Western Wear– *209 8th Ave. SW.;* ✆*403-255-0272 or 877-526 6537. www.lammles.com.* This Alberta chain offers ranch wear, boots and hats. Locations are found in numerous locations throughout Alberta & B.C.

Riley & McCormick Western Wear – *220 8th Ave. S.W.,* ✆*403-228-4024 or 800-661-1585, www.realcowboys.com.* In business since 1901, this flagship store stocks boots, hats, jeans, shirts and other western accessories. A second store location is at the main terminal at the Calgary airport.

ROYAL CANADIAN PACIFIC TRAIN

Ultra-Luxury train travel reached its peak in the late 19C and early 20C in the railcars built specially for Canadian Pacific executives. Long retired, these cars have returned to the rails for leisurely tours through the Rockies. Departing from downtown Calgary, the Royal CP train is pulled by historic locomotives through spectacular mountain scenery. Seven day/six night excursions feature luxurious staterooms, gourmet meals & fine wines in the well-appointed dining cars, and overnight stops in such popular destinations as Banff and Lake Louise, AB and Golden, BC. Limited summer and fall schedule. *Unique memory value.For information:* ✆*403-508-1400 or 877-665-3044. www.royalcanadianpacific.com.*

SPRUCE MEADOWS

Southwest of downtown via MacLeod Trail, then west along Hwy. 22X. RR 9. ✆*403-974-4200. www.sprucemeadows.com.* One of the finest show-jumping facilities on earth, Spruce Meadows is an oasis of perfect turf on the city outskirts. The 120 ha/300 acre site encompasses outdoor rings, indoor arenas, stables for 700 horses and a three-storey tournament centre. Major annual events include The Masters (Sep), the world's richest show-jumping tournament in prize money ($2M), attracting some 50,000 spectators daily and a television audience of millions. Other outdoor tournaments are the National *(second week of Jun)*; Canada One *(last weekend of Jun)*; and the North American *(early Jul)*, coinciding with the Calgary Stampede.

Cardston

Alberta

This small town was founded in 1887 by **Charles Ora Card**, a son-in-law of Brigham Young, leader of the Church of Jesus Christ of the Latter-Day Saints, also known as Mormons, who established Salt Lake City in 1847.

SIGHTS
👥 Remington Carriage Museum★★

623 Main St. 🦽 🕐 *Open Jul–Labour Day daily 9am–5pm. Rest of year daily 10am–4pm.* 🕐 *Closed Jan 1, Easter Sunday, Dec 24-25.* ✗ 🅿 ⊗ *$13 (child $9).* 📞 *403-653-5139. www.remington-carriagemuseum.com. Carriage rides (⊗$7) seasonally.*

This fascinating museum of transportation houses some 240 horse-drawn vehicles, the largest such collection in North America. Many of the conveyances are displayed within re-created scenes typical of the Western frontier such as a prairie camp or a firehouse. Highlights include a late-19C bull wagon, a sheepwagon and a Concord stagecoach. Carriages are overhauled in the **restoration shop**.

▸ **Population:** 3, 580.

🛈 **Info:** Tourist Information, 67 3rd Ave. W. 📞 403-653-3366 or 888-434-3366. www.cardston.ca.

▶ **Location:** Cardston lies in southwest Alberta, 25km/16mi north of the Montana (US) border.

🕐 **Timing:** Allow 2 hours for a visit to the Remington Carriage Museum.

👥 **Kids:** Carriage rides at the Remington Carriage Museum.

Cardston Alberta Temple

348 Third St. W. ⌐ *Temple not open to the public. Visitor centre* 🦽 🕐 *open mid-May–Labour Day daily 9am–9pm.* 🅿 📞 *403-653-3552.*

This imposing white granite structure was completed in 1923 and is one of the few Mormon temples in Canada.

The Mormon doctrine is based on the Bible, the *Book of Mormon* and the writings of Joseph Smith (1805-44). After Smith's death, most of his followers moved to Utah, under the leadership of Brigham Young.

The Mormons in Alberta built irrigation canals, which helped Cardston and surrounding communities to thrive agriculturally.

Remington Carriage Museum

© Michael Wheatley/age fotostock

Churchill★★

Manitoba

Canada's most northerly deep-sea port, Churchill is bleak in winter, but during the summer months, a carpet of wildflowers covers the tundra. In autumn, polar bears wander near, and sometimes into, the townsite on their seasonal migration northward, and in early July **beluga whales** arrive to feed and calve in the river. The Aurora Borealis here is the most intense in the world, drawing researchers and thousands of tourists.

A BIT OF HISTORY

In 1717, after a false start, the Hudson's Bay Company (HBC) established a fur-trading post on the Churchill River, named for the governor of the company, **John Churchill**, the future Duke of Marlborough and ancestor of Winston Churchill. Prompted by demands for a Prairie port, the railway was built in 1929 and port facilities soon after.

The Hudson Bay and Strait are navigable only four months a year *(mid-Jul–mid-Nov)*, when trains arrive constantly and ships take on Prairie grain.

SIGHTS
The Town

One airline offers regularly scheduled flights from Winnipeg. Calm Air International ℰ204-778-6471 or 800-839-0100 (Canada & US). www.calmair.com. Charter helicopter flights from Hudson Bay Helicopters – (204) 675-2575. Also accessible from Winnipeg by VIA Rail (♿see Planning Your Trip).

Churchill consists of a dozen paved streets filled with houses, shops and hotels; the grain elevator towers over the town. Health and recreational facilities, a library, cafeteria, theatre, high school, and business offices are housed in the **Town Centre Complex** (1976), which offers good **views** of the bay. The Parks Canada **visitor centre** is located at the train station (♿🕐*call for seasonal hours ℰ204-675-8863; www.pc.gc.ca)*. It offers information on area

▶ **Population:** 1,013.

Info: Town of Churchill, ℰ204-675-8871 or 888-389-2327. www.everything churchill.com.

Location: Churchill lies on Hudson Bay, the east side of the estuary, 1000km/625mi north of Winnipeg.

Parking: You can't drive to Churchill, but you can rent a truck or van (♿*see the Churchill website)*.

Don't Miss: From Prince of Wales Fort, you can view many types of wildlife.

Timing: The Churchill website has a thorough list of tour companies, stores, transport, accommodation and other information.

wildlife and history, including Prince of Wales Fort (♿ *see p184)* and **York Factory National Historic Site**, the remains of an earlier HBC trading post located 240km/149mi to the southeast, near the mouth of the Hayes River *(accessible only by canoe or charter plane)*. Kelsey Boulevard runs through town to the **Arctic Trading Co.**, a charming store filled with northern crafts, clothing and souvenirs. The **Churchill Northern Study Centre**, located east of town *(24km/15mi)*, offers courses on Arctic ecology, ornithology and other subjects *(ℰ204-675-2307; www.churchill science.ca)*.

Eskimo Museum★★

242 LaverendryeAve., Beside the Roman Catholic church. 🕐Open Jun–early-Nov Mon 1pm–5pm, Tue–Sat 9am–noon & 1pm–5pm. Rest of the year reduced hours. 🕐Closed major holidays. Contribution requested. ℰ204-675-2030.

This museum houses a fine **collection** of Inuit carvings in stone, ivory and bone collected over 50 years by the Oblate fathers. Many of the pieces refer to Inuit legends. A recorded commentary describes some of the works.

© Canadian Tourism Commission

Polar Bears Up Close

Abruptly, the large white bear sat down, completely upright in the snow, to nurse her cubs. Scanning the horizon, she stopped from time to time to poke her nose into the air and check for scents. Cameras whirred. "Ahhhh!" chorused the human observers who had come from far and wide to see these massive creatures (adult females weigh 300kg/660lbs on average, males 600kg/1,300lbs).

These observers were enclosed within heated, bathroom-equipped Tundra Buggies®—wide, rectangular "buses" equipped with 6ft-high all-terrain tires to keep windows (and passengers) out of reach of curious bears. From the vehicle's rear viewing platform, visitors can photograph polar bears as they chew on the tires, curl up behind a boulder or splay themselves on the snow.

In spring, these great sea bears float along the western coastline on huge ice floes blown by prevailing winds. The bears spend the summer on shore dozing and eating grass and seaweed. From mid-October to mid-November, the water normally freezes first on the points and capes near Churchill, where polar bears congregate, making this the perfect viewing point. One operator, Frontiers North Adventures, offers a tour that includes accommodations in the **Tundra Buggy Lodge**, a trainlike series of sleeping, dining and utility cars, linked by viewing decks.

Travel Manitoba and the Churchill Chamber of Commerce maintain lists of tour operators. Tundra Buggy Lodge program: contact Frontiers North Adventures based in Winnipeg ℘204-949-2050 or 800-663-9832; www.tundrabuggy.com).

Prince of Wales Fort★

Across Churchill River estuary from town. Access by helicopter or by boat. ☛ *Visit mid-Jun-mid-Aug for self-guided tours, and guided tours (1hr) only, mid-Oct-mid-Nov daily.* ⊛$8. ℘204-675-8863. www.pc.gc.ca.
This stone Hudson's Bay Company (HBC) fortress (1771) took 40 years to complete. In 1782 commander Samuel Hearne surrendered to a French fleet without a shot being fired; the fort was later returned to the British, but was never again used by the HBC. The walls are nearly 12m/40ft thick; 40 huge cannon are on the site. The boat trip to the fort is an excellent way to see beluga whales *(Jul–Aug).*
See 18C stone battery at **Cape Merry National Historic Site.** point for wild-liewing *(℘204-675-8863).*

Cypress Hills ★★
Alberta-Saskatchewan

These verdant hills, watered by lakes and streams, rise prominently in the midst of otherwise unbroken, sunbaked, short-grass prairie. On their heights grow the tall, straight lodgepole pines favored by Plains First Nations for their teepees or lodges—thus the name. The trees were probably mistaken by early French voyageurs for the jack pines (cyprès) of eastern Canada. A bad translation further compounded the error, and Cypress Hills was born.

A BIT OF GEOGRAPHY

Straddling the Alberta/Saskatchewan boundary, 70km/43mi north of Montana, the plains give way to rolling, forested hills cut by coulees, valleys, lakes and streams. The highest elevations in Canada between Labrador and the Rockies, they rise to nearly 1,500m/5,000ft.

A 200sq km/80sq mi area was untouched by the last Ice Age, which covered the rest of this vast area with ice more than 1km/.6mi deep. The hills form a divide between two great watersheds: Hudson Bay and the Gulf of Mexico. Streams flow south to the Missouri-Mississippi system and north to the South Saskatchewan River, Lake Winnipeg and Hudson Bay. The flora and fauna of the hills offer remarkable diversity.

A BIT OF HISTORY

In 1859 John Palliser, touring the western domains for the British government, described this area as "A perfect oasis in the desert we have travelled." Later, settlers found the hills ideally suited for **ranching**, a vocation the area maintains today.

In the early 1870s several trading posts were established in the Cypress Hills by Americans from Montana. In exchange for furs, they illegally traded "firewater," an extremely potent brew. During the winter of 1872-73, Assiniboine Indians camped near two of these posts were joined by a party of Canadian and American wolf-hunters, whose horses had been stolen by Cree raiders. Thinking the Assiniboines were the thieves, the drunken "wolfers" attacked the Indian camp, killing 36 people.

When news of the **Cypress Hills Massacre** reached Ottawa, Prime Minister Sir John A. Macdonald acted quickly. He created the **North West Mounted Police** (renamed the **Royal Canadian Mounted Police** in 1920) and dispatched them to the Northwest to stop such border incursions and end the illegal whisky trade.

The perpetrators of the massacre were arrested but later acquitted for lack of evidence. However, the fact that white men had been arrested impressed the Indians and helped establish the force's reputation.

SIGHTS

Cypress Hills Interprovincial Park★★

In Alberta, 65km/40mi southeast of Medicine Hat by Trans-Can Hwy. and Hwy. 41 South. Park office at Elkwater Lake. For road conditions check at park office ℘403-893-3833 (Alberta) or 306-662-5411 (Saskatchewan). Park ⏱ open year-round. Visitor centre ✕ ⟐ ⏱ open mid-May–Aug daily 10am–5pm; Closed Mon & Tue. ℘403-893-3833. www.cypresshills.com.

ℹ Info: Parks Canada and Alberta-Saskatchewan operate visitor centres. ⟐ *See below.*

▶ **Location:** Cypress Hills lies on the Alberta/Saskatchewan border, 70km/43mi north of the state of Montana.

⟳ **Don't Miss:** The highest point in Saskatchewan, 1468m/4,816 ft.

🕐 **Timing:** The park is a detour off the TransCanada Highway.

👥 **Kids:** Farwell's Trading Post at Fort Walsh re-creates frontier life.

Cypress Hills Interprovincial Park

© Michael Wheatley/age fotostock

The Cypress Hills area covers 2,500sq km/965sq mi. This park encompasses the highest part of the Cypress Hills, with 204sq km/79sq mi on the Alberta side and 182sq km/70sq mi on the Saskatchewan side. **Hiking trails** of varying difficulty take visitors through the woodlands and along streams. **Swimming** is permitted at Elkwater Lake (Jul–Aug); and there are boat and bike rentals. The park holds a general store, a cafe and the Elkwater Lake Lodge and Resort with rooms, cabins and condos. (www.elkwaterlakelodge.com).

From Elkwater Lake an interesting drive (40km/25mi) leads past **Horseshoe Canyon** to **Head of the Mountain,** which affords pleasant views of coulees and hills as far as the Sweet Grass Hills and Bear Paw Mountains of Montana. The drive proceeds to Reesor Lake and the park boundary. This road continues to Fort Walsh, approximately 18km/11mi south.

👥 Fort Walsh National Historic Site★

In Saskatchewan, 52km/32mi southwest of Maple Creek by Hwy. 271. ✕ ♿ ⏰ Open mid-May–Jul Tue-Sat, Jul-Labour Day daily 9:30am–5pm. Rest of Sept daily, call for hours. ⓢ$9.80 (child $4.90). ✆306-662-3590. www.pc.gc.ca. Access from Cypress Hills Provincial Park or from Maple Creek, this North West Mounted Police post, named for its builder, James Walsh, lies near the site of the Cypress Hills Massacre. From 1878 to 1882 it was the force's headquarters. The **Visitor Centre** has displays and films. The fort can be reached by foot or by park bus service. Log buildings include barracks, stables and the commissioner's residence. At **Farwell's Trading Post★** (2.5km/1.5mi south of the fort, access by park bus; ▪▪ visit by 45min guided tour only), costumed guides depict historical figures of the post's past.

Sitting Bull in Canada

In 1876 a force of Sioux warriors under their great chief, Sitting Bull, exterminated an American army detachment under Gen. **George Custer** on the Little Big Horn River in southern Montana. Fearing reprisals from the enraged Americans, Sitting Bull crossed into Canada with nearly 5,000 men. Inspector **James Walsh** of the North West Mounted Police was given the difficult task of trying to persuade the Sioux to return, in order to avoid war between the Sioux and their traditional enemies, the Cree and the Blackfoot, who inhabited the region. Riding into the sizable Sioux encampment near Wood Mountain (350km/217mi east of Fort Walsh) with only four constables and two scouts, he informed Sitting Bull that he must obey Canadian law. Although this act of bravery won the respect of the chief, it was four years before Sitting Bull consented to return to the US to live on a reservation.

Edmonton★★

Alberta

The capital of Alberta, long associated with the energy and agricultural industries, today enjoys a more diversified economy, marked by manufacturing and advanced technologies. Edmonton prides itself on its lively cultural scene, with museums, theatres and festivals as well as the dazzling attractions of the West Edmonton Mall, largest mall in North America.

A BIT OF HISTORY

From Post to Provincial Capital – By the end of the 18C, posts near present-day Edmonton were trading blankets, guns and other goods to Cree and Blackfoot Indians in exchange for animal pelts. In 1821, **Edmonton House** emerged as the Hudson Bay Company's most important post in the West. The settlement grew as goods arrived by York boat from York Factory or overland from Winnipeg by Red River cart.

The decision of the Canadian Pacific Railway Co. to route its line through Calgary was a blow, but other rail lines were built at the end of the century. During the Klondike Stampede of 1896-99, Edmonton became a "gateway to the North." Due to its strategic location between central farmland and northern energy resources, the city became Alberta's capital in 1905.

Petroleum Centre – Edmonton might have remained a quiet administrative centre had oil not been discovered in 1947 in **Leduc**, a small community to the south, followed by other discoveries. The city is the major service and distribution centre for the vast Athabasca Tar Sands to the north. The largest percentage of the province's producing oil wells are concentrated in the Edmonton area.

DOWNTOWN

Edmonton's downtown centres on Sir Winston Churchill Square and Jasper Avenue. The square is surrounded by modern buildings including **City Hall**,

▶ **Population:** 1,159,869.

ℹ **Info:** Edmonton Welcome Centre, 9797 Jasper Ave. (Shaw Conference Centre). ☎780-496-4620 or 800-463-4667. edmonton.com.

▷ **Location:** Edmonton spans the valley of the North Saskatchewan River in the centre of Alberta; downtown lies on the steep northern bluffs.

🅿 **Parking:** Meters charge from $1-$3.50/hr depending on day. Sundays is free.

👁 **Don't Miss:** Fort Edmonton is a must-see for Western history.

🕐 **Timing:** Visit during city's many festivals.

👪 **Kids:** The West Edmonton Mall; Telus World of Science; Royal Alberta Museum; Fort Edmonton Park.

the **Court House**, the Art Gallery, the elegant glass and brick **Citadel Theatre** (**A** *on map*), the attractive **Stanley A. Milner Library** (**B** *on map*), and Edmonton City Centre with its shops, restaurants and offices.

Two blocks south, the steel and glass structure of Edmonton's **Shaw Conference Centre** rises opposite Canada Place, which houses offices of the federal government.

Art Gallery of Alberta★

Interim location: Enterprise Square, 2 Winston Churchill Sq. 🕐*Open year-round Tue–Sun 11am–5pm (Wed 9pm).* 🕐*Closed major holidays.* 💰*$12.50.* ☎*780-422-6223. www.artgallery ofalberta.com.*

Completely renovated in 2010 and back to its previous location on Sir Winston Churchill Square, the striking architecture of Randall Stout doubled the gallery's previous exhibition space, allowing more displays from its 6,000-item permanent collection.

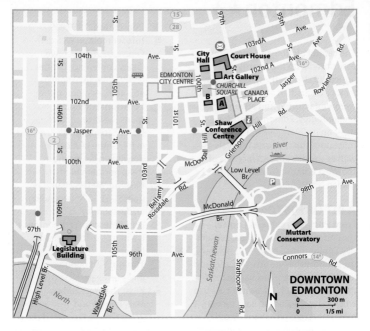

DOWNTOWN
EDMONTON

N

0   300 m
0   1/5 mi

Muttart Conservatory★

9626-96A St. ✕✆🅿⏰*Open year-round daily 10am–5pm, Thu until 9pm* ⏰*Closed Dec 25.* 👓*$12.50.* 📞*780-442-5311. http://www.edmontonattractions.com/muttart_conservatory/.*

The four glass pyramids of this striking architectural ensemble shelter some 700 plant species and act as the city's iconic landmark.

Legislature Building★

Visitor services at 10800 97th Ave. ✕✆🅿🚌 *Visit by guided tour (45min) only, May–mid-Oct Mon–Fri hourly 10am–noon, every 60 min 9am–4pm, weekends 9am–5pm. Rest of the year Mon–Fri tours hourly 9am–noon, every 30 min 12:30–4pm, weekends hourly noon–4pm.* ⏰*Closed Jan 1, Good Friday & Dec 25.* 📞*780-427-7362. www.assembly.ab.ca.*

Set in pleasant gardens overlooking the North Saskatchewan River, the yellow sandstone Alberta Legislature building (1912) occupies the original site of Fort Edmonton.

ADDITIONAL SIGHTS
🧍🧍 Fort Edmonton Park★★

7000 143rd Street. ✕✆🅿⏰*Open mid-May–mid-Jun Mon–Fri 10am–4pm, weekends & holidays 10am–6pm.* 👓*$26.20 w/Unlimited Rides Pass (child $20.90 w/pass).* 📞*780-496-7381. www.fortedmontonpark.ca.*

Rambling along the ravine of the North Saskatchewan River, this park re-creates the history of settlement in Edmonton. Board the vintage train *(free; continuous service)* to reach **Fort Edmonton**, the 1846 fur-trading post. Dominant is the Big House, the four-storey residence of the governor of the fort.

Among other reconstructed buildings is the chapel built for Rev. **Robert Rundle**, the first missionary in Alberta, who spent the years 1840 to 1848 at Fort Edmonton. Wagon tours available on the hour *(⏰Mon–Sat 11am–3pm).*

The **prerailway village** contains a reconstruction of Jasper Avenue in 1885. The McDougall Church, built in 1873 by Rev. **George McDougall,** was the first Protestant church in Alberta.

The village gradually becomes **1905 Street**, which shows Edmonton at a time of great growth. A street car *(free, continuous service)* runs down the middle of the road, which is lined with a penny arcade. Eventually 1905 Street becomes **1920 Street**, which represents a period of prosperity for Edmonton.

👥 West Edmonton Mall

8882-170th Street. 🚻♿🅿🕐*Shopping hours Mon–Sat 10am–9pm, holidays 10am–6pm, Sun 11am–6pm. Hours and fees vary for waterpark and rides.* ☎*780-444-5321. www.wem.ca.*
Covering over 483,000sq m/5.3 million sq ft, this leviathan of a shopping/ entertainment complex is the largest in the world, designed after the ancient Persian markets. The mall encloses an amusement park with more than 24 thrill rides such as a triple-loop rollercoaster (there's an interactive playground for small children), a full-size skating rink, a waterpark with two-dozen rides and activities, movie theatres, a casino, two hotels and more than 800 stores and 100 restaurants. There is even a Chinatown with its own market.

Royal Alberta Museum★★

103A Avenue, between 97th St. and 99th St., beside the CN Building across from Law Courts. 🚻♿🅿🕐*Opening late 2017. Check website for hours/ admission.* 🕐*Closed Dec 24–25.* ☎*780-453-9100. www.royalalbertamuseum.ca.*
One of the largest in the country, this new museum structure is a showcase in itself, leading to an interior narrative of human and natural history.

Fort Edmonton Park

© Travel Alberta

Ralph Applebaum designed the Human History and Natural History suite of galleries, as well as the exhibits in the main foyer. Lee H. Skolnick Architecture and Design Partnership are designing the Children's Gallery and the Bug Gallery, must-sees for the whole famiy. The extraordinary **Syncrude** Gallery of Aboriginal Culture details the life of the Plains Indians in western Canada with some 3,000 artifacts.

The **Natural History Gallery** encloses the **Bug Room**, filled with live creatures; the Bird Gallery, featuring the largest collection of mounted birds in the country; Reading the Rocks, which explains geological forces; and Treasures of the Earth, a display of gems and minerals.

Klondike Days

Every year in July, Edmonton stages a frenzied, citywide celebration of the great **Klondike Stampede**, when gold prospectors came through Edmonton to begin their trek north to Dawson City, Yukon. Officially called the Capital City Exhibition, or **K-Days**, the celebration attracts entertainment from far and wide, such as acrobats from China, as well as home-grown glitter.

Bedecked in costumes of the 1890s, residents and visitors alike strut in the kick-off parade and Sunday Promenade and in general whoop it up for 10 days. Chuckwagon races, a big midway, a food fair, a craft show, musical performances, and nightly vaudeville shows and fireworks are traditions. Many activities, such as Fun Town Farm & the **Mach-3** ride are aimed at families and children.

📱 ☎*780-471-7210 or 888-800-7275. www.k-days.com.*

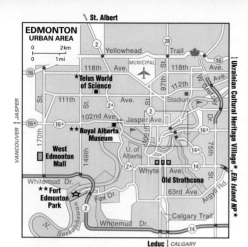

Map labels:
- EDMONTON URBAN AREA
- St. Albert
- 0 2km / 0 1mi
- Yellowhead Trail (28)
- 118th Ave.
- MUNICIPAL
- 118th Ave.
- ★Telus World of Science
- 111th St.
- 102nd Ave.
- Stadium
- Jasper Ave.
- ★★Royal Alberta Museum
- U. of Alberta
- West Edmonton Mall
- 149th
- Whyte Ave.
- Old Strathcona
- Whitemud Dr.
- ★★Fort Edmonton Park
- Fox Dr.
- 63rd Ave.
- Calgary Trail
- N. Saskatchewan
- Whitemud Dr.
- VANCOUVER ↑ JASPER
- 170th St.
- 16A
- 97th St.
- 112th St.
- W Gretzky Dr.
- 75th St.
- Argyll Rd.
- Ukrainian Cultural Heritage Village★ · Elk Island NP ★
- 14A
- 14
- Leduc | CALGARY

👥 Telus World of Science Edmonton★

11211 142 St.NW ✕⚙🅿🕐*Open late Jul–Labour Day daily 10am–8pm. Rest of the year daily 10am–5pm.* 🕐*Closed Dec 24–25.* 👁 *$27 (child $19.95).* 📞*780-451-3344. www.telusworldof scienceedmonton.com.*

Resembling a large spaceship, the centre houses an IMAX theatre and a planetarium, in addition to exhibits on the environment, the body, space, and forensics. Exhibits are designed particularly for young people.

Housed separately, an **observatory** offers a close-up view of the stars and planets *(weather permitting, call for hours)*.

EXCURSIONS
St. Albert

19km/12mi north by Rte. 2.

In 1861 a Roman Catholic mission was founded here on the banks of the Sturgeon River by Father **Albert Lacombe** (1827-1916).

The simple log **chapel** is the oldest building in Alberta (*St. Vital Ave.;* ⚙🅿🕐*open mid-May–Labour Day daily 10am–5pm;* 👁*admission by donation;* 📞*780-459-7663; www.culture.alberta. ca*). The crypt of the modern-day church contains the tombs of Father Lacombe and Bishop **Vital Grandin** (1829-1902), whose adjoining residence can also be visited.

Elk Island National Park★

On Hwy. 16, about 35km/22mi east.

⚙🕐 *Open daily 24 hrs-per day year-round. Hiking, camping, canoeing, cross-country skiing, golfing.* 👁*$7.80.* 📞*780-922-5790. www.pc.gc.ca. Visitor Centre* 🕐 *open daily 9:30am-4:30pm.*

One of the smallest of Canada's national parks, the 194sq km/75sq mi Elk Island nevertheless abounds with wildlife. Herds of plains bison stand or sit in the road in the early hours of the day; elk, moose, beaver and coyote are routinely sighted. At Tawayik Lake myriad waterfowl crowd the skies, and the rare trumpeter swan has been seen at Astotin Lake. Some 100km/60mi of nature trails punctuate the park's wetlands, aspen forests and meadows. New oTENTik camping structures available for overnights.

Ukrainian Cultural Heritage Village★

On Hwy. 16, about 50km/30mi east. ✕🅿🕐*Open mid-May–Labour Day daily 10am–5pm. Closed Sep-May*

Ukrainian Cultural Heritage Village

© Ryan Jackson/Travel Alberta

except special events. $15. ✆780-662-3640. www.history.alberta.ca. *Wheelchairs and scooters available for the physically challenged.*

Some 30 historic buildings have been moved to this living history site, which showcases Ukrainian settlement in east central Alberta from 1892 to 1930. Visitors can tour the village grounds on foot or ride in a horse-drawn wagon. Displays in the **Visitor Centre** focus on the mass migration of Ukrainian people to the Canadian Prairies. The village has a rural community and an early town that includes a train station, an operating grain elevator, a provincial police post, a domed Orthodox church, a spired Catholic church, a sod hut, a blacksmith shop and a hotel. Costumed interpreters and a Village Diner and food kiosk with Ukrainian traditional dishes enhance the visit.

ADDRESSES

STAY

$$$ Union Bank Inn – *10053 Jasper Ave.* ✆780-423-3600 or 888-423-3601. www. unionbankinn.com. 34 rooms&suites. ✕ℙ⚌. Housed in a 1910 Italianate building downtown, the inn bespeaks elegance inside and out. Rooms have a fireplace, goose-feather duvet, fleece robes and windows that open, while suites offer whirlpool baths. **Madison's Grill ($$$)** serves breakfast from 7am, dinner until 10pm *(no lunches)*, with elk, wild boar and salmon on the dinner menu.

$$$$ Fairmont Hotel Macdonald – *10065 100th St.* ✆780-424-5181 or 866-540-4468. www.fairmont.com. 199 rooms. ✕ᵫℙ⚌. This 1915 château-style landmark exudes Edwardian splendour. Guest rooms, though a bit small, are sumptuous. A tiled pool, fitness centre, staffed business centre and afternoon tea are added appeals. The **Harvest Room ($$$)** serves breakfast, lunch and dinner, but the Sunday brunch in the **Empire Ballroom** is a special treat not to be missed.

⚑ EAT

$$$ Hardware Grill – *9698 Jasper Ave.* ✆780-423-0969. www.hardwaregrill.com. *Dinner from 5pm Mon-Sat. Closed Sun & major holidays.* **Canadian.** Located downtown in Edmonton's historic Goodridge Block, this restaurant is known for its regional and staunchly seasonal Canadian cuisine. Bison carpaccio is a popular choice. Or, you may want to try the cedar-plank salmon with chanterelles. Ask about the Chef's Table.

$$$ RGE RD – *10643 123 St.NW, 780-447-4577. www.rgerd.ca.* Open Mon-Sat from 5pm until late. Untamed. To match the spirit of the wild West, owners Blair Lebsack and Caitlin Fulton, aim to captivate with fresh and original culinary dishes, set inside a cosy, redux farmhouse setting. Protein served are all sourced in Alberta, including three types of fish, and for those who want the full adventure - try the RGE RD Trip, culinary surpises from the chef for each course. Try Nature's Green Acres Pig Roast.

SHOP AND SIP

Old Strathcona – *#202, 10345 Whyte Ave.* ✆780-437-4182; www.oldstrathcona.ca. This vibrant 10-block hub is packed with coffeehouses, restaurants, pubs and some 300 shops. Look for Fair Trade handicrafts at **Ten Thousand Villages** *(10432-82nd St.;* ✆780-439-8349).

For a break, enjoy an Italian lunch at **Chianti** *(10501 82nd Ave.;* ✆780-439-9829) in the Old Post Office. **O'Byrnes Irish Pub** *(10616 82nd AveNW.;* ✆780-414-6766) is a fine place to sample Irish beers and whiskies. **The King & I** *(8208 107th St.;* ✆780-433-2222) serves excellent Thai cuisine—the Rolling Stones have stopped in; and **Blues on Whyte** *(10329-82nd Ave.NW;* ✆780-439-3981) live blues nightly.

EvelineCharles Salon and Spa – *Second level, near the ice palace in West Edmonton Mall. #2151 8882 170 St.* ✆780-424-5666. www.evelinecharles.com. Tired shoppers may want to head for this spacious spa, offering a full slate of aesthetic services. Stop in for a 45min neck and back massage or a pedicure. *Reservations suggested (required for packages).*

Fort Macleod★

Alberta

This small town was the site of the first North West Mounted Police post in the West. In 1874 Col. James Macleod and his men were dispatched to stop the illegal whisky trade and border incursions, such as the one leading to the Cypress Hills Massacre. Today Fort Macleod is an agricultural community. Grain is grown, and cattle are raised on the ranch land of nearby Porcupine Hills.

SIGHTS

👥 Fort Museum★

219 Jerry Potts Blvd.,. 🦽⏰Open May–Jun Mon–Fri 9am–5pm, Jul–Labour Day daily 9am–6pm. Rest of Sept–mid-Nov Wed–Sun 10am–4pm. 🎫$10 (child $5). 📞403-553-4703 or 866-273-6841. www.nwmpmuseum.com.

Set within a palisade of sharpened stakes, this museum re-creates life in and around police posts during the early settlement of Alberta. Inside the wooded palisaded walls, stand a number of log structures, including a reconstructed church and a lawyer's office.

▶ **Population:** 3,117.

ℹ **Info:** 📞403-553-4425 or 877-622-5366. www.fortmacleod.com.

◉ **Location:** Fort MacLeod lies on the Oldman River, 165km/102mi south of Calgary.

🅿 **Parking:** Both sights have designated parking.

👥 **Kids:** The Musical Ride at the Fort should thrill children.

The **Kanouse Trading House**, with its sod roof, evokes the hardships of the early settlers in the region.

The Mounted Police Building houses a model of the original fort and exhibits about the police. The **Centennial Gallery** contains a sizable collection of native arts and crafts.

In summer riders dressed in the police uniforms of 1878 (red jackets, black breeches, white pith helmets) perform a **musical ride** *(Jul–Labour Day daily 10am, 11:30am, 2pm & 3:30pm, weather permitting).*

Head-Smashed-In Buffalo Jump

© Roth & Ramberg/Travel Alberta

Teepee Camping

Always wondered what it would be like to sleep in a teepee? Here's your opportunity to find out. Overnight and two-night teepee camping is available mid-May through mid-September at Head-Smashed-In Buffalo Jump. The site is remote enough to assure a starry night, if the weather is clear. Bring your own sleeping bag or rent one there ($15/night). Canvas teepees, air mattresses, camping stoves are supplied, and showers are available at the interpretive centre. You'll help set up a teepee, dine on buffalo burgers and buffalo stew with bannock, listen to Blackfoot legends around the campfire, and take a guided walk before a breakfast of fry bread and Saskatoon jam. Lunch and a guided hike to a nearby archaeological dig site revealing aboriginal petroglyphs are included in the two-night package *(90-day advance reservations requested; for information ☎403-553-2731 or http://history.alberta.ca/headsmashedin).*

Head-Smashed-In Buffalo Jump★★

18km/11mi northwest by Hwy. 785 (Spring Point Rd.) ✕♿☉*Open daily 10am–5pm. Closed Jan 1, Easter Sunday, Dec 24–25.* ☞*$15 (child $10). history.alberta.ca/headsmashedin/.* ☎*403-553-2731.*

Designated **UNESCO World Heritage Site** in 1981, this buffalo jump has the most extensive deposits of butchered bones (11m/33.5ft deep) of any jump in North America.

For over 5,500 years, buffalo were driven to their deaths over this cliff. The buffalo provided most of the necessities of life for the Plains Indians— meat, hides for clothing and shelter, and bones for scrapers and needles.

Built into the sandstone cliff, a dramatic **Interpretive Centre** contains excellent displays on five floors about the history and culture of the Blackfoot people,

based on archaeological evidence. A film *(10min)* on buffalo hunting is shown. In the cafeteria, traditional native food such as buffalo stew and fried bannock bread is served.

Outside, paths lead to the top of the cliff, where visitors are afforded a spectacular **view★★** of the largely treeless surroundings; at the bottom, visitors can follow another trail to the area where the buffalo were skinned. Archaeological work on this rich site remains in progress and visitors can observe active digs.

During the summer, **drum and dancing** performances *(Jul–Aug; call for days and hours)* are held on the plaza at the Interpretive Centre. Year-round workshops and activities offer visitors the opportunity to try their skill at native handicrafts; registration is required, but there is no charge for classes, except for materials, if needed. It is possible to stay overnight in a teepee (*❧see box above).*

Lethbridge★

Alberta

Lethbridge was founded in 1870, after coal deposits were discovered in the valley. Today widespread irrigation and relatively mild winters moderated by the warm chinook winds have made cultivation of grain and vegetables, especially canola and sugar beet, profitable. Livestock are also raised here. Constructed into the side of Oldman riverbed are the striking buildings of the University of Lethbridge. The High Level Railway Bridge rises 96m/314ft above the riverbed.

SIGHTS

Nikka Yuko Japanese Garden★

In Henderson Lake Park, on Mayor Magrath Dr. ♿ ⏰*Open Jul–Aug daily 9am–8pm; early May–Jun & Sept–mid-Oct daily 9am–5pm.* ⊜$9. ✆403-328-3511. www.nikkayuko.com.

The city built this lovely garden in 1967 as a symbol of Japanese-Canadian amity (*Nikka Yuko* means "Japan-Canada friendship"). When Canada declared war on Japan in 1941, about 22,000 Japanese-Canadians living on the West Coast were placed in internment camps in British Columbia and Alberta. About 6,000 of them were resettled in Lethbridge, where they chose to stay after the war.

Nikka Yuko Japanese Garden

© Hubert Kang/Travel Alberta

- ▶ **Population:** 98,828.
- **Info:** City offices 910-4th Ave S. ✆403-329-7355. www.lethbridge.ca
- **Location:** Lethbridge is in southern Alberta, 216km/134mi southeast of Calgary, overlooking the wide riverbed of the Oldman River.
- **Parking:** Permitted parking times vary in the downtown area; check signage.
- **Don't Miss:** Lethbridge has lovely parks, trails and walking paths.
- **Timing:** Lethbridge is a pleasant place to stop for a night.
- **Kids:** Don't miss Wear"M" Out indoor playground and café (2-12 yrs).

👪 Fort Whoop-Up★

In Indian Battle Park, by the river, access from Hwy. 3. ♿ ⏰*New operator being selected at press time to operate site annually from May-Sept. Check website for updates.* www.fortwhoopup.com.

In the deep valley of the Oldman River stands a replica of the once-notorious whisky trading post founded by Americans from Fort Benton, Montana. It attracted Indians from afar to trade buffalo skins, furs and almost anything for a particularly lethal brew of chewing tobacco, red peppers, Jamaican ginger, black molasses and alcohol. Such illegal liquor forts sprang up in Southern Alberta and Saskatchewan in the early 1870s. The creation of the North West Mounted Police and forts Macleod and Calgary ended the illegal trade and brought law and order to the West. Wooden buildings form a fortified enclosure, defended by cannon. Interactive exhibits convey fort life. The **visitor centre** presents a video (*20min*) on the history of the post.

Moose Jaw ★

Saskatchewan

The city is reputedly named for a sharp turn in the Moose Jaw River that resembles the protruding jaw of a moose, but the Cree word *Moosegaw,* meaning "warm breezes," is a more credible source for the name. Moosejaw is an important railway junction and industrial centre; some 30 murals recall its colourful past. It is home to the Snowbirds, the precision flying team of the Canadian Air Force.

SIGHTS
City Tour
May–Sept daily. $13. Moose Jaw Trolley Co. 306-693-8097.
Board a replica of a 1911 streetcar for a guided tour of the city.

Tunnels
18 Main St. N. Tours year-round. 306-693-5261. www.tunnelsof moosejaw.com.
During Prohibition, Moose Jaw became the rum-running capital of the Prairies: its tunnels, carved beneath Main Street to stoke the furnaces of town businesses, were used, among other purposes, for bootlegging.

Western Development Museum ★
50 Diefenbaker Dr. Open Apr–Dec daily 9am–5pm. Rest of the year Tue–Sun 9am–5pm. Closed Jan 1, Dec 25-26. $9. Railway rides mid-May–Labour Day $2. 306-693-5989. www.wdm.ca.*
One of four provincial museums on Western development (North Battleford, Saskatoon, Yorkton), this one is devoted to transportation. Displays include a Canadian Pacific locomotive, a reconstructed train station and a 1934 Buick converted to run on rails and used as an inspection vehicle for 20 years; several Canadian planes, including a 1927 Red Pheasant; and the Snowbird gallery, highlighting the history of this renowned aerobatics team.

▶ **Population:** 32,526.

Info: Tourism Moose Jaw, 450 Diefenbaker Dr. 306-693-8097 or 866-693-8097. www.moosejaw.ca.

Location: Southern Saskatchewan, Moose Jaw lies 71km/44mi due west of Regina via the Trans-Canada Highway.

Parking: Parking meters cost only $0.75- $1.50/hr.

Don't Miss: The Kinsmen International Band and Choral Festival in May.

Timing: You will need a full day to enjoy the city.

Kids: Saskatchewan Burrowing Owl Interpretive Centre.

Saskatchewan Burrowing Owl Interpretive Centre
In Exhibition Grounds, 250 Thatcher Dr. E. Open mid-May–LabourDay daily 10am–6pm. Rest of the year by appointment only. Donation requested. 306-692-8710. www.skburrowingowl.ca.
Visitors can walk through a giant reconstructed burrow and an open field to see this endangered species in captivity as well as in the wild. Ask about their Adopt-an-Owl Program.

Sukanen Ship Pioneer Village and Museum
13km/8mi south on Hwy. 2. Open mid-May–mid-Sept Mon–Sat 9am–5pm, Sun noon–6pm. $10. 306-693-7315. www.sukanenmuseum.ca.*
Some 30 original and re-created buildings comprise a village depicting life in the early 1900s. Highlight is restored ship built by Finnish settler Tom Sukanen. A replica of the pioneer dwelling of **John George Diefenbaker,** Prime Minister of Canada from 1957 to 1963, is an on-site must-see.

ADDRESSES

SHOPPING

Yvette Moore Gallery – *76 Fairford St. W. Mon–Sat 10am–5pm. ℘306-693-7600 or 866-693-7600. www.yvettemoore.com.* Housed in a heritage building, this gallery sells Ms. Moore's paintings of Prairie life and landscapes, as well as regional crafts. The tiny **Gallery Café ($)** serves soups, beef loaf and vegetarian pies, plus Saskatoon berry pie, at lunch. Café open 11am-4pm.

TAKING A BREAK

$$$ Temple Gardens Hotel & Mineral Spa – *24 Fairford St. E. ℘306-694-5055 or 800-718-7727. www.templegardens.sk.ca. 181 rooms.* . *After a day of sightseeing, soak in a* mineral pool, filled with hot water drawn from ancient seabeds 1,350m/4,500ft below the earth. Extensive spa treatments available, plus Bogart's Lounge, Marnngside Café, and Harwood's Dining Room to pamper, relax, and nourish traveling guests.

Prince Albert National Park★

Saskatchewan

This large park is a fine example of Canada's southern boreal plains, an area where the aspen forest of the south mixes with the true boreal wilderness. Bison roam in isolated pockets of grassland near the southern boundary that also support prairie animals–coyotes, badgers and ground squirrels. The northern forests are home to wolves, moose, elk, black bears, beavers, red foxes and a small herd of woodland caribou. In the extreme north, white pelicans nest on Lavallée Lake, the second-largest white pelican colony in North America.

- **Info:** Northern Prairies Field Unit, Waskesiu Lake. ℘306-663-4522. www.pc.gc.ca.
- **Location:** The park sits in central Saskatchewan, 80km/50mi north of the city of Prince Albert by Hwys. 2 and 264.
- **Parking:** On-site parking available.
- **Don't Miss:** Either a hike in the park or one of the interpretive boat tours.
- **Timing:** You will surely need to spend the night in the park, where there is a range of campgrounds. The nearby motels and hotels outside the park are also an option.
- **Kids:** Older children will enjoy a hike to Grey Owl's hideaway.

VISIT

Open year-round. Hiking, camping, canoeing, swimming, cycling, golf, tennis, winter sports. $7.80/day. Map available at visitor centre (open mid-May–Labour Day daily 8am–8pm, rest of the year hours vary; ℘306-663-4522; www.pc.gc.ca) Accommodations and services available in the town of Waskesiu Lake (Chamber of Commerce, Waskesiu Lake ℘306-663-5410, www.waskesiulake.ca).

The **Nature Centre (t306-663-4522)** in Waskesiu Lake provides an introduction to the park, as well as information about day hikes and paddle trips in the area (*Lakeview Dr.; open mid-May–Sept daily 10am–5pm*). Roads follow both shores of Waskesiu Lake. Waskesieu Marina Adventure Centre for watercraft rentals, interpretive tours and canoes (*℘306-663-1999 in summer or 306-763-1278 in winter; www.waskesiumarina.com*).

Hiking trails and canoe routes crisscross the park. One hike leads to the cabin and grave of **Grey Owl** (*see box opposite*), situated on the shores of Ajawaan Lake *(19km/12mi)*.

Grey Owl

"Grey Owl," who posed as an Indian, dressing in buckskins and wearing his long hair in braids, travelled throughout North America and Europe with a conservation message, even lecturing to the British monarch George VI in 1937. Trying to reestablish beaver colonies, he worked for Canada's national park service, living first in Riding Mountain National Park with his pet beavers Rawhide and Jelly Roll, and then in Prince Albert. At his death in 1938, he was exposed as an Englishman, **Archie Belaney**, who had taken the Indian name Wa-Sha-Quon-Asin ("the Grey Owl") in about 1920. Though an impostor, Grey Owl remains one of Canada's finest nature writers and among the first to promote preservation of the wilderness. His most famous books are *Tales of an Empty Cabin*, *Pilgrims of the Wild* and *Sajo and Her Beaver People*. A 1999 film, *Grey Owl*, directed by Richard Attenborough and starring Pierce Brosnan, is a respectful tribute.

Regina★★

Saskatchewan

Set in an extensive, fertile wheat-growing plain and located on the main line of the Canadian Pacific Railway and the Trans-Canada Highway, this provincial capital has long been an important agricultural centre. For more than 50 years, Regina was the headquarters for the former Saskatchewan Wheat Pool, one of the largest grain cooperatives in the world, and now the city is riding the high-tech wave of development.

A BIT OF HISTORY

Pile O' Bones –In the early 1880s, the Canadian Pacific Railway Co. (CPR) decided to build its line across the southern plains. The Dominion government, in collaboration with the CPR, chose to locate the new territorial capital at a place where the rail line would cross a creek long favored by Indians and Métis for running buffalo into pounds to slaughter them, hence the Cree name Oskana, translated as "pile o' bones." In August 1882 when the first train arrived, Princess Louise, wife of Canada's Governor-General, rechristened it Regina ("Queen" in Latin) after her mother, Queen Victoria.

Queen City of the Plains – When Saskatchewan became a province in 1905,

- ▶ **Population:** 237,800.
- **Info:** ☎306-789-5099 or 800-661-5099. www.tourismregina.com.
- **Location:** Regina lies on the Trans-Canada Highway, in south central Saskatchewan.
- **Parking:** Meters operate Mon-Fri 8am until 6pm, and cost $2 par hour. On Sat, 2 free hrs, Sun parking is free.
- **Don't Miss:** The RCMP Heritage Centre.
- **Timing:** Allow at least a day to enjoy this city.
- **Kids:** Wascana Centre offers parks, Science Centre, IMAX, art gallery, even a skateboard plaza.

Regina became the capital. As immigrants poured in, the city burgeoned. To solve the water problems, Wascana Creek was dammed, creating an artificial lake. Trees were planted and carefully nourished, defying the notion of a treeless wilderness. Though the city's development in the 20C was precarious, Regina has experienced steady growth since World War II. The downtown core has been revitalized, and imposing buildings constructed. Today, Regina rises above the flat, treeless prairie like a mirage, the "Queen City of the Plains."

First Nations Gallery, Royal Saskatchewan Museum

Royal Saskatchewan Museum

Completed in 1912, this graceful building of Tyndall stone occupies a fine **site** overlooking gardens and Wascana Lake. Tours take in the legislative chamber and library, rotunda and art galleries.

👥 Wascana Centre★

2900 Wascana Dr. 🅿️🕐*Open daily year-round. Picnicking, swimming, boating, skateboarding & IMAX.* 📞*306-522-3661. www.wascana.sk.ca. Park information centre at Wascana Place (off Broad St.) within the park.*

This 930ha/2,300 acre park, Regina's pride and joy, is reputedly the largest urban park in North America. Formal gardens of beautiful flowers and trees surround the western part of the artificial Wascana Lake. **Willow Island** is a picnic site accessible by ferry *(Victoria Day–Labour Day Mon–Fri noon–4pm;* 🎫*$4; reservations requred for evenings and weekends* 📞*306-522-3661).*

DOWNTOWN
Royal Saskatchewan Museum★★

2445 Albert St. 🅿️♿🕐*Open May–Labour Day daily 9am–5pm.* 🕐*Closed Dec 25.* 🎫*$5 contribution requested.* 📞*306-787-2815. www.royalsaskmuseum.ca.*

This long, low building of Tyndall stone houses one of the finest museums of natural history in Canada.

On the upper level, the **Life Sciences Gallery** features remarkable dioramas that depict the wildlife and habitats of Saskatchewan. Exhibits in the **Earth Sciences Gallery** showcase dinosaurs and woolly mammoths, volcanoes and glaciers from the province's geological beginnings. The **First Nations Gallery** displays art and artifacts of the native cultures of the region; especially of interest is the winter encampment, which features a bison-hide teepee. T-Rex Discovery Centre is located in the town of Eastend and worth the visit if you like dinosaurs and meteorites.

Legislative Building★

2405 Legislative Dr. ✕♿🅿️🍽️*Visit by guided tour (30min/free) only, mid-May–Labour Day daily 8am–9pm. Rest of the year daily 8am–5pm.* 🕐*Closed Jan 1, Good Friday & Dec 25.* 📞*306-787-5358. www.legassembly.sk.ca.*

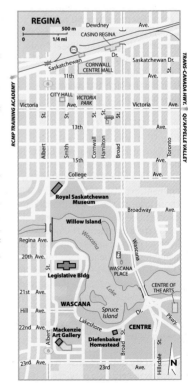

Historic Court Case of Louis Riel

After the defeat of the Northwest Rebellion in 1885, the Métis leader Louis Riel was taken to Regina for trial. The court immediately became a centre of controversy. To Quebeckers, Riel—a Catholic Métis who had studied for the priesthood in Montreal—was a patriot. To Ontarians, he was a common rebel who had gone unpunished after murdering Thomas Scott during the Red River Rebellion. Defence counsel pleaded that Riel was insane: he had spent several years in asylums and had wished to set up a new Catholic state on the Saskatchewan River, with Bishop Bourget of Montreal as Pope. Riel himself rejected the plea and convinced the jury he was sane. But if sane, he was guilty: the verdict was death by hanging. Prime Minister Sir John A. Macdonald was inundated with petitions from both sides. The sentence was delayed while doctors studied Riel's mental health. The prime minister weighed the political consequences of hanging Riel and decided the sentence had to be carried out. Riel lost his life on November 16, 1885.

Every summer the Schumiatcher Theatre at the MacKenzie Art Gallery (&*see opposite*) is the setting for a dramatic reenactment of the **Trial of Louis Riel**, based on actual court transcripts (🕐*last 3 weeks in Jul Wed–Fri 7:30pm; $15; tickets available at door or by reservation by calling* 📞*306-728-5728; www.rielcoproductions.com*).

MacKenzie Art Gallery★

3475 Albert St. ♿🅿🕐*Open year-round Mon,Wed,Fri&Sat 10am–5:30pm, Sun 12pm-5:30pm.* 🕐*Closed Tue, Jan 1, Good Friday, Dec 25–26.* 📞*306-584-4250. www.mackenzieartgallery.ca.*
Occupying the western end of the T.C. Douglas Building in Wascana Centre, this expansive art gallery features seven viewing rooms devoted largely to Canadian historical and contemporary art.

ADDITIONAL SIGHTS
Royal Canadian Mounted Police Training Academy★

RCMP Academy, Depot Division, 5600 11th Ave., west of downtown by Dewdney Ave. 📞*306-780-5900. www.rcmp-grc.gc.ca. Sunset Retreat Ceremony Jul–mid-Aug Tue 6:30pm (45-min. show).*
Visitors may no longer wander the academy grounds, but the nearby **Heritage Centre★** (*5907 Dewdney Ave.;*♿🅿🕐*open mid-May–Labour Day daily 11am–5pm;* 💰*$10;* 🕐*closed Jan 1, Dec 25;* 📞*306-522-7333 or 866-567-7267; www.rcmpheritagecentre.com*), opened in 2007, brings the history of the Mounties up to date with exhibits on

community policing, counter-terrorism activities and forensics. The vivid past of the force is not neglected, with exhibits on favourite characters such as Sitting Bull and the Mad Trapper of Rat River.

EXCURSION
Qu'Appelle Valley★

See Map of Principal Sights.
The Qu'Appelle ("*kap-PELL*") Valley cuts a deep swath across the otherwise flat prairie. As much as 120m/400ft deep in places, with several sparkling lakes, the valley presents a complete contrast to the surrounding plains. The name derives from Indian lore.

The Fishing Lakes★

73km/45mi east of Regina by Trans-Can Hwy., northeast by Rte. 10.
This route drives beside the Qu'Appelle River where it forms the fishing Lakes of Pasqua, Echo, Mission and Katepwa. North of Lake Echo, Route 56 leads to **Echo Valley Provincial Park★**, which is a delightful place to camp (♿🕐*open year-round, campgrounds closed in winter; visitor centre open May–Labour Day, hours vary;* 💰*$7/day vehicle fee;* 📞*306-332-3215; www.tpcs.gov.sk.ca*).

Riding Mountain National Park ★★

Manitoba

This diverse park is a rolling plateau of aspen parkland, bogs, grasslands and hardwood forests that attract the province's heaviest concentrations of wildlife.
Given the large populations of moose and elk, sightings of these creatures, as well as of bears or foxes, are highly probable.

GEOLOGY

The park rises 457m/1,500ft above the surrounding countryside (756m/2,480ft above sea level).

Early fur traders named it "Riding" Mountain, the place where they exchanged canoes for horses to continue west. It is part of the **Manitoba Escarpment,** a jagged 1,600km/1,000mi ridge winding across Manitoba, Saskatchewan and North Dakota.

The park is also a crossroads where northern, western and eastern environments and habitats meet. High areas are covered with an evergreen forest of spruce, pine, fir and tamarack. Lower sections support a deciduous forest of hardwoods, shrubs, vines and ferns. In the west wildflowers thrive on meadows and grassland *(Jul and Aug)*, forming some of the only true prairie left on the continent.

VISIT

Open daily year-round. Hiking, camping, boating, fishing, biking, horseback riding, golf, winter sports. Visitor centre ✕ & Open late Jun–Labour Day daily 9:30am–8pm; mid-May–mid-Jun & rest of Sept–mid-Oct daily 9:30am–5pm. Map available at visitor centre. $7.80/day. *204-848-7275. www.pc.gc.ca. Accommodations available in* **oTENTiks** *onsite ($100 per night peak season) or nearby the park in Wasagaming.*

Info: Park Office, Wasagaming. *204-848-7275. www.pc.gc.ca.

Location: The park lies in southwestern Manitoba, 197km/122 mi west of Winnipeg via the Trans-Canada Highway, *then 91km/56mi north of Brandon by Rte. 10.*

Parking: Do not get out of the car to approach wildlife on the roads.

Don't Miss: At Lake Audy you can see a bison herd.

Timing: To find out about accommodation, events and services, contact the Wasagaming Chamber of Commerce *204-848-2742 (May–Oct).* www.discoverclearlake.com.

Kids: The park visitor centre offers an excellent introduction to the park's geology and wildlife.

The **Visitor Centre** in Wasagaming features excellent displays and films on the park's geological history, habitats and native wildlife. Trails attract hikers and cyclists in summer, and cross-country skiers in the winter. Birders will see great grey owls, songbirds and others (some 260 species) that converge here. Wolf howls and elk-bugling trips are organized by the park office; on these group excursions, guides imitate wolf howls or use high-pitched bugles to coax the animals into view.

Near Lake Audy *(47km/29mi from Wasagaming)*, a herd of bison roams a large enclosure *(accessible by Lake Audy Rd. off Rte. 10).* From an interpretive viewpoint above the Audy plain, these animals can be seen in their true prairie environment. There are good **views★** of the Manitoba Escarpment from an observation tower off Route 10 near the park's north gate.

ADDRESSES

WHAT TO DO

National Ukrainian Festival –
In Selo Ukraina, 60km/36mi north of Wasagaming and 12km/7mi south of Dauphin, near intersection of Hwys. 5 and 10. Ukrainian Festival, 1430 Man St.South, Dauphin. 204-622-4600 or 877-474-2683. www.cnuf.ca. Held annually late July/early Aug near Riding Mountain National Park, this three-day celebration includes traditional and contemporary Ukrainian dancing, music and food. Among the festival highlights are a parade, street dances, arts and crafts displays, a bread-baking contest, beer gardens and a children's fest. On-site camping is available (*reservations essential*) and there are bus transport packages from Saskatchewan, Alberta and Winnipeg.

Elkhorn Resort Spa & Convention Centre – *3 Mooswa Dr. E., Onanole. 204-848-2802. www.elkhornresort.mb.ca. Open all year. Reservations required.* Riding stables offer 30–35 minute trail rides in the immediate vicinity of the ranch or within the park itself with guides. Two golf courses tempt players, while Solstice Spa starts visitors journey to wellness with a large menu of treatments, and foot care. **($$$) Mountain Grill & Bar** nourishes with hearty food & drink.

Saskatoon★

Saskatchewan

The largest city in Saskatchewan, this manufacturing and distribution centre is set in a fertile wheat-growing area, amid the province's vast potash reserves. Surrounding prairie landscape is dominated by the "heights" of Mount Blackstrap (91m/300ft), an artificial ski hill rising south of the city (40km/25mi).

A BIT OF HISTORY

Founded in 1883 by Methodists from Ontario, the city was named for the Saskatoon, a small purplish berry native to the region. Starting in 1908, German, Scandinavian, Ukrainian and British settlers arrived by the new train line and transformed the city. Today the settlers are honoured once a year in July during Pioneer Days.

SIGHTS
Remai Modern Museum★

Saskatoon South Downtown. ✕ ♿ 🅿 Open year-round as of 2017, check website for exact hours. Closed Dec 25. 306-975-7610. www. remaimodern.org. Located at the confluence of the Saskatchewan River and downtown, this stunning work

▸ **Population:** 305,000.

🚹 **Info:** 101-202 Fourth Ave. N. 306-242-1206 or 800-567-2444. www.tourism saskatoon.com. Visitor centre, Ave. C N. & 47th St. W. *(open May–Sept).*

▸ **Location:** On the banks of the South Saskatchewan River, Saskatoon lies 259km/161mi northwest of Regina.

🅿 **Parking:** Parking meters operate Mon–Sat 9am–6pm. Time limits vary from 30min to 3hrs.

◉ **Don't Miss:** The Wanuskewin Heritage Park.

🕐 **Timing:** Allow at least 2 days in town and 1 day for the excursion.

👪 **Kids:** Boomtown at the Western Development Museum.

of architect Bruce Kuwabara reflects the prarie topography, while melding nearby city elements, such as the exterior cladding of copper, borrowed from the nearby Bessborough Hotel. The museum's contemporary interior

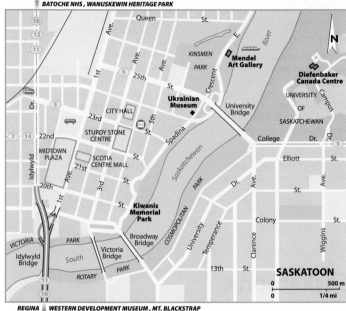

BATOCHE NHS , WANUSKEWIN HERITAGE PARK

REGINA , WESTERN DEVELOPMENT MUSEUM , MT. BLACKSTRAP

is a blend of design concepts from the imagination of Hjalti Karlsson and Jan Wilker, together with art direction by Sandra Shizuka. This project was made possible by a $30M donation from Frank and Ellen Remai Foundation. A must-see for all.

Ukrainian Museum

910 Spadina Crescent E. &○*Open year-round Tue–Sat 10am–5pm, Sun & holidays 1pm–5pm.* ○*Closed Jan 7 & Orthodox Easter Friday & major holidays.* $6. *306-244-3800. www.umc.sk.ca or www.tourism saskatoon.com.*

This museum presents displays of traditional costumes, tapestries, pioneer tools, musical instruments, wood-inlaid objects, and other handicrafts. Mannequins are garbed in male and female Ukrainian folk attire, including headdresses and footwear. Gift Shop open during museum hours.

Boat Trip

The Saskatoon Princess departs from Shearwater Docks (behind Mendel Art Gallery) &○*mid-May–Labour Day*

daily 4pm & 6:30pm (dinner cruise), plus Sat/Sun at 2pm, Sunday Brunch Cruise departs at noon . Round trip 1hr. $24. *Shearwater River Cruises Ltd., 888-747-7572 (Canada/US). www.shearwatertours.com. Reservations recommended.*

This cruise on the South Saskatchewan River is a pleasant way to discover the scenic beauty of the area and view the city from the waterside.

Diefenbaker Canada Centre★

University of Saskatchewan, 101 Diefenbaker Pl. &🅿○*Open year-round Mon–Fri 9:30am–4:30pm (Thu til 8pm), Sat–Sun and holidays noon–4:30pm.* $5 ($2 Thu evening). *Guided tour (30min) $7.* ○*Closed Jan 1, Dec 25-26, Good Friday, Remembrance Day.* *306-966-8384. www.usask.ca/diefenbaker.*

The 13th Prime Minister of Canada, John G. Diefenbaker (1895-1979) left his papers and collections to the university. A lawyer by training, well known for his defence of the "little man," "Dief" was a strong proponent of Western Canadian ideas in the Conservative Party. Elected party leader in 1956, he served as Prime Minister from 1957 to 1963, remaining influential in federal politics until his death. In addition to displays on his life and works, the centre features a replica of the office of the Prime Minister and the cabinet chamber as they existed in the Diefenbaker era.

▲▲ Western Development Museum★★

In Prairieland Exhibition Grounds, 8km/5mi south of downtown by Rte. 11/16. 2610 Lorne Ave. S. ✕ & P *Open Apr–Dec daily 9am–5pm. Jan–Mar Tue–Sun 9am–5pm. Closed major holidays.* ✎ *$10 (child $3).* ✆ *306-931-1910. www.wdm.ca.*

The grand attraction of the Saskatoon branch of this museum (other branches in North Battleford, Moose Jaw and Yorkton) is **Boomtown**, a faithful reconstruction of an entire street of 1910 vintage, complete with its Western Pioneer Bank, garage, stores, Chinese laundry, school, pool hall, theatre, hotel and railway station.

The church, moved here in 1972, is the only original structure on the street, which is lined with period cars and horse-drawn vehicles. Separate halls house automobiles and agricultural equipment, including steam tractors.

Have yourself photographed in a vintage costume in the Boomtown Studio and enjoy a light meal or piece of pie in the Victorian-styled Boomtown Cafe.

Wanuskewin Heritage Park★★

5km/3mi north of downtown by Hwy. 11. RR#4 Penner Rd. Open mid-May–Labour Day daily 9am–9pm. Rest of the year Mon–Fri 9am–4:30pm, Sat 11am–3pm. Closed Dec 25–Jan 1. ✎ *$8.50.* ✕ & P ✆ *306-931-6767 or 877-547-6546 (Canada/US). www.wanuskewin.com.*

Translated from Cree as "seeking peace of mind," *Wanuskewin* was a meeting place and hunting ground for nomadic Indians for more than 6,000 years until their removal to reserves in the 1870s. Several trails in the 307ha/760-acre park link the prehistoric sites, including a **buffalo jump** and the remains of a rare **medicine wheel**. A **visitor centre** features displays and demonstrations of native culture and allows observation of archaeological excavations.

In the heritage park's **restaurant** overlooking the park, you can sample First Nations' food, such as bison sausage or barbecued bison steak; grilled pickerel and whitefish are also on the menu. The traditional bread called bannock and a variety of soups are available too.

Wanuskewin Heritage Park

© Grambo/age fotostock

The Northwest Rebellion

The seeds of the last armed conflict on Canadian soil were sown in Manitoba's Red River Valley early in the 19C when the Métis learned that land did not necessarily belong to them. The uprising led to Louis Riel's provisional government of 1869, the formal creation of the Province of Manitoba (1870) and the allocation of 567,000ha/1.4 million acres of land for the Métis settlement.

Unfortunately, the Métis, left leaderless when Riel was banished for five years, were prey to speculators who bought their land for a fraction of its worth. Many moved northwest to the valley of the South Saskatchewan River, hoping to lead traditional lives and to avoid European settlers. However the Métis again found they had no right to the land they farmed. The Dominion government consistently ignored their petitions. In 1884, they sent for Riel.

Riel hoped to repeat his earlier victory at Red River. He allied the Métis with the Cree Indians, also discontent with changes in their lifestyle. An unfortunate incident resulting in the deaths of some members of the North West Mounted Police at **Duck Lake** destroyed all hope of a peaceful solution. A military force was quickly dispatched to the West under Maj. Gen. **Frederick Middleton.**

Under their military leader, **Gabriel Dumont** (aka **Poundmaker),** an experienced buffalo hunter, the Métis made a stand at Batoche. It was a heroic defence against overwhelming force that lasted four days, May 9–12, 1885. Riel surrendered and was taken to Regina to stand trial for murder. He was found guilty and hanged. Dumont fled to the US, though he was later pardoned and returned to Batoche. The struggle was not in vain, however, for in the wake of the rebellion, the Métis were offered the land title they had sought for such a long time.

For dessert, try the Saskatoon berry dessert with muskeg tea. The museum shop has a first-rate sampling of aboriginal crafts and clothing, including moosehide bags, beaded jewellery and Cree moccasins.

A special treat is a performance by the Wanuskewin International Dance Troupe, which presents both traditional and contemporary styles. *Call ahead for schedule 306-931-6767, and bring your cameras.*

EXCURSION
Batoche National Historic Site★★

88km/55mi northeast of Saskatoon by Rte. 11 to Rosthern, Rte. 312 E. and Rte. 225 N. ✕♿⊙Open mid-May–late-Jun Mon–Fri 9am–5pm, late-Jun–Sept daily 9am–5pm. ⊚$7.80. 306-423-6227. www.pc.gc.ca.

This quiet and beautiful **setting** on the South Saskatchewan River was the site of final stand of the Métis in 1885 (♿*see Northwest Rebellion, above).* Today the site is a poignant tribute to the **Métis,** descendants of mixed-blood parents, (primarily British, French and Scottish) men and their First Nations wives.

Little remains of the village except the white, steepled **church** (1896) dedicated to St. Anthony of Padua, the **rectory** with its bullet holes, and a cemetery of Métis graves, including Gabriel Dumont's burial place. The restored buildings, including a farm house (c.1895), contain historic artifacts. The **Visitor Centre** offers features displays on Métis history and culture.

Return trip to Saskatoon can be made by the St.-Laurent cable ferry *(10km/6mi north of Batoche),* past the small community of Duck Lake on Route 11, where the rebellion had its beginnings.

Winnipeg★★★
Manitoba

For more than a century, Winnipeg was the traditional first stop for immigrants to the West. Although challenged by Vancouver, Calgary and Edmonton in recent years, it retains the huge International Commodities Exchange (the most important in Canada), vast stock and railway yards, a manufacturing industry and headquarters of the Hudson's Bay Company.

Winnipeg is rich in cultural institutions—the Manitoba Theatre Centre, the Winnipeg Symphony Orchestra, the Manitoba Opera Company, Royal Winnipeg Ballet, and the new Canadian Museum for Human Rights.

A BIT OF HISTORY

Named for the large and shallow lake to the north called *win-nipi* ("muddy water") by the Cree, Winnipeg's future was assured when the Canadian Pacific Railway Co. chose the site as a major maintenance and repair centre and built a rail line through town. Waves of immigrants poured in by train. The city's skyline, dotted with spires, towers and domes of Catholic, Protestant and Orthodox churches, reflects this diversity. Every August the city's varied

▶ **Population:** 759,600.

Info: Visitor Centre, #300-259 Portage Ave., ℘204-943-1970 or 855-734-2489. www.tourismwinnipeg.com.

Location: Winnipeg, "Where the West begins," sits at the geographic heart of Canada, on the banks of the Red and Assiniboine rivers.

Parking: Solar-powered city parking meters issue a ticket that you leave in the windshield. In no-parking periods, meters display a menacing tow-truck.

Don't Miss: The grounds of The Forks; the Manitoba Museum; Canadian Museum for Human Rights.

Timing: Plan to take in at least one event if you can.

Kids: Assiniboine Park & zoo, Canadian Museum for Human Rights; the Manitoba Museum.

cultural background is celebrated in **Folklorama,** a festival held in pavilions throughout Winnipeg. The Folk Festival held in July is also a popular event.

The Forks National Historic Site

© Tourism Winnipeg/Juncutta Int'l/Canadian Tourism Commission

DOWNTOWN

The intersection of **Portage Avenue** and **Main Street** has traditionally been considered the centre of Winnipeg. It was said these streets were wide enough for 10 Red River carts to rush along side by side. Today this corner, long known as the windiest in Canada, is dominated by tall buildings, all connected underground by an attractive shopping area, **Winnipeg Square**. Extending for three blocks to the west, between Vaughan and Carlton streets, is **Portage Place★**, a shopping and office complex with restaurants, movie theatres, a giant-screen IMAX theatre and the Prairie Theatre Exchange.

Just south of the intersection at Portage and Main, in a small park below the Fort Garry Hotel, stands a stone gateway, all that remains of **Upper Fort Garry**, once the local headquarters of the Hudson's Bay Company. The present-day headquarters (**A** on map) rises a block away. **The Forks**, 26ha/65 acres of riverfront property refurbished by the city, includes the **Canadian Museum for Human Rights**, a **public market** housed within former stables, restaurants, shops, a children's museum and a waterside walkway (boat rentals). Riverboat cruises on the Red River contact Splash Dash Boat Tours & Rentals, *204-783-6633, www.splashdash.ca*. Walking tours (2hrs) of the downtown area depart from the ViaRail station (*late May–Sept Fri by appointment;*

$15 cash only; 204-898-4678; www.squarepegtours.ca; call for reservations & ask about their Ghost Tours).

North of the intersection lies the historic **Exchange District**, which has some remarkable examples of early 20C architecture (*1hr30min walking tours depart from Old Market Sq., look for sign; daily May–Labour Day 10am–4pm; specialty tours (90 min) at noon; $10; 204-942-6716; www.exchangedistrict.org*), and boutiques and restaurants around the **Old Market Square** (King, Albert and Bannatyne Sts.). Close by is **Centennial Centre**, a complex enclosing a concert hall, theatre, museum and planetarium. Just north lies Winnipeg's **Chinatown**.

Another interesting area for shopping and dining is **Osborne Village**, which sits south of the Assiniboine River between River and Stradbrook avenues.

⚤ Manitoba Museum★★★

190 Rupert Ave., across from City Hall.
Open daily 10am–5pm. $11–$26 (3-area pass) (child$7.50–$17.50). 204-956-2830.
www.mantobamuseum.ca.

On entering this remarkable museum, the visitor sees the magnificent diorama of a Métis rider, his spear poised, chasing several bison.

The **Earth History Gallery** includes an explanation of the geological creation of Manitoba.

Manitoba Museum

© Canadian Tourism Commission

Canadian Museum for Human Rights

The Canadian Museum for Human Rights (*https://humanrights.ca*) beckons visitors from across town and the surrounding plains. This captivating and curious structure has already won the National Cultural Tourism Award from the Travel Industry Association of Canada (TIAC), and has quickly become the city's iconic landmark. Izzie Asper's lifelong dream acts like a magnet for visitors to architect Antoine Predock's astounding exterior design, modelled after ice, clouds and stone, and set in a field of sweet grass at the legendary Forks of the Red River.

Venture indoors where internationally renowned museum designer Ralph Applebaum's amazing interactive installations highlight First Nations culture in a mesmerizing journey through time and geography, language and tradition. For over one hundred years, the Indian Residential School system in Canada abused the human rights of First Nations, Inuit and Métis youth. Canada's Truth and Reconciliation Commission (TRC) of 2008 sought the truth, and ways to begin healing and reconciliation. This museum offers six exhibits exploring this tragic story and legacy of Residential Schools, which is among Canada's most pressing human rights concerns. The museum's goal: keep the conversation current.

The **Arctic/Subarctic Gallery** is devoted to the northernmost part of the province. In the **Boreal Forest Gallery**, dioramas present the area's indigenous animals.

The highlight of the museum is the **Nonsuch Gallery**, a large, walk-through diorama with a replica of the *Nonsuch*, which sailed from England to Hudson Bay in 1668 in search of beaver pelts. The successful expedition led to the creation of the Hudson's Bay Company two years later. Relics of Sir John Franklin's ill-fated Arctic expedition are also on view.

The **Grasslands Gallery** focuses on Manitoba's south, with displays about the Assiniboine Indians and first European settlers, and an example of the famous pioneer **Red River cart**. The **Urban Gallery** captures a fall evening in Winnipeg in the 1920s.

A **planetarium** *(daily shows;* $11, child $7.50) and the **Science Gallery** *(same hours as museum;* $11, child $7.50) are located on the lower level.

Ukrainian Cultural and Educational Centre★

184 Alexander Ave. E. ☐☐*Open year-round Mon–Sat 10am–4pm (Sun 1pm–4pm Jul–Aug).* ☐*Closed major holidays.* ☎*204-942-0218. www.ukrainianwinnipeg.ca.*

The **museum** *(5th floor)* features exquisite examples of Ukrainian traditional embroidery, wood carving, ceramics and beautifully painted *pysanky* (Easter eggs). The centre includes an art gallery, library, archives and museum shop.

Costume Museum of Canada★

374 Donald St., 4th Fl. ☐☐☐*Open for shows/exhibitions and by appointment only.* ☎*204-989-0072. www.costumemuseumcanada.com.*
This non-profit museum, located downtown near the Manitoba Museum, illustrates 400 years of North American apparel via mannequin-filled *tableaux*. The 35,000-piece collection *(seasonally displayed)* spans 400 years of costumes worn by ordinary Canadians, as well as those made by great couturiers.

Winnipeg Art Gallery★

300 Memorial Blvd. ☐☐☐*Open daily Tue–Thu 11am–5pm (Fri til 9pm) Sat/ Sun 11am–5pm.* $12. ☎*204-786-6641. www.wag.ca.*
Designed by Winnipeger Gustavo Da Roza, this unusual wedge-shaped structure contains a beautiful art gallery. The gallery is best known for its **Inuit art** and for the Lord and Lady Gort Collection of Gothic and Renaissance panel paintings *(displayed periodically).*

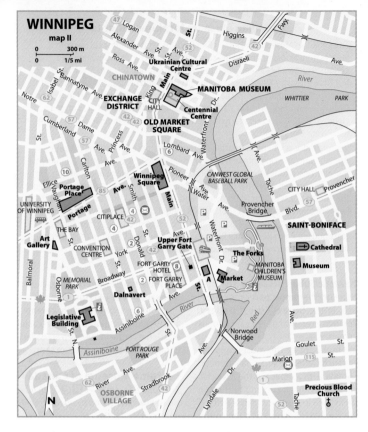

Legislative Building★

450 Broadway. ♿🅿🕐*Open year-round daily 8am–8pm.* 🕐*Closed Dec 25.* 👣*Guided tours available hourly Jul–Labour Day 9am–4pm. Rest of year by appointment.* 📞*204-945-5813. www.gov.mb.ca/legtour.*

This harmonious Neoclassical building stands in an attractive park, close to the residence of the Lieutenant-Governor. Completed in 1920, the Tyndall stone building forms an "H" with a dome at its centre. Above the dome stands the **Golden Boy**, cast by Charles Gardet, a bronze gold-plated statue clutching a sheaf of wheat. Guided tours take in the horseshoe-shaped legislative **assembly chamber** and two reception rooms. The statues around the building and in the park represent important figures in Manitoba history. Across Assiniboine Avenue stands a striking **statue** of Louis Riel by Miguel Joyal. Don't miss the rotunda.

Dalnavert Museum and Visitors Centre

61 Carlton St. 🅿👣*Visit by drop-in tour Fri–Sat 10am–4pm, group guided tour (7 or more $50).* 🎟*Admission $6.* 📞*204-943-2835. www.mhs.mb.ca.*

This beautifully restored Victorian house was built in 1895 by Sir Hugh John Macdonald, the only son of Sir John A. Macdonald, Canada's first Prime Minister. It was equipped with numerous luxuries for the times, including electric lighting, indoor plumbing and central hot-water heating.

Saint-Boniface★

In 1818 Fathers Provencher and Dumoulin arrived from Quebec to establish a Roman Catholic mission on the banks

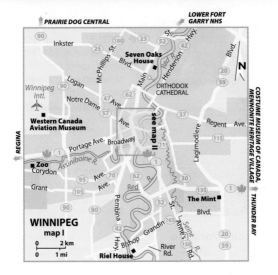

see map II

WINNIPEG
map I

0 2 km
0 1 mi

of the Red River. Saint-Boniface retains its distinctive French character.

Every February a **Festival du Voyageur** is held, celebrating the early fur traders. This is Western Canada's largest winter festival. *Walking tours of St. Boniface in summer (Tourisme Riel, 219 Provencher Blvd., 204-233-8343 or 866-808-8338, www.tourismeriel.com).*

St. Boniface Museum★

494 Ave. Taché. ⚭◷Open daily Mon–Fri 10am–4pm, Sat noon–4pm. Closed Sun. ⚭$6.75. ⚭Guided ours available by reservation only ($50 min). 204-237-4500. www.msbm.mb.ca.
The oldest building in Winnipeg, this convent, built for the Grey Nuns in 1846, holds mementos of Saint-Boniface residents, in particular of Louis Riel.

Cathedral

Six churches have stood on this site since 1818. Designed by Étienne Gaboury, the new cathedral features an attractive wooden interior. The **cemetery** contains the grave of Louis Riel.

Precious Blood Church

Also the work of Gaboury, this brick, shingle-roofed church is built in a shape that resembles a teepee.

ADDITIONAL SIGHTS
Royal Canadian Mint★

Trans-Can Hwy. at Hwy. 59. 520 Lagimodière Blvd. ⚭⚭◷Open Tue-Sat 9am–5pm. Reservations recommended. Tours Tue–Sat 9am–4pm◷Closed major holidays. ⚭$6. 877-974-6468 or 204-983-6429. www.mint.ca.
Visitors to this spectacular half-pyramid structure of rose-coloured reflecting glass can view the coin-minting process.

Riel House

330 River Rd., St. Vital. ⚭⚭⚭Visit by guided tour (30min) Jul 1–Labour Day daily 10am–5pm. ⚭ $3.90. 204-983-6757; www.pc.gc.ca.
Built in 1881, the tiny wooden house was occupied by the Riel family until 1968. Although Louis Riel never actually lived in the house, his body lay in state there after his execution in November 1885.

Seven Oaks House Museum

50 Mac Street. ⚭◷Open mid-May–Labour Day daily 10am–5pm. ⚭Contribution requested. 204-339-7429. www.travelmanitoba.com.
This nine-room log structure, believed to be the oldest remaining habitable house in Manitoba, was completed in 1853 by John Inkster, a wealthy merchant. It lies near the site of the Seven Oaks Massacre of 1816.

Assiniboine Park Zoo

© William Au Photography/Canadian Tourism Commission

👤👤 Assiniboine Park Zoo

2595 Robin Blvd.,. ✕ ♿ 🅿 🕒 Open mid-Apr–mid-Oct 9am–5pm. Rest of the year daily 9am–4pm. ⊜$19.75 (child $6.40). ☎204-927-6000. www.zoosociety.com.

This large and pleasant zoo offers a **tropical house,** home to a variety of monkeys and birds, and the Leatherdale International Polar Bear Conservation Centre, where it is possible to view polar bears up close in a walkthrough protected pool. Not far from the zoo, and within Assiniboine Park, the **Leo Mol Sculpture Garden** includes the Winnie the Bear sculpture (named for Winnipeg), said to be the inspiration for A.A. Milne's character Winnie the Pooh.

👤👤 Western Canada Aviation Museum★

At the airport, Ellice and Ferry Rds., Hangar T-2, 958 Ferry Rd. ♿ 🅿 🕒 Open year-round Mon–Fri 9:30am–4:30pm, Sat 10am–5pm, Sun noon–5pm. 🕒Closed major holidays. ⊜$7.50. ☎204-786-5503. www.wcam.mb.ca.

Over 20 aircraft are on display, ranging from early bush planes to jets. A second-floor observation deck allows visitors to see the airport runways.

EXCURSIONS
Lower Fort Garry National Historic Site★★

32km/20mi north of Winnipeg by Hwys. 52 and 9. ✕ ♿ 🅿 🕒 Open Jul 1 –Labour Day daily 9am–5pm, other seasons vary. ⊜$7.80. ☎204-785-6050 or 888-773-8888. www.pc.gc.ca.

Completed in 1847 by the Hudson's Bay Company, this stone fort remained an important post until 1911, receiving goods from the York Factory warehouse by **York boats**, an example of which is on the grounds. The highlight is the **fur loft**, with its fine collection of furs.

Mennonite Heritage Village★

In Steinbach, 61km/38mi southeast of Winnipeg by Trans-Can Hwy. and Hwy. 12. ✕ ♿ 🅿 🕒 Open May, Jun & Sept Mon–Sat 10am–5pm, Sun noon–5pm, Jul & Aug Mon–Fri 10am–6pm, Sun noon–6pm, rest of year Mon–Fri 10am–4pm. ⊜$10. ☎204-326-9661 or 866-280-8741. www.mennonite heritagevillage.com.

This village presents the life of Manitoba's first Mennonites who settled here in 1874. Two groups of Mennonites exist in Canada: the Swiss-Germanic of Ontario and the Russian Mennonites of the West. Extreme pacifists, both are descended from the Protestant sect led by **Menno Simons**.

Note the farmhouse built in characteristic style with the kitchen and stove in the centre (to heat all rooms) and a barn on one end. The **Livery Barn Restaurant ($)** serves borscht, a Russian Mennonite vegetable soup (no beets) ; _pluma moos_, a cold soup made from dried fruits; _perogies_; and for dessert, rhubarb platz.

Prairie Dog Central

Departs from Inkster Junction (1km/.6mi north of Inkster Blvd. between Sturgeon Rd. & Metro Rte. 90) 🕒mid-May–late Oct Sat–Sun call for schedule. ⊜$27.95-$41.95. Reservations required. ☎204-832-5259 or through Ticketmaster ☎204-253-2787. www.pdcrailway.com.

This vintage steam train, with its late-19C coaches, makes weekly excursions from Winnipeg to Warren, stopping at small towns so visitors can browse at local markets.

ADDRESSES

🛏 STAY

$ Beechmount B&B – *134 West Gate. Minimum two-night stay Jun–Aug.* 📞*204-775-1144 or 866-797-0905. www.beech mount.ca. 3 suites.* 🅿🛏🖥. Shady elms and oaks surround this riverbank 1890s Victorian mansion in a quiet yet central neighbourhood just west of Osborne Village. Large suites (one with detached bathroom) and an outdoor pool in a garden setting make this an attractive lodging. Generous breakfast.

$ Hostel Royal Plaza – *330 Kennedy St.* 📞*204-783-3000. http://www.hotelroyal plaza.ca. 120 beds.* ✖🚹. This hostel/hotel is located in downtown Winnipeg, near The Forks, the museums, the shopping and nightlife. All rooms have washroom and shower and air conditioning. Family rooms are available. Restaurant and bar.

$$ Best Western Charter House Hotel –*330 York Ave.* 📞*204-942-0101 or 888-670-7234. www.bwcharterhouse.com. 90 rooms.* ✖🚹🅿. This five-storey hotel, half a block from the Winnipeg Convention Centre and not far from The Forks, features friendly service and well-equipped, if conventional, rooms. The **Rib Room Restaurant ($$)**, whose affordable menu includes prime rib and a variety of seafood dishes, attracts the downtown business crowd. Café Bella & Lounge serves breakfast, lunch & dinner in a more family setting.

$$ The Columns B&B – *5 East Gate.* 📞*204-510-4803 or 877-772-1626. www.thecolumns.ca. 4 rooms. 2-wk advance reservations required in summer.* 🅿🖥. Situated in a quiet residential neighbourhood, this grand porticoed mansion (1906) is richly appointed with hardwood floors and oak panelling. Guest rooms have flat-screen TV, wireless Internet, ensuite bathrooms and bathrobes.

$$ Delta Winnipeg – *350 St. Mary's Rd.* 📞*204-942-0551 or 888-890-3222. www. deltahotels.com. 393 rooms.* ✖🚹🅿🛏. A great location across from shops and restaurants in Cityplace and the connecting skywalk to Winnipeg Convention Centre make this a favourite for conference delegates and travellers alike. The Delta has two pools (indoor and outdoor) as well as high-speed internet access and 24-hr Room Service.

The **Blaze Bistro ($$)** offers a well-priced menu, while the pub, **The Elephant & Castle ($)**, offers British pub fare and a game of darts.

$$ Inn at the Forks – *75 Forks Market Rd. www.innattheforks.com.* 📞*204-942-6555 or 877-377-4100. 115 rooms.* ✖🚹🅿 🆂🅿🅰 This modern, boutique hotel rises above the popular riverfront complex The Forks. Rooms sport contemporary furnishings and complimentary WiFi. Deluxe rooms have a spa shower or soaker tub; the waterfront suite offers views of downtown. Amenities include an on-site spa and fitness room. The **Smith ($$)** restaurant serves up Canadian cuisine and features live Canadian music sounds on weekends.

$$ River Gate Inn B&B – *186 West Gate.* 📞*204-489-5817 or 888-775-0166. www.rivergateinn.biz. 5 rooms.* 🅿🛏🖥 This Tudor-style house sits in a well-established neighbourhood. Upon entering, guests are asked to remove shoes for slippers. They are free to use the parlour, library, billiard room, and heated pool. One guest room has a semi-private bathroom; the others have ensuite bathrooms. Breakfast can be enjoyed outdoors in nice weather.

$$$ Fairmont Winnipeg – *Two Lombard Pl.* 📞*204-957-1350 or 866-540-4466. www.fairmont.com. 340 rooms.* ✖🚹🅿 🆂🅿🅰🛏. Winnipeg's premier downtown hotel towers over the famous corner of Portage and Main. Well-appointed, spacious rooms provide views of the historic Exchange District and connect to the Convention Centre & MTS Centre underground. **The VG (Velvet Glove) ($$$)** offers specialities like Beef Tenderloin, or Cold Water Seared Scallops, and desserts like Deconstructed Cheescake or Frozen Peaches & Cream.

$$$ Fort Garry Hotel – *222 Broadway.* 📞*204-942-8251 or 800-665-8088. www. fortgarryhotel.com. 246 rooms.* ✖🚹🅿🛏 🆂🅿🅰🖥. A few blocks south of Portage and Main, this imposing landmark has graced Winnipeg since 1913. A five-minute walk from The Forks, shopping areas and the major business district, the hotel offers spacious rooms, a fitness centre and spa, an indoor pool and a 24-hour deli. The **Palm Lounge ($$)**, which serves lunch and dinner, is known for its Sunday brunch and nightly live entertainment covering all styles of music.

⑂ EAT

$ East India Company – *349 York Ave.* *☎204-947-3097. www.eastindiaco.com.* ♿ **Indian**. Awash with rich tapestries and carvings from India, this exotic restaurant offers a buffet at lunch and dinner that comes with a salad bar and dessert bar and brims with traditional fare that includes curries, biryanis and vegetarian dishes. Customers may also order à la carte from the menu.

$ Resto Gare – *630 Des Meurons (at Provencher), St. Boniface.* ♿ *☎204-237-7072. www.restogare.com. No lunch Sun.* **French**. Housed in a converted train station in the city's French Quarter, this swank space is done up with bold red accents and vivid furnishings. The adjoining 1914 rail car is perfect for intimate parties. Bistro fare ranges from crêpe St. Jacques to bourguignon made with angus beef.

$$ Fusion Grill – *550 Academy Rd., ☎204-489-6963. www.fusiongrill.mb.ca. Open daily lunch & dinner. Closed Sun–Mon.* **New Prairie Cuisine (Canadian)**. Sleek eatery supports area producers & local artists, whose works adorn the walls. Arctic char, bison and grass-fed beef, to white truffle perogies (made with Yukon Gold potatoes, white truffle oil and duck sausage) or wild boar scallopini with creamed oyster mushrooms, tempting choices abound in this Cuvee Award-winning eatery. There's a wide selection of wines from Okanagan and Niagara.

$$$ Amici – *326 Broadway. ☎204-943-4997. www.amiciwpg.com.* **Northern Italian**. For more than two decades, the Tuscan-inspired dishes here have been a downtown draw for business people as well as celebrities. In an elegant linen-and-silver ambience, savour an inspiring menu of antipasti, pasta and risotto, and roasted veal, lamb or fowl with imaginative sauces and vegetable dishes. Downstairs at the ever-popular and less expensive **Bombolini** Wine Bar (**$$** *☎204-943-5066)*, enjoy pizza, pasta and simple meat dishes.

$$$ Café La Scala – *725 Corydon Ave. ☎204-474-2750.* **Italian**. Art brightens the walls of this narrow restaurant, bar and popular dance spot. Start with La Scala's portabella mushroom dumplings with cilantro chili garlic sauce or mussels Sambuca, and move on to a pasta course such as vermicelli with tiger shrimp in black bean sauce. Arugula salad with Asiago cheese, pine nuts and a balsamic vinegar reduction wins consistent raves.

$$$ The Gates on Roblin – *6945 Roblin Blvd. (Hwy. 241), Headingley. ☎204-224-2837. www.thegatesonroblin.com.* ♿ **Canadian.** Foodies from Winnipeg and beyond make the drive to the country to dine here. Dine on the likes of prime rib, Manitoba-raised pork, braised bison ribs or smoked salmon inside the elegant Dutch Colonial manor. Outdoor dining is seasonal. Reservations strongly suggested on weekends and holidays. Atrium overlooks spectacular view and horse corrals.

$$ Deer & Almond – *85 Princess St., 204-504-8562. Open 11am-3pm, 5pm-11pm, closed Sun.* **Fusion.** Tastes from the Mediterranean and Asia dominate an attractive space decorated with metal, wood, and original art. Dishes to be loved by Vegans and meat eaters alike, such as tahini-roasted eggplant and smoked tomato, or tender pork bellies and leeks. Surprises abound, and it's well worth the adventure to dine on such delicious fare.

SHOPPING

Winnipeg's Little Italy – An eight-block stretch of Corydon Avenue between Stafford and Osborne is filled with shops and a restaurant row.

Winnipeg Outfitters, *250 McPhillips St. ☎204-775-9653 or-800-665-0193. www.outfitters.ca.* A stuffed musk-ox greets browsers at this rambling brick building, five minutes west of downtown. The 30-year-old-plus exchange catalogs 7,000 items of outdoor, hunting, and extreme cold-weather wear and equipment.

Yorkton

Saskatchewan

In 1882 farmers from York County, Ontario, first settled near a river two miles north of present-day Yorkton. When the rail line was extended to the area in 1889, the community moved to be near it.

Other nationalities, especially Ukrainians, soon arrived by train. Today Yorkton is known as a manufacturing centre for agricultural equipment and for its stockyards.

▶ **Population:** 15,669.

Info: Visitor Centre, Junction Hwys. 9 & 16. 306-783-8707. www.tourismyorkton.com.

Location: Yorkton lies 187km/116mi northeast of Regina on the Yellowhead Highway.

Parking: Yorkton has metered parking.

Don't Miss: The Western Development Museum.

Timing: Allow at least a half day to explore Yorkton and the Western Development Museum.

SIGHT
Western Development Museum★

Hwy. 16 W. ♿ ⏰*Open Tue–Fri 9am–5pm, Sat–Sun noon–5pm.* ⏰*Closed major holidays.* ⬜$10. 306-783-8361. www.wdm.ca.

The Yorkton branch of this museum (other branches in North Battleford, Moose Jaw and Saskatoon) is devoted to the various ethnic groups found in Saskatchewan. There are displays on the native inhabitants, and dioramas of Ukrainian, German, Scandinavian, English and American pioneer homes. In addition, there is a collection of antique steam and gas-traction engines as well as other agricultural equipment on exhibit outdoors.

A Sampling of Canada's Collections of First Nations Culture and Art

- **Banff** Buffalo Nations Luxton Museum★
- **Calgary** Glenbow Museum★★
- **Churchill** Eskimo Museum★★
- **Edmonton** Royal Alberta Museum★★
- **Fort Macleod** Head-Smashed-In Buffalo Jump★★
- **Ottawa Canada Goose Museum at Nature Mueum**
- **'Ksan** Gitksan artifacts collection★★
- **Midland** Huron Indian Village★
- **Montreal** McCord Museum ★★
- **Prince Rupert** Museum of Northern British Columbia★★
- **Queen Charlotte** Haida Gwaii Museum★★
- **Regina** Royal Saskatchewan Museum★★
- **St. John's** The Rooms
- **Toronto** Royal Ontario Museum★★★
- **Vancouver** UBC Museum of Anthropology★★★; Museum of Vancouver ★★
- **Victoria** Royal BC Museum★★★
- **Winnipeg** Manitoba Museum★★★; Winnipeg Art Gallery★
- **Yellowknife** Prince of Wales Northern Heritage Centre★★

ONTARIO

Canada's richest and most populous province (13,792,052 inhabitants), Ontario is the country's industrial, economic, political and cultural heartland. Stretching from the Great Lakes in the south to Hudson Bay in the north, the province encompasses a spectacular menu and variation of scenery, the majority of its natural beauty spots being in or near water. Possessing nearly 200,000sq km/70,000sq mi of lakes, Ontario takes its name from the Iroquoian word meaning "shining waters."

Info: Ontario Tourism Marketing, 10 Dundas St. E., Suite 900, Toronto. ☎800-668-2746. www.ontariotravel.net.

Location: Ontario sits between Quebec and Manitoba, stretching from the Great Lakes to Hudson's Bay. To the south lie the US states of New York, Pennsylvania, Ohio, Michigan and Minnesota.

Don't Miss: Ontario's vast system of lakes and rivers offers any number of attractions for vacationers, but Toronto and Ottawa are also well worth your while.

Timing: Ontario has many interesting sights, but distances are vast; plan your itinerary realistically.

Geography

A Land Shaped by Glaciers – When North America's last Ice Age receded about 10,000 years ago, it left the region that is now Ontario scarred and completely reshaped. Great holes gouged out of the earth had gradually filled with water and over much of the land the geological core of the continent was revealed. The Precambrian rocks of this forested, lake-filled terrain known as the **Canadian Shield** are still exposed over a large part of the province today, producing a landscape of rock, water and rock-clinging trees. Only in the north and in the extreme south have sedimentary deposits allowed more varied surface features.

The Great Lakes – These vast expanses of freshwater are one of the most extraordinary legacies of the glaciers. **Lake Superior,** the largest, deepest and coldest of the lakes, was created before the ice ages by a fault in the Shield. The other

Horseshoe Falls, Niagara Falls

	JANUARY		JULY	
	Low	High	Low	High
Ottawa	−15°C/5°F	−6°C/21°F	15°C/59°F	26°C/79°F
Toronto	−7°C/18°F	−1°C/30°F	17°C/63°F	27°C/81°F
Thunder Bay	−21°C/-6°F	−8°C/16°F	11°C/52°F	23°C/75°F
Windsor	−9°C/16°F	−1°C/30°F	17°C/63°F	28°C/82°F

four (Lakes **Huron, Michigan, Erie** and **Ontario**) were formed by erosion of the original sediment over millions of years. Today their waters flow northeast down the St. Lawrence River to the Atlantic. All but Lake Michigan border Ontario, giving the province a freshwater shoreline of 3,800km/2,360mi, which greatly affects its climate.

The North – The large region north of an imaginary line from the Ottawa River to Georgian Bay via Lake Nipissing is referred to as "Northern Ontario." Sparsely populated except in areas of rich mineral deposits, the land rarely rises above 460m/1500ft. Northern Ontario provides wood for the pulp and paper mills, and its many lakes have created a sportsman's paradise.

The South – The smaller region south of the Ottawa River–Georgian Bay dividing line is the most densely populated and industrialized part of Canada, especially the area at the western end of Lake Ontario, known as the **Golden Horseshoe**.
To the east lies a small agricultural triangle in the forks of the Ottawa and St. Lawrence rivers. To the west are the fertile farmlands of the Niagara Peninsula and the region called **Southwestern Ontario**.

Climate – The climate varies widely in this province. Northern Ontario experiences long, bright but cold winters, and sunny summers with hot days and cool nights. In the south the winters are less severe because of the moderating influence of the Great Lakes. The summers are longer than in the north but much more humid, again due to the Great Lakes.

A Bit of History

Before the Europeans – Northern Ontario was inhabited by First Nations tribes, whose subsistence lifestyle was similar to that of the tribes in the Northwest Territories. The south, on the other hand, was the realm of Algonquian and Iroquoian language groups known as the **Eastern Woodlands culture** (see Introduction to Canada). These tribes generally lived a fairly sedentary life in organized villages around which fields of beans, corn and squash were cultivated. Every 10 or so years when the land was exhausted, the village was moved to a new site. The men hunted and fished extensively, never staying away long from their palisaded villages. Iroquoian society was matrilineal (descent was from the mother), and the women of these tribes wielded considerable power, selecting the male chiefs, for example. In contrast Algonquin society was patrilineal.

Composed of five tribes (Mohawk, Onondaga, Seneca, Cayuga, Oneida), the **League of the Iroquois** warred repeatedly with the early French settlers and defeated and dispersed the **Huron**, another Iroquoian group.

Part of New France – What is now Ontario was crisscrossed by most of the 17C and 18C French explorers, many in pursuit of furs. First to visit was **Étienne Brûlé,** followed by **Champlain, Radisson** and **Groseilliers** in their search for a route to Hudson Bay; Marquette and Jolliet in their search for a river flowing west from Lake Superior; and **René-Robert Cavelier, Sieur de La Salle** on his famous trip down the Mississippi.

ONTARIO

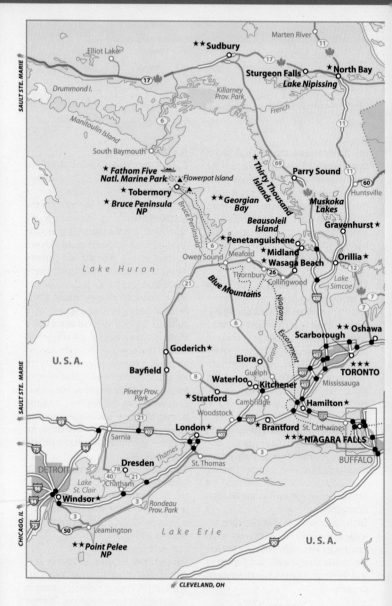

In 1639 the **Jesuits** established a mission on the shores of Georgian Bay to convert the Huron to Christianity. In 1650 the settlement succumbed to attacks by the Iroquois, who martyred five of the Jesuit fathers. In the early 18C, farms were laid out on the shores of the Detroit River in Southwest Ontario. At the same time, the **Hudson's Bay Company** was establishing itself in the province's northern section. In 1673 a post was founded at **Moosonee** on James Bay, which claims to be Ontario's oldest settlement.

Arrival of the Loyalists – When the American colonies revolted against British rule in 1775, many refused to join the rebels. Called Loyalists (or "Tories," to

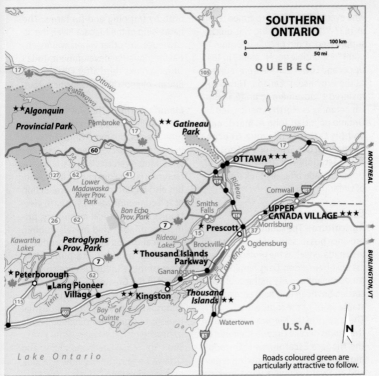

SOUTHERN ONTARIO

QUEBEC

★★ **Algonquin Provincial Park**

★★ **Gatineau Park**

OTTAWA ★★★

Cornwall

UPPER CANADA VILLAGE ★★★

Morrisburg

★ **Prescott**

Brockville

Ogdensburg

★ **Thousand Islands Parkway**

Gananoque

★ **Peterborough**

■ **Lang Pioneer Village**

★★ **Kingston**

Thousand Islands ★★

Watertown

U.S.A.

Lake Ontario

Roads coloured green are
particularly attractive to follow.

Kawartha Lakes

Petroglyphs ▲ Prov. Park

Rideau Lakes

Smiths Falls

Lower Madawaska River Prov. Park

Bon Echo Prov. Park

Pembroke

Ottawa

MONTREAL

BURLINGTON, VT

Bay of Quinte

Trent

N

SYRACUSE, NY

use the American term), most fled after the Revolution.

An estimated 80,000 Loyalists settled in Canada—in Nova Scotia, New Brunswick, Prince Edward Island, the Eastern Townships of Quebec, the St. Lawrence Valley and the Niagara Peninsula. Among the Loyalists in Ontario were Indians of the Six Nations **Iroquois Confederacy** (the Tuscarora joined the five-nation Iroquois league in 1722) who, under their great chief **Joseph Brant**, had fought for the British. The arrival of such a great number of people created, almost overnight, the province of Upper Canada (Lower Canada being present-day Quebec).

American Invasion – In 1812 the Americans, infuriated by British high-handedness on the open seas, declared war and invaded Canada, hoping to seize it quickly while the British were preoccupied fighting Napoleon in Europe. The ensuing war was fought mainly in Upper Canada. Naval encounters occurred on the Great Lakes, during which Toronto was looted and burned. There was fighting in the Niagara Peninsula, where **Isaac Brock** and **Laura Secord** established their names in Canadian history, and along the St. Lawrence, particularly at **Crysler's Farm** (⟳ see *UPPER CANADA VILLAGE*).

Toward Confederation – The British government encouraged immigration to Upper Canada to bolster the population against further American attack. Approximately 1.5 million people crossed the Atlantic from 1820 to 1840 to seek a better life in Ontario.

Fresh from a struggle to promote electoral reform in England, immigrants found Canada backward. Real political power lay with the governor and a council dominated by several well-connected groups known as the **Family Compact.** Opposition to this system was led by a fiery Scot, **William Lyon Mackenzie**, who eventually resorted to armed revolt in 1837. While the uprising was quickly suppressed, it did persuade Britain to grant "responsible government." In 1841 Upper and Lower Canada were reunited as the Province of Canada. This union fostered a movement to unite all British colonies in North America, led by Ontario politician **John A. Macdonald** and his Quebec colleague **George-Étienne Cartier.** When union (Canadian Confederation) was achieved in 1867, Upper Canada officially took the name of Ontario.

Economy

Agriculture – The southern part of the province boasts some of the richest soil in Canada as well as the province's longest frost-free season. Dairy farming is the predominant activity in the southeast corner. Soybean and field corn are the staple crops of the southwest.

The section of the Niagara Peninsula on the shores of Lake Ontario sheltered by the Niagara Escarpment is Ontario's most important **fruit-growing** region and an award-winning **wine-making** industry thrives.

Mining – No other province is as rich in minerals as Ontario, one of the world's largest suppliers of nickel, and a major producer of gold, silver, platinum, uranium, zinc, copper and a range of structural materials. The **Sudbury Igneous Complex** is the largest single source of nickel in the world. Platinum, copper, cobalt, silver, gold, selenium, sulphur compounds and tellurium are also extracted from the ore.

Forests, Fishing, Furs and Hydroelectricity – The province is still largely covered with forest, despite harvesting in the last century. Today pulp, paper and sawn lumber are the main products, and Ontario ranks third after British Columbia and Quebec in the value of total production. Ontario leads the rest of Canada in the value of fish taken from inland waters, thanks to the province's 250,000 lakes, and four of the Great Lakes. Fur production is still carried on

both by trapping and fur farms. The harnessing of the Niagara River, the St. Lawrence and other waters was essential for industrial development. Today Ontario ranks third after Quebec and British Columbia in hydroelectric output.

Manufacturing – The provincial economy is still dominated by the manufacturing sector, but more Ontarians work in the service sector than on assembly lines. Motor-vehicles and parts manufacturing is a major industry in Ontario, but also important are the production of telecommunications systems, electronics and electrical machinery, primary and fabricated metals, rubber, chemical goods and food products, as well as printing and publishing. Most of these industries are concentrated in the Greater Toronto Area and along the Highway 401 corridor from Windsor to Kingston. Other industrial regions of significance include Sarnia (petrochemicals), Niagara (auto parts), Sault Ste. Marie (steel and paper) and Ottawa-Carleton (telecommunications, high technology).

Great Lakes/St. Lawrence Seaway System – Completed in 1959, this network of lakes, rivers, locks and canals extends 3,790km/2,350mi from the Atlantic Ocean to the western end of the Great Lakes. Cheap water transportation on this system has been of great importance to the development of Ontario.

The New Economy – Ontario's services sector composes 70 percent of the overall economy. The province accounts for about half of Canada's $120 billion trade in services. Several Ontario-based companies are world leaders in the **telecommunications** equipment market. Ontario's biotechnology and communications technologies are centred in Toronto and Ottawa. Toronto is a leader in new media and in **film and television** production as well. Tourism in Ontario is the country's largest such industry; the province attracts 48 percent of visitors to Canada and generates 37 percent of the nation's income from this source.

PRACTICAL INFORMATION
GETTING THERE

BY AIR – Flights to Toronto's Pearson International Airport *(25km/15mi west of downtown; Terminal 1 ℘416-247-7678, Terminal 3 ℘416-776-5100 or 866-207-1690; www.gtaa.com)* are available via major domestic and international carriers. **Air Canada** *(℘888-247-2262 Canada/US; www.aircanada.com)* and its affiliates provide connections to regions throughout the province. **Public transportation** (bus and subway) links the airport to the greater metropolitan area *(℘416-869-3200 or 888-438-6646. www.gotransit.com)*. **Taxis** generally offer a flat rate to downtown *(about $50-$75)*. Union Pearson Express **shuttle** rail **service** from Union Station every 15 minutes between 5am-1am, $12 one-way (www.upexpress.com). Major **car rental** agencies also at the airport.

BY BUS AND TRAIN – The major intercity **bus** line is Greyhound *(℘416-594-1010 or 800-661-8747 Canada or 800-231-2222 US; www.greyhound.ca)*. **VIA Rail,** Canada's national passenger service, links many cities within the province *(℘888-842-7245 Canada/US; www.viarail.ca)*.

GENERAL INFORMATION
ACCOMMODATIONS AND VISITOR INFORMATION

The government tourist office produces annually updated regional guides that list accommodations, camping facilities, attractions and travel centres. Contact **Ontario Tourism Marketing**, *10 Dundas St. E., Suite 900, Toronto. ℘800-668-2746. www.ontariotravel.net*. This website has a wealth of useful information for travellers to Ontario.

ROAD REGULATIONS – The province has good paved roads. Speed limits, unless otherwise posted, are 100km/h (60mph) on freeways and the Trans-Canada, and 80km/h (50mph) on most highways and rural roads. The speed limits in cities and towns range from 40km/hr to 60km/h (25–40mph). **Seat belt** use is mandatory. For listings of the **Canadian Automobile Assn. (CAA)**, consult the local telephone directory or the website *(www.caa.ca)*.

TIME ZONES – Most of Ontario is on Eastern Standard Time. Daylight Saving Time is observed from the second Sunday in March to the first Sunday in November. In the western third of the province (west of longitude 90°) Central Standard Time applies.

TAXES – In addition to the national 5% GST, Ontario levies an 8% provincial retail sales tax (RST), a 10% alcoholic beverages tax and a proposed new hotel room tax being debated at press time. Non-residents can request rebates of the RST (a receipt must total $50 or more) within 30 days of purchase (but not for alcohol or tobacco) from Retail Sales Tax Office *℘866-668-8297 or www.fin.gov.on.ca*.

LIQUOR LAWS – The legal drinking age is 19. Liquor is sold in government stores.

PROVINCIAL HOLIDAY
Civic Holiday: 1st Monday in August

RECREATION
OUTDOOR ACTIVITIES

Water sports – Scenic routes to explore by boat are the Rideau Canal and lakes from Ottawa to Kingston, and the Trent-Severn system from Trenton to Georgian Bay via the Kawartha Lakes and Lake Simcoe. **Canoeing** is one of the most popular outdoor activities, ranging from lake and river to white-water canoeing. Many outfitters offer an array of excursions that include transportation, lodging, equipment and the service of experienced guides. The best-known regions are **Algonquin Provincial Park** *(℘705-633-5572, www.algonquinpark.on.ca)*, which has 1,500km/900mi of canoe routes, and **Quetico Provincial Park** *(℘807-597-2735, www.ontarioparks. com)*, through which the Boundary

Waters Fur Trade Canoe Route passes with 43 portages along 523km/325mi. For additional information, contact Paddle Canada in Kingston (℘888-252-6292, www.paddlingcanada.com).

Hiking – The Bruce Trail follows the Niagara Escarpment for 692km/430mi across the southern part of the province. Hikers pass through wilderness on the Coastal Trail along the shores of Lake Superior in **Pukaskwa National Park** (℘807-229-0801; www.pc.gc.ca).

Fishing – Ontario is a fisherman's paradise, particularly in the north, where many fly-in lodges arrange expeditions. Nonresidents must obtain a license, available from local sporting good stores. For information on seasons, catch and possession limits contact the Natural Heritage Information Centre, (℘800-667-1940, www.mnr.gov.on.ca).

Skiing – Thunder Bay, Blue Mountain (Collingwood), and the Gatineau Hills (Ottawa) are popular alpine skiing and snowboarding areas. Cross-country skiing is practiced in parks and centres across the province. Contact the Ontario Snow Resorts Association ℘705-443-5450. www.skiontario.ca.

SPECIAL EXCURSIONS

Several **white-water rafting** excursions, led by experienced guides, are available on the Ottawa River *(May–Sept; round-trip 4-6hrs; from ⊜starts at $89, including equipment & meal; accommodations extra; reservations required; Wilderness Tours* ℘613-646-2291 or 888-723-8669, www.wildernesstours.com).

A fascinating all-day train trip, the **Polar Bear Express Train**, takes the traveller across terrains of giant forests, bushland and muskeg through the Arctic watershed to Moosonee on Hudson Bay. Arriving at midday, visitors have ample time to tour Ontario's oldest English settlement, founded by the Hudson's Bay Co. in 1673. *Departs from Cochrane late Jun–late Aug Sun–Fri 9am, returns to Cochrane 11pm. Reservations required. Round trip ⊜$104.90.* ✕ ♿ 🅿. *Ontario Northland* ℘800-268-9281. www.ontarionorthland.ca.

Luxury steamboat cruising can be enjoyed aboard **MV Canadian Empress**. Cruises include shore visits to historic sites and to Ottawa, Montreal, Quebec City and other cities. Trips of 4–7 days available. *Depart from Kingston, Ottawa or Quebec City. Late-May–late Oct. Reservations required. Lawrence Cruise Lines, Inc.* ℘613-549-8091 or 800-267-7868. www.stlawrencecruiselines.com).

PRINCIPAL FESTIVALS

Feb	**Winterlude**, *Ottawa*
Mar	**Maple Syrup Festival**, *Elmira*
Apr–Nov	**Shaw Festival**, *Niagara*
May	**Ottawa Tulip Festival**,
May–Nov	**Stratford Festival**, *Stratford*
Jun	**Luminato**, *Toronto*
Jul	**Bluesfest International**, *Windsor*
	Great Rendezvous, *Thunder Bay*
	Honda Indy, *Toronto*
Jul–Aug	**Caribana**, *Toronto*
	Three Fires Homecoming Pow-Wow *Hagersville*
	Summerfolk, *Owen Sound*
Sept	**Internatonal Film Festival**, *Toronto*
	Niagara Wine Festival, *St. Catharine*
Nov	**Royal Agricultural Winter Fair**, *Toronto*
Nov–Jan	**Winter Festival of Lights**, *Niagara Falls*

White-water rafting on the Ottawa River

© Ontario Tourism Marketing Partnership Corporation

Brantford ★

Named for Six Nations Chief Joseph Brant, this manufacturing city, located on the banks of the Grand River, is famous as the family home of inventor **Alexander Graham Bell** and birthplace of hockey great **Wayne Gretzky.**

A BIT OF HISTORY

Brantford stands in the valley of the Grand River on land given to the Six Nations Indians in 1784 by the British government. Led by Chief **Joseph Brant** (1742-1807), these Native Americans, like other Loyalists, fled the US after the Revolution. European settlers purchased land from the First Nations in 1830, and the present city was founded, retaining the old name, Brant's Ford. The First Nations reserve to the south is the scene every August of the **Six Nations Fall Fair**.

SIGHTS
Bell Homestead
National Historic Site★

94 Tutela Heights Rd. From downtown, take Colborne St. West across Grand River, turn left on Mt. Pleasant St. and left again on Tutela Heights Rd. ✕ ♿ 🅿
☙ *Visit by guided tour (45-60min) only year-round Tue–Sun 9:30am–4:30pm.*
🕐 *Closed Feb18, Apr 18–20, Dec 24– Jan 1, Good Friday, Easter Sunday & Mon.* ⊘ *$6.25.* ☏ *519-756-6220. www.bellhomestead.ca.*
In 1870 **Alexander Graham Bell** (1847-1922) left Scotland and took a job in Bos-

▶ **Population:** 93,650.
🚗 **Michelin Map:** p242.
ℹ **Info:** Visitor & Tourist Centre, 399 Wayne Gretzky Parkway, ☏519-751-9900 or 800-265-6299. www.discoverbrantford.ca.
▶ **Location:** Brantford lies southwest of Toronto, on Hwy. 403 between Hamilton in the east and Woodstock in the west.
👁 **Don't Miss:** Bell Homestead National Historic Site.
🕐 **Timing:** Allow a day to leisurely enjoy the sights of Brantford.
👪 **Kids:** The Wayne Gretsky Sports Centre (👁 *see box "The Great Gretzky").*

ton as a teacher of the deaf. While trying to reproduce sounds visibly for his deaf pupils, he discovered how to transmit speech along an electrified wire, hence the telephone. The first "long distance" call was made from his parent' home in Brantford when Bell, in Paris, Ontario *(about 11km/7mi away),* was able to hear his father's voice.
This house (1858) is furnished much as it would have been in Alexander Graham Bell's day. Next door is an early telephone exchange and displays on the development of the telephone.

The Great Gretzky

Born in Brantford, Ontario, **Wayne Gretzky** (b.1961) is revered in Canada and beyond as the National Hockey League's greatest player. A backyard ice-skater at age two, first coached by his father, he went on to become NHL's most valuable player eight years in a row. For four seasons in the 1980s, he led his team, the Edmonton Oilers, to victory in Stanley Cup competitions. For seven consecutive years, he was awarded the leading NHL scorer trophy. His native city adores him: Wayne Gretzky Parkway, the annual Wayne Gretzky International Hockey Tournament, and the **Wayne Gretzky Sports Centre** 👪 are all named in his honour. The centre has three ice rinks, an Olympic swimming pool and many other facilities.

Woodland Cultural Centre

184 Mohawk St. ♿🕐*Open year-round Mon–Fri 9am–4pm, Sat–Sun 10am–5pm.* 🕐*Closed major holidays.* 🎫*$7 (museum).* ✆*519-759-2650. www.woodland-centre.on.ca.*

The highlight of the **museum** is the Constitution of the League of Five Nations (1452) made of shell beads and string. The interior of a 19C longhouse depicts the life of the Eastern Woodlands Indians.

A short drive away stands the oldest Protestant church in Ontario, **Her Majesty's Royal Chapel of the Mohawks** (*301 Mohawk St;* ♿🕐*open daily May-Sept 10am-4pm; Closed Mon; Services held summer Sun 10:30am* 🎫*contribution requested;* ✆*519-756-0240; www.mohawkchapel.ca).*

ADDRESSES

🍽/EAT

$$ The John Peel Restaurant – *48 Dalhousie St.* ✆*519-753-7337. www.johnpeel.ca. No lunch Sat. Closed Sun.* **Steakhouse.** A culinary fixture in downtown Brantford since 1974, The John Peel serves fine steaks and seafood along with a selection of more than 150 wines. Hot apple beignets with ice cream or crème caramel tempt diners for dessert.

$$$ Olde School Restaurant – *Paris Road West at 687 Powerline Rd. 2km off Hwy 403.* ✆*519-753-3131 or 888-448-3131. www.theoldeschoolrestaurant.ca. Lunch Mon–Fri from 11:30am; Dinner Mon–Sun from 5pm; Sun Brunch 11am–3pm.* ♿🅿. **Canadian.** This 19C brick school building is now a popular eating spot, awash in Victorian details like stained-glass windows and ornate light fixtures. It is a bit out of the way, toward the town of Paris, but the Queen visited in 1997. The chef specials come with soup or salad, sides.

Dresden

The country around this small manufacturing centre was first settled by black slaves who fled the US for freedom in British North America. One of these slaves was **Josiah Henson**, arriving in Ontario with his family in 1830. with the aid of donations from Britain, he purchased land in the Dresden area, established a refuge for other fugitives and founded a school. Unable to write, Henson dictated the story of his life (*The Life of Josiah Henson—Formerly a Slave*), which so impressed **Harriet Beecher Stowe** that she used him as the model for her influential novel *Uncle Tom's Cabin.*

SIGHT
Uncle Tom's Cabin Historic Site★

1.6km/1mi west off Hwy. 21 at 29251 Uncle Tom's Rd. ♿🕐*Open mid-May–Oct*

♿ **Michelin Map:** p216.
📋 **Info:** www.dresden.ca.
▶ **Location:** Dresden is in southwestern Ontario, between Windsor and London. Leave Hwy. 401 (Trans-Canada Hwy.) at Exit 101, and follow signage to Hwy. 21, then to Dresden. Dresden is about an hour from London.

Tue–Sat 10am–4pm, Sun noon–4pm (Jul–Aug open daily). 🎫*$7.* ✆*519-683-2978. www.uncletomscabin.org.*

This collection of wooden buildings includes Henson's house (Uncle Tom's Cabin), a simple church of the same era as the one in which he preached and a fugitive slave's house. In the museum there are items recalling the era of slavery such as posters advertising slave sales and slave whips. Henson's grave lies outside.

Georgian Bay★★

Named for George IV of England, this immense bay off Lake Huron is a popular vacation spot; summer cottages line its shores and islands. More than a resort area, however, the region supports considerable light industry. Owen Sound, Collingwood, Midland, Port McNicoll and Parry Sound are fair-size ports with grain elevators.

GEOGRAPHY

Immortalized by the Group of Seven painters, the eastern and northern shorelines are wild and rocky with thousands of islands. The western and part of the southern shores form a section of the **Niagara Escarpment;** this ridge of limestone crosses Ontario from Niagara Falls, mounts the Bruce Peninsula, submerges and then resurfaces to form Manitoulin and other islands, and ends in Wisconsin. In contrast, the coast along the western side of the Midland Peninsula has long sandy stretches, especially in the region of Wasaga Beach. In the southeast corner of the bay is Georgian Bay Islands National Park, established in 1929.

A BIT OF HISTORY

Étienne Brûlé, one of Champlain's men, visited Georgian Bay in 1610. Fur traders and Jesuits soon followed, arriving via the 1,300km/800mi canoe route from Quebec. Jesuits built a mission post called Sainte-Marie near the present site of Midland in 1639. At this time, the Huron were under attack from the Iroquois tribes to the south. Caught in the middle, several Jesuit fathers were killed after suffering incredible torture. The atrocities led to the abandonment of Sainte-Marie in 1649.

After the Jesuits' return to Quebec and the Huron's defeat, peace was restored until the early-19C when warfare erupted between the British and Americans over control of the Great Lakes.

- ⚲ **Michelin Map:** p216.
- ▯ **Info:** Visitor Information Centre, Tobermory. ℰ519-596-2452. www.tobermory.org.
- ◖ **Location:** The Georgian Bay is almost a lake in itself, cut off from the rest of Lake Huron by the Bruce Penninsula and Manitoulin Island.
- ⊘ **Don't Miss:** One of the cruises around the islands.
- ◔ **Timing:** You will need a few days to tour the bay area.
- ♟ **Kids:** Wasaga Beach Festival in June.

HISTORICAL SIGHTS
MIDLAND★

This busy city on the bay is well known for its numerous historical and natural attractions.

Sainte-Marie among the Hurons★★

Hwy. 12 E. ✕ ▯ ◔ *Open mid-May–mid-Oct daily 10am–5pm. Early May and Oct, Mon–Fri 10am–5pm.* ☞*$12.* ℰ*705-526-7838. www.saintemarie amongthehurons.on.ca.*

Consisting of 22 structures enclosed within a wooden palisade, the mission established by the Jesuits in 1639 and destroyed by them before their retreat in 1649 has been reconstructed.

An audiovisual presentation *(17min)* explains the mission's history and should be viewed before the rest of the visit. The chapel, forge, saw pit, carpentry shop, residences and native area are peopled by guides in 17C costume.

Beside Sainte-Marie is the **Wye Marsh Wildlife Centre**, with nature trails, a boardwalk and an observation tower *(16160 Hwy. 12 East, Midland)* ♿◔*open daily year-round 9am–5pm;*☞*$11;* ℰ*705-526-7809; www.wyemarsh.com).*

Martyrs' Shrine★

5km/3mi east of Midland on Hwy. 12 near Wildlife Centre. ✗ & ◑ *Open daily 8:30am–9pm, Shrine Café 10am–4pm.* ⊛ *$5.* ✆ *705-526-3788 or Toll-Free 855-526-3788. www.martyrs-shrine.com.*

This twin-spired stone church was built in 1926 as a memorial to the eight Jesuit martyrs of New France killed by the Iroquois between 1642 and 1649 and declared saints in 1930. On the front portico stand **statues** of Jean de Brébeuf and Gabriel Lalemant.

The church has a striking **interior** with wood panelling and a roof of sandalwood from British Columbia.

Huron Wendat Village★

549 Little Lake Park. & ◑ *Open May–Oct daily 9am–5pm. Rest of the year Mon–Fri 9am–5pm.* ◑ *Closed Good Friday & Dec 25–26.* ⊛ *$12 (including museum).* ✆ *705-526-2844. www.huroniamuseum.com.*

This village is a replica of a 16C Huron community. A wooden palisade surrounds examples of the long, rectangular, bark-covered frame houses in which the Huron lived communally.

The **Huronia Museum** is located beside the village *(same hours as the village)*.

PENETANGUISHENE★

12km/8mi west of Midland by Rtes. 12 and 93.

The southern entrance to this town, which has a large French-speaking community, is guarded by two angels symbolizing the harmony between the English and French cultures.

Discovery Harbour★

93 Jury Dr. ✗ 🅿 ◑ *Open late-May–Labour Day daily 10am–5pm. Closed Victoria Day.* ⊛ *$7.* ✆ *705-549-8064. www.discoveryharbour.on.ca.*

On a pleasant site above Penetang harbour stands this reconstruction of a British Naval dockyard and military garrison established here after the War of 1812. Costumed interpreters evoke the life of the commanding officer and his staff in the naval house and dockyard. At the wharf are replicas of 19C schooners.

WASAGA BEACH★

This popular resort is well known for its 14km/9mi stretch of white sand, the longest fresh water beach in the world.

Nancy Island Historic Site★

In Wasaga Beach Provincial Park, on Mosley St. off Hwy. 92. 11-22nd St. N. & ◑ *Open mid-Jun–Labour Day daily 10am–6pm. Late May–mid-Jun Sat–Sun only 10am–6pm. Rest of Sept–early-Oct Sat–Sun 10am–5pm.* ✆ *705-429-2728,* ✆ *705-429-2516 (off-season). www.wasagabeachpark.com.*

The museum stands on a small island near the mouth of the Nottawasaga River created by silt collecting around the hull of a schooner, the **Nancy**. During the War of 1812, the vessel was sunk by the Americans. In 1927 her hull was recovered from the silt and is now displayed in the museum.

NATURAL SITES

Thirty Thousand Islands★

An excellent way to see the natural beauty of Georgian Bay and its many islands is one of three boat cruises.

From **Midland** town dock *(*✗ & ◑ *departs May–Oct daily 1:45pm, additional cruises late Jun–mid-Sept; round-trip 2hrs 30min;* ⊛ *$30; reservations suggested; Midland Tours Inc.* ✆ *705-549-3388 or 877-668-2286; www.midlandtours.com).*

From **Parry Sound** town dock *(*✗ & ◑ *2hr morning cruises Jul–Aug departs daily 10am* ⊛ *$30; and 3hr afternoon cruises Jun–mid-Oct daily 1pm;* ⊛ *$40; reservations required; 30,000 Island Cruise Lines Inc.* ✆ *705-746-2311 or 800-506-2628/Canada & US; https://islandqueencruise.com).*

Tobermory★

This small village, located at the tip of the Bruce Peninsula, surrounds its double harbour known as Big Tub and Little Tub. The clear blue-green waters, underwater rock formations and number of old shipwrecks also attract divers. Visitors can stroll around the marina and follow the lakeside boardwalk.

The vessel **MS Chi-Cheemaun**, 110m/365ft-long, provides regular ferry service to Manitoulin Island. The ship accommodates some 143 vehicles and 638 passengers and offers full meal service in its cafeteria. ✕&ⓇDeparts late Jun–Labour Day daily 7am, 11:20am, 3:40pm & 8pm. May–mid-Jun & rest of Sept–mid-Oct daily 8:50am & 1:30pm; additional departure Fri 6:10pm. One-way 1hr 45min. ⌾$36.95/car plus $16.50 adult.Owen Sound Transportation Co. ☏800-265-3163/Canada & US. www.ontarioferries.com).

Bruce Peninsula National Park★

Tobermory.

&🅿Ⓡ Open daily year-round. Visitor centre Jul–Labour Day daily 8am–8pm, Sept–Oct daily 10am–5pm (Sat 8am–5pm). Closed Tue & Wed. Admin office Mon–Fri 8am–4:30pm. ⌾$4.90 admission &11.70/car (parking) ☏519-596-2233. www.pc.gc.ca.

Established in 1987, this national park is known for its trails along the spectacular Niagara Escarpment. There is a large campground at Cyprus Lake, 15km/9mi south of Tobermory. Don't miss 15-minute film about this and Fathom Five National Park.

Fathom Five National Marine Park★

Ⓡ Same conditions as Bruce Penninsula National Park.

This "underwater" preserve, Canada's first National Marine Park, encompasses 20 islands and the treacherous waters off Tobermory. The remains of 22 wrecks of mid-19C to 20C sail and steam vessels can be seen up-close with scuba-diving or snorkeling equipment. Some of the islands and two of the wrecks can be seen on Canada's largest **glass-bottomed boat tour**(✕&🅿 contact Blue Heron Co. ☏519-596-2999 or 855-596-2999; www.blueheronco.com).

Tiny **Flowerpot Island** was at one time completely covered by the waters of Lake Huron. Caves high up on the cliffs and two rock pillars, known as the

Kayaking along Bruce Peninsula

© Ontario Tourism Marketing Partnership Corporation

flowerpots, can be closely approached by boat or on foot (⌾$5.80 day-use fee) from the island. The tour boats afford good views of the flowerpots. Cruises cost $38.94 plus tax & park entrance fee.

Beausoleil Island

Part of the Georgian Bay Islands National Park. Access by private boat or water taxi only from Honey Harbour (about 40km/25mi northeast of Midland via Rte. 12, Hwy. 400 and Rte. 5). Ⓡ Open daily year-round. ⌾$5.80 day-use fee (mid-May–early Oct). Contact the park office, 901 Wye Valley Rd. ☏705-527-7200. www.pc.gc.ca.

There are walking trails, a picnic area, camping, Rustic Cabins rental and a visitor kiosk (&Ⓡ open Jul–Labour Day Mon–Thu 9am–5pm, Fri–Sun 9am–7pm) on this island.

The Blue Mountains

56km/35mi from Wasaga Beach to Meaford by Rte. 26.

The waters of Georgian Bay lie on one side of the road and the Blue Mountains, the highest part of the Niagara Escarpment, on the other.

ADDRESSES

🏨 STAY

$ Thurso House B&B – *167 Pine St., Collingwood.* ℰ705-444-4476. *www. thursohouse.com. 3 rooms.* 🅿️ 🛏️. Guest rooms come with en suite bath at this 1902 Romanesque Revival house.

$$ Blue Bay Motel – *32 Bay St., Tobermory.* ℰ519-596-2392. *www.bluebay-motel.com. 16 rooms. 2-night minimum Sat–Sun Jul–Sept.* 🅿️. Clean, simple rooms at this motel overlook Little Tub Harbour. Wireless Internet.

$$ Grandview Motel – *8 Earl St., Tobermory.* ℰ519-596-2220. *www.grand view-tobermory.com. 18 units.* ✗🅿️. This motel has comfortable rooms. A large 3000 sq.ft. fully equipped cottage also available to rent with fireplace.

$$ Harborside Motel – *24 Carlton St., Tobermory.* ℰ519-596-2999. *www.blue heronco.com. 36 units.* From your patio, watch boats in Little Tub Harbour. Some rooms have kitchenettes.

$$ Saga Beach Resort – *88 Main St., Wasaga Beach.* ℰ705-429-2543 or ℰ800-263-7053. *www.sagaresort.com 16 motel rooms, 17 cottages.* 🅿️🛏️. This year-round compound is close to the main Wasaga beach. All lodgings have kitchens; some have no telephone.

🍽️ EAT

$ Leeside Restaurant – *3 Eliza St., Tobermory.* ℰ519-596-8375. *www.leeside restaurant.com.* **Canadian.** Whitefish dinners, hamburgers and breakfast from 5am (summer).

$$ SiSi Trattoria – *27 Bruce St.South, Thornbury.* ℰ519-599-7769. *www.sisi trattoria.com.* **Italian.** *Closed Monday.* Pasta, pizza, fish and much more fine dining at this renovated local star.

Crownsnest Pub, *5 Bay St., Tobermory.* ℰ519-596-2575. *http://crowsnestpub.ca.* Grilled local whitefish, hearty burgers, pizza and live music wekends.

Goderich★

This town was founded in 1828 as the terminus of the Huron Road, a right-of-way built in the early 19C to encourage settlement. The town has wide, tree-lined residential streets that radiate like the spokes of a wheel from central, octagonal **Court House Square**. On a visit Queen Elizabeth II called Goderich "the prettiest town in Canada." It has the advantage of a lovely harbour and beaches on the western short of Lake Huron.

SIGHTS
The Waterfront

Follow West St. from Court House Sq. In 1984 dredging deepened the lake to provide entry into the harbour for full-cargo vessels. Small craft berth at the city marina and a fleet of tugboats service freighters. 👫 *Tugboat harbour tours cancelled during 2014, for an update contact MacDonald Marine* ℰ519-524-

▶ **Population:** 7,521.

⛣ **Michelin Map:** p216.

🏢 **Info:** 57 West St. ℰ519-524-8344 or 800-280-7637. www.goderich.ca.

⬤ **Location:** The town sits on a bluff above the point where the Maitland River joins Lake Huron, midway between Port Elgin and Sarnia.

✪ **Don't Miss:** The Queen of England called this "the prettiest town in Canada." Take time to stroll and admire the big houses and three beaches.

🕐 **Timing:** Allow one day for sights and the excursion.

👫 **Kids:** The Huron Historic Gaol; harbour tugboat tours.

Convictions and Penalties

Here's a sampling of charges and resulting fines for the quarter ending in June 1879, in the County of Huron, from the Clerk of the Peace's Office:

Nature of Charge	Amount of Penalty, Fine or Damage
Vagrancy	$ .25
Insulting Language	$1.00
An Affray	$2.00
Disorderly Conduct	$1.00
Telling Fortunes	$2.00
Fast Driving over Brussels bridge	$1.00

9551. www.mactug.com. Residents and visitors alike are drawn to the sandy beaches, snack bars and extensive **boardwalk**.

Huron County Museum

110 North St. &🕐Open May 1 – Dec 31 Tue–Sat 10am–4:30pm, Thu til 8pm, Sun 1pm–4:30pm. 👓$7.50 museum & gaol). 📞519-524-2686. www.huroncountymuseum.ca.
This museum, part of which is housed in an 1856 school, was originally the project of an avid collector. It has been enlarged and modernized. Agricultural implements, military artifacts, and furniture are on view over two floors.

Huron Historic Gaol

181 Victoria St. N. 🕐Open May 1– late-Oct Mon–Sat 10am–4:30pm, Sun 1pm–4:30pm. Rest of Sept–Oct Sun–Fri 1pm–4pm, Sat 10am–4:30pm. 👓$7.50 museum & gaol. 📞519-524-6971. www.huroncounty.ca/gaol.
This unusual 150-year-old octagonal stone structure housed the county jail (gaol is the British spelling) from 1841 until 1972. It was built as a modern, humane facility during a period of prison reform in North America. It is now a National Historic Site. Visitors may enter the cells, library, kitchen, laundry room and outdoor yards. The top floor served as the courtroom (👓see sidebar of sample penalties). The adjoining house of the prison governor may be toured.

EXCURSION
Bayfield

21km/13mi south by Hwy. 21.
This small village near Lake Huron has a short but colorful main street, shaded by tall trees and lined with interesting shops, restaurants, inns and places of worship. Surrounding tree-lined residential streets hold vacation cottages, well-kept houses, manicured gardens and trailered boats.

ADDRESSES

🏨 STAY AND ⍾ EAT

$$$ The Little Inn – 26 Main St., Bayfield. 📞519-565-2611 or 800-565-1832. www. littleinn.com. 26 rooms & suites. ✕🅿️ Spa
A former coach stop, this charming inn, operating since 1832, offers guests modern amenities such as whirlpools and working fireplaces. Rooms are decorated with country antiques. The cuisine in the airy **dining room ($$$)** is regionally based. Dining 8am-9pm.

$$$$ The Red Pump Inn – 21 Main St., Bayfield. 📞519-565-2576 or 888-665-2576. www.theredpumpinn.com. 7 suites.
Equipped with a fireplace and balcony, each suite is well-appointed with crisp white linens atop comfortable beds. Enjoy contemporary cuisine in the first gourmet **dining room in the area ($$$)**, or in the pub, or garden in season. Gift and Fashion Boutique open onsite with unusual range of fashions and surprises.

Gravenhurst★

This attractive town with its tree-lined streets, elegant houses, and opera house (now a performing-arts centre) lies on picturesque Lake Muskoka, with its indented shoreline and numerous islands. A former logging settlement, Gravenhurst today serves as the gateway to the Muskoka Lakes area. It is also the birthplace of Dr. **Norman Bethune** (1890-1939), surgeon, inventor, advocate of socialized medicine and a national hero in China.

▶ **Population:** 12,055.
◔ **Michelin Map:** p216.
▤ **Info:** 3-5 Pineridge Gate
 ✆705-687-3412.
 www.gravenhurst.ca.
◖ **Location:** Gravenhurst lies at the southern end of the Muskoka Lakes, east of the Georgian Bay, on Hwy. 11 between Orillia and Bracebridge.
◉ **Don't Miss:** A lake cruise will help you appreciate the Muskoka area's reputation as Ontario's most popular vacation region.
◕ **Timing:** Spend at least two days in Gravenhurst and the Muskoka Lakes area. One week in cottage country is ideal.

SIGHTS
Bethune Memorial House National Historic Site★

235 John St. N. ✆Visit by guided tour (1hr) only, ◔Open Jul–Oct daily 10am–4pm. Sept–Oct Sat–Wed 10am–4pm, Jun Wed–Sun 10am–4pm. ☞$3.90. ✆705-687-4261. www.pc.gc.ca.

The son of a Presbyterian minister, **Norman Bethune** (1890-1939) studied medicine in Toronto, then practised in Detroit. Between 1928 and 1936, he worked as a chest surgeon in Montreal but, disillusioned with the lack of interest in socialized medicine in Canada, he departed for Spain to fight on the Republican side in the civil war. In 1938 he went to China and worked as a surgeon with the Chinese Communists fighting the Japanese, dying of blood poisoning late in 1939. Fame in his own country stemmed from Bethune's status as a hero to the Chinese.

The doctor's birthplace contains several rooms restored to their 1890s appearance, and an excellent **interpretive display** in three languages (English, French and Chinese) on his life and importance.

COTTAGE COUNTRY

Visitors to Ontario will inevitably hear references to "cottage country"—and for most Toronto residents that means the Muskoka Lakes and Georgian Bay. Other Ontarians think of area between Georgian Bay and the Ottawa River, all the way north to Algonquin Park. Some 1,600 lakes litter this largely forested landscape. During cottage season (Victoria Day to Thanksgiving) families abandon their homes to dwell in cabins, small houses and mansions (all called "cottages" by Canadians) around these deep-blue waters. Amenities range from the bare essentials to grandiose furnishings, a float plane and a watercraft or two. Purchase the latest in cottage couture at **Muskoka Store** *(Hwy. 11 N. of Gravenhurst; ✆705-687-7751; www.muskokastore.com)*. Purveyor of stocks wooden furniture (including the Muskoka chair), casual clothing, canoes and kayaks, kitchen utensils, gardening tools and just about anything else cottagers need to enjoy their vacations.

Steamship Cruises

Muskoka Steamship & Historical Society, 185 Cherokee Lane. ✕🚻🕐*Depart from Muskoka Wharf Jun–mid-Oct daily. Call for times & specialty cruise details. Round trip 1hr–4hrs. Reservations required.* ➽*$20–$100.*
🕿 *705-687-6667 or 866-687-6667. www.realmuskoka.com.*

Visitors can board the **RMS Segwun** at Gravenhurst's wharf to appreciate the beauty of the lakes and see some of the summer homes along their shores.

EXCURSION
Algonquin Provincial Park★★

About 100km/60mi northeast of Gravenhurst by Rtes. 11 and 60. ✕🕐*Open daily year-round.* ➽*Vehicle permit $17.* 🕿*705-633-5572. www.algonquinpark.on.ca.*

Encompassing 7,725sq km/2,983sq mi of forested wilderness in the eastern portion of the province, Algonquin is Ontario's third largest park. It is a popular recreation spot because of its hiking trails, canoe routes, camping facilities, fishing and swimming holes, winter ski runs and resident wildlife.

Known as the Parkway Corridor, Route 60 traverses the southern portion of the park for 56km/35mi. Information centres are located at each entrance, and the **Logging Museum★** (late Jun–mid-Oct) near the East Gate features area history of the industry. Situated 13km/8mi northwest of the East Gate is the park's **Visitor Centre★**, containing a cafe, bookstore, theatre, exhibits and an outdoor viewing deck. Two rustic resorts with dining rooms are the **Killarney Mountain Lodge** (*Lake of Two Rivers, Killarney;* 🕿*705-287-2242 or 800-461-1117 US/Canada; www.killarney.com*) and **Arowhon Pines** (*Little Joe Lake, Huntsville;* 🕿*705-633-5661, winter 416-483-4393) or 866-633-5661; www.arowhonpines.ca*).

Hamilton★

The city of Hamilton has a fine landlocked harbour bounded on the lakeside by a sandbar. A canal has been cut through the bar to enable ships of the seaway to reach port with their loads of iron ore for Hamilton's huge steel mills. The sandbar is crossed by Burlington Skyway, part of the **Queen Elizabeth Way (QEW)**, which connects Toronto with Niagara Falls. Hamilton is set on the Niagara Escarpment, which swings around the end of Lake Ontario at this point, rising steeply to 76m/250ft in the city. Known locally as "the mountain," it provides pleasant parks and views.

SIGHTS
City Centre★

Downtown Hamilton has (*along Main St. between Bay and James Sts.*) several attractive buildings, in particular City Hall; the Education Centre; the Art Gal-

▸ **Population:** 781,000 CMA.

Michelin Maps: p216 and p230.

Info: Tourist Office, 28 James St. N. 🕿905-546-2666 or 800-263-8590 or www.tourismhamilton.com.

Location: Western end of Lake Ontario, southwest of Toronto.

🅿 **Parking:** Parking meters enforced Mon–Sat, 8am–6pm. There are also 19 lots and 2 covered garages.

Don't Miss: The Royal Botanical Gardens offer lovely landscapes and pleasant restaurants.

🕐 **Timing:** Hamilton deserves at least a day of your time.

Kids: The African Lion Safari Park.

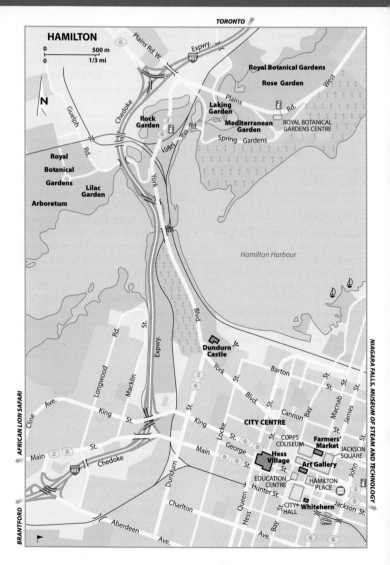

HAMILTON

Royal Botanical Gardens

Rose Garden

Laking Garden

Rock Garden

Mediterranean Garden

ROYAL BOTANICAL GARDENS CENTRE

Plains Rd.

Spring Gardens

Royal Botanical Gardens

Lilac Garden

Arboretum

Hamilton Harbour

Dundurn Castle

Barton

CITY CENTRE

COPPS COLISEUM

Farmers' Market

JACKSON SQUARE

Hess Village

Art Gallery

EDUCATION CENTRE

HAMILTON PLACE

CITY HALL

Whitehern

AFRICAN LION SAFARI

BRANTFORD

NIAGARA FALLS, MUSEUM OF STEAM AND TECHNOLOGY

---

lery; and Hamilton Place, a cultural centre with two theatres.

A few blocks west is **Hess Village★** *(junction Hess and George Sts.),* a district of older homes converted to fashionable boutiques, restaurants and cafes.

Also in the vicinity is the **farmers' market** (35 York Blvd; ⟨open year-round Tue, Thu, Fri, Sat early mornings until 6pm; ✆905-546-2096), one of Ontario's largest indoor markets, selling the produce of the Niagara Peninsula.

Art Gallery★

123 King St. W. ⟨Open year-round Tue–Sun from 11am-6pm, til 8pm Thu. Closed Mon. Free first Fri of month 4pm-8pm⟨$10. ✆905-527-6610. www.artgalleryofhamilton.com

This distinctive structure stands across a plaza from City Hall. Changing exhibits from the permanent collection of more than 9,000 works of European, Canadian and contemporary art are displayed as well as visiting shows.

Whitehern Historic House and Garden (A on map)

41 Jackson St. W. ⌛Visit by guided tour (1hr) only. ◷*Tue-Sun 12pm-4pm.* ◷*Closed Jan 1, Good Friday & Dec 25–26.* ✆*$7.* ✆*905-546-2018. www.whitehern.ca.*

In small but pleasant gardens surrounded by Hamilton's city centre, this Georgian house was the residence until 1968 of three generations of the McQuesten family, who inspired such projects as the Royal Botanical Gardens and the Niagara Parkway.

Dundurn National Historic Site★

610 York Blvd. ⌛Visit by guided tour (1hr) only, ✖◷*Tue–Sun 12pm–4pm.* ◷*Closed Jan 1, Good Friday & Dec 25-26.* ✆*$11.* ✆*905-546-2872. www.museumsontario.ca.*

This grand stone house with its Neoclassical portico entry stands on a hill in Dundurn Park, with a good **view** of the bay and city. The residence was completed in 1835 by Sir **Allan Napier MacNab**, Prime Minister of the Province of Canada from 1854 to 1856. Of particular interest is the basement, the domain of an army of servants.

Royal Botanical Gardens★

680 Plains Rd. W. ✖◷*RBG Centre open daily 10am–8pm. Outdoor gardens open May–mid-Oct.* ◷*Closed Jan 1 & Dec 25.* ✆*$16.* ✆*905-527-1158 or 800-694-4769. www.rbg.ca. Free shuttle bus May–Oct.*

These gardens occupy 1,000ha/2,700 acres of land at the western tip of Lake Ontario. Several gardens are worth seeing *(car required)*. The **Mediterranean** garden has vegetation from five regions of the world with a Mediterranean climate. Also visit the **Larking garden**, the **rock garden** and the **lilac garden**.Greenhouse Café serves daily 11:30-3pm, Turner Pavilion Tea House 11am-5pm, or The Rock Garden Café 11:30am-3pm.

Museum of Steam and Technology★

900 Woodward Ave. Just south of Queen Elizabeth Way (QEW). ◷*Open Tue–Sun noon–4pm.* ◷*Closed Jan 1, Good Friday, Dec 25-26.* ✆*$7.* ✆*905-546-4797. www.hamilton.ca.*

Hamilton's 1859 water-pumping station provides an example of 19C steam technology. Two Gartshore steam-powered beam engines are in working order.

EXCURSION

🚶 African Lion Safari★

1386 Cooper Rd. ✖♿◷*Open May-Oct daily 10am–4pm (Sat-Sun til 5pm).* ✆*$30.95 (child $21.95).* ✆*519-623-2620 or 800-461-9453 (US/Canada). www.lionsafari.com.*

Drive your car through enclosures of African and North American free-roaming animals. This zoo is internationally recognized for its excellent breeding program of endangered species. There are more than 30 cheetahs, numerous elephants, hippos, lions and tigers, plus zebras, bison, giraffe, and plenty of others, including raptors. Over 100 species total. Dining options onsite.

ADDRESSES

⊘/ EAT

$ Rock Garden Café – *In RBG Centre at the Royal Botanical Gardens.* ✆*905-527-1158, ext 540. www.rbg.ca. Open for lunch only 11:30am–3pm daily.* **Canadian**. This pleasant restaurant on the grounds of the Royal Botanical Gardens overlooks Spicer Court with its seasonal plantings. Sandwiches, soups and salads and seasonally changing entrées.

$$$ Ancaster Old Mill Inn – *548 Old Dundas Rd., Ancaster. Exit Mohawk Rd. from Hwy. 403 W.* ✆*905-648-1828. www. ancasteroldmill.com.* **Contemporary**. In Ancaster, just west of Hamilton, an 18C stone mill has been converted into an upscale restaurant with seven dining rooms, the most popular of which overlooks a waterfall through floor-to-ceiling windows. Two prix-fixe menus are prepared daily, with a selected wine for each course. A variety of breads made on the premises accompany the meal.

Kingston and the Thousand Islands★★

This onetime capital of Upper Canada, and first capital of the united Canadas owes its political and economic development to its location at the junction of Lake Ontario and the St. Lawrence River. The former colonial stronghold is home to several military colleges.

KINGSTON★★

A French fur-trading post established here in 1673 was abandoned when New France fell. The settlement established by Loyalists soon became an important British naval base and dockyard, and a fort was built to protect it during the War of 1812. The Rideau Canal increased the town's importance. Kingston served as capital of the Province of Canada from 1841 to 1843.

Today the **Royal Military College** (Fort Frederick), the Canadian Army Staff College and the National Defence College are located here. Kingston is a pleasant city, with tree-lined streets, parks, and public buildings constructed of local limestone. Among these is the handsome **City Hall★** in Confederation Park

- ⌖ **Michelin Map:** p217.
- **Info:** Tourist Office, 209 Ontario St. ℘613-548-4415 or 888-855-4555. www.cityofkingston.ca.
- ▶ **Location:** The city of Kingston lies on the north shore of Lake Ontario, where the St. Lawrence River leaves the lake in a channel full of islands.
- **P** **Parking:** Meters operate downtown Kingston Mon–Sat 9:30am–5:30pm, 2-3hr limit, $1-1.50 per hour. In city lots with attendants, the first hour is free.
- **Don't Miss:** Music in the Park concerts in summer.
- ⏱ **Timing:** Cruise the waters near Kingston through Thousand Isl.

on the harbour; the **Court House★** with a small dome similar to that of City Hall; the **Cathedral of St. George,** which is reminiscent of Christopher Wren's London churches; the **Grant Hall** building of Queen's University; and some of the buildings of the Royal Military College.

City Hall

© Ontario Tourism Marketing Partnership Corporation

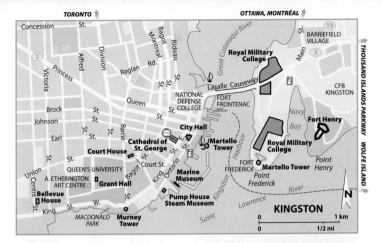

SIGHTS

MacLachlan Woodworking Museum

2993 Hwy 2 East, Grass Creek Park,
○Open May-Sept Tue-Sun 10am-5pm
☞$5. ☏613-542-0543.
http://woodworkingmuseum.ca
Started as a Centennial project in 1967 by Sandy MacLachlan, an 1855 log house was moved to Princess Street and operated as a private museum for over a decade. In 1998, City of Kingston purchased the museum, and moved it again. This facility holds the largest collection of woodworking tools in Canada.

Pump House Steam Museum

23 Ontario St. ○Open mid-May–Sep
Tue–Sat 10am–5pm, Thu until 8pm,
Sun noon–6pm, rest of year times vary.
☞$5. ☏613-546-4291.
www.steammuseum.ca.
To pay tribute to Canada's steam age, two enormous 1897 steam pumps once used in Kingston's 1849 pumping station have been restored.

Murney Tower

West of harbour at King W. & Barrie Sts.
○Open mid-May–Labour Day daily
10am–5pm. ☞$5. ☏613-572-5181.
www.kingstonhistoricalsociety.ca.
This 1846 squat stone tower in a pleasant park beside the lake is one of Kingston's Martello towers, a National Historic Site. Inside, living quarters of the garrison have been re-created.

Bellevue House

© Pamela Delaney/Michelin

Bellevue House National Historic Site★

35 Centre St. ♿○Open Jul–Labour Day
daily 10am–5pm. May-Jul & Sept–Oct
Thu–Mon 10am–5pm, closed Tue & Wed.
☞$3.90. ☏613-545-8666.
www.pc.gc.ca.
From 1848 to 1849 this 1840 Italian-styled villa was the residence of Canada's first prime minister, Sir **John A. Macdonald** (1815-91), who spent much of his youth in Kingston and opened his first law office in the city in 1835. The house is furnished to reflect Macdonald's time of residence.

The Thousand Islands

© Merrithew/Ontario Tourism Marketing Partnership Corporation

Fort Henry★★

1 Fort Henry Dr. ✕🕐*Open late-May–mid-Sept daily 10am–5pm.* ✆*$18.* 🕿*613-542-7388. www.forthenry.com. or www.pc.gc.ca.*

Completed in 1837, this stone fortress is set on a peninsula above Lake Ontario. Restored in 1938 and now a National Historic Site, it is best known today for the **Fort Henry Guard**, a troop of students who re-create the life of the 19C British soldier and guide visitors. In particular, the **garrison parade** *(daily)* should not be missed.

THE THOUSAND ISLANDS★★

🛈 *1000 Islands Tourist Office.* 🕿*315-482-2520 or 800-847-5263. www.visit1000islands.com.*

As it leaves Lake Ontario, the St. Lawrence River is littered, for an 80km/50mi stretch, with about 1,000 islands. All of the islands are of Precambrian rock, the remnants of the **Frontenac Axis**, which links the Canadian Shield with the Adirondacks of New York state. The international border passes among them.

VISIT
Boat Trips★★

Several companies offer cruises (dinner too) among the islands.

From Kingston: *Kingston 1000 Islands Cruises* 🕿*613-549-5544 or 800-848-0011. www.1000islandscruises.ca.*

From Gananoque *or* **from Ivy Lea**: *Gananoque Boat Line* 🕿*613-382-2144 or 888-717-4837. www.ganboatline.com.*

From Rockport: *Rockport Boat Line* 🕿*613-659-3402 or 800-563-8687. www.rockportcruises.com.*

Thousand Islands Parkway★

Begins 3km/1.8mi east of Gananoque at Interchange 648 (Hwy. 401). 37km/23mi to Interchange 685 (Hwy. 401), south of Brockville.

This scenic drive follows the shore of the St. Lawrence River, offering many good views. **1000 Islands Tower** (♿🕐 *open early-May–mid-Oct daily 9am–dusk;* ✆*$10.62;* 🕿*613-659-2335; www.1000islandstower.com*) on Hill Island provides a fine **view**★ of the islands. At Mallorytown Landing is the visitor centre for **Thousand Islands National Park** *(2 County Rd. 5;* ♿

ⓘ *visitor centre open mid-May–Labour Day daily 10am–4pm;* 🚗 *Parking $7/ day.* ☎*613-923-5261; www.pc.gc.ca).* Beside the visitor centre, a hut encloses the remains of the wreck of an early 19C gunboat. Ask about their new oTENTik camping option.

ADDRESSES

🛏 STAY

$$ Hotel Belvedere *–141 King St. E.* ☎*613-548-1565 or 800-559-0584. www. hotelbelvedere.com. 20 rooms.* 🅿 ⬜. This well-situated hotel, built in 1880, exudes Edwardian elegance throughout. Guest quarters are fireplace- and duvet-equipped. On the patio are umbrella-shaded tables and seasonal plantings.

$$ Rosemount Inn and Spa – *46 Sydenham St. S.* ☎*613-531-8844 or 888-871-8444. www.rosemountinn.com. 2-night minimum on weekends. 11 rooms.* 🅿 Spa ⬜. Guests at this stately Italianate stone house (c.1848) enjoy its porch, gardens, gourmet breakfasts and spa offers massages, facials & wraps. All bedrooms have en suite bathrooms and ceiling fans.

$$ Trinity House Inn – *90 Stone St. S Gananoque.* ☎*613-382-8383 or 800-265-4871. www.trinityinn.com. 8 rooms.* 🅿✕⬜. Off the main street, this 1859 brick mansion offers comfortable rooms with packageplans, including B&B, and the Prince Regent Jacuzzi Suite. Buffet breakfast in garden or veranda.

$$$ Gananoque Inn and Spa – *550 Stone St. S. Gananoque.* ☎*613-382-2165 or 800-465-3101. www.gananoqueinn.com. 57 rooms.* 🅿✕Spa. This hotel has welcomed guests since the 1890s. Five buildings include two century-old houses with suites. The spacious waterfront **dining room ($$)** offers French cuisine carefully prepared with seasonal produce locally produced, while Muskie Jake's Tap and Grill serves pub fare.

🍴 EAT

$ Chez Piggy–*68-R Princess St.* ☎*613-549-7673. www.chezpiggy.com.* **International**. In a restored livery stable, Piggy's offers lunch, dinner and Sunday brunch, served indoors or on the popular garden patio. The delicious bread comes from the owners' next-door Pan Chancho bakery.

$$ Le Chien Noir Bistro – *69 Brock St.* ☎*613-549-5635. www.lechiennoir.com.* **French.** This bistro serves up honest French fare for lunch, dinner and Sunday brunch. One surprise: a gourmet version of *poutine*, the Québécois snack staple.

$$$ Casa Domenico – *35 Brock St.* ☎*613-542-0870. www.casadomenico.com.* **Italian.** Open for lunch and dinner, this fine-dining restaurant serves a varied version of traditional Italian dishes. The friendly dining room features exposed masonry walls.

AFTER HOURS

The Kingston Brewing Company – *34 Clarence St.* ☎*613-542-4978; www.kingstonbrewing.ca. Open daily 11am–2am.* Behind the Victorian storefront, is Canada's oldest wine-producing brewpub.

$ Tir nan Og Irish Pub *–200 Ontario St.* ☎*613-544-7474. www.primepubs.com Tue–Sun 11am until very late.* Here you'll find Irish beer, food and song, plus breakfast, lunch & dinner.

SHOPPING

Earth to Spirit Trading Company – *340 King St. E.* ☎*613-536-5252. www.earthtospirit.com.* Fair-trade baskets, crafts, jewellery and other gift items from around the world.

LEISURE

Dolce Bella Spa – *8 Cataraqui St.* ☎*613-544-1166 or 877-424-4417. www.dolcebellaspa.com.* Inside a restored woolen mill overlooking the Cataraqui River, this polished day spa and hair salon provides treatments for men and women.

Thousand Islands Playhouse – *185 South St., Gananoque.* ☎*613-382-7020 or 866-382-7020. www.1000islands playhouse.com. Open May–early Nov.* Around the corner from the Gananoque Inn. New and classic plays, children's theatre, concerts and stand-up comedy are presented.

Kitchener - Waterloo

Orderly and clean, these twin industrial cities in Southern Ontario reflect their German heritage. The skills and industriousness of their immigrant founders created a diverse economy still evident today. Every fall there is a nine-day **Oktoberfest** featuring German food and drink, oompah-pah bands and dancing *(www.oktoberfest.ca).*

SIGHTS
Woodside National Historic Site
528 Wellington St. N., Kitchener.
Open year-round 10am-5pm.
$3.90. 519-571-5684 or 888-773-8888. www.pc.gc.ca.
This 1853 brick Victorian house was the boyhood home of **William Lyon Mackenzie King**, Prime Minister of Canada 1921-30 and 1935-48. The house has been restored to reflect the period of King's residence in the 1890s. The influence of his grandfather, the rebel leader William Lyon Mackenzie, is of particular note.

Joseph Schneider Haus Museum
466 Queen St. S., Kitchener. Wed–Sat 10am–5pm, Sun 1pm–5pm.Closed Easter Monday $6. 519-742-7752. http://josephschneiderhaus.com
This Georgian frame house was built around 1816 by Kitchener's founder, Joseph Schneider. It has been restored and furnished to the period of the mid-1850s. An added wing displays decorative arts and German folk art.

👥 Doon Heritage Crossroads
About 3km/2mi from Hwy. 401. Take Exit 275 and turn north. 10 Huron Rd., Kitchener. Hazel's Café self serves. Open May–Labour Day daily 9:30am–5pm. $10. 519-748-1914. www.waterlooregionmuseum.com.
This site depicts a small rural Waterloo village c.1914. The two-storey frame house at the **Peter Martin Farm**, originally constructed c.1820, permits an overview of Mennonite family life on a 60-acre spread of land. The village comes to life as costumed animators weave history and lore into their colorful descriptions of life on the family farm.

EXCURSION
Elora
About 37km/23mi northeast via Regional Rds. 22 and 18.
Welcome Centre, 9 Mill St. E.
877-242-6353. www.elora.info.
In this charming 19C mill town on the Grand River, stone buildings house shops and cafes. The main attraction is its 21m/70ft **gorge**, perched above Elora Mill Inn (*see Addresses*). In summer villagers enjoy a dip in the cold waters of the **Elora Quarry**, just east of the village *(318 Wellington County Rd. 18; 519-846-5234; open mid-Jun–Labour Day; $6)*. The **Elora Festival** is held Jul-mid-Aug *(www.elorafestival.com).*

▶ **Population:** 507,096.

Michelin Map: p216.

Info: Kitchener Tourism, 260 King St. W., Suite 201, Kitchener. 519-745-3536 or 800-265-6959. www.explorewaterloo region.com.

Location: Kitchener and Waterloo are separate cities that, together with the town of Cambridge, form an urban agglomeration. They lie southwest of Toronto, between Toronto and London.

Parking: www.kitchener .ca/parking

Don't Miss: The farmers' market in St. Jacobs is Canada's largest year-round Farmer's Market.

Timing: 2-3 days w/Elora.

👥 **Kids:** Doon Heritage Crossroads.

The Mennonites in St. Jacobs Country

The first settlers in this area, the **Mennonites** were members of a Protestant sect that grew out of the Anabaptist movement (whose members believed in adult baptism) during the reformation of 16C Europe. The Mennonites were persecuted in Europe and began coming to America in the early 18C. Many emigrated to Pennsylvania, but during the American Revolution the group's commitment to nonviolence (members refused to serve in any army) made them unpopular. Some Mennonites moved North with the Loyalists, settling in the Kitchener area. Old Order Mennonites eschew electricity, modern machinery, cars and telephones. They can sometimes be seen in the country near Kitchener–Waterloo, driving horse-drawn buggies that display a fluorescent triangle on the back as a safety precaution. Mennonite men wear black suits and wide hats; the women wear ankle-length black dresses and small bonnets. To learn more about Ontario's Mennonites and their way of life, see the 15min video at the Visit Centre in St. Jacobs *(1386 King St. N., St. Jacobs; ℘519-664-1133; www.stjacobs.com).* Contact the centre about tours of Mennonite country. ☺ Please bear in mind that Mennonites are not a tourist attraction; they want to stay separate from "English" life.

© Lissia/Ontario Tourism Marketing Partnership Corporation

ADDRESSES

⦿/ EAT

$ Remi's Place *–45 Mill St. W. (Mews), Elora. ℘519-846-8442. www.eloramews. com/shops/jennys.html.* **Canadian**.Enjoy an ice-cream cone or a light meal at this eatery near the bridge. In summer, dine outdoors on the patio in the courtyard.

$ The Baden Hotel *– 39 Snyder's Rd. W., Baden. ℘519-634-5711. www.badenhotel. com.* **German**. This restaurant, built as a hotel in 1874, dishes up schnitzel fries, baby back ribs and local Oktoberfest sausage, as well as pub grub. 18 beers on tap.

$ Kennedy's Restaurant *– 1750 Erb's Rd. W., St. Agatha. ℘519-747-1313 or 800-250-5953. www.kennedycatering.ca.* **German**. This old-fashioned Irish pub is known for its rolled ribs, pigtails, and cabbage rolls. Pub fare served too.

$ Olde Heidelberg Restaurant & Tavern *– 3006 Lobsinger Line, Heidelberg. ℘519-699-4413. www.oldhh.com.* **German**. This 1860 stage coach stop near the St. Jacobs market serves hearty fare. Photos of dishes and has a tavern and motel to serve travelers too.

$$ Elora Mill Inn, Hotel & Spa *– 77 Mill St., Elora. ℘905-648-1088. www. landmark-group.ca.* **Contemporary**. Renovated with loving care (re-opening late 2017), guests hear the rush of the waterfall below, while dining on creative dishes inside stone walls. Patio dining overlooks the river. 32 **guest rooms ($$$)** have antique furnishings; some have a fireplace.

MARKETS

Farmers' markets offer fresh produce, local German and ethnic specialties.

Kitchener *– 300 King St. W. ℘519-741-2287. www.kitchenermarket.ca. Year-round Sat 7am–2pm. Shops and restaurants Tue–Fri 8am–3pm and Sat 7am–2pm.*

St. Jacobs *– At Weber St. N. and Farmers' Market Rd., north of Waterloo. ℘519-747-1830. www.stjacobs.com. Year-round Thu & Sat 7am–3:30pm, mid-Jun–late-Aug Tue 7am–3:30pm.*

London★

In 1792 **John Graves Simcoe**, lieutenant-governor of Upper Canada (now Ontario), named the site for the British capital and called the river on which it stood the Thames. Today London is a bustling industrial and insurance centre, but with quiet tree-lined streets, attractive houses and expansive green spaces, notably **Springbank Park**, a hub of outdoor activity west of the downtown core, offers an oasis. The University of Western Ontario, one of Canada's most distinguished, is located here.

▶ **Population:** 474,786 CMA.
🜲 **Michelin Map:** p216.
🯅 **Info:** Tourist Office, 696 Wellington Rd. S. ✆519-661-5000 or 800-265-2602. www.londontourism.ca.
▶ **Location:** London lies between Toronto and Windsor on Hwy. 401, in the rich agricultural south of Ontario.
🅿 **Parking:** Parking in the downtown core and on the campus can be difficult. In city parking lots, time limits are strictly enforced.
☻ **Don't Miss:** Museum London.
🕑 **Timing:** Allow one day for the sights and one for excursions.
👥 **Kids:** Children's Museum. londonchildrensmuseum.ca.

SIGHTS
Museum London★★
421 Ridout St. N. ✗🜲🕑*Open year-round Tue–Sun noon–5pm.* ⊛*Contribution requested.* ✆*519-661-0333. www.museumlondon.ca.*
Set in a park overlooking the river Thames, this spectacular museum is remarkable chiefly for its design by Toronto architect Raymond Moriyama. The structure of concrete barrel vaults contains skylights which provide indirect natural lighting without damaging the art. The collection includes portraits by London's native son Paul Peel, who maintained a studio on Richmond Street.

The museum's restaurant **The River Room ($$)** is a popular London dining spot, especially for Sunday brunch *(lunch & dinner from 11am Tue–Fri; brunch only Sun;* ✆*519-850-2287.*

Eldon House★
481 Ridout St. N. 🕑*Open Jun thru Sep Tue–Sun noon–5pm, Jan–Apr Sat–Sun noon–5pm. May & Oct–Dec Wed–Sun noon–5pm.* ⊛*By donation.* ✆*519-661-5169. www.eldonhouse.ca*
Just north of a series of restored Georgian houses stands London's oldest house, constructed in 1834. The library and drawing room are particularly noteworthy.

👥 Springbank Park
Springbank Dr.
This 140ha/300-acre green space bordering the Thames River is a hub of outdoor activity west of the downtown core. There are picnic facilities, ball fields, playgrounds for children and miles of walking trails. You can ride the park's merry-go-round or mini-train in season (⊛*$2.25;* 🕑*open May–Oct)*. But the park's highlight is **Storybook Gardens** *(1958 Storybook Lane;* 🅿🕑*open mid-May–Jun Mon–Thu from 10:30am, Sat/Sun til 6pm; Jun–Sep daily 10am–5:30pm;* ⊛*$6;* ✆*519-661-5770; www.storybook.london.ca)*, an assortment of fanciful constructions based on nursery rhymes that house animals and games and rides for youngsters.

Specific highlights in Storybook Gardens, to the delight of kids of all ages, are a water park, an island for pirates, a farm with barnyard animals and an enchanted forest sheltering peacocks, owls, hawks and other birds.

EXCURSIONS
👥 FANSHAWE PIONEER VILLAGE

In Fanshawe Conservation Area, 15km/9mi northeast. 2609 Fanshawe Park Rd. E. ✕🕐*Open mid-May–mid-Oct Tue–Sun and holiday Mon 10am–4:30pm.* 👓*$7.* 📞*519-457-1296. www.fanshawepioneervillage.ca.*

This reconstructed 19C Presbyterian community is set in a park beside Fanshawe Lake. The village has an Orange Lodge. A Protestant fraternity founded in Ireland in 1795 and named for William III (of Orange), the militantly Protestant **Orange Order** had considerable influence in the founding of Ontario. Costumed guides lend life to the village.

Ska-Nah-Doht Iroquoian Village

In Longwoods Road Conservation Area, 32km/20mi southwest by Hwy. 401, then Hwy. 402, Exit 86. 8449 Irish Dr., RR#1, Mount Brydges. ⛄🕐*Open mid-May–Labour Day daily 9am–4:30pm. Rest of the year Mon–Fri 9am–4:30pm.* 🕐*Closed major holidays.* 👓*$3.50.* 📞*519-264-2420. www.lowerthames-conservation.on.ca.* 😷*Insect repellent recommended.*

This village is a re-creation of the type inhabited by Iroquois in Ontario 800 to 1,000 years ago. The park visitor centre at the entrance features audiovisual programs and displays. The village is surrounded by a wooden palisade with a complicated entrance to make it easy to defend.

ADDRESSES

🛏 STAY

$ Parkview B&B – *131 Victoria St.* 📞*519-858-4170 or cell 519-854-4628. www. parkviewbb.ca. 2 rooms & 1 apartment.* 🖂 Sitting on lovely landscaped grounds in North London, this lodging provides a hot breakfast (*24hr notice required*) and wireless Internet.

$$ Idlewyld Inn – *36 Grand Ave.* 📞*519-432-5554. www. idlewyldinn.com. 21 rooms.* 📶⛄✕. After renovations in 2014, this stately manor now features spa, restaurant, patio, meeting rooms, and beautifully appointed guest rooms.

$$ Windermere Manor – *200 Collip Circle.* 📞*519 858-1391 or 800-997-4477. www.windermeremanor.com. 48 rooms.* 📶⛄✕🖂. Located near the University of Western Ontario, this large hotel offers modern accommodations in a historic setting. Breakfast included.

$$$ Elm Hurst Inn & Country Spa – *415 Harris St. in Ingersoll.* 📞*519-485-5321 or 800-561-5321. www. elmhurstinn.com. 46 rooms & 3 suites.* 📶⛄✕🗖🖂. Guest rooms in this Gothic mansion have duvets; some premium rooms have a fireplace, a terrace and Jacuzzi. The on-site spa, fitness centre and wireless Internet are added amenities. Dining is divine too.

🍽 EAT

$ Dave's Pub & Grill at Oakwood Resort – *70671 Bluewater Hwy, Grand Bend.* 📞*519-238-2324.www.oakwoodinnresort.com.* Serves lunch or dinner or just a drink overlooking the first tee from an oversized terrace. Affordable choice.

$$ Michael's on the Thames –*1 York St.* 📞*519-672-0111. www.michaelsonthe thames.com.* **International**. This smart dining room overlooks the river. Extensive menu of steaks, lamb and duck and veal, as well as Italian pastas.

$$ Villa Cornelia – *142 Kent St.* 📞*519-679-3444. www.villacornelia restaurant.com.* **Canadian.** Turreted 1892 Queen Anne house is a romantic setting for main courses of meat, fish, duck and (surprise!) Russian blinis with smoked salmon. Vegetarian dish too.

$$$ Garlic's of London – *481 Richmond. 519-432-4092 www.garlicsoflondon.com.* **Canadian.** For the best take on classic dishes with a twist, this eatery serves consistent fare for breakfast, lunch, and dinner. Try their slow-roasted namesake garlic bisque, scallop & chorizo cioppino, or Muscovy duck. Regionalism reigns here, so this is likely the best farm-to-table example in the region. Sunday Brunch is an absolute must for the salmon brioche.

Niagara Falls★★★

Roughly halfway along its course from Lake Erie to Lake Ontario, the Niagara River suddenly plunges over an immense cliff, creating one of earth's great natural wonders. These famous falls are the most visited in the world, attracting more than 12 million people a year. The Province of Ontario and the State of New York have created beautiful parks full of flowers on both sides of the river adjacent to the falls.

GEOGRAPHY

Two Cataracts – There are, in fact, two sets of falls separated by tiny Goat Island, which stands at their brink. The **American Falls** (on the US side of the river) are 300m/1,000ft wide and more than 50m/160ft high. The Canadian or **Horseshoe Falls** (named for their shape) are nearly 800m/2,600ft wide, about the same height, and contain 90 percent of the water allowed to flow down the river. It is the Horseshoe Falls that people think of as Niagara.

Diverting the Waters – The river's water volume varies by hour and season. Major power developments divert up to 75 percent of the water above the falls and the flow of water over the falls is reduced at night when additional electricity is needed to illuminate them. In winter so much water is diverted that the falls partially freeze—a spectacular sight. Visitors should consider today's water diversion and try to imagine the cataract's appearance in 1678 when **Louis Hennepin** was the first European to view them. Hennepin heard such a mighty noise on Lake Ontario that he followed the river upstream to discover its source.

Erosion of the Falls – In geological terms the falls are not old. At the end of the last Ice Age, the waters of Lake Erie created an exit channel for themselves over the present-day Niagara

◉ **Michelin Map:** p216.

▣ **Info:** INFO Niagara, 5400 Robinson St. ☎905-356-6061 or 800-563-2557. www.niagarafalls tourism.com.

◐ **Location:** The falls are found in the eastern Niagara Peninsula, between Lakes Ontario and Erie.

🅿 **Parking:** Free parking outside main Falls/Queen Victoria area, or $25 per day Parking Pass or consider using WeGo People Mover bus system at $7.50 per day.

◉ **Don't Miss:** Drive at least one way along the Niagara Parkway.

◔ **Timing:** Visit the falls at night to see them illuminated. There are also fireworks displays summer and winter. Contact the Tourist Office.

👪 **Kids:** Scary but fun, the White Water Walk. The Botanical Gardens, especially the Butterfly Conservatory.

Escarpment into the old Lake Iroquois. The water's force immediately began to erode the underlying soft shale, creating a gorge.

Today the Niagara River has cut a gorge some 11km/7mi back from the edge of the escarpment at Queenston to the present position of the falls. In another 25,000 years or so, the gorge will extend back to Lake Erie and, unless we find a solution, and the falls as we know them will practically cease to exist.

GETTING AROUND

So you can fully enjoy the Falls, take the new WEGO handicapped accessible bus system year-round. Operated by the Niagara Parks Commission & City of Niagara Falls, these buses stop at over 15 sites, and feature four different

Journey Behind the Falls, Niagara Falls

lines meeting at Niagara Parks beside Horseshoe Falls.

🕐 For times call 📞 905-356-1179 or visit www.WEGOniagarafalls.com. Tickets available at Niagara Falls Visitor Centre locations at Queen Victoria Park. This service replaces the former PeopleMover system which ran here for over 26 years.

📷 $7.50 (24hr boarding throughout the day. includes Falls Incline Railway). Parking available in summer at Rapids View Parking Lot 📷 $10/car, rest of the year at Falls Parking Lot 📷 $18/car.

NIAGARA FALLS
map III

THE FALLS★★★

The falls can be viewed from the riverbank level, from the water level at the bottom of the cataract and from the summit of various viewing towers.

The Walk from Rainbow Bridge to Table Rock★★★

About 1.6km/1mi.

From Rainbow Bridge visitors can wander along the bank beside the river, passing **Queen Victoria Park**. The American Falls are in view, and it is possible to stand on the brink of Horseshoe Falls at Table Rock. In Table Rock House, elevators descend to enable visitors to walk along **tunnels** to see this immense curtain of falling water (&⌚*open daily 9am, closing hours vary;* ⌚*closed Dec 25.* 👓*Wonder Pass $16.75;* 📞*877-642-7275 Canada/US, www.niagaraparks.com).*

Hornblower Niagara Cruises

5920 Niagara Pkwy. 1-905-NIAGARA. Board the Niagara Falls Boat Tour on River Road.

Experience the full sensory impact of one of the world's greatest sights from aboard the new Hornblower 700-passenger Catamaran cruise boats. Early Morning, Sunset, Dinner, and Fireworks cruises. Don't forget to buy the **Audio Guide** to maximize the memory and understand the site to the fullest.

The View from Above★★★

Three towers in Niagara Falls provide a spectacular elevated view of the cataract. The best view is afforded from the **($$)Skylon** revolving restaurant (*5200 Robinson St.;* ✕&⌚*open Jun–Oct daily 8am–10pm;* 👓*free ride to the top when dining at Revolving Restaurant or Summit Suite Buffet; $15.02 for just Ride-to-the-Top.* 📞*905-356-2651; www.skylon.com),* which visitors ascend in exterior elevators known as yellow bugs.

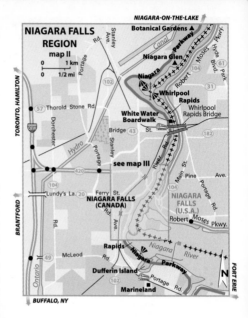

NIAGARA FALLS REGION
map II

NIAGARA-ON-THE-LAKE
Botanical Gardens
Niagara Glen
Niagara
Whirlpool Rapids
Whirlpool Rapids Bridge
White Water Boardwalk
see map III
NIAGARA FALLS (CANADA)
NIAGARA FALLS (U.S.A.)
Rapids
Dufferin Island
Marineland
TORONTO, HAMILTON
BRANTFORD
BUFFALO, NY
FORT ERIE

NIAGARA PARKWAY★★
(North)

This route follows the river north to its junction with Lake Ontario. From the falls the parkway passes under Rainbow Bridge, through a pleasant residential area and past the Whirlpool Bridge.

👥 White Water Walk★★

⌚*Open daily Apr–late fall, 9am–closing times vary.* 👓*$8.75 (child $5.15).* 📞*877-642-7275 (Canada/US). www.niagaraparks.com.*

Elevator descends to bottom of gorge where visitors see some of the world's most hazardous water thundering, roiling and rising into huge **rapids**. Wheelchair accessible.

The Whirlpool Aero Car★★

A colourful antique Spanish aerocar (*weather permitting,* ⌚*opens Apr–mid- Nov daily 10am; late Jun–mid-Oct 9am; closing times vary;* 👓*$12.25 (child $8).* 📞*877-642-7275 Canada/US. www. niagaraparks.com)* crosses the gorge high above the river, with excellent **views★★** as it swirls around the whirlpool and the rocky gorge. This ride is not wheelchair accessible.

Niagara Glen★

There is a view of the river from above. Trails lead to the water's edge *(15min to descend, 30min to ascend)*.

👥 Niagara Parks Botanical Gardens★

✕♿🕐*Open year-round daily 10am–dusk.* 🕐*Closed Dec 25.* ✆*877-642-7275 (Canada/US). www.niagaraparks.com.* Beautiful plantings of flowers, shrubs and trees are maintained by students of Niagara Parks Commission School of Horticulture. The rose garden is especially lovely in early June. The 1,022sq m/11,000sq ft **butterfly conservatory** shelters some 2,000 butterflies in climate-controlled comfort (🕐*open late Jun–Aug 10am–7pm; rest of the year hours vary;* 🕐*closed Dec 25;* ⊜*free admission; parking is $5; horse & carriage tours mid-May–mid-Oct 10am–5pm $18.50).*
About 1.6km/1mi from the botanical gardens, across the river on the US side, the immense **Robert Moses Generating Station** can be seen. Later, on the Canadian side, the **Sir Adam Beck Generating Station** is visible. Both stations use water diverted from the river above the falls to generate electricity.

Queenston Heights★

🕐*Open daily year-round.*
These heights are part of the Niagara Escarpment and were once the location of Niagara Falls. Today they are a pleasant park that provides good views of the river. In the park stands a monument to Gen. Sir **Isaac Brock**, the British military hero of the War of 1812. The heights were captured by the Americans during the war. Brock was killed while leading a successful charge to recapture them.

EXCURSIONS FROM QUEENSTON TO NIAGARA-ON-THE-LAKE

12km/7mi

Queenston★

This village at the foot of the escarpment has attractive houses and gardens.

Laura Secord Homestead

29 Queenston St. 🚶*Visit by guided tour (30min) only early May–early Sept daily 10am–5pm. Mid-Sept–early Oct Wed–Sun 10am–5pm.* ⊜*$9.50.* ✆*877-642-7275 (Canada/US). www.niagaraparks.com.*
In 1813 Laura Secord walked 30km/19mi from her home in enemy-held Queenston to warn the British of a surprise attack planned by the Americans.
Her rather plain house has been restored by the candy company named after this Canadian heroine.

For the remainder of the drive to Niagara-on-the-Lake, there are several parks with picnic tables, and occasional

NIAGARA FALLS
EXCURSIONS
map I

fine views of the river. In summer, stalls selling the produce of the Niagara Peninsula line the route.

Niagara-on-the-Lake★★

12km/7mi. 🛈 *Chamber of Commerce, 26 Queen St. www.niagaraonthelake.com.*
Pleasant shops, restaurants, teahouses, hotels and the **Niagara Apothecary**, an 1866 pharmacy (&🕐*open Mother's Day–Labour Day daily noon–6pm, Jul & Aug from 11am, Sept–mid Oct Sat–Sun noon–6pm; www. niagara apothecary.ca)* line a wide, main thoroughfare, **Queen Street★**, with a clock tower at its centre. Niagara-on-the-Lake is also a cultural centre, home to the **Shaw Festival**, a season (*Apr–Oct*) of theatre featuring the works of the Irish playwright **George Bernard Shaw** (1856-1950). Other works are also performed. *Box office:* ☎*800-511-7429 (Canada/US). www.shawfest.com.*

Fort George★

On River Rd. near the theatre. 26 Queen St. &🕐*Open May–Oct daily 10am–5pm, Apr & Nov Sat–Sun 10am–5pm.* ⊗*$11.70.* ☎*905-468-6614. www.friendsoffortgeorge.ca. or www.pc.gc.ca.*
Built by the British in the 1790s, this fort played a key role in the War of 1812. Costumed staff demonstrate activities of the period.

WELLAND CANAL★★

From Niagara-on-the-Lake, take Niagara Stone Rd. (Rte. 55) to its end; turn left on the south service road, right on Coon Rd. to Glendale Ave.; turn right and cross the canal. From Niagara Falls, take Queen Elizabeth Way (QEW) to St. Catharines; exit at Glendale Ave. interchange, follow Glendale Ave. and cross the canal by the lift bridge; turn right or left on canal service road (Government Rd.).
Navigation of large watercraft between Lakes Ontario and Erie was impossible until canals and locks were built in the 19C. The present canal, which is part of the St. Lawrence Seaway system, is 45km/28mi long, crossing the Niagara Peninsula between St. Catharines and Port Colborne. The canal's eight locks raise ships 99m/326ft.

The Drive along the Canal★★

About 14km/9mi from Lake Ontario to Thorold on Government Rd.
Fine views of huge ships negotiating seven of the eight locks of this section. North of lift bridge at Lock 3, find **St. Catharines Museum** at the Welland Canal Centre (✕&🕐*open daily 9am-5pm;* 🕐*closed Dec 24–Jan 5;* ⊗*donation;* ☎*905-984-8880 or 800-305-5134; www.stcatharineslock3museum. ca)* includes a **viewing platform** of the seaway.

FROM THE FALLS TO FORT ERIE

32km/20mi
The Niagara River is impressive, revealing its **rapids★★** as it prepares to plunge over the cliff.
Niagara Parkway (South)★ crosses to **Dufferin Islands**, which connect by walkways (🕐*open year-round;* ☎*877-642-7275; www.niagaraparks.com)* plus hiking trails, streams and swimming area. **Old Fort Erie**, where the Peace Bridge crosses the river to **Buffalo**, has great **views★**.

Old Fort Erie

✕🕐*Open early May–early Oct daily 10am–5pm. Rest of the year, call for hours.* ⊗*$12.25.* ☎*905-871-0540. www.niagaraparks.com.*
Reconstruction of third fort is set at mouth of Lake Erie. Visitors enter by drawbridge, tour barracks, a guardhouse and powder magazine. Students in early 19C uniforms perform manoeuvres and serve as guides.

North Bay ★

This resort centre on the shores of Lake Nipissing was located on the old canoe route to the West. North Bay is still the centre of a rich fur-trapping industry. Each year (May & Jun) beaver, mink, muskrat and other furs are auctioned at Fur Harvesters Auction, Inc., which ranks among the largest in the world (1867 Bond St., ℘705-495-4688, www.furharvesters.com).

SIGHTS

Farmers Market, Oak Street Parking Lot#10, behind the North Bay Bus Terminal, every Sat from 8:30am-1:00pm and Wed from 10am-3pm rain or shine. Farm fresh produce, homemade preserves, baked goods and local artwork. No better place to soak up the ambiance of the community character, taste traditional flavours, and interact with the residents.

The Waterfront ★
Memorial Dr. below Main St.
The sidewalk bordering Memorial Drive bustles with joggers, walkers, cyclists, and tourists. From the government dock, there are scenic **cruises** aboard the 300-passenger, twin-hulled *Chief Commanda II* on Lake Nipissing around the Manitou Islands. ✕🚻⏰*Depart mid-May-late-Sep. Call for departure times. Round trip 1.5hrs. Reservations required.* 👓*$25. Georgian Bay Cruise Co. ℘705-494-8167 or 866-660-6686. www.chief-commanda.com.*

EXCURSION
Sturgeon Falls
37km/23mi west by Hwy. 17. Follow the signs.
Southwest of this community is the **Sturgeon River House Museum** 👥, which tells the story of the fur-trapping industry in Northern Ontario (*250 Fort Rd.;* 🅿️🅿️⏰*open Jul–Labour Day daily 9am–5pm; rest of the year Mon–Fri 9am–4pm;* ⏰*closed major holidays.* 👓*$3;* ℘705-753-4716; www.sturgeonri-verhouse.com). Exhibits include a Hudson's Bay Company trading post. Nature trails thread the riverside property.

▶ **Population:** 64,043.
👓 **Michelin Map:** p216.
🅱 **Info:** Tourist Office, 200 McIntyre St. E. ℘705-474-0400.
◐ **Location:** North Bay lies on Lake Nipissing, between the Georgian Bay and the Quebec border.
⊛ **Don't Miss:** A cruise on Lake Nipissing aboard the *Chief Commanda II* (👓*see Waterfront below).*
⏰ **Timing:** North Bay has a vibrant cultural life, with festivals, theatre and events. Check with the tourist office for specifics.
👥 **Kids:** The Sturgeon River House Museum has programs for children.

ADDRESSES

🍴 EAT

$$$ Churchills – *631 Lakeshore Dr.* ℘705-476-7777. www.churchills.ca. **Canadian.** This fine dining restaurant includes pan-fried pickerel as well as house specialities beef tenderloin and prime rib. Upstairs is Chumbolly's bar, while Winnie's Pub onsite offers the Winnie Burger, fish & chips and ribs.

$$ My Thai Palace. *236 Main St. West.* 705-474-1234. *Asian.* www.mythaipalace.ca. Menu led by their famous Volcano of Seafood, but so many great dishes here, the best way to savor the merits of the kitchen is to order different dishes and share. Try their crispy fish platters, curry shrimps, or garlic sauce Pad Khing. Vegan and gluten-free options also available.

Orillia★

Set on the narrows between Lakes Simcoe and Couchiching, this small resort town has a reputation out of all proportion to its size. Orilla served as the model for "Mariposa" in *Sunshine Sketches of a Little Town* by famed humourist and author **Stephen Leacock** (1869–1944). One of Canada's best-known literati, this professor of political economics at McGill University spent his summers here, finding inspiration for some of his finest works.

SIGHT
Stephen Leacock Museum★
50 Museum Dr. Near Old Brewery Bay off Hwy. 12 Bypass at 20 Museum Dr. ✕ ⏰*Open May–Sept daily 8:30am–4:30pm. Rest of the year Mon–Fri 9am–5pm.* ⬤*$3 donation recommended.* ☎*705-329-1908. www.leacockmuseum.com.*

▶ **Population:** 30,586.
⏱ **Michelin Map:** p216.
🈳 **Info:** 50 Andrews St. S., Suite 300. ☎705-325-1311. www.city.orillia.on.ca.
▶ **Location:** Ortillia is set on the narrows between Lake Couchiching and Lake Simcoe.
✺ **Don't Miss:** The Leacock Museum.
🕐 **Timing:** Take time to stroll around Orillia, a picturesque town with lovely walking paths.

Set amid pleasant grounds overlooking Brewery Bay, Leacock built home in 1928, and renovated in 2014. Waterfront café Fri-Sun 11am-3pm.

Oshawa★★

This industrial city on the north shore of Lake Ontario is a centre of Canada's automobile industry. Its name has long been synonymous with industrialist and philanthropist **Robert S. McLaughlin** (1871–1972), who had a key role in that industry.

SIGHTS
Parkwood Estate★★
270 Simcoe St. N. 4km/2.5mi north of Hwy. 401. ✕☞⬤*Visit by guided tour (2hrs) Jun–Aug Tue–Sun 10:30am–5pm. Rest of the year Tue–Sun 1:30pm–4pm.* ⏰*Closed major holidays.* ⬤*Donations requested.* ☎*905-433-4311. www.parkwoodestate.com.*
This gracious, imposing residence was built in 1917 by Robert S. McLaughlin, who converted his father's carriage business into a motor company, and used an American engine in his famous **McLaughlin Buick**.
In 1918 he sold the company to the General Motors Corp. of the US, but

▶ **Population:** 356,177 CMA.
⏱ **Michelin Map:** p216.
🈳 **Info:** Tourist Information ☎905-436-3311 or 800-667-4292. www.oshawa.ca.
▶ **Location:** Oshawa lies on the north shore of Lake Ontario, 39km/24mi east of Toronto.
🅿 **Parking:** All the sights have designated parking.
✺ **Don't Miss:** The Canadian Automotive Museum, for rare cars.
🕐 **Timing:** Save time for lunch at Parkwood Estate in the Garden Teahouse Restaurant.

remained chairman of the Canadian division, whose main plant is in Oshawa. The house contains priceless antiques from all over the world and is set in beautiful **gardens**, with statuary and fountains. A **teahouse** sits beside a long pool with fountains.

Canadian Automotive Museum★

99 Simcoe St. S. Open year-round Mon–Fri 9am–5pm, Sat–Sun 10am–6pm. Closed Dec 25. $10 (child$5). 905-576-1222. www.oshawa.ca

About 70 automobiles (1898-1981) in mint condition are on display, including 1903 Redpath Messenger, 1912 McLaughlin Buick and 1923 Rauch and Lang electric car.

Robert McLaughlin Gallery

72 Queen St., Civic Centre. Open year-round Mon–Fri 10am–5pm (Thu til 9pm), Sat–Sun noon–4pm. Free parking after 6pm & weekends. Closed Jan 1, Easter Sunday, Dec 24–26. Contribution requested. 905-576-3000. www.rmg.on.ca.

Built in 1969, the expanded gallery designed by Arthur Erickson displays the works of the **Painters Eleven**, a group of artists who united in the 1950s to exhibit abstract art.

Ottawa★★★

This seat of national government sits on the south bank of the **Ottawa River** at the point where it meets the **Rideau River** from the south and the **Gatineau River** from the north. The Ottawa River marks the boundary between the provinces of Ontario and Quebec, but the National Capital Region spans the river, encompassing a large area that includes both the cities of Ottawa and Gatineau. The city charms visitors with its handsome rivers, expansive parklands, miles of bicycle paths, colourful springtime tulips and the world's longest skating rink: the Rideau Canal.

A BIT OF HISTORY

The First Settler – In the winter of 1800, American **Philemon Wright** travelled by oxcart on frozen waterways from New England and harnessed the **Chaudière Falls** to power gristmills and sawmills on the Quebec side of the river. He floated the first raft of squared timber to Quebec in 1806, beginning what was to become a vast industry.

The Rideau Canal – The War of 1812 exposed the dangers of using the St. Lawrence as a military communications and supply route from Montreal to Upper Canada. After the war the **Duke of Wellington** sent men to Canada to look for a safer passage. The route selected followed the Ottawa, Rideau

> ▶ **Population:** 870,250.
> **Michelin Map:** p217.
> **Info:** Tourist Office; 130 Albert St., Suite 1800. 613-237-5150 or 800-363-4465. www.ottawatourism.ca.
> ▷ **Location:** The capital lies due west of Montreal, about 160km/100mi upstream from the confluence of the Ottawa and St. Lawrence rivers.
> **P Parking:** No public parking on Parliament Hill. Pay lots and metered parking are available in the downtown area south of Wellington Street. Many museums and other sights provide parking lots, as do hotels.
> **Don't Miss:** The walking and bicycle trails along the Rideau Canal, skating during winters and 150th Canada Birthday events.
> **Timing:** Ottawa's truly spectacular natural setting is best appreciated through the Scenic Drives such as Ottawa River Parkway and Rideau Canal drive, which take at least two hours.
> **Kids:** Science and Technology Museum; Museum of Nature; Agriculture Museum.

Rideau Canal in winter, Parliament Buildings in the background

© Philippe Renault/hemis.fr

and Cataraqui rivers and a series of lakes to reach the Royal Navy base at Kingston on Lake Ontario. Construction of the canals and locks was entrusted in 1826 to Lt.-Col. **John By** of the Royal Engineers, who established his base at the present site of Bytown (now Ottawa). By 1832 the canal was completed, but its cost was so great that By returned to England unemployed and penniless.

Lumbertown – The completion of canal construction did not signal the end of Bytown's boom. Using the power of Chaudière Falls, residents built sawmills on the Bytown side of the Ottawa River. Having never been used militarily, the Rideau Canal blossomed briefly as a means of transporting the lumber south to the US. Bytown became a rowdy centre for lumberjacks and rivermen skilled at negotiating the rapids.

Westminster in the Wilderness – The 1850s saw great rivalry among Montreal, Toronto, Kingston and Quebec City over selection as the capital of the newly united Canada. The government asked **Queen Victoria** to decide the issue. She chose Bytown, which had hastily changed its name to Ottawa as more suitable for a capital. Begun in 1859, the Parliament Buildings were completed enough by 1867 to be used by representatives of the new confederation, for which Ottawa was now the capital.

Ottawa Today – A city of parks, scenic roads and bicycle paths, Ottawa is also a city of flowers, especially in May when thousands of tulips bloom—a gift from the Dutch, whose future queen spent the war years in Ottawa. It is a city that has capitalized on the cause of its founding—the **Rideau Canal**. Flanked by tree-lined drives, this waterway is a recreational haven: canoeing, boating, jogging, strolling, biking in summer, and ice-skating and cross-country skiing in winter, when little "chalets," set on the ice, offer food and skate rentals. The canal can be followed its entire 200km/125mi length to Lake Ontario through picturesque countryside with lovely lakes. Scenic roads follow the Ottawa and Rideau rivers.

High rises contain government departments and ministries, the most dominant being **Place du Portage** across the river in Gatineau.

Finally, Ottawa is a cultural centre, with a fine selection of museums, and music, dance and drama at the **National Arts Centre**. The city is particularly lively during the winter festival titled **Winterlude** *(Feb)*, the **Canadian Tulip Festival** *(May)* and **Canada Day** celebrations *(late Jun–early Jul)* on Parliament Hill.

In 2001, the City of Ottawa absorbed 12 former municipalities to become a megacity, overseen by one mayor, one city manager and nearly two dozen city executives.

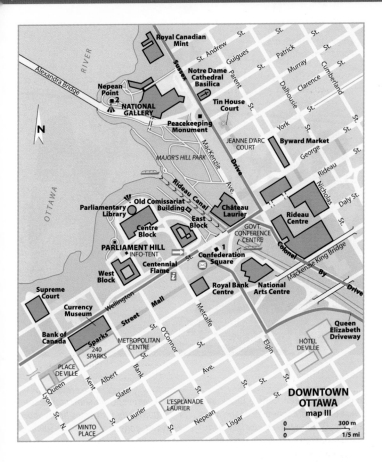

DOWNTOWN
OTTAWA
map III

0   300 m
0   1/5 mi

PARLIAMENT HILL AND AREA★★

With its three Gothic-style Parliament Buildings, Parliament Hill dominates the northern side of **Confederation Square**. In the middle of the square stands the towering granite archway of the **National War Memorial** *(see map)*, which was dedicated in 1939 by King George VI. Neighbouring "the Hill," as it is familiarly known, is the Fairmont **Château Laurier**, a distinguished hotel recognizable by its turrets and steeply pitched copper roofs. The Government Conference Centre stands opposite. Bordering the southern tip of Confederation Square is the National Arts Centre. The Parliament Buildings stand on the hill. **East Block**, with its whimsical windowed tower that looks like a face, and

West Block, both designed by Strent and Laver, were completed in 1865. The **Parliamentary Library**, designed by Thomas Fuller and Chilion Jones, was finished only in 1877. **Centre Block**, also by Fuller and Jones, was opened in 1866 but rebuilt in 1920 after a fire in 1916. The **Peace Tower** at its centre was added in 1927 as a monument to Canadians killed since Confederation. Today Centre Block contains the Houses of Parliament—the Commons and the Senate. West and East blocks contain parliamentary offices.

Visiting Parliament Hill

Since Parliament Hill's tourist activities are numerous during peak season *(mid-May to Labour Day)*, it is advisable to stop first at the large white tent **(Info-tent)**

Changing of the Guard, Parliament Buildings

© Destination Canada/Ontario Tourism Marketing Partnership Corporation

located between Centre Block and West Block for a schedule of the day's events (⏰*mid-May–Labour Day, 9am–5pm, til 8pm weekdays late Jun–Labour Day*) Information is also available at the Capital **Info Kiosk** at 90 Wellington St., *directly opposite Parliament (*⏰*open daily 9am–5pm;* ⏰*closed Jan 1 & Dec 25–26,* ☎*844-878-8333 or 800-465-1867, www.ottawatourism.ca*).

Parliament Hill is "guarded" by the Mounties—members of the Royal Canadian Mounted Police, attired in ceremonial uniforms of stetsons, red tunics, riding breeches and boots *(summer only)*. Regiments of Foot Guards wearing bearskin caps, scarlet tunics and blue trousers are also stationed on the Hill in summer. Resembling the ceremony held outside Buckingham Palace, a **Changing of the Guard★★** is performed in summer *(late Jun–late Aug 10am)* and a seasonal, bilingual **Northern Lights** *(30min)* presents Canada's history (♿⏰*early Jul–early Sept nightly at 10pm in July, 9:30 in August and 10pm*

in Sept; in case of rain, show may be cancelled). Nightly Christmas lights show early Dec–early Jan; ☎613-239-5000).

Ottawa River Boat Trip★★

✕♿⏰*Departs from Ottawa locks mid-May–mid-Oct daily 11am, 2pm, 4pm, evening cruises 7:30pm late Jun–Labour Day. Cruise departs from Gatineau dock (Gatineau) 30min earlier. Round-trip 1hr 30min.* 💳*$25 ($15 child). Paul's Boat Lines.* ☎*613-225-6781. www.paulsboatcruises.com.*

This is an excellent trip, especially at dusk, affording close-up views of Parliament Hill, the Rideau Falls and the houses along Sussex Drive overlooking the river, in particular the Prime Minister's residence. The sheer size and force of the Ottawa River are impressive.

Centre Block★

♿🚭*Visit by guided tour (20min–1hr, depending on Parliament's sessions) only, year-round daily usually 9am–8:30pm (but call to confirm hours). Rest* of the year daily 9am–4:30pm (call to confirm). ◐Closed Jan 1, Jul 1 & Dec 25. ✆613-996-0896 or 800-465-1867. www.parl.gc.ca.

Tours enable visitors to enter the Senate, the House of Commons (unless in use) and the Parliamentary Library, the only part of the original structure to escape the 1916 fire. The wood-panelled library is modelled on the reading room of the British Museum.

Parliamentary proceedings are open to the public if the House or Senate is in session. Each sitting begins with the **Speaker's Parade.**Separately, the Peace Tower can be ascended for a **view★** of the capital.

East Block★

♿🕐Visit by guided tour (45min) only, Jul–Labour Day daily 10am–5:15pm. Same-day tickets at 90 Wellington St. across from Parliament. ◐Closed Jul 1. ✆613-239-5000 or 800-465-1867. www.parl.gc.ca.

Interior of mid-19C building has been restored to its 1872 appearance. In summer students role-play historical figures to enliven the visit.

The Grounds

In front of the Parliament Buildings is a low-lying fountain called the **Centennial Flame (A** on map) because of the natural gas always burning at its centre. Symbolizing the first 100 years of Confederation, it was lit at midnight on New Year's Eve, 1966.

The walk around Centre Block is pleasant, affording **views★** of the river and of Gatineau. A notable collection of statues, many by Quebec sculptor **Louis-Philippe Hébert** (1850-1917), commemorates Canadian Prime Ministers, Queen Victoria and Queen Elizabeth II.

Rideau Canal★

Heritage Canal, Ottawa River.
In 2007 this 202km/126mi-long canal, with a total of 45 locks, was designated a UNESCO World Heritage Site. It is the only early 19C canal on the continent still functioning along its original route.

From Wellington Street visitors can descend into the small gorge where the Rideau Canal begins.

Eight **locks** raise boats from the Ottawa River to the top of the cliff. There is also a **boat trip** on the canal (♿🕐departs from Rideau Canal Dock, behind Conference Centre, May–mid-Oct daily 10am, 11:30am, 1:30pm, 3pm & 4:30pm; late Jun–Labour Day cruises also at 7:30pm, round-trip 1hr 15min, ⊕$25.Paul's Boat Lines ✆ 613-225-6781, www.paulsboatcruises.com).

Beside the locks stands the **Old Commissariat Building** (see map), completed by Colonel By in 1827, which now houses the **Bytown Museum**, with a display on the canal builders. ◐Open late May–early Oct daily 10am–5pm (Thu til 8pm, free admission after 5pm), Oct–May Tue–Sun 11am–4pm. ⊕$6.50 (child $3). ✆613-234-4570. www.bytownmuseum.com.

Above the canal, the Fairmont Château Laurier Hotel(◐see Addresses) anchors the corner of Rideau Street and MacKenzie Avenue. South of Wellington and facing the canal, the handsome **National Arts Centre★** contains theatres and a celebrated cafe with an outdoor terrace located beside the waterway (✖♿🅿🕐call for tour information;✆613-947-7000; www.nac-cna.ca). Across the canal stands the **Rideau Centre**, a hotel, convention and shopping complex.

ByWard Market★

✖🅿🕐Open May–mid-Oct daily 7am–6pm (some shops open til 8pm Thu & Fri). Rest of the year daily 8am–5pm. ◐Closed Jan 1 & Dec 25. ✆613-562-3325. www.bywardmarket.com.

Stretching over several blocks, this colourful market (primarily indoors in winter) has existed since 1846. The ByWard Market Building holds restaurants, craft shops and coffeehouses.

Tin House Court★

Completely renovated cobblestone square, bordered by stone buildings and graced by a fountain, is home to Art Price's 1973 sculpture, once part of the actual façade of tinsmith Honoré Foisy's whimsical house. Note #7 Clarence Street, a new building housing the NCC's Confederation Pavilion celebrating the nation's 150th Anniversary as of 2017. To the south, across Clarence Street, Nunavut artist Pauta Saila's bronze sculpture of a dancing bear energizes cobblestoned Jeanne d'Arc Court.

Notre Dame Cathedral Basilica★

385 Sussex Dr. ♿ 🅿 🕒 *Open Mon–Fri 9am–5pm, summer til 4pm.* ☎*613-241-7496. www.notredameottawa.com.*
This church with twin spires is a Roman Catholic cathedral built between 1841 and the 1880s. To the right of the basilica, there is a statue of Joseph-Eugene Guigues, the first bishop of Ottawa. The very fine **woodwork** of the interior was carved in mahogany by Philippe Parizeau. Around the sanctuary there are statues crafted in wood by Louis-Philippe Hébert, which have been painted to look like stone.

Peacekeeping Monument

Across the street, and adjacent to the basilica, is a prominent memorial to Canadians who have served as international peacekeepers. Titled *The Reconciliation*, the monument was dedicated in 1992, and designed by Jack Harman.

Nepean Point★

Situated high above the river beside Alexandra Bridge, this point offers a splendid **view★★** of Parliament Hill, Gatineau and the Gatineau Hills across the river. Overlooking the river facing west is a statue of **Samuel de Champlain (2** *on map)*, who paddled up the Ottawa River in 1613 and 1615.

Sparks Street Mall

South of Parliament Hill stretches this pleasant pedestrian mall with trees, seating and cafe tables between the shops. Note the **Royal Private Banking Centre** and, at the opposite end of the mall, the attractive **Bank of Canada★**, designed by Arthur Erickson and opened in 1980. Outside the east tower

in a small park stands a bronze sculpture by Sorel Etrog titled *Flight* (1966).

Supreme Court

301 Wellington St. ♿ 🍴 *Visit by guided tour only, May–Aug daily 9am–5pm; tours continual throughout day; English on the hour/French on the half-hour. Sept–April Mon–Fri 9am–5pm, book tour in advance.* ☎*613-995-5361. www.scc-csc.gc.ca.*
Canada's Supreme Court occupies a building with green roofs overlooking the Ottawa River. The court itself consists of nine judges, five of whom constitute a quorum. Visitors can listen to a hearing of an appeal if the court is in session, and see the building's interior.

THE MUSEUMS★★★

Several of Ottawa's numerous fine museums are concentrated within the city core. Others, such as the Aviation Museum and the Agriculture Museum, are on the outskirts of the city proper.

National Gallery of Canada★★★

380 Sussex Dr. 🍴♿🕒 *Open May–Sept daily 10am–5pm (Thu til 8pm). Rest of the year Tue–Sun 10am–5pm (Thu til 8pm); open Mon when holiday.* 🕒*Closed Jan 1, Good Friday & Dec 25.* 💰*$12, free Thu after 5pm (special exhibits additional fee).* ☎*613-990-1985 or 800-319-2787. www.gallery.ca.*
This magnificent glass, granite and concrete building (1988, Moshe Safdie), capped by prismatic glass "turrets," rises on the banks of the Ottawa River across from the Gothic parliament buildings. The newly created Canadian and Indigenous Galleries celebrate Canada's 150 years as a country.
The affiliated **Canadian Museum of Contemporary Photography** is housed in the National Gallery (🕒*same hours and phone as National Gallery,* ♿ *see above;* 💰*entrance included in National Gallery admission fee; http://cmcp.gallery.ca)* and features changing exhibits of works by Canadian photographers.

National Gallery of Canada

© Joey Panetta/Ontario Tourism Marketing Partnership Corporation

Canadian Art
Level 1.

Both the **garden court**, with its colourful plantings, and the restful **water court** add grace and beauty to the transition from gallery to gallery. Highlights include the reconstructed **chapel** of the Convent of Our Lady of the Sacred Heart (1888); early Quebec religious art; the works of Paul Kane and Cornelius Krieghoff; paintings by Tom Thomson and the Group of Seven, Emily Carr, David Milne, Marc-Aurèle Fortin, Jean-Paul Lemieux, Alfred Pellan *(On the Beach)*, Goodridge Roberts, Guido Molinari and Claude Tousignant. Modern and contemporary works are also featured.

Indigenous Gallery includes Inuit art featuring originals by artists such as Jessie Oonark and Pudlo.

European and American Art
Level 2.

Among the highlights are Simone Martini's *St. Catherine of Alexandria*, Lucas Cranach the Elder's *Venus*, Rembrandt's *The Toilet of Esther*, El Greco's *St. Francis and Brother Leo Meditating on Death*, Bernini's fine bust of *Pope Urban VIII* and Benjamin West's *Death of General Wolfe*. Impressionists and 20C Masters are well represented.

Canadian Museum of History (formerly Museum of Civilization★★★ (Quebec)
See Entry Heading Gatineau.

Canada Aviation and Space Museum★★★
Rockcliffe Airport, 11 Aviation Pkwy.
✕ ♿ 🅿 🕐*Open May–Labour Day daily 9am–5pm. Rest of the year 10am–5pm, Closed Tue. Closed Dec.25.* ✎*$13 (child $8).* ☎*613-993-2010 or 800-463-2038. www.aviation.technomuses.ca.*

This museum is devoted to the history of aviation from pioneer days to the present, with special emphasis on Canadian contributions. Highlights include a replica of the *Silver Dart*, the first aircraft to fly in Canada, fighters and bombers used in both world wars, and early "bush" float planes like the De Havilland Beaver, first flown in 1947. The **RCAF Hall of Tribute** honours men and women of the Royal Canadian Air Force.

Canada Aviation and Space Museum

© Canadian Tourism Commission

👥 Canadian Museum of Nature★★

240 MacLeod St. ✕🚹🅿🕐*Open Jun–Labour Day daily 9am–5pm (Wed & Thu til 8pm). Rest of the year Tue–Sun 9am–5pm (Thu til 8pm).* 🕐*Closed Dec 25 & 2nd week in Jan.* ∞*$13.50 (child $9.50).* 𝒫*613-566-4700 or 800-263-4433. www.nature.ca.*

The museum has exhibits on the creation of oceans and continents, particularly North America, and an outstanding display on **dinosaurs**. The new Canada Goose Art Gallery presents the Canadian Arctic's abundant natural biodiversity and its important connections to humans as focused in this permanent gallery open June 2017. Children will enjoy the hands-on **Discovery Zone**, where they can examine specimens and watch movies *(30min)* about nature.

Bank of Canada Museum★★

234 Laurier Ave. W., 🚹🕐*Check new website for latest hours and fees.* 🕐𝒫*613-782-8914.*
www.bankofcanadamuseum.ca.

On 2 July 2013, the Currency Museum closed its doors after more than 30 years of continuous operation, and reopening in 2017 as the new Bank of Canada Museum. Designed, constructed and opened as an element of the new 836,000 square foot Bank of Canada's Ottawa head office complex, made of granite, steel & glass.

Called the Bank of Canada Museum, it is housed beneath the plaza at the corner of Bank and Wellington streets in downtown Ottawa. Sharing an impressive glass entrance with the Bank's conference centre, the new facility will feature a gift shop, an educational space, a bright and open visitor centre as well as temporary and permanent exhibition halls.

👥 Canada Science and Technology Museum★★

1867 St. Laurent Blvd. ✕🚹🅿
🕐*Re-opening fall of 2017. Check for new times and entrance fees on website.* 𝒫*613-991-3044.*
www.sciencetech.technomuses.ca.

Renovations and the creation of the new Space Park are the order of the day here. Visitors will be treated to a totally new set of innovative experiences as of fall 2017.

Integrating the hall of **steam locomotives** will be impressive because of the sheer size of the vehicles. Exhibits on early automobiles (1900-30) in Canada and the ocean liner *Titanic* may also be featured. Canada's contribution in physics, communications, astronomy and other fields is explored in additional exhibits.

Canadian War Museum★★

1 Vimy Place. ✕🚹🕐*Open May–mid-Oct Mon–Fri 9:30am–5pm (Thu til 8pm & Jul–Labour Day Fri til 8pm), Sat–Sun 9:30am–6pm. Rest of the year Tue–Fri 9:30am–5pm (Thu til 8pm), Sat–Sun 9:30am–5pm.* 🕐*Closed Dec 25.* ∞*$15. (free Thu 4pm-8pm).* 𝒫*819-776-8600 or 800-555-5621. www.warmuseum.ca.*

This museum honours the nation's military involvements and peacekeeping efforts over the ages. Don't miss paths over the museum's roof, allowing superb **views★** of the Ottawa River. The **Military History Research Centre** (🕐*open May–mid–Oct Mon–Fri 9am–4:30pm; rest of the year Tue–Fri 9am–4:30pm;* 🕐*closed major holidays;* 𝒫*819-776-8652)* includes national collections documenting Canada's military history.

Royal Canadian Mint

320 Sussex Dr. Don't miss your 45-minute tour of this renovated star of Ottawa museums. 𝒫*613-993-8990 or 800-276-7714. www.mint.ca.*

Canada's circulating money is created at the the Royal Canadian Mint in Winnipeg. Commemorative and collector (numismatic) coins are made at this regenerated Ottawa location built in 1908.

Library and Archives Canada

395 Wellington Street. 613-996-5115 or 866-578-7777 www.bac-lac.gc.ca. 🕐*Open daily Mon-Fri 6am-11pm, Sat & Sun 10am-6pm.*

The collected heritage of Canadians, this museum of Canadiana contains materi-

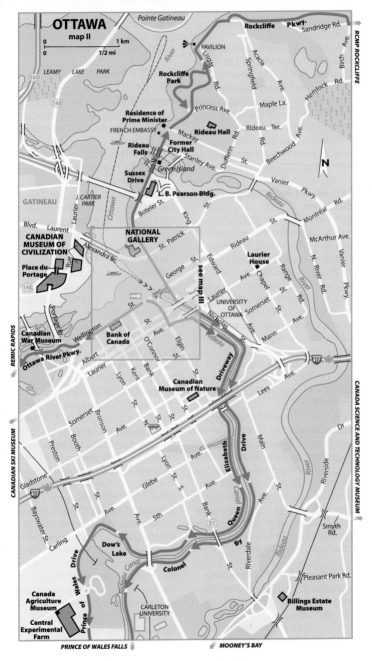

OTTAWA
map II

Pointe Gatineau

Rockcliffe Pkwy.   Sandridge Rd.

PAVILION

Rockcliffe Park

LEAMY LAKE PARK

Princess Ave.

Residence of Prime Minister

FRENCH EMBASSY

Rideau Hall

Mackay

Rideau Falls

Former City Hall

Stanley Ave.

Sussex Drive

Green Island

L. B. Pearson Bldg.

Boteler St.

GATINEAU

J. CARTIER PARK

Vanier Pkwy.

McArthur Ave.

CANADIAN MUSEUM OF CIVILIZATION

NATIONAL GALLERY

St. Patrick St.

Rideau St.

Place du Portage

Alexandra Br.

George St.

see map III

Laurier House

Laurier Ave.

UNIVERSITY OF OTTAWA

Somerset St.

Nicholas

Canadian War Museum

Wellington St.

Bank of Canada

Ottawa River Pkwy.

Albert St.

Laurier Ave.

O'Connor St.

Elgin St.

Driveway

REMIC RAPIDS

Somerset St.

Bronson Ave.

Lyon St.

Kent St.

Bank St.

Canadian Museum of Nature

Lees Ave.

Gladstone Ave.

Booth St.

Preston St.

Lyon St.

Glebe Ave.

Elizabeth Drive

Main St.

CANADIAN SKI MUSEUM

Bayswater St.

Carling Ave.

Bank St.

5th Ave.

Queen

By

Riverdale

Riverside Dr.

Smyth Rd.

Dow's Lake

Colonel

Pleasant Park Rd.

Canada Agriculture Museum

CARLETON UNIVERSITY

Billings Estate Museum

Central Experimental Farm

Prince of Wales Drive

Rideau Canal

PRINCE OF WALES FALLS

MOONEY'S BAY

CANADA SCIENCE AND TECHNOLOGY MUSEUM

RCMP ROCKCLIFFE

als in all types of formats from across Canada and around the world that are of interest to Canadians. Also connects with the Canadian **Museum for Human Rights in Winnipeg**.

Laurier House★

335 Laurier Ave. E. 🚶*Visit by guided tour (1hr) only, Jul–Labour Day daily 10am–5pm. Rest of year 10am–5pm but closed Tue & Wed.* 🚫*Closed Easter*

holidays. $3.90. &613-992-8142.
www.pc.gc.ca.
In 1897 Canada's first French-speaking
Prime Minister, **Sir Wilfrid Laurier**, in
office from 1896 to 1911, moved into the
house. Canadian Prime Minister **William
Lyon Mackenzie King,** grandson of the
rebel William Lyon Mackenzie, resided
here until his death in 1950.
The visit includes a reconstruction of the
study of **Lester Bowles Pearson,** Prime
Minister from 1963 to 1968.

Canada Agriculture Museum★

861 Prince of Wales Dr. &Main
*exhibition area open Feb–Oct daily
9am–5pm. Closed Mon & Tue. Barns
open all year round 9am–5pm, except
Dec 25.* $10 (child $7). &613-991-
3044 or 866-442-4416.
http://cafmuseum.techno-science.ca
The machinery, the techniques and
the smells evoke farming in times past.
Old breeds of sheep, cattle, pigs and
horses can be seen (*guided tours
of animal barns year-round; reserve in
advance;* &613-991-3053). Visitors can
take Tally-Ho wagon rides on-site (*Jun–
Sept Sat–Sun;* $4).
The 425ha/1,050-acre **Central Experimental Farm** is the headquarters of
Canada's Agriculture and Agri-Food
department. On the grounds are splendid ornamental gardens. There is also
a tropical greenhouse and the large
Dominion Arboretum bordering the
Rideau Canal (*grounds open year-
round daily dawn–dusk; greenhouse open
year-round daily 9am–4pm; call Friends
of the Farm* &613-230-3276).

Billings Estate Museum★

2100 Cabot St. &Open May–late-
Oct Wed–Sun 10am–5pm. Guided
tours Wed–Sun noon–5pm; $6.15
&613-247-4830. *http://www.ottawa.
ca/museums. High tea service on the
lawn from May–Labour Day from
11am–4pm rain or shine $13. Boxed
lunches also served for $6.50, plus
homebaked goodies.*
This attractive home on 8 acres was built
in 1829; it is the oldest frame house in

Ottawa. Refurbished rooms are full of
artifacts, photographs and furniture
relating to the Billings family.

DRIVES AROUND THE CAPITAL★★

Ottawa is well known for its lovely
drives beside the river, along the canal
and in the Gatineau Hills to the north.

Sussex Drive and Rockcliffe Parkway★★

8km/5mi from Confederation Square.
This drive along the river and through
the residential area of Rockcliffe passes
the Basilica of Notre Dame, the Canadian War Museum and the **Lester B.
Pearson Building**, which houses the
Department of Foreign Affairs and International Trade. The road then crosses
the Rideau River to Green Island past
Ottawa's former **city hall**, designed
by Moshe Safdie, the architect of the
National Gallery of Canada.

Rideau Falls★

Park beside the French Embassy.
On both sides of Green Island, the
Rideau River drops over a sheer cliff into
the Ottawa River. The falls are said to
resemble a curtain, hence their name,
which means "curtain" in French. To see
the second set of falls, visitors can cross
the first set by a bridge. There are good
views of the Ottawa River and Gatineau.
Along Sussex Drive, the entrance to the
Official Residence of Canada's Prime
Minister, **24 Sussex Drive**, is seen on
the left. Around the corner is the gate
to **Rideau Hall,** official residence of the
Governor General. The grounds can be
visited (*open year-round daily 8am–
one hour prior to sunset;* guided
*tours late-Jun–Sep 10am–4pm: call for
reservations* &613-991-4422 or 866-842-
4422). There are **tours** of the residence
(*45min guided tours: call for schedule and to reserve* &866-842-4422; www.
gg.ca). The road then passes through
Rockcliffe Park via a one-way route.
The steepled church in Pointe Gatineau
is St. François de Sales, built in 1886.
Rockcliffe is an area of large stone
mansions, tree-lined streets and lovely

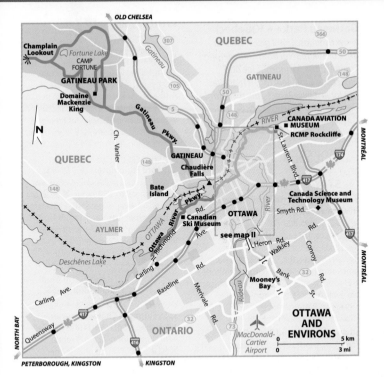

OTTAWA
AND
ENVIRONS

5 km
3 mi

gardens. The drive ends at **RCMP Rockcliffe** (Royal Canadian Mounted Police), where members of the famous **musical ride** (*30 min*) and their horses are trained. When the troop is not on tour (*generally May – Oct*), the horses can be seen in training (&⊘*open May 1–Aug 31 daily 9am–3:30pm; Sept–Apr Tue & Thu 10am–1:30pm; ✆613-998-8199; www. rcmp-grc.gc.ca*).

Rideau Canal Driveways★
Each drive is about 8km/5mi from Confederation Square.
The **Queen Elizabeth Driveway** follows the canal's west bank; the **Colonel By Drive** parallels the east bank. The University of Ottawa is soon passed on the left. Later on, Carleton University is also seen. At **Dow's Lake**, where the canal widens out, canoes and paddleboats can be rented. At this point the two drives diverge, the Colonel By continuing along the canal, the Queen Elizabeth entering the Central Experimental Farm. From Colonel By Drive, there are views of Prince of Wales Falls and the

Rideau Canal locks before the drive ends at Hog's Back Road.

Prince of Wales Falls★
Free parking in Hog's Back Park.
Mooney's Bay marks the end of the Rideau Canal; thereafter, the Rideau River is navigable. After leaving the bay, the river drops over these falls and rushes through a small gorge. The dam was built by Colonel By in 1829. Mooney's Bay (*access from Riverside Dr.*), is one of Ottawa's main recreational areas.

Ottawa River Parkway★
1km/7mi from Confederation Square.
Wellington Street passes the parliament buildings, the Bank of Canada and the Supreme Court, and becomes the parkway just south of Portage Bridge. The drive beside the Ottawa River offers several lookout points for the Remic Rapids. The best view is from **Bate Island★** (*take Champlain Bridge to Gatineau and exit for island*). The parkway continues, affording other good viewpoints.

Gatineau Park★★ (Quebec)

www.canadascapital.gc.ca. Circular drive of 55km/34mi from Confederation Square. Cross Portage Bridge and proceed to Gatineau; turn left on Rte. 148 for just over 2km/1.2mi, then turn right on the Gatineau Pwky. & *See GATINEAU.*

ADDRESSES

🏠 STAY

$ Hostelling International Ottawa: Hi-Ottawa Jail Hostel– *75 Nicholas St. ℰ613-235-2595/800-663-5777. www. hihostels.ca. 154 beds.* ▣. Housed in the 1863 Carleton County Gaol near ByWard Market, this hostel offers beds in renovated jail cells, as well as dormitories and semi-private rooms. Rooms for couples are available, as are laundry facilities, lockers and Internet access. Historic tours show off the gallows and the cells.

$$ Angela's Bed and Breakfast. *166 Glebe Ave. 613-769-3794. http:// angelasbedandbreakfastottawa.com. 3 rooms. LGBT-friendly & eco-conscious.* Multi-generational household located in the heart of the Glebe, this ideally situated house is a short walk to Bank St. commercial district, parks, pedestrian/ cycling paths and historic Rideau Canal.

$$ Auberge The King Edward – *525 King Edward Ave. ℰ613-565-6700 or 800-841-8786. www.kingedwardottawa.com 3 rooms.* ▣ ⌑. Asymmetrical turrets and bull's-eye windows characterize this Victorian terrace house in Sandy Hill, with a restored interior featuring moldings, archways, fireplaces and bay windows. Spacious guest quarters feature 3m/10ft ceilings, antique furnishings, air-conditioning and wireless Internet. Framing the grounds is a cast-iron fence built in the 1870s to deter cows and pigs.

$$ Gasthaus Switzerland Inn – *89 Daly Ave. ℰ613-237-0335 or 888-663-0000. www.gasthausswitzerlandinn.com. 22 rooms.* ▣ ⌑. East of the city centre in Sandy Hill, this heritage limestone house (1832) sits adjacent to Ottawa University, close to cinemas and theatres. Guests enjoy well-lit rooms with duvets, large windows, wireless Internet and some w/ fireplace. In summer, have breakfast in the garden. Green Key Eco-Rating from Hotel Association of Canada.

$$ McGee's Inn – *185 Daly Ave. ℰ613-237-6089 or 800-262-4337. www.mcgeesinn.com. 12 rooms.* ▣ ⌑ This sprawling brick mansion (1886) in Sandy Hill was built for John McGee, brother of Thomas D'Arcy McGee, a Father of Confederation assassinated in Ottawa in 1868. Two themed rooms, one with a canopy bed, have gas fireplaces and double Jacuzzis. Every room has air conditioning, Internet access, a small fridge and cable television.

$$$ Lord Elgin Hotel – *100 Elgin St. ℰ613-235-3333 or 800-267-4298. www. lordelginhotel.ca. 359 rooms.* ✕ & ▣ ⌑ Named for James Bruce, 8th Earl of Elgin and governor general of British North America from 1847–54, this Ottawa institution near Confederation Square is well located for sightseeing and shopping. Exensive fitness facilities. Guest rooms are decorated in warm tones. The restaurant, **GRill 41 ($$$)**, offers breakfast, lunch and dinner.

$$$$ Fairmont Château Laurier – *1 Rideau St. ℰ 613-241-1414 or 866-540-4410. www.fairmont.ca. 429 rooms.* ✕ & ▣ ⌑ ⌑. Named after former Canadian Prime Minister Sir Wilfrid Laurier, this massive limestone chateau has been an Ottawa landmark since 1912 and enjoys an enviable location next door to Parliament. Immense leaded-glass windows pierce the oak-panelled lobby and adjoining rooms. Make your reservations before Dec 2017, when a huge renovation/expansion begins. A favourite local meeting spot, **Wilfrid's ($$$)** restaurant serves regional Canadian cuisine. High tea until 5:30pm.

🍴 EAT

$ Blue Cactus – *2 ByWard Market. ℰ613-241-7061. www.bluecactusbarand grill.com.* & **Contemporary.** Sample some of Ottawa's best margaritas, the house-blend Sangria, or choose from a selection of nine regional micro-brewed beers while you ponder the large menu at this marketside cafe. Start with the ever-popular Blue Cactus nachos, or the Voodoo Chicken with searing Creole mustard sauce, or the bison burger, seared tuna, or vegetarian options.

$ Yang Sheng – *662 Somerset St. W. ℰ613-235-5794.* **Chinese**. This casual eatery is always crowded with a local Asian clientele, students among them. Yang Sheng's spicy cuisine includes dim sum, and ample servings of delicacies like hot and sour soup, barbecued duck and spicy Szechwan eggplant.

$$ Canal Ritz – *375 Queen Elizabeth Dr. ✆613-238-8998. www.canalritz.com* **Italian.** ♿ Patrons can paddle here by canoe, tie up at the dock and drop in at this renovated boathouse perched on a bend in the Rideau Canal. The floor-to-ceiling windows and patio place diners seemingly atop the canal. The specialty is thin-crust pizza, but their grill is active, pasta dishes abound, and Sunday Brunch is very popular.

$$Feleena's – *742 Bank St. ✆613-233-2010. www.feleenas.ca.* **Mexican.** A favourite in the upscale Glebe district, Feleena's offers a comfortable adobe-toned interior with Diego Rivera-style murals. Authentic dishes predominate, but salmon with cilantro or vegetarian enchiladas cater to the less adventurous palate. On weekends brunch starts at 11:30am. Summer terrace.

$$ Festival Japanese – *149 Kent St. ✆613-234-1224.www.festivaljapan.ca.* **Japanese.** Traditional setting of screens, polished wood and bamboo, this restaurant is a relaxing place in Ottawa's busy centre. The extensive menu includes all principal types of Japanese food, from sushi to sukiyaki-for-two cooked tableside and Udon or Soba noodles. The fish dishes are especially nicely presented.

$$ Mystiko – *281 Kent St., ✆613-233-3626. www.mystikogreekkitchen.com. No lunch weekends.* **Greek.** A sleek interior greets diners, but the food is reliably traditional. Popular appetizers include the calamari and octopus, while the slovaki (lamb, pork or beef) tops the choice for entrées. Moussaka and grilled quail are signature dishes.

$$$ Le Café – *In National Arts Centre, 53 Elgin St. ✆613-594-5127. www.nac-cna.ca. No lunch Sat in winter.* **Canadian.** ♿ Overlooking the Rideau Canal, this upscale restaurant is known for its well-presented regional Canadian cuisine, typified by such entrées as the cinnamon roasted duck breast, New Brunswick salmon or Alberta beef.In summer, patrons enjoy the airy patio and the passing parade of "canalites."

$$$ Metropolitan – *700 Sussex Dr. ✆613-562-1160. www.empiregrill.com.* **Contemporary.** A patio spilling out onto bustling streets in summer, a palatial bar and comfortable indoor contemporary tavern-cum-brasserie entices patrons to linger at this friendly, busy bistro. The focus is on Alberta Angus beef grilled to perfection, but their codfish, tagliatelle, and mussels are excellent. The offers brunch on Sat, Sun & holidays.

$$$$ Beckta Dining & Wine – *150 Elgin St. ✆613-238-7063. www.beckta.com. Dinner only. Closed some holidays.* **Canadian.** Beckta sits in a redbrick Victorian a few blocks south of Parliament Hill, but the interior is streamlined and plush. The spotlight here is on game, fish and beef from Canada: halibut from British Columbia, Quebec peninsula char and Alberta beef tenderloin. A five-course tasting menu is offered with optional wine pairings. International in scope, the wine list includes a few Niagara wines.

$$$$ Signatures Restaurant – *453 Laurier Ave. E. ✆613-236-2499 or 888-289-6302. www.signaturesrestaurant.com. Dinner only. Closed Sun-Mon.* **French.** ♿ If you have occasion to splurge, do it here, on the premises of the Le Cordon Bleu Ottawa Culinary Arts Institute. The dining rooms in the Tudor-style mansion are elegant; the service is superb. Signatures' classic French cuisine is highly praised. Beyond seasonal à la carte menu, a seven-course tasting menu is offered.

PUBS APLENTY

Heart and Crown and Peter Devine's – *67 Clarence St. ✆613-562-0674. www.irishvillage.ca.* Serves shepherd's pie and Guinness beef stew in a lively, casual Irish pub setting. 16 taps promise a wide selection of brews. In summertime the pub's outdoor tables afford great people-watching in the heart of the market. Live music here every night.

D'Arcy McGee's Irish Pub – *44 Sparks St. ✆613-230-4433. www.primepubs.com.* The high-gloss wood interior, with detailed scrollwork around the bar, was hand-carved in Ireland for authenticity's sake. Draft beer and a fine array of Irish whisky, Cuban cigars and, well, plenty of *craic* (good times and fun) compliment the corned beef and cabbage. Open daily til the wee hours with entertainment Wed and weekends: Celtic, blues, and more.

Peterborough

This pleasant city is set on the Trent Canal, part of the Trent-Severn Waterway, which links Lake Ontario with Georgian Bay. Boating, especially canoeing, is a popular activity in the region, particularly on the Kawartha Lakes to the north and farther north, along the canoe routes in **Algonquin Provincial Park**. The area is also known for its sizable font of petroglyph First Nation relics.

SIGHTS
Lift Lock★

In operation mid-May–mid-Oct. This hydraulic lift lock built in 1904 is one of only eight in the world. Its operation is explained in the **Visitor Centre** of the **Trent-Severn National Historic Site** (&P*open daily late Jun–Labour Day from 10am; closed Good Friday; $0.90; 705-750-4900 or 888-773-8888; www.pc.gc.ca).* Visitors can experience the lift lock by taking the **boat cruise★**. *Departs from Peterborough Marina, 92 George St.N. Jul–Aug 3 times daily; mid-May–Jun & Sept–mid-Oct twice daily. $26.50. Reservations suggested. Liftlock Cruises 705-742-9912 or 888-535-4670. www.liftlockcruises.com).*

Canadian Canoe Museum★

910 Monaghan Rd. P&Open Mon–Sat 10am–5pm, Sun noon–5pm. Closed Jan 1, Dec 25–26. $12. 705-748-9153 or 866-342-2663. www.canoemuseum.net.
A former factory houses this fascinating array of more than 600 canoes, kayaks and rowing craft of all types and construction—reputedly the largest collection of paddled craft in the world. One exhibit is devoted to the paddling accoutrements of the late Prime Minister of Canada Rt.Hon.**Pierre Elliott Trudeau**. The newest display features two canoes by Canadian artist Alex McKay, including the "Treaty Canoe," based on treaties between Canada and First Nations Peoples.

▶ **Population:** 135,000.
Michelin Map: p217.
Info: Peterborough and the Kawarthas Tourism, 1400 Crawford Dr. 705-742-2201 or 800-461-6424. www.thekawarthas.ca.
Location: Peterborough lies between Toronto and Kingston on the Otonabee River where it widens into Little Lake.
Don't Miss: 4th Line Theatre performances.
Timing: Allow at least one day to visit the sights and two days to take the excursions.
Kids: Lang Pioneer Village for make-believe.

EXCURSIONS
Lang Pioneer Village

104 Lang Rd., Keene. 16km/10mi southeast of Peterborough by Rte. 7 and Country Rd. 34. Open late May–mid Jun Mon–Fri 10am–3pm. Late Jun–Labour Day daily 10am–4pm. Visit by guided tour only, early–mid-Sept Mon–Fri hourly 10am–4pm. $8 (child $4). 705-295-6694 or 866-289-5264. www.langpioneervillage.ca.
In a delightful rural setting, this 19C village contains reconstructed buildings and an original gristmill (1846), still in working order. Costumed staff demonstrate daily chores and trades.

Petroglyphs Provincial Park

55km/34mi northeast of Peterborough via Hwy. 28. &Open mid-May–mid-Oct daily 10am–5pm. $10.75/car. 705-877-2552. www.ontarioparks.com.
The largest concentration of First Nations petroglyphs anywhere in Canada is protected in this park, located near Stony Lake. About 900 carvings of between 500 and 1,000 years of age can be seen.

Point Pelee National Park★★

This park is one of the few places where the true deciduous forest of eastern North America still exists. Well known to ornithologists across the continent, the southernmost tip of the Canadian mainland possesses a unique plant and animal life, largely due to its latitude of 42°N, the same as that of Rome.

GEOLOGY

The peninsula took its shape 10,000 years ago when wind and lake currents deposited sand on a ridge of glacial till under the waters of **Lake Erie**. The sand spit today is mantled with a lush forest of deciduous trees. Beneath them, many species of plants thrive, including the prickly pear cactus with its yellow flower. **An Ornithologist's Paradise** – Point Pelee's location at the convergence of two major flyways, its extension into Lake Erie and its lack of cultivation have combined to foster large bird populations. In spring and fall migrations, as many as 100 species have been sighted in one day. September is the month of the southern migration for the monarch butterfly. Visitors can see trees covered with these beautiful insects.

- ⏱ **Michelin Map:** p216.
- ℹ **Info:** Visitor Centre, 407 Monarch Lane, Leamington. ℘519-322-2365. www.pc.gc.ca.
- ▶ **Location:** Point Pelée lies on a pointed peninsula extending into Lake Erie, south of Windsor near the Michigan border.
- 🅿 **Parking:** There are several parking areas. Cars parked on the roads are towed.
- ⊛ **Don't Miss:** Junior Naturalist Program for kids during July & August.
- 🕐 **Timing:** You need a full day to enjoy this park.

VISIT

About 10km/6mi from Leamington. Follow the 🦫 (beaver) signs. ✕🚹🕐*Open year-round May–Sep 6am–10pm (5am during May migration). Rest of the year daily 7am–sunset. Hiking, fishing, canoeing,*

Northern Oriole

R. Corbel/MICHELIN

Rose-Breasted Grosbeak

R. Corbel/MICHELIN

Eastern Kingbird

R. Corbel/MICHELIN

bicycling (bicycle & canoe rentals), swimming, ski trails, ice-skating, & birdwatching. ☜$7.80/day. ✆519-322-2365 or 888-773-8888. www.pc.gc.ca. **Visitor Centre** – 7km/4mi south of park entrance. ♿ ○ open Jul–Labour Day 9am–7pm; 1st 3 wks May daily 7am–5pm; Jun & rest of Sept daily 10am–6pm, Oct & April daily 10am–5pm. Rest of the year Sat–Sun only 10am–5pm. Be sure to buy a Checklist of Birds at the Visitor Centre to keep track of birds you see.

Shuttle-to-the-Tip of peninsula departs from Visitor Centre (every 20min, Apr–Nov, starting at 6 or 7am in May and Sept for seasonal migration). Paths lead in both directions along the park's 19km/11mi of fine sandy beaches (swimming prohibited at the tip; swimming beaches accessible from picnic areas). Marshland between the sandbars can be toured by a **boardwalk** (1km/.6mi), where two lookout towers provide **panoramas★** of the marsh.

Prescott★

This small industrial town on the St. Lawrence is the only deepwater port between Montreal and Kingston. Prescott is an old Loyalist town, with heritage buildings, a renovated waterfront and walking paths. It was the site of the **Battle of the Windmill** in 1838 when rebel supporters of William Lyon Mackenzie were dislodged from a windmill on the riverbank. Today an international bridge spans the river near the town, one of 13 linking Ontario with the US.

▶ **Population:** 4,284.
Ġ **Michelin Map:** p217.
⊟ **Info:** Town of Prescott ✆613-925-2812. www.prescott.ca.
◐ **Location:** Prescott lies halfway between Kingston and Cornwall.
⊛ **Don't Miss:** Fort Wellington & RiverWalk
○ **Timing:** Spend a half day here, see the town and fort.
▲± **Kids:** See the Redcoats at the fort.

Fort Wellington
© JF Bergeron/Ontario Tourism Marketing Partnership Corporation

SIGHT
▲± Fort Wellington

On Hwy. 2, just east of town. ○Open Canada Day (Jul 1)–Labour Day daily 10am–5pm. ☜$3.90. ✆613-925-2896. www.pc.gc.ca.
Built during the War of 1812, this small earthen fort includes officers' quarters and a three-storey stone **blockhouse**. Costumed interpreters include those attired in British regimental uniforms of the period.

East of the fort (1.5km/1mi), between Highway 2 and the river, stands the **windmill** of battle fame. It features displays on the battle and offers a pleasant **view** of the river (picnic tables).

Sault Ste. Marie★★

Connected to Michigan's city of the same name by road and railway bridges, this Ontario city is an industrial centre with huge steelworks and a pulp mill. The "Soo," as it is commonly called [as in the pronunciation Soo Sainte Mar-EE], lies on the north side of **St. Mary's River**, the international boundary and waterway that connects Lakes Superior and Huron, forming an important link in the Great Lakes/**St. Lawrence Seaway** system.

▶ **Population:** 79,800.

Info: Tourism office, 99 Foster Dr. ℘705-759-5442 or 800-461-6020. www.saulttourism.com.

Location: Sault Ste. Marie lies between lakes Huron and Superior.

Don't Miss: The train tour through Agawa Canyon.

Timing: To take the drive and the rail excursion as well as see the city's sights, it would be best to allow a minimum five days for a visit.

A BIT OF HISTORY

Étienne Brûlé visited the rapids in 1622, as did many of the great explorers of New France: Nicolet, Radisson, Groseilliers, Marquette, Jolliet, La Salle, the La Vérendrye family and others. In 1668 Père Marquette established a mission here, calling it Sainte Marie du Sault (sault means "rapids" in French). Gateway to the wild and uninhabited Algoma wilderness, a favoured subject of the Group of Seven painters, Sault Ste. Marie is also the birthplace of Canada's first woman astronaut, **Roberta Bondar**, for whom several city properties are named.

SIGHTS

Sault Ste. Marie Canal National Historic Site★

Visitor Centre at 1 Canal Dr. Lock ◐open early Jun–Labour Day daily 10am–5pm, mid-May– late Jun Mon–Fri 10am–5pm & early Sept–mid-Oct Mon–Fri 10am–4pm. ⟿Guided tours Jul–Aug daily 11am & 2pm for a nominal fee; Entrance $5.80. ℘705-941-6262. www.pc.gc.ca. The enormous ships of the Great Lakes bypass the rapids through four parallel locks on the American side of the river, one of the busiest sections of the entire seaway system. A lock on the Canadian side handles recreational craft (mid-May–mid-Oct). At the base of Huron Street, there is a reconstruction of the first lock (A *on map*). **Heritage Teas** will again be served in the **Superintendant's Residence** on Sundays in July and August after completion of the major renovation of the site in 2017. Live music, costumed interpreters, fancy sandwiches, tea and desserts. Served on select Sundays at 2pm. Check Visitor's Centre for details. Tickets must be purchased in advance.

Riverfront★

Sault Ste. Marie has a pleasant riverfront area dominated by its attractive **Civic Centre**, built of copper-coloured reflecting glass. Nearby stands the permanently berthed **MS Norgoma (B** *on map)*, the last overnight passenger ship used on the Great Lakes *(docked next to Roberta Bondar Pavilion; ◐open Jun–Labour Day daily 11am–7pm; presently being refurbished, so call first; $6. ℘705-256-7447; www.norgoma.org).*

Ermatinger/Clergue House★

800 Bay Street. ◐Open mid-May–early Jun & rest of Sept–Oct Mon–Fri 9:30am–4:30pm. Mid-Jun–Labour Day daily 9:30am–4:30pm. Dec by appointment. ⟿$7. ℘705-759-5443. www.ssmcoc.com. This attractive Georgian stone house was built in 1814 by Charles Oakes Ermatinger, a partner in the North West Company, and his Ojibway wife, Charlotte.

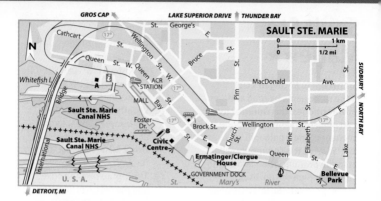

Bellevue Park

Near corner of Lake St. and Queen St. E.
From this park on the river, there are fine **views★** of the ships using the locks and of the bridge to the US.

EXCURSIONS
Gros Cap★

26km/16mi west by Hwy. 550.
From this headland there is a good **view★** of Lake Superior and the beginning of the St. Mary's River.

Train Trip to Agawa Canyon

183km/114mi. Departs from Bay St. depot in Sault Ste-Marie. ✕&🕐*Late Jun–mid-Oct daily 8am, return 6pm. New GPS-triggered tour narration (5 lang). Round-trip 10hrs.* ⊚*$84.07 (summer), $101.77 (fall). Also 2 & 3-day overnight packages available . Reservations required. Algoma Central Railway Inc.* ☏*705-946-7300 or 800-242-9287 (Canada/US). www.agawacanyontourtrain.com.*
At a stopover in Agawa Canyon *(2hrs)*, travellers can climb to a lookout for a fine view★ of the canyon and the Agawa River.

Lake Superior Drive★★

Map of Principal Sights. 230km/143mi by Trans-Can Hwy. (Rte. 17) to Wawa.
The road cuts through some of the oldest rock formations in the world, the Canadian Shield. The drive is especially fine around **Alona Bay** *(viewpoint after 108km/67mi)* and **Agawa Bay** *(viewpoint after 151km/94mi)*. Lookouts have been built beside the road.

For 84km/52mi the road passes through **Lake Superior Provincial Park** *(swimming, hiking, camping, boat rentals;* 🅿🕐*open daily May–late Oct;* ⊚*$14.50/vehicle;* ☏*705-856-2284; www. lakesuperiorpark.ca).* The park is known for its Indian **pictographs**—rock paintings. After 153km/95mi a side road leads to a parking lot from which a rugged trail descends to the lake.

A series of pictographs can be found on **Agawa Rock**, a sheer rock face rising out of the water *(accessible only when lake conditions are favourable; extreme caution advised)*. The **view★** of the lake is excellent.

Roberta Bondar, Astronaut

Born in Sault Ste. Marie in 1945, Roberta Bondar later became a neurologist and biologist and trained as a pilot. In 1992 Dr. Bondar crewed on the American space shuttle *Discovery*, becoming Canada's first woman in space. *MacLean's* magazine included her in 1998 among the top 10 heroes in the history of the nation. A popular public speaker and avid environmental photographer, Dr. Bondar has seen her photos exhibited in the Canadian Museum of Nature in Ottawa and the Royal Ontario Museum in Toronto. Her birthplace has named a city park, marina and government office building in her honour.

Stratford★

This community is home to the annual **Stratford Festival**, a major theatrical event that attracts people from all over North America. Though the focus is Shakespearean, the festival offers a wide variety of drama and music as well as behind-the-scenes tours, lectures and workshops.

A BIT OF HISTORY

In 1952 local journalist **Tom Patterson** dreamed of creating a festival to celebrate the works of the Bard. The festival has since grown to a seven-month season *(May–Nov)* in three theatres—the Festival, the Tom Patterson and the Avon. Offerings have branched out from Shakespeare, and standards are very high.

For performance schedule & reservations, contact the Stratford Festival box office ☎800-567-1600 (Canada/US); www.stratford shakespearefestival.com.

FESTIVAL THEATRE

This modern interpretation of the Elizabethan stage used in Shakespeare's day was revolutionary in the 1950s (but much copied since) because no elaborate scenery could be used, and no member of the audience was more than 20m/65ft from the stage.

The theatre is set at the edge of a pleasant park that stretches down to the river, dammed at this point to form **Victoria Lake**, the home of many swans.

Before evening performances in the summer, the beautifully manicured lawns and the small island in the lake are covered with picnicking theatregoers. At intermission audience members wander among the formal flower beds and over the lawns surrounding the theatre.

▶ **Population:** 30,886.

⚐ **Michelin Map:** p216.

▪ **Info:** Tourism Alliance, 47 Downie St. ☎519-271-5140 or 800-561-7926. www.welcometostratford.com.

◖ **Location:** Stratford lies north of London and west of Kitchener, a 2hr drive west from Toronto.

▣ **Parking:** There is a parking lot at the Festival Theatre and at the Tom Patterson Theatre. There is free parking along Lakeside Drive and along the circular drive in Upper Queen's Park. No overnight parking is permitted on city streets.

◉ **Don't Miss:** Take in a play. See the swans in Victoria Lake.

◕ **Timing:** Book ahead for your restaurant.

ADDRESSES

⊘/EAT

$ Festival Café – *In the Festival Theatre's South Lobby atrium.* Offers sandwiches, beverages and ice cream 2 hrs before performances and at intermissions.

$$ The Old Prune – *151 Albert St. ☎519-271-5052. www.theprune.com. Closed Mon & Nov–Apr.* **Contemporary.** Four cozy dining rooms include the Garden Room, which overlooks a serene reflecting pool. The intriguing menu two, three, & four-course prix-fixe dinners with a new adjusted price point. Whole poached lobster, Angus rib steak, and black cod dishes reflect a new chapter of excellence for Chef Brian Steele.

$$$$ Revival House– *70 Brunswick St. ☎519-273-3424. www.revival.house.com. Closed Mon & Jan–Mar.* **French.** Three plush rooms where menus are sophisticated, with entrées centred on lamb, beef, fish and local produce. REvival is the main venue, Chapel an upstairs gastrolounge, and Confession, described by owners as Straford's VIP hideaway.

FESTIVAL TOURS

Costume Warehouse Tour – *Meet at 350 Duoro St. Mid-May–mid-Oct Wed–Sat.* ✆*$8.* Hundreds of stored costumes and props. **Garden Tour** –*Meet at Festival Theatre's William Shakespeare sculpture.Early.*

✆*$8.* ☏*519-273-1600 or 800-567-1600. Call for times. Advance reservations advised.*
A guided stroll through the landscaped grounds of the Festival Theatre.

Sudbury★★

Located on the largest single source of nickel in the world, Sudbury is the biggest and most important mining centre in Canada. The city is also a principal centre of francophone culture in Ontario; about a quarter of the population of the region is Franco-Ontarian. Laurentian University, which serves the northeastern part of the province, is bilingual. The Sudbury region is typical Canadian Shield country, with beautiful lakes, rivers, rocks and trees. A number of lakes are encompassed within city limits, including Lake Ramsey, which has yellow pickerel (walleye), and beaches just a short walk from the civic centre.

SIGHTS
♟♟ Science North★★★

About 1.5km/1mi south of Trans-Canada Hwy. From Hwy. 69 bypass, take Paris St. to Ramsey Lake Rd. 100 Ramsey Lake Rd. ✕&◷*Open late Jun–Labour Day & late Dec daily 9am–6pm. Apr–mid-Jun & rest of Sept–mid-Dec daily 10am–4pm.* ◷*Closed Dec 24–26 & 31.* ✆*$21 (child $17).* ☏*705-522-3701 or 800-461-4898 (Canada/US). www.sciencenorth.on.ca.*

Perched on a rock outcropping on the shores of Lake Ramsey, this dramatic science centre was designed by Raymond Moriyama in association with local architects. A hexagonal exhibit building resembling a snowflake (to represent the glacial action that shaped Northern Ontario) is set over a cavern blasted out of the rock (to represent the probable creation of Sudbury Basin by a meteor).

> ▸ **Population:** 160,274.
> ⚲ **Michelin Map:** p216.
> ▮ **Info:** Sudbury Tourism, City Hall, 200 Brady St. ☏705-674-4455 ext 7718 or 866-451-8525. www.sudburytourism.ca.
> ◗ **Location:** Sudbury lies east of Georgian Bay, between North Bay and Sault Ste. Marie, at the edge of a vast wilderness.
> ⊗ **Don't Miss:** Science North, a modern science centre with dramatic exhibits.
> ♟♟ **Kids:** Dynamic Earth.

Visitors enter a large admissions area and proceed to the centre proper via a **rock tunnel**. Raw rock is exposed as it is in the impressive **rock cavern** (9m/30ft high by 30m/100ft in diameter), where a 3-D film and laser shows highlight geological history on a giant screen.

Exhibit floors are reached via an ascending spiral ramp that zigzags over the **Creighton Fault**. This fault, a geological fracture within the Canadian Shield active more than 2 billion years ago, left a groove 4m/13ft deep at this point.

Hanging over the fault is a 23m/72ft fin whale skeleton, weighing 1800kg/4,000 pounds, recovered from Anticosti Island. The glass walls of the ramp permit views of Lake Ramsey outside. Nature Exchange allows anyone to swap possessions for items from the centre's nature collection. There are exhibits about the weather and fossils, among others, and in the Discovery IMAX Theatre and Planetarium, science shows

Science North

© Goh Iromoto/Ontario Tourism Marketing Partnership Corporation

are presented regularly. From the dock **boat tours** of the lake can be taken (♿⏱*depart mid-May–late-Sept daily; round-trip 1hr; ☞$14.95, child $11.95; William Ramsey Cruise ☎705-523-4629 or 800-461-4898 Canada/US).*

Dynamic Earth★★

5km/3mi west of Science North by Regent and Lorne Sts. 122 Big Nickel Mine Drive. ⏱*Open late Jun–Labour Day Mon–Fri 9am–6pm, weekends 9am–6pm; mid-Mar–late-June Mon–Fri 10am–4pm, weeknds until 5pm.* ☞*$20 (Play All Day Passport adds all other selection including Science Centre North, IMAX and Planetarium for $35 (child $27). ☎705-522-3701.*

Descend into Big Nickel Mine to learn about how mining shaped this part of Northern Ontario. Exhibits explain the mining of gold. Long a Sudbury landmark, the **Big Nickel**, a 9m/30ft-high replica of the 1951 Canadian commemorative five-cent piece, has stood near the mine for more than 50 years.

ADDRESSES

▯/EAT

$$ Pasta è Vino –118 Paris St. ☎705-674-3050. **Italian**. In a century-old house, traditional pasta, seafood and other dishes are prepared with an inventive flair. **$$ Alexandria's** –211 Shaughnessy St. ☎705-688-1453. *Closed Sun*. **Mediterranean**. Quiet stop focuses on foods of Greece, Italy, Spain, & France, but local pickerel too. **$$ Apollo** –844 Kingsway. ☎705-674-0574. **Greek**. Crowd-pleasing dishes like moussaka, spanakopita & baklava.

Sudbury's Strata

The nickel-bearing rock strata are part of the **Sudbury Igneous Complex**, a geological formation about 60km/37mi long and 27km/17mi wide located within a 200km/125mi wide crater created by a meteor or comet impact 1.85 billion years ago. The area's wealth (platinum, copper, cobalt, silver and gold, in addition to nickel) was discovered in 1883 during construction of the Canadian Pacific Railway. Today the discovery is commemorated by a plaque *(on Hwy. 144 near the Murray Mine)*, and Sudbury claims the world's largest integrated nickel mining, smelting and refining complex. Built in 1970 to reduce the local impact of emissions of sulphur dioxide, **Super Stack**, an enormous smokestack rising 380m/1,250ft above the surrounding countryside, tops the complex. Some 90 percent of the sulphur in the ore is successfully contained.

Thunder Bay★★

Situated almost in the centre of Canada on the shores of Lake Superior, Thunder Bay is the largest city on Lake Superior. As a major inland port and the Canadian western terminus of the Great Lakes/St. Lawrence Seaway system, the city receives some 400 ships annually. Prairie grain, coal, potash and other goods arriving by rail or truck are transshipped to lakers bound for ports to the east.

SIGHTS
The Waterfront★

To appreciate the impressive port, and the sheer size of the grain terminals and ships, view them from **Marina Park** (end of Red River Rd.; ◷open daily year-round). The largest of these ships is 222m/728ft by 23m/75ft, capable of carrying up to a million bushels of grain—the yield of 20,650ha/51,000 acres of land. The breakwater protecting the harbour from the storms of Lake Superior can also be seen.

Waves can reach 12m/40ft in height in autumn. In summer the lake is calmer, and sailboat races are held weekly within and outside of the breakwater. The park itself is the venue for summer festivals and events, and lies near the shops of the CN railroad station.

▶ **Population:** 108,359.

ℹ **Info:** Tourism Thunder Bay, P.O. Box 800, 53 South Water St. ✆807-983-2041 or 800-667-8386. www.thunderbay.ca. Info centres at the Pagoda (cnr. of Water St. and Red River Rd., Jun–Labour Day) and at site of Terry Fox Monument & Lookout (year-round).

◑ **Location:** Except for Fort William, attractions lie mostly along the lake to the east of the city.

☺ **Don't Miss:** The harbour as seen from Marina Park is an awesome sight.

◷ **Timing:** Reserve four to five days to enjoy this area.

👪 **Kids:** Fort William offers a look at the life of fur traders and explorers. In July, the "Great Rendezvous" is re-enacted (℄see below).

Viewpoints★

Thunder Bay is surrounded by the hills of the Canadian Shield. The city is hemmed in across the bay by a long peninsula that forms a cape called **Sleeping Giant** because it resembles the prone figure of a man.

The Great Rendezvous

The exchange of goods and transportation is not the result of the St. Lawrence Seaway's construction. For many years the area was the linchpin of the fur trade. Every summer brigades of canoes left the widespread posts of the North West Company to transport a year's collection of furs to a trading post called Fort William. There these "wintering" partners (so named because they spent the winter in the wilds) met the Montreal partners who had made the long canoe trek through the Great Lakes with the trading goods their counterparts would need for the next year. Lasting about six weeks, the **"rendezvous"** was a time of wild celebration, as well as serious discussion of trading policy and strategy against the rival Hudson's Bay Company, which took its furs to market by way of the great bay. When the two fur-trading companies merged in 1821, Fort William lost its position as the place of the great rendezvous, but it remained a fur-trading post until late in the century. In 1970 the communities of **Fort William** and **Port Arthur** were amalgamated to create the city of Thunder Bay. The fort has been re-created as it was at its peak, and every July the rendezvous is reenacted.

Kakabeka Falls

© Ontario Tourism Marketing Partnership Corporation

Mount McKay★

At end of Mountain Rd., on Fort William First Nation Reserve.

This prominent flat-topped peak is the highest (488m/1,600ft) of the Norwestern Chain. From a ledge 180m/600ft high, there is a fine **view** on clear days of the city, port and Sleeping Giant.

Hillcrest Park★

High St. between Red River Rd. and John St. Rd.

Located on a cliff above Port Arthur, this park provides a good **view** of the port, elevators, ore dock and, in the distance, Sleeping Giant and the islands that close the harbour mouth.

♣♣ Fort William Historical Park★★

16km/10mi south by Broadway Ave. 1350 King Rd. ✕ ♿ ⏰*Open mid-May–mid-Oct daily 10am–5pm. Rest of the year by* 💬*guided tour only, Mon–Fri 11am & 2pm.* 💲*$14 (child $10).* ☎*807-473-2344. www.fwhp.ca.*

Located on the Kaministikwia River, part of the trade route to the northwest, the fort of the Great Rendezvous has been superbly reconstructed.

From the visitor centre, visitors can walk through the woods to the palisaded fort.

Inside is a large square of log buildings, two raised above the ground on stilts (the river still floods, as recently as 2006). Some 40 structures represent all aspects of early 19C fur-trade society.

Costumed guides help re-create fort life. The North West Company partners can be seen discussing business in the council house; birchbark canoes, tinware and barrels are being crafted by hand.

EXCURSIONS
Kakabeka Falls★★

29km/18mi west by Trans-Canada Hwy. (Rte. 17). Provincial park ⏰*open year-round. Park* ⏰*open to vehicles mid-May–early Oct daily;* 💲*$10.75/vehicle. Hiking, camping, fishing, canoeing.* ☎*807-473-9231. www.ontarioparks.com.*

The Kaministikwia River, crossed by a bridge, plunges 39m/128ft over a cliff around a pinnacle of rock into a narrow gorge. The falls were the first obstacle negotiated by the fur traders of the North West Company when they left Fort William to return to the northwest.

North Shore Lake Superior★★

211km/131mi to Schreiber by Trans-Canada Hwy.

This route passes several interesting features northeast of Thunder Bay.

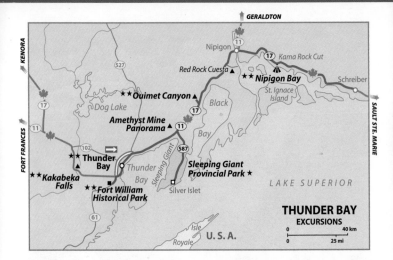

Terry Fox Monument and Scenic Lookout

1km/.6mi east of Hodder Ave.

The fine bronze monument commemorates the heroic efforts of **Terry Fox** to raise money to fight cancer. Deprived of his right leg by the disease at age 18, he undertook a cross-Canada run in 1980, starting in Newfoundland. Two months later, he was forced to abandon his run close to this spot because of recurring cancer from which he died in 1981. The monument overlooks Lake Superior.

Sleeping Giant Provincial Park★

After 51km/32mi, take Rte. 587.
&。○*Open daily late May–mid-Oct. Cross-country ski trails accessible Jan–Mar.* ⊛*$10.75/car.* ℘*807-977-2526. www.ontarioparks.com.*

Occupying most of the peninsula that has the Sleeping Giant at its end, this pleasant park features trails, high cliffs, fine **views★** of Lake Superior and the remains of the village of Silver Islet. This community was formed in 1868 when a rich silver vein was discovered on the tiny islet offshore.

Amethyst Mine Panorama

After 56km/35mi, take E. Loon Rd. for 8km/5mi. &。○*Open Jul–Aug daily 10am–6pm. Mid-May–Jun & Sept–mid-Oct daily 10am–5pm.* ☜*Guided tours daily.* ⊛*$8.* ℘*807-622-6908. www.amethystmine.com.*

At this open-pit mine, pieces of amethyst can be collected *(charge per pound)* and polished stones purchased.

Ouimet Canyon★★

After 76km/47mi, take road for 12km/8mi. ○*Open mid-May–mid-Oct daily dawn–dusk.* ⊛*$10.75.* ℘*807-977-2526. www.ontarioparks.com.*

This incredible canyon was gashed out of the surface of the Canadian Shield during the last Ice Age. It is 100m/330ft deep, 150m/500ft across and more than 1.6km/1mi long. Just after the Red Rock turnoff on the Trans-Canada Highway is a cliff of layered limestone coloured red by hematite, the **Red Rock Cuesta**, nearly 210m/690ft high and about 3km/2mi long.

Nipigon Bay★★

88km/55mi from Nipigon to Schreiber.

After crossing the Nipigon River, the Trans-Canada Highway runs along the shore of this bay, offering **views★★** of rocky islands covered with conifers and rocks worn smooth by Lake Superior. The **view★★** of Kama Bay through the Kama Rock Cut *(27km/17mi from Nipigon)* is particularly fine. Rock such as this posed problems during the construction of this highway in 1960, and in the building of the Canadian Pacific Railway.

Toronto★★★

The country's largest metropolis, the capital of Ontario enjoys a buoyant economy driven by finance, telecommunications, biotechnology, aerospace, film and television production and media. Major Canadian corporations have their head offices here.

A vibrant, multicultural city with a liveable downtown core, Toronto offers a vigourous cultural scene, professional sports teams, great shopping, and many recreational activities. The city possesses a fine harbour, punctuated with a chain of offshore islands that provide the city with its major parkland and second airport.

BIT OF HISTORY

"Toronto Passage" – Prior to 1600, the **Huron** and **Petun** peoples abandoned their north shore lands to the warlike **Iroquois Confederacy**, which dominated the fur trade. The Iroquois in turn ceded to French traders control of the "Toronto Passage" of trails and canoe routes between Lakes Huron and Ontario.

The French Regime – As early as 1615 the site of Toronto was visited by **Étienne Brûlé**, one of Champlain's men. Years later French traders met native and English traders on the Humber River in what is now Toronto, a Huron word for "meeting place." The French began construction in 1720 of forts around Lake Ontario; remains of **Fort Rouillé** have been found in Toronto's Exhibition Grounds. The Seven Years' War (1756-63) brought an end to French presence in the area.

York – In 1787, **Sir Guy Carleton**, the Governor of British North America, arranged to buy land from the **Mississaugas**, who had occupied the Toronto area after the Iroquois. Loyalists fleeing the US had also settled along the lake; their demands for English law led to the formation of Upper Canada

▶ **Population:** 6,054,091. (Metropolitan GTA area).

⌖ **Michelin Map:** p216.

🛈 **Info:** Toronto Visitors Centre, 207 Queens Quay W. ☎416-203-2500 or 800-499-2514. www.seetorontonow.com. ●*The symbol indicates a subway station.*

◑ **Location:** Set on the north shore of **Lake Ontario**, Toronto is the hub of the **Golden Horseshoe**, the 60km/100m-wide arc from Oshawa to Hamilton, where at least a quarter of Canada's manufacturing is based. The **Humber River** borders Toronto to the west, and the **Don River** to the east.

🅿 **Parking:** Street metered parking is available but hard to find; timed parking (signed) and permit-only parking is strictly enforced. It is prudent to park in lots. Museum parking, when available, must be paid for, often in cash only.

😊 **Don't Miss:** CN Tower and the Royal Ontario Museum. And, since this is Canada, why not visit the Hockey Hall of Fame?

🕐 **Timing:** Public transportation (Toronto Transit Commission or "TTC" as locals call it) with its network of subway trains, buses, and streetcars (trams) is efficient, safe and inexpensive. When driving, avoid the crowded north-south artery, Yonge St.; try Avenue Road, Bathurst or Don Valley Parkway.

👫 **Kids:** The Ontario Science Centre, LEGOland, and of course the Toronto Zoo and Playdium.

(now Ontario) in 1791. Colonel **John Graves Simcoe**, Lieutenant-Governor of the new territory, chose the site for a temporary capital, because of its fine harbour and distance from the American border. It was called **York**, after the Duke, a son of George III. In 1813 an American fleet set fire to the legislative and other buildings. In retaliation, the British set fire to part of Washington, DC, including the White House, in 1814.

The Family Compact – After 1814, immigrants flooding in from Britain began to challenge the power of what was called "the Family Compact," a small group of weathy men who dominated the government of York and Upper Canada. An outspoken Scot named **William Lyon Mackenzie** (1795-1861) attacked the group in his newspaper, *The Colonial Advocate*. He was elected to the legislative assembly (although not allowed to take his seat) and in 1835 was elected the first mayor of the City of Toronto (the name was changed as the Duke of York continued to lose in battle). In 1836, Gov. **Sir Francis Bond Head** dissolved the legislature.

The Rebellions of 1837 – Mackenzie turned to armed rebellion in 1837. When Toronto's garrison was away in Lower Canada, he gathered supporters and marched toward the city. British reinforcements arrived under Col. Allan MacNab, the revolt collapsed and Mackenzie fled to the US. Although two of Mackenzie's men were publicly hanged, the revolt was effective in that "responsible government" was granted and the United Province of Canada was created. Mackenzie was permitted to return in 1849.

Montreal was the site of an armed rebellion, also in 1837, against British rule. Although crushed, the insurgence subsequently resulted in representative government for Quebec.

A City of Neighbourhoods – As late as 1941 Toronto was 80 percent Anglo-Saxon, but since World War II, the city has opened its doors to immigrants from around the world. Today Toronto benefits from a stimulating mix of cultures. **Kensington Market** *(Kensington Ave., west of Spadina and north of Dundas)* is the realm of the Portuguese, East Indian and Jamaican communities *(best time to visit is Mon–Sat mornings)*. One of the largest Chinese districts in North America, **Chinatown** *(Dundas St. from Elizabeth to Spadina)* is also vibrant with street vendors. The **Italian** districts *(College St. and St. Clair Ave., west of Bathurst)* evoke the mother country. **Greektown** *(Danforth Ave. between Coxwell and Broadview; ●Chester)* offers numerous cafes, specialty shops and fruit markets featuring Greek food. The **India Bazaar** on on Gerrard St. E. offers restaurants, produce, art, clothing and street food from Southeast Asia. **Koreatown** on Bloor St W. is renowned for barbecue and karaoke. **Roncesvalles Village** is the place where the Polish community comes to shop and eat. Particularly active between Spadina and Bathurst, **Queen Street West** has become a colourful area of trendy bistros, and boutiques.

Toronto Today – With a municipal population of nearly 2.6 million, the metropolis is now the fifth largest on the continent. One project defining the city is **Harbourfront Centre**, a multimillion-dollar development of a somewhat derelict waterfront. Highlights of the mega-project include the creation of new city-core neighbourhoods, a waterfront park, promenade, $25 million dollar underwground parking facility, and most significantly, reconfiguration of the elevated Gardiner Expressway, a 1950s eyesore that divided the city from its waterfront.

At the corner of Dundas and Yonge streets, **Dundas Square**, opened with great fanfare in May 2003, has become one of Toronto's top visitor destination. The centrepiece is an "urban beach," an array of 10 fountains that people can walk around or through. High-tech signage rather controversially surrounds the square.

Toronto waterfront with CN Tower

©Peter Spiro/iStockphoto.com

On the southwest corner of the intersection, **Toronto Eaton Centre**, is Canada's largest entertainment and retail complex, including 250 brand-name shops, specialty stores, restaurants, and much more. (*www.torontoeatoncentre.com*).

High-rise construction continues, especially along the waterfront. **Queen's Quay Terminal** is a massive mixed use community devlopment stretching from Bathurst to Jarvis and including the **Martin Goodman Trail** for cyclists, as well as a new pedestrian **Waterfront Trail** all the way to the **Beaches** area.

As with all big, bustling cities, not everything looks bright and rosy. Toronto's downtown streets are often gridlocked, homelessness is visible and parking is expensive and often scarce. Still, Toronto is a great city to live in or to visit.

THE WATERFRONT★★

Built largely on land reclaimed in the mid-19C to mid-20C for the city's growing port installations, the areas adjacent to Front Street contain Toronto's foremost landmarks–CN Tower, Rogers Centre, Air Canada Centre, and Fairmont Royal York Hotel– and its largest lakefront revitalization; Harbourfront. Several quays were overhauled to house colourful shops, galleries, performance arenas, restaurants, sailing schools and the pre-eminent outdoor stage venue known as Molson Amphitheatre at Ontario Place. The grounds of Union Station, CN Tower and Rogers Centre can be reached on foot from Union Station by **Skywalk,** a large, glass-enclosed walkway containing eateries and souvenir shops as part of the **PATH** network, the Guinness Book's "largest underground shopping complex in the world."

CN Tower★★★

301 Front St. W. Entrance at Front and John Sts. ●*Union, then via Skywalk.* ✕&◷*Open 364 days 9am–10:30pm. Hours adjusted seasonally.* ◷*Closed Dec 25.* ↠*From $45* ☏*416-601-3848. www.cntower.ca.*

The city's most prominent landmark, this concrete structure reaches 180 storeys (over 553m/1,815ft in height), the tallest freestanding structure in North America. It attracts some 2 million visitors a year.

In only 58 seconds visitors are "beamed up" 346m/1,136ft (nearly the height of the Empire State Building) in one of six exterior glass-front elevators to the **look-out level**, a seven-storey-tall, circular steel "turban." From its observation decks, **views★★** of the

Caribana Dancer

R. Corbel/MICHELIN

Entertainment Galore

The centre of English-language culture in Canada, Toronto boasts first-rate companies and venues. The Four Seasons Centre for the Performing Arts is home to the Canadian Opera Company. The Toronto Symphony, the Mendelssohn Choir, the National Ballet of Canada, Toronto Dance Theatre and Harbourfront Centre's Fleck Dance Theatre offer regular performances. The St. Lawrence Centre for the Arts, the Royal Alexandra, Princess of Wales Theatre, and the Elgin and Winter Garden Theatre Centre stage new and traditional plays and musicals.

Every fall, city hosts one of the world's premier film festivals called TIFF, while summer brings a variety of outdoor entertainment. Several annual events draw visitors: the **Canadian National Exhibition** *(at the Exhibition Grounds late-Aug–Labour Day)*, reputedly the world's largest exhibition; **Luminato**, Toronto's festival of arts and creativity *(Jun)*; the **International Dragon Boat Festival**, a Chinese celebration *(Jun)*; and **Caribana**, a West Indies festival of steel bands and floating nightclubs on the lake *(mid-Jul–early Aug)*.

Spectator sports include Toronto Blue Jays baseball, horse shows *(Royal Agricultural Winter Fair)*, TorontoFC pro soccer and auto racing. The Air Canada Centre hosts Toronto Raptors basketball and Maple Leafs hockey.

city and suburbs, the lake and shoreline are superb *(panels identify buildings and parks)*. One floor down, intrepid visitors can stand or sit on the **glass floor**, a section of thick glass panels that permit an impressive view 342m/1,122ft straight down to the ground below. There's also the revolving **360 The Restaurant** *(reservations recommended; ℘416-362-5411)*.

The sweeping **views★★★** of the cityscape and Lake Ontario from the **Skypod**, a windowed ring 447m/1,465ft above the ground, are spectacular. If visibility is good, Niagara Falls and Buffalo, 120km/75mi away, can be seen.

Rogers Centre★★

●Union, then via Skywalk. ✕&🅿
℘416-341-2770. www.rogerscentre.com.
This huge, domed sports/entertainment complex next to CN Tower is home to American League Baseball's Toronto Blue Jays, and the Canadian Football League's Toronto Argonauts. Designed

by architect Roderick Robbie and engineer Michael Allen, the centre was built (1989) by a private consortium in partnership with local and provincial governments for over $570 million. The multipurpose stadium hosts rock concerts, conventions and trade shows as well as a variety of sports. Projecting from the Front Street façade 5m/16ft above street level, **Michael Snow's** 14 painted-fibreglass sculptures *(The Audience)* tower over arriving visitors. Rogers Centre boasts a 3ha/8-acre **retractable roof**, the 348-room **Renaissance Hotel** overlooking the playing field *(℘416-341-7100 or 800-237-1512)*, and you will find several restaurants and underground parking.

Harbourfront Centre★★

Info desk at York Quay Centre, 235 Queens Quay West. Access from York, Spadina and Bathurst Sts. ●Union or Spadina, transfer to 510 LRT to York Quay Centre. ✕&🅿🕒*Open mid-*

Kayaking between Toronto Islands

© HonestTraveller/iStockphoto.com

Apr–mid-Oct daily 10am–11pm (Sun & holidays til 9pm). Rest of the year daily 10am–9pm. Box office open Tues–Sat 1pm–6pm (til 8pm if an evening performance). ℘416-973-4000. www.harbourfrontcentre.com.

A focal point of the city's cultural life, especially in summer, Harbourfront is also the scene of year-round recreational, educational and commercial activities. **Queen's Quay Terminal** (1927), with its imposing clock tower, accommodates airy offices, plush living spaces, fashionable boutiques and eateries, the 450-seat Fleck Dance Theatre and on the fourth floor, the offices of Tourism Toronto. Nearby, **York Quay Centre** houses an architecture gallery, a craft studio and a theatre. Next is the **Power Plant Contemporary Art Gallery (A** on map) (♿ ⊙ open year-round Tue–

Sun 10am–5pm, Thu til 8pm; ⊙ closed Mon except holidays open noon–6pm; ⊕ free admission ℘416-973-4949; www.thepowerplant.org), the multipurpose **Enwave Theatre (B** on map), with its glass-faceted foyer, evolved from a 1920s icehouse. The **Westjet Stage (C** on map), an open-air 1,750-seat concert facility, occupies the southwest corner of the quay.

Toronto Islands★★

Three ferries depart from Queen's Quay in summer (Centre Island, Ward's Island and Hanlan's Point mid-Apr–mid Oct) and two in winter (Ward's Island and Hanlan's Point mid-Oct–mid-Apr). One also departs from the foot of Bathurst Street to Billy Bishop Airport on the islands. Wards Island year-round daily 6:35am–11:15pm (11:45pm Sat–Sun

GREEK ON DANFORTH

One of Toronto's most enjoyable walking neighbourhoods, the Danforth Avenue section known as Greektown (www.greektowntoronto.com) is lined with designer shops and restaurants, many with sidewalk patios. Popular eateries include (♿ see Addresses) The Friendly Greek at 551 Danforth, t416-469-8422 or **Pappas Grill** (440 Danforth Ave. ℘416-469-9595), best known for appetizers such as hummus and *tzatziki* dips

and lamb. Specialty store **iQ Living** (542 Danforth Ave. ℘416-466-2727) is a Canadian enterprise selling furnishings, hardware, accessories, kitchen utensils, storage products and other items for the home. For great family fun, catch the annual **Taste of the Danforth** (2nd weekend in Aug.; www.tasteofthedanforth.com), which turns this busy thoroughfare into a pedestrian walkway bursting with live entertainment, food stalls, music and fashion shows.

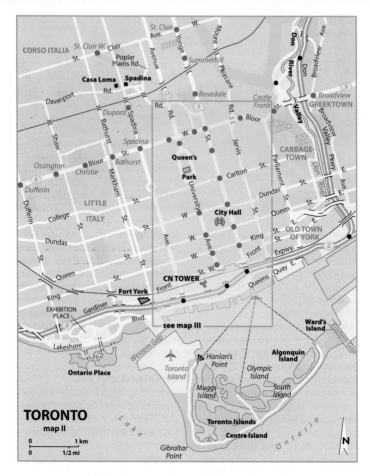

TORONTO
map II

& holidays), other islands hours vary, consult schedule. ⇒$7.50 round-trip. ♿ 𝒞416-392-8193. www.toronto.ca/parks/island.

These islands function as Toronto's principal public parkland. Extending 6km/4mi from end to end, they offer expansive lawns, age-old shade trees, sandy beaches, marinas and splendid **views★★** of downtown Toronto. Attractions on Centre Island include restaurants, cafes, a beach (on the Lake Ontario side), a delightful **amusement park** 👥 for youngsters (🕐open Jun–Labour Day, daily 10:30am, closing hrs vary; May & rest of Sept Sat–Sun 10:30am, closing hrs vary; 𝒞416-203-0405; www.centreisland.ca). Visitors can explore the islands on foot or by bike

(motor vehicles prohibited on the islands; bike rentals available), particularly **Algonquin** and **Ward's** Island, whose quaint roads lined with small, privately owned cottages have a decidedly rural charm. Near **Billy Bishop Airport** on the islands' western end is **Hanlan's Point**, renowned for its **views** of the city (a trackless train operates continuously between Centre Island and Hanlan's Point). The hour-long **Inner Harbour & Island Cruise** offers fine **views** of downtown (Departs from Pier 6, Queen's Quay West, York St. Jun–Aug every 30 min 10am-6pm, every hour from 6pm–9pm (summer); round-trip 1hr fully narrated; ⇒$25.95. 🅿Toronto Harbour Tours: 𝒞416-203-6994; www.torontotours.com).

Fort York★

250 Fort York Blvd. Access by Bathurst streetcar or by car: from Lakeshore Blvd. take Strachan St. just before Princes' Gate entrance to Exhibition Grounds, then right on Fleet St. and left on Garrison Rd. (under Gardiner Expressway). 🅿️🕐*Open late-May–Labour Day daily 10am–5pm. Rest of the year daily 10am–4pm (Sat–Sun 5pm)* 🕐*Closed weekend before Christmas until Jan 2.* ♿*$9 (child $4.25).* 📞*416-392-6907. http://www.fortyork.ca.*

Constructed in 1793, Fort York was devastated in 1813 during American capture. It was rebuilt, but peace meant its military importance diminished.

The **officers' barracks** is furnished to show the lifestyle of senior officers of the period. Costumed staff conduct tours and, in summer, stage military manoeuvres *(Jul–Aug)*. Events on Canada Day (July 1) and Simcoe Day (Aug 1) offer fife & drum, musketry and cannons.

👥 Ontario Place★★

955 Lakeshore Blvd. W. Access from Exhibition Grounds. ✖♿🅿️🕐*Boasting a new look for Canada's 150th birthday celebration in 2017, the redevelopment of this site results in a multi-use urban destination and public waterfront park.* 📞*416-314-9900. www.ontarioplace.com.*

This sprawling, innovative leisure complex designed by Eberhard Zeidler originally emerged from an extraordinary setting of lagoons, marinas and man-made islands on the lakefront bordering the CN Exhibition Grounds. With an emphasis on family entertainment and recreation, facilities include a water park, pedal and bumper boats, a motion-simulator ride, mini-golf, restaurants & 240 marina slips.

Resembling a giant golf ball, **Cinesphere** features IMAX 3D films on a screen six storeys high. The **Molson Amphitheatre** is still in use for a variety of musical productions. The Froster Soak City **water park** features four water slides, lounge pools with water jets and a giant tipping bucket.

OLD TOWN YORK★

Although little dates from the 1793 plans of Lieutenant-Governor Simcoe, some structures date from the early 19C, including an active marketplace, the **South Saint Lawrence Market** *(92 Front St. E. at Jarvis St;* ●*King;* ✖♿🕐*open year-round Tue–Thu 8am–6pm, Fri to 7pm, Sat 5am–5pm;* 📞*416-392-7219; www.stlawrencemarket.com)*, a cavernous brick building sheltering a two-storey food hall. The market is especially lively on Saturday morning when early-bird shoppers converge on fruit stands, bakeries, meat counters, and delicatessens. The market encases the surviving portion of the **Second City Hall** (1845-99). The former second-floor council chamber houses the **Market Gallery** of the City of Toronto Archives, which presents rotating exhibits of historical documents and artifacts *(♿🕐 open year-round Tue–Thu 10am–6pm, Fri 10am-7pm, Sat 9am–5pm, Sun 10am-4pm.* 🕐*closed major holidays;* 📞*416-392-7604; www.stlawrencemarket.com/gallery).*

Directly across the street will be the newly designed glass atrium version of the **North St. Lawrence Market**, is a bustling farmers' market with many specialty vendors, open from dawn until 5pm. 📞*416-392-7219. www.stlawrencemarket.com.* The new glass structure boasts great views from each of its four floors, to the west for example, Toronto's **Flatiron Building**, the Gooderham (1892) on Wellington Street, against a backdrop of the towers of Brookfield Place.

Just behind the market via a charming walkway is the 1850 Neoclassical **St. Lawrence Hall** *(King and Jarvis Sts.)*, distinguished by its domed cupola. It now houses various commercial enterprises.

Just opposite is lovely St. James Park, a small manicured expanse that offers rest to passers-by.

Farther east sits **Toronto's First Post Office★** *(*👥*260 Adelaide St. E;* 🕐*open year-round Mon–Fri 9am–4pm, Sat–Sun 10am–4pm;* 🕐*closed major holidays;* 📞*416-865-1833; www.townofyork.com*

Gooderham Building

© Pietro Canali/Sime/Photononstop

com), opened in 1834. Costumed staff demonstrate quill-and-ink letter-writing. Kids can write and post a letter the old-fashioned way for $1.

DOWNTOWN

Containing the city's formidable financial core, Toronto's downtown

TAKING THE FIFTH

It has that Prohibition feel, but don't let the back-alley entrance fool you. The **Fifth Social Club** (225 Richmond St. W.; ℘416-979-3000; www.thefifth. com), still known as Easy and the Fifth, is a swank nightclub. Housed in a renovated factory in the city's buzzing Entertainment District, this popular spot, with the air of an upscale loft, attracts young professionals (ages 25 to 45) for weekend drinks and dancing. The Black Betty rock n' roll lounge bar appeals to a boisterous, blue-jean-clad crowd. **The Fifth Grill ($$$)** is one of the city's best restaurants, with white linens, live piano music, and delicious steaks and seafood. In summer, enjoy your meal along with skyline views outside on **The Terrace,** a pretty rooftop patio. *Restaurant reservations are a must.*

exudes a sense of momentum and prosperity. Site of the country's leading banks, legal, insurance and brokerage firms, and the Toronto Stock Exchange, the area of King and Bay streets constitutes Canada's "Wall Street."

The skyscrapers are connected by the largest **underground city** of shops, eateries, banks and concourses in the world, extending eight blocks from Union Station and the Fairmont **Royal York Hotel** to City Hall, Eaton Centre and on up to Dundas Street. The PATH network of walkways, clearly marked, covers 10km/6mi.

One of the best-known and longest roads (1,896km/1,178mi) in Canada is **Yonge Street**, the city's east-west dividing line. Laid out by Simcoe in 1795 as a military route, this thoroughfare is lined with fancy boutiques, colourful flower stands, trendy restaurants, interesting stores and antiques shops.

FINANCIAL DISTRICT★★

●*King or St. Andrew*

A stunning ebony-coloured ensemble covering an entire city block, the **Toronto-Dominion Centre★★** was the first component of the current financial district. A fine example of the International style, the spartan black-glass towers, known locally as the TD Centre, reflect the design of eminent

20C architect Mies van der Rohe, consultant for the project. The complex now includes five towers. Fronting Bay Street, the Ernst & Young tower (1992) incorporates the former Art Deco Stock Exchange Building (1937) within its base. On view throughout the centre are works by contemporary artists, predominantly Canadian.

The downtown abounds in other skyscrapers by noted architects, among them the adjacent **Royal Bank Plaza★** (**D** on map), designed by Boris Zerafa. Completed in 1976, the 41-storey and 26-storey gold reflecting-glass towers are linked by a 40m/130ft-high glass-walled banking hall, entry point to the underground city. A suspended sculpture of 8,000 aluminum tubes, the work of renowned Venezuelan artist Jesus Rafael Soto, dominates the interior of the hall.

The tiered, aqua-glass towers of **Brookfield Place** (formerly BCE Place), was designed by Spanish architect Santiago Calatrava, abut a lower central building bisected into matching office wings by an elaborate arched, aluminum **atrium.** The complex is also the home of the **Hockey Hall of Fame★** 👥 (**E** on map). Here, the original Stanley Cup is on display in the stately, domed lobby (1886) of the former Bank of Montreal building (*take the escalator to lower level;* ♿ 🕐 *open daily Mon–Sat 9:30am–6pm, Sun 10am–6pm; rest of year varies;* 🕐 *closed Jan 1, Nov 9 & Dec 25;* 🎟 *$18, Youth $12;* 📞*416-360-7765; www.hhof.com.* Four buildings (1931 to 1972) form **Commerce Court**, a 57-storey stainless-steel tower, head office of the Canadian Imperial Bank of Commerce, designed by famed architect I.M. Pei.

Opposite Commerce Court, an "erector-set" canopy marks the entrance to the slender 68-storey **Scotia Plaza** (1988) by Boris Zerafa. It is distinguished by a V-shaped wedge at its summit. **First Canadian Place** consists of a 72-storey white tower (1975) housing the Bank of Montreal and the 36-storey tower (1983) containing the **Toronto Stock Exchange (F** *on map*). Connecting

the towers is a three-level plaza with elegant shops and an attractive water wall. Under Adelaide Street, the PATH walkway leads to a grouping of shops known as the Lanes and another called the Plaza Shops, which extend to Sheraton Centre.

Designed by Boris Zerafa, the multi-faceted glass towers of **Sun Life Centre★** (1984) frame the east and west sides of University Avenue at King Street. Near the entrance to the 28-storey east tower, an outdoor sculpture by Sorel Etrog suggests a massive wheel-based tool.

Roy Thomson Hall★★

60 Simcoe St. ●*St. Andrew.* ♿ 📞*416-593-4255. www.roythomson.com.*
Resembling a large inverted bowl, this glass-sheathed concert hall, named for Canadian newspaper magnate Roy Thomson anv designed by **Arthur Erickson**, dominates the corner of King and Simcoe streets. Opened in 1982 and the home of the Toronto Symphony, the hall retains is acoustical superiority.

To insulate the performance area, a thick circular passageway with entry doors at intervals creates a "sound lock." Transparent at night when illuminated, the diamond-shaped exterior panels shimmer in daylight, their blue cast a reflection of the sky.

On Front Street, south of Roy Thomson Hall, the concrete box-shaped 10-storey **Canadian Broadcasting Centre**, built in the Deconstructivist style in 1992, was designed by Philip Johnson.

City Hall Area★

●*Osgoode or Queen.*
With its crescent-shaped towers and mushroomlike council chamber, **City Hall★**, completed in 1965, was the symbol of Toronto until supplanted by icons the CN Tower and Rogers Centre. The masterpiece by Finland's **Viljo Revell** remains a landmark nevertheless. Spacious **Nathan Phillips Square** (named for a former mayor), with its wide, arch-covered reflecting pool, attracts crowds of ice-skaters in winter. Henry Moore's outdoor bronze sculpture *The Archer* led to the sizable collection

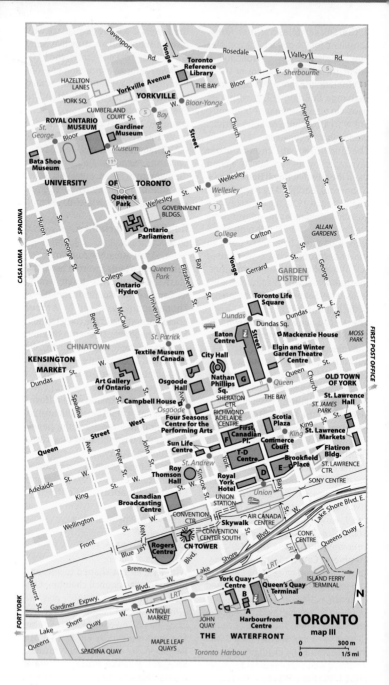

TORONTO
map III

of his pieces in Toronto's Art Gallery of Ontario.

Occupying the east side of the square, **Old City Hall★ (G** *on map*), designed by Toronto-born **Edward J. Lennox** (1855-1933), houses the provincial courts. Extending several blocks on Yonge Street between Queen and Dundas

Ice skating at Nathan Phillips Square, City Hall in the background

© www.torontowide.com/Toronto Tourism

streets is **Eaton Centre★** (●Queen; ✕ ♿ 🅿 🕐 open year-round Mon–Fri 10am–9:30pm, Sat 9:30am–9:30pm, Sun 10am–7pm; ☎416-598-8560; www.torontoeatoncentre.com), a five-level office/shopping complex with trees, fountains and natural lighting designed by Eberhard Zeidler. The Hudson's Bay Company ("The Bay") is reached by a covered walkway across Queen Street.

Elgin and Winter Garden Theatre Centre★

189 Yonge St. Opposite Eaton Centre north of Queen St. ●Queen. ♿ ☞ Visit by guided tour (1hr 30min) only, Thu 5pm, Sat 11am. ☺$12. Box office Tue–Sat 11am–5pm, or until show time. 🕐 Closed Dec 25. ☎855-622-2787 or 416-314-2871. www.heritagetrust.on.ca.

This National Historic Site houses one of the few remaining double-decker theatres in the world. Designed by Thomas Lamb, the 1,500-seat Elgin and 1,000-seat Winter Garden opened in 1913 and 1914 respectively as vaudeville, and later, silent-film houses. The Elgin theatre is reached through a gilded lobby of Corinthian pilasters and arched mirrors. A seven-storey marble staircase leads to the fanciful Winter Garden, with its ceiling of hanging beech boughs.

Mackenzie House★

82 Bond St. ●Dundas. 🕐 Open May–Labour Day Tue–Sun noon–5pm. Rest of Sept–Dec Tue–Fri noon–4pm, Sat–Sun noon–5pm. Rest of the year Sat–Sun noon–5pm. 🕐 Closed major holidays. ☺$6.19. ☎416-392-6915. www.toronto.ca.

This 19C brick row house was the last home of William Lyon Mackenzie, the rebel leader and publisher. Rooms on the three floors have been restored to the 1850s period. In the modern annex at the rear is a replica of his **print shop** with a hand-operated flatbed press.

Osgoode Hall★

130 Queen St. W. ●Osgoode. Quiet is necessary, since courts may be in session. ☞ Guided tours (45min) Jul–Aug only, Mon–Fri 1 pm. ☎416-947-3300 or 800-668-7380. www.lsuc.on.ca.

Home to the Supreme Court of Ontario and the Law Society of Upper Canada, this stately Neoclassical edifice is set on expansive lawns west of Nathan Phillips Square.

Erected in 1867 allegedly to keep cows out, an ornate cast-iron fence surrounds the judicial bastion. The two-tiered, arched interior courtyard induces admiration, as does the magnificent **Great Library**.

North of Osgoode Hall stands the provincial **Court House (J** on map), with its circular rotunda.

Four Seasons Centre for the Performing Arts★★

145 Queen St. W. ●Osgoode.
✈*Guided tours (90 min) on select Sundays (check website calendar for dates).* ⊜*$20.* ✆*416-363-8231. www.fourseasonscentre.ca.*
Opposite Osgood Hall rises Toronto's long-awaited venue for the Canadian Opera Company and National Ballet of Canada. The multi-storey glass and structural steel building (2006) was designed by Jack Diamond.

Campbell House★

160 Queen St. W. (University Ave. at Queen St.) ●Osgoode. ✈*Visit by guided tour (30min) only, May–mid-Oct Tue–Fri 9:30am–4:30pm, Sat–Sun noon–4:30pm. Rest of the year Tue–Sat 9:30am–4:30pm.* ○*Closed major holidays.* ⊜*$6.* ✆*416-597-0227. www.campbellhousemuseum.ca.*
Once belonging to Sir **William Campbell** (1758-1834), chief justice of Upper Canada from 1825 to 1829, the Georgian brick mansion (built 1822) was moved to this site in 1972 from historic York. The restored rooms contain period pieces and portraits of the his family.

The headquarters of Canada Life Assurance Co. rise just behind Campbell House. A prominent landmark, the building is distinguished at night by its tower, the lights of which indicate the barometer reading.

Art Gallery of Ontario★★

317 Dundas St. W. ●St. Patrick.
✕&○*Open year-round Tue–Sun 10am–5:30pm (Wed & Fri til 9pm). Closed Jan 1, Dec 25.* ⊜*$19.50.* ✆*416-979-6648 or 877-225-4246. www.ago.net.*
The museum reopened in 2008 after a massive $276 million transformation designed by Toronto-born architect **Frank Gehry**. Major elements include a new façade in glass and wood for the Dundas Street entrance, a new south wing for contemporary art, a large new social gathering space, a two-level museum store, a new restaurant and a cafe, and space for temporary exhibits. Art viewing space has been increased by 47 percent.

The museum closed in late 2007 in order to re-hang its collection in the new space. The project was propelled by the late businessman Kenneth Thomson's donation of nearly 2,000 works and $70 million.

The gallery retains the world's largest public collection of works by renowned

Art Gallery of Ontario, transformed and designed by Frank Gehry

© Christian Heeb/hemis.fr

British sculptor **Henry Moore** (1898-1986). The permanent collection ranges from 15C European paintings to international contemporary art and includes 11,000 years of Canadian art.

Henry Moore Sculpture Centre★★

Level 2. The centre owns more than 900 of Moore's works, including 712 prints, 140 original plasters and bronzes and 77 drawings. Many were donated by the artist when he learned that the museum intended to devote a gallery to him. The centre was designed by the artist to use natural light from the glass-panelled roof. At night, the effect of artificial lighting, with its interplay of shadows on the sculpted shapes, is stunning.

Permanent Collection★★

The **European Collection** covers the Old Masters, Impressionism and early-20C movements. Displayed in several galleries *(level 2)*, the **Canadian Collection** features 18C to contemporary works. Selections from the gallery's African and Oceanic collection are also on view *(level 2)*. Contemporary **Inuit art** on exhibit dates from the early 1900s to the present. Contemporary art and 20C art are displayed primarily in galleries on levels 4 and 5.

The Grange★

Entrance through the art gallery's Tannenbaum Sculpture Atrium.

This Georgian brick mansion (c.1817) was the home of lawyer, politician and Family Compact stalwart, **D'Arcy Boulton Jr.** (1790-1870). In 1875 The Grange became the home of well-known scholar **Goldwin Smith**, Regius Professor of History at Oxford, who made it a centre of intellectual pursuits and progressive ideas.

The mansion is meticulously furnished to give the aura of Family Compact days. Of special interest is the beautiful, curved staircase in the entry hall. The basement contains kitchens typical of a 19C gentleman's house.

The residence faces lovely Grange Park *(open to the public via street access),*

COLLEGE STRIP

If you want to know where U of T and Ryerson students hang out, College Street *(between Bathurst and Shaw Sts.)* is the place. Quirky boutiques beckon during daylight hours, while lively clubs and pubs draw in late-night revellers. **Motoretta** (no.554) sells vintage Vespas in flashy colours along with related paraphernalia (*416-925-1818. www.motoretta.ca).* Diner-style **Café Diplomatico** *(no. 594)* is a combo coffeehouse/ice-cream haunt (*416-534-4637; www. cafediplomatico.ca; open Sun–Thu 8am–1am, Fri/Sat til 2am).* Party nightly at College Street Bar (no.574) and Hype Hip-Hop Fridays from 10pm. www.collegestreetbar.com

from which visitors can appreciate the mansion's gracious façade.

Textile Museum of Canada

55 Centre Ave. ●*St. Patrick.* ♿🕐*Open year-round daily 11am–5pm (Wed til 8pm).* 🕐*Closed major holidays.* 👓*$15.* *416-599-5321. www.textilemuseum.ca.*

Occupying two floors of a high-rise hotel/condominium complex, the only Canadian museum devoted exclusively to textiles features global traditional and contemporary works.

QUEEN'S PARK★

Based on E.J. Lennox's landscape scheme of 1876, this oval-shaped park is the setting for Ontario's Parliament and nearby government buildings. To the west and east sprawls the **University of Toronto**, Canada's largest university, perhaps best known for its medical school where, in 1921, **Frederick Banting** and **Charles Best** succeeded in isolating insulin.

To the south, the mirrored, multistoried headquarters of **Ontario Hydro** (1975, Kenneth R. Cooper) rises above the surroundings. The building has no furnace or heating plant; instead, energy given off by artificial lighting, equipment and people is stored in thermal reservoirs in the basement and recirculated.

Ontario Parliament★

●*Queen's Park.* ✗&⚫◄ *Tours (30min) leaving from information counter at front doors Victoria Day–Labour Day every hour on the half-hour from 9:30am–5pm, lunhour tour each Fri at 12:30. View legislature in session (call to ensure government is in session) from public galleries.* ⊙*Closed major holidays.* &416-325-0061. *www.ontla.on.ca.*

Dominating the south end of the park, the imposing sandstone 1893 **Legislative Building** (also called Parliament Buildings) typifies Richardsonian Romanesque architecture.

The ponderous exterior belies the interior's elegant beauty, particularly the white-marbled **west wing**, rebuilt after a fire in 1909, and the stately **legislative chamber** with its rich mahogany and sycamore. On view is the 200-year-old mace *(ground floor)*, a ceremonial gold "club" mandatory at House proceedings. Taken by the Americans during their 1813 assault on York, it was returned years later by President F.D. Roosevelt.

Gardiner Museum of Ceramic Art★★

111 Queen's Park (across from the Royal Ontario Museum). ✗&⚫⊙*Open year-round Mon–Thu 10am–6pm (Fri til 9pm), Sat–Sun 10am–5pm.* ⊙*Closed Jan 1.* ⌾*$15 ($7.50 Fri 4pm–9pm).* &416-586-8080. *www.gardinermuseum.on.ca.*

Located in a modern granite building, this museum, the project of collectors George and Helen Gardiner, features pottery and porcelain from a variety of countries and cultures.

The Pottery Gallery *(ground floor)* showcases works of the **Ancient Americas**, specifically from Mexico, and Central and South America dating from 2000 BC to about AD 1500— primarily figurines, vessels and bowls of Olmec, Toltec, Aztec and other cultures.

Also included is 15C and 16C **Italian majolica** and 17C English tin-glazed **delftware**.

The Porcelain Gallery *(2nd floor)* features **18C porcelains** of Du Paquier, Sèvres (characterized by bright yellows), the great English companies—Worcester, Derby, Chelsea–and others. Highlights are the Meissenware pieces.The new Bell collection of blue-and-white Chinese porcelain, attractively presented in glass wall cabinets, contains close to 200 pieces.

The museum restaurant, called **à la Carte at the Gardiner** offers homemade soups, gourmet originals, sandwiches, delectable sides, knockout desserts and espresso. Brunch on weekends is popular.

ROM

100 Queen's Park (Main entrance on Bloor Street West). ✗&⊙*Open year-round daily 10am–5:30pm (Fri til 8:30pm).* ⊙*Closed Dec 25.* ⌾*16, child $13 (discount prices Fri after 4:30pm).* &416-586-8000. *www.rom.on.ca.* *The museum's floor plan, available at the admissions desk in the entrance lobby, is most useful.*

Renowned for extensive research, this enormous museum, commonly referred to as the ROM, is housed in a five-floor building at Avenue Road and Bloor Street. Maintaining over 20 departments in art, archaeology and the natural sciences, the museum, known especially for its East Asian holdings, possesses a remarkable collection of six-million-plus artifacts and artworks from around the world.

The original H-shaped building (1914) has been propelled into the 21C with the completion of the striking Michael Lee-Chin Crystal, designed by Daniel Libeskind, and opened to the public in mid-2007. It includes a dramatic new entrance off Bloor Street West, a cavernous main lobby, a spacious new **museum shop**, seven permanent galleries and the new restaurant on the top level.

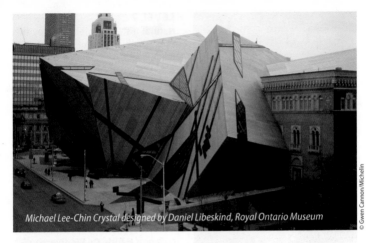

Michael Lee-Chin Crystal designed by Daniel Libeskind, Royal Ontario Museum

© Gwen Cannon/Michelin

ROYAL ONTARIO MUSEUM (ROM)★★★
●Museum

▶ **Location:** Southwest corner of Bloor Street & Avenue Road, ROM is best reached by foot or subway.

🅿 **Parking:** Municipal lot (height restriction) at 9 Bedford Rd., (one block west of Avenue Rd., offers discount for minimum 3-hour stay (get discount voucher from ROM admissions desk). Metered parking spaces difficult to find nearby.

🚫 **Don't Miss:** First Peoples Gallery and the Centres of Discovery.

🕐 **Timing:** Plan to spend at least 3–4 hours.

👫 **Kids:** Kids Gallery, Life Drawing for Kids & Hands-On Centre.

LEVEL 1

The spacious new entrance off Bloor Street West on Level 1 ushers visitors into the crystalline-shaped **Michael Lee-Chin Crystal**, a striking addition evocative of the gems and minerals in the museum's collection. Its five components of glass and brushed aluminium are interlocked to form a massive architectural prism. From the lobby and new court, visitors pass into the Samuel Hall Currelly Gallery of the original building, named for **Charles**

Trick Currelly (1876-1957), whose world travels provided the first treasures for a collection. To the east, two **totem poles** rise above the stairwells. Crafted of red cedar by the Nisga'a and Haida peoples of British Columbia in the 19C, the totem poles are so tall that their upper sections can be viewed from the second and third floors. The taller pole depicts the family history of the chief who owned it. Just beyond is the original vaulted **rotunda**, with an exquisite domed **ceiling** of golden mosaic tessarae. Flanking the rotunda are the **Sigmund Samuel Gallery of Canadiana**, which presents paintings and decorative arts from Canada's past (note in particular the panelled room from the Bélanger House c. 1820) and the superb **First Peoples Gallery**, filled with works by the Inuit and First Nations Peoples. Enter it to explore a multifaceted history of Canada's indigenous people whose creativity, resourcefulness and endurance are evident in a wealth of artifacts, from a birchbark canoe and Inuit kayak, beaded clothing, caribou parkas, tools, weapons and Ojibway pottery to a model of an Iroquoin longhouse. Sitting Bull's headdress and the war-record robes are highlights. Lining the west side of this floor are galleries exhibiting the ROM's incredible Asian holdings. The outstanding exhibit is the **Chinese Collection**, one of the largest and most important of its kind

Golden mosaics on the ceiling of the rotunda

© www.torontowide.com/Toronto Tourism

outside China. Spanning nearly 7,000 years, the exhibits date from the Shang dynasty 1523 BC (the Chinese Bronze Age) to the overthrow of the Qing or Manchu dynasty (1644-1911).

The collection is noted for its clay **tomb figures,** small replicas of people and animals buried with the dead as their "servants," and dating from the 3C AD. The star attraction, however, is the **Ming Tomb,** the only complete example in the Western world. It is reportedly the burial place of Zu Dashou, a 17C general who served the last Ming emperors and lived into the Qing period.

Remarkable for its ink and colour clay wall paintings, the **Bishop White Gallery** simulates the interior of a Chinese temple. Life-size polychromed and gilded statues of *bodhisattvas* (those enlightened, compassionate individuals destined for Buddha status) of 12-14C stand in the centre.

The Herman Herzog Levy Gallery is a dimly lit room displaying light-sensitive **East Asian** works of art (12-14C), including murals and paintings on scrolls. In the gallery of **Korean Art**, decorative arts include a variety of ceramic pieces; note the women's hairpins. In the gallery devoted to Japanese works, a c.1800 suit of armour of the Edo period is especially interesting.

LEVEL 2

Natural history exhibits occupy this floor, the highlight of which are the magnificent, reassembled **dinosaurs** 👥. Many of these skeletons come from field expeditions in the Alberta Badlands.

The CIBC **Discovery Gallery** is an innovative space with interactive exhibits for children. The glass atrium of the **Bird Gallery** is filled with Canadian geese, turkeys, owls, ducks and an assortment of smaller birds. The **Bat Cave** 👥 is a lifelike reconstruction of the St. Clair Cave in Jamaica, complete with hundreds of handmade bats.

The Patrick and Barbara Keenan Family Gallery of **Hands-On Biodiversity** 👥 is an interactive gallery that lets visitors crawl into a simulated wolf's den; identify leaves, sounds and tracks; and touch antlers, horns, bones, skulls and skins, among other activities.

The central section houses the new **Schad Gallery of Biodiversity**, featuring "Life in Crisis", with rhinos, hammerhead and blue sharks, endangered leatherback turtles and the extinct dodo bird, among other animals. It also features live displays of a coral reef and a colony of leafcutter ants.

On the opposite side, a host of interactive exhibits and presentations compose the **Earth's Treasures** section, including specimens and rocks that can be touched and examined. A highlight is the **Gallery of Gems and Gold**, where exquisite collections of smaller gems and jewellery are on view. The **Canadian Mining Hall of Fame** features photographs and films of noted pioneers in the development of the nation's mining industry.

LEVEL 3

This level is devoted to world cultures, with special emphasis on the ancient world. The **Gallery of Africa, the Americas and Asia-Pacific** showcases the rich culture of indigenous peoples from Africa, the American continents, the Asia-Pacific region and Oceania.

The **Ancient Egypt** exhibit depicts daily life via tools, utensils, jewellery

Foot Notes

England's Edward II is credited with initiating the measurement of the "foot" in 1320. His own foot measured 36 barley corns; each corn was a third of an inch, making the total of 12 inches equal to one foot. In England in the 14C, the length of a shoe's pointed toe was regulated by law and depended upon the wearer's social status. The height of a shoe's heel also conveyed the social importance of the wearer. Thus, the wealthy were, and still are, termed "well-heeled." The origin of calling someone a "square" is said to derive from the wearing of square-toed shoes long after they were in fashion.

Source: *Bata Shoe Museum*

"Shoes are such a personal artifact. They tell you about the owner's social status, habits, culture and religion. That's what makes them special."

Sonja Bata, founder, Bata Shoe Museum

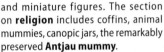

and miniature figures. The section on **religion** includes coffins, animal mummies, canopic jars, the remarkably preserved **Antjau mummy**.

The **Punt wall reliefs**, sculptural casts from the temple of Queen Hatshepsut (1503-1482 BC), illustrate her trade mission along the Nile. In the **Gallery of Greece**, sculptures of marble, terra-cotta figurines, coins and exquisite jewellery evidence Greek creativity from 500 BC to 31 BC. In the Ancient Cypress Gallery, myriad Cypriot artifacts testify to the creativity of the Bronze Age through the Hellenistic period (c. 2200–30 BC).

In the east wing, the **Samuel European Galleries** concentrate on decorative arts from the Middle Ages to the present. The gallery's two wings showcase topics and themes such as culture and context, as well as a Judaica collection celebrating Jewish life and culture.

The **Lee Collection** assembles medieval and Renaissance wares of gold and silver. **Culture and Context** presents partial-room reconstructions, such as a Victorian parlour (1860-85).

ADDITIONAL SIGHTS
Bata Shoe Museum★★
327 Bloor St. W. ●St. George.
&⊙Open year-round 10am–5pm (Thu 8pm). ⊙Closed Dec 25, Good Friday. ☎$14 (Thu 5pm–8pm Pay What You Can). ✆416-979-7799. www.batashoemuseum.ca.

Bata Shoe Museum

© Clifton Li/Toronto Tourism

Housed in a five-storey building designed by renowned architect **Raymond Moriyama** to resemble a shoebox, this unique museum draws on its 10,000-piece collection to illustrate a 4,500-year history of shoemaking and mankind's footwear. Shoes in the permanent exhibit range from 3,550-year-old Theban funerary slippers and 1,500-year-old Anasazi sandals to Mahatma Gandhi's leather chappals (c.1940s), Princess Di's fuchsia kid pumps, and traditional Arctic footwear.

Yorkville★
●Bay.
Once the hub of creatives fashioning the music of the 60's, Yorkville today represents all that is chic in Toronto—

ALL THE BEST

*446 Summerhill, 1054 Mt.Pleasant, &
483 Church St,(midtown).* ℘ *416-921-
2714. www.allthebestfinefoods.com.*
A Toronto institution for nearly 25
years, **All the Best** gourmet food
shop has freshly made dinner items
to go, exotic sauces and artisanal
cheeses, many of which are imported
or made by organic *fromagerie* houses
in the region. Baked goods include
berry crisps, tarts, cheesecakes,
breads and pastries. For table settings,
snazzy table linens, candles, cultlery,
and cookbooks galore on sale.
When you tire of shopping, head back
to your hotel or B&B and contact The
Food Dudes *(24 Carlaw Ave, ℘647-
340-3833).* Their unique and delicious
combo deals are original, delicious
and moderately priced. Just order
a main dish with your choices, then
a dessert option, and their delivery
partner, "Foodee" brings it to you.
www.fdpantry.com

and a remarkable transformation.
Between Yonge Street and Avenue
Road, **Yorkville Avenue** presents
charming Victorian houses converted
into expensive boutiques or trendy cafes
sporting the latest architectural façades
and underpinnings.
In York Square at the corner of Avenue
Road and Yorkville Avenue, shops
surround an interior brick courtyard
where summer dining is alfresco.
Behind the square lies posh Hazelton
Lanes *(open during business hours)*,
a labyrinthian shopping/office/
condominium complex (1978) designed
by Boris Zerafa.

On the other side of Yorkville Avenue,
Cumberland Terrace is a rambling
enclosure of a few shops, eateries and
offices, with a passageway to Cumberland Street.

Toronto Reference Library★

789 Yonge St. ●Bloor-Yonge.
&♿Open Jul–Aug Mon–Thu
*9am–8:30pm, Fri 9am–6pm, Sat & Sun
9am–5pm. Rest of the year also Sun
1:30pm–5pm.* ℘416-393-7131.
www.torontopubliclibrary.ca.
An architectural gem designed by
Raymond Moriyama, this massive brick
and glass building contains Canada's

most extensive public library with 10 million items, 50 miles of stacks, 5 floors, and over 25 million virtual visits.

Rising from a wide, light-filled centre, the tiered balconies are bordered by solid undulating balustrades.

In a cozy corner on the fifth floor is a tiny room *(access from 4th floor)* brimming with the **Arthur Conan Doyle Collection**—famed Sherlock Holmes stories, Sherlockian criticism, Doyle's autobiography, historical novels, poetry and other writings. Worn Victorian furnishings complement mementos of the great detective's presence.

Casa Loma★★

1 Austin Terrace. ●*Dupont, then climb steps.* ✕ 🅿 🕐*Open year-round daily 9:30am–5pm (last admission 4pm).* 🕐*Closes 1pm Christmas Eve, closed Dec 25.* ⊜*$25.* ✆*416-923-1171. www.casaloma.org.*

This enormous sandstone castle, completed in 1914, was the lavish 98-room residence of prominent industrialist Sir **Henry Pellatt**, known as the Crooked Knight. Maintained since 1937 by the Kiwanis Club, the Medieval mansion is a popular tourist attraction.

Seven storeys in height, the castle boasts two towers—one open-air, the other enclosed—which offer good views of the city; secret passageways; and a 244m/800ft underground tunnel to the magnificent **carriage house** and stables. The palatial residence includes 21 fireplaces, a **great hall** (22m/70ft ceiling), a marble-floor conservatory, an oak-panelled drawing room and a library for 10,000 books. Especially well appointed are the **Round Room** with its exquisite Louis XV tapestry furnishings, the **Windsor Room** and Lady Pellatt's suite.

Spadina Museum★

285 Spadina Rd. ●*Dupont, then climb steps.* ♿⟳ *Visit by guided tour (1hr) only, Apr–Labour Day Tue–Sun & holiday Mon noon–5pm. Rest of Sept–Dec Tue–Fri noon–4pm, Sat–Sun noon–5pm. Rest of the year Sat–Sun noon–5pm.* 🕐*Closed Jan 1, Good Friday & Dec 25–26.* ⊜*$7.96.* ✆*416-392-6910. www.toronto.ca.*

Spadina Museum is a historic house and garden that overlooks its 2.5ha/6-acre grounds in a fashionable residential district. The 50-room brick mansion was home to businessman **James Austin** and his heirs.

In 1866 Austin, a successful grocer who eventually headed Consumers' Gas and founded the Dominion Bank, acquired the estate. His son added the spacious billiard room in 1898 and, in 1907, the terraces and porte-cochere. The third floor, with its hipped roof and pedimented dormers, was built in 1912. Reflecting the grandeur of Victorian and Edwardian styles, the spacious **drawing room** with its matching striped seating, and the airy wicker-furnished **palm room** show the comforts the Austin family expected.

METRO SIGHTS
👥 Ontario Science Centre★★★

770 Don Mills Rd. 11km/7mi from downtown (22km/14mi by car via Don Valley Pkwy. to Eglinton Ave.). ●*Eglinton then no. 34 East bus (to Don Mills Rd. stop).* ✕♿🅿 🕐*Open daily*

Casa Loma

Ontario Science Centre

© Ontario Science Centre

10am–4pm, Sat 10am–8pm, Sun & holidays 10am–4pm . ⏰Closed Dec 25. 🎟️$22 (with IMAX $28). ☎416-696-1000. www.ontariosciencecentre.ca. Demonstrations and Omnimax films daily. For times and locations, check notice board at the bottom of escalator, level C.

Cascading down the Don River ravine, this sizable complex, designed by Raymond Moriyama, takes full advantage of its natural site. Consists largely of interactive exhibits on science and technology, & **OMNIMAX** theatre. There are ten exhibitions designated by numbers. Highlights are the **Space Hall**, which displays moon rocks and meteorites; there's even a cloud chamber. The **Planetarium** is on this level as is **KidSpark**, an interactive gallery where children *(8 years & younger)* learn by doing. Highlights continue with the **Living Earth** exhibit, where visitors explore a limestone cave and experience an indoor rain forest; the **Science Arcade**, with humorous electricity demonstrations; and the **Weston Family Innovation Centre** (aka **HotZone**) visitors can make a shoe, conduct an orchestra, make a soundtrack and engage in other creative activities. Level 6 is the **AstraZeneca Human Edge** exhibit about the human body.

👥 Toronto Zoo★★★

361A Old Finch Ave, Scarborough. 35km/22mi from downtown. ●Kennedy, transfer to bus 86A or Toronto Zoo Shuttle from Union Station. ✖♿🅿⏰*Open mid-May–Labour Day daily 9am–7pm. Early Mar–mid-May & rest of Sept–early Oct daily 9am–6pm. Rest of the year daily 9:30am–4:30pm.* ⏰*Closed Dec 25.* 🎟️*$28 (child $18).* ☎*416-392-5929. www.torontozoo.com. Site map available at entrance. Begin by boarding the narrated shuttle, the Zoomobile (daily 9:30am–5:30pm; 🎟️$8), which provides an excellent overview of main attractions; disembark at the Serengeti station and continue on foot.*

Opened in 1974, this world-class zoological park features a remarkable variety of wildlife on 287ha/710 acres of tableland and forest. The 5,000 animals are divided into six "zoogeographic" regions: Africa, Australasia, Eurasia, the Americas, Indo-Malaya and Canada. Among the 460 species represented are numerous endangered or rare animals such as **Er Shun** and **Da Mao**, the two spectacularly popular panda bears, or the Siberian tiger, snow leopard, Malayan tapir, pygmy hippopotamus and the Indian rhionoceros. Designed by Raymond Moriyama, harmoniously integrated glass and wood pavilions provide shelter for animals unadapted to Canada's climate.

The popular **Africa Pavilion**, abundant with tropical vegetation and exotic birds, is home to lowland gorillas and other primates as well as Canada's largest herd of African elephants. The **Edge of Night** exhibit *(in the Australasia Pavilion)* provides a journey into a nocturnal world inhabited by seldom-seen species like the Tasmanian devil.

Seasonal rides and special activities for kids include: Tundra Trek ride *($12)*, Gorilla Climb Ropes Course *($8)*, Zoomobile *($8)*, and Conservation Carousel *($3)*.

Giant Panda Bear, Toronto Zoo

© Gordon Fisher/age fotostock

👥 Black Creek Pioneer Village★★

1000 Murray Ross Pkwy. 29km/18mi northwest of downtown. ●Yonge and Finch, transfer to Steeles bus no. 60. ✕🅿🕐*Open Jul–Labour Day Mon–Fri 10am–5pm, Sat–Sun & holidays 11am–5pm. Rest of year varies.* 🕐*Closed Dec 25–26.* 🎟$15 (child $11). ✆416-736-1733. www.blackcreek.ca. Site plan is distributed at the entrance.*

The village comprises 40 buildings, including 5 from the original farm established between 1816 and 1832 by Pennsylvania-German settlers, and 19C structures moved to the site.

EXCURSIONS
👥 Canada's Wonderland

9580 Jane St., Vaughn. 30km/19mi north by Hwy. 400 and Rutherford Rd. GO TRANSIT from ●Yorkdale or York Mills. ✕🔊🅿🕐*Open mid-May–Labour Day daily; call or consult website.* ✆905-832-8131. www.canadaswonderland.com.*

This theme park features 200 attractions, including rides like **Wonder Mountain's 4D Guardian**, with lots of activities for children. The park boasts The Behemoth, Canada's fastest and tallest roller coaster. There is **Splash Works**, an outdoor water park, as well as shows, events and concerts.

McMichael Canadian Art Collection★★

10365 Islington Ave. Kleinburg. 40km/25mi north. Hwy. 400 to Major Mackenzie Dr., then west 6km/4mi to Islington Ave., then north 1km/.6mi. 🕐✕🔊🅿*Open year-round daily; call to confirm hours).* 🕐*Closed Dec 25.* 🎟$15. ✆905-893-1121 or 888-213-1121 (Canada/US). www.mcmichael.com.*

Housed in log and fieldstone buildings, this gallery features paintings by the first truly Canadian school — the**Group of Seven**. The gallery also owns sizable collection of contemporary First Nations and Inuit art.

Tom Thomson (1877-1917) died before group was formed, but his influence was substantial. Original members were **Lawren Harris, A.Y. Jackson, J.E.H. MacDonald, Franklin Carmichael, Arthur Lismer, Frederick Varley** and **Frank Johnston**. **A.J. Casson** joined group in 1926. In 1952 **Robert** and **Signe McMichael** bought land in rural Kleinburg, decorating their home with Group of Seven paintings. In 1965 they donated the collection and property to Ontario. Influenced artists include; **Clarence Gagnon, Emily Carr** and **David Milne**, are also displayed, plus Clifford Maracle, **Norval Morrisseau, Daphne Odjig** and **Arthur Shilling**.

Spa Getaways

Hidden in the countryside an hour north of Toronto, **($$) High Fields Country Inn & Spa** *(11568-70 Concession 3, in Zephyr; ℘905-473-6132; www.highfields. com. Check website for updated rates.)* commands a hilltop overlooking Ontario's farmlands. A winding road leads to a large barn with horse pastures (polo lessons) and the inn, complete with outdoor pool and tennis court. Paths groomed for guided nature walks or cross-country skiin thread the expansive property. Rambling main house holds guest quarters, a dining area and treatment rooms. New-age techniques such as chakra and Japanese Reiki along with facials, wraps, massages and hydrotherapies. Breakfast included with room, lunch and dinner **($$$)** by reservation. Tucked away on 400 acres in the idyllic Northumberland Hills, one hour east of city, **Ste. Anne's Spa ($$$$$)** *(1009 Massey Rd., in Grafton; ℘905-349-2493 or 888-346-6772; www. haldimandhills.com)* welcomes guests to its grand porticoed mansion & spa cottages, appointed with Irish antiques, and surrounded by lushly landscaped grounds. Amenities include an outdoor pool, fitness room, sauna, chef-staffed kitchen, and diningroom. Body treatments abound. Overnight lodging is available at inn or 7 spa cottages lavishly decorated.

PRACTICAL INFORMATION
AREA CODES
Since the Greater Toronto Area has several area codes, you will need to dial all 10 digits (area code plus the phone number) when making local calls. For more information: ℘1-800-668-6878 or www.bell.ca.

GETTING AROUND
BY PUBLIC TRANSPORTATION –
The Toronto Transit Commission (TTC) operates an extensive public transit system of buses, streetcars and subway lines. Hours of operation: **Subway** Mon–Sat 6am–1:30am, Sun 9am–1:30am. **Buses and trams** daily 6am–1am (Sun 9am), reduced service Sat–Sun. Blue Night buses and trams daily 1:30am–5am. Adult cash fare $3.25 one way for unlimited travel with no stopovers. Day Pass $12. Tokens three for $8.70. Purchase tickets & tokens in subway stations. Free transfers between buses & streetcars. System maps & timetables available free of charge. Route information ℘416-393-4636 or www.ttc.ca.
BY CAR – Use of public transportation or walking is strongly encouraged within the city as streets are often congested and street parking may be difficult to find. Toronto has a strictly enforced tow-away policy. Motorists should park in designated **parking** areas which are identified by a sign with a green 'P'; there is a 3hr limit; public, off-street parking facilities are located throughout the city.
For a free map and information about parking fees, call ℘416-393-7275. *www.toronto.ca. The website, www. greenp.com, is devoted to finding parking lot space, parking services, and latest parking news.*
CAR RENTALS – Avis ℘416-777-2847. Hertz ℘416-979-1178. National ℘800-227-7368.
BY TAXI – Co-op ℘416-504-2667; *www.co-opcabs.com.* Diamond ℘416-366-6868; *www.diamondtaxi.ca.* **Beck Taxi** ℘416-751-5555; *www.beck taxi.com.*
BY MOTORCOACH – Gray Line Tours ℘647-789-5267 or 800-594-3310. *www.grayline.ca.*

GENERAL INFORMATION
ACCOMMODATIONS – For a listing of suggested hotels, see the Addresses in this chapter. For **hotels/motels** contact Tourism Toronto (℘416-203-2600 or 800-499-2514, Canada & US.

Reservation services: Hotels.com ☏800-246-8357. Downtown Toronto Assn. of B&B t416-410-3938; www.bnbinfo.com.

CITY PASS – Ask about CityPass wherein five major attractions are packaged together (CN Tower, Royal Ontario Museum, Casa Loma, Ripley's Believe It Or Not, Ontario Science Centre or Toronto Zoo) for a lower total price *($57.45)*. ☏888-330-5008; www.citypass.com.

LOCAL PRESS – **Daily:** *Toronto Star, Toronto Sun, The Globe and Mail, The National Post.* **Weekly:** *L'Express* (Francophone news), *Now (weekly; www.nowtoronto.com);*

Monthly: *Toronto Life* magazine and free guides to entertainment, shopping, and restaurants *(www.torontolife.com); Where (monthly; www.wheretoronto.com).*

Entertainment – Consult the arts and entertainment supplements in local newspapers (Thursday edition) for schedules of cultural events and addresses of principal theatres and concert halls. **Ticketmaster** *(☏416-870-8000 for concerts or 416-872-1111; www.ticketmaster.ca.)* sells tickets for theatre and the arts. HIP TIX *(☏416-536-6468; www.whatsontonight.ca)* for tickets for theatrical, dance and musical events sold by TAPA, the Toronto Alliance for the Performing Arts. Royal Alexandra and Princess of Wales theatres: ☏416-872-1212, *www.mirvish.com.*

USEFUL WEBSITES – www.torontolife.com (current events, restaurant and nightlife guide), www.beforelastcall.ca (overview of trendy restaurants, clubs and pubs).

SPORTS – **Toronto Blue Jays** (baseball): season Apr–Oct at Rogers Centre *(☏416-341-1234 or 888-654-6529; www.bluejays.com).* **Toronto Maple Leafs** (ice hockey): season Oct–Apr at Air Canada Centre *(☏416-815-5500, schedules; ☏416-872-5000, Ticketmaster; www.theaircanadacentre. com.)* **Toronto Argonauts** (football): season mid-Jun–Nov at Rogers Centre

Watching Toronto Blue Jays, Rogers Centre

© Jeffrey Carlson/Toronto Tourism

(☏416-341-2700, schedules; ☏416-341-2746, tickets; www.argonauts.ca; ☏416-872-5000, Ticketmaster). In Dec 2008 the US football team the **Buffalo Bills** played against the Miami Dolphins, another National Football League team, at the Rogers Centre, thus initiating the Bills Toronto Series, which included a regular-season game through 2013, and intermittent preseason games. **Toronto Raptors** (basketball): season Nov–Apr at Air Canada Centre *(☏416-815-5500, schedules; ☏416-872-5000; www.nba.com/raptors).*

USEFUL NUMBERS

Police: 911 (emergency) *or* 416-808-2222 **(non-emergency)**
Travellers Aid Society 416-366-7788
VIA Rail 888-842-7245
Toronto Coach Terminal – *610 Bay St.* 416-393-7911
Toronto Pearson International Airport – Customer Service: 416-776-9892 *Terminal 1 & 3:* 416-247-7678 (Terminal 2 now part of Terminal1).
Canadian Automobile Assn.: 800-268-3750.
CAA Emergency Road Service (24hr): 416-222-5222 or 800-222-4357
Shoppers Drug Mart (24hr pharmacy) *various locations:* 416-979-2424
Post Office Station A – *52B 66 Wellington St. W.* 866-607-6301
Road Conditions – 416-599-9090
Weather (24hr) – 416-661-0123

ADDRESSES

🏠 STAY

$ Uof T Housing – *214 College, Room 293. ℘416-978-8045.www.housing.utoronto. ca. Check for rates.* For inexpensive accommodations in the heart of the city, select "Temporary Housing" from the website and choose from B&Bs, guest house residences, corporate hotels, or inns. Includes Trinity College, Innis College, and St Michael's College options.

$$ Hotel Victoria – *56 Yonge St. ℘416-363-1666 or 800-363-8228. www.hotelvictoria-toronto.com. 56 rooms.* ✖&🄿. Situated only a few blocks from theatres, shopping and restaurants, this small boutique hotel is dwarfed by Yonge Street skyscrapers. Small standard rooms, nicely decorated in dark woods and warm peach and grey tones, include standard amenities and high-speed Internet access as complimentary newspaper.

$$ Strathcona Hotel – *60 York St. ℘416-363-3321 or 800-268-8304. www. thestrathconahotel.com. 194 rooms in 11 styles.* ✖🄿. Situated across the street from Union Station, in the middle of the Financial District, the Strathcona has a pleasant lobby facing busy York Street. Standard rooms are on the small side, but are sleek and comfortable, with modern amenities; corporate rooms are equipped with data ports and dual-line phones. Guests here have access to a nearby GoodLife Fitness club and spa.

$$$ InterContinental Toronto Yorkville – *220 Bloor St. W. ℘416-960-5200. www. ichotelsgroup.com. 208 rooms.* ✖&🄿🏊 Sitting opposite the Royal Ontario Museum, this high-rise hotel offers convenience to Yorkville/Bloor Street shopping and attractions. Pleasant guest rooms have spacious baths, plush robes, in-room safes and windows that open. A complimentary newspaper comes to your door. **Signatures Restaurant ($$$)** serves up excellent contemporary cuisine headlined as "global fusion": entrées from steak and seafood to pork belly are exquisitely prepared and presented.

$$$ DoubleTree by Hilton Hotel Toronto Downtown – *108 Chestnut St. ℘416-977-5000 or 800-668-6600. www. metropolitan.com. 427 rooms.* ✖&🄿🏊 New owners lead a sleek, clean lined updated version with Asian influences at this fine downtown hotel. Guest rooms have blond woods, glass, and neutral colour schemes as well as down duvets, Italian linens, in-room safes, Internet access and windows that open. **Hemispheres ($$$)** restaurant, serves some of the best cuisine in the city beginning at 6:30am and serving until 10pm. 24-hour fitness centre.

$$$$ Fairmont Royal York – *100 Front St. W. ℘416-368-2511 or 866-540-4489. www.fairmont.ca. 1,365 rooms.* ✖& 🄿🏊 Spa. Its noble façade a familiar part of the city skyline, Toronto's landmark hostelry is palatial. From its imposing chandeliered lobby to its grand ballrooms, the hotel exudes an aura of majesty. Kings, Prime Ministers, three generations of Britain's Royal Family, not to mention countless celebrities, have stayed here. Elegant guest rooms offer all the amenities, including high-speed wireless Internet. Tunnel to trains.

$$$$ Omni King Edward – *37 King St. E. ℘416-863-9700 or 800-843-6664. www.omnihotels.com. 298 rooms.* ✖&🄿. The "King Eddie" dates to 1903 saluting King Edward VII. Recently completely renovated, features marble pillars, vaulted ceilings, artwork and lavish floral arrangements decorating the public areas. Guest-room decor is fit for a king, with mahogany furnishings and marble baths, but with modern amenities including wireless Internet. Decorated with wall art, **Victoria's ($$$)** attracts for fine dining, afternoon high tea, or Sunday Brunch.

$$$$$ Trump International Hotel & Tower Toronto – *325 Bay St. 416-306-5800 or 855-888-7867. www.trumpcollection.com. 261 rooms.* Winner of 5 stars from Forbes, and Top Hotel in Toronto from Tripadvisor, this 65-storey stone, steel & glass creation of the notorious Donald Trump features the finest collection of amenities. Heated indoor inifinity salt water lap pool, 24-hour in-room dining, Trump Kids, Quartz Crystal Spa, and nanny services astound. (**$$$$**) America Restaurant & bar onsite beckons the chic & famous.

$$$$$ Windsor Arms – *18 St. Thomas St. ℘416-971-9666 or 877-999-2767. www.windsorarmshotel.com. 28 rooms.* ✖&🄿🏊 Spa. Near Bloor Street and neighbouring Yorkville, this high-end boutique hotel occupies a 1927 Gothic

Revival structure. Inside, luxury meets high-tech in spacious guest suites outfitted with Jacuzzi tubs, limestone baths and Frette linens as well as wireless Internet. The celebrated Russian Red Tea Room serves "high tea," afternoons . In the **Living Room ($$$$)** impeccable service complements fine continental cuisine from 7am until 2am.

⍩/EAT

$ Shopsy's Deli – *96 Richmond St.W. ℘416-365-3333. www.shopsys.ca.* ♿ **American.** A Toronto institution since 1921, this breakfast-lunch-dinner spot is famous for its all-beef hot dogs and corned beef sandwiches enjoyed in the Sheraton Centre Toronto Hotel. There's a dynamic range of sandwich platters, burgers and salads as well as catering and even a food truck. Walls are lined with celebrity photos and caricatures.

$ Spring Rolls – *40 Dundas St. W @ Yonge. Four other locations in Ontario. ℘416-585-2929. www.springrolls.ca.* **Asian.** Sleek Asian decor and tasty, affordable Vietnamese, Chinese and Thai dishes attract students, a local office crowd and tourists. Entrée specials change daily and include soup and salad. Pad Thai, Thai red curry and stir-fries with Szechwan or black bean sauce top the list of the most popular dishes. And don't forget the spring rolls!

$$ The Red Tomato Pizza Pasta Wine Bar – *321 King St. W. ℘416-971-6626. www.redtomato.ca.* **International**. One of many popular, bustling restaurants in the King Street entertainment district, this cozy lower-level eatery (its higher-priced sister, **Fred's Not Here**, (occupies the main floor) offers soups, salads, dim sum, pasta and other dishes.

$$ John and Sons Oyster – *56 Temperance St. ℘416-703-5111. http:// johnandsonsoyster house.com.* **Seafood**. Daily selection of different oysters and seafood. The house specialty is fresh oysters presented on the half shell with a choice of condiments, including homemade pepper sauces. A meal here is a night of memorable maritime goodies.

$$ Le Papillon on Front – *69 Front St. E. ℘416-367-0303. www.papillononfront. com.* **French**. This stylish brasserie serves an inventive menu from ash covered goat cheese and New York steak, to tuna tartare, seafood crepes and smoked duck breast within its inviting exposed brick walls. The French and Québécois fare also includes onion soup, *tourtière* (a Québécois meat pie baked with seasoned pork, beef and veal) and *steak au poivre*.

$$ Megas – *402 Danforth Ave. ℘416-466-7771. www.megasrestaurant.com.* **Greek**. One of the friendliest restaurants in Greektown, Megas is a real neighborhood eatery with unassuming decoration. A Mediterranean-style menu is available inside or on the sidewalk patio in summer. Entrées include homemade soups, melizano & octopus, while mains are classic with grilled lamb & seafood platters very popular.

$$$ Sassafraz – *100 Cumberland St. ℘416-964-2222. www.cafesassafraz.com.* **French.** This trendy eatery on one of Yorkville's prime corners *(Cumberland & Bellair Sts.),* has a bistro menu at lunchtime—steak-frites, salade Niçoise—available inside or on the sidewalk patio facing busy Cumberland Street. Inside, the sunny yellow garden room blooms year-round with herb trees under a 40ft atrium. Here you'll dine on creative cuisine such as venison ossobucco, or Quebec duck with sweet potato and much more. **S-Café Bar** onsite attracts Bohemian-style set.

$$$ Southern Accent – *595 Markham St. Dinner only. ℘416-536-3211. www. southernaccent.com.* **Cajun/Creole.** Housed in a former Victorian residence, this funky Mirvish Village restaurant attracts a mixed crowd to its outdoor patio and small, mood-lit rooms on different levels. Start your meal with a Cajun martini, made with jalapeno pepper-infused gin or vodka. Favourites include Creole jambalaya and Bourbon Street chicken. Everything is à la carte, including the side dishes and yummy corn bread.

$$$$ Canoe – *66 Wellington St. W. ℘416-364-0054. www.oliverbonacini.com.* ♿ **Canadian.** Overlooking the harbour and the Toronto Islands from its perch on the 54th floor of the Toronto Dominion Bank Tower, this perennial hot spot combines haute Canadian cuisine with excellent service. Signature dishes include maple-cured BC salmon, seared la Ferme foiegras and barbecue-spiced organic quail. Minimalist decor mixes country pine and polished concrete.

Bloor/Yorkville neighbourhood

© Clifton Li/Toronto Tourism

$$$$ Piano Piano – *88 Harbord St.* ☏*416-929-7788. www.pianopianotherestaurant. co. Dinner only.* ♿. **Italian**. This Annex neighbourhood restaurant offers a delicious contemporary spin on the Italian restaurant ideal. From Gnocchi Fritti and Foie Toast, to Beef Carpaccio, Pretty Woman Pizza and Bone-In Veal Parmesan, diners must exercise restraint to allow for desserts such as Ginger Carrot Cake (for two). Gluten-free and dairy-free options available.

TEA TREATS

Three historic hotels in downtown Toronto offer afternoon tea.

At the posh **Windsor Arms** hotel *(☏see STAY)*, a high-style afternoon tea is served in daily sittings *(Mon–Wed 1pm & 3pm, Thu–Sun 12:45pm, 3:30pm & 6pm)* in the parlourlike Tea Room or next to the fireplace in the sumptuous purple room.

The landmark **Omni King Edward Hotel** *(☏see STAY)* offers a gracious tea service *(Wed–Sun 2:30pm–5pm)* in its **Victoria's** restaurant, a space that is comfortably contemporary and appointed with works of art.

A fabulous tea at the grande dame of hotels, **The Fairmont Royal York** *(☏see STAY)*, is served in EPIC, a sleek, modern restaurant *(late May–early Sept Sat–Sun only 12:30pm–4pm)*. A tour of EPIC's rooftop garden is included.

SHOPPING

Whether your taste is chic or edgy, you'll find it in Toronto's many shopping districts. The upscale shops at **Bloor/Yorkville** *(Bloor and Cumberland Sts., Yorkville and Hazelton Aves.)* carry top designs—and the highest price tags. Offering evening attire to frumpy weekend wear, **Yonge and Eglinton** caters to the yuppie crowd. Boutiques along **Queen Street West** *(west to Bathurst St.)* show off the latest fashion trends, while up-and-coming designers occupy **West Queen West** *(Bathurst west to Shaw St.)*, a bargain-filled bohemian hub where sophisticated buyers find haute couture at affordable prices. Finally, **College Street** *(Bathurst to Shaw St.)* attracts college students for cutting-edge clothes, gear & more. *(www.toronto.ca/shoptoronto)*.

SPAS

Award-winning women-only Sweetgrass Spa is located at 111 Queen Street East, at the very the core of downtown, offering a dynamic daily menu of treatments, products and packages to pamper the contemporary or traditional women's physical needs. t647-986-5300. www. sweetgrassspa.ca. The Duchess of York and Jennifer Lopez are a few of the celebrities who have been pampered here. With just seven treatment rooms, **The Spa at Windsor Arms** *(☏see STAY; ☏416-934-6031; www.windsorarmshotel. com)* is as exclusive as the hotel itself. One unique treatment is Abhyanga Ayurvedic, a deep, whole body massage stemming from an ancient East India holistic approach. The adjacent pool area with a fireplace offers relaxation. In the InterContinental Toronto Centre, **The Spa** *(225 Front St. W., 3rd floor; ☏416-646-5838; www.thespaintercontinental. com)* ushers patrons into a calm Aveda space concept and offers aesthetics and therapeutic packages for men and women. After your treatment, take a dip in the Himalayan salt hot tub or the saline swimming pool; then sun on the outdoor deck beneath the CN Tower. Highly trained staff uses the Aveda Elemental Natural Questionaire to determine personal needs to suite each customer's detailed profile.

Upper Canada Village★★★

Part of the newly formed Saint Lawrence Parks Commission, stretching almost 200 km (120 miles) from Kingston to the Quebec Border, Upper Canada Village reflects 1860s life in rural Ontario. This 27ha/66-acre living museum was created in the late 1950s when plans were made to flood some 20,000 acres of farmland during construction of the St. Lawrence Seaway and the control dam at Cornwall. More than 500 houses, churches, offices, shops and other structures were moved to higher ground. Today two dozen of these heritage buildings can be visited in Upper Canada Village.

ACCESS

11km/7mi east of Morrisburg. From Hwy. 401, take Exit 758 (Upper Canada Rd.) and travel south. Turn left onto County Rd. 2 and continue east 2km/1.2mi to the village. 🅿 *Parking lot is just past Crysler Farm Battlefield Park.*

VISIT

👥✕🚻🕐 *Open mid-May–early-Oct daily 9:30am–5pm. Horse-drawn transportation (free) on premises.* 🎟 *$19 (child $12).* ✆ *613-543-4328 or 800-437-2233. www.uppercanadavillage.com.*

- 🅖 **Michelin Map:** p217.
- 🅘 **Info:** Saint Lawrence Parks Commission, 13740 County Road 2, Morrisburg. ✆613-543-4328 or 800-437-2233. www.parks.on.ca.
- ◕ **Location:** The village is located in Morrisburg, on the St. Lawrence upriver from Cornwall on Hwy 401. It is south of Ottawa, on Hwy 31.
- 🅿 **Parking:** Leave your car at the large parking lot near the entrance.
- 👁 **Don't Miss:** Beach's sawmill to see water-powered sawing of logs into boards; draft horses and oxen being used at Louck's Farm.
- 🕐 **Timing:** Plan to spend 3–4 hours, but one- and two-hour tours are possible.
- 👥 **Kids:** The costumed interpreters include children, so visiting kids can interact with their own ages.

Costumed "inhabitants" walk the sawn boardwalks or are drawn by horses on sandy roads. They make cheese and bread, quilt, operate the mills and

Pastor's house, Upper Canada Village

© Maxim Bulat/iStockphoto.com

complete farm chores, among other activities.

Note in particular the elegant refinement of the **Robertson House**, a middle-class residence; the solid prosperity of the **Loucks Farm**, and **Crysler Hall** with its Greek Revival architecture. There are also churches and schools, a village store, a doctor's surgery, a print shop and a tavern. At **Montgomery House**, patrons may enjoy authentic 1860s-style log cabin living with surprising modern amentities. It also gives guests close proximity to the Upper Canada Golf Course, Crysler Beach, Prehistoric World, the Upper Canada Migratory Bird Sanctuary and Crysler Park Marina. (&see ADDRESSES below). There's also the cafeteria-style Village Cafe (May–mid-Sep) and the Harvest Barn Restaurant. The **sawmill,** flour mill and **woollen mill** operate on water power. The flour mill features a steam engine that dates to 1865. A **children's activity centre** housed in a large barn offers educational activites.

NEARBY ATTRACTIONS
Battle of Crysler's Farm Monument.
Beside Upper Canada Village in the park. Battle Visitor Centre &$5.

Battlefield Monument

© Pamela Delaney/Michelin

This monument commemorates the **Battle of Crysler Farm** in 1813, when British and Canadian troops routed a much larger American force. It stands beside the St. Lawrence River **view**.

Long Sault Parkway
5km/3mi east of Upper Canada Village between Ingleside and Cornwall via Rte. 2.

This scenic drive traverses a chain of connected islands in the St. Lawrence River. Activities along the way include fishing, boating *(canoe rentals available)*, picnicking and bird-watching. Bicycle and walking trails abound, and there are sand swimming beaches. Three campgrounds are administered by the St. Lawrence Parks Commission. *Information and reservations:* &613-543-3704.

ADDRESSES

🛏 STAY

$$$ Upper Canada Guest House – *C/o Upper Canada Village, 13740 County Rd.2, Morrisburg.* &*613-543-4328 or 800-437-2233. Minimum 2-night stay Jun–Aug.* Upper Canada Village visitors rent this internationally renown two-storey, two bedroom, two bathroom, refurbished farmhouse. Families and groups of up to six people will enjoy modern amenities in this late-19C dwelling. Grassy point locale assures guests of excellent views of St. Lawrence River.

🍴 EAT

$$ Willard's Hotel – &*613-543-0660. http://www.bafoodservices.ca.* Willard's Hotel prepares authentic 19C fare for visitors at lunch and tea time 11:00am–5pm May–mide-Sep. Delectables such as pan-fried perch in Rosemary and Robert's sauce, and sirloin steak smothered in wine-rich gravy. Homemade apple pie, bread pudding and lemon syllabub are good dessert choices. Afternoon tea is served upstairs on the wide front porch well shaded by the hotel's ample eaves, or indoors, in the upstairs parlour.

Windsor★

Like Detroit, this industrial centre is a major automobile manufacturer and a port on the Great Lakes/St. Lawrence Seaway system. Today Windsor is one of Canada's busiest points of entry. Every year the multi-day **International Freedom Festival** is celebrated to include the national holidays of both countries: July 1st and July 4th.

A BIT OF HISTORY
The area was first settled by the French. In 1701 **Antoine de la Mothe Cadillac** built a post on the north side of the Detroit River that became the headquarters of the French fur trade in the Great Lakes/Mississippi River area. Captured by the British in 1760, the fort and town were handed over to the Americans after the Revolution, and the Detroit River became the international border.

SIGHTS
Dieppe Gardens★
The outstanding attraction of this park, which stretches several blocks along the river west of the main thoroughfare (Ouellette Ave.), is its **view★★** of the Detroit skyline across the water. It is also a good vantage point from which to watch the huge ships of the seaway.

Art Gallery of Windsor★
401 Riverside Dr. W. ✕🚻♿🕐Open year-round Wed–Sun 11am–5pm. ⊛Free admission. 𝒫519-977-0013. www.agw.com.
Exhibits from the gallery's permanent collection of more than 3,000 works of Canadian art dating from 1750 to the present include paintings from the Group of Seven.

EXCURSIONS
Fort Malden★
100 Laird Ave., Amherstburg. 25km/15mi south via Rtes. 2 and 20. ♿ 🕐Open May–Labour Day daily 10am–5pm, Sept–Oct Wed–Sun 10am-5pm. ⊛$3.90. 𝒫519-736-5416. www.pc.gc.ca.

▶ **Population:** 335,000.
🚗 **Michelin Map:** p216.
ℹ **Info:** Tourist Office, 333 Riverside Dr. W., Suite 103. 𝒫519-255-6530 or 800-265-3633. www.visitwindsoressex.com.
◐ **Location:** The city of Windsor lies on the south side of the **Detroit River,** opposite the American city of Detroit. Ambassador Bridge and Detroit/Windsor Tunnel connect the cities.
🅿 **Parking:** US quarters are accepted at parking meters and pay/display machines. Check signage carefully for overnight parking.
👁 **Don't Miss:** Boat watchng at Dieppe Gardens.

Now a National Historic Site, this fort, built by the British at the end of the 18C, occupies a fine **site** overlooking the seaway. In the **Visitor Centre** a video (6min) explains the fort's role in the War of 1812 and the Rebellions of 1837. Earthworks and a restored barracks can be toured.

Route 50
31km/19mi from Malden Centre to Kingsville.
This quiet road through the flat farmland that borders Lake Erie affords opportunities to view marshland birds and colourful market gardens.

Jack Miner's Migratory Bird Sanctuary
360 Road 3 West, Kingsville; south of Hiway 401, just noth of town. 🕐Open year-round Mon–Sat 8am–5pm, building times vary. 𝒫519-733-4034 or 877-289-8328. www.jackminer.com.
Visit this sanctuary founded by conservationist **Jack Miner** (1865-1944) when an estimated 10,000 geese and ducks land to feed (Nov-Dec).

This vast province encompasses an area of 1,540,680sq km/594,860sq mi, or one-sixth of Canada's total landmass. More than 75 percent of its population of 7.5 million is Francophone. The **Québécois** have maintained their own culture and lifestyle, creating a unique society in a North American milieu. About 8 percent of the population claims British origin and is concentrated largely on Montreal Island. Approximately 1 percent claims native ancestry, primarily First Nations as well as Métis and Inuit, who live in small settlements in the Great North. A growing segment of Quebec's population hails from a wide variety of ethnic origins.

Info: Tourisme Québec. 877-266-5687 or 514-873-2015 (Canada/US). www.quebecoriginal.com.

Location: East of Ontario, west of New Brunswick, Quebec borders Maine, Vermont, New Hampshire and New York to the south.

Don't Miss: Montreal and Quebec City are essential, but plan at least one day by the side of one of the thousands of lakes here.

Timing: Quebec City is about three hours from Montreal. Both cities are never more than 1 hr from forests, rivers or mountains.

Geography

Regional Landscape – Stretching almost 2,000km/1,240mi from the US border to Hudson Strait, Quebec is Canada's largest province. Three main physiographic regions can be distinguished in Quebec. The northern tundra and vast forested area lie on the **Canadian Shield**, a rocky expanse of extensive plateaus interrupted by a few mountain massifs. The extreme south of the province and the Gaspé Peninsula, on the other hand, are part of the **Appalachian Mountains**. These chains reach heights of 972m/3,188ft in the Eastern Townships and 1,288m/4,227ft in the Gaspé Peninsula. Lodged between these two regions, the **St. Lawrence Lowlands**, a triangular wedge graced with fertile soils and a moderate climate, support most of the province's agricultural production. Stretching some 1,197km/742mi in

length, the **St. Lawrence River** flows in a northeasterly direction along Ontario and through Quebec to the Gulf of St. Lawrence and into the Atlantic Ocean.

Climate – Snowfall can accumulate up to 150cm/5ft in much of the central interior. Summer in the southern regions is hot and humid. Sometimes, in late October or early November, "Indian summer" returns briefly for a last fling.

January temperatures in Montreal average −9°C/16°F, with an average of 254cm/8ft of snowfall for the entire winter season. Located farther north, Sept-Îles registers the heaviest recorded snowfall in eastern Canada. In July Montreal registers maximum means of 26°C/79°F, Quebec City 25°C/77°F and Sept-Îles 20°C/68°F. Temperatures in excess of 32°C/90°F are not uncommon.

A Bit of History

Birth of New France – Before the arrival of Europeans, Quebec's territory was inhabited by First Nations of the **Eastern Woodlands** culture, including Algonquins and Montagnais. During the 15C Basque fishermen came to fish off the coast. French navigator **Jacques Cartier** (1491-1557) landed on the Gaspé Peninsula in 1534 and claimed this new land for the king of France. In 1608, **Samuel de Champlain** founded Quebec City. The **Iroquois Wars** (until 1701) and France's lack of interest in the colony, kept settlement to a minimum.

A Vast Empire – During the mid-17C the *coureurs des bois* (fur traders) and missionaries from New France explored the continent. Étienne Brûlé, Jean Nicolet and Nicolas Perrot reached Lake Superior. In the 1650s Pierre Radisson and the Sieur des Groseilliers travelled

Cap Bon-Ami, Parc national du Canada Forillon, Gaspésie

©Jean-Pierre Huard, ATRG

north perhaps as far as Hudson Bay. The greatest explorers were the **La Vérendrye family**. Pierre Gaultier de Varennes explored Manitoba and Saskatchewan between 1731 and 1738, setting up trading posts. His sons François and Louis-Joseph reached the Rockies in present-day Montana in 1742.

Treaty of Paris – On September 13, 1759, British Gen. **James Wolfe** (1728-59) defeated French Gen. **Louis-Joseph de Montcalm** (1712-59) on the **Plains of Abraham** in Quebec City, signalling the end of the French colony. The colony was ceded to England in 1763 by the Treaty of Paris.

A British Colony – Faced with a Roman Catholic, French-speaking population, the new governor, **Sir Guy Carleton**, decided to recognize the rights of the Roman Catholic church, the seigneurial system and French civil law as a basis for government. These rights were enshrined in the **Quebec Act** of 1774. In 1791, the British divided the colony into Upper and Lower Canada. Public frustration over limits to self-government led to the **Rebellions of 1837** in both colonies.

Led in Quebec by **Louis-Joseph Papineau** (1786-1871), the **Patriots** were defeated, but full representative government was granted.

In 1867 the British North America Act established **Canadian Confederation,** the foundation of modern Canada.

A Sovereign State – During the 1960s, under Premier **Jean Lesage** (1912-1980) a climate of social, economic and political change, labelled the "Quiet Revolution," emerged in Quebec. Spearheaded by the leader of the Parti Québécois (1968), **René Lévesque** (1922-87), Quebec sovereignty became a hotly debated topic. In 1980 and again in 1995, the PQ lost referendums on Quebec sovereignty, but the emotionally charged issue of the province's relationship to the rest of the country will likely dominate the political scene for some time.

Economy

Since the opening of the **St. Lawrence Seaway** in 1959, Quebec's economy has been tied to that of the US. Over 50 percent of the province's manufactured goods are exported, 80 percent to the US. Quebec is the Canadian leader in production of **pulp and paper**, manufacturing a third of the country's total output of **newsprint**. Abitibi and Témiscamingue contain large deposits of **copper**. The province has abundant **hydroelectric resources**. This low-cost energy has spurred the province's electro-metallurgic industries. Quebec has become a major producer of **aluminum**. **Agriculture** predominates in southern Quebec, and the major **fishing** centres are Gaspé Peninsula and Côte-Nord.

PRACTICAL INFORMATION
GETTING THERE

BY AIR – International and domestic flights arrive at **Montreal's Pierre Elliott Trudeau International Airport** (*22km/14mi west of downtown, in the town of Dorval, ℘514-394-7377 or 800-465-1213, www.admtl.com*) and **Quebec City's Jean Lesage airport** (*℘418-640-3300, www.aeroportdequebec.com*).

Montreal's Mirabel airport (*55km/34mi north of downtown, ℘514-394-7377 or 800-465-1213*) is used for cargo flights. **Air Canada**: (*℘514-393-3333 or 888-247-2262 (Canada/US), www.aircanada.com*). Affiliated carriers offer connections to many cities within Quebec. Major car rental agencies are located at the airports.

BY BUS AND TRAIN – Intercity bus service and connections throughout the Montreal–Quebec City–Gaspésie corridor are offered by **Autocars Orléans Express Inc.** (*℘514-395-4000, 418-525-3043 or 888-999-3977, www.orleansexpress.com*). **Amtrak** links Montreal and the US with daily connections from Washington, DC, via New York City. For information in the US: *℘800-872-7245 or www.amtrak.com*.

VIA RAIL – train service is extensive within the province: *℘514-989-2626, or 888-842-7245 (Canada/US), www.viarail.com*.

BY BOAT – The province has an extensive **ferry** boat system. For schedules contact Tourisme Québec (*Ⓒsee below*).

GENERAL INFORMATION
ACCOMMODATIONS AND VISITOR INFORMATION

Tourism Québec publishes vacation brochures, regional guides and road maps that can be downloaded from the website or ordered free from: **Tourisme Québec** (*℘514-873-2015 or 877-266-5687 (Canada/US), www.quebecoriginal.com*).

Major hotel chains can be found in urban areas. Small hotels and bed-and-breakfast lodgings offer quality accommodations at moderate prices throughout the province.

Farm holidays may be especially appealing to families. Available in French only, the guide *Gîtes et Auberges du Passant au Québec* (*$28.85 within Canada, $35.10 mail to US, $42 to Europe*) is available from **Fédération des Agricotours du Québec** in Montreal (*℘514-252-3138; www.terroiretsaveurs.com*).

Hôtellerie Champêtre in Montreal (*℘514-861-4024 or 800-861-4024; www.hotelleriechampetre.com*) lists numerous inns, condo-hotels, villas and resorts in Quebec and has online reservations.

LANGUAGE – The official language of Quebec is French, spoken by 82% of the population. The second language is English. Many Quebecers in urban areas are bilingual. Tourist information is generally available in both languages. Telephone operators are bilingual. Road signs, except on the TransCanada Hwy, are in French. *Ⓐ Quebec websites appear initially in French, but an "English" button gives you an English version.*

ROAD REGULATIONS – Quebec has a network of highways (*autoroutes*) and secondary roads. Road signs are in French only. The speed limit on highways, unless otherwise posted, is 100km/h (60mph), on secondary roads 90km/h (55mph), and 50km/h (30mph) within city limits. Turning right on red is prohibited off the island of Montreal. **Seat belt** use is mandatory. **Canadian Automobile Assn. (CAA),** Quebec City *℘418-624-2424 or 800-686-9243 (Quebec only); www.caaquebec.com*).

TIME ZONES – Quebec is on Eastern Standard Time, except the Magdalen Islands, which are on Atlantic Standard Time (1hr ahead of the rest of Quebec). Daylight Saving

Time is observed from the second Sunday in March to the first Sunday in November.

TAXES – Canada's 5 percent GST has a local sales tax of 9.975 percent added for all goods and services. No GST is levied if the item is shipped directly by a Canadian business to the non-resident's home (*902-426-5150 in Halifax; www.cra-arc.gc.ca/visitors*). The Quebec sales tax is not refunded to visitors as it once was.

LIQUOR LAWS – The legal drinking age is 18. The sale of wine and liquor is regulated by the provincial government and sold in "Société des Alcools" stores. Beer and wine are also sold in grocery stores.

PROVINCIAL HOLIDAY
Québec National Holiday: June 24

RECREATION
OUTDOOR ACTIVITIES
Parks Canada (*www.pc.gc.ca*) operates three **national parks** in Quebec (Forillon, La Mauricie, Mingan Archipelago) and the province operates 27 **provincial parks** (confusingly also called national parks) which offer year-round outdoor activities. For details: www.bonjourquebec.com.

Canoeing is practised on most of the rivers. **Kayaking** is popular in the northern regions of Saguenay and Nunavik, at camps & resorts. Ranch vacations that include **horseback riding** are prevalent in the Eastern Townships, Gaspé Peninsula and Bas-Saint-Laurent. Contact *514-252-3126 or 800-932-3735. www.loisirquebec.qc.ca*. Major areas offer **skiing** are the Laurentians (*Mt. Tremblant *866-356-2233 or 819-681-2000, overseas; www.tremblant.ca*), the **Eastern Townships** (*Bromont *450-534-2200; Mt. Orford *819-843-6548; Owl's Head *450-292-3342; Sutton *450-538-2545*) and Quebec City region (*Mt. Ste-Anne *418-827-4561; www.mont-sainte-anne.com*). For a list of resorts, go to www.quebecoriginal.com or www.onthesnow.com/quebec.

Snowmobiling is a popular sport. A registration card is required to operate a snowmobile: contact the **Fédératon des Clubs de Motoneigistes in Montreal** *514-252-3076. www.fcmq.qc.ca*. For **hunting** and **fishing**, contact the **Ministère des Ressources naturelles et de la Faune** (*418-627-8600 or 866-248-6936; www.mrnf.gouv.qc.ca/English/wildlife*). For a free publication on outfitters' lodges: **Fédération des pourvoiries du Québec** (*418-877-5191 or 800-567-9009; www.fpq.com*).

SPECIAL EXCURSIONS
Canoeing, rafting, horseback riding, biking or hiking tours in the Montreal/Ottawa region are offered through **New World Centre** (*800-361-5033; www.newworld.ca*). Rock climbing, dogsledding, canoeing and kayaking can be arrranged through **CÉPAL** (*418-547-5728 or 800-361-5728. www.cepalaventure.com*). **The Zoological Society of Montreal** arranges field trips of 1- to 2-days to different areas of Montreal (*514-845-8317l; http://zoologicalsocietymtl.org*).

PRINCIPAL FESTIVALS

late Jan	**Quebec Winter Carnival**, *Quebec City*	
Feb	**Winterlude**, *Gatineau*	
Mar	**Maple Sugar Festival**, *Saint-Georges*	
Jun	**Quebec Song Festival**: *Tadoussac*	
Jun-Jul	**International Jazz Festival**, *Montreal*	
Jul	**World Folklore Festival**, *Drummondville*	
	International Summer Festival, *Quebec City*	
Jul-Aug	**Blueberry Festival**, *Mistassini*	
Aug	**Hot Air Balloon Festival**, *Saint-Jean-sur-Richelieu*	
	World Film Festival, *Montreal*	

Vauréal waterfall

©Gilles Rigoulet/Hemis/Photoshot

Île d'Anticosti★★

Some 222km/138mi in length and 56km/35mi at its widest point, Anticosti Island is mantled with coniferous forests, crisscrossed by rivers teeming with Atlantic salmon and trout, and known by deer hunters for its game. French industrialist **Henri Menier** purchased Anticosti for in 1895, and transformed it into his private paradise, importing white-tailed deer and other animals. The Quebec government acquired it in 1974; it is now part of a reserve (4,575sq km/ 1,766sq mi).

ACCESS

From Montreal, Quebec City or Sept-Îles contact SÉPAQ ℘418-890-6527 or 800-665-6527 (US/Canada) www.sepaq.com. Boat service available through Relais Nordik Inc., from Rimouski and Havre-Saint-Pierre ℘418-723-8787 or 800-463-0680. www.quebecmaritime.ca. Reservations 30 days in advance. A four-wheel-drive vehicle is very handy on the island.

VISIT

A tour of the island from **Port-Menier**, the island's only remaining permanent settlement, leads past such scenic wonders as the **Chutes de Kalima-**

- **Info:** Association touristique régionale de Duplessis, 312 av. Brochu, Sept-Îles. t418-962-0808 or 888-463-0808 (Canada/US). www.tourisme duplessis.com.
- **Location:** The island lies at the point where the St. Lawrence widens into the Gulf, downriver from Sept-Iles.
- **Don't Miss:** Port Menier is the only town. Tourist office: ℘418-535-0311.
- **Timing:** You will need at least two or three days for a visit.

zoo and **Caverne à la Patate; Chute et canyon de la Vauréal★★**, with a 70m/230ft waterfall; and **Baie de la Tour★★**, renowned for its spectacular limestone cliffs that plummet dramatically into the sea.

West of Port-Menier, **Baie-Sainte-Claire** provides an ideal setting for observing **white-tailed deer**, sometimes seen in herds of up to 100. At nearby **Pointe de l'Ouest** *(1km/.6mi south)*, remains of the **Calou**, shipwrecked in 1982, can be seen.

Bas-Saint-Laurent★★

On the south shore of the St. Lawrence River, between Quebec City and the Gaspé Peninsula, this region is characterized by peaceful farmlands along the shore, divided into long, narrow strips perpendicular to the river. To the north, the Laurentian Mountains plunge into the St. Lawrence.

SIGHTS
Lévis★
250km/155mi east of Montreal by Rte. 20 or Rte. 132. A ferry connects Lévis to Quebec City.
Located opposite Quebec City, this city is noted for its port and its wood industries. The city is also the headquarters of the Desjardins cooperative savings and loan company (*Caisse populaire Desjardins*), founded in 1900 by journalist Alphonse Desjardins (1854-1920). The white clapboard **Maison Alphonse-Desjardins★** displays artifacts relating to Desjardins and the cooperative movement (*6, rue du Mont-Marie; & P visit by guided tour only year-round Mon–Fri 10am–noon & 1pm–4:30pm, Sat–Sun noon–5pm; closed Jan 1-2, Dec 25-26 & 31; 418-835-2090 or 866-835-8444; www.desjardins.com*).

- **Michelin Map:** pp306-307.
- **Info:** Tourism Bas-St-Laurent, 148, rue Fraser, Rivière-du-Loup. 418-867-1272 or 800-563-5268 (Canada/US). www.basstlaurent.ca.
- **Location:** Route 132 passes through the principal communities of this region, affording superb views of the St. Lawrence.
- **Don't Miss:** Kamouraska is one of the prettiest towns in Quebec.
- **Timing:** You can cross the river on ferries at Rivière du Loup, Trois Pistoles and Rimouski.

HOW DO YOU EEL?
In the town of Kamouraska, take a guided tour at the Site d'Interprétation de l'Anguille de Kamouraska (*205 Ave. Morel; 418-492-3935*) and discover the secrets of traditional eel fishing. End the experience by sampling a smoked version of the snakelike fish, considered a delicacy by many cultures.

Canada Geese and Snow Geese, Parc du Bic
© Barrett & MacKay/All Canada Photos/age fotostock

Lieu historique national du Canada des Forts-de-Lévis★ (Lévis Forts National Historic Site of Canada)

41 du Gouvernement Rd. ♿ 🅿
🕐*Open late-Jun–late Aug daily 10am–5pm. By reservation other times.* ☎ *$3.90.* 📞*418-835-5182 or 888-773-8888. www.pc.gc.ca.*
Forming an irregular pentagon, the fort (1865-72) stands atop Pointe-Lévis, the highest point on the south shore of the St. Lawrence.

Lieu historique national du Canada de la Grosse-Île-et-le-Mémorial-des-Irlandais★ (Grosse-Île and the Irish Memorial National Historic Site of Canada)

2 d'Auteuil St. 🗡🅿🕐*Open mid-May–mid-Oct Mon–Sun hours vary.* 📞*418-248-8888. www.pc.gc.ca. Ferry from Berthier-sur-Mer contact Les Croisières Lachance.* 📞*418-692-1751 or 855--268-9090. www.croisiereslachance.com. From Quebec City, Lévis, Ste-Anne-de-Beaupré and Île-d'Orléans, contact Les Croisières Le Coudrier* 📞*418-692-0107 or 888-600-5554. www.croisierescoudrier.qc.ca. Reservations required. Visit & ferry* ☎ *From $73.50. Boards 10am/ returns 5pm.*

Increasing European immigration prompted establishment, in 1832, of a quarantine station on Grosse-Île to limit the spread of cholera into Canada. **Route 132** continues through **L'Islet-sur-Mer**, the birthplace of famed Arctic explorer Capt. Joseph-Elzéar Bernier (1852-1934), and through **Saint-Jean-Port-Joli★**, the craft and wood-carving capital of Quebec.

La Pocatière★

60km/37mi northeast of Montmagny.
This community is a centre for agricultural research. The **Musée François-Pilote★** is a research centre for Quebec domestic architecture (*100 4th Ave.;* 🅿🕐*open daily mid-May until Thanks-giving (early-Oct) 10am–5pm; rest of year Thu–Sun 10am–5pm*☎*$6;* 📞*418-856-3145*).

Route 132 passes across a wide flood-plain, affording views of the Laurentian Mountains. From the pleasant community of **Kamouraska★**, lines of eel traps can be seen in the tidal flats.

Rivière-du-Loup★

72km/45mi northeast of La Pocatière.
Situated between Quebec City & Gaspé Peninsula, this town is a commercial and resort centre. Downtown are the imposing Gothic Revival **St. Patrick's Church and Presbytery**, surrounded by verandas, and the **Viatorian Clerics' Residence**. A new **whale-watching**

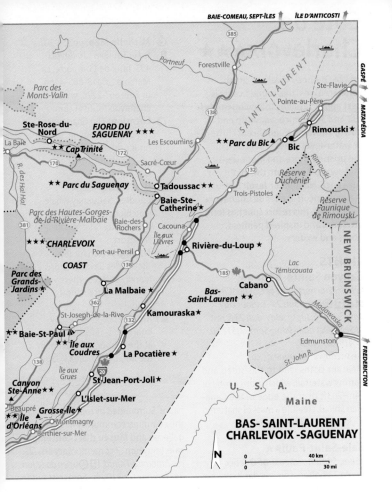

boat (www.quebecmaritime.ca/aml), Le Coudrier de l'Anse, accommodates 194, with onboard bilingual guides, bar & two washrooms.

Parc du Bic★ (Bic Park)
81km/50mi from Rivière-du-Loup.
This provincial conservation park *(www. sepaq.com)* has both deciduous and boreal forests. The small town of **Bic** is known for its spectacular **setting**★★ on the St. Lawrence River.

Rimouski★
25km/16mi northeast of Bic Park.
This industrial city is a major metropolis of eastern Quebec. Note the **Maison Lamontagne**★, one of the few remaining examples of masonry half-timbering in North America *(707, boul. du Rivage;* ✕ P ◷ *open late Jun–Labour Day daily 9am–6pm;* ❧$4; ✆418-722-4038; www. maisonlamontagne.com).

Located 10km/6mi from town, the **Musée de la mer et lieu historique national du Canada du phare de Pointe-au-Père**★ (Maritime Museum and Pointe-au-Père Lighthouse National Historic Site) at Pointe-au-Père display artifacts recovered from the wreck of the *Empress of Ireland*, the "Titanic of the St. Lawrence": 1,012 people died when she sank *(1000 rue de la Phare;* ✕ P ◷ *open late-May–early Oct daily 9am–6pm;* ❧$12 (Empress & lighthouse); ✆418-724-6214; www.shmp.qc.ca).

Côte de Charlevoix★★★

One of Quebec's loveliest, most varied regions, this rugged coast is best appreciated by following Routes 138 and 362, which weave up and down, affording magnificent clifftop or water-level views of forested hills, the pristine shore and mountains that sweep down into the mighty St. Lawrence. Named for Jesuit historian Pierre-François-Xavier de Charlevoix (1682-1781), this resort spot has long attracted and inspired painters, poets and writers.

SIGHTS

Canyon Sainte-Anne★★

52km/32mi northeast of Quebec City. ✕ ♿ 🅿 ⏱ *Open Jun 24–Labour Day daily 9am–5:30pm. May–Jun 23 & rest of Sept–Oct daily 9am–5pm.* 💰*$12.50.* 📞*418-827-4057. www.canyonste-anne.qc.ca.*
Pleasant paths lead to this steep and narrow waterfall, which drops a total of 74m/243ft over the edge of the Canadian Shield, creating a mass of shattered rocks and whirlpools at its base.

Baie-Saint-Paul★★

95km/59mi northeast of Quebec City. Route 138 offers spectacular **views**★★ on the descent to this celebrated artists'

La Malbaie

© R. Chiasson/All Canada Photos/Getty Images

♿ **Michelin Map:** pp306-307.

🅸 **Info:** Tourism Charlevoix, 495, boul de Comporté, La Malbaie. 📞418-665-4454 or 800-667-2276. www. charlevoixtourism.com.

▶ **Location:** The Charlevoix region lies about an hour's drive down the St. Lawrence northeast of Quebec City.

👁 **Don't Miss:** Ile aux Coudres, Saguenay whale-watching, Baie-St.Paul art community & Le Massif ski resort.

⏱ **Timing:** Watch for the "Route des Saveurs" signs marking places where you can eat or obtain local produce.

👪 **Kids:** Children will enjoy boarding a 1939 schooner at the Schooner Museum in the Île-aux-Coudres village.

---

haunt. Surrounded by rolling green hills, the charming community has many art galleries and **Musée d'art contemporain** (museum of contemporary art) *(23, rue Ambroise-Fafard;* 🅿 ⏱*open daily Jun 24–Labour Day 10am–5pm; rest of the year 11am–5pm;* ⏱*closed Dec 25/26;* 💰*$8* 📞*418-435-3681; www.macbsp.com).* Departing by Route 362, visitors will find an overlook that provides another splendid **view**★★ of the town, the St. Lawrence and the south shore.

Île-aux-Coudres★★

Free ferry service departs from Saint-Joseph-de-la-Rive Jun–Sep daily 6:30am–11:30pm every hour. Rest of the year daily 7:30am–11pm frequently. ♿. *Société des traversiers du Québec* 📞*418-643-2019. www.traversiers.gouv.qc.ca.*
Named by Jacques Cartier in 1535 for its abundant hazel trees *(coudriers),* this enchanting island occupies a spectacular offshore **site**. A tour

of the island (21km/13mi) by car or bicycle offers views of the north and south shores of the St. Lawrence. The **Musée les voitures d'eau★** (Schooner Museum) presents the region's maritime history (📇🕐open mid-Jun–early Sept daily 10am–5pm; mid-May–early Jun & mid-Sept–mid-Oct weekends 10am–5pm; ∞$3; ☏418-438-2208). **Les Moulins de l'Isle-aux-Coudres★** (Île-aux-Coudres Mills; 📇🕐open Jun 24–mid-Aug daily 9am–6:30pm; late May–Jun 23 & mid-Aug–mid-Oct daily 10am–5pm;∞$8; ☏418-760-1066; www. tourismeisleauxcoudres.com) provide a rare opportunity to compare the mechanisms of a windmill and a water mill. Mid-May until mid-Oct take the family on the **Treasure Hunt** ($10) to win up to $500 in cash.

La Malbaie-Pointe-au-Pic★
26km/16mi northeast of Île aux Coudres. Occupying a beautiful **site**, this resort community was named "Malle Baye" (bad bay) by de Champlain in 1608, when his ships ran aground. **Fairmont Manoir Richelieu** (in Pointe-au-pic) is a grand reminder of the 19C resort hotels.

Baie-Sainte-Catherine★
74km/46mi northeast of La Malbaie. **Whale-watching cruises★★** are popular, just as in Tadoussac across the fjord. A lookout tower in **Saguenay-St. Lawrence Marine Park** offers glimpses of the mammals in the water below (182 rue de l'Église, Tadoussac; interpretation centre, Pointe Noire ♿📇🕐open mid-Jun–Labour Day daily 9am–6pm; rest of Sept–early Oct Fri–Sun 9am–5pm; ∞$5.80; ☏418-235-4703; www.pc.gc.ca & www.parcmarin.qc.cq).

Côte-Nord★

Long known as an untamed wilderness of forests with occasional fishing villages, Côte-Nord underwent gradual industrialization with the development of **pulp mills** in the 1920s and 30s and later, with the discovery of rich **iron-ore** deposits. In the 1960s the region's enormous hydroelectric potential was harnessed, prompting another surge of economic growth.

SIGHTS
Complexe Manic-Outardes
Manic-5 is located 210km/130mi north of Baie-Comeau (422km/262mi northeast of Quebec City) on Rte. 389. Begun in 1959, the harnessing of the Manicouagan and Outardes rivers took 20 years to complete. The first power plant of the complex to produce electricity was **Manic-2★** (📇👣visit by 1hr 30min guided tour only, Jun 24–Aug 31 daily at 9:30am, 11:30am, 1:30pm & 3:30pm; ☏866-526-2642; www.hydro-quebec.com). The spectacular **Daniel Johnson Dam★★** of **Manic-5★★** is the

- ℹ **Info:** Association touristique régionale de Manicouagan, 337, boul. LaSalle, bureau 304, Baie-Comeau. ☏418-294-2876 or 888-463-5319. www.tourismecote-nord.com.
- ▶ **Location:** The Côte-Nord, or North Shore, of the St. Lawrence River extends from the mouth of the Saguenay River north to the Labrador border.
- 🐾 **Don't Miss:** A drive along Route 138 leads through desolate stretches of pristine, rocky landscape, interrupted by developing towns and hydroelectric plants. Look out for whales, too!
- 🕐 **Timing:** The northernmost part, between Havre St-Pierre and Blanc-Sablon, is accessible only by boat or plane.

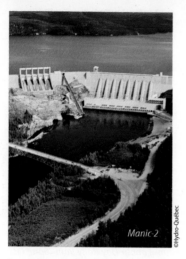

Manic-2
©Hydro-Quebec

largest arch-and-buttress dam in the world (*same schedule and contact information as for Manic-2, but tour is 2hr*).

Sept-Îles★

640km/397mi northeast of Quebec City by Rte. 138.

Occupying a superb **site★★**, Sept-Îles has a deepwater port that enables ocean-bound vessels to transship coal and iron ore throughout the year. The old wharf gives views of the magnificent bays and the seven islands.

Le Vieux-Poste (Old Trading Post) pays tribute to the region's first inhabitants, the Montagnais *(500, boul. Laure;* 🅿️🕐*open Jun 24–Labour Day daily 9am–5pm; rest of year Tue–Fri 10am–noon & 1pm–5pm, Sat–Sun 1pm–5pm;* 🎫 *$7;* ☏ *418-968-2070; www.mrcn.qc.ca)*. Offshore, the **Parc régional de l'Archipel des Sept-Îles★** (Sept-Îles Regional Park) offers an introduction to the Côte-Nord.

The community of **Havre-Saint-Pierre** marks the end of Route 138. The ferries for the **Mingan Archipelago★★**, a national park reserve, and for Anticosti Island depart from the wharf. Havre-Saint-Pierre is also the departure point for the boat trip *(3 days)* to Blanc-Sablon, situated 1.5km/1mi from the Labrador border. ♿*For more information, consult the Michelin GREEN GUIDE Quebec.*

Cantons de l'est★★

The **Eastern Townships** (sometimes called *Estrie*) is an area of lush rolling hills east of Montreal. After the American Revolution, Loyalists settled here. The towns and villages reflect their New England heritage. Today the population is predominantly Francophone.

TOPOGRAPHY

This area of deep valleys, tree-covered hills rising nearly 1,000m/3,280ft, and beautiful lakes such as Brome, Memphrémagog, Magog and Massawipi is a popular retreat for Montrealers.

The Eastern Townships has some of Quebec's best farmland; agritourism is a major activity. East of the Townships, the flat fertile farmland referred to as the **Beauce★** contains the greatest

♿ **Michelin Map:** pp312-313.

🛈 **Info:** Tourism Cantons-de-l'est, 20 rue Don-Bosco Sud, Sherbrooke. ☏819-820-2020 or 800-355-5755. www.easterntownships.org.

▶ **Location:** The Eastern townships sit in the southwest corner of the province, along the US border.

🕭 **Don't Miss:** A cruise on Lake Memphrémagog.

🕐 **Timing:** There are lots of lovely restaurants, inns, art galleries and beaches, so plan to spend several days here.

👪 **Kids:** The Granby Zoo is popular with all ages.

Abbaye de Saint-Benoît-du-Lac

concentration of maple groves in Quebec. In spring, sugaring-off parties are a popular pastime.

SIGHTS

Sherbrooke★

150km/93mi east of Montreal by Rtes. 10 and 112.

At the confluence of the Saint-François and Magog rivers, this city is the principal community of the townships. The **Musée des Beaux-Arts** (Museum of Fine Arts) exhibits a fine collection of Quebec art *(241, rue Dufferin; ♿🅿🕑open daily late Jun–Labour Day 10am–5pm; rest of the year Tue–Sun noon–5pm; 🕑closed Dec 25–26 & Jan 1-2; ⊜ $10; ☏819-821-2115; www.mbas. qc.ca)*. Standing atop the Marquette Plateau, the imposing Gothic Revival **cathedral★**, offers a **view★** that encompasses the entire city.

Magog★

124km/74mi east of Montreal by Rte. 10.

This popular resort community enjoys a splendid **setting** on the shores of Lake Memphrémagog, which stretches over 50km/31mi, crossing the border into Vermont. **Scenic cruises★** afford great views of Mt. Orford, Sugar Loaf and Owl's Head *(✕♿🅿🕑depart from Quai Magog Jun–Oct beginning 2010 Wed–Sun; 2hr*

⊜ $37, 3hr (with meal) $69–72; reservations required; Escapades Memphrémagog ☏819-843-7000 or 888-422-8328; www.escapadesmemphremagog.com).

Abbaye de Saint-Benoît-du-Lac★ (Saint-Benoît-du-Lac Abbey)

20km/12mi south of Magog by Rte. 112 west, follow signs. 🕑*Open year-round daily; call during hours listed on website to reserve your visit.* ♿🅿 ☏*819-843-4080. www.st-benoit-du-lac.com.*

The pleasant drive to this Benedictine monastery offers lovely glimpses of the sparkling lake waters. The monks are famous for their Gregorian chants and for their cheese (L'Ermite and Mont-Saint-Benoît).

Parc du Mont-Orford★ (Mount Orford Park)

116km/72mi east of Montreal by Rte. 10 (Exit 115) and Rte. 141. Park 🕑*open daily year-round. Le Cerisier Interpretation Centre* ✕♿🅿⛺. ⊜*$7.50.* ☏*819-843-9855 or 800-665-6527. www.sepaq.com.*

This provincial park is dominated by Mt. Orford (881m/2,890ft), a well-known ski centre. Follow a short path around the television tower at the summit for a sweeping **panorama★★**.

Centre d'Arts Orford
(Orford Arts Centre)

3165, ch. du Parc. ✕🅿🕐*Open year-round daily 9am–4:30pm (extended hrs in summer).* ☎*819-843-3981 or 800-567-6155. www.arts-orford.org.*
The centre is renowned for its annual summer music festival (Festival Orford).

Compton

172km/107mi east of Montreal by Rtes. 10, 143 and 147.
This quiet village is the birthplace of **Louis-Stephen Saint-Laurent** (1882-1973), who served as Canada's 12th prime minister. He fought to establish a distinct Canadian identity during his years in office (1948-57).

Lieu historique national du Canada Louis-S.-St-Laurent★
(Louis-S. St.-Laurent National Historic Site of Canada)

Rue Principale (Rte. 147). ♿🕐*Open late-Jun–late-Sep 10am-5pm* ⬿*$3.90.* ☎*819-835-5448 or 888-773-8888. www.pc.gc.ca.*
The general store that belonged to the Prime Minister's father has been re-created, and is stocked with replicas of the goods sold here in the late 19C. The simple clapboard house has been restored to represent various periods of the prime minister's life. A **multimedia presentation** (*20min*) highlights Saint-Laurent's life and career.

Granby

80km/50mi southeast of Montreal by Rte. 10 (Exit 68) and Rtes. 139 and 112.
Set on the banks of the Yamaska River, Granby is especially known for its zoo, one of the largest in Canada.

♟ Granby Zoo★

Blvd. Bouchard. ✕♿🅿🕐*Open late May–mid-Jun daily 10am–5pm. Late Jun–Aug daily 10am–7pm. Early Sept–Nov 1 Sat–Sun only 10am–5pm.* ⬿*$23.25–32.99 (child $12.95–21.49).* ☎*450-372-9113 or 877-472-6299. www.zoodegranby.com.*
This popular zoo houses more than 1,000 animals from all over the world.

Highlights include the cave of nocturnal creatures, the Bear Mountain, Cats Pavilion, and the **Red Pandas**.
In the Reptiles House, visitors can see turtles, iguanas, anacondas and rattlesnakes, among other inhabitants. The water park features a heated wave pool, a river for tubing and a water games area.

Valcourt

130km/81mi east of Montreal by Rte. 10 (Exit 90) and Rtes. 243 and 222.
Joseph-Armand Bombardier (1907-64) developed in 1959 the **Ski-Doo**—the snowmobile that went on to transform life in the north during the winter.

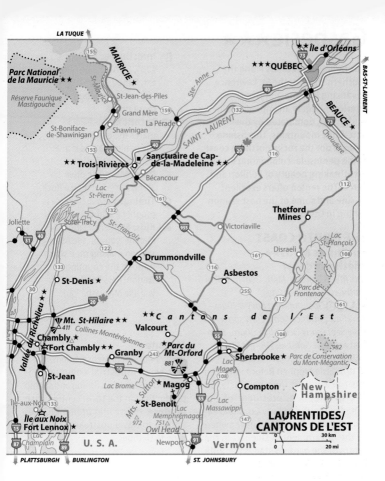

LA TUQUE

MAURICIE

155

Parc National
de la Mauricie ★★

Réserve Faunique
Mastigouche

St-Jean-des-Piles

Grand Mère

159

St-Boniface-
de-Shawinigan

153

55

★★ Trois-Rivières ★★

Shawinigan

La Pérade

Bécancour

161

132

40

Ste-Anne

SAINT-LAURENT

★★ ★ Île d'Orléans

★★★ QUÉBEC

BAS-ST-LAURENT

BEAUCE ★

Chaudière

116

20

Sanctuaire de Cap-
de-la-Madeleine ★★

112

Lac
St-Pierre

Joliette

31

40

Sorel-Tracy

122

133

St-Denis ★

30

55

133

Vallée du Richelieu

Mt. St-Hilaire ★★

411

Collines Montérégiennes

Chambly ★

☆Fort Chambly ★★

Granby ★

243

10

St-Jean

Île-aux-Noix 133

☆ Île aux Noix
Fort Lennox ★

15

St-François

355

Drummondville

116

Victoriaville

Disraeli

161

Asbestos

255

Thetford
Mines

Lac
St-François

108

Parc de
Frontenac

161

★★ C a n t o n s   d e   l' E s t

Valcourt

★ Parc du
Mt-Orford

881

55

Lac
Memphrémagog

972

751

Owl Head

Magog

★ St-Benoît

Lac
Brome

Mts. Sutton

Sherbrooke ★

Lac
Magog

108

Compton

982

Parc de Conservation
du Mont-Mégantic

Lac
Massawippi

147

New
Hampshire

**LAURENTIDES/
CANTONS DE L'EST**

U. S. A.

Newport

Vermont

30 km

20 mi

87

89

Île aux
Champlain

⚓ PLATTSBURGH   BURLINGTON   ST. JOHNSBURY

**👤👤 Musée J.-Armand Bombardier★
(J.-Armand Bombardier Museum)**

1001 Ave J.-A. Bombardier. ♿🅿⏰*Open
May–Labour Day daily 10am–5pm.
Rest of the year Tue–Sun 10am–5pm.*
⏰*Closed Jan 1–2, Dec 24–26 & Dec 31.*
👓*$7 (add $5 factory tour).* 📞*450-532-
5300. www.museebombardier.com.*
This fascinating museum highlights the
life and work of Valcourt's native son.

EXCURSION
Drummondville

*110km/68mi east of Montreal by
Rte. 20 (Exit 177).*
Founded as a military outpost after the
War of 1812, this community in Centre-
du-Québec is today an important indus-
trial hub for the garment industry.

**👤👤 Village québécois d'antan★
(Québécois Village of Olden Times)**

1425 Rue Montplaisir. Exit 181, Rte. 20.
✕🅿⏰*Open early Jun–mid-Jun Wed–
Sun 10am–5:30pm. Late Jun–early Aug
daily 10am–5:30pm. Early Sept–late
Sept Fri–Sun 10am–5:30pm.* 👓*$25.01
(child $23.27).* 📞*819-478-1441 or 877-
710-0267. www.villagequebecois.com.*
About 70 authentic buildings were relocated to this pleasant site to re-create
life in the region between 1810 and
1910. The reconstructed **church** models
Drummondville's St. Frederick Church
(1822), and the two-room schoolhouse
has one room for boys and one for
girls. Costumed interpreters explain the
daily life of the former villagers (*English
limited*).

Gaspésie★★★

This peninsula extends along the southern shore of the St. Lawrence, advancing into the gulf. The interior is largely an impenetrable wilderness, dominated by the **Chic-Choc** mountains. Tiny fishing villages dot the rocky northern coast of the peninsula, culminating in the breathtaking beauty of Forillon and Percé. The region offers excellent cuisine and some of the best salmon fishing in Quebec.

THE NORTH COAST
Jardins de Métis★★ (Métis Gardens)

200, Rte 132, Grand-Métis. 350km/217mi southeast of Quebec City.
✕&🅿🕐*Open Jul–Aug daily 8:30am–8pm (last entrance 6pm). Early Jun & early Sept–early Oct daily 8:30am–6pm (last entrance 5pm).* ⬮*$18.* ✆*418-775-2222. www.refordgardens.com.*

In 1918 Elsie Stephen Reford inherited this tract of land from her uncle, Sir George Stephen, president of the Canadian Pacific Railway Co. She created magnificent gardens, now owned by the government of Quebec. In the centre of the gardens stands the **Villa Reford**. The first floor houses dining facilities and a craft shop.

- 🛈 **Info:** Quebec Maritime, #205, 84 rue Saint-Germain Est, Rimouski. ✆418-742-7889. www.quebec maritime.ca.
- ▶ **Location:** Percé Rock marks the eastern tip of the peninsula and is a popular destination.
- 👁 **Don't Miss:** The drive along the coast; Percé Rock.
- 🕐 **Timing:** Matane to Percé is roughly a 5-hour drive.
- 👪 **Kids:** At the fish ladder in Matane, you can see Atlantic salmon making their way through the counting station. Fossil enthusiasts will like Miguasha Park.

Matane

55km/34mi east of Métis Gardens.
This small industrial community is known for its salmon fishing and shrimp production. In the town centre, a **fish ladder★** (*passe migratoire*) enables salmon to travel upstream from mid-June to October.

Parc de la Gaspésie★ (Gaspésie Park)

1981, Rte. du Parc, Saint-Anne-des-Monts. 103km/64mi east of Matane.
✕&🅿🕐*Open daily year-round.*

Jardins de Métis

©Tourisme Gaspésie

Rocher Percé

© Cynthia Ochterbeck/MICHELIN

Hiking, fishing, camping, canoeing, cross-country skiing. ☞ $7.50. ✆ 418-763-7494 or 800-665-6527. www.sepaq.com.

The **Mont Albert Sector** reflects vegetation characteristic of the northern tundra. In the **Lake Cascapédia Sector**, the ridges of the Chic-Choc Mountains offer spectacular **views★★** of the Appalachians. From the summit of Mt. Jacques Cartier an expansive **view★★** extends to the McGerrigle Mountains. The **information centre** presents exhibits, films, lectures and slide shows (🕐 *open mid-May–mid-Oct daily 8am–8pm; late Dec–early Apr daily 8:30am–4:30pm*).

Scenic Route★★

Past Gaspésie Park, Route 132 follows the contours of the coastline, affording splendid views. Of particular interest are the impressive shale cliffs around **Mont-Saint-Pierre** and the expansive views of the gulf from the bustling fishing village of **Rivière-au-Renard**.

Parc national Forillon★★ (Forillon National Park)

122 Gaspé Blvd., Gaspé. 217km/135mi east of Gaspésie Park.

🅿🕐 *Open daily year-round. Visitor centres open daily May 31–mid-Oct.* ☞ $7.80. ✆ 418-368-5505 or 888-773-8888. www.pc.gc.ca.

Located on the eastern tip of the peninsula, this 245sq km/95sq mi park includes limestone cliffs towering over the

sea, forested mountains, wildflower meadows, and sandy beaches. A road leads to **Cape Bon Ami**, providing magnificent **views★★** of the sea, limestone cliffs, and sometimes whales. At **Cape Gaspé★**, a pleasant walk affords **views★** of the Bay of Gaspé and Île Bonaventure. Nearby in the former fishing village of **Grande-Grave★**, several historic buildings have been restored.

Gaspé★

42km/26mi south of Forillon National Park.

Housed in a new building (2009), the **Musée de la Gaspésie★** highlights historical events such as Jacques Cartier's discovery of the peninsula in 1534, the Mi'kmaq Indian population and regional geography (*80, boul de Gaspé; ♿🅿🕐 open daily 9am–5pm;* ☞ *$10;* ✆ *418-368-1534; www.museede-lagaspesie.ca*). Completed in 1969 the **Cathédrale du Christ-Roi★** (Cathedral of Christ the King) is distinguished by its cedar exterior that blends harmoniously with the environment.

THE SOUTH COAST
Percé★★★

76km/47mi south of Gaspé.

This bustling tourist town was named for the massive offshore rock pierced (*percé*) by the sea. The landscape features reddish-gold limestone and shale, folded into a variety of cliffs, bays and hills.

Rocher Percé★★ (Percé Rock)

This mammoth rock wall measures 438m/1,437ft long and 88m/289ft high, and is connected to **Mont Joli★★** by a sandbar, accessible at low tide.

The Coast★★★

The shoreline along Route 132 offers spectacular **views★★** of the area. **Cape Barré** permits a view to the west of cliffs known as Trois-Sœurs ("Three Sisters"). South of Percé, **Côte Surprise** offers another superb view. Rising 320m/1,050ft above Percé, **Mont Sainte-Anne** features extraordinary red-rock formations. Lookouts allow increasingly expansive **views★★★** of Percé rock, the village and surrounding area. Along the sheer cliff on the west side of Mt. Sainte-Anne, another trail provides views of the **Great Crevasse**, a deep fissure in the rock.

Parc de l'Île-Bonaventure-et-du-Rocher-Percé★ (Île Bonaventure and Percé Rock Park)

✕ ❷ ⓧ *Open late May–mid-Oct daily 9am–5pm.* ☜*$7.50.* ☎*418-782-2240 or 800-665-6527. www.sepaq.com.*
North America's largest **gannet** colony lives here, with some 60,000 birds. A pleasant **boat trip** leads past Percé Rock and then around the island, affording superb views (♿ ❷ ⓧ *departs from Percé wharf mid-May–late Oct daily 9am–5pm; round-trip 1hr 15min; reservations required;* ☜*$25, whale-watching $50; Les Bateliers de Percé Inc.* ☎*418-782-2974 or 877-782-2974; www.infogaspesie.com).*

Bonaventure

131km/81mi southwest of Percé.
Founded in 1760 by Acadians, this village is home to the **Musée acadien du Québec**, which depicts their influence on Quebec's culture (*95, av. Port-Royal;* ✕♿❷ⓧ*open Jun 24–mid-Oct daily; call for hours.* ☜*$8;* ☎*418-534-4000; www.museeacadien.com).* A new **biopark** (*www.quebecmaritime.ca/bioparc*) offers overniting with Wolves & estuary boat tours.

Carleton

63km/39mi west of Bonaventure.
From the 558m/1,830ft summit of **Mont Saint-Joseph**, the **panorama★★** encompasses Chaleur Bay from Bonaventure to the Miguasha Peninsula and south to New Brunswick.

Parc de Miguasha★ (Miguasha Park)

231, Rte. Miguasha Ouest. 24km/15mi west of Carleton. ✕♿❷ⓧ*Open Jun–late Aug daily 9am–6pm. Rest of year times vary.* ☜*$3.50 (park), $12.25 (park & museum).* ☎*418-794-2475 or 800-665-6527. www.sepaq.com.*
This park lies on an escarpment jutting out into Chaleur Bay, which contains fossils from the Devonian Period (400 million years ago). The **natural history museum** shows fossils found on-site.

Lieu historique national du Canada Bataille-de-la-Restigouche (Battle of the Restigouche National Historic Site of Canada)

Rte. 132, in Pointe-à-la-Croix 44km/27mi from Miguasha Park. ♿❷ⓧ*Open Jun–early Oct daily 9am–5pm.* ☜*$3.90.* ☎*418-788-5676 or 888-773-8888. www.pc.gc.ca.*
France's attempt to save its colony from British domination was thwarted in the estuary of the Ristigouche River in 1760. A **visitor centre** displays the hull and anchor of the French warship *Le Machault.*

ADDRESSES

⌂ STAY

$$ Auberge du Centre d'art Marcel Gagnon – *564 Route de la Mer, Sainte-Flavie.* ☎*418-775-2829 or 866-775-2829. www.centredart.net. 10 rooms.* ✕❷
Simple, clean, comfortable rooms are located on the upper floor of this art centre. At the **restaurant** (**$$**) on the ground floor, the main attraction is Marcel Gagnon's composite sculpture *Le grand rassemblement (The Great Gathering).*

$$$ Auberge Au Pirate 1775 – *169 Rte.
132 Ouest, Percé.* ✆*418-782-5055. 5 rooms.
Reservations advised.* ✖🅿. Wonderfully
comfortable rooms with coffee maker,
fridge and beautiful views of Percé Rock
await you at the Pirate's House. The
dining room (**$$$**) attracts visitors from
around the country with an imaginative
dinner menu featuring local seafood.

$$$ Gîte du Mont-Albert – *2001 Route
du Parc, Sainte-Anne-des-Monts.* ✆*418-
763-2288 or 866-727-2427. www.sepaq.com.
60 rooms, 20 cabins and two suites in
Caribou Lodge.* ✖🕭🅿. Located within
the Parc de la Gaspésie, this stately hotel
provides a pleasant base for the park's
seasonal activities. Clean, cozy rooms, all
with views of Mont-Albert & Wi-fi. Cabins
have a fireplace and wood stove; 15 have
kitchens. Heated outdoor pool/sauna.

$$$ Hôtel la Normandie – *221 Rte. 132
Ouest, Percé.* ✆*418-782-2112 or 800-463-
0820. www.normandieperce.com. 45 rooms.*
✖🅿. A waterfront hotel in the most
traditional sense, the Normandie offers
tastefully decorated rooms, most with
views of the ocean and Percé Rock.

The **dining room** (**$$**) features buffet
breakfast and a *table d'hôte* (fixed-price)
dinner. Seafood, meat or poultry choices.
French fine cuisine and extensive
wine list.

♀/ EAT

$$ Chez Pierre – *96 Boul. Perron Ouest,
Sainte-Anne-des-Monts (Tourelle).* ✆*418-
763-7446.* 🕭 **Seafood.** To appreciate the
bounty of the St. Lawrence River, take
time for a meal at Chez Pierre. Order
from the menu or try the *dégustation
poissons* (fish sampler). Efficient service,
and a nice view of the water.

$$ La Maison du Pêcheur – *155 Place
du Quai, Percé.* ✆*418-782-5331.
www.maisondupecheur.ca. Closed mid-
Oct–May.* **Quebecois.** Located next to
the public pier, the Fisherman's House
serves breakfast, lunch and dinner.
For dinner, choose from bistro classics or
Québécois seafood specialties like
lobster flavoured with maple syrup.
Locals favour the seaweed soup
(*potage aux algues marines*).

Gatineau★

Gatineau functions primarily as an
annex to Canada's federal capital
city of Ottawa in Ontario.
The downtown area has witnessed
a great deal of change, including the
construction of two large federal
government complexes and the
creation of a new campus for the
University of Quebec.

SIGHTS

👥 Canadian Museum of History
(Children's Museum & IMAX)
100 Rue Laurier. ✖🕭🅿🕐*Open Jun–
Labour Day Mon–Fri 9:30am–6pm (Thu
til 8pm), Fri–Sun 9:30am–6pm. Rest
of the year, call or see website for hrs.*
👓*$13 (1 museum) (child $8).*
✆*819-776-7000 or 800-555-5621.
www.historymuseum.ca*
The sweeping curves of the two large
buildings designed by **Douglas Cardi-
nal** evoke the emergence of the North
American continent and its subsequent

> ▶ **Population:** 265,349.
> 📋 **Info:** ✆*819-246-0222.
> www.gatineau.ca or www.
> tourismeoutaouais.com.*
> ◖ **Location:** Gatineau lies
> on the Québec side of the
> Ottawa River. Roads on the
> Gatineau side are narrow
> and winding.
> 🅿 **Parking:** Metered street
> parking is available; city
> and private lots (*fee applies*).
> 🕐 **Timing:** Plan to spend
> at least half a day at the
> newly-named Canadian
> Museum of History (aka
> Museum of Civilization).

molding by wind, water and glaciers.
The northern **curatorial wing** houses
administrative offices and conserva-
tion laboratories, while the southern
wing, the **museum building**, provides
25,000sq m/270,000sq ft of exhibit halls.

Canadian Museum of History

Harry Foster/Canadian Museum of Civilization

The **First Peoples** exhibit greets arriving visitors. In the **Canada Hall** artifacts and reconstructed buildings recreate 1,000 years of Canadian heritage. The **children's museum** encourages young people to explore the world, from a Mexican village to a Pakistani street.

Parc de la Gatineau★★ (Gatineau Park)

33 Scott Rd., Chelsea. ⏱*Park open daily year-round, visitor centre open daily May–Nov 9am–5pm; rest of year varies. Parkways closed from first snowfall until early May, visitor centre closed Christmas morning.* ✕&🅿⚠ ⇝*$11/car.* 📞*819-827-2020 or 800-465-1867. www.ncc-ccn.gc.ca.*
Covering 356sq km/137sq mi, this park nestles between the valleys of the Ottawa and Gatineau rivers. **Champlain Lookout** offers a magnificent **panorama★★** of the Ottawa Valley.

Domaine Mackenzie-King★ *(Mackenzie King Estate).* ⏱*Open May 15–mid-Oct weekdays 10am–5pm (except Tue when museum is closed but grounds and Tea Room are open, Sat–Sun & holidays 11am–6pm.* ✕&🅿 ⇝*$8/car.* 📞*819-827-2020. www.ncc-ccn.gc.ca.*
Moorside, the residence of **William Lyon Mackenzie King** (1874-1950), Canada's tenth prime minister, features exhibits and a tea room.

ADDRESSES

🍴/EAT

$$$ Soif Wine Bar (by **Veronique Rivest**) – *88 Rue Montcalm, Gatineau.* 📞*819-934-9919.* **International**. Operating within the converted Le Twist burger joint, international Canadian wine connossieur Veronique Rivest has set up shop to create a new wine savouring experience. Waiter service, tapas, patio, groups welcome.

$$$ Restaurant Le Sans-Pareil – *71 Blvd. Saint-Raymond, Gatineau.* 📞*819-771-1471. www.lesanspareil.com. No lunch Sat. Closed Sun.* **Belgian**. This Belgian outpost features a classic seasonal menu with Canadian touches. For dinner, a four-course prix-fixe meal **($$)** and a four-course surprise selection **($$$)** are available.

Cycling in the Parc de la Gatineau

© hojun yu/iStockphoto.com

Laurentides★★

Stretching along the north shore of the St. Lawrence, this range of low, rounded mountains rises to an altitude of 1,166m/3,825ft at **Mont Tremblant**. Part of the Canadian Shield, the Laurentians (*Laurentides* in French), formed more than a billion years ago in the Precambrian era, are among the oldest mountains in the world. The area north of Montreal between Saint-Jérôme and Mt. Tremblant is especially noted for its string of resort towns that offer an attractive blend of recreational activities and fine cuisine.

SIGHTS
Sainte-Adèle★
68km/42mi north of Montreal by Rtes. 15 and 117.
Occupying a lovely **site** on small Lake Sainte-Adèle, this town is dominated by the luxurious **Hôtel Chantecler** *(1474, chemin Chantecler; ℘888-916-1616, US/ Canada; www.lechantecler.com)*, which has its own ski hill. Frequented by artists and writers, the village features numerous restaurants and charming country inns.

Sainte-Agathe-des-Monts★
18km/11mi north of Sainte-Adèle by Rte. 117.
Set on the shores of **Sables Lake★★**, this town is the capital of the Lauren-

- ⓘ **Michelin Map:** p312.
- ▯ **Info:** Tourisme Laurentides ℘450-436-8532. www.laurentides.com or www.hautes-laurentides. com. Information bureau on Hwy. 15, Exit 51 (La Porte du Nord).
- ◖ **Location:** Hwy. 15 (the Laurentian Autoroute) takes you north from Montreal to Ste-Agathe. Resorts in all directions.
- ◉ **Don't Miss:** Take the ski life to the top of Mt. Tremblant for great views.
- ◷ **Timing:** It is a 2 hour drive from downtown Montreal to Mont-Tremblant, over Hwy. 15 to Ste-Agathe, then Hwy. 117 north.
- ⚮ **Kids:** Maple syrup treats at Cabane à sucre Millette *(see Addresses).*

tians region. A **scenic cruise** takes in the lake and houses lining its shores (♿▣◷*boat departs from dock at foot of Rue Principale mid-May–late Oct daily 11:30am, 1:30pm, 2:30pm & 3:30pm; additional departures Jun 25–late Aug 5pm & 7:30pm; round-trip 50min; ⬭$17; Les Croisières Alouette ℘819-326-3656; www. croisierealouette.com).*

Lac Monroe, Parc du Mont Tremblant

Parc du Mont Tremblant★
(Mt. Tremblant Park)

About 140km/87mi north of Montreal. Park ✕⛄♿️🅿️🕐open daily. 🕐Sections of the park's roads are closed during winter. 👁️*$7.50.* ☎️*819-688-2281 or 800-665-6527. www.sepaq.com.* Quebec's oldest park abounds in lakes and hiking trails, and visitor services to maximize outdoor fun. New bus service from City of Mt.Tremblant to La Diable Visitors Centre.

St.Lin-de-Laurentides

62km/38mi north of Montreal by Rte. 15, then east on Rte. 158.

This town is the birthplace of Sir **Wilfrid Laurier** (1841-1919), prime minister of Canada (1896-1911). The **Lieu historique national de Sir-Wilfrid-Laurier** is sited on his presumed birthplace *(945 12th Ave., St-Lin-Laurentides; ♿️🅿️🔦📷🔊 visit by 1hr guided tour Jun 21–Labour Day daily, see website for hours;* 👁️*$3.90;* ☎️*450-439-3702; www.pc.gc.ca).*

ADDRESSES

🏨STAY

$$$$ Fairmont Tremblant – *3045 Chemin de la Chapelle, Mont-Tremblant.* ☎️*819-681-7000 or 866-540-4415 (Canada & US). www.fairmont.ca/tremblant. 314 rooms.* ✕♿️🅿️🏊♨️. Reigning above Mont-Tremblant Village, this resort hotel exudes rustic comfort inside. Rooms feature dark wood furnishings and warm colours. Watch skiers from heated outdoor pool or enjoy a spa treatment. **($$$) Windigo** nourishes with fine dining and wine cellar.

🍴/EAT

$$$$ Restaurant La Forge – *3041, ch. de la Chapelle, Mont-Tremblant Resort.* ☎️*819-681-4900. www.laforgetremblant.com.* **Canadian.** This inviting two-level restaurant, with a bistro on the main floor, is located at the base of the ski lifts. The open kitchen prepares steaks, lamb or veal grilled over wood.

$$ La Tablée des Pionniers – *1357 Rue St-Faustin, Saint-Faustin–Lac Carré.* ☎️*819-688-2101 or 855-688-2101. www.latableedespionniers.com.* **Quebecois**. ♿️ Tour the syrup-making facilities, then enjoy an all-you-can-eat meal of maple-syrup smoked ham, sausages in maple syrup, potatoes, baked beans and bread. End with the sugar pie.

PARC LINÉAIRE LE P'TIT TRAIN DU NORD

Access by Rte. 15 and/or Rte. 117 from St-Jérôme or any of the 23 towns and villages that lie along the park. Open Dec–Apr for cross-country skiing and snowmobiling, May–Oct for hiking and bicycling. Biking no charge; skiing $12/daily. ☎️*450-224-7007 or 800-561-6673 (US/Canada). www.laurentides.com/parclineaire.* For more than 70 years, the railway line P'Tit Train du Nord brought skiers to the Laurentians. Today, hikers, cyclists, cross-country skiers and even snowmobilers like the "linear park" for its 200km/124mi of maintained pathways. Val-David and Mont-Tremblant are the most popular of the 23 village access points. Former train stations are now service centres.

SNOWSHOES AND SAUNAS

Opportunities for exercise don't wane much in winter. **La Source Aquaclub** (☎️*819-681-5668. www.tremblant.ca*) is a fitness centre that features an indoor pool with waterfalls. Diversions include **snowshoe** excursions or **dogsledding** (☎️ *819 681-4848. www.tremblantactivities.com*) at a neighbouring forest trail.

For muscle-bruised skiers, the nearby **Le Scandinave** (☎️*819-425-5524 or 888-537-2263; www.scandinave.com*) offers a spa experience alongside Rivière du Diable. The idea is to slowly raise your body temperature in a cycle of heat, cold and rest while working up the nerve to jump into the hole cut in the frozen river! The Finnish sauna, Jacuzzi and Norwegian steam baths are joined by outdoor heated sidewalks. Compared to the river, the bracing Nordic waterfall seems tame. Swedish massages are offered here too.

Îles de la Madeleine★★

Located in the Gulf of St. Lawrence, these eight islands plus islets are connected by sand spits that form a hook-shaped mass about 72km/45mi long. In 1755 they became a refuge for **Acadians** deported from Nova Scotia, ancestors of today's Madelinots. Supplemented by agriculture, logging and tourism, fishing remains the primary economic activity of the archipelago.

Access

Ferry *from Souris, PEI, to Cap-aux-Meules (5hrs). Call for times. One-way* ⊕*$49.75, additional* ⊕*$92.80/car. Reservations. Cruises from Montreal.* ✕&◻ *CTMA Ltd.* ℰ*418-986-3278 or 888-986-3278. www.ctma.ca.*
Flights *between Montreal and Havre aux Maisons Island on Air Canada Jazz (* ℰ*888-247-2262; www.aircanada.com) and Pascan Aviation Inc. (* ℰ*450-443-0500 or 888-313-8777; www.pascan.com).*

SIGHTS

Île du Cap-Aux-Meules★★ (Cap aux Meules Island)
Cap-aux-Meules' highest point, **Butte du Vent**, affords **views★★** of the entire chain of islands. The western coast features dramatic **rock formations**. This is the commercial heart of the archipelago, and the main port.

▶ **Population:** 13,062.
🈳 **Info:** Tourist Office, 128, ch. Principal, Cap-aux-Meules. ℰ418-986-2245, 877-624-4437 or www.tourismeiles delamadeleine.com.
◑ **Location:** The islands are near Cape Breton Island, Nova Scotia, and Prince Edward Island.
◔ **Timing:** The islands are on Atlantic time.

Île du Havre Aubert (Havre Aubert Island)
The **Musée de la Mer★** (Maritime Museum) acquaints visitors with the maritime history and culture of the Magdalen Islands *(1023, Rte. 199;* &◻◔*open Jun 24–Labour Day Mon–Fri 9am–6pm, Sat–Sun 10am–6pm; rest of the year call for hours;* ⊕*$8;* ℰ*418-937-5711; www. tourismeilesdelamadeleine.com/en).* The historic site of **La Grave★** has stores, ironworks, *chaufauds* (sheds where cod was dried), boutiques and warehouses.

Île du Havre aux Maisons★ (Havre aux Maisons Island)
Examples of local architecture include the **baraque**, designed to shelter hay. At **Dune du Sud★** a beach and rock formations attract visitors.
On **Île de la Grande Entrée★** (Grande Entrée Island), coastal hiking trails afford **views★★★** of jagged cliffs, tidal pools and twisted trees. To the northeast the **Grande Échouerie Beach★★** is considered the archipelago's loveliest.

Red cliffs at La Belle Anse, Île du Cap-aux-Meules

© Egmont Strigl/age fotostock

Montreal★★★

Canada's second-largest metropolis after Toronto occupies a large island in the St. Lawrence River, some 1,000 miles from the Atlantic. This cosmopolitan city has long been the leading industrial, commercial and financial centre in Canada. Home to the world's largest Francophone population outside Paris, Montreal offers visitors a wealth of cultural attractions, a diversity of urban settings, and Mount Royal at its downtown core.

A BIT OF HISTORY

Early Exploration – While searching for a route to the Orient in 1535, Jacques Cartier visited the Mohawk village of **Hochelaga** on the Island of Montreal. In 1611, Samuel de Champlain, founder of Quebec City settlement, sailed upriver onto the nearby island of St. Helen. However, European habitation of Montreal proper only began in 1642 with Paul de Chomedey, **Sieur de Maisonneuve** (1612–76), who is considered the founder of Montreal.

Under the French Regime – In the 17C the Sulpician order in France chose de Maisonneuve to sail across the Atlantic and establish the mission of **Ville-Marie** (City of Mary), present-day Montreal. Amid fighting between the Iroquois Indians and the French settlers, Ville-Marie developed into a commercial centre, and was renamed Montreal in the early 18C. French fur-trading forays across the Great Lakes brought astounding wealth, and when Montreal surrendered to the British in 1760, it had become a thriving community. Most of the French nobility returned to France, while a large number of Scots, attracted to the fur trade, and an influx of Loyalists from the US swelled the anglophone population.

From Rebellion to Confederation Montreal was the centre of one of the **Rebellions of 1837**, a political uprising which, in Quebec, contested the power

▶ **Population:** 3,824,221.
◉ **Michelin Map:** pp326-327
🛈 **Info:** Tourisme Montreal. Infotourist Centre, 1255 Peel St. Suite 100 ✆514-873-2015 or 877-266-5687. www.tourisme-montreal.org. *The ● symbol indicates a subway station.*
▶ **Location:** The main downtown area sits at the foot of the southeast slopes of Mont-Royal. The Montreal Métro system can move you quickly and safely around the city. Signage is in French, but pictographs are often used.
🅿 **Parking:** Downtown parking meters are computerized; you note the number of your meter, pay at a nearby automatic kiosk, and keep your coupon. Later, you can "feed" your meter from any kiosk.
◎ **Don't Miss:** Old Montreal's cobblestone streets, especially around Place Jacques-Cartier; the Olympic Park area, with the Biodôme, Jardin Botanique, & Planetarium.
🕐 **Timing:** In the evening, return to the city centre to take in the night life in Old Montreal and on Crescent and St. Denis streets.
👫 **Kids:** The Biodôme, Insectarium, & Planetarium in the Olympic Park are perfect for kids. In the Old Port area, don't miss iSci, with its interactive exhibits.

held by the Crown-appointed governor and his council. Led by Louis-Joseph Papineau, George-Étienne Cartier and other French Canadians, the **Patriots** engaged British troops several times. Although the insurgents were defeated,

Montreal skyline with Marché Bonsecours

© Philippe Renault/hemis.fr

the British government granted Quebec a representative government.

By the time of Canada's Confederation as a nation in 1867, Montreal stood at the forefront of railway development, claiming the world's largest grain port. Financial institutions along St. James Street (Rue St-Jacques in French) supported Montreal's dominance of Canada's financial sector until the 1970s.

Montreal Today – Following a period of slow growth after the Great Depression, Montreal emerged in the 1960s as an international centre of commerce and culture. In addition to hosting the 1967 World Fair (**Expo '67**), the **1976 Olympic Games** and the **1980 International Floralies**, the city celebrates annual international festivals in jazz, film and comedy, attracting millions of visitors. Montreal's premier cultural neighborhood **Quartier des Spectacles** (bounded by Saint-Hubert on the east, City Councillors on the west, Sherbrooke on the north and René-Lévesque on the south) is crowned by **Place des Arts★★**, the core venue for international entertainment shows, and home to the Montreal Opera. Les Grands Ballets Canadiens has just moved across the street to the newly opened Espace Dance in the renovated Wilder Building. The new **Maison Symphonique** is now home to the Montreal Symphony Orchestra, on the Place des Arts site. The city remains a major centre of Francophone culture, with numerous cafés, restaurants and bistros, especially along Rue Saint-Denis and Boulevard St.Laurent, an infamous nightlife, as well as fashionable shops, boutiques and promenades.

VIEUX-MONTRÉAL★★★ (OLD MONTREAL)

●*Place d'Armes.*

Bounded by the Old Port, Saint-Jacques, Rue Berri and Rue McGill, Montreal's historic core was originally enclosed within imposing stone walls erected in the early 1700s. During the 19C the settlement expanded and Montrealers moved outside the fortifications. Warehouses and commercial buildings gradually replaced stone dwellings and gardens, and the area fell into decline. Interest in Old Montreal revived in the 1960s: the surviving 18C homes were renovated, warehouses were transformed into apartment buildings and condominiums, art galleries, restaurants and shops thrive now.

▶ Horse-drawn carriages (calèches) depart from Rue Notre-Dame, Place d'Armes, Rue de la Commune and Place Jacques-Cartier.

Place d'Armes★

Designed in the 17C by the Sulpician Dollier de Casson, is the second oldest public site in the city. A **monument★** *(see map)* by sculptor Louis-Philippe

PRACTICAL INFORMATION
GETTING AROUND
BY PUBLIC TRANSPORTATION –
Local subway (Métro) and bus service are provided by the Société de transport de Montréal (STM) (*514-786-4636 + option 4; www.stm.info*). The **MÉTRO** system operates from 5:30am; check website for last train (*lines 1, 2 & 4*) or 12:15am (*line 5*). Each Métro line is designated by a number & color. The **BUS** service has 220 daytime and 23 night routes, as well as commuter trains to the far suburbs. Rechargeable "smart cards" for paying fares are in use. Passengers may also buy disposable cards, such as the Unlimited Weekend Pass ($13.75) or pay a single fare ($3.25) in cash in a bus (exact fare only) or in a Métro station. Cards are on sale in stations and at many conveniences stores. Weekly passes for travelers (*$25.75*) or a monthly pass ($83.00) amount to large savings. Lost and found: *514-786-4636+ option 8+ option 6+ option 2.*
BY CAR – Rental agencies include: Avis *514-866-2847*, Budget *514-866-7675*, Discount *514-849-2277*, Hertz *514-342-8813*, Thrifty *514-845-5954*. **BY TAXI** – Co-Op *514-725-9885*, Champlain *514-273-2435*, Pontiac Hemlock *514-766-TAXI (8294) and there is uber.com.*

GENERAL INFORMATION
ACCOMMODATIONS AND VISITOR INFORMATION
Infotourist Office: 1255 Peel St. (corner Peel and Ste-Catherine) ●Peel or 174 Notre-Dame E. in Old Montreal ●Champ-de-Mars.
The Montreal Museums Pass gives free access to 30 museums for $75 over 3 days within 30 days of your first paid visit. For another $5, you can get public transit as well. The pass can be purchased online or at any participating museum. *www.montrealmuseums.org.*
Local Press: Daily newspapers: English – the *Gazette.* French– *Le Journal de Montréal, Le Devoir, La Presse.*

Entertainment: For current schedules and for addresses of principal theatres and concert halls, consult the free alternative publication Cult Montreal (www.cultmontreal.com) (English) and *Voir (www.voir.ca)* (French) or the Journal Métro de Montréal (French) found in all Métro stations, or the weekend arts and entertainment supplements in local newspapers.
Tickets may be purchased from Admission *855-790-1245 or 877-528-0786. www.admission.com;* Ticketpro *888-311-9090. www.ticketpro.ca;* Billets.ca *514-935-9999 or 800-935-9962. www.billets.ca;* and Place des Arts *514-842-2112 or 866-842-2112. www.placedesarts.com.* Sports:
Montréal Canadiens (National Hockey League) season Oct–Apr at the Bell Centre (●Lucien-L'Allier) *514-790-2525 or 877-668-8269. http://canadiens.nhl.com.* **Montreal Alouettes** (Canadian Football League) season Jun–Nov at Percival Molson Stadium (●McGill or Square Victoria; shuttle service to stadium 2hrs before games) *514-871-2266. http://en.montrealalouettes.com.*
Montreal Impact (United Soccer League) season May–Sept at Saputo Stadium, corner Sherbrooke and Viau (●Viau) *514-328-3668. www.montrealimpact.com.* Every August, Montreal hosts the **Rogers Cup Canadian Open**, a Tier 1 tennis tournament that draws the world's best players. Montreal and Toronto (Rexall Centre) alternate hosting the men's and women's events. Uniprix Stadium (●de Castelnau) *855-836-6470 ext 2. www.tenniscanada.com.*

USEFUL NUMBERS
AREA CODES 514, 450, 438 & 579.
Dial all 10 digits (area code + no.)
♦ **Police–Ambulance–Fire**: **911** (Emergencies only)
♦ **Tourisme Montréal**: 800-230-0001. *www.tourisme-montreal.org*
♦ **Tourisme Quebec**: 514-873-2015. *www.quebecoriginal.com.*
♦ **Central Train Station**

(Bonaventure Station) (VIA Rail): 895 Rue de la Gauchetière Ouest. 514-989-2626 or 888-842-7245. *www.viarail.ca*

♦ **Keolis Canada (bus service within Quebec)**: 514-395-4000 or 888-999-3977. *www.orleansexpress.com*

♦ **Greyhound** (bus service Canada and US): 514-287-1580 or 800-661-8747. *www.greyhound.com.*

♦ **Station Centrale d'Autobus**: 1717 rue Berri. 514-842-2281. *gamtl.com*

♦ **Montréal-Trudeau International Airport**: 514-633-3333 or 800-465-1213. *www.admtl.com*

♦ **Canadian Automobile Assn.**: 1180 Drummond St. 514-861-5111. *www.caa.ca*

♦ **Jean Coutu Drugstore** (open 24 hours): 305 Rue Sherbrooke W. (●Place de Arts) 514-285-2646

♦ **Pharmaprix Drugstore** (open 24hrs): 5122 Côte des Neiges, H3T 1X8 (●Côte des Neiges) 514-738-8464

♦ **Road Conditions** (24hrs): 1-888-355-0511 (in French and English)

♦ **Weather** (24hrs): 514-283-4006

Hébert in the centre honours the founder of Montreal, Paul de Chomedy, sieur de Maisonneuve, who, according to legend, killed the local First Nations chief on this site during a 1644 battle. Today Place d'Armes is home to some of the most prestigious buildings in the city. The north side of this busy square is dominated by the **Banque de Montréal★** (1847), a fine example of the Neoclassical style.

The financial heart of Canada until the 1970s, **Rue Saint-Jacques★**, extending west, is lined with elegant 19C and 20C edifices. Note the Canadian Imperial Bank of Commerce *(no. 265 Ouest)*, with façade of fluted Corinthian columns, and **Banque Royale du Canada★** (Royal Bank of Canada) *(no. 360 Ouest)*, whose tower distinguishes the city's skyline. The **Le Centre de Commerce mondial de Montréal** (World Trade Centre Montreal), opened in 1992 at 380 Rue St-Antoine Ouest, fuses the façades of 11 historic buildings; its glass atrium incorporates a remnant of the former wall, Ruelle des Fortifications, and cascading natural light from the magnificent glass roof, creates a welcoming atmosphere adding to the site's elegance.

Basilique Notre-Dame★★★ (Notre-Dame Basilica)

Rue Notre-Dame Ouest. ●*Place d'Armes.* &⊙*Open year-round Mon–8am–5pm, Tue-Sat 8am–8pm, Sun 12:30pm –4pm.* ✆*514-842-2925 or 866-842-2925. www.basiliquenddm.org.*

Interior, Basilique Notre-Dame

© Susanne Kremer/Sime/Photononstop

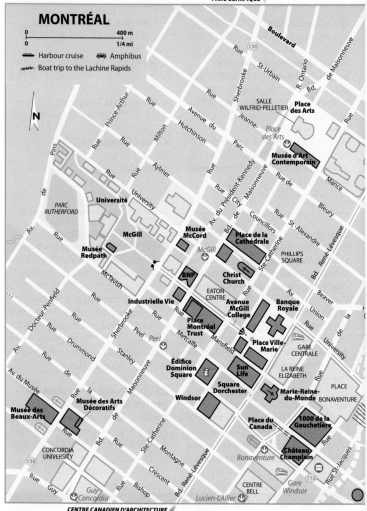

MONTRÉAL

0 ——————— 400 m
0 ——————— 1/4 mi

🚢 Harbour cruise 🚌 Amphibus
🚤 Boat trip to the Lachine Rapids

Boulevard

Rue

St-Urbain

R. Ontario

Bd.

de Maisonneuve

Rue

Avenue du

Hutchinson

Rue

Milton

Prince-Arthur

Rue

Rue

Rue

Aylmer

University

Rue

Parc

SALLE
WILFRID-PELLETIER

**Place
des Arts**

Jeanne-

Place
des Arts

**Musée d'Art
Contemporain**

Av. du Président-Kennedy

Rue de

Maisonneuve

Rue de

Mance

Bleury

N

Pins

de

Rue

**PARC
RUTHERFORD**

Av.

Rue

Université

McGill

University

McGill

**Musée
Redpath**

McTravish

**Musée
McCord**

McGill Ⓜ

**Place de la
Cathédrale**

St-Alexandre

Councillors

Rue

Bd. René-Lévesque

PHILLIPS
SQUARE

Ste-Catherine

Rue

Beaver

BNP

**Christ
Church**

EATON
CENTRE

Industrielle Vie

Docteur-Penfield

Rue

Rue

Sherbrooke

Peel

Peel

Rue

Rue

Drummond

Stanley

Maisonneuve

Metcalfe

Mansfield

**Avenue
McGill
College**

**Place
Montréal
Trust**

**Banque
Royale**

Union

Rue

de

University

la

Av

GARE
CENTRALE

**Place Ville-
Marie**

Av. du Musée

Rue

de

la

Rue

Ste-Catherine

de

Montagne

**Édifice
Dominion
Square**

ℹ

**Sun
Life**

**Square
Dorchester**

Windsor

LA REINE
ELIZABETH

**Marie-Reine-
du-Monde**

PLACE
BONAVENTURE

**Musée des
Beaux-Arts**

**Musée des Arts
Décoratifs**

Rue

Bd.

Rue

**Place du
Canada**

**1000 de la
Gauchetière**

Rue

St-Jacques

CONCORDIA
UNIVERSITY

Crescent

Bishop

Bd. René-Lévesque

Bonaventure Ⓜ

**Château-
Champlain**

112

Rue

Guy

Guy Ⓜ
Concordia

Rue

Lucien-L'Allier Ⓜ

CENTRE
BELL

Gare
Windsor

This twin-towered basilica rises on the south side of Place d'Armes. Completed in 1829, the Gothic Revival structure is renowned for its magnificent **interior**, with sculptures, wainscoting and gilt-work typical of provincial religious architecture. As visitors enter, eyes are drawn to the imposing **reredos** that stands out against the background's soft blue hues. The massive black walnut **pulpit**★ is the work of Louis-Philippe Hébert. Don't miss the beautiful rear Sacred Heart Chapel, also known as the "Wedding Chapel."

Vieux Séminaire de Saint-Sulpice★ (Old Sulpician Seminary), the oldest structure in the city, stands beside the basilica.
Note the façade **clock,** installed in 1701, believed to be the oldest public time-piece in North America.

Place Jacques-Cartier★★

Lined with outdoor cafes and flower parterres, this charming cobblestone square is especially lively in summer. Marking the north end of the plaza, a **statue** *(see map)* of Horatio Nelson

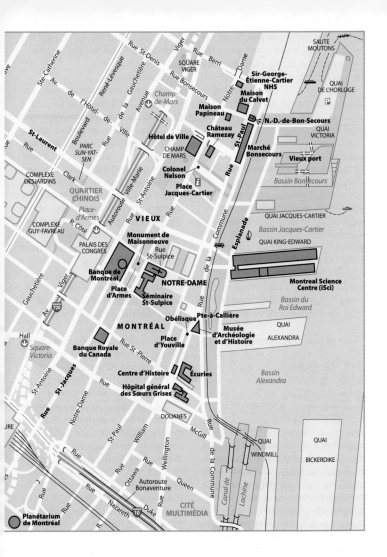

(1809) commemorates the British general's victory at Trafalgar.

Montreal's **Hôtel de Ville★** (City Hall), an imposing Second Empire building, stands at 275 Rue Notre-Dame ●*Champs de Mars (main hall &. ◐open Mon–Fri 10am–4pm; ⬤⬤ 1hr guided tours Jun–mid-Aug by reservation; ◐closed major holidays; ℘514-872-0077; www.old.montreal.qc.ca)*. The south end of the square leads to **Rue Saint-Paul★★**, lined with 19C buildings housing shops, inns, galleries and artists' studios, and on to Rue de la Commune and the Vieux-Port.

Vieux-Port★ (Old Port)

Stretching along the St. Lawrence River, at the foot of Place Jacques-Cartier, the former port has been transformed into a bustling waterfront park with bike and walking paths; a skating rink; exhibition spaces; quays for private yachts, eve a beach with sand, and **iSci★ ▲▲**, the **Montreal Science Centre** (●*Champs de Mars; ✕&.🅿 ◐open year-round Mon–Fri 9am–4pm, Sat–Sat 10am–5pm; ⬤$14.50, child $8.50; ℘514-496-4724 or 877-496-4724; www.centredessciencesdemontreal. com)* with its IMAX cinema (additional *fee)*. To enjoy scenic **views★** of the city and the majestic river, stroll along the wide boardwalk or take a **harbour cruise★** (✕&🅿*departs from King Edward Pier May–Oct daily cruises, packages, and fireworks departures; Croisières AML; 📞514-842-9300, or 866-856-6668; www.croisieresaml.com).*

Expéditions dans les rapides de Lachine (Lachine Rapids Jet Boat)

Depart Quai de l'Horloge (Clock Tower) Jun–Sept 5 times daily 10am–6pm, every 2hrs. Round-trip 1hr. Reservations required. ⊜*$67.* &🅿 *(fee) Lachine Rapids Tours/Saute-Moutons★★.* ●*Champ de Mars.* 📞*514-284-9607. www.jetboatingmontreal.com.*

Passengers get wet on this exciting voyage, whisked upriver through the ferocious Lachine Rapids. V**iews★★** of Montreal and surrounds are spectacular.

Château Ramezay Museum★

280 Rue Notre Dame Est. ●*Champs de Mars.* ✕&🕐*Open Jun 1–early Oct daily 9:30am–6pm. Rest of the year Tue–Sun 10am–4:30pm.* 🕐*Closed Jan 1 & Dec 23–25 & 30.* ⊜*$11.* 📞*514-861-3708. www.chateauramezay.qc.ca.*

This squat, fieldstone residence (1705) was constructed for Claude de Ramezay, 11th Governor of Montreal. It served as the British gubernatorial residence until 1849. The highlight of the **museum** is the exquisite, hand-carved 1725 mahogany **panelling** from Nantes, France. Outside is a herb and kitchen garden, and there are breadmaking workshops for the whole family.

Lieu historique national de Sir George-Étienne Cartier★ (Sir George-Étienne Cartier National Historic Site)

458 Rue Notre-Dame. &🕐*Open mid-Jun–Labour Day Wed-Sun 10am–5pm, rest of Sept–mid Dec Wed–Sun 10am–5pm.* ⊜*$3.90.* 📞*514-283-2282 or 888-773-8888. www.pc.gc.ca.*

This mansard-roofed structure, composed of two adjoining houses, was the home of **George-Étienne Cartier** (1814-73), one of the Fathers of Con-

federation. Period rooms illustrate the lifestyle of 19C middle-class society.

Rue Bonsecours

This attractive cobblestone street leads from Rue Notre-Dame to Rue Saint-Paul. At no. 440 stands the **Maison Papineau** (Papineau House), topped by a steeply pitched roof pierced by two rows of dormer windows. It was home to six generations of the Papineau family, including Louis-Joseph, leader of the Patriots during the 1837 Rebellions. The **Maison du Calvet★** (Calvet House) (1798), at the corner of Rue Saint-Paul, is a traditional 18C urban residence turned auberge and restaurant as **Hotel Pierre du Calvet** (www.pierreducalvet.ca).

Chapelle Notre-Dame-de-Bon-Secours★ (Chapel of Our Lady of Perpetual Help) *400 Rue Saint-Paul Est.* ●*Champs de Mars.*

This small church, topped by a copper steeple, with statue of the Virgin facing the port, stands on the site of a wooden edifice commissioned by Marguerite Bourgeoys in 1657 and destroyed by fire in 1754. Climb the observatory, accessible from the tower, to enjoy a panorama of the river, Old Montreal and the Old Port. Located in the basement, the **Musée Marguerite Bourgeoys** (&🕐*open May–early Oct Tue–Sun 10am–6pm, Mar–Apr & mid-Oct–mid-Jan Tue–Sun 11am–4pm;* ⊜*$12;* 📞*514-282-8670; www.marguerite-bourgeoys.com)* depicts the life of Bourgeoys (1620-1700), who came to Montreal with de Maisonneuve in 1653 to found the Congregation Notre-Dame. She was canonized in 1982. Near the church, on Rue Saint-Paul, stands the **Marché Bonsecours★** (*350 Rue St-Paul St. Est;* ✕&🅿🕐*open daily 10am, closing hrs vary;* 📞*514-872-7730; www.marchebonsecours.qc.ca),* a large Neoclassical stone structure crowned by a lofty dome and constructed to house Montreal's first interior market. It served as the city hall from 1852 to 1878, and even Canada's Parliament briefly. Today it is home to many local artisan crafts and design shops and leases temporary exhibit space.

Place d'Youville

●*Square Victoria.*

Brick structures surrounding this square reflect Dutch Baroque architectural style, as the **Centre d'Histoire de Montréal★** (Montreal History Centre & former firehall) presents the city's rich past (*335 Place d'Youville; & ◯Open summer daily Tue–Sun 10am–5pm, winter Wed-Sun 10am-5pm; ෧$6; ℘514-872-0238; http://ville.montreal.qc.ca/chm*). To the east of the square stand the **Écuries d'Youville** (Stables), an ensemble of grey stone structures (1828) enclosing a lovely garden courtyard. Spanning the block between Saint-Pierre and Normand Streets, the **Hôpital général des Soeurs Grises** (Grey Nuns Convent) t.514-842-9411 was erected in 1693 and extended in 1753 by Marie d'Youville, founder of the Grey Nuns order.

Pointe-à-Callière

A 10m/33ft **obelisk** *(see map)* commemorates de Maisonneuve's landing in May 1642. Opened in 1992, the **Musée d'Archéologie et d'Histoire de Montréal★★** (Montreal Museum of Archaeology and History) presents Montreal's fascinating history (*350 Place Royale; ●Place d'Armes; ╳ & ◯open Mon–Fri 10am–5pm, Sat/Sun11am–6pm; ◯closed major holidays; ෧$20, $8 youth; ℘514-872-9150; www.pacmusee.qc.ca*).

DOWNTOWN★★

●*Rue Peel.*

The city's commercial heart lies to the west of Old Montreal. A walk along Sherbrooke Street, one of the prestigious arteries of the city, reveals a lively retail sector alongside choice residences of the former *Golden Mile.* Rue Sainte-Catherine Ouest (West) is home to major stores (Ogilvy, Simons, The Bay) and commercial centres, while Avenue McGill College is lined with 20C skyscrapers leading to the university and Mount Royal.

Dorchester Square★

Long considered the centre of the city, the square is surrounded by a group of remarkable buildings, including the imposing Renaissance Revival **Dominion Square Building★** (1929) and **The Windsor★**, formerly an elegant hotel, now restored as an office building, with mansard roof pierced by dormer and œil-de-bœuf windows. The **Sun Life Building★★**, an imposing Beaux-Arts edifice erected in 1913, dominates the east side of the square. Facing Dorchester Square is **Place du Canada,** a small green plaza bordered by the **Hôtel Marriott Château-Champlain** (1967), marked by convex, half-moon windows.

Cathédrale Marie-Reine-du-Monde★★ (Mary Queen of the World Cathedral)

Main entrance on Blvd. René-Lévesque. 1085 Rue de la Cathédrale. ●*Bonaventure. & ◯Open daily. ℘514-866-1661. www.cathedralecatholique demontreal.org.*

Consecrated in 1894, cathedral is modelled after St. Peter's in Rome. Inside is the gold-leaf **baldachin** (1900), a replica of the 16C ornamental canopy created by Bernini for St. Peter's Basilica. On the left side of the nave, a **mortuary chapel** (1933) contains tombs of noted clergy. Behind the cathedral at **1000 de la Gauchetière** (1992), is the perpetual indoor skating rink.

Place Ville-Marie★★

Dominating the complex is I.M. Pei's 42-storey **Banque Royale Tower★** (1962), a cruciform structure sheathed in aluminum. A concrete esplanade affords an unparalleled **vista★** north to McGill University and Mt. Royal.

Extending from Place Ville-Marie to McGill University, **Avenue McGill College** is a showplace for the city's post-Modern architecture. Completed in 1989, the enormous **Place Montréal Trust★★** *(no. 1500)* features a pastel blue glass cylinder encased in a square base of rose marble and glass. Across the street *(no. 1981)* rises the sprawling, metallic-blue twin towers of the **Tours de la Banque Nationale de Paris/ Banque Laurentienne★** (National Bank of Paris/Laurentian Bank Towers).

The granite-clad **Tour l'Industrielle Vie** (Industrial Life Tower) *(no. 2000)* presents an elegant exterior enlivened by **The Illuminated Crowd** sculpture.

Christ Church Cathedral★

Entrance from Rue Sainte-Catherine between Rue University and Ave. Union. 1444 Av. Union. ●*McGill.* &🕙*Open year-round daily 8am–6pm.* ☎*514-843-6577 ext.236. www.montrealcathedral.ca.*
Handsome edifice (1859) exemplifies the Gothic Revival style. Graceful interior has magnificent stained-glass windows and a beautifully carved stone **reredos**. Behind the church rises the **Place de la Cathédrale★**, a modern office tower featuring a massive underground shopping promenade.

Musée McCord★★ (McCord Museum)

690 Rue Sherbrooke Ouest. ●*McGill.* ✗&🕙*Open summer Mon–Fri 10am–6pm, Wed & Thur til 9pm, Sat–Sun 10am–5pm, end of Sept-end May closed Mon, Tue-Fri 10am-6pm, Wed til 9pm.* ☜*$20 (kids free)* ☎*514-398-7100. www.mccord-museum.qc.ca.*
One of Canada's foremost historical museums, the McCord's holdings, including an outstanding compilation of 1,250,000 photographs, providing a fascinating insight into Canadian history.

Decorative Art Gallery, Montreal Museum of Fine Arts

Montreal Museum of Fine Arts, Decorative Arts and Design, Photo Marc Cramer

McGill University★

End of Ave. McGill College. ●*McGill.*
Set on the slopes of Mt. Royal, Canada's oldest university (1821) today claims an enrolment of 32,000 students.
Housed in a large structure designed in the style of an antique temple, the **Musée d'histoire naturelle Redpath★** (Redpath Museum of Natural History) displays vertebrate and invertebrate fossils, minerals, zoological artifacts, African art objects and Egyptian antiquities (🕙*open year-round Mon–Fri 9am–5pm, Sun 1pm–5pm;* 🕙*closed Sat & major holidays;* ☎*514-398-4086; www.mcgill.ca/redpath). Suggested contribution $10 (kids free).*

Musée des Beaux-Arts de Montréal★★ (Montreal Museum of Fine Arts)

1380 Rue Sherbrooke Ouest. ●*Peel* ✗&. 🕙*Open year-round Tue 11am–5pm, Wed–Fri 11am–9pm, Sat–Sun 10am–5pm.* 🕙*Closed Jan 1 & Dec 25.* ☜*$20 ($12 permanent collection; half price Wed after 5pm).* ☎*514-285-2000 or 800-899-6873. www.mbam.qc.ca.*
Beaux-Arts main edifice (1912) presents Canadian art, decorative arts and antiquities; newer pavillion, created by **Moshe Safdie** (1991), displays temporary exhibits and international art. Buildings are linked by underground galleries of Ancient and Oceanic art. In late 2016, the Michal and Renata Hornstein Pavilion for Peace opened, housing the Hornstein's generous donation of Old Master paintings. The museum also preserved the failing Romanesque **Erskine and American Church**, turning it into the **Bourgie Hall** *(1339 Sherbrooke)* for live music concerts. The $40 million **Claire and Marc Bourgie Pavilion** displays over 3,000 works of Canadian art, including 500 Inuit sculptures & 180 Amerindian artifacts in one-of-a-kind collection.

Musée des Arts décoratifs de Montréal★ (Montreal Museum of Decorative Arts)

2200 Rue Crescent.
🕙*Admission included in entrance fee*

to Montreal Museum of Fine Arts; same hours and phone number).
Formerly located at Château Dufresne, the international design collections moved in 1997 to exhibit space next to the Museum of Fine Arts: a passageway connects the two museums.

Centre canadien d'architecture★ (Canadian Centre for Architecture)

1920 Rue Baile. ●*Guy-Concordia.* ♿🅿🕐*Open year-round Wed–Sun 11am–6pm (Thu til 9pm).* 🕐*Closed Jan 1 & Dec 25.* 👛*$10 (free for all Thu after 5:30pm.* 📞*514-939-7026. www.cca.qc.ca.*
Designed by Peter Rose & Phyllis Lambert, CCA (1989) is an acclaimed museum and research facility as well as an example of post-Modern design. Forming the core of the building is **Shaughnessy House,** a Second Empire mansion built in 1874. Also open to the public are the Shaughnessy House reception rooms and the delightful **conservatory** and tiny **tea room.**Across Boulevard René-Lévesque is an **architectural garden** by Melvin Charney.

Musée d'art contemporain de Montréal★★ (Museum of Contemporary Art of Montreal)

185 Rue Sainte-Catherine Ouest. ●*Place-des-Arts.* 🕐*Open year-round Tue 11am-6pm, Wed–Fri 11am–9pm, Sat–Sun 10am–6pm. Closed Mon.* ♿🅿🍽 *Guided tours available.* 👛*$15 (half-price Wed 5pm–9pm).* 📞*514-847-6226. www.macm.org.*
Housed in the Place des Arts complex, this museum presents contempary art works across a wide array of materials used and formats, including live and electronic.

Planétarium Rio Tinto Alcan (Montreal Planetarium)

4801 ave. Pierre-De Coubertin. ●*Pie-IX.* ♿🅿🕐*Open daily from 9am with two shows running back-to-back: Continuum, in English at 11:30, noon, 12:30, 2:30, 3, 5:30 & 6pm, and From the Earth to the Stars at 12:30, 3:30 &* 6:30pm. 👛*$19.75, $10.00 (child)* 📞*514-868-3000. http://espacepourlavie.ca.*
Newest member of the Olympic Park **Espace Pour La Vie** (Space for Life) concept, this planetarium joins Biodome, Insectarium & Botanical Gardens in a site attracting guests for days of fun and fascination, action and education.

Grande Bibliothèque de Montréal (Grand Library of Montreal)

475 blvd. De Maisonneuve Est. ●*Berri-UQAM.* ♿🕐*Open Tue–Thu 10am–10pm, Fri–Sun 10am–6pm.* 📞*514-873-1100 or 800-363-9028 (Quebec only). www.banq.qc.ca.*
The new Montreal central library opened in 2005, housing 4 million items. An unusual façade sports green-glass panels on vertical copper supports. The interior has plenty of reading spaces, collections of movies, recordings, and rare documents, and even a **Presse Café** for counter sandwiches, salads, sweets & coffees during library hours.

MONT-ROYAL AND SURROUNDINGS★★

Rising abruptly from an otherwise flat plain, the 233m/764ft Mont-Royal forms part of the Monteregian Hills, a series of eight peaks located between the St. Lawrence and the Appalachians. To the west of Mt. Royal lies the town of **Westmount**, once largely Anglophone and still one of the city's choicest residential areas. On the hill's northern flank is the borough of **Outremont,** home to Montreal's Francophone bourgeoisie.

Parc du Mont-Royal★★ (Mount Royal Park)

Drive up Voie Camillien-Houde or Chemin Remembrance to parking areas or walk from Rue Peel at Ave. des Pins. ●*Mont-Royal.* ✕♿🅿 *($9/day)* 🕐*Open daily 6am–midnight.* 📞*514-843-8240. www.lemontroyal.qc.ca.*
Opened in 1876, the park was designed by American landscape architect **Frederick Law Olmsted**, creator of New York City's Central Park. It covers 470 acres, and reaches 764 feet above sea level.

There are three peaks and three belvederes. **Lac-aux-Castor** (Beaver Lake) is a favourite stopping point for walkers, a popular skating venue in winter, and **($$$) Le Pavillion** (French), together with **($$) Smith House** (Bistro/Café) nearby, offer delicious food, beverages & services throughout the year, and on holidays.

Viewpoints

The terrace fronting **Belvédère du Kondiaronk** (Chalet Lookout) affords a splendid **view★★★** of bustling downtown and the Monteregian Hills. The trail around the summit leads to the **cross**, a 36.6m/120ft metal structure, illuminated at night, commemorating a wooden cross that was once placed here by founder Paul Chomedy, sieur de Maisonneuve.

From popular **Belvédère Camillien -Houde** *(accessible by vehicle on the Voie Camillien-Houde)*, the superb **view★★** of eastern Montreal is dominated by the Olympic Stadium & St.Lawrence River.

Oratoire Saint-Joseph★★ (St. Joseph's Oratory)

Entrance at 3800 Chemin Queen- Mary. ●*Côte-des-Neiges.* ✕♿🅿*$5.* 🕐*Open daily, guided tours at 10am, 1:30pm and 3pm ($5). $3 admission.* ✆*514-733-8211. www.saint-joseph.org. Overnight at Jean XXIII Pavilion $55 per night.* ✆*514-733-8216 ext.2640. Family rooms available.*

The oratory's origin was a small chapel erected in 1904 by Alfred Bessette, known as Brother André, who gained a reputation as a healer.

Today the shrine, with its colossal dimensions and octagonal, copper-clad dome (largest outside Rome), draws a million pilgrims annually. From the wide terrace is an excellent **view** of northern Montreal and the Laurentian Mountains. Within the complex are the **Musée du Frère André** *(same hours as the oratory)* and the **chapelle du Frère André**. The **Stations of the Cross★** are located in a hillside garden.

Boulevard Saint-Laurent

Established in 1672, this artery long formed Montreal's principal passageway, hence its nickname "the Main." During the 19C, Chinese settled in the southern section, giving rise to a lively **Quartier chinois★** (Chinatown) *(at Rue de la Gauchetière)*. Succeeding waves of immigrants & the chic club scene have given the area its reputation for vibrant commercial activity to this day. http://boulevardsaintlaurent.com

Musée des Hospitalières de l'Hôtel-Dieu de Montréal (Hospitallers Museum)

201 Ave. des Pins Ouest. ●*Sherbrooke. Entrance on Ave. des Pins.* ♿🕐*Open mid-Jun–mid-Oct Tue–Fri 10am–5pm, Sat–Sun 1pm–5pm. Rest of the year Wed–Sun 1pm–5pm.* 🕐*Closed Good Friday, Easter Monday & Dec 25–Jan 1.* ☞*$10.* ✆*514-849-2919. www.museedeshospitalieres.qc.ca*

This museum traces the history of the Hospitallers of St. Joseph (religious order devoted to caring for the sick) at Hôtel-Dieu Hospital and their presence in Montreal.

OLYMPIC PARK AREA★★★ Parc Olympique★★ (Olympic Park)

●*Pie-IX, or by car (entrance to the parking lot from 3200 Rue Viau)* 🅿 *($17/ day, $20 during major events at Olympic Stadium). Information desk and ticket office at base of tower.*

Velopousse Maisonneuve: tourist bicycle shuttle tour with 3 pickup points, including Station In Vivo at the Olympic Park. ($20) Family $35. ✆*514-523-2400 ext 234.*

Constructed for the 1976 Olympic Games, this gigantic sports complex includes a stadium, tower and an updated sports centre with six pools, Biodome, Insectarium, Planetarium, Botanical Gardens and Saputo Stadium (MLS Soccer). The **Olympic Village**—two 19-storey towers lodged 11,000 athletes during the Games—now contains a residential and commercial complex. Begun in 1973, the stadium wasn't completed until 1987 and at great cost ($1.2 billion). It is known locally as "The Big Owe."

Olympic Stadium

●Pie-IX. ✗♿✈Visit by guided tour (60min) only, mid-Jun–Labour Day daily. English tours 10am–5pm. Rest of the year 5 bilingual tours daily 11am–3:30pm. ✆Price varies with season. ✆514-252-4141 or 877-997-0919. http://parcolympique.qc.ca.

Immense concrete structure consists of 34 cantilevered ribs crowned by a structural ring and dominated by the world's tallest inclined tower, originally designed with a retractable roof. Hovering at a 45 degree angle above the stadium, the 175m/574ft **tower** has a funicular elevator (🕐open Tue-Sun 9am–8pm; Mon 1–8pm; ✆$23.25). From the observation deck, the **panorama**★★★ extends as far as 80km/50mi, weather permitting.

Biodôme★

✗♿🕐Open daily 9am–5pm, extended hours during summer. 🕐Closed Dec 24–25 & Mon mid-Sept–late Dec. ✆$19.75, $10 (child). ✆514-868-3000. http://espacepourlavie.ca.

Opened in 1992, this museum occupies a **velodrome** constructed as an Olympic cycling venue. Re-created habitats support plants and animals indigenous to a tropical forest, Laurentian forest, the St. Lawrence basin and the Arctic region.

👥 Jardin botanique de Montréal★★ (Montreal Botanical Garden)

4101 Rue Sherbrooke Est. ●Pie-IX. ✗♿🅿 ($10). 🕐Open May 15 to June 22: daily, 9 a.m. to 6 p.m. June 23 to August 31: Sun-Wed, 9am-6 p.m., Thu-Sat, 9am-7pm, Sep 1: 9am-6 pm, Sep 2-Oct 31: daily, 9am- 9 pm, Nov 1-May 14: Tue-Sun, 9am-5pm. ✆ $19.75 (child $10). ✆514-872-1400. http://espacepourlavie.ca.

Founded in 1931, this garden is one of the world's finest horticultural facilities. The Chinese Greenhouse, called the "Jardin céleste," displays a superb **Wu Collection** of penjing, or "landscape in a pot." Opened in 1991, the **Jardin de Chine** (Chinese Garden) is a replica of a typical Ming dynasty (14-17C) garden from southern China. The 2.5ha/6.2 acre **Jardin japonais** (Japanese Garden) and the **Japanese pavilion** include a Zen garden, a tea garden and a collection of **bonsais** (on view seasonally).

Other sections not to be missed include the **Rose Garden,** the **Marsh and Bog Garden**, and **Arboretum** with 10,000 tree specimens. The **Biodiversity Centre**, features a gold standard LEED building for research, collection, and training the next generation of scientists. Near the Rose Garden, **Insectarium** is built in the shape of a giant bug (hours same as Botanical Garden).

Tower of the Olympic Stadium viewed from Parc Maisonneuve

New Dufresne-Nincheri Museum★

2929 av. Jeanne-d'Arc. ●Pie-IX. South corner of Rue Sherbrooke and Blvd. Pie-IX. ♿🕐 Open year-round Wed–Sun 9:30am–5pm. ☎$14. ✆514-259-9201. www.chateaudufresne.com.

Completed in 1918, this 44-room Beaux-Arts mansion evokes lifestyle of Montreal's moneyed class in the 20s and 30s, and now represents the oldest stained glass studio in Quebec with the opening of the Nincheri Studio.

OTHER AREAS OF INTEREST
Île Sainte-Hélène★

Access by car on Jacques-Cartier or Concordia Bridge. ● Jean-Drapeau.

Southeast of Montreal, this beautiful island, which Samuel de Champlain named for his wife, Hélène Boulé, is home to **Biosphère**, North America's only museum of the environment, and the **Stewart Museum**, celebrating Europe in the New World.

Vieux-Fort (Old Fort)

✗🅿🕐 Open Wed–Sun 10am–5pm. ☎$10. Family $20. ✆514-861-6701. www.stewart-museum.org.

Located in the Old Fort, the **Musée David M. Stewart★** presents the history of European settlement in Quebec. A geodesic dome designed by Buckminster Fuller, the **Biosphère★ 🏛**, was constructed as the US pavilion at the 1967 World Fair. (*160 Chemin Tour de l'Île; ✗♿🅿; ✆514-283-5000; http://biosphere.ec.gc.ca).* **Six Flags Park La Ronde 🏛**, Montreal's major amusement park (40 rides), occupies a pleasant site on the north end of the island (*✗♿🅿$10 🕐open Jul–Aug 11am–9pm; call for other hrs; ☎$63.99, $46.99 (child); ✆514-397-2000; www.laronde.com).* The road skirting the island's western edge provides **views★** of Old Montreal, the port installations and the **Cité du Havre** peninsula, which links city to St. Helen's Island via Concordia Bridge (Pont de la Concorde). **Habitat★** a modular apartment complex built for Expo '67, dominates the peninsula.

Île Notre-Dame★ (Notre Dame Island)

Access by car on Concordia Bridge or by free bus service from Jean-Drapeau Métro station on Île Sainte-Hélène.

This artificial island, created in 1959 and enlarged in 1967, contains a Formula 1 racetrack, beach, waterpark and **Floralies gardens, plus venues hosting live music festivals such as Osheaga and Ile Soniq.** *(✗♿🅿🕐open year-round daily 6am–midnight; ✆514-872-6120; www.parcjeandrapeau.com).* The Expo '67 French pavilion houses **Casino de Montréal** (Montreal Casino). http://casinos.lotoquebec.com

Cosmodôme★★

Located in Laval, 12km/7mi north of city, at 2150 Autoroute des Laurentides. From Montreal, take Rte. 15 north (Exit 9) and follow signs. Space Science Centre ✗♿🅿🕐open Jun 24–Labour Day daily 9am–5pm. Rest of the year daily 10am–5pm. Closed Jan 1 & Dec 25. ☎$From $11 for a senior on one mission to $100 for a family on 3. ✆450-978-3600. www.cosmodome.org

Opened in 1994 to promote space science and technology, a replica of the Ariane rocket fronts this ultramodern complex. In the **Space Science Centre**, interactive exhibits, replicas and models, as well as mural panels and videos, introduce visitors to the history and exploration of space. **Space Camp Canada** offers space-oriented educational activities for children and adults *(some programs necessitate overnight stays).*

Sault-au-Récollet

Located 12km/7mi north via Rte. 138 between Christophe-Colombe & Papineau avenues, this area was a portage site for First Nations. Gouin blvd. runs east.

Set on rapids beside Rivière-des-Prairies, Sault-au-Récollet is best known for its **Église de la Visitation-de-la-Bienheureuse-Vierge-Marie★** (Church of the Visitation of the Blessed Virgin Mary), the oldest religious structure on the island. The edifice boasts an elaborate **interior★★**. Of particular interest are the turquoise/gold vault and the **pulpit,** a beautiful piece of liturgical furniture. The neighbourhood itself is charming. Blvd. Gouin is lined with vintage homes.

ADDRESSES

🛏 STAY

$ HI-Montreal Youth Hostel – *1030 Rue Mackay. ℘514-843-3317 or 866-843-3317. www.hostellingmontreal.com. 243 beds.* ✕ This Hosteling International affiliate in downtown Montreal offers a non-smoking environment, kitchen services, a television room, wireless Internet service, a laundromat and washrooms with each room. Private and group rooms available.

$$ Hôtel de l'Institut – *3535 Rue St-Denis. ℘514-282-5111or 800-361-5111 (Canada/U.S.). www.ithq.qc.ca. 42 newly renovated rooms.* ✕&🅿. Occupying the top floors of this designer-friendly structure housing the province's tourism school. This training hotel is where Prince William & Catherine stayed and took culinary workshops, and is a perfect hotel to watch the fireworks on the buildings south facing upper rooms. Delicious onsite dining room (**$$**) overlooking St.Louis Square just north of Sherbrooke St. is a must.

$$$ Auberge de la Fontaine – *1301 Rue Rachel Est. ℘514-597-0166 or 800-597-0597. www.aubergedelafontaine.com. 21 rooms.* &🅿☺. This 19C Victorian mansion sits facing beautiful La Fontaine Park. Colourful contemporary rooms, wireless Internet, access to the kitchen for snacks and beverages, and a breakfast buffet served in the sunny dining room make for a restful stay.

$$$ Château Versailles – *1659 Rue Sherbrooke Ouest. ℘514-933-3611 or 888-933-8111. www.versailleshotels.com. 65 rooms & suites.* ✕&🅿☺. Composed of four interconnected 19C Victorian town houses, this hotel offers excellent service and convenient location at the western edge of downtown. Amenities include complimentary afternoon tea, WiFi, business station, and babysitting.

$$$ Fairmont The Queen Elizabeth – *900 Blvd. René-Lévesque Ouest. ℘514-861-3511 or 866-540-4483. www.fairmont.ca. 982 rooms/91 suites.* ✕&🅿☺. The stately Queen Elizabeth, reopening in June 2017 after major renovations, enjoys a convenient location above Montreal's underground city and VIA RAIL's Gare Centrale train station. Check out the redesign details at: fairmontmontreal.com

$$$$ Hostellerie Pierre du Calvet – *405 Rue Bonsecours. ℘514-282-1725 or 866-544-1725. www.pierreducalvet.ca. 10 rooms.* ✕🅿☺. This 1725 merchant's house sits on a cobblestone street in Old Montreal. Décor is opulent, with ornate antiques and Oriental rugs. Rooms have original stone walls, fireplaces, canopy beds and all amenities. American-style breakfast is served. Dinner is offered nightly in plush **Les Fille du Roy ($$$)** restaurant ℘514-849-3535.

$$$$ Hôtel Place d'Armes – *55 Rue Saint-Jacques Ouest. ℘514-842-1887 or 888-450-1887. www.hotelplacedarmes.com. 135 rooms.* ✕&🅿 Spa ☺. This charming boutique hotel is located on Place d'Armes in the centre of Old Montreal. Rich furnishings and amenities include spacious bathrooms, wireless Internet and rooftop **Terrasse Place D'Armes**. . The restaurant, **Suite 701 ($$$)** offers a very up-market take on Quebec cuisine, while **Kyo Bar Japonais** delights with sushi and more.

$$$$$ Hôtel Le Germain – *2050 Rue Mansfield. ℘514-849-2050 or 877-333-2050. www.hotelgermain.com. 101 rooms.* ✕&🅿. Sumptuous bedding and amenities include wireless Internet, CD players, plush bathrobes and the morning newspaper. Newly renovated, the hotel boasts the famed **($$$) Laurie Raphael** restaurant. The Germain Group's sister hotel **Alt Hotel Griffintown** (*www.althotels.ca*) leads robust redevelopment of this former industrial neighborhood within walking distance of Old Montreal.

🍽 EAT

$ Bagel, Etc – *4320 blvd. St.Lauent ℘514-845-9462. No dinner.* **American**. If you want breakfast up until late afternoon, come to this popular eclectic diner. Bagels, eggs, smoked salmon, bacon, fluffy taters, and blueberry pancakes are the main attractions at this eatery in the on The Main. Great hot sauce collection.

$ Rotisserie Le Chalet BBQ – *℘514-489-7235. 5456 Sherbrooke St.West at Decarie. www.chaletbbq.com.* **BBQ**. Renowned for its simple inexpensive barbequed chicken, this no frills landmark has been

> **BYOW** Restaurants that don't have a liquor license allow patrons to bring your own vintages. Many BYOW *(apportez votre vin)* eateries are located in the Plateau Mont-Royal and Mile End quarters.
>
> **Table d'hôte** These fixed-price meals typically include a three-course menu consisting of a starter, main dish and dessert.

delighting since 1944, and the floor show is worth the visit alone.

$ Eatalie – *18, 45th Avenue, Lachine (waterside near airport).* 514-447-7970. *Open daily 8am to 7pm. www.eatalie.ca.* **Italian**. This neighborhood gem is located near Lakeshore Drive, not far from the airport, on your way into the city. Eating here is like sitting down with your Italian friend's family, where there is always the smell of fresh cooking, someone laughing, and delicacies made with wholesome ingredients. Best pizza on the Island of Montreal leads a menu of Italian soups, sandwiches, lasagna, meatballs, espresso coffee and desserts like fresh cannoli.

$$ Café Saigon – *1280 rue St.André, just south of rue Ste.Catherine Est.* 514-849-0429. *Open daily BYOB.* Asian best-kept secret in town, this family-run lunch/dinner jewel serves amazing Imperial rolls, Tonkinese soups, dreamy good grilled shrimp & scallops, General Tao chicken, and more inexpensive dishes.

$$ Stash Café – *200 Rue Saint-Paul Ouest.* 514-845-6611. *www.stashcafe.com.* **Polish**. Near Place d'Armes, patrons share polished old tables and enjoy savoury dishes such as *bigos* (sauerkraut with sausages and mushrooms) or *plaki* (potato pancakes with apple and sour cream). Try their apple square for dessert.

$$$ Primo & Secondo – *7023 Saint-Dominique.* 514-908-0838. *Open Tue–Sun 5:30pm–10pm.* **Italian**. Located beside the Marché Jean Talon, chef creates magic using freshest ingredients. Classic blackboard lists daily temptations such as grilled milk-fed veal chop served with rosemary potatoes, spinach and roasted red peppers drizzled with white truffle oil.

$$$ Sinclair – *414 Saint-Sulpice, Vieux-Montréal.* 514-284-3332. *www.restaurantsincliar.com.* **Contemporary**. Inside the Hotel Saint-Sulpice, and literally

attached to the Notre-Dame Basilica, this eatery is led by a true master of the culinary arts in a very competitive food city. Boasting the most appealing outdoor patio in Old Montreal, this eatery is famous too for their $25 prix-fixe lunch specials. Discovery Menu leads the offerings.

$$$ Gibby's – *298 Place d'Youville.* 514-282-1837. *www.gibbys.com. Open daily from 5:30pm.* **Steakhouse**. Set in the most historical quarter of the city, this cozy stone building is famous for steaks and seafood. Whether your taste is for grilled rib eye, filet mignon, Arctic char, or rack of lamb, this diningroom delivers consistently.

$$$$ Maison Boulud – *1228 rue Sherbrooke Ouest.* 514-842-4224. *www.ritzmontreal.com.* **French**. Legendary chef Daniel Boulud casts gastronomic spell on diners at this newly renovated structure. This is the original North American Ritz, with a famed garden dining venue. The menu features local and artisanal products celebrated by this 3-star Michelin chef.

AROUND TOWN

$$ Espace La Fontaine: Bistro Culturel – *3933 ave. du Parc Lafontaine.* 514-280-2525. *http://espacelafontaine.com.* To truly connect with Montreal residents; come here for the height of city's typical fresh market cuisine, live music concerts, indoor/outdoor films, workshops, art exhibitions & patio.

$$ Maison Smith – *1250 chemin Remembrance.* ●*Mont-Royal, then Bus #11.* 514-843-8240. *http://www.lemontroyal.qc.ca.* Les Amis de la Montagne (Friends of the Mountain) occupies an original farmhouse as a non-profit dedicated to protecting the city's largest asset. The onsite café/bistro serves homemade gourmet fresh soups, sandwiches, desserts & good coffee. Wonderful terrasse, onsite Mt. Royal exhibition & giftshop.

NIGHTLIFE

New City Gas – *950 rue Ottawa.* 514-879-1166. *http://newcitygas.com.* If you like to dance to the newest sounds, this mammoth supperclub is a must visit. Few clubs can boast a history back to 1839, but this former gasworks brick edifice has been given new life and is winning fans.

CYCLING

BIXI - 514-789-BIXI (2494). *https://montreal.bixi.com.* Public bicycle sharing system ($) operates sites 24/7 in city.

Nunavik★★

Officially recognized in 1988, after creation in 1986 by referendum, as the homeland of Quebec's Inuit population, the province's northernmost region offers the adventurous visitor a unique travel experience. Located on the Ungava Peninsula, this vast territory also encompasses numerous offshore islands and part of the James Bay region to the west. The lack of vegetation is characteristic of regions with harsh climates. In fact, most of the peninsula is under permafrost, reaching 275m/902ft in depth in Nunavik's northernmost areas.

A BIT OF HISTORY

The region's first inhabitants were hunters from Asia who are believed to have crossed the Bering Strait some 4,000 years ago. Today the majority of the Inuit population of 11,000 inhabits 14 coastal villages and has access to schooling and professional training.

VISIT

The largest among the 14 villages, **Kuujjuaq★** is the seat of regional government offices. Located to the west, **Inukjuak** serves as headquarters for the Avataq Cultural Institute, a nonprofit organization devoted to the preservation and development of the Inuit heritage in Nunavik. The northeasternmost villages of **Kangiqsujuaq** and **Salluit** are especially remarkable for their spectacular **sites★★**, surrounded by rugged mountains and jagged cliffs. Located on the western shore, **Puvirnituq** has gained recognition as a centre for Inuit sculpture. Situated on the Hudson Bay, just north of James Bay, **Kuujjuarapik** is home to a sizable number of Cree Indians and to most of Nunavik's non-native population.

A wide sandy beach stretches from the mouth of the Great Whale River to the opposite side of this southernmost village, where high dunes provide good views.

🛈 **Information:** Nunavik Tourism Association, Kuujjuak. ℘888-594-3424. www.nunavik-tourism.com.

▶ **Location:** Nunavik lies north of the 55th parallel, with Hudson Bay to the west, Ungava Bay and the Hudson Strait to the north and Labrador to the east.

😊 **Don't Miss:** Some 50 species of birds nest high on the Ungava Penninsula. There are also polar bears, musk oxen, seals, walruses, whales and great herds of caribou.

🕐 **Timing:** The season in which you visit will determine what you can see.

PRACTICAL INFORMATION
GETTING THERE

The 14 villages lining Nunavik's eastern and western shores are accessible by airplane only. Contact **First Air** (℘800-267-1247; www.firstair.ca), Air Inuit (℘514-905-9418 or 800-361-2965; www.airinuit.com) or **Air Creebec** (℘819-825-8355 or 800-567-6567 www.aircreebec.ca) for schedules and flight information.

ACCOMMODATIONS AND VISITOR INFORMATION

For information on outfitters, accommodations and events, contact: **Nunavik Tourism Association** ℘819 -964-2876 or 888-594-3424. www.nunavik-tourism.com.

SEASONS

In summer, come prepared even for snow: pack long underwear along with insect repellent; snow attire is necessary for the winter season.

Québec★★★

Quebec City

Built atop the Cape Diamant promontory jutting into the St. Lawrence River, Quebec's capital has delighted visitors for centuries with its multitude of historic and religious monuments, fortifications and narrow cobblestone alleys. The distinctive French flavour is enhanced by fine restaurants, outdoor cafes and a lively nightlife. In 1985 the city became the first urban centre in North America to be inscribed as a UNESCO's World Heritage Site.

A BIT OF HISTORY

Birthplace of New France – Long before Jacques Cartier's arrival in 1535, First Nations hunters and fishermen inhabited the area of the village of Stadacona. In 1608 **Samuel de Champlain** constructed a rudimentary wooden fortress, known as the **Habitation.** The first European settlers arrived in Quebec during the 17C. Primarily craftsmen and merchants attracted to the profitable fur trade, they erected houses in the Lower Town, which became the centre of commercial activity. Religious institutions and the colonial administration settled in the Upper Town, within fortifications.

18C and 19C – Quebec City's location atop the 98m/321ft-high Cap Diamant (Cape Diamond) promontory provided the colony with a naturally fortified area. Nevertheless, the French city was repeatedly attacked—first by the Iroquois, then by the British. The Battle of the Plains of Abraham precipitated the British Conquest of 1759.
Following the Treaty of Paris in 1763, Quebec City became capital of the new British dominion. Owing mainly to its busy port activities, the city maintained a competitive position with Montreal until the mid-19C.

Quebec City Today – Since the turn of the 20C, most jobs have been related to public administration, defence and

▶ **Population:** 806, 359.

▸ **Info:** Quebec City Tourism, 399 Rue Saint-Joseph Est. ☏418-641-6290 or 877-783-1608. www.quebecregion.com.

▶ **Location:** Québec City is 255km/158mi northeast of Montreal, on the north bank of the St Lawrence River. It is divided into an Upper Town and Lower Town. The city of Lévis lies on the opposite bank, linked by two bridges as well as ferries.

▣ **Parking:** Municipal lots and street parking throughout the city. In winter, respect snow clearing times: cars will be towed if in the way of snow clearing.

☺ **Don't Miss:** Château Frontenac, "the castle on the cliff" overlooking the St. Lawrence River, is Quebec City's iconic landmark.

⏱ **Timing:** Plan to walk within and below the walls of the city— ☺ but be aware that you'll be climbing or descending stairs frequently.

👥 **Kids:** Fortifications of the Citadel; the Musée du Fort, with its lively Sound and Light show.

the service sector. The growth of the provincial government in the past 25 years has provided the capital city with renewed vitality. Throughout its turbulent history, the city has remained a bastion of French culture in North America. Comprising half the population in 1861, Anglophones have steadily moved away over the past century, giving the city a distinctly Francophone character. The main metropolitan event is the famous winter **Carnival** *(Feb)*, which attracts millions of visitors.

Château Frontenac and the Old Town seen from the St. Lawrence River

©Tony Tremblay/iStockphoto.com

PRACTICAL INFORMATION
GETTING AROUND
BY PUBLIC TRANSPORTATION –
Local **bus** service is provided by
the **Réseau de transport de la
Capitale** (RTQ) (*℘418-627-2511; www.
rtcquebec.ca*). Regular buses operate
from 5:30am–1am. Tickets may be
purchased in local tobacco shops &
newsstands (*$2.95*) or onboard the
bus (*$3.50, exact change required*). Day
passes are also available (*$8.25/day*).
A bus terminal is located in Old
Quebec at Place d'Youville. Several
city buses also leave from the Train &
Bus Station (Gare du Palais).
BY CAR – Rental agencies: Avis
℘418-523-1075. Budget *℘418-692-
3660*. Hertz *℘418-694-1224*. Enterprise
℘418-523-6661.
BY TAXI – Taxi Coop Québec *℘418-
525-5191*. Taxi Québec *℘418-525-8123*.
Taxi Coop Sainte-Foy Sillery *℘418-
653-7777*.

GENERAL INFORMATION
LOCAL PRESS – Daily newspapers:
English – *The Chronicle Telegraph
(North America's oldest newspaper
(1764 (weekly)*. French– *Le Journal de
Québec, Le Soleil*.
ENTERTAINMENT – Consult the free
tourist publications *Québec Scope* and
Voila Quebéc and the weekly cultural
newspaper *Voir* (French*)* or the *Voice
of Quebec (English): www.veq.ca*.
Purchase tickets through each venue
or through **Billetech** *℘418-643-8131
or 877-643-8131; www.billetech.com*.

SPORTS
Hockey: Remparts de Quebéc
(Quebec Major Junior Hockey League)
QMJHL, season Sept–Mar at Centre
Videotron. *℘418-525-1212; www.
remparts.qc.ca*. **Baseball**: Capitales
de Quebéc (Can-Am League) at Stade
Municipal. *℘418-521-2255; www.
capitalesdequebec.com*.

USEFUL NUMBERS
Police–Ambulance–Fire:
911 (Emergencies only)
Health Info 24hr answering service
provided by registered nurses:
418-648-2626.
Brunet Drugstore, *57 Rue Dalhousie
(in Old Port)*: *418-694-1262.*
Canadian Automobile Assn.:
Member services: *800-686-9243.*
Emergency 24hr road service:
800-222-4357. www.caa.ca.
Road conditions: *888-355-0511.*
Weather (24hr/day): *418-648-7766.*

VIEUX-QUÉBEC★★★
HAUTE-VILLE★★★
(UPPER TOWN)

The site of Samuel de Champlain's Fort Saint-Louis (1620) on massive Cap Diamant, the Upper Town retained its administrative and religious vocation for more than two centuries.

It was only during the 19C that elegant residential neighbourhoods evolved along the Rues Saint-Louis, Sainte-Ursule and d'Auteuil, and Avenues Sainte-Geneviève and Saint-Denis. Today the Upper Town is considered the central core of Old Quebec and still functions as the city's administrative centre.

Place d'Armes and Vicinity★★★

Bordered by prestigious buildings and restaurants, this compelling square, once used for military drills and parades, forms the heart of Old Quebec. It is dominated by the city's most prominent landmark, **Château Frontenac★★**. Erected in 1893 by the Canadian Pacific Railway in the distinctive Chateau style, this renowned hotel stands on the site of the former Governor's residence. (*guided tours*). Next to the chateau, the Governors' Garden features the **Wolfe-Montcalm Monument (1** *on map*) (1827), a joint memorial to the two enemies who died in combat.

Located behind the chateau, **Terrasse Dufferin★★★**, a wide wooden boardwalk, is perched 671m/2,200ft above the majestic St. Lawrence, offering breathtaking **views★★** of Lower Town and the river. A **monument (2** *on map*) to Samuel de Champlain marks the northern end of the terrace. At the southern end, a flight of steps ascends to the **Promenade des Gouverneurs★★** (Governors' Walk) (*closed in winter*), precariously suspended along the steep cliff that leads from the terrace to the National Battlefields Park.

In the narrow **Rue du Trésor**, a quaint pedestrian street off Place d'Armes, artists exhibit sketches of city scenes.

Musée du Fort★
(Fort Museum) (M[1]*on map*)

10 rue Sainte-Anne. Open late Mar-early Nov daily 10am–5pm. Rest of the year check website for exact hours. $8 (child under 10 free). 418-692-2175. www.museedufort.com.

This museum features a sound and light presentation (*30min*) that traces the city's military and civil history.

Basilique-cathédrale
Notre-Dame-de-Québec★
(Notre Dame-de-Quebec
Basilica-Cathedral) (B *on map*)

16 Rue de Baude. Open daily. Late Jun–Labour Day Mon–Sat 7:30am–8:30pm, Sun 8:30am–3:45pm. Rest of the year call or go online for hrs. Guided tours available $5. 418-692-2533. www.notre-dame-de-quebec.org.

The original 1674 cathedral was destroyed during the battles of 1759. It was reconstructed between 1768 and 1771 by Quebec's distinguished family of architects, Jean and François Baillargé and in the next generation, Thomas, who designed the 1843 façade. Destroyed by fire in 1922, the church was rebuilt in its original appearance.

The majestic **Hôtel de ville de Québec** (Quebec City Hall) dominates the Place de l'Hôtel de ville across from the basilica. In the square stands a **monument (3** *on map*) to Elzéar Alexandre Taschereau, the first Canadian cardinal. North of the basilica, the **Quartier Latin★** (Latin Quarter) is the oldest residential district in Upper Town, and features the world famous rue de Trésor artist street for original keepsakes and artisan souvenirs. www.ruedutresor.qc.ca.

Séminaire de Québec★★
(Quebec City Seminary)

1, rue des Remparts. ($11/day) Guided tours available in summer. 418-692-3981. www.patrimoine-religieux.com.

Founded in 1663 by Msgr. François de Laval to train priests, this institute of higher learning is the oldest in Canada. In 1852 the seminary was granted a university, Université Laval, which moved to the Sainte-Foy campus in 1950.

The **Vieux-Séminaire** (Old Seminary) comprises three sections arranged around an inner court. The sundial on the façade of the **Procure Wing** dates to 1681. Highlights of the tour include the **Msgr. Olivier Briand Chapel★**, noteworthy for the fine wood panelling on its walls, and the **Congregational Chapel**, featuring a statue of the Virgin Mary crafted by Thomas Baillairgé.

Operated since 1995 as part of the Museum of Civilization, the **Musée de l'Amérique Française★** (Museum of French America) **(M²on map)** presents France's historic, cultural and social heritage in North America *(2 Côte de la Fabrique; ◷open Jun 24–Labour Day daily 9:30am–5pm; rest of the year Tue–Sun 10am–5pm; ⊗$8; ℘418-692-2843; www.mcq.org/en/maf).*

Monastère de l'Hôtel-Dieu de Québec★ (Augustine Monastery)
32 Rue Charlevoix.t855-780-4800
Founded by Augustinian nuns in the 1640s, this monastery is best known for its hospital, the Hôtel-Dieu, which still operates today. The **church** *(◷same hours as museum, below)*, designed by Pierre Émond in 1800, features a Neo-classical façade adorned with a sculpted Ionic portal.

The **Musée des Augustines de l'Hôtel-Dieu de Québec (M³on map)** (Augustine Museum) traces the Augustinian Nuns' history *(♿ ◷open year-round Tue–Sat 10am-6pm, Sun 10am–5pm; ◷closed major holidays; ℘418-692-2492; www.patrimoine-religieux.com).* The museum includes one of the foremost collections of **paintings★** dating back to the time of New France.

Rue Saint-Louis
The 1736 **Maison Maillou★ (C** *on map)* (Maillou House), located next to the Château Frontenac, now houses the Quebec City Chamber of Commerce. The offices of the Consulate General of France occupy the adjacent house, the

Maison Kent (D) (Kent House), dating from the 1830s. Standing at the corner of Rue des Jardins is the 1674 **Maison Jacquet★ (E** *on map)* (Jacquet House). Reputedly the oldest house in Quebec City, it is occupied today by a restaurant specializing in Quebec cuisine.

Monastère des Ursulines★ (Ursuline Monastery)
6 Rue Donnacona.
Founded in 1639 by Madame de la Peltrie and Marie Guyart (Mère Marie-de-l'Incarnation), the monastery has transitioned from the oldest educational institution for young women in North America, to a 65-room wellness retreat, featuring contemporary monastic "cells" or modern ensuite rooms, plus complete packages including meals, massages, and yoga. *℘844-694-1639. www.augustines.ca.*

The **chapel** (1902) is remarkable for its **interior decoration** *(◷open Jun–Oct Tue–Sat 10am–11:30 & 1:30pm–4:30pm, Sun 1pm–5pm; Closed Nov-Jun; ⊗$6, includes admission to Ursuline Museum; ℘418-694-0694).*

The **Musée des Ursulines★★ (M⁴** *on map)* (Ursuline Museum) (#12 rue Donnacona) occupies the site of the house of Madame de la Peltrie, the order's benefactrice, in the 17C *(◷open May–Sep Tue–Sun 10am–5pm, Oct–Apr Tue–Sun 1pm–5pm; ⊗$8; ℘418-694-0694; www.museedesursulines.com).* Reflecting the occupations of the nuns, the collection includes furnishings, paintings, sculptures and **embroideries★**.

Price Building★
65 Rue Sainte-Anne, Québec QC, G1R 3X5
This 16-storey 1930 Art Deco edifice, Quebec City's first skyscraper, was the head office of the Price Brothers, who introduced the pulp and paper industry to the Saguenay region.

Cathédrale anglicane de la Sainte-Trinité★ (Holy Trinity Anglican Cathedral) (F *on map*)
31 Rue des Jardins.
Modelled after London's Church of St. Martin-in-the-Fields, this edifice (1804)

was the first Anglican cathedral built outside the British Isles. King George III provided the funding and sent English oak from the royal forests of Windsor for the pews. In summer, the courtyard is a gathering place for artists.

BASSE-VILLE★★★ (LOWER TOWN)

From Dufferin Terrace, take the steep Frontenac stairway to Lower Town. Follow Côte de la Montagne down the hill to the Casse-Cou stairway on the right descending to Rue du Petit-Champlain. A funicular (cable car) also connects Dufferin Terrace to the Lower Town (○In service daily 7:30am–11:30pm; ✆$2.50; ℘418-692-1132; www.funiculaire-quebec.com).

This narrow stretch of land dominated by Upper Town was the site of Champlain's **Habitation**. As port activities declined in the 1860s, the neighbourhood fell into decay. In 1970 the Quebec government began restoring the area. The archaeological and restoration work continues today. Lined with shops, art galleries, eateries, and a live theatre, the cobblestone pedestrian **Rue du Petit-Champlain★** reflects the quarter's 18C appearance.

A Night at the Capitole

972 Rue Saint-Jean. Box office ℘418-694-4444 or 800-261-9903. www.lecapitole.com. Located near Porte St-Jean, this century-old building houses one of Quebec's most prestigious theatres. With a seating capacity of 1,300, the sumptuous interior lends itself to large-scale productions as well as more intimate concerts. Before or after the show (or even for breakfast), stop in at **Restorante Il Teatro ($$$)** (*℘418-694-9996; www.lecapitole.com*), which serves fine Italian cuisine in a modern setting. In summer the terrace offers a wonderful view of Rue Saint-Jean.

Maison Chevalier★ (Chevalier House)

60, rue du Marché-Champlain. ○*Open Jun 24–Labour Day daily 9:30am–5pm. Closed until June 24, 2017.* ℘*418-646-3167 or 866-710-8031.* ✆*Free admission. www.mcq.org/en/informations/mhc.*

This imposing stone structure is composed of three separate buildings. The west wing was built in 1752 for a wealthy merchant, Jean-Baptiste Chevalier. The house now serves as part of the Museum of Civilization and features exhibits on traditional Quebec architecture and furniture.

Batterie Royale (Royal Battery)

At the end of Rue Sous-le-Fort and Rue Saint-Pierre. ♿○ *Open daily year-round.* ℘*418-646-3167.*

Constructed in 1690, this thick, four-sided earthen rampart was destroyed during French-British fighting in 1759 and gradually buried. Archaeologists unearthed it in 1972. It has been reconstructed and replicas of 18C cannon are positioned in the 11 embrasures.

Bilodeau

20 Rue du Cul-de-Sac. ○*Open throughout the year, call for hrs.* ℘*581-742-6595. https://bilodeaucanada.com*

Since 1997, this family-run artisan shop specializing in all things fur, serves locals and world as a leading furrier, bootmaker, taxidermist, and member of the Economusem network. *http://qc.economusee.com*

Place Royale★★

This important cobblestone square was the hub of the city's economic activity until the mid-19C. Bordered by typical 18C stone houses, the square features a bronze bust of King Louis XIV as its centrepiece, and the beautiful Église Notre-Dame-des-Victoires. The **interpretation centre** offers guided tours of the area (*29, rue Nôtre Dame;* ○*open 24 Jun–Labour Day daily 9:30am–5pm; rest of the year Tue–Sun 10am–5pm;* ✆*$7;* ℘*418-646-3167 or 866-710-8031; www.mcq.org/en/informations/mpr*

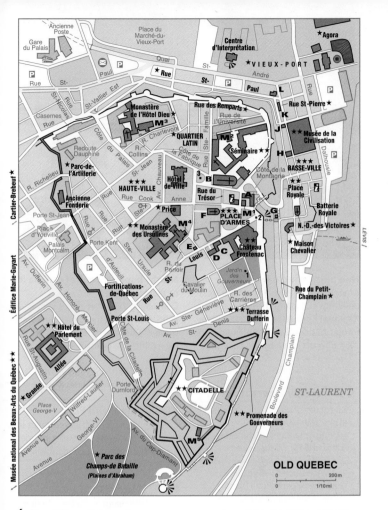

Église Nôtre-Dame-des-Victoires★ (Church of Our Lady of the Victories)

32, rue Sous-le-Fort. ⏱*Open May–mid-Oct daily 9:30am–5pm. Rest of the year Mon–Sat 10am–4pm.* ☎*418-692-1650 & 418-692-2533.*

Completed in 1723, this stone edifice topped by a single spire stands on the site of Champlain's "Habitation." Inside, the magnificent **retable** represents the fortified city.

Musée de la Civilisation★★ (Museum of Civilization)

85 Rue Dalhousie. ✕&🅿⏱*Open Mon-Sun daily 10am–5pm. Closed Dec*

25. ☞*$16.* ☎*418-643-2158 or 866-710-8031. www.mcq.org.*

Designed by **Moshe Safdie**, the museum is housed in two angular buildings crowned by copper roofs and a glass campanile. A monumental staircase links them and leads to a terrace overlooking an inner court and the 1752 **Maison Estèbe** (Estèbe House).

Among the permanent exhibits, **This Is Our Story: First Nations and Inuit in the 21st Century,** documents the history and culture of the First Nations that inhabit Quebec, delving into what it means to be aboriginal in the 21st Century; worldviews, beliefs, & traditions.

Place Royale

© Juliane Martini / Michelin

Rue Saint-Pierre★

Among the noteworthy commercial buildings still lining the street are the **National Bank (H** *on map*) (no. 71); the former **Molson Bank (J** *on map*) (no. 105), now occupied by the post office; and the **Imperial Bank of Canada (K** *on map*) (nos. 113-115).

Dominating the corner of rues Saint-Paul and Saint-Pierre, is the former **Canadian Bank of Commerce (L** *on map*), which exemplifies the Beaux-Arts style.

Rue Saint-Paul★ is renowned for its antique shops, art galleries & inns.

Vieux-Port★ (Old Port)

Created by the federal government in the 1980s, the **Agora★** complex includes an amphitheatre, a wide boardwalk on the river and a marina.

FORTIFICATIONS★★

Much of the charm of Quebec City stems from its city walls. **Lord Dufferin**, governor general of Canada between 1872 and 1878, refurbished the fortified enceinte, rebuilt the gates to the city and cleared the ramparts.

La Citadelle★★ (Citadel)

Entrance at end of Côte de la Citadelle. ♿ 🅿 🚻 *Visit by guided tour (1hr) only May–Sep daily 9am–5pm, Oct–Apr 10am–4pm.* 🎫*$16. Free 2hr outdoor parking & bike racks available.* ℘418-694-2815. www.lacitadelle.qc.ca.

Some areas of the Citadel are off-limits, as it is still a military base for the Royal 22nd Regiment. Erected between 1820 and 1832, this massive fortress is typical

of star-shaped fortifications. Occupying the old powder magazine, the **Musée du Royal 22e Régiment (M⁵ on map)** contains a collection of military objects dating from the 17C to the present.

Lieu historique national des Fortifications-de-Québec (Quebec Fortifications National Historic Site)

2, rue D'Auteil. ♿🕐*Open early May–early Oct daily 10am–5pm. Rest of the year by reservation.* ☞*$3.90.* 📞*418-648-7016 or 888-773-8888. www.pc.gc.ca/fortifications.*

The **interpretation centre** presents the history of Quebec's defence systems. Visitors can stroll south along the ramparts over the **Porte Saint-Louis** (St. Louis Gate) and the Kent and St-Jean gates to Artillery Park.

Site patrimonial Parc-de-l'Artillerie★ (Artillery Park Heritage Site)

The main entrance at 2 Rue d'Auteuil is located near St-Jean gate. ♿🕐*Open May-Oct daily 10am–5pm.* ☞*$3.90.* 📞*418-648-4205 or 888-773-8888. www.pc.gc.ca/artillery. Ask about their "Ambassador" privilege.*

Commemorating three centuries of military, social and industrial life in Quebec City, this huge site includes barracks, a redoubt and an old foundry. Housed in the **old foundry,** the interpretation centre has a remarkable **scale model★★** of Quebec City, produced between 1806 and 1808 by British engineers.

Rue des Remparts★

A pleasant stroll down the street allows visitors to recapture the atmosphere of the old fortified city.

OUTSIDE THE WALLS
Grande Allée★

Departing from the St. Louis Gate and extending southward from Old Quebec, this wide avenue is to the city what the Champs-Élysées is to Paris. Lined with restaurants, bars, outdoor cafes, boutiques and offices, the thoroughfare is an elegant setting for the city's nightlife.

Hôtel du Parlement★★ (Parliament Building)

✕♿🅿🗣 *Guided tour only(30min), Mon–Fri 9am–4:15pm Sat/Sun 10am–4:15pm. Visitors enter via Door No. 3 (corner Grande-Allée & rue Honoré-Mercier).* 📞*418-643-7239 or 866-337-8837. www.assnat.qc.ca.*

Overlooking the Old City, this majestic edifice is the finest example of Second Empire architecture. Note the imposing **façade,** which presents a historic tableau commemorating Quebec history. (**$$**) **Le Parlementaire** serves typical local fare from 8am–2:30pm, such as grilled cheese, French toast and BBQ chicken. Complete meals from $8.t418-643-6640.

Parc des Champs-de-Bataille★ (Battlefields Park)

🕐*Open daily year-round.* 📞*418-648-4071/418-638-3506. www.ccbn-nbc.gc.ca.*

A large section of the park occupies the former **Plains of Abraham**, where the French and British armies fought a major battle (1759) that sealed the fate of the French colony. Don't miss the **Discovery Pavilion of the Plains of Abraham★**, which presents the history of the Plains of Abraham through multi-media displays *(835 Av. Wilfred-Laurier;* ✕♿🅿🕐*open Jul 1–Labour Day daily 8:30am–5:30pm; rest of year til 5pm;* ☞*$15 Includes Martello Tower, Odyssey exhibit, Abraham's Bus tour of grounds;* 📞*418-648-4071; www.ccbn-nbc.gc.ca).*

Musée national des Beaux-Arts du Québec★★ (Quebec Museum of Fine Art)

Entrance is located between the two buildings, on ground level. In Battlefields Park. ✕♿🅿🕐*Open Jun–Labour Day daily 10am–6pm (Wed til 9pm). Rest of year Tue–Sun 10am–5pm (Wed til 9pm).* ☞*$18.* 📞*418-643-2150 or 866-220-2150. www.mnba.qc.ca.*

This three-building complex provides an overview of Quebec art from the 18C to the present. Jean-Paul Riopelle, Jean-Paul Lemieux and other great Quebec artists are represented here.

Observatoire de la Capitale/ Édifice Marie-Guyart (Observatory of the Capital, in the Marie Guyart Building)

1037 Rue de la Chevrotière, 31st floor. ♿⏰*Open Feb–mid-Oct daily 10am–5pm. Rest of the year Tue–Sun 10am–5pm.* ✆*$14.* ☎*418-644-9841 or 888-497-4322. www.observatoirecapitale.org.* The observatory occupying the 31st floor of this administrative building provides a splendid **view**★★ of Old Quebec, plus the spectacular St.Lawrence River Valley and Laurentian Mountain range beyond.

Lieu historique national du Cartier-Brébeuf★ (Cartier-Brébeuf National Historic Site)

175 Rue de l'Espinay. 3km/2mi from St. John Gate by Côte d'Abraham, Rue de la Couronne, Drouin Bridge and 1re Ave. ♿🅿⏰*Open June 24–Labour Day daily 10am–5pm.* ✆*$4.90.* ☎*418-648-7016. www.pc.gc.ca.* This park commemorates **Jacques Cartier**, who wintered on this spot in 1535-36, and **Jean de Brébeuf**, a Jesuit missionary killed by the Iroquois.

EXCURSIONS
Côte de Beaupré★★ (Beaupré Coast)

Bordering the St. Lawrence, this narrow stretch of land extends from Quebec City to Cap Tourmente, site of annual snow geese migration. Drive along Route 360 through charming communities dating from the French Regime.

Parc de la Chute-Montmorency★★ (Montmorency Falls Park)

10km/6mi east of Quebec City. 🏊♿🅿 ⏰*Open year-round daily.* ☎*418-663-2887. www.sepaq.com (click on resorts).* Montmorency River cascades over a high cliff creating falls 83m/272ft high. **Montmorency Manor** (1780) houses a restaurant with a panoramic terrace view. Don't miss their hot bread pudding with maple sugar syrup. (⏰ *May–Oct)* and **Visitor Centre** that presents the

area's heritage (🍴♿🅿⏰*open daily 9am–5pm;* ☎*418-663-3330).* The **upper lookout** conveys the falls' height and force. At **lower lookout**, visitors can approach the falls' base *(rain gear is advised)*. An **aerial tram** returns visitors to upper level (⏰ *Jun–Sep daily 8:30am–7:30pm;* ✆*$11.25, child $5.75;* ☎*418-663-3330; Charlevoix Train* ☎*877-536-2774; http://www.lemassif.com).*

Sainte-Anne-de-Beaupré Shrine★★

Sainte-Anne-de-Beaupré. 35km/22mi east of Quebec City. ♿🅿⏰*Open year-round daily 6:30am, closing hrs vary.* ☎*418-827-3781. www.ssadb.qc.ca.* This imposing, Medieval-style basilica was consecrated in 1934. Divided into five naves separated by huge columns, the interior is lit by 240 **stained-glass windows**. Glimmering **mosaics** adorn the barrel vault above the main nave.

Église Saint-Joachim★★ (St. Joachim Church)

172 Rue de l'Eglise, Saint-Joachim. 40km/25mi northeast of Quebec City. ⏰*Open mid-May–mid-Oct daily 9am–5pm.* ☎*418-827-4020.* The small church (1779) is known for its magnificent **interior,** completed in 1825 by François and Thomas Baillairgé.

Île d'Orléans★★

10km/6mi northeast of Quebec City. Route 368 runs 67km/41mi around this river island with splendid scenery & fine **views**★★ of artisan agricultural community known as the "Breadbasket of Quebec". The village of **Saint-Laurent**★claims the island's only marina. In **Saint-Jean**★, **Manoir Mauvide-Genest**★exemplifies architecture under the French regime *(1451 Chemin Royal;* ♿ 🅿 ⏰*May 14–Oct 15 l0am–5pm;* ✆*$6;* 🍴*entrance w/ guided tour $8;* ☎*418-829-2630; www. manoirmauvidegenest.com).* The community of Sainte-Famille is best known for its tri-steepled **church**★★ (1748), dating from the French Regime.

ADDRESSES

🏨 STAY

$ Auberge internationale de Québec – *19 Rue Ste-Ursule.* ☎418-694-0755 or 888-694-0950. www.cisq.org. *275 beds.* ✕&
Located within the walls of the Old City, this youth hostel is a member of Hostelling International. Open year-round, it offers rooms that accommodate two to 5 people, some with private bathrooms, plus dormitory. The Café Bistrot and kitchen are onsite.

$$ Hôtel Belley – *249 Rue St-Paul.* ☎418-692-1694 or 888-692-1694.www. hotelbelley.com. *8 rooms.* ✕&🅿. Brick walls, exposed beams, original art and a great location in Vieux-Port make for a comfortable and reasonably priced stay. Downstairs is the **Belley Tavern ($)**, which serves salads and sandwiches. The hotel also rents apartments across the street for longer stays.

$$$ Château Bonne Entente – *3400 Chemin Ste-Foy.* ☎418-653-5221 or 800-463-4390. www.lebonneentente.com. *160 rooms including 60 suites.* ✕&🅿 Spa
Occupying a wooded site convenient to both Old Quebec and the airport, this five-star hotel offers stunning gardens with complete amenities of a modern eco-minded resort. Pamper yourself at the Amérispa Health & Beauty Centre, then settle in front of the fireplace in the Tea Room, for tea and petit-fours. Family suites feature bunk beds and toys for the kids.

$$$ L'Hôtel Le Germain Dominion– *126 Rue St-Pierre.* ☎418-692-2224 or 888-833-5253. www.germaindominion.com. *60 rooms.* &🅿⌨. Located in a nine-storey commercial building constructed in 1912 for Dominion Fish and Fruit, Ltd., this boutique hotel sits in the heart of the Old Port district. Stained glass and ironwork highlight the exquisitely decorated lobby and reading room. Natural light floods the spacious, ultramodern guest rooms equipped with goose-down duvets, pillows and bathrobes, and the hidden patio is a wrll-kept local secret. Rate includes a continental breakfast.

$$$ L'Hôtel du Vieux Québec – *1190 Rue St-Jean.* ☎418-692-1850 or 800-361-7787. www.hvq.com. *45 rooms.* ✕&🅿⌨
A good choice for families and student groups, this carefully restored century-old brick hotel in the Latin Quarter boasts lovely rooms with sofas, private baths and mini-refrigerators; some have kitchenettes. Rates include a continental breakfast and pets are accepted from May to October.

$$$$ Auberge Saint-Antoine – *8 Rue St-Antoine.* ☎418-692-2211 or 888-692-2211. www.saint-antoine.com. *95 rooms.* &🅿. A renovated 1822 warehouse and an adjoining 1720s English merchant's house now compose one of the city's finest hotels. Many rooms and suites in this Relais & Châteaux property have the original stone walls and hand-hewn beams, along with amenities such as heated bathroom floors. **Panache ($$$)** located in a vintage maritime warehouse onsite serves French Canadian fare at lunch and dinnertime. Wine cellar boasts 700 listings of wine and champagne.

$$$$ Fairmont Le Château Frontenac – *1 Rue des Carrières.* ☎418-692-3861 or 866-540-4460. www.fairmont.ca. *611 rooms and suites.* ✕&⬈🅿 Spa. The regal 1893 copper-roofed château towers above Old Québec. Queen Elizabeth, Winston Churchill, and the rich and famous have stayed here. New Chateau Boreal Program has hotel planting a tree in guest's name if they forego daily cleaning of room. Amenities include a large gym & indoor pool, babysitting, limo service & WiFi. **Restaurant Champlain ($$$$)** serves French/Quebecois dishes celebrating produce from the *terroir* (region).

$$$$ Hôtel de Glace (Ice Hotel) – *1860 boulevard Valcartier. Open before Christmas–late Mar weather permitting.* ☎418-623-2888 or 877-505-0423.👓 *Tour $18.25.* www.hoteldeglace-canada.com. *44 suites.* ✕⌨. Entirely redesigned for 2017, iconic site fashioned from tons of snow and ice. Cozy sleeping bags nestled on deer pelts keep off the chill. One-night stay includes access to Nordic spa, full-course dinner, breakfast, free parking, plus access to Valcartier Vacation Village. http://valcartier.com

🍴 EAT

$$$ Aux Anciens Canadiens – *34 Rue Saint-Louis.* ☎418-692-1627. www.aux ancienscanadiens.qc.ca. **Québécois**. Situated in a historic white house with red trim (1675), this venerable restaurant offers a delicious introduction to *la cuisine québécoise*. Traditional favourites include pea soup and *tourtière* (meat pie) as well as game and seafood. For dessert, try maple-syrup pie drizzled with cream.

$$ Le Café du Monde – *84 Rue Dalhousie.* ✆*418-692-4455. www.lecafedumonde.com.* **French**. Typical Parisian bistro fare of *steak frites* (steak and French fries), *magret de canard* (breast of duck) and *moules* (mussels), a cozy atmosphere and gregarious waiters in white aprons make for a pleasant dining experience portside.

$$ Paillard – *1097 Rue St-Jean.* ✆*418-692-1221. www.paillard.com.* **Bakery/Diner**. 🕭 No trip here is complete without savouring both the fresh typical bakery goods and specialties served by Yves Simard and his team. Fresh breads, pastries, sandwiches, ice cream, pizzas, & convivial atmosphere.

$$ La Playa – *780 Rue St-Jean.* ✆*418-522-3989.* **International**. Latin, Cajun and Thai flavours pepper La Playa's shrimp, fish and poultry specialties. Try one of the 60 exotic martinis. In summer ask for a table on the terrace.

$$ Portofino Bistro Italiano – *54 Rue Couillard.* ✆*418-692-8888. http://portofino. ca/en.* **Italian**. 🅿. In this 1760 stone home, you can choose from more than 20 varieties of homemade pasta and 30 different wood-fired pizzas,

complimented by a good Italian wine. Or sample specialties such as veal scallopini and rack of Quebec lamb. The atmosphere is exuberant, with nightly musicians.

$$ Bistro Les Bossus – *620 blvd. St.Joseph Est.* ✆*418-522-5501. www.lesbossus.com. Serves breakfast/ lunch/dinner.* **Contemporary**. Brick backdrop enlivens black and white tiles, long counter, and designer globe-lit banquettes. Great atmosphere gets better with *confit de canard, burger portobello, great soups & truffes maison.*

$$$ Le Continental – *26 Rue St-Louis.* ✆*418-694-9995. www.restaurantle continental.com.* **Contemporary**. 🕭 One of the oldest restaurants in the city, this local favourite near Château Frontenac serves classic specialties such as rack of lamb and duckling *à l'orange* as well as seafood and steak. Dark blue walls and wood panelling impart a simple elegance to the dining room.

$$$$ Le Saint-Amour – *48 Rue Sainte-Ursule.* ✆*418-694-0667. www. saint-amour.com.* **Québécois**. Dine in casual elegance in the tile-floored Winter Garden, the Saint-Amour's cheery atrium. *Foie gras de canard du Québec* (Quebec duck foie gras), *saisie de caribou des Inuits aux baies de genièvre* (caribou steak with juniper berries) and *crème brûlée à la mure* (blackberry crème brûlée) typify the traditional cuisine crafted with a nouvelle twist by chef Jean-Luc Boulay. Treat yourself to the nine-course *menu découverte,* with accompanying wines.

SHOPPING

Lambert & Co. – *1 Rue des Carrières.* ✆*418-694-2151.* This diminutive boutique inside the Fairmont Le Château Frontenac Hotel sells cold-weather necessities. Woolen stockings, plus soaps, maple products, and smoked-salmon pâté prepared onsite.

Boutique des Métiers d'Art – *29 Rue Notre-Dame.* ✆*418-694-0267.* Specializing in Quebec artisans, features a broad selection of art objects incorporating an enormous variety of materials. At the rear of the gallery you'll find lovely glass sculptures, ceramics, and leaded-glass windows in vibrant colours.

© R. Chiasson/All Canada Photos/Getty Images

Rue du Petit-Champlain

Vallée du Richelieu★★

Some 130km/81mi long, the majestic Richelieu River flows north from its source in Lake Champlain (New York) to join the St. Lawrence at Sorel. The region remains one of the richest agricultural areas in the province. A popular weekend retreat for Montrealers, the valley attracts legions of tourists every summer, winter, spring and fall.

A BIT OF HISTORY

Samuel de Champlain discovered the waterway in 1609; it was named later for **Cardinal Richelieu,** chief minister of Louis XIII. The river served as an invasion route and was heavily fortified during the French regime. The forts at Chambly, Saint-Jean-sur-Richelieu, Lennox and Lacolle were built initially to protect Montreal against attacks by Iroquois, and later by British and American troops. To facilitate transportation between the US and Quebec, an extensive canal system was built along the Richelieu River in the mid-19C.

SIGHTS
Chambly★

30km/19mi from Montreal by Rte. 10.
A pleasant walk along the river in this residential suburb of Montreal leads past the canal and Fort Chambly to **Rue Richelieu★,** lined with sumptuous 19C residences.

Lieu historique national du Fort-Chambly★★ (Fort Chambly National Historic Site)

2 Rue de Richelieu. Beside the river. ♿🅿
🕐 *Open mid-May–June 20 & Sep 3–Oct 13 Wed–Sun 10am–5pm, Jun 21–Sep 1 daily 10am–5pm.* 🎫*$5.65.* 📞*450-658-1585 or 888-773-8888. www.pc.gc.ca.*
Located in a magnificent park on the Chambly Basin, this fort, erected between 1709 and 1711, is the only remaining fortified complex in Quebec dating back to the French Regime. The fort is laid out in a square with bastions

- 🕐 **Michelin Map:** p313.
- ℹ **Info:** Quebec Tourism/ Montérégie Region. 📞514-873-2015 or 877-266-5687. www.quebecoriginal. com or www.tourisme-monteregie.qc.ca.
- ◖ **Location:** The valley of the Richelieu lies between Montreal and New York state. Many small towns here have tourism kiosks.
- ◈ **Don't Miss:** In summer, colourful hot air balloons often drift through the sky.
- 🕐 **Timing:** In the autumn, the valley is famed for its apples and its icewine, made from grapes frozen on the vine.
- 👪 **Kids:** Go to Safari Park to see exotic animals up close.

at each corner. A **visitor centre** explains the history of the fort and the restoration project. Located near the fort, the 1814 **guard house** *(corps de garde)* exemplifies the Palladian style adopted by the military throughout the British colonies. The small fieldstone **St. Stephen's Church**, built in 1820, served as the garrison's place of worship.

Fort Chambly National Historic Site

© MikeyGen73/iStockphoto.com

Centre de la nature du mont Saint-Hilaire★★ (Mt. Saint-Hilaire Nature Centre)

23km/14mi north of Chambly. 422 Chemin des Moulins, Mont-Saint-Hilaire. ✕♿🕐*Open year-round daily 8am–1hr before dusk.* ✇*$6.* ☎*450-467-1755. www.centrenature.qc.ca.*

Rising abruptly above the valley, Mt. Saint-Hilaire (411m/1,348ft) is the most imposing of the Monteregian Hills. Several trails (hiking, snowshoeing and cross-country skiing) crisscross the lush forests and lead to the summit, which affords sweeping **views★★** of the Richelieu Valley. The **Visitor Centre** explains the topography of the region (🕐*open Mar–Oct daily 9am–5pm; rest of the year daily 8:15am–4:15pm).*

Saint-Denis-sur-Richelieu★

33km/20mi north of nature centre.

This agricultural community was the site of a Patriot victory in 1837. At the **Maison Nationale des Patriotes★** (Patriots' National House) displays and an audiovisual presentation *(23min)* explain *(in French only)* the background of the uprising *(610 Chemin des Patriotes;* ♿🅿🕐*open May–Sept Tue–Sun 11am–6pm, Oct–Dec 23 Wed–Sun 1pm–5pm, reservations other times;* ✇*$8;* ☎*450-787-3623; www.mndp.qc.ca).*

Saint-Jean-sur-Richelieu

40km/25mi southeast of Montreal by Rtes. 10 and 35.

Known today for its mid-August annual **Hot Air Balloon Festival** (www.ballooncanada.com) and manufacturing centre for pottery and ceramics, this city once formed part of the chain of fortifications erected by the French along the Richelieu River. The **Musée du Fort Saint-Jean** (Fort Saint-Jean Museum) contains a collection of weapons, uniforms and other military artifacts *(15 Rue Jacques-Cartier Nord;* ♿🕐*call to reserve visit;* ✇*$4;* ☎*450-358-6500, ext. 5769; www.museedufortsaintjean.ca).* After seeing the museum, visitors can tour the remains of the old ramparts on the grounds.

Île-aux-Noix

48km/30mi south of Montreal by Rtes. 10, 35 and 223.

Situated near the US border, this 85ha/210 acre island was fortified by the French in 1759 and captured by the British the following year. The island is now preserved as a National Historic Site.

Lieu historique national du Fort-Lennox★ (Fort Lennox National Historic Site)

1 Av. 61. ✕♿🅿🕐*Open Jun–Labour Day daily 10am–6pm (til mid-Jun weekdays 5pm). Mid-May–late May & rest of Sept–mid-Oct Sat–Sun 10am–6pm.* ✇*$7.80 (ferry & visit of fort).* ☎*450-291-5700 or 888-773-8888. www.pc.gc.ca.*

Erected in the 1820s, this bastion-type fortress occupies a pleasant **site** overlooking the Richelieu River. The Neoclassical stone buildings have been restored to re-create life on a British army base in the mid-19C.

👥 Parc Safari★★ (Safari Park)

63km/39mi south of Montreal by Rtes. 15 and 202. ✕♿🅿🕐 *Open late Jun–late Aug daily 10am–7pm.* ✇*$40 (child $22).* ☎*450-247-2727. www.parcsafari.com.*

This zoological park is renowned for its animals roaming freely in large enclosures. Required to remain in their vehicles, visitors can follow the **Car Safari** *(4km/2.5mi)* while taking photos, or ride the **Expedition Express** ($20) to save possible damage on your car from the animals. Highlights include The Labyrinth, an interactive maze for everyone. Rides on elephants or ponies and a petting zoo complete the visit.

Fjord du Saguenay★★★

Located at the southern tip of the Saguenay region, the immense, saucer-shaped Lake Saint-Jean empties into the Saguenay River. Measuring 155km/96mi in length, this river flows into the southernmost fjord in the world, the majestic Saguenay Fjord, which discharges its waters into the St. Lawrence. The region is famous for the landlocked salmon known as **ouananiche**; the wild **blueberries**, or bleuets, found on the north shore of the lake; and the famous nine-day **International Swim Marathon** held in July. The spectacular, natural **Parc du Saguenay★★** (Saguenay Park) has been created to preserve part of the shoreline (*91 Notre-Dame, Rivière-Éternité;* ✗ 🅿 🕐 *open daily year-round,* 👁 *$8.50;* ✆ *418-272-1556 or 800-665-6527; www.sepaq.com).*

🚻 **Michelin Map:** pp306-307.

🚹 **Info:** Regional Tourism Association, 412 Boul. Saguenay E, Office 100, Chicoutimi. ✆418-543-9778 or 877-253-8387. www.saguenaylacsaintjean.ca

▶ **Location:** The Saguenay extends from Lac Saint-Jean past the towns of Alma, Jonquière, and Saguenay, to enter the St. Lawrence River at Tadoussac/Baie Ste-Catherine at the north edge of the Charlevoix region.

👁 **Don't Miss:** The fjords of the Saguenay and whales of the St. Lawrence at Tadoussac are best seen by cruises. There are several operators in the Tadoussac area.

🕐 **Timing:** The ideal wildlife viewing time is dusk or dawn.

👫 **Kids:** The zoo at St. Felicien.

A BIT OF HISTORY

The Lake Saint-Jean area remained unsettled until the mid-19C, when the first sawmills were built and the rivers were harnessed for electricity. Hydro-electric power plants, pulp mills and aluminum smelters still line the shores of the lake and the Upper Saguenay. Beyond Saint-Fulgence, the deep river channel was gouged out of Precambrian rock by glaciers in the last Ice Age. Lined by rocky cliffs, the channel is 1,500m/4,920ft wide in places, with an average depth of 240m/787ft. The untamed beauty of the southern section has attracted visitors for years. Most choose to take a scenic river cruise, but the fjord can also be enjoyed by exploring the villages along its shores.

Fjord du Saguenay

© Picavet/Photolibrary/Getty Images

SAGUENAY FJORD★★★
Tadoussac★★

*220km/136mi northeast of Quebec City
by Rtes. 40 and 138.*

The oldest trading post in North America occupies a magnificent **site** at the mouth of the Saguenay on the cliffs and dunes lining the St. Lawrence River.

Founded in 1540 by Basque fishermen, in 1600 Pierre Chauvin built Canada's first fur-trading post here. Settlers moved into the area in the mid-19C, and the community developed into a vacation spot.

Today Tadoussac's main attractions are whales that swim up the St. Lawrence to the mouth of the Saguenay .

The village is dominated by the red roofs of the **Hotel Tadoussac** (1941). Facing the hotel, a boardwalk extends along the river, connecting a reconstruction of Chauvin's trading post and a tiny Indian chapel (1747). A short walk to the wharf affords fine views of the area.

Sainte-Rose-du-Nord

94km/58mi inland from Tadoussac on north shore of Saguenay River.

Founded in 1838, this charming village occupies an exceptional **site★★** in a cove nestled between two rocky escarpments. The small **nature museum** contains a collection of nature's oddities *(199 Rue de la Montagne;* ◐*daily 9am–9pm* ☞*$5;* ✆*418-675-2348; www. ste-rosedunord.qc.ca.*

Saguenay★

200km/124mi north of Quebec City by Rte 175.

The former town of Chicoutimi has, since 2002, been a borough of the town of Saguenay; the other boroughs are Jonquière and La Baie. Meaning "to the edge of deep waters" in the local Montagnais language, Chicoutimi has long been considered the point at where the river becomes a spectacular fjord.

La Pulperie★
(Regional Museum)

300 Rue Dubuc, Chicoutimi. ♿◐*Open Jun 24–early-Sept daily 9am–6pm (last entry 5pm). Rest of the year Wed–Sun*

10am–4pm. ◐*Closed Jan 1 & Dec 24-25 & 31.* ☞*$14.50.* ✆*418-698-3100 or 877-998-3100. www.pulperie.com.*

This former pulp and paper mill (1896) was one of the most important industrial complexes in Quebec in the early 20C. The former workshop has been converted into an **interpretation centre** that features an audio-visual presentation on the mill and the lumber industry in general (plus audio guides for trails nearby). In Building 1921 of the pulp mill, the **Maison Arthur-Villeneuve** (Arthur Villeneuve House) was the home of painter Arthur Villeneuve (1905-90), who worked as a barber while painting in his spare time.

The simple dwelling was relocated to this site, and is decorated with his colourful (and sometimes terrifying) murals.

LAC SAINT-JEAN★★
Péribonka

270km/167mi north of Quebec City by Rtes. 175 and 169.

After spending a few months in this community in 1912, the French author Louis Hémon (1880-1913) wrote his well-known novel *Maria Chapdelaine, récit du Canada français*. Informative exhibits at the **Musée Louis-Hémon★** (Louis Hémon Museum) trace the life and work of the author *(700 Rte. Maria-Chapdelaine, Peribonka;* ♿◐ *open Jun 24– Labour Day daily 9am–5pm; rest of the year Mon–Fri 9am–4pm;* ☞*$8;* ✆*418-374-2177. www.museelh.ca).*

Saint-Félicien

67km/42mi west of Péribonka by Rte169.

Located on the western shore of the lake, this agricultural community is known for its **Zoo Sauvage (wild zoo)** ★★ ▲▲ *(6km/4mi at 2230 Blvd. du Jardin;* ✗♿🅿️◐ *open Jun–Aug 9am–6pm, mid-Jul–mid-Aug til 8pm, May & Sept–Oct daily 9am–5pm;* ☞*$53.49 (includes Anima Lumina one-hour nightime light experience);* ✆*418-679-0543 or 800-667-5687; www.zoosauvage.org).*

A train takes visitors through the zoo, allowing them to admire a variety of animals roaming in natural sur-

Scenic Cruises★★

Tadoussac – *Depart Jun–Oct daily 9:45am from Tadoussac pier to Baie-Éternité in the Saguenay Fjord. Round-trip 3hrs. Reservations advised.* ✕ ♿ 🅿 ⛴$69.95. *Croisières AML ☏855-351-3289or 866-856-6668; www.croisieresaml.com.*
A boat trip is the most spectacular way to see the fjord. Éternité Bay is a cove dominated by twin cliffs Cap Éternité and Cap Trinité. Rising some 518m/1,700ft, **Cap Trinité★★** holds a statue of the Virgin Mary 180m/590ft above the water.

Saguenay – *Depart Jul–Sept daily from dock in Chicoutimi at 9am return 5pm by bus. Several cruises offered downriver towards Sainte-Rose-du-Nord. Reservations required.* ✕ 🅿 ⛴$77. *Croisières du Fjord Saguenay. ☏418-543-7630 or 800-363-7248. www.croisieremarjolaine.com.* On the return trip, the views of Ha! Ha! Bay and of the city itself are equally magnificent.

Whale-watching Cruises★★

Tadoussac – *Depart from Tadoussac marina Jun–mid-Sept daily 9:45am & 1pm (& 4:15pm summer). Rest of the year, call for hours. Round-trip 3hrs. Reservations required.* ✕ ♿ 🅿 ⛴$69. *Croisières AML. ☏418-692-1159 or 800-563-4643. www.croisieresaml.com.*

Les ecumers de St.Laurent offers cruises daily from Les Escoumin at 7:30am (10% discount), 9:30am, 12:00, 2:30pm, 5pm and on request. $48 (children under 14 $37. ☏418-233-2141 or 1-888-817-9999.

At Tadoussac the St. Lawrence is some 10km/6mi wide. The most common species sighted on cruises are the **fin, minke** and **beluga** (white whales) and occasionally, a **humpback** or even the huge **blue whale**.

roundings. Of particular interest is the **Nature Trails Park★★**, inhabited by some 950 animals native to Canada.

Roberval
25km/15mi south by Rte 169.
Located on the southwestern shore of Lake Saint-Jean, this community is today an important service centre for the area. It is also the finish point of the annual International Swim Marathon.

Musée Amérindien de Mashteuiatsh (Native Museum of Mashteuiatsh)
9km/6mi north of Roberval by Blvd. Saint-Joseph. 1787 Rue Amishk, Mashteuiatsh (Pointe-Bleue). ♿🕐*Open mid-May–mid-Oct daily 9am–6pm (til 7pm early Jul–late Aug Wed–Sat. Rest of the year Mon–Fri 8am–4pm.* ⛴*$10. ☏418-275-4842 or 888-875-4842. www.museeilnu.ca.*
Located in Mashteuiatsh, a First Nations site created in 1856, this museum traces the history of the Montagnais. A small shop offers handicrafts created in the area.

Val-Jalbert Historic Village★
9km/6mi south of Roberval by Rte. 169. The village can be visited on foot or by tram. ✕♿🅿🕐*Open mid-Jun–mid-Aug 9am–6pm, mid-Aug–mid-Oct 10am–5pm.* ⛴*$23.48. ☏418-275-3132 or 888-675-3132. www.valjalbert.com.*
Today a ghost town, Val-Jalbert was once the site of a thriving pulp mill built in 1902. By the late 1920s, stiff competition led to the mill's closing and the village gradually fell into ruins. Some older homes have been renovated, and are available to visitors as rental units year-round. The **Vieux Moulin** (Old Mill), standing on the Ouiatchouan River, now contains an exhibit on the mill's operation. A steep stairway *(400 steps; cable car ascent* ⛴ *$3)* leads to the top of an impressive waterfall on the Ouiatchouan River. From this vantage point, the **view★★** encompasses Lake Saint-Jean and the surrounding area.

Trois-Rivières★★

Capital of the Mauricie Region, this industrial centre is located on the north shore of the St. Lawrence River at the mouth of the Saint-Maurice. Just before joining the St. Lawrence, the Saint-Maurice River branches around two islands, creating the three "rivers" for which the city is named.

A BIT OF HISTORY

Sent by Champlain, **Sieur de Laviolette** established a fur-trading post here in 1634. Home to many great explorers, including Pierre Radisson, Sieur des Groseilliers and Sieur de la Vérendrye, the city flourished. In the 1850s a thriving pulp and paper industry took root in the area.

By the 1930s Trois-Rivières was the world capital for the production of newsprint, a distinction it holds to this day. This bustling city is also the location of a University of Quebec campus.

SIGHTS
Rue des Ursulines★

This charming street is lined with some of the oldest structures of the city, which survived a fire in 1908.

Distinguished by a gracious dome and large wall sundial, the **Monastère des Ursulines** (Ursuline Monastery) is the jewel of Trois-Rivières' old quarter. Inside, the **museum** features fine collections of ceramics, silver, books and furniture *(734 Rue des Ursulines; ⏱open May–Nov Tue–Sun 10am–5pm, late-Jun–Labour Day daily10am–5pm, Mar–Apr Wed–Sun 1pm–5pm. ∞$5; ✆819-375-7922; www.musee-ursulines. qc.ca)*. Other buildings of interest on this street include St. James' Church, erected in 1742 by the Récollet Brothers, and the Gannes and Hertel de la Fresnière Houses.

Parc Portuaire★ (Waterfront Park)

This attractive tr--level terrace affords superb **views** of the river and Laviolette Bridge, erected in 1967. At the eastern

- ▶ **Population:** 141,529.
- ⚐ **Michelin Map:** p 313.
- 🛈 **Info:** Office de Tourisme et des Congrès, 1457 Rue Notre-Dame Centre. ✆819-375-1122 or 800-313-1123. www.tourisme troisrivières.com.
- ▷ **Location:** Trois-Rivières lies about half-way between Montreal and Quebec City on Hwy 40. The town of Nicolet is on the south shore.
- 🅿 **Parking:** The city now has computerized parking meters (⚐see Montreal). The cost is $1/hr 9:30am–5pm Mon–Wed and to 9pm Thu-Fri. Sat–Sun are free.
- ⊛ **Don't Miss:** The Quebec Museum of Popular Culture has fascinating and unexpected exhibits about the province's French and First Nations culture.
- ⏱ **Timing:** A river cruise offers a look at both nature and the industrial development along the shores.
- 👪 **Kids:** The Forges du Saint-Maurice Ironworks.

end of the park, a monument commemorates Sieur de la Vérendrye, the first European to reach the Rockies. At the **Borealis Centre**, displays an introduction to the dominant pulp & paper industry here. (200, ave. des Draveurs; ✕⚐⏱open daily 10am–6pm, Wed-Sat 10am-8pm; winter 10am-5pm∞$13.25; ✆819-372-4633. www.borealis3r.ca) 5S Passage stimulates the five senses: hearing, smell, taste, touch and sight. Through three stations, we offer you an experience that perfectly combines modern technology and ancient artefacts Onsite dining at Aux Confluents is known as "Most beautiful terrace between Montreal and Quebec City, overlooking the St.Lawrence River and St.Maurice River.

Musée québécois de culture populaire★ (Quebec Museum of Popular Culture)

200 Rue Laviollette. At the intersection with Rue Hart. ✕&⟲*Open Jun 24–Labour Day daily 10am–6pm. Rest of the year Tue–Sun 10am–4pm. Closed Jan 1–2 & Dec 24–26 & 31.* ✆*$13.* ✆*819-372-0406. www.culturepop.qc.ca.*

This museum offers an excellent look at Quebec culture. Exhibits display selections from a permanent ethnography collection of more than 80,000 objects and an archaeological collection of more than 20,000 artifacts of Amerindian and European cultures.

Adjoining the museum is the **Vieille Prison** (Old Jail Museum), an imposing stone structure completed in 1822 and closed in 1986. The building houses an interpretation centre.

EXCURSIONS

Cap-de-la-Madeleine (Our Lady of the Cape Shrine)★★

5km/3mi east of Trois-Rivières by Rtes. 40 and 755 (Exit 10). 626 Rue Notre-Dame Est. &⟲*Open May–mid-Oct daily 7am–8pm (mid-Aug 10pm). Rest of the year daily 8am–7pm.* ✆*819-374-2441. www.sanctuaire-ndc.ca.*

In the mid-19C Father Luc Désilets decided his growing congregation needed a new church to replace the one built on this site in 1717. The priest vowed to preserve the existing church in exchange for a miracle. In March 1879, ice appeared on the river, remaining just long enough for parishioners to take the stones across.

The imposing octagonal basilica is adorned with magnificent **stained-glass windows** designed in the Medieval style by Dutch oblate father Jan Tillemans. Set in attractive grounds beside the basilica, the original stone church now serves as a votive chapel. The miraculous statue stands above the altar.

Mauricie Region★

Surrounding the valley of the Saint-Maurice River, this region is stocked with industrialized forestry operations. Hugging the river, the drive along Route 155

affords **views★** of the river and the rocky cliffs lining its sides. Located northwest of Grand-Mère, the **Parc national de la Mauricie★★** (Mauricie National Park) offers a landscape of dense forests interspersed with lakes and rivers (✕&⟲*open year-round but southeast sector only in winter; check website;* ✆*$7.80;* ✆*819-538-3232 or 888-773-8888; www.pc.gc.ca).*

Lieu historique national des Forges-du-Saint-Maurice★★ (Les Forges-du-Saint-Maurice Ironworks National Historic Site)

13km/8mi from Trois-Rivières by Blvd. des Forges. 1000 Boul des Forges. &☐⟲*Open Jun 21–Labour Day daily 10am–5pm.* ✆*$3.90.* ✆*819-378-5116 or 888-773-8888. www.pc.gc.ca.*

Established in 1729, these ironworks produced stoves, guns, ploughshares and dumbbells until 1883, when the iron ore and wood of the region were depleted. At the **blast furnace** *(haut fourneau),* displays explain the smelting process. Beside the river a spring known as **Fontaine du Diable** (Devil's Fountain) is a source of natural gas.

Battered by the Atlantic Ocean on one side and washed by the calmer Gulf of St. Lawrence on the other, Canada's four Atlantic seacoast provinces (New Brunswick, Nova Scotia, Prince Edward Island, and Newfoundland and Labrador)—also known as Atlantic Canada—lie on the eastern side of the continent. They share the pervasive influence of the sea, which has molded, in great measure, their economic, political and cultural development.

ⓘ Info: Atlantic provinces and major cities have a tourist office. Contact information at the head of each section.

▶ Location: New Brunswick, Prince Edward Island and Nova Scotia, accessible by car, either by land or over bridges. Newfoundland can be reached only by air or ferry, while remote Labrador, while part of the mainland, is only accessed by air or boat.

◉ Don't Miss: Whales & birds are abundant here.

◷ Timing: Two weeks is barely enough to see the major sights.

👥 Kids: Prince Edward Island's northern shores and southern Northumberland Strait feature beaches, safe swimming, dunes & more.

Geography

Landscape – Parts of the region, notably northern New Brunswick and Cape Breton Island, are hilly, lying near the end of the **Appalachian Mountain** chain. In the western part of Newfoundland, the **Long Range Mountains** (average height 610m/2,000ft) are part of this chain. Barren and rocky by the sea while densely forested inland, the landmasses possess some fertile areas—the Saint John River Valley, the Annapolis Valley and Prince Edward Island. Their indented coastlines are studded with bays, inlets, cliffs and coves. The **Bay of Fundy** produces a phenomenal tidal bore. The highest recorded tide in the world occurred at **Burncoat Head** on the Nova Scotia shore: a difference of 16.6m/54ft between high and low tides.

Climate – The sea largely determines the climate of this region. Moving south down the Atlantic coast, the cold **Labrador Current** enters the Gulf of St. Lawrence by the Strait of Belle Isle. Meeting warmer air currents moving in off the continent to the west, the cold waters of the current cause regular fogs along both Newfoundland and Nova Scotia coasts.

Winters are stormy along the Atlantic but milder than inland. Summers are cooler and less humid than in Ontario and Quebec at the same latitude. The coast is cooler than inland.

In general, precipitation is evenly distributed throughout the year. Snow falls in all the provinces, but is heaviest in northwestern New Brunswick. Labrador experiences a more severe climate with more extreme temperatures but less precipitation.

Population – Almost 2.3 million people live in the Atlantic provinces, with Nova Scotia the most populous (942,926), followed by New Brunswick (753,171). Prince Edward Island has the lowest population (146,400). The most homogeneous of any province, Newfoundland and Labrador sustains a population of 527,800 with 98 percent declaring English as their mother tongue. The French-speaking minority (largely Acadians) is concentrated on Prince Edward Island (17 percent of the population) New Brunswick (33 percent). Nearly 30 percent of Nova Scotia's population is of Scottish origin. The Mi'kmaq are the most populous of the First Nations in Newfoundland, New Brunswick and Nova Scotia. Inuit and Montagnais-Naskapi Indians are found primarily in Northern Labrador. Less than 1 percent of the region's inhabitants, the African-Canadian population is concentrated primarily in the towns within Nova Scotia and New Brunswick.

A Bit of History

First Nations Cultures – Before the arrival of Europeans, the Atlantic provinces were inhabited by First Nations Peoples of the **Eastern Woodlands** culture: **Mi'kmaq** in New Brunswick, Nova Scotia and Prince Edward Island lived by hunting and fishing; **Maliseets** cultivated the land in southern New Brunswick like their Iroquoian brothers in Ontario; and the **Beothuk** in Newfoundland also fished and hunted. The Beothuk's belief that all goods were held in common increased hostilities with the early European fishermen who frequently found their supplies missing. Mass murder and European diseases diminished these people greatly. The last known surviving Beothuk died in St. John's in 1829.

The First Europeans – Although he is credited as the first European arrival, **John Cabot** (1450-98)—an Italian navigator on a 1497 voyage of discovery for England's Henry VII—was not the first European to set foot in the region. Archaeological remains prove that the Norse settled on the Newfoundland coast about the year 1000. There is reason to believe the **Irish** reached the province's shore in the 6C, and it is possible that **Basques** fished the North Atlantic as early as the 15C. At Red Bay in Labrador, archaeologists have discovered the presence of a large 16C Basque whaling port. Cabot's importance lies in his publicizing the region's rich fisheries. The Basques, English, French, Portuguese and Spanish came for the cod, abundant off Newfoundland's Grand Banks. By the end of the 16C, English fishermen established small colonies along the coasts.

In 1583 Newfoundland was proclaimed the territory of Elizabeth I at St. John's. **Jacques Cartier** had claimed Prince Edward Island for France in 1534, renaming it Île-St.-Jean. Pierre Du Gua

Fortress of Louisbourg, Nova Scotia

© Ron Watts/age fotostock

de Monts and Samuel de Champlain established **Port Royal** in Nova Scotia in 1605.

"New Scotland" – In 1621 James I granted present-day Nova Scotia, Prince Edward Island and New Brunswick to **Sir William Alexander** to establish a "New Scotland" there (both men were Scots)—hence the Latin name *Nova Scotia* used on the original charter. In 1632 Charles I returned the region to the French.

"l'Acadie" (Acadia) was what the French called a vague area covering much of Nova Scotia, Prince Edward Island, New Brunswick and Maine. The Acadians are descendants mainly of 17C French colonists.

British Regime – The English Crown granted a few charters in the 17C for colonies on Newfoundland, but authority for local law and order, granted in 1634 by Charles I, belonged largely to the **fishing admiral**—master of the first British ship to enter a harbour. French claims to the region ended in 1713 when, by the Treaty of Utrecht, France retained **Saint-Pierre** and **Miquelon**.

Nova Scotia Again – The Treaty of Utrecht gave Acadians the choice of

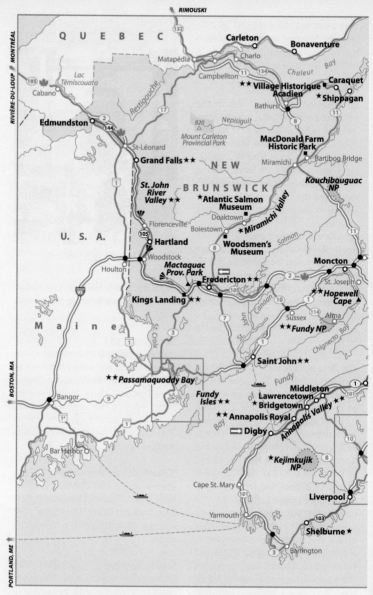

leaving British territory or becoming British subjects. The Acadians stated they would take the oath with exemption from military service. Then, in 1747, nearly 100 New England soldiers billeted in the village of Grand Pré were killed, as they slept, in a surprise attack by a French force from Quebec. Treachery among the Acadian inhabitants was suspected.

Acadian Deportation – Fear of future attacks hardened the British toward the Acadians, especially after 1749 when Halifax was founded with 2,500 English settlers who could provision the army. In 1755 Gov. **Charles Lawrence** delivered his ultimatum—take an unqualified oath of allegiance or be removed from Nova Scotia. When the Acadians refused, Lawrence quickly

GULF OF ST. LAWRENCE

★★*Îles de la Madeleine*
(Québec)
Cap-aux-Meules

Cape North

PRINCE EDWARD ISLAND

★★ *Cape Breton Highlands NP*

Cabot Trail ★★

ARGENTIA, NL

Summerside
Shediac

★ **Baddeck**   ●**Sydney**   Glace Bay

●**Charlottetown** ★★

19

☆ **Fort Beauséjour** ★★
Amherst
Tatamagouche
■ **Steam Mill**
Pictou

Bras d'Or Lake
105
St. Peters

★★★ **FORTRESS OF LOUISBOURG**

CAPE BRETON ISLAND

★ **Springhill**
104
■ **Balmoral Mills**
Antigonish

104

2
▼ *Cape Split*
215
○ **Truro**
16
Canso

Grand-Pré ★
Burncoat Head
Maitland ★
St. Marys

N O V A   S C O T I A

★ **Sherbrooke** ★

7

○ **Windsor**
102
■ **Uniacke Estate** ★

★ **Wolfville**

○ **Dartmouth** ★
HALIFAX ★★★

ATLANTIC OCEAN

South Shore ★★

MARITIME PROVINCES

0 ——— 100 km
0 ——— 50 mi

N

issued the Deportation Order. Over the next eight years, 14,600 Acadians were forcibly deported. Unwelcome in the colonies, the Acadians were able to establish a new community only in Louisiana and, as **Cajuns,** survive to this day. Some escaped to Saint-Pierre et Miquelon. Others fled to Île-St.-Jean until 1758, when the island was captured by a British expedition under **Lord Rolo,** and later annexed by Nova Scotia. Left untouched was a small settlement in the Malpeque area, the origins of Prince Edward Island's French-speaking population today. When peace was restored between England and France in 1763, most exiles returned to settle mainly in New Brunswick, where their descendants live to this day.

ATLANTIC PROVINCES

Scots, Loyalists and Other Settlers – After Deportation, the British offered free land to anyone willing to settle in Nova Scotia. New Englanders from the south, groups from the British Isles and from the German Rhineland, and Scottish Highlanders accepted the offer.

After 1776, when revolution erupted in the American colonies, Nova Scotia was transformed by 30,000 Loyalists who fled the new U.S. A separate administration was set up in 1784 and called New Brunswick for the German duchy of Braunschweig-Lüneburg, governed by England's George III. Other Loyalists settled in Prince Edward Island, named in 1799 for Queen Victoria's father.

Confederation – In September 1864, representatives of Nova Scotia, New Brunswick and Prince Edward Island met with a delegation from Canada (then only Ontario and Quebec) to discuss British union in North America. This historic conference paved the way for Confederation in 1867. Newfoundland chose not to join, holding out until 1949, when it became Canada's 10th province.

Economy

Fishing Industry – In the late 1990s cod stocks on the **Grand Banks** off Newfoundland collapsed due to overfishing, and the Canadian government in 2003 declared a moratorium on cod fishing, ending a 500-year-old industry.

The most valuable catch for the Maritimes is **lobster, with crab and lobster on the rise**. Prince Edward Island is famous for **mussels** and Malpeque **oysters;** and Nova Scotia for Digby **scallops.** In New Brunswick and in Nova Scotia, north of Dartmouth, **aquaculture** focuses on the cultivation of mussels, clams and oysters.

Agriculture – Agriculture is the backbone of Prince Edward Island, most famous for its **potatoes.** Farms exist in Newfoundland on **Avalon Peninsula** and in **Codroy Valley,** but they supply local markets only.

Forest Products – New Brunswick's **pulp, paper** and **lumber** industries easily outdistance agriculture in domestic production. Newfoundland now includes mining and manufacture based on forest resources in its economic mix. Offshore oil production and tourism are among its leading industries.

Mining and Energy – The **iron ore** mines of the **Labrador Trough** in western Labrador are the major source of Canada's iron ore products. The discovery in 1993 of nickel in Voisey Bay, Labrador, opened a new source of wealth. Copper and gold are also mined in Newfoundland.

One of the world's largest base metals (zinc, lead and copper) mines is located in New Brunswick. Antimony is mined near Fredericton and two potash mines are situated near Sussex. **Coal** continues at Minto-Chipman. In Nova Scotia coal, gypsum and salt are mined. New Brunswick's electric power resources are significant. A **nuclear power** station is located at Point Lepreau on the Bay of Fundy. Nova Scotia's tidal power plant at Annapolis Royal supplies 20 megawatts at peak production.

The importance of provincial **oil and natural gas** is seen in the huge Sable Offshore Energy Project off Nova Scotia, and in the Irving Oil Refinery at Saint John, Canada's largest. Labrador's **hydroelectric** potential is enormous. Virtually all the power produced by the huge generating station at **Churchill Falls** goes to the province of Quebec. **Hibernia**, off St. John's, is the most productive oil well in Canada, now given a new future via satellite discovery of the Hibernia South Extension, giving another 20-30 years of oil.

Manufacturing – The food sector dominates Atlantic Canada's manufacturing. Some 300 companies engage in pharmaceutical and medical research, telecommunications and advanced technologies such as satellite remote sensing and ocean mapping. Music, filmmaking, and plastic arts are also growing.

Recreation

For specific information on activities below, contact provincial tourism office: see NEW BRUNSWICK, NOVA SCOTIA, PRINCE EDWARD ISLAND, and NEWFOUNDLAND and LABRADOR.

Parks – All four provinces have excellent national and provincial parks with camping facilities and activities. Washed by the warm waters of the Gulf of St. Lawrence, Prince Edward Island National Park has lovely beaches. Miles of sand dunes are part of New Brunswick's **Kouchibouguac National Park**. Hiking trails abound in Fundy National Park, Mactaquac Provincial Park and Mt. Carleton Provincial Park, as they do in Nova Scotia's National Park in Cape Breton's highlands and Newfoundland's national parks.

Water Sports – Water temperatures are surprisingly warm off Prince Edward Island's northern shores and New Brunswick's Northumberland Strait, in the vicinity of Shediac's Parlee Beach Provincial Park. On the beautiful Saint John River, where **houseboats** can be rented by the week. **Kejimkujik National Park** has several canoeing routes, and sailing and canoeing opportunities in Newfoundland's abundant lakes and rivers. **Sea kayaking** is offered along Nova Scotia's eastern shore, off Cape Breton in particular. **Windsurfing** is practised on the bays and off the north shore beaches of Prince Edward Island (especially Stanhope Beach), in the Eel River Bar of New Brunswick's Restigouche region and off the Acadian Peninsula.

Fishing – Trout, salmon and cod fishing in Newfoundland and Labrador are probably the best in eastern North America. Watch the salmon leap *(Aug)* is **Squires Memorial Park** near Deer Lake. Atlantic **salmon** are found in the Margaree Valley in Nova Scotia and Miramichi and Restigouche valleys of northern New Brunswick. **Fly fishing** is the only legal method for anglers to catch salmon in Nova Scotia. **Deep-sea fishing** is popular in the Maritimes chartered boats.

Whale Watching – Whales usually can be seen throughout the summer *(Aug and Sept, especially)* off the coasts of Newfoundland, New Brunswick and Nova Scotia. Cruises are available in Newfoundland near St. John's, Terra Nova National Park, Trinity and Twillingate. Deer Island, Grand Manan Island and St. Andrews are departure points for whale-watching voyages in New Brunswick. Nova Scotia cruises depart from northern Cape Breton Island and from Digby Neck.

Bird Watching – The bird population of **Grand Manan Island** drew James Audubon to its shores to sketch its many species. In Nova Scotia, south of Liverpool, the **Seaside Adjunct** of Kejimkujik National Park protects a breeding grounds for piping plovers. Yarmouth harbors cormorants and black-backed gulls. The **Bird Islands** attract a variety of sea birds to their protected sanctuaries and McNab's Island in Halifax Harbour provides a nesting site for osprey. At its three famous sea-bird colonies—**Cape St. Mary's, Witless Bay** and **Funk Island**—gannets, murres, kittiwake gulls, razor-billed auks, puffins, guillemots and dovekies can be observed. Bald eagles, and even occasionally a golden eagle, are sighted along the south coast.

Other Activities – **Adventure tours** on foot, by riverboat, dogsled or **snowmobiles** are offered in Newfoundland and Labrador. Operating mainly from Halifax, wilderness expeditions include backpacking and cross-country skiing. March trips to see baby harp seals on ice floes in the Gulf of St Lawrence, are organized by Chateau Madelinot in Fatima, Magdalen Islands. *855-986-2211 www.hotelsaccents.com.*

New Brunswick

Bounded by the US on the west and Quebec to the north, New Brunswick is the Atlantic provinces' connection to the continental mainland. The province is linked to Nova Scotia by the Isthmus of Chignecto. Although the Northumberland Strait separates New Brunswick from Prince Edward Island, since 1997 the two provinces have been connected by the 13km/8mi-long Confederation Bridge.

▶ **Population:** 753,900.
⟳ **Michelin Map:** pp358-359.
▤ **Info:** Tourism and Parks, Campbellton. *℘*800-561-0123. www.tourismnew brunswick.ca.
◷ **Timing:** Allow at least one week to visit New Brunswick.
▲▲ **Kids:** The beaches along the Acadian coast are among the warmest north of Virginia.

GEOGRAPHY

An extensive coastline faces Baie de Chaleur (Heat Bay) in the north, the Gulf of St. Lawrence to the east and the Bay of Fundy in the south. Extending into the bay are the three **Fundy islands** of Deer, Campobello and Grand Manan. The interior consists of mountainous uplands, central highlands, the Saint John River Valley, and a plain east to Chaleur Bay. This 673km/418mi Saint John River flows northeast from northern Maine along the US/New Brunswick border to empty into the Bay of Fundy. Turbulent at Grand Falls gorge, the river cascades over 25m/76ft cataracts and 18m/59ft at Beechwood—both sites of hydroelectric dams. After the provincial capital of **Fredericton,** it

gradually broadens, traversing picturesque farmland. At its mouth, the river is thrown back by the mighty Fundy tides in a gorge called **Reversing Falls.** Fredericton and the major port city of **Saint John** are situated on the river's banks.

A BIT OF HISTORY

Era of Wooden Ships – Saint John became one of the world's great shipbuilding centres by the mid-19C. Skilled craftsmen perfected clipper ships, schooners, brigs and barques.

By Confederation in 1867, New Brunswick was wealthy, and in the late 19C, the province was the most prosperous in Canada. However, by 1900 steam had replaced sail power and steel hulls superseded wooden ones; the age of prominence was over.

Cultural Heritage – The social fabric of New Brunswick was woven by a diverse population of Mi'kmaq and Maliseet Indians, New England Loyalists, Acadians, Scots, Irish, Germans, Danes and Dutch. The richness of place names stems from original Indian designations. The Acadians' yearly "Blessing of the Fleet," Canada's largest Irish festival, an annual folk music celebration and a Francophone festival illustrate the cultural variety of the province. Acadian potato and clam pie, a Loyalist dish of fish chowder, and buckwheat pancakes topped with maple syrup hint at the diversity of cuisine.

© BRIAN G. ATKINSON/New Brunswick Tourism

Shediac Lobster Festival

PRACTICAL INFORMATION
GETTING THERE
BY AIR – Air Canada and its affiliates provide direct air service to Saint John and Fredericton (*888-247-2262 Canada/US; www.aircanada.com)*.

BY TRAIN – VIA Rail serves Moncton via Montreal, with connecting bus service to Saint John (*888-842-7245. www.viarail.ca).*Service between Montreal and New Brunswick daily except Tuesday and Saturday. Service is in jeopardy to the Maritimes, so call to confirm.

BY BOAT – Government-operated ferries *(free)* provide service in the lower Saint John River area and to islands in the Bay of Fundy. Ferries *(toll)* connect the province with Nova Scotia and Quebec. For information, contact New Brunswick Tourism (*see below)*.

GENERAL INFORMATION
ACCOMMODATIONS AND VISITOR INFORMATION
Annual tourist guide gives info on history, attractions and events. Order or download from website. Government-inspected hotels and motels, B & B lodgings and country inns, farm vacations and campgrounds are also listed. Contact **New Brunswick Tourism** 800-561-0123. *www.tourism newbrunswick.ca.*

LANGUAGE – New Brunswick is officially bilingual; approximately 35 percent of the population speaks French. All road signs are in English and French.

ROAD REGULATIONS – The province has good paved roads. Speed limits, unless otherwise posted, are 100km/h (60mph) on provincial highways and 50km/h (30mph) in cities. **Seat belt** use is mandatory.

Canadian Automobile Assn. (CAA) 378 Westmorland Rd., Saint John. 506-634-1400 or 800-561-8807. www.caa.ca/maritimes.

TIME ZONE – New Brunswick is on Atlantic Standard Time. Entering from the US or Quebec, set your watch ahead 1hr. Daylight Saving Time is observed from the second Sunday in March to the first Sunday in November. Taxes – In New Brunswick, taxes are combined to form a Harmonized Sales Tax (HST). The HST for New Brunswick is 15% (some items are exempt).Nonresidents may be entitled to a rebate on tour packages only: for details access www.cra-arc.gc.ca.

LIQUOR LAWS – The legal drinking age is 19. Liquor is sold in government stores. Some privately owned stores sell liquor as agencies for the provincial liquor corporation.

PROVINCIAL HOLIDAY
New Brunswick Day:
1st Monday in August

RECREATION
Hiking trails abound in Fundy National Park, Mactaquac and Mt. Carleton provincial parks. **Windsurfing** is practised on the Eel River Bar of the Restigouche region and off the Acadian Peninsula. **Fishing** for Atlantic salmon is rewarding in the Miramichi and Restigouche valleys. Bird watching is popular on Grand Manan Island. The province has some 46 **golf** courses; for details go online to www.golfnb.

PRINCIPAL FESTIVALS

May–Jun	**Salmon Festival**, *Campbellton*
Jul	**Lobster Festival**: *Shediac*
	Irish Festival: *Miramichi*
Jul–Aug	**Foire Brayonne**, *Edmundston*
	Bon Ami Festival, *Dalhousie*
Aug	**Festival Acadien**, *Caraquet*
Sept	**Harvest Jazz and Blues Festival**, *Fredericton*
Oct	**Fall Frolic**, *Doaktown*

Fort Beauséjour★★

Overlooking the Cumberland Basin (an arm of Chignecto Bay), the Missiguash River Valley and the Tantramar Marshes, this former French fort is exceptional for its impressive **panorama★★** of the surrounding country *(fog or rain may hamper visibility)*.

A BIT OF HISTORY

In 1672 the Acadians first settled in this area, which they called Beaubassin, reclaiming it from the sea by an extensive system of dikes. After the Treaty of Utrecht ceded mainland Nova Scotia to Britain in 1713, they found themselves in the middle of a border conflict. The British built Fort Lawrence on their side of the isthmus; the French built Fort Beauséjour on their side. Captured in 1755 by a British force under Col. **Robert Monckton**, Fort Beauséjour was renamed Fort Cumberland. The Acadians were removed under the Deportation Order of that same year. Strengthened by the British, the fort withstood an attack in 1776 by New England settlers sympathetic to the American Revolution. In 1926 the fort, rechristened Fort Beauséjour, was designated a National Historic Site.

- **Michelin Map:** p359.
- **Infor:** Fort Beauséjour-Fort Cumberland National Historic Site, 111 Fort Beauséjour Road, Aulac. ☎506-364-5080. www.pc.gc.ca.
- **Location:** The fort is situated in Aulac near Nova Scotia border, just off Trans-Can Hwy., Exit 550A. It stands on the Chignecto Isthmus, a narrow strip of land joining New Brunswick and Nova Scotia, southeast of Moncton.

VISIT

Open Jun–mid-Oct daily 9am–5pm. ☎$3.90. ☎506-364-5080. *www.pc.gc.ca.*
The **Visitor Centre** houses displays on the site. Three restored underground casemates can be visited, and the earthworks are in good repair.

Fredericton★★

Set on a bend in the Saint John River, this quiet city is the capital of New Brunswick. Largely due to the munificence of **Lord Beaverbrook** (1879-1964), Fredericton is the cultural centre of the province.

A BIT OF HISTORY

Fredericton's true beginning came, like Saint John's, with the arrival of the Loyalists in 1783. Upon the formation of the province in 1784, the settlement they founded, complete with a college that is now the **University of New Brunswick,** was chosen as the capital and named Fredericton after the second son

- ▶ **Population:** 56,224.
- **Michelin Map:** p358, p365.
- **Info:** Fredericton Tourism, 397 Queen St., ☎506-460-2129 or 888-888-4768 or www.tourismfredericton.ca.
- **Parking:** Inquire at the Service Centre at City Hall (back door) at 397 Queen St. for a free three-day visitors' parking pass. ☎506-460-2019.
- **Timing:** Use Fredericton as a base for visiting other sights.

Lord Beaverbrook

Born **William Maxwell Aitken** in Ontario, and reared in Newcastle, New Brunswick, Lord Beaverbrook (1879-1964) was a successful businessman in Canada before leaving for England in 1910. After entering politics he was elevated to the peerage in 1917, adopting his title from a small New Brunswick town. Having established Beaverbrook Newspapers, he built a vast empire on London's Fleet Street. Influential in the government of **Winston Churchill,** he held several key cabinet posts during World War II. Although absent from the province most of his life, Beaverbrook never forgot New Brunswick. In addition to gifts to Newcastle, he financed, in whole or in part, an art gallery, a theatre and several university buildings in Fredericton.

of George III. By the 20C most of the population worked for the provincial government or the university. The 21C, however, has seen more diversification, with rapid growth in the information technology industry in particular.

SIGHTS

Stretching along the southern bank of the Saint John River is a strip of parkland known as **The Green★**.

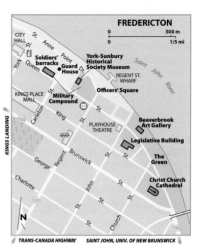

Beaverbrook Art Gallery★★

703 Queen St. ♿ ☉Open summer 7 days per week 10am-5pm, Sun noon-5pm. Rest of the year closed Mon, open rest of week 10am-5pm, closed Dec 25. ⊛$10. ✆506-458-2028 or 877-458-2028.
www.beaverbrookartgallery.org.
The gallery features Lord Beaverbrook's collection of British, European and Canadian art. The collection of **British art** is the most comprehensive in Canada. The **Canadian Collection** features works by most of the country's best-known artists, including Cornelius Krieghoff.

Legislative Building★

♿ ☉*706 Queen St., Open daily late-Jun–late-Aug 9am–5pm, rest of the year Mon–Fri 9am–5pm. ☉Closed major holidays. ✆506-453-2527.*
www.gnb.ca.
Opposite the art gallery stands the 1880 Georgian seat of provincial government, with its classical dome. Visitors may view the assembly chamber.

Christ Church Cathedral★

168 Church St. ☉Open year-round Mon–Fri 8:45am–noon & 1pm–4:45pm, and Sun for services. ✆506-450-8500.
www.christchurchcathedral.com.
Completed in 1853 the stone church is an example of decorated Gothic Revival architecture. The interior has a hammer-beam wooden pointed **ceiling**.

Military Compound★

Changing of the guard: 571 Queen St. Jul–Aug daily 11am & 4pm (also 7pm Tue & Thu). ✆506-460-2041.
Now a pleasant park known as **Officers' Square,** the old parade ground is the site of the former British **officers' quarters,** a three-storey stone building with white arches, constructed in 1839, with additions in 1851. A few blocks to the west, the **Guard House** (map p365), built

in 1827, stands adjacent to the **soldiers' barracks** *(map p365)*, a stone building with red-painted wooden terraces. Both buildings have been restored and furnished, and offer free summer outdoor theatrical shows and concerts .

York-Sunbury Historical Society Museum (M *on map*)

571 Queen St. In officers' quarters. ◷*Open Jul–Labour Day Mon–Sat 10am–5pm & rest of Sept–Nov Tue–Sat 1pm–4pm. Rest of the year by appointment.* ⊕*$5.* ☎*506-455-6041. www.yorksunburymuseum.com.* This museum provides a portrait of the area from its settlement by the Native American population to the present.

ADDRESSES

🛏 STAY

$$ The Colonel's Inn – *843 Union St.* ☎*506-452-2802 or 877-455-3003. www.thecolonelsin.com. 3 rooms.* 🅿︎⚊. Impeccably maintained, this 1902 residence is just across the river from downtown Fredericton, accessible by shuttle boat or a walking trail. The air-conditioned bedrooms have a private bath, TV/DVD, wireless Internet and a hot, homemade breakfast included.

$$ Crowne Plaza Fredericton Lord Beaverbrook – *659 Queen St.* ☎*506-455-3371 or 866-444-1946. www.cpfredericton.com. 169 rooms including*

12 suites. ✗⚐🅿︎⚊. This Crowne Plaza hotel has an unbeatable location in the downtown core (the art gallery is next door). Spacious guest rooms have modern amenities, including a sleep CD. Three fine-dining restaurants serve contemporary cuisine.

$$ On the Pond – *20 Rte. 615, Jewett Mills.* ☎*506-363-3420 or 800-984-2555. www.onthepond.com. 8 rooms.* 🅿︎ Spa. Guest quarters at this English-cottage style lodge 20min east of Fredericton are done in a woodland theme. Downstairs you'll find a cozy great room with a stone fireplace. Spa packages are available.

$$$ Quartermain House B & B – *92 Waterloo Row,* ☎*506-206-5255 or 855-758-5255. www.quartermainhouse.com* Three traditional spacious rooms loaded with TV's, phones, desks, Wifi, air conditioners, hair dryers, irons, clocks, plush Turkish robes and even slippers. Five star comfort riverside.

🍴 EAT

$$ The Blue Door – *100 Regent St.* ☎*506-455-2583. www.thebluedoor.ca. No lunch.* **Contemporary**. Enjoy a martini outside on the patio, then dine on seafood amid exposed brick walls, bold paintings and artsy plantings. Try Buck-a-Shuck Fridays for oyster lovers.

$$ BrewBakers – *546 King St.* ☎*506-459-0067. www.brewbakers.ca.* **International**. This well-frequented eatery contains dining rooms on several levels, with enough nooks and hideaways to afford privacy and quiet to couples. The menu roams from pizza and pasta to seared haddock sandwich, to roasted lamb panini and beyond.

$$ The Palate Restaurant – *462 Queen St.* ☎*506-450-7911. www.thepalate.com.* **International.** This casual bistro boasts an open kitchen, local art on the walls, background jazz and such dishes as giant sea scallops and banana rum yellow curry. Patio dining also.

$$ Brass Rail– *1315 Regent St.* ☎*506-455-1430 or 800-561-8777. www.frederictoninn. nb.ca.* **Canadian.** This hotel restaurant has all bases covered for the travelling public, serving breakfast, lunch, and dinner from early til late. Try their popular inexpensive noon buffet , or Sunday brunch from 10:30am (kids under-12 eat free).

Fredericton

© BRIAN G. ATKINSON/New Brunswick Tourism

Fundy National Park★★

Extending 13km/8mi along the Bay of Fundy's steep cliffs, this rolling parkland is interrupted by deep-cut rivers and streams in deep valleys. Created by 9m/29ft or higher tides, the vast tidal flats, explorable at low tide, contain a wealth of marine life.

VISIT

✕ ♿ ⏱ *Open year-round. Camping, golf, fishing, boat rental, swimming pool, playgrounds, tennis, mountain biking, hiking, cross-country skiing, snowshoeing.* ⏱ *Visitor Centre (east entrance) open mid-Jun–Labour Day daily 8am–9:45pm; mid-May–mid-Jun & Labour Day–early Oct daily 8am–4:30pm.* ⌾ *$7.90 entry fee.* ✆ *506-887-6000. www.pc.gc.ca.* ♿ *Note: views described may be obscured by fog.*

Eastern Park Entrance

From the park gate there is a fine **view★** of the tranquil Upper Salmon River, the hills to the north, the small fishing village of Alma, Owl's Head and the bay. To appreciate the contrast, visit at both low and high tides.

Herring Cove

11km/7mi from entrance.

♱ **Michelin Map:** p358.
🛈 **Info:** ✆506-887-6000. www.pc.gc.ca.
▶ **Location:** The park is located near Alma, on Rte.114, which follows the coast south of Moncton. This is not the spot for the famed Fundy tidal bore; that can be seen from Bore Park in Moncton.
👥 **Kids:** The tidal pools at Point Wolfe will intrigue children.

At the end of the road, a path leads down to a cove that has tidal pools brimming with limpets, barnacles, sea anemones and other life at low tide.

👥 Point Wolfe★★

10km/6mi from entrance.
The road crosses Point Wolfe River by a covered wooden bridge, below which is a small gorge forming the river's entry into Wolfe Cove. To collect logs floated downstream, a dam was constructed. Schooners loaded the sawed wood at wharves built in the coves. Today only the bridge and dam remain.
At low tide the sand and rock **pools** are alive with sea creatures.

Point Wolfe,
Fundy National Park

© aprott/iStockphoto.com

Miramichi Valley★

The name Miramichi has long been associated with fine salmon fishing. A major spawning ground for Atlantic salmon, the river has two branches (the Southwest Miramichi and the Little Southwest Miramichi), which together traverse the province. The area is also lumber country; Miramichi (formerly Newcastle and Chatham), near the river's mouth, is known for its shipbuilding past. Joseph Cunard, founder of the famous shipping line, lived in Chatham.

- **Michelin Map:** p358.
- **Info:** ✆800-561-0123. www.tourismnew brunswick.ca.
- **Location:** The valley is found in east central New Brunswick. Drive north from Fredericton on Hwy. 8.
- **Don't Miss:** The towns of Carqaquet and Shippagan are pleasant stops.
- **Timing:** Allow 2 days to see the major sights.
- **Kids:** The Aquarium and Marine Centre at Shippagan; the Village historique acadien.

SIGHTS
Atlantic Salmon Museum★

263 Main St., Doaktown. 94km/58mi northeast of Fredericton by Rte. 8.
♿⏰*Open early Jun–mid-Oct Mon–Sat 9am–5pm (also Sun 1pm-4:30pm Aug).* ✆$5. ✆506-365-7787 or 866-725-6662. www.atlanticsalmonmuseum.com.
Overlooking a series of pools on the Miramichi River, this museum is devoted to the area's famed Atlantic salmon.

Central New Brunswick Woodmen's Museum

6342 Rte. 8, Boiestown. 68km/42mi north of Fredericton by Rte. 8 in Boiestown. ⏰*Open mid-May–mid-Oct daily 9:30 am–5pm.* ✆$6. ✆506-369-7214. www.woodmensmuseum.com.

This museum presents life in a lumber camp. On display is a sawmill with its original equipment and a range of tools from axes to chain saws. The re-created bunkhouse and cookhouse evoke the flavour of camp life. A small **train** *($3)* runs continuous tours around the site.

MacDonald Farm Provincial Historic Site

600 Rte.11, Bartibog Bridge. 13km/8mi east of Miramichi on Rte. 11. ⏰*Open mid-Jun–early Sept daily 10am-4pm. Late May–mid-Jun Mon–Fri 9:30am–4:30pm.* ✆$4. ✆506-778-6085. www.macdonaldfarm.ca.
Overlooking the Miramichi estuary, this old stone farmhouse (1820) has been restored to the period when Alexan-

Caraquet

Just east of Village Historique Acadien lies the town of Caraquet (11km/7mi), home of the 1891 **Hôtel Paulin ($$$)** *(143 Blvd. Saint-Pierre W.* ✆506-727-9981 or 866-727-9981. www.hotelpaulin.com).* Located on the second and third floors, the guest rooms have a country look with quilts or floral bedspreads, hardwood floors and rustic furniture. Downstairs features an open sitting area and a public **dining room ($$),** where the focus is on seafood and upscale Acadian-style cuisine. Overnight guests can help themselves to a continental breakfast in the morning.

You'll want to visit Caraquet in August, when the town hosts its annual Acadian Festival, opened by a **blessing of the fleet,** symbolic of Christ's benediction to the fishermen of Galilee.

der MacDonald and his family lived in it. Visitors can participate in domestic farm chores and learn traditional crafts.

EXCURSIONS
Shippagan★
104km/65mi N/E of Bartibog Bridge.
This town on the Acadian peninsula has a **boardwalk** along the harbour offers views of the wharves. From Lameque Island a bridge crosses to Miscou Island, which has fine beaches on the Gulf of St. Lawrence.

♣♦ Aquarium and Marine Centre★
108 Aquarium St. ✕☐🕒*Open 15 Jun–Sept daily 10am–6pm.* 👓*$9.15 (child $6.11).* 📞*506-336-3013. www.aquariumnb.ca.*
In a series of aquariums, outdoor seal pool and touch tank, fish native the St.

Lawrence River and New Brunswick's lakes and rivers are on view. Visitors can enter the cabin of a reconstructed trawler.

♣♦ Village Historique Acadien★
311 Rte 11, Caraquet. 47km/29mi west of Shippagan on Rte. 11.
✕☐🕒*Open summer daily 10am–6pm.* 👓*$20/2 days (child $16).* 📞*506-726-2600 or 877-721-2200. www.villagehistoriqueacadien.com.*
This reconstructed village depicts the life of the Acadians from 1780 to 1890, after their return from Deportation. Staffed by Acadians wearing traditional costumes, the village extends along a road nearly 1.6km/1mi long. Ask about overnight Hotel Chateau Albert package deal w/breakfast for $149.95.

Moncton

Set on a bend of the Petitcodiac River, Moncton is famous for its tidal bore, which rushes up the river from the Bay of Fundy. The first settlers in the area were German families from Pennsylvania, but they were joined by Acadians returning to British territory after Deportation. Today one-third of the population is French-speaking.

SIGHT
Tidal Bore★
In the open ocean, the ebb and flow of the tide is barely noticeable, but in certain V-shaped bays or inlets, the tide enters the broad end and literally piles up as it moves up the bay.
This buildup occurs in the **Bay of Fundy**, 77km/48mi wide at its mouth, narrowing and becoming shallower along its 233km/145mi length. Thus, the tide is squeezed as it travels the bay, a ripple increasing to a wave several feet high as it enters the rivers emptying into the bay. This wave is known as a "bore," a tidal wave of unusual height.

▶ **Population:** 138,644.
⚲ **Michelin Map:** p358.
🛈 **Info:** Visitor Information Centre, Resurgo Place, 20 Mountain Rd., 📞506-853-3597 or 800-363-4558. http://tourism.moncton.ca.
▶ **Location:** Moncton sits at the southeastern edge of the province.
🅿 **Parking:** Moncton has electronic meters, fed by coin or by a card purchased at city hall. Finding a space is generally not a problem.
🕒 **Timing:** Moncton's sights take 2 days, but take extra for Hopewell Rocks. Before you go to see the tidal bore, check tidal times in advance online at www.waterlevels.gc.ca.
♣♦ **Kids:** Take them to TidalBore Park to watch the world's largest tidal change.

Rocks at Hopewell Cape

New Brunswick Tourism

At Moncton the bore varies from a few inches to nearly two feet. The highest bores occur when the earth, moon and sun are aligned.

👥 Tidal Bore Park★

Off Main St. at the corner of King St. schedules available from the Tourist Office at City Hall or from website. Arrive 20min prior to view lowest level and return later to see high tide. ♿ 🖉*506-853-3590. http://tourism. moncton.ca.*

The tidal bore and changing levels of the Petitcodiac River are best viewed from the park. A small stream at low tide, the river lies in the centre of a bed of red mud. At high tide the river widens to 1.6km/1mi and the water level increases by up to 7m/23ft.

EXCURSIONS
Monument Lefebvre National Historic Site★

480 Rue Centrale, Memramcook. 20km/12.5mi southeast by Rte. 106 in St.-Joseph. ♿🕐*Open Jun–mid-Oct daily 9am–5pm.* 💲*$3.90.* 🖉*506-758-9808 (summer). www.pc.gc.ca.*

Located in the Lefebvre Building of the **College St.-Joseph,** the first Acadian institution of higher learning,

the site chronicles the history of this French-speaking culture.Founded by Rev. Camille Lefebvre in 1864, the college trained Acadian leaders for nearly 100 years before its amalgamation with the Université de Moncton.

The small museum has displays on the Memramcook Valley, where the Acadians maintained continuous settlement, despite Deportation. A recent exhibit traces the Acadians' odyssey from 1755 to the present.

Hopewell Cape★★

35km/22mi south of Moncton by Rte. 114. Directional signs en route.
☺ *Be sure to climb stairs at the posted time to avoid the 10m/32ft tides.*
Near this little village overlooking She-pody Bay is an interesting phenom-enon known as **The Rocks.** Sculpted by tidal action, wind and frost, these red sandstone formations, some as tall as 15m/50ft, stand on the beach, cut off from the cliffs. Tiny tree-cov-ered islands at high tide, these shapes become "giant flowerpots" at low tide, their narrow bases widening to support balsam fir and dwarf black spruce at the top. Visitors can walk around them when the tide is out and look at crevices in the cliffs that will become new flowerpots.

Passamaquoddy Bay/Fundy Isles★★

This inlet of the Bay of Fundy between Maine and New Brunswick is dotted with islands and indented with harbours, and includes the estuary of the **St. Croix River.** A popular resort, the area is also famous for its lobster and an edible seaweed known as **dulse,** a regional delicacy that is served in a variety of ways.

A BIT OF HISTORY

In 1604 Samuel de Champlain chose the bay as the site of his first settlement and wintered on St. Croix Island (today in Maine). Loyalists, arriving in 1783, settled the communities of St. Stephen, St. Andrews and St. George, and of Deer and Campobello islands.

Fog and cold weather occur even in summer, particularly on the islands.

SIGHTS
St. Andrews★

506-529-5120. www.standrewsbythe sea.ca, www.townofstandrews.ca.
Founded by Loyalists, St. Andrews became a prosperous mercantile and fishing town. In 1842 some of its century-old houses were floated intact across the estuary when the Webster-Ashburton Treaty declared the Canadian/US border to be the St. Croix River—and some Loyalists discovered they were on the "wrong" side of it. The town is home to the Blockhouse, a National Historic Site. The town's quaint main thoroughfare, **Water Street**, mixes boutiques and cafes.

▲▲ HMSC Aquarium-Museum (Fundy Discovery Aquarium)★

1 Lower Campus Road, St. Andrews.
Open mid-May–mid-Oct daily 10am til 5pm. $14.24 (child $10). Seal feedings at 10:15am & 3:30pm.
506-529-1200.
www.huntsmanmarine.ca.
This interesting little aquarium with the huge display area, has fish tanks and

- **Michelin Map:** p358, p372.
- **Info:** *800-561-0123. www.tourismnew brunswick.ca or www.st andrewsbythesea.ca.*
- **Location:** St. Stephen, the largest town on the Canadian side, lies about 90 minutes west of Saint John. St Andrews sits on a small peninsula just south.
- **Don't Miss:** Campobello, home of Franklin D. Roosevelt.
- **Timing:** Plan your itinerary around ferry times.
- **Kids:** The HMSC Aquarium-Museum.

St. Andrews

Brian Atkinson/New Brunswick Tourism

exhibitions on the marine ecosystems of the Bay of Fundy and neighbouring Atlantic waters. A family of harbour seals performs for visitors. Films are shown regularly in the theatre, on-site academic study projects abound, and there is a giftshop and café as well.

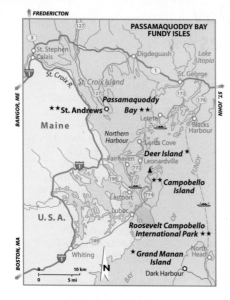

Map labels: FREDERICTON, PASSAMAQUODDY BAY FUNDY ISLES, St. Stephen, Calais, Digdeguash, Lake Utopia, St. Croix R., St. Croix Island, St. George, Passamaquoddy Bay, ★★St. Andrews, Letete, Blacks Harbour, Maine, Northern Harbour, Lords Cove, Fairhaven, Deer Island ★, Leonardville, ★★Campobello Island, Eastport, Lubec, U.S.A., Roosevelt Campobello International Park ★★, Whiting, ★Grand Manan Island, North Head, Dark Harbour, BANGOR, ME, ST. JOHN, BOSTON, MA, FUNDY BAY, 10 km, 5 mi, N

St. Andrews Blockhouse

454 Whipple St. On Joe's Point Rd.
◷Open Jun 1st–Sept 1st daily
10am–6pm. ⊜$1. ✆506-529-4270 or
506-636-4011. www.pc.gc.ca.
Built to protect New Brunswick's western frontier from American invasion during the War of 1812, this is the only blockhouse remaining of the original 14 erected.

Deer Island★

Car ferry departs from late-Jun–Sep
daily 9am–6pm. ⊜Free from Town of
Letete. ✆506-662-3724 or 888-747-
7006. www.gnb.ca. From Eastport,
Maine (www.eastcoastferriesltd.com.)
late Jun–mid-Sept daily 8:30am–
6:30pm, hourly. ⊜$16/car & driver, $4
per passenger. ℗ ✆506-747-2159 or
877-747-2159. Note: ferries operate on
first-come, first-served basis. Lines form
on weekends and at peak times.
This Fundy island is inhabited primarily by fishermen. The world's largest lobster pound is located on its western side. A pleasant **trip★** is the ferry ride to the island from Letete, among the smaller islands covered with birds. In the narrow inlet of **Northern Harbour,** a corral for lobsters has been built with nets and fences. At the southern end of the

island, a large whirlpool forms when the Fundy tides are running strong. Called **"Old Sow"** for the noise it makes, this vortex is the largest tidal whirlpool in the western hemisphere.

Campobello Island★★

Car ferry departs from Deer
Island– Campobello Island late
Jun–mid-Sept 8:30am–6:30pm,
hourly. ⊜$16/car & driver, $4 pp. ℗
✆506-747-2159. www.eastcoastferries.
nb.ca. Accessible by bridge from
Lubec, Maine. American and non-
Americans need a valid passport for
border crossing; unless both parents
accompany their children, proof of
custody is required.
◷New Brunswick is 1hr ahead of
Maine; set watch forward.
Known as the "beloved island" of US President **Franklin D. Roosevelt** (1882-1945), the site is a summer resort. First settled in the 1770s, Campobello was named for **William Campbell,** the governor of Nova Scotia, and for its beauty *(campo bello* means "beautiful pasture" in Italian). By the end of the 19C, it had become a retreat for wealthy Americans. FDR spent summers on Campobello with his parents and later with his wife, Eleanor. In 1921, FDR contracted polio and left the island for 12 years. In 1964 the Canadian and American governments jointly established the park to commemorate him.

Roosevelt Campobello International Park★★

On Campobello Island. ♿◷Grounds
open year-round dawn-to-dusk. Visitor
Centre open late May–Oct daily 9am–

Cottage at Roosevelt Campobello International Park

New Brunswick Tourism

5pm EDT. ℘*506-752-2922 or 877-851-6663. www.fdr.net.*

The southern part of the island is natural parkland crisscrossed by several lovely **drives.** Note the view of Passamaquoddy Bay from Friar's Head (*turn right at picnic area sign just south of visitor centre*), and of Herring Cove from Con Robinson's Point (*follow Glensevern Rd. East*). Built in the Dutch Colonial style, the red-shingled, green-roofed **cottage** (*late May–mid-Oct*) with 34 rooms belonged to FDR. Films on the life of Roosevelt are shown in the **visitor centre.** North of the visitor centre, **East Quoddy Head Lighthouse** (*12km/7mi by Wilson's Beach and gravel road to the Point*) overlooks Head Harbour Island.

Grand Manan Island★

✕&⊙*Car ferry departs Blacks Harbour late Jun–mid-Sept daily 7:30am, 9:30am, 1:30pm, 5:30pm & 9pm (no departure Sun 7:30am). Rest of the year approximately 4 crossings daily. 1hr 30min.* ☞*$35.80/car, $12/person.* ℘*506-662-3724 or 855-882-1978. http://grandmanan.coastaltransport.ca.*

The largest of the Fundy islands, Grand Manan is noted for its rugged scenery, picturesque harbours and sizable bird population. On the island's rocky west coast, **Dark Harbour** is a processing centre for **dulse**, which grows on submerged rocks in the Bay of Fundy. Collected at low tide and dried in the sun, dulse can be added to soups and stews and eaten raw or toasted.

ADDRESSES

🛌 STAY

$$$ Marriott's Algonquin Resort – *184 Adolphus St.* ℘*506-529-8823 or 855-529-8693. 217 rooms and 16 suites.* ✕&🅿🛆 Spa. This sprawling 1889 railroad hotel rises from a carpet of lawn and trees on a bluff overlooking St. Andrews. The lobby has an adjoining front porch; a cozy library, spa facilities and a golf course are added perks. Rooms are appointed with handsome fabrics and period reproduction or contemporary furniture. The **Braxton's Restaurant (\$\$\$)**, serves American-style fine dining.

❟ EAT

$$ Rossmount Hotel, Restaurant & Bar – *4599 Rte. 127.* ℘*506-529-3351. www.rossmountinn.com.Dinner only.* **Canadian**. Menu changes daily, features seafood & fresh vegetables from their garden. The restaurant remains one of St. Andrews' better dining values. Ask about overnight inn/dining packages.

Saint John★★

New Brunswick's largest city, this industrial centre and major port is fondly called "fog city" due to the dense sea mists rolling in off the Bay of Fundy. Its rocky, hilly site at the mouth of the Saint John River, at the junction with the bay, has resulted in a city with few straight roads and many cul-de-sacs.

A BIT OF HISTORY

Part of Acadie – In 1604 Samuel de Champlain and Pierre Dugua, Sieur de Mons landed briefly at the mouth of the river. Another Frenchman, **Charles de Saint-Étienne de La Tour,** built a trading fort in 1630 on the site of present-day Saint John, which a compatriot burned down. The trade rivalry among the French in Acadia was compounded by the Anglo-French struggles. The area was ceded by the 1763 Treaty of Paris to the English.

The Loyalists Arrive – In 1783 some 14,000 Loyalists disembarked at the mouth of the river. They possessed few pioneering skills, but they created a prosperous city of shipyards. Thriving on trade and shipbuilding, Saint John was known as the "Liverpool of America" during the 19C.

Decline and Renewal – From 1860 to 1880, however, Saint John began to decline: demand for wooden ships was decreasing; an international depression had set in by early 1874; and in 1877 more than half the city was destroyed by a great fire. After a century of decline, the city began to revive in the 1960s.

Martello Towers

Not one of the Martello towers constructed in British North America between 1796 and 1848 was ever attacked. Of the total 16 (Halifax 5, Kingston 6, Quebec City 4 and Saint John 1), 11 remain to this day.

▶ **Population:** 127, 761.
◔ **Michelin Map:** p358, p375.
▣ **Info:** ✆866-463-8639. http://discovesaintjohn.com
◔ **Location:** Saint John lies opposite Annapolis Royal in Nova Scotia; a ferry crosses the bay.
🅿 **Parking:** Parking is ample downtown: metered, in city lots and garages.
🚷 **Don't Miss:** Reversing Falls is so famous you have to see it.
🧍‍♂️ **Kids:** Stonehammer UNESCO Global Geopark.

Today, high tech, oil and tourism are bringing prosperity. A new sports and entertainment venue, Harbour Station, has been constructed and the Imperial Theatre features a symphony, two live theatre companies.

Every July the city recalls its founding with a celebration known as **Loyalist Days.** Inhabitants dress in 18C costumes and re-enact the landing of 1783.

DOWNTOWN★★

Saint John's downtown has been revitalized, making it a pleasant area for visitors to explore on foot (contact tourist office for designated walks).

Market Square Area★★

The square contains an attractive shopping mall with a central atrium and several levels, a hotel, convention centre and the New Brunswick Museum.

A row of late-19C warehouses fronts a pleasant plaza around the **market slip** where Loyalists landed in 1783. In summer there are outdoor cafes and concerts in the plaza.

On the plaza's south side stands an 1867 clapboard structure with gingerbread decoration, **Barbour's General Store (A** on map), a museum stocked with merchandise of the period (🅿⊙open Jun–Nov daily 10am–6pm; ✆506-658-2939; http://discoversaintjohn.com). Over

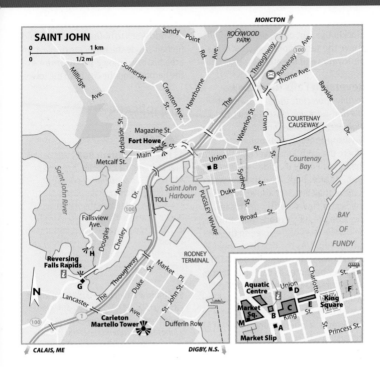

SAINT JOHN

0   1 km
0   1/2 mi

CALAIS, ME   *DIGBY, N.S.*

St. Patrick Street a pedestrian bridge links the square with the Canada Games **Aquatic Centre** (*www.aquatics.nb.ca*) and **City Hall (B** *on map*). **Brunswick Square (C** *on map*) is a complex of shops, offices and a hotel.

👥 New Brunswick Museum★

(**M** *on map*) Market Square. ♿ ⊙*Open mid-May–early Nov Mon, Tue, Wed, Fri 9am–5pm (Thu til 9pm), Sat 10am–5pm, Sun noon–5pm. Rest of the year Tue–Fri 9am–5pm, Sat 10am–5pm, Sun noon–5pm.* ⊙*Closed major holidays.* 👝*$10.* 📞*506-643-2300 or 888-268-9595. www.nbm-mnb.ca.*
The museum has excellent examples of Indian birchbark, quillwork and bead-work. The gallery of natural science features displays of the province's animal life and geological specimens.

Loyalist House (D *on map*)

120 Union St. ⊙*Open Jul–mid-Sept daily 10am–5pm. Mid-May–Jun Mon–Fri 10am–5pm. Rest of the year by appointment.* 👝*$5.* 📞*506-652-3590. www.loyalisthouse.com.*

One of the oldest structures in the city, this house was built in 1817 by David Merritt, a Loyalist who fled New York state in 1783. One of the few buildings to escape the fire of 1877, the house has a shingled exterior on two sides and clapboard on the other. The plain exterior belies the elegant and spacious Georgian interior.

King Square Area

Generally considered the centre of Saint John, this square has trees, flowerbeds arranged in the form of the Union flag and a two-storey bandstand, a tip og the hat to the original benfactors, the City Coronet Band of 1908. In one corner stands the old **city market (E** *on map*), where a variety of New Brunswick produce can be bought, including dulse. On the other side of the square, the **Loyalist burial ground (F** *on map*) can be seen.

ADDITIONAL SIGHTS
Fort Howe Lookout

From Main St., take Metcalf St., then make a sharp right turn onto Magazine St. From this wooden blockhouse (not open) on a rocky cliff above the surrounding hills, there is a **panorama**★ of the area.

Reversing Falls Rapids★★

To fully appreciate the rapids, visit at low tide, slack tide (see below) and high tide. Check tides online at www.tourismsaintjohn.com.
Where the Saint John River empties into the Bay of Fundy the tides are 8m/28ft high. At high tide when the bay water is more than 4m/14ft above river level, the water flows swiftly upstream. At low tide the bay is more than 4m/14ft below the level of the river, so the river rushes into it. As the tide rises, the rush of river water is gradually halted and the river becomes as calm (slack tide) before gradually being reversed in direction. The narrow bend just before the river enters the bay creates rapids and whirlpools, a phenomenon known as "reversing falls rapids."

Reversing Falls Bridge Lookout (G *on map*)

Parking at west end of bridge.
Visitor centre open mid-May–mid-Oct daily 8am–8pm. 506-658-2937. www.tourismsaintjohn.com.
Take steps to roof. From this lookout fine **views**★★ of the changing river current are afforded. Visitors unable to stay for the tidal cycle may enjoy the **film** *($2)*, which condenses the 24-hour event.

Falls View Park Lookout (H *on map*)

Parking at end of Falls View Ave.
The **views**★ of the rapids from the park are not as dramatic as those from the bridge.

Carleton Martello Tower★

454 Whipple St. W. Open late-Jun–late-Oct daily 10am–5:30pm. $3.90. 506-636-4011. www.pc.gc.ca.
Today a National Historic Site, this Martello tower was built in 1813 as a defence for the city. It was used during the 19C and in both world wars. A two-storey steel and concrete structure was added in World War II to house anti-aircraft and firehall. Inside the tower are displays on area history. Enjoy a **panorama**★★of the harbour and the city from the tower.

ADDRESSES

STAY

$$ Homeport Historic B&B – *80 Douglas Ave. 10 rooms. 506-672-7255 or 888-678-7678. www.homeport.nb.ca.*
On a ridge offering views across downtown to the bay, this Italianate manor dates to 1858. Opened as a B&B in 1997, it offers sizable guest rooms with Victorian-era antiques gleaned from local shops and auctions. Breakfasts include a hot dish, fresh fruit and homemade granola.

$$ Shadow Lawn Inn – *3180 Rothesay Rd. 506-847-7539 or 800-561-4166. www.shadowlawninn.com. 9 rooms and 2 longstay apartments.* Located in the outlying village of Rothesay. Rooms are furnished with a mix of antiques and period reproductions. Continental breakfasts included. The inn's **restaurant (\$\$\$)** serves Canadian fare in an upscale setting.

EAT

$ Taco Pica – *96 Germain St. 506-633-8492.* **Mexican.** Opened in 1994 by Guatemalan immigrants, serves traditional black bean soup, soft tacos, fajitas and Latin staples like *pepian* (spicy Guatemalan-style beef stew).

$$ Billy's Seafood – *49-51 Charlotte St. (City Market). 506-672-3474. www.billysseafood.com.* **Seafood.** A fish shop and eatery, Billy's also serves lunch. Order plain boiled lobster, pan-seared scallops, or the bouillabaisse.

$$ Magnolia Café/Bourbon Quarter – *112 Prince William St. 506-642-1885. www.bourbonquartersj.com.* **International.** This 2-for-1 location serves breakfast, lunch, and dinner with live .music at Magnolia, plus fine dining at Bourbon Quarter.

Saint John River Valley★★

Communities sprang up throughout the valley when some 4,000 of the Loyalists who arrived in 1783 settled here. In the 19C numerous steamboats moved among these communities.

FROM FREDERICTON TO EDMUNDSTON
285km/177mi

Fredericton★★
See FREDERICTON.

▷ Leave Fredericton on the Trans-Canada Hwy. (Rte. 2).

The highway follows the river upstream to the Mactaquac Dam, New Brunswick's largest power project. On the north bank of the head pond lies **Mactaquac Provincial Park**, a haven for sports enthusiasts. The Trans-Canada Highway travels the south side of the pond with fine **views★** as the country becomes increasingly rural.

👥 Kings Landing Historical Settlement★★
20 Kings Landing Rd., Kings Landing.
✕🕐*Open early Jun–mid-Oct daily 10am –5pm.* 💰*$17.99 (child $12.41)* 📞*506-363-4999. www.kingslanding.nb.ca.*
This restored riverside village provides a glimpse of life from 1783 to 1900.

- 👆 **Michelin Map:** p358.
- ℹ **Info:** 📞800-561-0123. www.tourism newbrunswick.ca.
- ▷ **Location:** The Trans-Canada Highway parallels the river valley for much of the river's length.
- 👁 **Don't Miss:** Grand Falls is a notable New Brunswick sight.
- 🕐 **Timing:** Allow 4 days to leisurely enjoy this driving tour.
- 👥 **Kids:** Kings Landing offers a look at old-fashioned life.

About 100 costumed interpreters explain aspects of 19C rural life. Beside the millstream is an operating water-powered **sawmill.** An example of a roadhouse of the period, the **Kings Head Inn** serves refreshments and homemade goodies such as New Brunswick Salmon Chowder, Ploughman's Lunch and Gingerbread and Whipped Cream. Moored at the wharf (the "landing") is a half-size replica of a 19C **wood boat.** Between Kings Landing and Woodstock, there are excellent **views★★** of the Saint John River traversing lovely rolling country of farms and forests.

▷ After Woodstock, leave Trans-Can Hwy. and take Rte. 103 to Hartland.

Kings Landing Historical Settlement

New Brunswick Tourism

Republic of Madawaska

Long contested among Ontario, Quebec, New Brunswick and the US, the land south of Lake Témiscouata in Quebec and New Brunswick, and the area north of the Aroostook River in Maine were once collectively called Madawaska. New Brunswick was left with the city of Edmundston and a thumb-shaped stretch of land. The long-standing dispute forged a spirited independence among the Madawaskans, who created a legend for themselves, rather than a political entity—the Republic of Madawaska. Known as the **Brayons** because they crushed flax with a tool called a brake, the Madawaskans have their own flag with an eagle and six stars and their own president, the mayor of Edmundston.

Hartland★

Settled by Loyalists, this town is known for the longest **covered bridge** in the world. Completed in 1901 and rebuilt in 1920, the 391m/1,282ft bridge crosses the Saint John River in seven spans, linking Routes 103 and 105.

Descending the hill on Route 103, note the good **view★** of the bridge. The woodwork construction can be appreciated only from the interior *(cars can be driven through; no trucks)*.

◗ Take Rte. 105 on the east bank to Florenceville and the Trans-Can Hwy. to Grand Falls. There are fine **views★** from highway of the river and farms north of Florenceville. The river gradually approaches the Maine border and enters the mountainous country of the north.

◗ Leave Trans-Can Hwy. and enter Grand Falls.

Grand Falls★★

Falls and Gorge Commission ✆506-473-6013 or 877-475-7769. www.grandfallsnb.com.

Fiddleheads

Harvested from the riverbanks of the Saint John in spring, edible fiddlehead ferns, boiled and topped with butter and lemon, are a New Brunswick delicacy.

A power plant has diverted much of the water of the falls, but there are two good vantage points from which to see the gorge.

Falls Park

Accessible from Malabeam information centre on Madawaska Rd. ✕&◷*Open Jun–early Aug daily 9am–9pm. Mid-May–late May & mid-Aug–mid-Oct daily 9am–6pm. ✆506-475-7788.* Park offers great **view★** of gorge/falls.

La Rochelle Centre★

In Centennial Park. Accessible from Malabeam reception centre on Madawaska Rd. ◷*Open daily July & Aug.* ⊜*$5. ✆506-475-7766.* Stairs descend into the gorge, which has walls as high as 70m/230ft in places. There are some deep holes in the rock called wells, but it is the **gorge★★** that is impressive.

◗ Continue north on Rte. 144. After Grand Falls the Saint John becomes wide and placid again, marking the Canadian/US border. The towns and villages seen across it are those in Maine.

Edmundston

City is dominated by twin-spired **Cathedral of the Immaculate Conception**. Residents are mainly French-speaking. **Madawaska Museum & Gallery***(195 Herbert Blvd.;* &◷*Daily Mon–Fri 10am–5pm, Sat/Sun 1pm–5pm;* ⊜*$5; ✆506-737-5282)* presents the history of this region.

Nova Scotia★★

Surrounded by the Gulf of St. Lawrence, Atlantic Ocean, Northumberland Strait and Bay of Fundy, Nova Scotia has 7,460km/ 4,625mi of serrated coastline. Proximity to the sea and natural harbours have defined its historical role as largely strategic.
The provincial capital, Halifax, has long served as a military stronghold.

GEOGRAPHY

The Peninsula – The mainland is largely flat terrain, except for a rocky, indented eastern shore and a forested interior **South Mountain** forms the northern border of this upland interior. Stretching from Cape Blomidon to the tip of Digby Neck, the **North Mountain** range parallels South Mountain for 190km/118mi along the Bay of Fundy shore. Sheltered between them is the fertile Annapolis and Cornwallis river valleys. The cropped 300m/984ft **Cobequid Mountain** extends 120km/74mi over Cumberland County, which borders the Isthmus of Chignecto.

▶ **Population:** 947,284.
◔ **Michelin Map:** p358-359.
▮ **Info:** Tourism Nova Scotia, ☏902-425-5781/ ☏800-565-0000. www.novascotia.com.
⊘ **Don't Miss:** Cape Breton Island and the Cabot Trail are spectacular.
◕ **Timing:** Halifax is a good base for seeing most sights. Allow 7 to 10 days to fully appreciate the province.
♟ **Kids:** Louisbourg offers costumed soldiers and lots of running space.

The Island – Northern **Cape Breton Island★★★** is mostly a wooded plateau. At the northern end is **Cape Breton Highlands National Park**. A vast inland sea 930sq km/359sq mi wide, **Bras d'Or Lake★** nearly bisects the island.

A BIT OF HISTORY

Acadie – In 1604 Samuel de Champlain established Port Royal, but French

PRACTICAL INFORMATION
GETTING THERE

BY AIR – **Air Canada** and its affiliates offer daily flights from the US and from Toronto and Montreal to Halifax, and connections within Atlantic Canada. ☏888-247-2262 (Canada/ US). www.aircanada.com. **Halifax Stanfield International Airport** ☏902-873-4422. www.hiaa.ca. JA Douglas McCurdy **Sydney Airport** ☏902-564-7720. www.sydneyairport. ca. **Yarmouth Airport** ☏902-742-6484. www.yarmouthairport.ca.
BY BUS AND TRAIN – Bus travel within the province is provided by **Maritime Bus** (SMT-Eastern) (*☏902-429-2029 or 800.575.1807; www. maritimebus.com*). **VIA Rail** connects Nova Scotia through Toronto and Montreal (*☏888-842-7245 Canada/US; www.viarail.ca*).

BY BOAT – The new CAT passenger and car ferry service connects **Portland** (5hrs), Maine, with **Yarmouth NS** (USD *$107 one-way/$194 return*). State of the art catamaran ferry makes daily roundtrips for 700 passengers and 200 cars. Features same hull structure as US Navy in its class of Joint High-Speed Vessels. Departs daily from Portland at 2:30pm and from Yarmouth at 8:30am with crossing time at five hours or half that of previous vessels. Expanded amenities onboard include Scotia Market Gif Shop, Little Mates Quarters Children Area, Movie Zone, Forchu Lounge, Sip Café, and Seaside Experiences (tastings, chef presentations, live music).
Saint John NB with **Digby NS**. Departs daily year-round. One-way

2hrs 45min. Reservations required. $92/vehicle, $77/passenger plus $20 fuel surcharge. For ferry schedules & reservations contact Bay Ferries (*877-762-7245 (Canada/US). www.bayferries.com*).

GENERAL INFORMATION
ACCOMMODATIONS AND VISITOR INFORMATION
For a free copy of a tourist guide and a map, contact **Tourism Nova Scotia** (*902-425-5781 or 800-565-0000, Canada/US; www.novascotia.com*).

CHECK-IN NOVA SCOTIA: Hotel and campground reservations, car rentals, tourist information. *800-565-0000.

ROAD REGULATIONS: Nova Scotia has good roads; some interior roads are loose-surface. Speed limits, unless are 100km/h (62mph) on the Trans-Canada Highway, 80km/h (50mph) on highways and 50km/h (30mph) in cities and towns. **Seat belt** use is mandatory. **Canadian Automobile Assn. (CAA)** (*Halifax* *902-443-5530 or 800-222-4357; www.atlantic.caa.ca*).

TIME ZONE: Nova Scotia is on Atlantic Standard Time. Daylight Saving Time is observed from second Sunday in March to first Sunday in November.

TAXES: In Nova Scotia, the national GST has been combined with the provincial sales tax to form the Harmonized Sales Tax (HST) levied at a single rate of 13% (some items are exempt). Nonresidents may be entitled to a rebate on tour packages: www.cra-arc.gc.ca.

LIQUOR LAWS: The legal drinking age is 19. Liquor is sold in government stores and in some retail outlets, and is served in licenced bars and restaurants. Licenced vineyards may also serve wine.

PRINCIPAL FESTIVALS
May–Jun	**Apple Blossom Festival**, *Annapolis Valley*
Jul	**Nova Scotia International Tattoo**, *Halifax*
	Highland Games and Scottish Festival, *Halifax*
	Antigonish Highland Games, *Antigonish*
	Gathering of the Clans, *Pugwash*
Aug	**Natal Day**, *Province-wide*
	Festival acadien de Clare, *Yarmouth & Acadian Shores'*
	International Busker Festival, *Halifax*
Sept	**Waterfront Seafood Festival**, *Lunenburg*
	Kentville Pumpkin People, *Kentville*
	Canadian Deep Roots Music Festival, *Wolfville*
Oct	**Celtic Colours Festival**, *Cape Breton*

claims to the region ended in 1713 (*see Introduction to Atlantic Provinces, History*).

Seafaring Nation – One great industry established by the Loyalists was **shipbuilding**, especially in the Napoleonic Wars (1803-15) when Britain needed wooden ships and ship parts. Sailors on Nova Scotia's renowned schooners were called **Bluenoses**, an American term of derision for people who could survive the region's cold climate. By 1900 shipbuilding waned; but boats are still crafted on the South Shore.

Preserving the Past – Nova Scotia boasts more historic sites than any province in Canada except Quebec. More than 20 historic sites are open to the public.

Genealogy is popular here: local museums, schools and universities, genealogical societies and churches have archival facilities for tracing one's roots. The province's food promotion, "**Taste of Nova Scotia**," is offered by more than 45 dining establishments. The **Gathering of the Clans** recalls the province's Scottish beginnings.

Annapolis Royal★★

One of Canada's oldest settlements, Annapolis Royal has a pleasant **site** overlooking the great basin of the Annapolis River. Acadians reclaimed the marshland by building a dam across the river with floodgates to control the water level. Twice a day the Bay of Fundy tides rush in, reversing the river's flow. This gracious town was the site of French-English battles and Acadian struggles.

A BIT OF HISTORY

The earliest settlement was a French colony at **Port Royal** under nobleman **Pierre du Gua, Sieur de Mons**, destroyed in 1613 by a force from Virginia. By 1635 the French governor **Charles de Menou d'Aulnay** had rebuilt the town. Over the next century the French settlement grew, forming the region called Acadia. In 1710 the fort fell to a New England expedition under Col. Francis Nicholson.

Renamed Annapolis Royal after England's **Queen Anne**, the town became the capital when the mainland was ceded to the British by the Treaty of Utrecht in 1713. However, it was subject to frequent French attack and in 1749 the capital was relocated to Halifax.

Much of the area's history is evident today: **Pierre du Gua, Sieur de Mons'** habitation has been reconstructed near Port Royal, Fort Anne has been partially re-created and the older buildings along **Lower Saint George Street** have been renovated.

SIGHTS
Fort Anne National Historic Site★

Grounds ⏱ *open year-round. Visitor Centre* ⚐🅿 *Open Jun & Sep Tue–Sat 9am–5:30pm, Jul–Aug daily.* 🎫*$3.90.* 📞*902-532-2397 (summer), 902-532-2321. www.pc.gc.ca. Check for 2-for-1 passes and the Candlelight Graveyard Tours (902) 532-3035.*

▶ **Population:** 481.
🚗 **Michelin Map:** p 358.
ℹ **Info:** Town Hall, 285 St. George St., 📞902-532-2043 or 877-522-1110. www.annapolisroyal.com.
▶ **Location:** Annapolis Royal lies opposite Saint John, NB, from which a ferry runs to nearby Digby.
🅿 **Parking:** There are three municipal lots, but no parking meters. Overnight parking on the street is tolerated.
👁 **Don't Miss:** The tidal generating station, one of the few in the world.
🕐 **Timing:** Allow at least two days to enjoy the town, including a day to explore Kejimkujik National Park, 48km/30mi from town.
👪 **Kids:** The Port Royal "habitation" is nicely sinister.

This fort was once the most fought-over place in Canada, suffering 14 sieges during the Anglo-French wars. In 1917 Fort Anne became the first National Historic Park (now Site) in Canada. In one of the bastions stands a stone **powder magazine** of the French period. From the earthworks there is a **view★** of the Annapolis Basin. Built in 1797 by order of Prince Edward, the **officers' quarters★**, now restored, house a **museum,** which includes a display on the fort's military history.

Historic Gardens★

On Upper Saint George St. (Rte. 8), just south of Fort Anne. ⚐⏱*Open May–Oct 9am–5pm, Jul–Aug til 8pm.* 🎫*$14.50.* 📞*902-532-7018. www.historicgardens.com.*
Overlooking Allain's River, a tributary of the Annapolis, this series of themed gardens exemplifies the horticultural diversity of the region's past as well as recent gardening technology.

The **Acadian Garden** has a traditional cottage and a replica of the dike system. The **Governor's Garden** is characteristic of formal 18C gardens. The **Victorian Garden** reveals a more natural setting. The **Rose Garden** traces the development of this ever-popular species.

Annapolis Tidal Power Generation Station★

On the Causeway (Rte. 1). Visitor Centre at 204 Prince Albert Rd. ♿🅿🕐*open mid-May–mid-Oct daily 9am–7pm.* 👓*Contribution suggested.* 👓*Guided tour* 👓*Free. Donations accepted.* ☎*902 -532-5454. www.annapolisroyal.com.* North America's first tidal power project, this station harnesses the enormous energy of the Bay of Fundy tides to produce electricity. The exhibit area explains the project and its construction. A causeway over the dam affords views of tidal activity and of the generating station.

EXCURSIONS
North Hills Museum★

5065 Granville Rd. in Granville Ferry (on road to Port Royal). ♿🕐*Open Jun–mid-Oct Mon–Sat 9.30am–5.30pm, Sun 1pm–5.30pm.* 👓*Free. Donations accepted.* ☎*902-532-2168. http://northhills.novascotia.ca.* Despite a series of modifications, this small wood-framed 18C house has retained a pioneer look. It provides a fitting setting for the predominantly 18C antique collection of a retired banker.

👥 Port-Royal National Historic Site★★

10km/6mi from Annapolis Royal Causeway.

This habitation (French word for "dwelling") is a replica of Canada's first European settlement of any permanence. The collection of dark, weathered, fortified buildings joined around a central courtyard was designed in a style reminiscent of 16C French farms by **Samuel de Champlain** (1567-1635), captain and navigator of the expedition of **Pierre du Gua, Sieur de Mons**. Destroyed in 1613 by English forces, the buildings were reconstructed in 1938 by the Canadian government, using Champlain's sketch and writings as guides.

Visit

🅿🕐*Open Jul–Aug daily 9am–6pm. Mid-May–Jun & Sept–mid-Oct Tue–Sat 9am–5.30pm.* 👓*$3.90.* ☎*902-532-2898 (summer), 902-532-2321. www.pc.gc.ca.* Over the gateway entry hangs the **coat of arms** of France and Navarre, ruled by King Henry IV.

C**olombage,** the term used in France for log-filled, wooden frame construction, was employed to form the walls. No nails or spikes join the timbers: they are mortised and tenoned and pinned together.

Kejimkujik National Park★★

Maitland Bridge. From Annapolis Royal 48km/30mi to park entrance, near Maitland Bridge. ♿🕐*Open mid-May–Labour Day from*

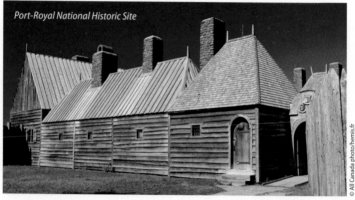
Port-Royal National Historic Site

© All Canada photo/hemis.fr

8.30am, during summer til 8pm.
$5.80. Hiking, camping, cycling,
swimming, canoeing, cross-country
skiing. Canoe & bicycle rental at Jakes
Landing. ☎902-682-2772.
www.pc.gc.ca.

For centuries the park's waterways
served the Mi'kmaq First Nations People and canoe routes still afford peaceful passage. The **Mill Falls** hiking trail
leads through fern-filled woods along
the ambling **Mersey River** to its foamy
rapids. The viewing tower *(on main park*
road, 10km/6mi from park entrance) permits an elevated **view★** of lovely Kejimkujik Lake.

Kejimkujik National Park

© PetrovVadim/iStockphoto.com

Annapolis Valley★★

Some of the earliest French colonists
settled in this region, only to be
deported by the British in 1755.
The Acadians built dikes to reclaim
the marshland for agricultural
production. In addition, the valley is
sheltered on both sides from heavy
wind and fog by the North and South
mountains, a feature that has nurtured
the valley's famed **apple orchards**.

🚗 DRIVING TOUR

DIGBY TO WINDSOR
213km/132mi

Digby
From this waterfront town, ferries cross
to New Brunswick. The harbour is often
busy with fishing fleets. Local restaurants feature **Digby scallops** prepared
in many ways (*see Addresses*).

▶ Take Hwy. 101 and then Rte. 1.

Highway 101 follows the shore of the
Annapolis Basin with pleasant views
until it turns inland at Deep Brook,
where Route 1 continues along the
shoreline.

- **Michelin Map:** pp 358-359.
- **Info:** ☎902-425-5781 or
  800-565-0000.
  www.novascotia.com.
- **Location:** Flowing to
  the sea, the **Annapolis
  River** widens into the
  Annapolis Basin, a tidal
  lake connected to the Bay
  of Fundy by a narrow outlet
  known as Digby Gut. The
  Annapolis Valley extends
  from Digby to Windsor
  on the Minas Basin.
- **Don't Miss:** The view of
  Annapolis Valley from
  the Look Off.
- **Timing:** Windsor, at the
  north end of the valley,
  connects to Halifax, which
  sits on the Atlantic side,
  via Hwy. 101.

Annapolis Royal★★
See ANNAPOLIS ROYAL.
Remains of the old French dike system
can be seen from the road. Route 1
crosses the river; wide meadows line
the riverbanks. At **Bridgetown★** elm-
shaded streets contain fine houses,
many built by Loyalists. **Lawrencetown**
and **Middleton** are similarly graced with
trees. Apple orchards line the hills, par-

ticularly between Kingston and Waterville, where fruit stands and "U-pick" farms are common.

▶ Continue 57km/35mi on Rte. 1 to junction with Rte. 358.

EXCURSION TO CAPE SPLIT★★

28km/17mi north by Rte. 358.

Prescott House Museum★

1633 Starr's Point Rd. in Starr's Point, off Rte. 358, about 5km/3mi north of Rte. 1. ⏱*Open Jun–Oct Mon–Sat 10am–5pm, Sun 1pm–5pm.* ▱*$3.90.* ♿ ✆*902-542-3984. http://museum.gov.ns.ca.*

This attractive whitewashed brick house, set amid lovely grounds, was built in the early 19C by **Charles Prescott**, legislator, merchant and acclaimed horticulturalist. On this estate Prescott experimented with new strains of wheat and of fruit. He is partly responsible for the development of the apple industry in this area.

The interior is attractively furnished with some original pieces. A pleasant **sun room** was added by Prescott's great-granddaughter. The **garden** is also worth visiting.

▶ Return to Rte. 358 and continue north.

The Look Off★★

Approximately 14km/9mi north of Starr's Point. Follow the signs on Rte. 358. Watch for paved pull-off with steel barricade.

Although there is no official marker for this site, one cannot pass by without stopping. The **view★★** of Annapolis Valley is magnificent. At least four counties are visible from this popular vantage point, some 200m/600ft above the valley floor.

About 8km/5mi north of The Look Off, as Route 358 descends into the tiny community of Scots Bay, there is a lovely **view★** of this bay, the Minas Channel and the Parrsboro Shore.

Cape Split★★

Rte. 358 ends. Hiking trail 13km/8mi through woods to tip of cape.

This hook of forested land juts into the Bay of Fundy, edged by magnificent cliffs. From road's end there are **views** of the wide bay, the shoreline of the cape and the Parrsboro Shore.

▶ Return via Rte. 358. After about 9km/6mi, take the unpaved road on the left (Stewart Mountain Rd.). At junction turn left. Road terminates at provincial park. Follow signs. Hiking trails for Cape Blomidon are shown on the panel in the visitor parking lot.

Beach at Cape Blomidon

Gwen Cannon/MICHELIN

Sam Slick

Thomas Chandler Haliburton became famous as the creator of the character Sam Slick, a fictitious Yankee peddler. His stories about Sam—22 in all—were first published in installments in the newspaper the *Novascotian*. In 1836 the newspaper's owner, Joseph Howe, published them as a book under the title *The Clockmaker; or, The Sayings and Doings of Samuel Slick of Slickville*. It was so popular, an estimated 80 editions were printed during the 19C. The book is basically a series of moral essays, made palatable by Haliburton's humour. A caricature of the proverbially dishonest 19C Connecticut salesmen who roamed rural areas, Slick travels all over Nova Scotia, making fun of its unenterprising inhabitants. Many of the epigrams he coined are still in use today: "six of one and half a dozen of the other," "an ounce of prevention is worth a pound of cure," "facts are stranger than fiction," "the early bird gets the worm," "as quick as a wink," and "jack of all trades and master of none" are among the most familiar.

Blomidon★

As the road leaves the woods and descends into flatlands, the first view of the **Minas Basin★★** is grand. Bright red barns and two-storey farmhouses dot the landscape, dominated by the red cliffs of Cape Blomidon.

From the end of the picnic area, the **views★★** in both directions of the wide red beach (at low tide), and the stratified pink cliffs, contrasted with the blue waters of the basin, are breathtaking, especially from Blomidon Provincial Park.

▶ At Blomidon junction, continue south via Pereau and Delhaven to Rte. 221.

About 2km/1.2mi south of the junction, there is a **view★** from Pereaux Small Crafts Harbour of the hole in a rock formation known locally as **Paddys Island,** fully visible at low tide.

▶ At the junction with Rte. 221, turn right to Canning for Rte. 358 back to Rte. 1.

Wolfville★

This charming town is home to **Acadia University**, founded in 1838. Several mansions have been converted into wayside inns (*see Addresses*).

Grand-Pré National Historic Site (UNESCO Heritage Site)★

Just north of Rte. 1, 4km/2.5mi east of Wolfville. &♿🅿🕐*Open daily after May 20 from 9am-5pm.* ⊗*$10.80, Youth $6.90, Family $27.13.* ✆*902-542-3631 or 866-542-3631. www.grand-pre.com.*

Before Deportation, Grand-Pré was the most important Acadian settlement in Nova Scotia, with about 200 farms along the edge of the Minas Basin. Residents who had moved here from Port Royal constructed a system of **dikes** to keep the sea out, while marsh water was allowed to escape through floodgates. The cultivated land soon supported crops, livestock and orchards. After Deportation, the farmlands were given to planters from New England, and later to Loyalists.

The American poet **Henry Wadsworth Longfellow** chose Grand-Pré as the setting for his poem *Evangeline*. Published in 1847, the work describes a young couple's separation during Deportation. On the site of the first church of Grand-Pré stands a small **chapel** (1930) constructed of local stone in a style reminiscent of churches in France. Inside, there are **displays** illustrating Acadian settlement, the British takeover and the final Deportation. A bronze **statue** of Evangeline by **Louis-Philippe Hébert** stands on the grounds. **Blacksmith** shop now open again.

Windsor

Famous as the home of writer Thomas Haliburton, one of the most prominent Nova Scotians of his day, the town is set at the confluence of the Avon and St. Croix rivers. The Avon is sealed off from Bay of Fundy by a causeway. The community was once the 18C Acadian settlement of Piziquid, taken over by New Englanders after Deportation and renamed Windsor.

Haliburton House Museum★

414 Clifton Ave. Follow signs from causeway. ○*Open Jun–Oct Mon–Sat 10am–5pm, Sun 1pm–5pm.* ⊙*$2.80.* *℘902-798-2915. http://haliburton-house.novascotia.ca.*

Built in 1836 on the tree-covered estate of **Thomas Chandler Haliburton** (1796-1865), judge, legislator and author, this mansion also houses Windsor's **Hockey Heritage Centre**. Haliburton, a lawyer and justice on the Provincial Supreme Court, was the first Canadian author to achieve international renown with *The Clockmaker; or, The Sayings and Doings of Samuel Slick of Slickville.*

Shand House Museum

389 Avon St. Street parking prohibited. Upon entrance to Windsor, watch for signs to separate parking area. ○*Uphill walk to the house.* ○*Open Jun–mid-Oct Mon–Sat 9.30am–5.30pm, Sun 1pm–5.30pm.* ⊙*$3.50.* *℘902-798-8213. http://shandhouse.novascotia.ca.*

The most imposing of the houses atop Ferry Hill overlooking the Avon River, this Victorian dwelling was completed in 1891. Furnishings are those of the original and only owners. Visitors can ascend the square tower.

Fort Edward National Historic Site

67 Fort Edward T., off King St. near causeway. ⊡○*Grounds open year-round. Blockhouse open late-Jun–late-Aug Tue–Sat 9:30am–5:30pm.* *℘902-798-4706 (late Jun-Sept), 902-532-2321. www.pc.gc.ca. Free admission.*

The blockhouse was built in 1750 as a British stronghold in Acadian territory. From the grassy fortification, there are **views** of the tidal river and Lake Pesaquid . Made of squared timbers, the **blockhouse** is the only remaining building of the fort. Inside are displays on the blockhouse defence system and the fort's history.

ADDRESSES

⌂ STAY

$$ Blomidon Inn – *195 Main St., Wolfville.* *℘902-542-2291 or 800-565-2291. www.blomidon.ns.ca. 31 rooms.* ✖⊡⊑. This elegant 19C sea captain's mansion sits on four acres near Acadia University. Rooms have antiques and include modern amenities; many have Jacuzzi tubs. Dine in one of two wood-panelled **dining rooms ($$)**, or enjoy afternoon tea on the terrace in summer.

$$ Woodshire Inn – *494 King St., Windsor.* ✖⌖⊡ *℘902-472-3300. www.thewoodshire.com. 6 rooms.* This brightly painted 19C house sports an inviting contemporary interior. Rooms have canopy beds, feather duvets, flat-screen TVs and ceiling fans. The sleek **bistro ($$)** offers lunch, a weekend brunch and dinner *(nightly).*

�$ EAT

Sample town's famous large scallops, prepared grilled, fried, stuffed, boiled, broiled, or rolled in cornmeal and sautéed in butter. Watch the town's inshore scallop fleet as you dine.

$ Captain's Cabin – *2 Birch St., Digby.* *℘902-245-4868. www.captainscabin.ns.ca.* Overlooks water. Seafood/steak.

$ Fundy Restaurant and Bar – *34 Water St., Digby.* *℘902-245-4950 or 866-445-4950. www.fundyrestaurant.com.* Breakfast, lunch and dinner on water.

$ Shore Line Restaurant – *78 Water St., Digby.* *℘902-245-2573. Closed Nov-Apr. www.shorelinerestaurantandgifts.ca/shoreline.html.* Serves breakfast, lunch and dinner.

Balmoral Mills★

This tiny community in central Nova Scotia is known for its operational 19C grist mill.

SIGHT
Balmoral Grist Mill Museum★

10km/6mi southeast of Tatamagouche by Rte. 311. 660 Matheson Brook Rd. 902-657-3016. http://balmoral gristmill.novascotia.ca. Grounds open year-round. Museum open Jun–Oct Mon–Sat 10am–5pm, Sun 1pm–5pm. $3.90 (child $2.80).

Standing beside Matheson Brook in a pleasant valley, this fully operational Balmoral Grist Mill was built in 1874. Although commercial use ceased in 1954, the mill has been completely restored.

When in operation *(a few hours daily)*, the mill is a hive of activity. Weighing over a tonne, the millstones (the runner stone is original; the bedstone was replaced in 2007) grind barley, oats, wheat and buckwheat into flour and meal *(for sale)*. Various milling processes are explained. Below the mill the revolving waterwheel can be seen.

- **Michelin Map:** p 359.
- **Info:** Northumberland Shore Region http://novascotia.com. 800-565-0000.
- **Location:** Tatamagouche lies between Amherst and New Glasgow along Hwy. 6 on the north coast. Balmoral Mills lies southeast of Tatamagouche.
- **Kids:** The display for children at the Sutherland Steam Mill.

EXCURSION
Sutherland Steam Mill Museum

In Denmark. 10km/6mi northeast by Rte. 311, minor road and Rte. 326. Open Jun–Oct Tue–Sat 10am–5pm, Sun 1pm–5pm. $3.90. 902-657-3016. http://sutherlandsteammill.novascotia.ca.

Alexander Sutherland built this sawmill in 1894. All machinery is in working order, and the mill "steams up" once a month *(phone ahead for schedule)*.There is a interactive **display** geared to children.

Balmoral Grist Mill Museum

© Wally Hayes/Nova Scotia Tourism, Culture and Heritage

Cabot Trail★★

Named for explorer **John Cabot**, who is reputed to have landed at the northern tip of Cape Breton Island in 1497, this romantic route is one of the most beautiful drives in North America. Opened in 1936, the paved, two-lane highway makes a spectacular tour of the northern part of the island not to be missed.

DRIVING TOUR

Round-trip of 301km/187mi from Baddeck.

BADDECK★

Overlooking Baddeck Bay, this charming village is the starting point of the Cabot Trail. The popular resort town has a lovely **site★★** on the north shore of **Bras d'Or Lake**. This immense inland sea's resemblance to a Scottish loch has attracted many settlers of Scottish origin. Among them was **Alexander Graham Bell** (1847-1922), humanitarian, researcher and prolific inventor.

Alexander Graham Bell National Historic Site★★

559 Chebucto Street, Baddeck.
♿🅿🕐*Open daily May–late-Oct 9am–5pm.* ✆*$7.80.* ✆*902-295-2069. www.pc.gc.ca.*
Bell's favourite shape, the tetrahedron, is used extensively in the design of this fascinating museum.
In 1885 Bell first visited Baddeck, where he was to conduct much of his aeronautical work. Eventually he chose the location for his summer residence, naming his home *Beinn Bhreagh*, "beautiful mountain" in Gaelic. The discovery of the telephone in 1874 had brought him fame and the capital to continue other research. In 1907, with other pioneer aviators, he founded the Aerial Experiment Assn. and sponsored the first manned flight in Canada when the **Silver Dart** flew across Baddeck Bay in 1909. His hydrofoil craft reach the incredible speed (for 1919) of 114kmh/70mph on Bras d'Or Lake.

⚬ **Michelin Map:** p 390.
🗐 **Information:** Destination Cape Breton Association. ✆888-562-9848. www.cbisland.com.
◖ **Location:** Cape Breton, an island off the north end of Nova Scotia, is connected to the mainland by the Canso Causeway.
🅿 **Parking:** There are places to pull over along the road; do not stop on the shoulder because traffic may not be able to avoid you.
◉ **Don't Miss:** The trail can be driven in either direction, but visitors may prefer clockwise travel for the security of hugging the mountainside during steep, curvy stretches.
🕐 **Timing:** You can make the circuit in one long day.
👪 **Kids:** The coal mining museum at Glace Bay.

There are models of the telephone, as well as many other ingenious devices. A highlight is the superb **photograph collection**, recording Bell's life and work. One wing of the museum is devoted to his hydrofoil, the HD-4. From the museum's rooftop garden, there is a **view** of the wooded headland across Baddeck Bay. Beinn Bhreagh (⚬*closed to the public*), can be seen among the trees.

FROM BADDECK TO CHÉTICAMP★

88km/55mi.
The Cabot Trail follows the valley of the Middle River, passes the Lakes O'Law and joins the Margaree River's verdant **valley★**.

North East Margaree

This tiny rural community has a museum of note.

Village of Chéticamp

© Gilles Rigoulet/hemis.fr

Margaree Salmon Museum★

&♿ &🕐*Open mid-Jun–mid-Oct daily 9am–5pm.* ☞*$2.* ✆*902-248-2848. www.margareens.com.*
This pleasant little museum features a large collection of colourful fishing flies and rods. The life cycle of the Atlantic salmon is illustrated.

The Cabot Trail parallels the Margaree River northward, affording pastoral **views★**. As the road descends, the **view★** of Margaree Harbour is lovely. The trail crosses the estuary of the Margaree River and heads north along the Acadian coast, with views of the Gulf of St. Lawrence.

Chéticamp

An enclave of Acadian culture, this fishing community lies opposite Chéticamp Island. A stone church dedicated to St. Peter distinguishes the town. Hand-hooked rugs are Chéticamp's claim to fame.

Acadian Museum

774 Main St. ✖♿🅿🕐*Open Jul–Aug daily 8am–9pm. May–Jun & Sept–mid-Oct daily 9am–5pm.* ✆*902-224-2170. www.inverness-ns.ca.*
Operated by a cooperative of Acadian women, the museum and gift shop feature hooked mats, rugs and other crafted items. There are demonstrations of hooking, spinning, carding and weaving. The on-site **restaurant** specializes in Acadian cooking (♿*see Addresses*).

FROM CHÉTICAMP TO CAPE SMOKEY
124km/77mi

Cape Breton Highlands National Park★★

Spanning coast to coast across northern Cape Breton, this 950sq km/367sq mi spectacular wilderness park combines seashore and mountains.
The west coast borders the waters of the Gulf of St. Lawrence. On the eastern side the Atlantic Ocean pounds the bare rocks with great force, yet there are several fine beaches throughout this preserve. Whales, and even bald eagles, can be found on either shore.

Visit

Cape Breton Highlands National Park (Ingonish Beach is both salt & fresh water). ♿🅿🕐*Open year-round.* ☞*$7.80 entry fee. Information centres (*🕐*Visitor Centres open mid-May–mid-Oct, spring & fall 9am-5pm, Summer 8:30am–7pm, centres located at park entrances north of Chéticamp and at Ingonish Beach (* ✆*902-224-2306). www.pc.gc.ca.*
From park entrance at Chéticamp River, Cabot Trail winds up Chéticamp Canyon

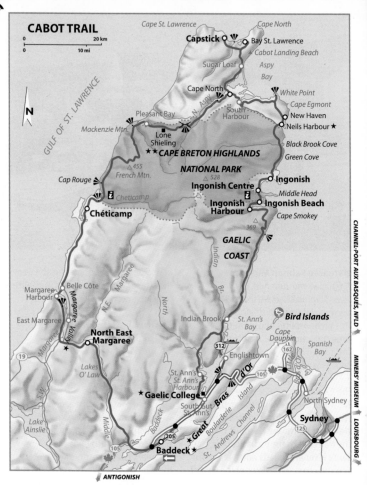

to emerge on the coast, parallel to the sea, affording fine **views★★**. From **Cap Rouge** lookout, there is an especially lovely **view★★**. The road gradually climbs French Mountain and heads inland across the plateau.

The road descends to Mackenzie Mountain. Then, by a series of switchbacks, it reaches Pleasant Bay with outstanding **views★★** on the descent. The **Lone Shieling** (about 6.5km/4mi from Pleasant Bay, then short walk) is a replica of a Scottish crofter's cottage. The road climbs North Mountain, descends steeply, affording pretty **views★**, and then enters the valley of the North Aspy River, which it follows to the village of **Cape North.**

Bay St. Lawrence★★

38km/24mi round-trip from Cape North. This scenic drive rounds Aspy Bay, affording views of its long sandbar, and then heads inland to St. Lawrence Bay at the north end of Cape Breton Island. At the end of the road is the tiny fishing village of **Bay St. Lawrence.** Near the approach to the village, a large white clapboard church (St. Margaret's) is prominent. From its grounds the **view★** of the bay community is picturesque.

◗ Upon leaving Bay St. Lawrence, turn right and continue 3km/1.8mi to Capstick.

Cabot Trail, Cape Breton Highlands National Park

© Jerry Whaley/age fotostock

Capstick

This hillside settlement consists of a few isolated houses above the seacliffs. The dramatic **views★** of the inlets through the scraggy pines are enhanced by the beauty of the water's color.

◗ Return to Cabot Trail. After South Harbour, take coast road.

After fine **views★** of Aspy Bay, its sand-bar and the long Cape North peninsula, the road turns south after White Point through the charming fishing villages of **New Haven** and **Neils Harbour★**.

◗ Rejoin Cabot Trail.

This section of the trail is an especially splendid drive along the coast, particularly after **Black Brook Cove**. Worn pink boulders stretch into the sea, while green forests cover the inlands. **Green Cove** is a lovely spot. From Lakie's Head lookout the narrow peninsula of **Middle Head** and towering Cape Smokey can be identified.

The Ingonishs

Ingonish Centre, Ingonish Beach, Ingonish Harbour and other Ingonish designations are popular resort spots. The bay itself is cut into two parts by Middle Head, the dramatic setting of the **Keltic Lodge,** one of Canada's best-known resort hotels. To the south **Cape Smokey** rises out of the sea.

THE GAELIC COAST: CAPE SMOKEY TO BADDECK
89km/55mi.

The trail climbs over Cape Smokey and then drops again, permitting several good **views★**.

Offshore are the **Bird Islands**, a sanctuary where vast numbers of seabirds nest in summer. The trail rounds St. Ann's Harbour, offering lovely views at South Gut St. Ann's.

Gaelic College★
In St. Ann's.

Founded in 1938 by Rev. A.W.R. MacKenzie, this school is the only one on the continent to teach the Gaelic language and Highland arts and crafts. Attracting youth from all over North America, the college offers such courses as bagpipe music, Highland dancing and hand weaving of clan tartans. During July and August, the college hosts a *ceilidh* [KAY-lee] featuring local performers *(Wed evening)*, a must-see event. N. B. Outsiders must be asked to dance by a local before hitting the floor.

Great Hall of the Clans
51779 Cabot Trail Rd., on campus.
♿🅿🕐*Open mid-May–early-Oct daily
9am–5pm.* ⬤*$8 (child $6, family $20)*
📞*902-295-3411. gaeliccollege.edu.*
Inside the large hall, wall **exhibits**,
some interactive, illustrate clan history
and life. At one end of the hall stands a
statue of Angus MacAskill (1825-63), the
236cm/7ft 9in-tall, 193kg/425-pound
"Cape Breton giant" who toured the US
with the midget Tom Thumb.

Alternative Route★
*22km/14mi by Rte. 312 and
Trans-Canada Hwy.*
This road enters St. Ann's Bay via a narrow spit of land that divides the bay
from St. Ann's Harbour. At the end of
the spit, a ferry crosses the outlet *(24hrs
daily, every 10min; Feb–Apr no crossing if
ice;* ♿ 📞*902-861-1911; www.gov.ns.ca).*

EXCURSIONS
Great Bras d'Or★
*18km/11mi northeast along Trans-Can
Hwy. from South Gut St. Ann's.*
The road ascends Kelly's Mountain with
a **view**★ from the lookout of the harbour. Crossing Cape Dauphin peninsula,
it descends to the Great Bras d'Or. There
are good **views**★ of this stretch of water,
and in the distance, of **Sydney,** Cape
Breton's principal city.

Bra d'Or Lakes Biosphere Reserve ★★
532 Chebucto St. 📞*902-674-2578.
www.blbra.ca.*
In 2011, this site was designated as Canada's 16th UNESCO Biosphere Reserve.
It encompasses a salt-water estuary
watershed "inland sea" with three pas-
sages to the Atlantic Ocean.

Miners' Museum★★
*42 Birkley St.,Glace Bay. 19km/12mi
northeast of Sydney. Follow museum
signs from town to Quarry Point.*
✖♿🅿🕐*Open mid-May–Sep daily
10am–6pm. Restaurant open Apr–late
Oct daily 11am–8pm.* ⬤*$6 (*🥾*guided
tour $15; protective clothing provided).*
📞*902-849-4522.
www.minersmuseum.com.*
Overlooking the Atlantic Ocean from its
6ha/15-acre site, this museum stands as
a monument to Cape Breton's coal-mining history, which ended in 1984.
The museum has exhibits on coal formation and mining methods. Retired
miners conduct **mine tours** *(30min),*
and a **miners' village** has been reconstructed. In addition to a store, a miner's
house of the period 1850-1900 has been
re-created. The restaurant *(hours vary)*
serves home-cooked specialties.

ADDRESSES

🛏 STAY
$$$ Keltic Lodge – *Middle Head
Peninsula, Ingonish Beach.* ✖🅿♨Spa
📞*902-285-2880 or 800-565-0444. www.
kelticlodge.ca. 74 rooms. 9 cottages. Closed
late Oct–mid-May.* This sprawling cliff-side
resort overlooks the Atlantic Ocean
from a forested promontory on Cape
Breton's east side. Guest rooms are richly
appointed, cottages have fireplaces, there
is a spa, and nightly music. The **Purple
Thistle ($$)** serves Canadian dishes and
the **Atlantic Restaurant ($)** offers steaks
and seafood. Heated outdoor pool, tennis
courts and 18-hole golf course.

🍽 EAT
$ Restaurant Acadien – *At the
Chéticamp Hooked Rugs Coopérative
Artisanale, Chéticamp.* 📞*902-224-2170.
http://www.inverness-ns.ca/acadian-
museum.html.* Authentic Acadian-style
foods served with an emphasis on the
locally fashioned hooked rugs and
other artisanal souvenirs. Also includes
examples of wood carving, spinning,
and weaving traditions. Operates as a
cooperative, so patronage is appreciated
and donations accepted.

Halifax★★★

The capital of Nova Scotia overlooks one of the finest harbours in the world. The deep outer inlet of the Atlantic Ocean narrows into a protected inner harbour called the **Bedford Basin**. The foot-shaped peninsula upon which the city was built is dominated by a hill, topped with a star-shaped citadel. These two factors—a natural harbour and a man-made fortress—were the basis of the city's founding.

A BIT OF HISTORY

Early History – Halifax came into being because of the existence of Louisbourg. New Englanders had successfully captured the French fortress in 1745, only to see it later returned to France. Responding to their anger, in 1749 the Governor of Nova Scotia, Col. **Edward Cornwallis,** and about 2,500 English settlers constructed a fortified settlement on the site of the present-day city. From its inception Halifax was shaped by the military—from the social gatherings of the nobility (officers in both services) to the presence of brothels along the wharves. Even law was martial; citizens had no power for nearly 100 years, until Halifax achieved city status.

The Royal Princes – Forbidden by their father to remain in England, two

- ▶ **Population:** 390,328.
- ◔ **Michelin Map:** p359, p394.
- ▤ **Info:** ; Destination Halifax, 1800 Argyle St.,Suite 802-422-9334. www. destinationhalifax.com.
- ▶ **Location:** Halifax lies on the east coast of Nova Scotia, at about the mainland's mid-point, facing the Atlantic Ocean.
- ℙ **Parking:** Downtown Halifax is quite congested and parking is difficult. Meters are colour-coded to indicate the maximum time you can park. Red means 30min, grey 90min, green 2hrs and yellow 3-5hrs. The rate is $1.50 an hour. There are also public and private lots.
- ☻ **Don't Miss:** The Citadel is historic w/ lovely views.
- ◷ **Timing:** Two days to see Halifax; it is a good base from which to tour area.
- ♟ **Kids:** Maritime Museum of the Atlantic has actual ships berthed alongside, and the Museum of Natural History has exhibits for children. Pier 21 has exhibits for kids.

Citadel Hill
© shaunl/iStockphoto.com

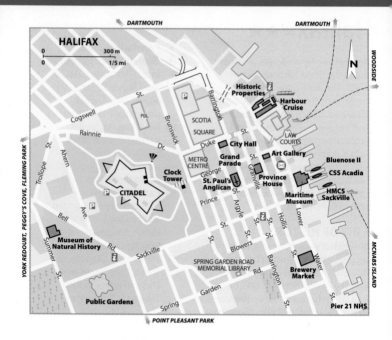

scapegrace sons of **George III** made Halifax their home. The future **William IV** spent his 21st birthday in wild revels off the port. His brother **Edward,** Duke of Kent, and later the father of Queen Victoria, served as Commander in Chief in Halifax from 1794 to 1800. Spending a fortune on defences, he made Halifax a member of the famous quadrilateral of British defences, which included Gibraltar and Bermuda. He installed the first telegraph system in North America by which he could relay orders to his men from Annapolis Royal or from Bedford Basin, where his mistress lived.

The City Today – Halifax is the largest city in the Atlantic provinces and the region's commercial and financial heart as well as a major seaport and the Atlantic base of the **Canadian Navy.** As a major port city, Halifax welcomes thousands of cruise ship passengers annually. It is also home to five universities. Halifax's hilly streets are stacked with colourful wooden houses. During the summer months, seaside restaurants and cafes bustle, boats from nearby yacht clubs fill the harbour and large cruise ships linger in port.

SIGHTS
Halifax Citadel National Historic Site★★

The present star-shaped citadel is the fourth fort since 1749 to crown the hill overlooking Halifax. Begun in 1828 at the order of the Duke of Wellington, the fort was completed in 1856. Although never attacked, it was occupied by the military until after World War II.

The Citadel's site offers **views★** of the city, harbour, Dartmouth, George's Island and the Angus McDonald suspension bridge. Note the attractive **clock tower,** the symbol of Halifax; the 1803 original was ordered by Prince Edward. The fortification contains a large central parade ground where soldiers attired in 19C uniforms perform military drills (mid-Jun–Labour Day daily).

Visit

✕🅿🕐Grounds open year-round. Citadel open Jul–Aug daily 9am–6pm; early May–Jun and Sept–Oct 9am–5pm. Rest of the year grounds open without services. 🕐Closed Dec. 25. ⊚$11.70 ($7.80 off-season) Parking $3.15. ✆902-426-5080. www.pc.gc.ca. Coffee bar & library.

PRACTICAL INFORMATION
GETTING AROUND
BY PUBLIC TRANSPORTATION –
The municipality operates public
transit buses and ferries. **Buses** run
Mon–Sun 6am–1am. **Ferries** run
frequently (12min Halifax-Dartmouth)
Mon–Sat 6am–midnight, Sun 6am–
6.30pm. Cash **fare** is $2.50. Bulk tickets
(20 for $32) available at drug stores,
bookstores, bus terminals, grocery
stores. Route information: *902-490-
4000 or 800-835-6428; www.halifax.ca/
metrotransit.*

Free rides downtown Jul–late Oct
through FRED service: *902-423-
6658; www.downtownhalifax.ns.ca.*
BY CAR – Rental agencies: **Avis**
902-492-2847. **Discount** *902-
468-7171.* **Budget** *902-492-7500.*
Enterprise *800-736-8222.*
BY TAXI – A frequent **airport shuttle**
from the airport to downtown
hotels costs about $20; a taxi from
the airport costs about $55. Cab
companies: Yellow *902-420-0000.*
Casino *902-425-6666.*

GENERAL INFORMATION
LOCAL MEDIA – **Daily** newspapers:
Halifax Chronicle Herald and *Globe and
Mail.* The *Metro* is a free local daily.
Weekly: *The Coast.* **Monthly**: *Where
Halifax magazine.*
ENTERTAINMENT – Consult the
supplements in local newspapers for
schedules. Purchase tickets through
Ticket Atlantic *902-451-1221.*
PERFORMING ARTS – Neptune
Theatre – *1593 Argyle St.* *902-429-
7070 or 800-565-7345. www. neptune*
theatre.com. *Sept–May, sometimes to
Jul.* Fresh compositions by new artists
as well as traditional favourites.
The Cohn – *6101 University Ave.*
902-494-3820. Dalousie University's
auditorium showcases local, national
and international music and theater.
NIGHTLIFE – **The Dome** – *1726-
1740 Argyle St.* *902-422-5453. www.
thedome.ca. Wed–Sun.* Large nightclub
with local and visiting DJs and six bars
(open til 3.30am).
The Maxwell's Plum – *1600
Grafton St.* ✕*902-423-5090. www.
themaxwellsplum.com.* Friendly pub
with 60 beers on tap and cheap eats.
Hearty weekend brunch.
The Split Cow – *1855 Granville St.* ✕
902-422-4366. Popular pub attracts
rockers, CEOs and students. Live "east
coast" music.
Reflections Cabaret – *5184 Sackville
St.* *902-422-2957.* Here 20- to
50-somethings dance and watch
talent shows.

USEFUL NUMBERS
Police–Ambulance–Fire: **911**
(Emergencies only)
Halifax Train Station (ViaRail) 1161
Hollis St. 888-842-7245; www.viarail.ca
Halifax International Airport 902-
873-4422; www.hiaa.ca
Canadian Automobile Assn. 3514
Joseph Howe Dr. 902-443-5530
Shoppers Drug Mart *(24hr pharmacy)*
902-429-2400
Road conditions: Dial 511;
www.weathernetwork.ca
Weather *(24hr)* : www.halifax.ca
(click on visitors).

Surrounded by a dry defensive ditch,
the complex houses a visitor centre, barracks, powermagazines and a museum.
Visitors can walk on the ramparts and
visit the outer ditches and ravelins. An
audiovisual presentation *(50min)*, **Tides
of History,** covers the history of Halifax
and its defences. Precisely at midday
every day, the **noon gun** is fired. Don't
miss the mock battles on the slope of
Citadel Hill Saturdays 10am-5pm & Sundays til 3pm.

Historic Properties and
the Harbour★
Off Upper Water Street, the pedestrian
area between Duke Street and the Cogswell interchange is called the Historic

Waterfront in the Historic Properties

© Reinhard Schmid/Sime/Photononstop

Properties. Several 19C stone ware-houses and wooden buildings house shops, studios, restaurants and pubs. From Historic Properties visitors can walk west through a series of restored buildings to the Granville Street Mall and Scotia Square. A **boardwalk** follows the harbourfront north around the Shera-ton Hotel and south past the Law Courts and the terminus of the passenger ferry to Dartmouth. North America's oldest farmer's market (1750) can be found at the southern end of the waterfront. Halifax Seaport Farmer's Market is at the base of Terminal Road. (℘902-492-4043)

Harbour Cruise★★

Departs from 1751 Lower Water St., May–mid-Oct daily 2pm (also 6.30pm dinner cruise in peak season). Round-trip dinner Cruise. ◎$71.99. 1hr Pirate Tour tour $21.99. Murphy's on the Water Tours ℘902-420-1015. www.murphysonthewater.com.

The Harbour Queen cruise provides a view of the installations around Halifax harbour. The cruise rounds Point Pleas-ant and enters the **North West Arm,** a lovely stretch of water extending along the peninsula's west side and bordered by expensive homes and yacht clubs.

Maritime Museum of the Atlantic★

1675 Lower Water St. Open May–Oct daily 9.30am–5pm (Tue til 8pm; Sun opens 1pm May & Oct). Rest of the year Tue–Sat 9.30am–5pm (Tue til 8pm), Sun 1pm–5pm. Closed Jan 1, Good Friday, Dec 25–26. ◎$9.25 (child $5); ℘902-424-7490. http://maritimemuseum. novascotia.ca.

Note the restored ship's **chandlery,** housed in an old warehouse. Other highlights include an extensive display on the *Titanic* and the recent acquisi-tion of Family Letters from the 1917 Halifax Explosion. Outside, moored at the museum's wharf, The **CSS Acadia,** a 200-foot steamship built in 1913 for the Canadian Hydrographic Service, can be boarded *(May –mid-Oct).*

In summer the **Bluenose II,** a replica of the schooner that held the Inter-national Fishermen's trophy for 17 years, offers **cruises** in Halifax Harbour when not visiting other ports *(departs from museum's wharf Jun–Sept; call Fisheries Museum of the Atlantic in Lunenberg for schedule & reservations ℘902-634-4794 or 866-579-4909.*

The restored **HMCS Sackville,** a World War II corvette that served in the Bat-tle of the Atlantic, can also be boarded *(Jun–Oct; ◎$5; ℘902-429-2132).*

Province House★

1726 Hollis St. &OOpen Jul–Aug Mon–Fri 9am–5pm, Sat–Sun & holidays 10am–4pm. Rest of the year Mon–Fri 9am–4pm. To book a tour, call 902-424-5982. http://nslegislature.ca. Visitors must secure a pass from the front desk.

This Georgian 1819 sandstone structure houses the Legislative Assembly of Nova Scotia, which has existed since 1758. Visitors can see the **Red Chamber,** where the Legislative Council used to meet, and observe debates in the **assembly chamber**. Once housing the provincial Supreme Court, the **legislative library** was the site, in 1835, of the self-defence of journalist **Joseph Howe** against a charge of criminal libel. His acquittal marked the beginning of a free press in Nova Scotia.

Art Gallery of Nova Scotia★

1723 Hollis St. &OOpen year-round Wed-Fri 10am–5pm (Thu til 9pm), Fri+Sat-10am-5pm, Sun noon–5pm. OClosed Jan 1 & Dec 24–26. $6. Call for tour. 902-424-5280. www.artgalleryofnovascotia.ca.

Housed in the stately Dominion Building and the adjacent Provincial Building, this modern museum exhibits Canadian art, including paintings of the **Group of Seven,** as well as international art. Regional **folk art**—painting, sculptures, paper and textiles—is a highlight. The museum possesses a small but excellent collection of **Inuit art.** Since 2006, a satellite branch is located in Yarmouth.

Grand Parade

Bordered by **City Hall** at one end and **St. Paul's Anglican Church** at the other, this pleasant square has been the centre of Halifax since its founding. The small, timber-framed church is the oldest Protestant church in Canada (1750).

⚑ Museum of Natural History★

1747 Summer St. &POOpen May–Nov Mon–Sun 9am–5pm (Wed til 8pm).

Fisherman's Cove

4, Government Wharf Rd., Eastern Passage NS (to end of Rte. 111 South from either harbour bridge, then Rte. 322 South). Visitor Information Centre, Bldg 24. 902-465-6093. www.fishermanscove.ns.ca.

On the Atlantic Ocean side of Dartmouth, this little cove is accessible by car or Taxsea from Halifax's Cable Wharf. Fishing boats bob in the water along the wharf and colourfully painted huts resemble fishermen's quarters. Crafts sold include fine Nova Scotian artwork and regionally published books. Try sharing the Admiral's Seafood Platter at **Boondock's Dining Room ($$)** *(6 Government Wharf Rd., 902-465-3474. www. boondocksdining.ca).* A raised boardwalk leads through the sea grass near the water's edge.

Rest of the year Tue–Sun 9am–5pm (Wed til 8pm). $6.230(child $4.05). 902-424-7353. http://naturalhistory. novascotia.ca.

Mi'kmaq exhibits and archaeological displays, natural-history dioramas and marine life, especially whales and sharks, can be viewed.

Kids especially will enjoy the saltwater touch tank and re-created beehive, and at the **nature centre,** snakes, frogs and turtles. Ask about their Wee Wild Ones Program, and say hello to Gus, the 90-year-old gopher tortoise.

Public Gardens★

Main entrance at corner of Spring Garden Rd. & South Park St. &OOpen daily Apr–Nov 8am–dusk. No entry fee. www.halifaxpublicgardens.ca.

Opened to the public in 1867, this 7ha/17-acre park is a fine example of a Victorian garden, with weeping trees, ponds, fountains, statues, formal plantings and an ornate bandstand. Note the massive wrought-iron entrance gate.

Bandstand in the Public Gardens

Pamela Delaney/Michelin

Point Pleasant Park★

ⓗ*Closed to traffic;* ⓟ*Parking on Point Pleasant Dr. at Tower Rd. and near container terminal.* ⓗ*Park open from 6am–midnight and office open Mon–Fri 8am–4pm.* ℘*902-490-4700. www.pointpleasantpark.ca.*

Situated at the southernmost point of the peninsula, this lovely 75ha/186-acre park has excellent **views★★** of the harbour and the North West Arm. In 2003, an almost direct hit by Hurricane Juan destroyed more than 75,000 trees in the park. An extensive two-year series of

Shubenacadie Park

Locks Rd., Dartmouth (Rte. 111 South from either harbour bridge, take the Waverley Rd. exit, watch for signs). ℘*902-462-1826.* Over a century ago, the historic Shubenacadie Canal linked Halifax Harbour with the Bay of Fundy through a series of connected lakes and rivers. Today part of the canal route cuts through a park with scenic walking and biking trails that edge two lakes. Restored canal locks lie along the trails, and there is an historical exhibit at the Fairbanks Centre. The park includes a campground, playground, swimming area and boat rentals (canoes, kayaks, paddleboats).

public consultations led to a long-term plan to renew this park leased from Britain on a 999-year lease.

Prince of Wales Tower

ⓗ*Grounds open year-round. Tower open Jul–Labour Day daily 10am–6pm.* ℘*902-426-5080. www.pc.gc.ca.*

The prototype of what came to be called a **Martello tower**, this circular stone structure was the first of its kind in North America.

Prince Edward ordered its construction in 1796, naming the tower for his brother—the future George IV.

Canadian Museum of Immigration at Pier 21★

1055 Marginal Rd. ♿ⓟ ⓗ*Open May–Nov daily 9.30am–5.30pm. Dec–Mar Tue–Sat 10am–5pm. Apr Mon–Sat 10am–5pm.* ⓢ*$11 (child $7).* ℘*902-425-7770 or 855-526-4721. www.pier21.ca.*

Over a million refugees, immigrants and war brides passed through this immigration shed from 1928 until 1971. The pier was also the departure point for World War II troops on their way to Europe. Displays recount the compelling story of the largely European influx. Children especially will enjoy the hands-on activities and the period railway car.

EXCURSIONS
McNabs Island★

Access by ferry from Halifax waterfront. For schedules: Metro Transit in Halifax ℘*902-465-4563 or 800-326-4563; www.mcnabsisland.com.*

Located in Halifax Harbour, east of Point Pleasant Park, the island has thick forests, colourful wildflowers and large pond. Old roads serve as walking and cycling trails that lead to the remains of Fort McNab *(at the south end),* sand beaches and good views, especially from the lighthouse.

Sir Sandford Fleming Park

5.5km/3mi by Cogswell St., Quinpool Rd. & Purcell's Cove Rd. (Rte. 253). ⓗ*Open year-round daily 8am–dusk. Walking trails, swimming, boating,* picnic area. ♿🅿️☎️902-490-4000 (Metro Transit routes).

This park, locally called "The Dingle" is a tribute to **Sir Sandford Fleming** (1827-1915), a Scottish engineer who helped build Canada's continental railway system, designed the nation's first postage stamp and urged the adoption of international standard time.

Walking trails lead to Frog Pond off Purcell's Cove Road. The long stretch of North West Arm can be seen in its entirety from the recenty repaired **Dingle Tower** (🕐open Jun–Oct daily 8am–5pm).

York Redoubt★

11km/7mi by Cogswell St., Quinpool Rd. & Purcell's Cove Rd. (Rte. 253).
🅿️🕐*Grounds open year-round from 8am, summer til 8pm.* ☎️*902-426-5080. www.pc.gc.ca.*

First constructed in 1793, the defences were strengthened by Prince Edward, who named the redoubt for his brother, the Duke of York. During World War II the redoubt was vital in the city's defence. At the north end are the remains of a stone tower. Gun emplacements face the harbour approach. At the south end the **command post** has displays on the defences, and from it *(weather permitting)* good **views★** of the harbour.

Dartmouth★

Site of a naval dockyard and research centre, Halifax's twin city across the inlet has a popular waterfront and shop-lined streets. Waterside park, a venue for summer concerts, features the **World Peace Pavilion**. Connected to Halifax by bridges, Dartmouth is serviced by the **ferry Christopher Stannix**. (♿🅿️🕐*departs from Lower Water St. daily; 🚫no service Jan 1, Good Friday, Easter Sunday & Dec 25. 12min;* ☎️*$2.50;* ☎️*902-490-4000; www.halifax.ca).*

The Quaker House

57 Ochterloney St. 🔍*Visit by guided tour only, Jun–Aug Tue–Sun 10am–1pm & 2pm–5pm.* ☎️*$5.* ☎️*902-464-2253. dartmouthheritagemuseum.ns.ca.*

A short stroll from the ferry terminal, this heritage house is the sole survivor of 22 dwellings built for a group of Quaker whalers who moved to the province from New England in 1785. Restored to the period, the house has a shingled exterior with paned windows, an off-centre door, exposed beams and a narrow winding staircase. An herb garden occupies the backyard.

Black Cultural Centre for Nova Scotia

10 Cherry Brook Rd. ♿🅿️🕐*Open daily 10am–4pm, Sat noon-3pm, Closed Sun.* ☎️*$6.* ☎️*902-434-6223 or 800-465-0767 www.bccns.com.*

This sizable museum, library and meeting hall foster the province's black history and culture. There is a memorial to naval hero **William Hall** (1827-1904), the first Nova Scotian and first black to be awarded the Victoria Cross, the Commonwealth's military medal for exceptional courage.

Uniacke Estate Museum Park★

758 #1 Hwy., in Mt. Uniacke, 40km/25mi northwest by Rtes. 7 and 1. Grounds 🅿️🕐*open year-round daily dawn–dusk. House open Jun–Oct Tue–Sat 10am–5pm, Sun 11:30am–5pm.*☎️*$4.* ☎️*902-866-0032. http://uniacke.novascotia.ca.*

This fine example of plantation-style Colonial architecture, completed in 1815, was the country home of Richard Uniacke, Attorney-General of Nova Scotia from 1797 to 1830.

The interior looks today as it did in 1815, including several mahogany pieces crafted by George Adams of London.

ADDRESSES

🛏️ STAY

$ Fountainview Guest House – *2138 Robie St.* ☎️*902-422-4169 or 800-565-4877. www.angelfire.com/id/fountainview. 8 rooms.* 🅿️.Situated across from Halifax Commons, this guest house lies close to restaurants and commercial services. Fountainview offers variously sized clean rooms with shared bathrooms. For an extra charge, a light breakfast can be served in your room.

$$$ Seawatch Bed&Breakfast – *139 Ferguson's Cove Road.* ℰ*902-477-1506. https://seawatch.ca*. Two nautical-themed suites provide the perfect perch to watch the sunrise, seals, whales, boats, and marine goings-on from the western shore of Halifax Harbour across from McNab's Island. Near Mauger's Beach Lighthouse, each suite has ensuite bathroom, and breakfast is served on deck or in suite.

$$ Hampton Inn by Hilton Downtown Halifax – *1960 Brunswick St.* ℰ*902-422 1391 or 800-426-7866. http://hamptoninn3.hilton.com.* ✕🅿🖾 Located on the edge of the downtown core, hotel is ideally located within walking distance of all of the downtown amenities. At the base of the Halifax Citadel National Historic Site, adjacent to the Metro Centre and the World Trade and Convention Centre.

$$ The Halliburton – *5184 Morris St.* ℰ*902-420-0658 or 888-512-3344. www. thehalliburton.com. 29 rooms.* ✕🅿🖾 Housed in three contiguous early 19C town houses, this downtown hostelry has a tasteful sitting room with wing chairs, oil portraits and a fireplace greets arriving guests. **Stories ($$$)** (ℰ*902-444-4400*) the hotel restaurant, is renowned for its inventive fusion-style entrées. A garden courtyard is also available for dining.

$$ The Lord Nelson Hotel and Suites – *1515 South Park St.* ℰ*902-423-6331 or 800-565-2020. www.lordnelsonhotel.com. 261 rooms.* Valet parking $40. ✕🅱🅿. Built by the Canadian Pacific Railway in 1928, handsome rooms in soothing colours overlook neighbouring Public Gardens. Ask about longstay. English pub-style **The Arms ($)** restaurant serves breakfast, lunch and dinner. .

$$ Prince George Hotel – *1725 Market St.* ℰ*902-425-1986 or 800-565-1567. www. princegeorgehotel.com. 203 rooms.* ✕🅱🅿🖾. Situated in the heart of downtown, the Prince George features a fitness centre with state-of-the-art exercise equipment and a heated indoor pool. The **Gio ($$$)** restaurant offers a sophisticated menu with local products (ℰ*902-425-1987*). Closed Sundays. For excursions, the hotel will pack lunches.

$$ Waverley Inn – *1266 Barrington St.* ℰ*902-423-9346 or 800-565-9346. www. waverleyinn.com. 34 rooms.* 🅱🅿🖾 Guest rooms in this historic 1870s inn are richly furnished with Victorian antiques,

massive wooden beds and modern amenities. Deluxe rooms have feather duvets and whirlpool baths. A hospitality suite provides snacks.

🍴 EAT

$ Bluenose II Restaurant – *1824 Hollis St.* ℰ*902-425-5092.* **Seafood/Greek**. For 25-plus years the Bluenose has been serving fresh seafood and Greek platters to locals and travelers. Daily specials include catch-of-the-day like haddock, plus lobster rolls, clams and chips.Their clam and corn chowders are delicious. www.bluenoseii.ca

$$ Il Mercato Ristorante – *1595 Bedford Hwy, Sunnyside Mall.* 🅱 ℰ*902-832-4531. www.il-mercato.ca.* **Italian**. This lively restaurant offers creative pasta, pizza and focaccia sandwiches and more.Favourites include ravioli stuffed with roasted chicken and linguine with grilled shrimp and lemon cream sauce.

$$ Economy Shoe Shop – *1661-1663 Argyle St.* ℰ*902-423-7463. www. economyshoeshop.ca.* **International**. A neon sign from an old cobbler's shop inspired this odd name. The Shoe Shop is a bar frequented by artistic types. Catering to the after-theatre and jazz crowds serving tapas, lobster flambé, pizzas and pastas, as well as seafood, steaks and chicken.

$ Tomavino's Ristorante – *5173 South St.* ℰ*902-425-7111. Italian.* Located at Hollis Street, this subterranean trattoria with brick walls and flickering candles features gourmet pizzas and pastas. Chicken fusilli (chicken breast in pesto, tomatoes and cream) is popular. Summer patrons patio dine.

$$$ da Maurizio Dining Room – *1496 Lower Water St.(inside Alexander Keith brewery). Closed Sun.* ℰ*902-423-0859. www.damaurizio.ca.* 🅱. **Italian**. Haligonians consider this restaurant one of the finest in the city. The menu is refined, imaginative and authentic Italian. Try their Prix Fixe menu.

Fortress of Louisbourg★★★

Guarding the entrance of the
St. Lawrence River, the approach
to Quebec, Louisbourg was once
the great 18C fortress of New
France, manned by the largest
garrison in North America. The
$25 million restoration of this
National Historic Site is the most
expensive preservation project
ever undertaken by the Canadian
Government.

Access

*37km/23mi south of Sydney by Rte. 22,
southwest of town of Louisbourg.*

A BIT OF HISTORY

A Bleak Beginning – When the French
lost the mainland of Nova Scotia in 1713,
they decided to construct a fortified
town on the eastern peninsula of Île
Royale (now Cape Breton); work began
in 1719.

The massive undertaking was riddled
with problems: a harsh climate, a boggy
site, scarce building materials and a few
corrupt French officials. Difficult living
conditions and lack of discipline among
the common soldiers contributed to a
mutiny in 1744.

A Not-So-Impregnable Fortress – In
1745, prior to completion, 4,000 New
Englanders attacked the "impregnable"
fortress. Less than two months later the
French surrendered. In 1748 the British
agreed to return the fort to the island
colony of King **Louis XV,** founding Halifax as a counter-fortress. Ten years later
Louisbourg surrendered again, this time
to British regulars. **James Wolfe,** the
second in command, went on to capture
Quebec City in 1759. To prevent further
threat, the British destroyed Louisbourg
in 1760.

Since 1961 one-quarter of the fortress
has been rebuilt according to the original plans and historical records.

VISIT

✕ ♿ 🅿 🕐 *Open Jul–Aug daily
9:30am–5pm, Mon-Fri 9:30am-4pm*

- ⚲ **Michelin Map:** p 359.
- 🛈 **Info:** Fortress of Louisbourg
National Historic Site,
Louisbourg: www.pc.gc.ca.
Town of Louisbourg: www.
louisbourgtourism.com.
- ◗ **Location:** The fort
dominates the town
of Louisbourg, on the
northeast coast of Cape
Breton Island.
- 🅿 **Parking:** Free parking at
the Visitor Centre; 7–10
minute bus ride to the
fortress.
- 🍴 **Don't Miss:** A meal in
one of the three period
restaurants, served on
earthenware and pewter
by costumed staff.
- 🕐 **Timing:** Bring what
you'll need for the visit:
returning to your car is
time-consuming.
- 👫 **Kids:** There is a Children's
Interpretive Centre at the
Rodrigue House in July–
August.

*early-Oct-late-May. Restaurants &
bakery open Jun–Sept. May & Oct
16–31, no costumed interpretors or
services; Visitor Centre closed;* 🚶 *tours
led by Parks Canada guide.* 🎫 *$17.60
Jun–Sept, $7.30 May & Oct.* ☎ *902-
733-3552. www.pc.gc.ca.* ☝ *Note: Be
prepared for cool temperatures, rain
and fog. Comfortable walking shoes
recommended.*

Models of the fortress and displays on
the history of Louisbourg provide orientation in the **visitor centre** *(departure
point for bus to fortress).* Visitors enter
the walled town through the elaborate
Dauphin Gate, manned by a sentry.
Over 50 buildings *(most open to the public)* are constructed of wood or rough-
cast masonry, some furnished to their
1740s appearance, others containing

themed exhibits. In the summer season, costumed staff portray 18C French society's leisure, landowner and working classes. Popular attractions include a **bakery,** where bread similar to the kind King Louis' troops lined up for in 1744 can be purchased. Along the quay stands the high wooden **Frédéric Gate,** the entrance through which important visitors to this once-bustling port were ushered from the harbour. The rich furnishings on the ground floor of the **Commissaire-Ordonnateur's residence** include a harpsichord of the period. Archaeological artifacts recovered during reconstruction are on display at various locations.

King's Bastion★★

Once one of the largest military strongholds in North America, King's Bastion is a symbol of reconstructed Louisbourg. The **governor's apartments** consist of 10 elegant rooms, lavishly furnished. Not as comfortable are the **officers' quarters.** The **soldiers' barracks** are drafty and spartan. The **prison** and a **chapel** can also be visited.

Maitland★

Maitland was once an important shipbuilding centre best known as the site of the construction of the largest wooden ship built in Canada, the **William D. Lawrence.**
Today Maitland's fine houses attest to the wealth created by the former industry.

SIGHT
Lawrence House Museum★

🅿 🕐 *Open Jun1–early-Oct Mon–Sat 9.30am–5.30pm, Sun 1pm–5.30pm.* ⊛*$4. ☎902-261-2628. http://museum.gov.ns.ca/lh.*
Surrounded by elm trees, this two-and-a-half-storey house is a splendid example of the grand residences of Nova Scotia's shipbuilders and sea captains. William Dawson Lawrence built this house (c.1870) to overlook his shipyard on the Shubenacadie River at the point where it joins Cobequid Bay. Believing he could double a ship's size without doubling its operating costs, Lawrence constructed an 80m/262ft ship that weighed 2,459 tonnes and had three masts, the highest being over 60m/200ft. Launched in 1874, the ship sailed all over the world.

- 🕭 **Michelin Map:** p 359.
- 🅱 **Info:** Lawrence House Museum, 8660 Hwy. 215. ☎902-261-2628. http://museum.gov.ns.ca/lh.
- 🅲 **Location:** Maitland overlooks Cobequid Bay in the Minas Basin, directly east of Saint John, NB.
- 🅿 **Parking:** There is parking near the museum.
- 🅐 **Don't Miss:** You can look through binoculars from the housetop to appreciate William Lawrence's view of his shipyard.
- 🕐 **Timing:** The Maitland-Truro area is an easy excursion from Halifax.

The house contains most of its original furnishings, including shipbuilding artifacts, pictures of 19C ships and a 2m/7ft model of the *William D. Lawrence.*
A lookout area across the road from the house affords visitors a good **view★** of the tidal flats.

Sherbrooke★

Once the location of a French fort (1655), the settlement was abandoned after capture by the English in 1669 until people were attracted by the rich timberlands in 1800. During the early 19C, sawmills sprang up and wooden ships were built. Gold was discovered in 1861, and for about 20 years the town flourished. Today it is a centre for sports fishing and tourism.

SHERBROOKE VILLAGE★★

This historic village is actually an extension of the town of Sherbrooke. Streets have been closed to traffic.

VISIT

🏛👥✕🚻🅿🕐*Open Jun–early-Oct daily 9.30am–5pm.* 🎟*$13.75 (child $4.75).* 📞*902-522-2400 or 888-743-7845 (US/Canada). http://museum.gov.ns.ca/sv.*
Built in 1862 with separate cells for men and women, the **jail** occupied half the jailer's house. Of particular interest is the **boatbuilding shop** where wooden boats are still constructed. Above Cumminger Brothers' general store, visitors can don 19C costumes and be photographed in the ambrotype **photography studio**. The hotel serves 1880s fare such as cottage pudding and gingerbread. Removed from the village is **McDonald Brothers' Mill** *(.4km/.3mi)*, an operational water-powered sawmill. A **lumber camp** of the 19C shows the living conditions of loggers nearby.

🧭 **Michelin Map:** p 359.

ℹ **Info:** Sherbrooke Village, Sherbrooke. 📞902-522-2400 or 888-743-7845 (US/Canada). http://museum.gov.ns.ca/sv.

▶ **Location:** Sherbrooke lies on the St. Mary's River, on the northeast coast of the mainland.

🅿 **Parking:** There is parking near the village.

📷 **Don't Miss:** Getting your photograph taken in a 19C costume.

🕐 **Timing:** Plan to spend at least two hours in the village.

👫 **Kids:** Unusually for a restored village, Sherbrooke is a real town, so children may find it particularly interesting, especially the jail.

Sherbrooke Village

© Wally Hayes/Nova Scotia Tourism, Culture and Heritage

South Shore★★

Known locally as the South Shore, Nova Scotia's eastern shore winds along miles of indented coast between Halifax and Barrington along the Atlantic Ocean. It is famous for its rugged coastline, granite coves, sandy beaches, pretty fishing villages and attractive tree-lined towns with elegant houses built from shipbuilding or privateering fortunes. The greatest concentration of quaint seaside communities is found south of Halifax.

- **Michelin Map:** pp 358-359.
- **Info:** Dept of Tourism, Halifax. ☎902-425-5781 or 800-565-0000. www.novascotia.com.
- **Location:** The route lies between Halifax and Liverpool to the south.
- **Don't Miss:** Lunenburg.
- **Timing:** This excursion requires about two days.
- **Kids:** The Ross Farm Museum offers rides and demonstrations of farm activities.

🚗 DRIVING TOUR

FROM HALIFAX TO LIVERPOOL
348km/216mi.

Halifax★★★
⚒*See HALIFAX.*

▶ Leave Halifax by Rte. 3. Turn left on Rte. 333.

As the coast is approached, the landscape becomes wild, almost desolate. Huge boulders left by retreating glaciers, and stunted vegetation give the area a lunar appearance. *Fog is least common mid-July to October but can occur anytime.*

Peggy's Cove★★
Immortalized by artists and photographers across Canada, this tiny village is set on a treeless outcropping of massive, deeply lined boulders. Its tranquil harbour, with colourful boats and fishing shacks built on stilts over the water, is indeed picturesque. The **lighthouse** stands alone on a huge granite slab pounded by the Atlantic Ocean.
Sudden high waves and slippery boulders have resulted in tragedy. Use extreme caution when walking in this area.

Tranquil Peggy's Cove

© Sandra Phinney/Michelin

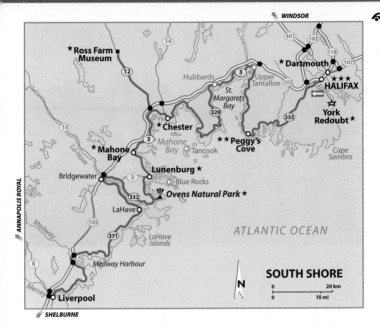

WINDSOR

Ross Farm Museum

Hubbards

Upper Tantallon

Dartmouth

★★★ **HALIFAX**

Chester

St. Margarets Bay

★★ *Peggy's Cove*

York Redoubt ★

Mahone Bay

Tancook

Mahone Bay

Cape Sambro

Bridgewater

Lunenburg ★

Blue Rocks

Ovens Natural Park ★

ANNAPOLIS ROYAL

LaHave

Medway

ATLANTIC OCEAN

LaHave Islands

SOUTH SHORE

N

Medway Harbour

0 ————— 20 km
0 ————— 10 mi

Mersey

Liverpool

SHELBURNE

Note the **carvings** of village residents done in the granite rock by William deGarthe (1907-83).

A dramatic **memorial** to Swissair Flight 111, which crashed offshore on Sept 2, 1998, killing 229 passengers and crew, is located at The Whalesback, 1km/.5mi northwest of Peggy's Cove.

The road follows the coast with views of the villages on **St. Margarets Bay.**

▶ Rte. 333 joins Rte. 3 at Upper Tantallon; follow Rte. 3 until Rte. 329 turns off after Hubbards. Tour the peninsula and rejoin Rte. 3 just before Chester.

Chester★

Perched on cliffs rising out of Mahone Bay, this charming town, founded by New Englanders in 1759, is a popular summer residence of Americans and retirement spot for Canadians.

▶ Take Rte. 12 North, 7km/4mi after Chester.

▲▲ Ross Farm Museum★

4568 Rte. 12, New Ross. 24km/15mi one way from the coast. ⏱*Open May–Oct daily 9.30am–5.30pm. Rest of the year*

Wed–Sun 9.30am–4.30pm. ⬡*$8 (child $3).* ✆*902-689-2210 or 877-689-2210. http://museum.gov.ns.ca.*

Cleared from wilderness in 1816 by William Ross, this farm belonged to five generations of his family before acquisition by the Nova Scotia Museum Complex.

Maintained as a living museum, the farm features coopering, candle making, forging, sheep shearing and other demonstrations that vary by season. Horse-drawn wagon rides are offered.

▶ Return to Rte. 3.

Mahone Bay★

Between 1756 and 1815 hundreds of small ships sailed from Nova Scotia ports to harass French, Spanish, Dutch and American vessels.

After obtaining a license, a privateer could attack only enemy ships. All prizes had to be taken to Halifax, where the Court of Vice Admiralty decided their legality. Profits were enormous and coastal communities prospered.

Upon approaching the town, there is a lovely **view**★ of the town's three neighbouring churches reflected in the water.

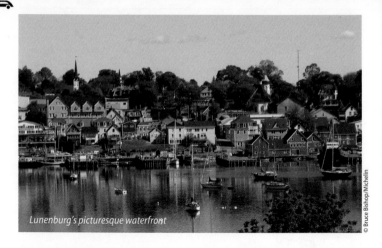
Lunenburg's picturesque waterfront

© Bruce Bishop/Michelin

▶ Follow Rte. 3 So uth 10km/6mi.

Lunenburg★★

Situated on a hilly peninsula with "front" and "back" harbours, picturesque Lunenburg is named for the northern German hometown (Lüneburg) of the first settlers who arrived in 1753.

Colourful historic houses grace the streets. **Old Town Lunenburg** was inscribed as a UNESCO World Heritage Site in 1995.

Once a pirates' haven, the town was sacked by American privateers in 1782. The **Bluenose**, constructed here, was undefeated champion of the North American fishing fleet and winner of four international schooner races from 1921 to 1938.

The *Bluenose II,* a replica of the original, was also constructed here in 1963 and offers seasonal **cruises** when in port *(departs from Fisheries Museum; ☜$40; contact Lunenburg Marine Museum Society for schedule & reservations ♿ 🄿 ✆902-634-4794 or 866-579-4909).* Every September the popular **Waterfront Seafood Festival** is celebrated in Lunenburg.

👥 Fisheries Museum of the Atlantic★★

68 Bluenose Dr., Lunenburg harbour.
✖♿🄿🕐*Open Jul–Aug Tue–Sat 9.30am–7pm, Sun–Mon 9.30am–5pm. May–Jun & Sept–Oct daily 9.30am–5.30pm. Rest of the year Mon–Fri 9.30am–4pm. ☜$12 (child $3.50). ✆902-634-4794 or 866-579-4909. museum.gov.ns.ca.*

This three-storey centre features exhibits ranging from the history of the *Bluenose* and the illicit "rum-running" trade during Prohibition to the banks fishery. Moored at the wharf, the **Theresa E. Connor,** Canada's oldest saltbank schooner to fish the Grand Banks, can be boarded. The steel-hulled side trawler **Cape Sable** can also be boarded.

▶ Follow Rte. 3 and turn left on Rte. 332 for 15km/9mi. Turn left at Feltzen South and right on Ovens Rd.

Ovens Natural Park★

✖🄿🕐*Open mid-May–Oct daily 8.30am–9pm. Rest of the year, call for hours. ☜$10 (child $5). ✆902-766-4621. www.ovenspark.com.*

This private park has a lovely site, which offers **views★** across Lunenburg Bay to Blue Rocks. Several sets of stairs lead to the ovenlike caves, cut into the cliffs by the action of the sea.

▶ Continue on Rte. 332 and then left on Rte. 3.

The road follows the wide and tranquil estuary of LaHave River, lined with frame houses and trees. The river is crossed at **Bridgewater,** a large, industrial town.

▷ Turn left on Rte. 331.

The road passes the town of **LaHave**, where Isaac de Razilly, Lieutenant-General of Acadia, built a fort in 1632. The road continues with many pleasant views, especially in the vicinity of **Medway Harbour.**

Liverpool
Founded in 1759 by New Englanders, Liverpool, like its great English namesake, is on the Mersey River.

Perkins House Museum★
105 Main St. P Q*Open Jun–mid-Oct Mon–Sat 9.30am–5.30pm, Sun 1pm–5.30pm. ∞$4. ✆902-354-4058. http://museum.gov.ns.ca.*
This New England frame house was built in 1767 for Col. Simeon Perkins, a merchant and ship owner from Cape Cod. On display next door in the Queens County Museum is a copy of the colonel's diary, which captures life in a colonial town from 1766 to 1812.

EXCURSION
Shelburne★
64km/38mi south by Hwy. 103 to Exit 25. Tourist centre on Dock St. ✆902-875-4547.
Founded by Loyalists in 1783, this small waterfront town was briefly one of the largest cities in North America.
Work continues at the barrel factory and in the **Dory Shop Museum** (P Q*11 Dock St.; open Jun–mid-Oct daily 9.30am–5.30pm. ∞$4. ✆902-875-3219. http://museum.gov.ns.ca).*

Ross-Thomson House Museum★
9 Charlotte Lane. Q*Open Jun–mid-Oct daily 9.30am–5.30pm. ∞$3.* P *✆902-875-3219. http://museum.gov.ns.ca.*
Veterans of the West Indies trade, sons of Scottish merchant opened this structure. In use by 1785 as a house, store and warehouse. Seasonal flower and herb gardens grace the front entrance.

Springhill★

This former town is famous for its coal-mine disasters. In 1891 an enormous blast in one of the mines followed by a flame killed 125 men. Then, in 1916, a subterranean fire caused much damage, though no deaths. An explosion and fire in 1956 caused 39 deaths. The next year a fire razed the business district of the town. Finally, in 1958, an underground upheaval, or "bump," killed 76 men. The mines closed in 1962.

> ▶ **Population:** 3,941.
> ⚲ **Michelin Map:** p 359.
> ▤ **Info:** Tourist Information Booth in Anne Murray Centre, 36 Main St.
> ▷ **Location:** Springhill is located inland on the "arm" of the peninsula, east of the Isthmus of Chignecto, just off the Trans-Canada Highway.

SIGHT
Miners' Museum★
145 Black River Rd. Follow signs along Rte. 2 (Parrsboro direction). Q*Open Jun–mid-Oct daily 9am–5pm. ∞$4.50. ✆902-597-3449. www.explorenovascotia.com.*
This museum commemorates the disasters and the bravery of the rescuers through displays such as newspaper clippings and mining equipment. The interesting **mine tour** is conducted by retired miners. Equipped with hard hats, rubber coats and boots, visitors descend about 270m/900ft into the old Syndicate Mine via a tunnel of regular height, rather than those along which the miners had to crawl. Both old and new mining methods are demonstrated.

Truro

Set on the Salmon River near its mouth, this city experiences the high tides of the Bay of Fundy and the tidal bore. Site of a thriving Acadian community called Cobequid before the Deportation, Truro was later settled by people from Northern Ireland and New Hampshire. Today this manufacturing centre is home to the Nova Scotia Agricultural College.

SIGHT
Tidal Bore★

Viewpoint: leave Hwy. 102 at Exit 14 and take Tidal Bore Rd. (left on Robie and left again on Tidal Bore Rd., if coming from Halifax). Before you go, obtain a tidal schedule from the welcome centre. Arrive at observation deck 15min prior and stay a full hour to see high tide.

Twice a day the tide rushes up the Salmon River from the Bay of Fundy, causing a wave that may vary from a ripple to several feet in height. What is more interesting than this tidal wave is the tremendous inrush of water and the rapid rise in water level immediately following it. In fact, high tide is reached just over an hour after the arrival of the bore. Bore rafting is popular in the area.

Joseph Howe falls, Victoria Park

© Matthew Singer/iStockphoto.com

▶ **Population:** 12,500.

⚅ **Michelin Map:** p 359.

🛈 **Info:** Welcome Centre, Victoria Square. ✆902-895-4484 (May–Oct). www.truro.ca.

▶ **Location:** Truro lies at the end of Cobequid Bay, a long finger of the Bay of Fundy.

🅿 **Parking:** Parking area near The Palliser restaurant.

🕐 **Timing:** Contact the Welcome Centre for time of next bore.

👥 **Kids:** Glooscap Heritage Centre.

Victoria Park

Brunswick St., downtown. 🕐*Open daily dawn–dusk.* ✆*902-893-2922.*

Created in 1887 this spacious urban park is situated near the Salmon River. It has since grown to 405ha/1,000 acres. Natural features include a brook, a spectacular gorge, and two waterfalls. Recreational amenities include tennis courts, a large swimming pool, picnic grounds and a playground.

👥 Glooscap Heritage Centre★

65 Treaty Trail. Take Exit 13A off Hwy. 102. 🕐*Open mid-May–late Oct daily 8am–5pm. Rest of the year Mon–Fri 8:30am–4:30pm.* 🕐*Closed late Dec–early Jan.* 🌐*$6 (child $3.50).* ✆*902-843-3493. www.millbrookheritage.ca*

The Mi'kmaq legend recounts that the first man on earth was **Glooscap**, born from a lightning bolt. The heritage centre of the Millbrook First Nations Reserve includes an exhibit gallery, gift shop and visitor information centre for the area. Outside the entrance stands an immense 12m/40ft bronze statue of Glooscap.

Inside, baskets, porcupine quillwork and intricate beadwork showcase the skills of Mi'kmaq artisans. Aboriginal tools, traditional clothing and artifacts are also on display.

Prince Edward Island

Canadian Confederation was born here 150 years ago, and Canada's smallest province, this crescent-shaped island is only 225km/140mi long. Iron oxides give the soil its characteristic brick red colour; and on summer days the landscape presents a kaleidoscope of green fields, blue sea and sky, red soil and puffy white clouds.

A BIT OF HISTORY

Île-St.-Jean and the Acadian Deportation – Jacques Cartier claimed the island for France in 1534, naming it Île-St.-Jean. In the 18C, French settlers founded **Port la Joye,** near the present site of Charlottetown. When in 1758 England removed the Acadians under the Deportation Order, about 30 families went into hiding.

Prince Edward and Confederation – In 1799 the colony was named Prince Edward Island in honour of a son of King George III of England.

The island was the site of the historic **Charlottetown Conference** in September 1864, the first of several meetings which led to Canadian Confederation in 1867.

- ▶ **Population:** 147,390.
- ○ **Michelin Map:** p 414.
- ▤ **Info:** Tourist Office, 6 Prince Street, Charlottetown. ✆902-473-8570or 800-463-4734 or www.tourismpei.com.
- ◑ **Location:** Separated from Newfoundland by the Gulf of St. Lawrence, the island lies just 14km/9mi from New Brunswick and 22km/14mi from Nova Scotia via Northumberlan Strait.
- ○ **Timing:** You can tour the island from a base in Charlottetown. Allow at least five to seven days.

The Island Today – Principal industries today are agriculture (especially **potatoes**), tourism and fishing.

Annually over 700,000 visitors are drawn to the unhurried pace of life; **farm vacations** are popular, and **lobster suppers**, held during the summer in church and community halls, provide a sampling of fresh regional seafood and abundant garden produce.

Confederation Bridge

© Tourism PEI/Stephen Desfoches

GETTING THERE

BY AIR – **Air Canada** and Air Canada Jazz provide direct flights from Toronto, Montreal and Halifax (*888-247-2262; www.aircanada.com*). **WestJet** (*888-937-8538; www. westjet.com*) and **Sunwing Airlines** (*800-761-1711; www.sunwing.ca*) offers flights from Toronto and Montreal, and **Delta** (*800-221-1212, Canada/US; www.delta.com*) from Boston.

Charlottetown Airport is less than 5km/3mi from downtown. *902-566-7997. www.flypei.com.* Taxis and major car rental agencies are at the airport.

BY CAR – The 13km/8mi two-lane **Confederation Bridge** links Borden/Carleton, Prince Edward Island (PEI), with Cape Jourimain, NB and takes approximately 12min to cross. A toll is collected at Borden/Carleton upon exiting the island (*$46.00/first two axles, $7.50 each additional*); Cash, debit card and major credit cards accepted; *888-437-6565; www.confederationbridge.com*).

BY BOAT – **Northumberland Ferries** connects Wood Islands with Caribou, NS. Check schedules online: *www.ferries.ca*. No service late Dec–Apr. One way 1hr 15min.

ADDRESSES

STAY

$ Heart's Content – *236 Sydney St. (at Weymouth), Charlottetown. 902-566-1799. www.stayincharlottetown.com. 4 rooms.* A downtown location within walking distance of waterfront and city attractions makes this B&B a good value for the money. The two bathrooms are shared. Tidy rooms, storage for bicycles and a continental breakfast.

$$ Warn House – *330 Central St., Summerside. 902-436-5242 or 888-436-7512. www.warnhousebandb.ca. 4 rooms.* This immaculately clean, centrally located bed and breakfast is tastefully furnished with Canadian art, antiques and modern fixtures. The friendly hosts prepare a hearty breakfast, which is served in the handsomely decorated dining room.

$$$ Briarwood Inn – *253 Matthew's Lane, Alberton. Jun–Nov. 902-853-2518 or 888-272-2246. www.briarwood.pe.ca. 22 rooms.* Located on the banks of the Dock River near Cascumpec Bay, this compound containing cottages, a lodge and a three-storey inn makes a heavenly hideaway for longer-stay vacations. Briarwood rooms are air conditioned.

$$$ The Great George Boutique Hotel, *96 Kensington Rd., Charlottetown. 902-566-3137 or 800-361-1118. http://mhgpei. com. 78 rooms.* Located near Province House in the heart of downtown, this inn is a cluster of 21 heritage buildings. Guests can choose from loft bedrooms and efficiency units, two-storey suites, and two-bedroom flats equipped with laundry facilities and kitchen. An exercise room, high-speed WiFi, and breakfast served in the cozy Pavilion lobby round out the amenities.

$$$$ Dalvay-by-the-Sea – *In Dalvay. North shore, near the east entrance to PEI National Park. Open Jun–late Sept. 902-672-2048 or 888-366-2955 (US/Canada). www.dalvaybythesea.com. 25 rooms, 8 cottages.* Former residence of oil magnate Alexander MacDonald, this gabled Queen Anne-style mansion now houses a prestigious resort. Breakfast and dinner are included in the rates. Dalvay's formal **MacMillan Dining Room ($$$)** provides contemporary cuisine featuring local seafood and farm products. Tennis, biking, croquet and lake boating available. No TVs, phones or radios.

$$$$ Fairholm Inn – *230 Prince St. (corner Fitzroy), Charlottetown. 902-892-5022 or 888-573-5022. www.fairholm inn.com. 7 luxurious suites.* Stately two-storey mansion (1839) has spacious

Island's lobsters

© Tourism PEI/Stephen Harris

high-ceilinged rooms equipped with marble fireplaces. Bathrooms feature clawfoot tubs, and two have Jacuzzis. Read in the sittingroom, relax in the cheerful sunroom, or breakfast in the formal diningroom.

$$$$ Inn at Spry Point – *Souris RR#4. On Rte. 310 (Spry Point Rd.) just off Rte. 2, Souris. &902-583-2400 or 844-583-2400. www.innatsprypoint.com. 15 rooms (summer cottages also available).* ✕🄿 A remote promontory above Northumberland Strait provides the setting for this large, airy inn. Trails cross the forests near the inn's grounds, and waves crash on the nearby sandy beach. All of the large rooms have private balconies or terraces that afford lovely views. Overlooking the ocean, the **dining room ($$$)** offers local produce, fresh fish and Island meats; the table d'hôte menu changes daily.

☐/ EAT

$$ Lobster on the Wharf – *2, Prince St., Charlottetown. &902-368-2888 or 877-919-9311. www.lobsteronthewharf.com.* **Seafood**. *Open May 1-Oct 30.* ♿ For an array of fresh seafood, head for this casual waterside eatery, where families can indulge indoors or out at checkered-cloth-covered tables. Lobster, snow crab, clams, scallops, shrimp, oysters, haddock and salmon are all on the menu, along with island lobster roll and fish-and-chips. Order online as well (shipping costs and taxes extra.)

$$ The Millin New Glasgow– *5592 on Rte. 13, New Glasgow. &902-964-3313; www.themillinnewglasgow.com. Closed Mon & Tue.* **Contemporary**. Built in 1896 as a community hall, this structure overlooking the Clyde River now houses a restaurant with three dining rooms. Seafood, meat and fowl are served with flair. Try the chocolate molton lava cake for dessert, with a specialty coffee.

$$ The Pilot House – *70 Grafton St., Charlottetown. &902-894-4800. thepilothouse.ca. Closed Sun & Mon.* **International**. Housed in a renovated 19C hardware building, a popular entrée are the seared scallops with citrus infused Israeli couscous. Steaks, prime rib, and seafood are also on the menu. The pub offers lower-priced dishes, or try outdoor dining at the Queue on their contemporary deck.

$$$ Inn at Bay Fortune – *Rte. 310, just off Rte. 2, Bay Fortune. Open late May–mid-Oct. Dinner only. &902 (or 888)-687-3745. www.innatbayfortune.com.* **Canadiana**. This upscale inn has a reputation for Maritime cuisine, local art, and onsite garden ingredients. Served in an airy glass-enclosed veranda, meals focus on the bounty of the island's forests, fields and waters (Island blue mussels, Colville Bay oysters). Inn's gardens form the basis of the daily menu. Reserve the Chef's Table in the kitchen.

Charlottetown★★

This gracious provincial capital is also a thriving commercial centre, its port serving as a funnel for the region's agricultural bounty. It is also the hub of retail services for the island. A lively arts and dining scene hums pretty much year-round. Named for the wife of King George III, Queen Charlotte, the city was founded in 1768, and hosted the Fathers of Conderation in 1867 when forming Canada.

▶ **Population:** 64,487.
⏣ **Michelin Map:** p 414.
▤ **Info:** Visitor Information Centre, 6 Prince St. ☎800-955-1864 or 902-629-1864. discovercharlottetown.com.
◐ **Location:** Charlottetown is located near the confluence of the West, North and Hillsborough rivers at Northumberland Strait.
🅿 **Parking:** Parking is metered, and often hard to find downtown; spaces are often the "nose-in" variety. Meters are rigourously enforced.

SIGHTS

Attractively situated along the water's edge, **Victoria Park** is home to the regal, Neoclassical **Government House**. From shore, expansive **views★** extend to Fort Amherst.

Province House National Historic Site★★

165 Richmond St. ⏣ Parks Canada has collaborated with the Confederation Centre of the Arts to create The Story of Confederation exhibit, while Province House is closed for conservation work until 2020. The CCA installation is a creative, true-to-life, duplicate of the Confederation Chamber in Province House National Historic Site, replete with reproduction pieces from the original structure. This amazing show illustrates where the Fathers of Confederation met for the Charlottetown Conference of 1864, to first discuss the idea of Canada.

Confederation Centre of the Arts★

145 Richmond St. Box office at 130 Queen St. ✕⏣◷Open Mon–Sat 10pm–8pm. Sun & Days of show 2.5 hrs before performance. ☎902-628-1864 or 800-565-0278. www.confederationcentre.com.
This national memorial arts centre (1964) houses theatres, the provincial archives and a restaurant. The **art gallery★★** features works by Canadian artists, most notably Robert Harris (1848-1919), a renowned portrait painter. The main theatre hosts the annual **Charlottetown Festival** musical *Anne of Green Gables*

St. Dunstan's Basilica

45 Great George St. ⏣◷Open year-round Mon–Fri 8:30am–5pm, Sat 9am-4:30pm, Sun 10:30-6pm. ☎902-894-3486. www.stdunstans.pe.ca.
The twin 61m/200ft spires of this Gothic edifice (1917) gracefully punctuate Charlottetown's skyline.

Nightlife

42nd Street Lounge – *125 Sydney St. ☎902-566-4620. www.offbroadwayrestaurant.ca. Closed Sun.*

This lounge above **Off Broadway Restaurant** (known for its steaks and fresh mussels) is a place to relax. Soft lighting, comfortable wing chairs and antique tables encourage conversation. In addition to wines and spirits, the lounge offers appetizers and desserts. It's a great place for after-dinner drinks or post-theatre snacking.

Charlottetown Circuit★★

This scenic drive encompasses the stunning white beaches of the north coast; charming Acadian fishing villages; sights related to *Anne of Green Gables;* and the red cliffs of the southern coast, bordered by Northumberland Strait.

🚗 DRIVING TOUR

190km/118mi circuit north and west from Charlottetown.

Prince Edward Island National Park★

In Cavendish, 24km/15mi northwest of Charlottetown. ♿🅿️🕐*Open year-round.* 👓*$3.90 ($7.80 summer). Cavendish Destination Centre open late Jun–Labour Day daily 8am–10pm; mid-May–mid-Jun & rest of Sept–mid-Oct daily 9am–5pm.* 📞*902-672-6350. www.pc.gc.ca.* 🛇*To preserve the dunes, use boardwalks & designated footpaths.*
One of Canada's smallest but most popular national parks stretches for about 40km/25mi along the north shore of the island, fringing the Gulf of St. Lawrence. Interspersed with boardwalks, the **Gulf Shore Parkway** offers lovely **beaches,** dunes, cliffs and salt marshes.

- 👓 **Michelin Map:** p 414.
- 🔖 **Info:** Information Centre, 6 Prince Street, Charlotte town. 📞800-463-4734. www.tourismpei.com.
- ▶️ **Location:** This popular drive circles most of Queens County and runs through central Prince Edward Island.
- 🛇 **Don't Miss:** The beaches of the Prince Edward Island National Park spread out under pink sandstone cliffs.
- 🕐 **Timing:** The tour takes a leisurely day.
- 👪 **Kids:** The Green Gables Haunted Trail is a must do at Green Gables Heritage Place at Silverbush.

👪 Green Gables Heritage Place

8619 Rte. 6 west of Rte. 13, in PEI National Park. ✕♿🅿️🕐*Open May–Oct31 daily 9am–5pm. Early Nov–early Dec & late Mar–Apr by appointment.* 🕐*Closed Easter weekend.* 👓*$3.90 ($7.80 summer), child $1.90 ($3.90 summer)* 📞*902-963-7874. www.pc.gc.ca.*
This small green and white farmhouse belonged to relatives of **Lucy Maud Montgomery**, author of *Anne of Green*

Cavendish beach and dunes

© Tourism PEI/Carrie Gregory

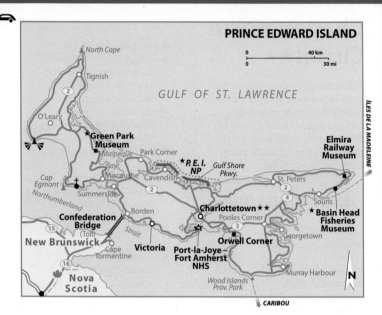

PRINCE EDWARD ISLAND

Gables. She used the house as a setting for the novel, which tells the story of an irrepressible orphan girl adopted by a strict but kindly brother and sister living at Green Gables farm.

▲▲ Anne of Green Gables Museum at Silverbush

In Park Corner at 4542 Rte. 20. ♿🅿🕐*Open late-May–late-Oct 11am–4pm, Jul & Aug 9am–5pm, off-season by reservation.* 👓*$5.50.* 📞*902-886-2884 (weekends) or 800-665-2663. www.annemuseum.com.*

Throughout her life, author Lucy Maud Montgomery visited relatives at this spacious house; her 1911 wedding was held in the drawing room.

Enjoy a **ride** (👓*$6; 1 hr*) in a horse-drawn surrey over the gentle hills to the lake.

Victoria-by-the-Sea

Overlooking Northumberland Strait, this tiny seaside community is undoubtedly the island's most picturesque hamlet, complete with an active wharf and a provincial park. Dominating the end of Main Street, the colourful **Orient Hotel Bed & Breakfast ($$)** (📞*902-658-2503 or 800-565-6743; www.theorienthotel.com*) welcomes overnight guests and offers packages (room, dinner at Landmark Café & theatre tickets). The **Seaport Museum** is housed in a lighthouse and houses a collection of photographs outlining the development of

Art Gallery-Cafe

The Dunes Studio Gallery & Café –*3622 Brackley Point Rd.* 📞*902-672-2586. www.dunesgallery.com.* Dramatic cedar and glass structure houses studio, gallery, gift shop and **café ($$)**. Canadian-made pottery, paintings, jewellery, blown glass, baskets and other crafts. The café serves creative cuisine on the gallery's attractive pottery. Floral arrangements of huge flowers grown on the premises add an artistic flair. Be sure to visit the tranquil garden, the deckside lily pond *(3rd floor)* and the top-floor lookout, accessible via a striking spiral wooden staircase.

Lobster Suppers

An island tradition, lobster suppers began some 40 years ago as a fund-raiser for the Junior Farmers Organization; the first meal cost $1.50. The summertime suppers have since been commercialized to cater to huge crowds. **St. Ann's Church** in Hope River offers daily afternoon and evening sittings in its large basement (*mid-Jun–late Sept Mon–Sat 4pm–8pm; ℘902-621-0635; www.lobster suppers.com*). **St. Margarets Lobster Suppers** (℘*902-687-3105*) serves lobster and ham dinners in its licensed dining room, and **New Glasgow Lobster Suppers** (*Jun–mid-Oct Mon–Sat 4pm–8:30pm; ℘902-964-2870; peilobstersuppers.com*) operates in a two-level, 500-capacity hall, with lobster pounds on-site. Paying a set price as they enter, patrons are seated at long wooden tables. The meal starts with fish chowder, followed by salads (potato, coleslaw and green). Steamed mussels follow. Next comes the lobster itself (1, 1-1/2 or 2 pounds, based on what you paid), served in the shell. Cake or pie with ice cream is often served as dessert. Ham or fish are often offered for those who don't like lobster.

the seaport and the history of former keepers. The **Victoria Playhouse** gives summer performances at Victoria Hall.

Port-la-Joye–Fort Amherst National Historic Site
In Rocky Point, on Blockhouse Point Rd. off Rte. 19. ✗ ◷ *Open daily Jun–Oct.*

Visitor Centre open Jul–Aug daily 9am–5pm. ⌕$3.90. ℘902-675-2220 *(summer). www.pc.gc.ca.*
The British captured this area from the French in 1758.

Eastern Shores★

Side roads lead through lush forests past small communities with names such as Cardigan, Greenfield and Glenmartin that hearken back to the province's British heritage.

⌕ **Michelin Map:** p 414.
🚩 **Info:** Information Centre, 6 Prince Street, Charlottetown. ℘800-463-4734. www.tourismpei.com.
▶ **Location:** The drive follows the deeply indented bays and harbours of the island's eastern coast.
◷ **Timing:** This drive takes most of a day.
👥 **Kids:** The Orwell Corner village in Vernon.

🚗 DRIVING TOUR

375km/233mi circuit from Charlottetown indicated by signs showing a white starfish on a blue and orange background designating the Points East Coastal Drive (www.pointseastcoastaldrive.com).

👥 Orwell Corner Historic Village
In Orwell, 30km/19mi east of Charlottetown on the Trans-Can Hwy. ✗ ℗ ◷ *Open mid-Jun–late-Oct daily 9:30am–5:30pm. Late May–late Jun Mon–Fri 9am–5pm. Rest of Sept–late*

Oct Sun–Thu 9am–5pm. ◷*Closed Labour Day.* ⌕$10.20. ℘902-651-8515. *www.orwellcorner.ca.*
This superbly restored crossroads village, settled in the early 19C by pioneers from Scotland and Ireland, retains the flavour of the island's agricultural origins.

Anne of Green Gables at Orwell Corner Historic Village

©AllCanadaPhotos/Photoshot

Basin Head Fisheries Museum★

Basin Head Road, 10km/6mi east of Souris on Rte. 16. ✕ ℗ ⏲ Open Jul–Aug Mon–Fri 9:30am–4:30pm. ⊜$4. ℘902-357-7233. www.peimuseum.com.

Boats, nets, hooks, photographs and dioramas illustrate the life and work of an inshore fisherman. Outside, small wooden buildings house a small boats exhibit.

Elmira Railway Museum

In Elmira, 16km/10mi east of Souris on Rte. 16A. ♿ ℗ ⏲ Open Jun–late-Sept daily 9:30am–5pm. ⊜$5. ℘902-357-7234. www.peimuseum.com.

Formerly end of the railway system linking island with the continent, this charming station houses a museum with exhibits and start of the Confederation Trail, a geocaching hotspot with over 1600 caches to discover.

Summerside Circuit★

Following the western part of the province, this scenic drive introduces the visitor to shipbuilding at Green Park; the Malpeque Bay, famed for its fine oysters; and fox farming, a major island industry from 1890 to 1939.

🚗 DRIVING TOUR

288km/179mi circuit northwest of Summerside indicated by signs showing a lighthouse with a setting sun for the North Cape Coastal Drive (www.tourismpei.com/north-cape-coastal-drive).

⚹ **Michelin Map:** p 414.

🅱 **Info:** Information Centre, 6 Prince Street, Charlottetown. ℘800-463-4734. www.tourismpei.com.

▶ **Location:** The picturesque landscape of western Prince Edward Island is fringed with capes and beaches.

⏲ **Timing:** The time needed depends on the museums you visit.

👫 **Kids:** The lighthouse is fun.

Acadian Museum of Prince Edward Island

In Miscouche, 8km/5mi west of Summerside, on Rte. 2. ♿ ⏲ Open May–Labour Day daily 9:30am–5pm (Jul–Aug 7pm).

Rest of the year Mon–Fri 9am–5pm, Sun 1pm–4pm. $4.50. 902-432-2880. http://museeacadien.org.

Erected in 1991, this modern facility for the preservation of Acadian heritage combines a historical museum with a documentation centre for genealogical research.

Green Park Shipbuilding Museum & Yeo House★

In Port Hill, 34km/21mi northwest of Summerside on Rte. 12.
Open Jun–late Sept daily 9am–5pm. $5.70. 902-831-7947 (summer) or 902-368-6600. www.peimuseum.com.

Formerly the grounds of an active shipyard, Green Park is today a provincial heritage site.

Yeo House (1865) is a large, steeply gabled Victorian structure restored to reflect the lifestyle of a prominent family of the period. Maps, photographs and tools on display in the **visitor centre** present the industry's 19C heyday.

West Point Lighthouse

In O'Leary, in Cedar Dunes Provincial Park on Rte. 14.
Open mid-Jun–Sept daily 9am–8:30pm. $3. 902-859-3605 or 800-764-6854.
www.westpointlighthouse.com.

This distinctive 30m/85ft striped lighthouse (1875) was automated by electricity in 1963. The tower contains numerous examples of lighthouse lenses and lanterns. From the observation platform at the summit, **views** stretch across the shoreline's dark red dunes. The lighthouse also serves as an inn, with a restaurant and museum open to the public.

Potato Museum

Off Rte. 142 at 1 Dewar Ln., in O'Leary, west of Rte. 2.
Open mid-May–mid-Oct Mon–Sat 9am–5pm, Sun 1pm–5pm. $9.98. 902-859-2039 (summer) or 844-849-1470 (farm tours).
www.peipotatomuseum.com.

Here, visitors can learn how Sir Walter Raleigh, Sir Francis Drake and even Thomas Jefferson promoted the versa-

tile tuber, first cultivated in Peru perhaps as early as 10,000 years ago. At the canteen, sample potato maple-butter tarts, potato fudge or even a potato dog. Ask about their new farm tours.

Our Lady of Mont-Carmel Acadian Church

In Mont-Carmel, on Rte. 11, east of Rte. 124.
Open Jun–Sept daily 8am–8pm. Rest of the year Sun 9am–5pm. 902-854-2789.

The Northumberland Strait's twin-steepled church (1896) replaces two earlier structures. The symmetrical façade and interior vaults are reminiscent of religious architecture in France's Poitou region, original home of most of the island's first Acadian settlers.

ADDRESSES

PEI Preserve Company – *2841 New Glasgow Rd., New Glasgow.* 902-367-3282 or 800-565-5267. www.preservecompany. com. Sample preserves, mustards and chutneys, and tea of the day. The cheery **Café on the Clyde ($)** (*New Glasgow;* 902-964-4301) serves breakfast, lunch and casual evening fare with views of the adjacent New Glasgow Country Gardens (902-964-4300), which have 2km/1.5mi of walking trails.

Cheeselady's Gouda Cheese – *Off Rte. 223 in Winsloe North.* 902-368-1506. View the short video on the Dutch way of making cheese and see the processing room. Then sample Gouda variations such as pepper and mustard.

Medallion Trading PEI – *28 Schuman St., Charlottetown.* 888-448-3001. www.medallionsmokedsalmon.com. Tour the smoking chambers and sample smoked eel, salmon cavier, trout with pepper and maple syrup, and other products, using traditions of Master Smokers from Europe, Scandinavia and local Mi'kmaq Indigenous Peoples. Their smoking process only uses alder trees from Prince Edward Island in their process.

Newfoundland and Labrador

The largest of the Atlantic provinces, Newfoundland and Labrador consists of the rocky island named Newfoundland and the mountainous mainland of Labrador, with a combined landmass of 405,720sq km/156,648sq mi. The remote shores and wilderness interior of Canada's easternmost province appeal particularly to nature lovers in search of adventure.

GEOLOGY

The Island – Called "The Rock" for its craggy profile, this island province has a beautiful, deeply indented 14,400 miles (23,200 km) coastline, studded with bays, coves and islands. In the north and west, the coast is grandiose with towering cliffs and deep fjords. From the heights of the **Long Range Mountains** in the west, a continuation of the Appalachians, the land slopes east and northeast. Parts of the interior are heavily forested; others are expanses of rocky barrens and boggy peat lands, a legacy of glaciers, as are the multitude of lakes and rivers.

Labrador – A rugged land of high mountains (Cirque Mountain, in the **Torngat Mountains** of the north, reaches 1,676m/5,500ft), Unlike the

> ▶ **Population:** 528,336.
> Ⓖ **Michelin Map:** p 420.
> 🔢 **Info:** Newfoundland and Labrador Tourism, St. John's. ✆709-729-2830 or 800-563-6353. www.newfoundland labrador.com.
> ▷ **Location:** Newfoundland lies at the eastern end of the Gulf of St. Lawrence. It is separated from Quebec and Labrador by the Strait of Belle Isle, and from Nova Scotia by the Cabot Strait. Labrador is part of Quebec's mainland and reaches north nearly to the Arctic.

island, Labrador forms part of the Canadian Shield. Its 26,728 people reside primarily along the coast and around the mines in its rich iron-ore belt.

Collapse of the Fishery – The "Banks" are vast areas of shallow water that lie in the Atlantic to the south and east of the province. For 500 years these waters have attracted fishermen to the fish-breeding grounds. The largest and richest of the grounds is the **Grand Banks,** where the cold Labrador Current meets the warmer Gulf Stream. Sinking

Parker's Cove, Burin Peninsula, Newfoundland

© Newfoundland and Labrador Tourism

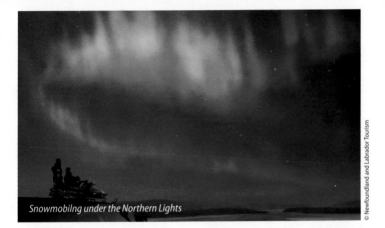

Snowmobilng under the Northern Lights

© Newfoundland and Labrador Tourism

below the warmer one, the cold current stirs up plankton on the seabed. The plankton rises to the surface, attracting great schools of fish.

In 1992, however, it became evident that cod stocks had collapsed due to over-fishing and the Canadian government placed a moratorium on commercial cod fishing; some 40,000 people lost their jobs. Ten years later, stocks had shown no signs of recovery and on April 24, 2003, the fisheries minister announced the closing of the Candian commercial cod fishery. The social and economic consequences might have been devastating but for the emergence of a new and far more profitable industry: mineral extraction, particularly oil and gas. Lately, scientists and fishermen alike note cod returning.

NEWFOUNDLAND TODAY

Offshore Oil – Completed in 1997, the **Hibernia oil platform**, secured to its drill site some 315km/200mi out in the Grand Banks, weighs over 1.2 million tonnes/1.3 million tons, heavy enough, it is projected, to withstand collision with the giant icebergs common in these waters.

Production began in 1997; output from one well is currently about 150,000 barrels of oil a day, and new wells are being developed.

In 2002 production began from the **Terra Nova** site, and in 2005 from the **White Rose** site, both some 350km/219mi off the coast. The two sites operate from innovative "floating production storage and off-loading" vessels that can be moved in case of inclement conditions.

Oral Traditions

Visitors to Newfoundland are captivated by the wealth of unusual idioms and wonderful accents of its inhabitants. Centuries of isolation have chiselled a character that is independent, individualistic and humorous. Where else are there localities named **Stinking Cove,** Useless Bay, **Jerry's Nose,** Cuckold Cove, **Come by Chance** and Happy Adventure, or local terms like *tickle* (a narrow waterway)? English is the first language of 98 percent of the islanders, but remarkably varied dialects enrich the provincial tongue. Some have definite Irish overtones; others are reminiscent of England's West Country (Dorset, Devon, Cornwall). Local expressions such as "to have a noggin to scrape" (a very hard task), "to be all mops and brooms" (to have untidy hair) and "long may your big jib draw" (good luck for the future) add color and humour to everyday conversations.

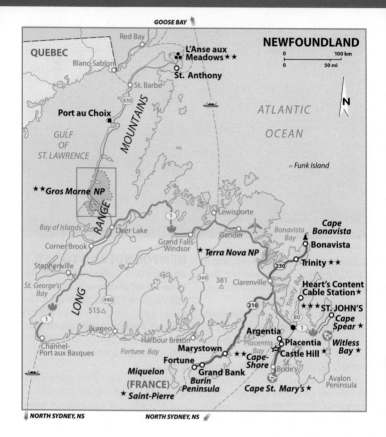

QUEBEC

NEWFOUNDLAND

GOOSE BAY

Red Bay

Blanc-Sablon

L'Anse aux Meadows ★★

St. Anthony

St. Barbe

Port au Choix

GULF OF ST. LAWRENCE

MOUNTAINS

ATLANTIC OCEAN

N

○ Funk Island

★★ Gros Morne NP

RANGE

Bay of Islands

Deer Lake

Lewisporte

Bonavista Bay

Cape Bonavista

Corner Brook

Grand Falls-Windsor

Gander

★ Terra Nova NP

Bonavista

Stephenville

Trinity ★★

St. George's Bay

LONG

515△

381 △

Clarenville

Heart's Content Cable Station ★

Trinity Bay

★★★ ST. JOHN'S

Cape Spear ★

Burgeo

Channel-Port aux Basques

Harbour Breton

Fortune Bay

Argentia

Placentia Bay

Placentia

Castle Hill ★

Witless Bay ★

Marystown

Fortune

Cape-Shore

St. Bride's

Miquelon (FRANCE)

Grand Bank

Burin Peninsula

Cape St. Mary's ★

Avalon Peninsula

★ Saint-Pierre

NORTH SYDNEY, NS

NORTH SYDNEY, NS

In addition, the Voisey's Bay Nickel Company is investing $3 billon to mine and process nickel from a site discovered in 1993 in Labrador. Thus, despite the disaster in the cod fishery, the outlook for the province is one of guarded euphoria.

Lifestyle and Food – About one-quarter of the island's population resides in the capital city of St. John's; the remain-der lives mainly in coastal fishing villages known as **outports,** tiny coastal settlements. With the traditional cod removed from the menu, arctic char, lobster, salmon, snow crab and halibut are favourite dinners, and **squid burgers** are an island peculiarity. Game includes caribou steaks and moose. Fruits of the region include blueberries, partridge-berries and yellow **bakeapples**.

PRACTICAL INFORMATION
GETTING THERE
BY AIR – St. John's International **Airport** (✆709-758-8500 or 866-758-8581; www.stjohnsairport.com). 10km/6mi to downtown.
Air Canada provides direct flights from Calgary, Toronto, Montreal and Halifax (✆888-247-2262; www.air

canada.com). **West Jet** (✆888-937-8538; www.westjet.com) flies directly from Calgary, Toronto and Halifax. United (✆800-231-0856; www.united. com) flies from Newark, NJ, and **Lufthansa** (✆800-563-5954; www. lufthansa.com.) from Toronto and Halifax. Air Canada Jazz (✆888-247-2262; flies into **Gander International**

Airport (Labrador) (*709-256-6668, or 709-256-6666; www.ganderairport. com*) in Gander, NL. **Air Labrador** (*709-896-6730 or 800-563-3042; www.airlabrador.com*) and **Provincial Airlines** (*709-576-1666 or 800-563-2800; www.provincialairlines.ca*) provide regular connections within the province and beyond.

BY BOAT – Passenger & car ferry service is available from North Sydney, NS, to Channel-Port aux Basques *(departs year-round twice daily; daytime crossings 4.5–6hrs, night 4.5-8hrs.* and to Argentia *(mid Jun–late Sept; once daily crossing 14–15hrs).* For schedules & reservations, contact **Marine Atlantic**, North Sydney, NS (*800-341-7981, Canada/US; www. marine-atlantic.ca).* Connecting bus service to inland destinations **DRL Coachlines** *709-263-2171 or 888-263-1854; www.drl-lr.com).*

Provincial Ferry Services (*709-729-2300 or 888-638-5454;www. hotfrog.ca/Products/ferry/NL)* serves seacoast towns in Newfoundland and eastern Laborador. **M/V Bella Desgagnés** accommodates 381 passengers with 459 plane-style seats, offers 160 berths/63 cabins with private facilities, including two for reduced mobility. Cafeteria & diningroom too. *Information: 800-463-0680 or www.quebecmaritime.ca. For ferry service to* **Saint-Pierre and Miquelon** *see SAINT-PIERRE AND MIQUELON.*

GENERAL INFORMATION
ACCOMMODATIONS AND VISITOR INFORMATION
Travel, hunting & fishing guides and road maps free of charge from **Newfoundland and Labrador Tourism**, St. John's. *709-729-2830 or 800-563-6353. www. newfoundlandlabrador.com.*

ROAD REGULATIONS – Trans-Canada Highway Rte.1 *(910km/565mi)* traverses Newfoundland from Channel-Port aux Basques to St. John's, and most secondary highways are paved. Gravel roads vary according to traffic and weather. Main roads passable during winter, but check with local authorities before departure (*see Tourism website above).* **Seat belt** use compulsory. Speed limits are 100km/h (60mph) on four-lane highways, 80km/h (50mph) on secondary highways and 50km/h (30mph) on gravel roads.

TIME ZONES – Most of Labrador observes Atlantic Standard Time. Newfoundland Standard Time is 30min ahead of Atlantic Standard Time and 1hr 30min ahead of Eastern Daylight Time. Daylight Saving Time is from second Sun in March to first Sun in November.

TAXES – Newfoundland and Labrador's Harmonized Sales Tax (HST) is levied at a single rate of 15 per cent. Nonresidents may be entitled to a rebate; for information visit www. cra-arc.gc.ca.

LIQUOR LAWS – Liquor and wine are available only from government stores except in remote areas where local stores are licensed. Beer is available in most convenience stores. The legal drinking age is 19.

PROVINCIAL HOLIDAY
The Queen's Birthday (Victoria Day): Closest Mon before May 24

PRINCIPAL FESTIVALS

mid-Feb	**Corner Brook Winter Carnival**: *Corner Brook*	
Jun	**St. John's Days**: *St. John's*	
Jul	**Point Leamington Festival**: *Point Leamington*	
Jul 14	**Bastille Day:** *St. Pierre*	
Jul– mid-Aug	**Stephenville Festival**: *Stephenville*	
Aug	**Labrador Straits Bake-apple Folk Festival**: *Point Amour*	
	Festival of Flight: *Gander*	
mid-Aug	**Labrador Straits Bakeapple Folk Festival**: *Point Amour*	

Burin Peninsula

This peninsula is the doorstep to the once-vast offshore fishing industry in the **Grand Banks.** Just off the "toe" are the island remnants of France's once-great empire in North America: Saint-Pierre et Miquelon.

🚗 DRIVING TOUR

203km/126mi south of Trans-Can Hwy. by Hwy. 210 to Fortune.

The drive on Highway 210 is long and deserted until **Marystown,** situated on Little Bay. Its huge shipyard, where fishing trawlers are built, has suffered with decline of the industry.

South of Marystown, Route 210 crosses the peninsula and descends to Fortune Bay, providing views of the southern coast of Newfoundland. Just before entering Grand Bank, there is a view of the south coast and Brunette Island. To the west the coast of the French island of Miquelon is just visible, weather permitting.

Grand Bank

199km/123mi south of Trans-Can Hwy. by Hwy. 210.

An important fishing centre, this community was once the home of the

- **Michelin Map:** p 420.
- **Info:** Newfoundland and Labrador Tourism. ℘709-729-0862 or 800-563-6353. www.newfound landlabrador.com.
- **Location:** On the southern coast of Newfoundland between Placentia and Fortune bays.
- **Kids:** Provincial Seamen's Museum's model ships.

famous "bankers." Some of the houses from that era are examples of the Queen Anne style with their widow's walks or small open rooftop galleries from which women could watch for the return of their men from the sea.

👥 Provincial Seamen's Museum★

54 Marine Dr. ℘709-757-8020. www.therooms.ca/psm. ◷May–Oct Mon–Sat 9am–4:30pm, Sun noon-4:30pm. ⊚$2.50.

This branch of the Provincial Museums network features displays and photographs of ships like the Titanic, plus fishing **models** & types of ships used.

Highway 210 to **Fortune**, another fishing community, is the departure point for ferries to the French islands of Saint-Pierre et Miquelon.

Grandy Dory, Provincial Seamen's Museum

© The Rooms Corporation of Newfoundland and Labrador

The Cape Shore★★

Newfoundland's most dramatic coastline, extending from Placentia to St. Bride's, delights visitors with its natural wonders and historic sites as well as magnificent ocean views and remnants of Europe's territorial struggles.

SIGHTS
Castle Hill National Historic Site★

In Placentia, 44km/27mi south of Trans-Can Hwy. by Rte. 100. About 8km/ 5mi from Argentia ferry. &⊘Grounds open year-round. Visitor Centre open Jun–Sept10am–6pm.⊛$3.90. ℘709-227-2401. www.pc.gc.ca.

This park contains the remains of France's early 17C Fort Royal, rebuilt and renamed Castle Hill by the British. Overlooking the small town of **Placentia**, the site affords a **panorama★★** of the city itself, Placentia Bay and **The Gut**—a small channel that separates the bay from two long, deep inlets.

During World War II, a large American base was built at nearby **Argentia,** the site of the famous 1941 offshore meeting between Churchill and Roosevelt that produced the **Atlantic Charter,** a statement of peace goals adopted in 1942 by the United Nations. An interesting **Visitor Centre** describes the French and English presence in the area. A pleasant pathway through evergreen forests leads to **Le Gaillardin,** a redoubt built by the French in 1692.

Cape Shore Drive★★

46km/29mi from Placentia to St. Bride's on Rte. 100. ⊛ Fuel and food available infrequently. Fog may hamper visibility.

Traversing a rugged, hilly coast, Route 100 provides spectacular **views**. Sparsely populated communities such as picturesque **Gooseberry Cove** *(25km/16mi south of Placentia)* dot the wide inlets. Colourful flat-topped

houses, woolly sheep and an occasional fishing boat anchored offshore are common scenes until the road turns inland at St. Bride's.

👥 Cape St. Mary's Ecological Reserve★

About 14km/9mi east of St. Bride's. Leave St. Bride's via Rte. 100. Turn right on paved road and continue 14km/8mi. ⊘Open year-round. Interpretive centre open daily May–Sep.

⊛ View the birds with free guided summer tours provided onsite. env.gov.nl.ca/env/parks/wer/r_csme/.

This sanctuary for seabirds is one of the largest nesting grounds in North America for **gannets,** relatives of the pelican family. Atop a dramatic shoreline alive with the sounds of over 70,000 birds, its pastoral **setting** is unique. Visitors can get within several feet of the birds. Providing **views★** of the rugged coast, a trail from the lighthouse and Interpretive centre leads to **Bird Rock,** the precarious domain of hundreds of gannets. Surrounding cliffs attract throngs of noisy black-legged kittiwakes, common murres and razorbills.

- 🕉 **Michelin Map:** p 420.
- 📖 **Info:** Newfoundland and Labrador Tourism, ℘709-729-0862 or 800-563-6353. www.newfound landandlabrador.com.
- ▶ **Location:** The Cape Shore lies on the southwest arm of the Avalon Penninsula, which extends off the east coast of the island.
- 👁 **Don't Miss:** The drive along the Cape Shore.
- ⊘ **Timing:** Start early; check the weather before heading out.
- 👥 **Kids: See legions of birds at** Cape St. Mary's Ecological Reserve.

Gros Morne National Park★★

This vast, pristine park, designated a UNESCO World Heritage Site in 1987, includes some of the most spectacular scenery in eastern Canada. Consisting of rock more than a billion years old, the flat-topped **Long Range Mountains** are the northernmost part of the Appalachians. Between them and the coast lies a poorly drained plain, sometimes high above the sea, with a variety of cliffs, sandy shores and little fishing communities.

> ♿ **Michelin Map:** p 425.
> ℹ **Info:** Parks Canada, Rocky Harbour. ☎709-458-2417. www.pc.gc.ca
> ▶ **Location:** The park covers 1,805sq km/697sq mi along the west coast of Newfoundland's **Great Northern Peninsula.**
> ⊙ **Don't Miss:** A guided boat tour on Trout River Pond.
> ⊙ **Timing:** Contact Visit Gros Morne at ☎709-458-3605 or 866-732-2759. www.visitgrosmorne.com

Access

44km/27mi northwest of Deer Lake. Take Rte. 430 from Deer Lake to Wiltondale, then Rte. 431 to park, 13km/8mi.

VISIT

⊙*Open year-round.* ⊛*$9.80 entry fee (May–Oct). Hiking, camping, cross-country skiing, fishing, kayaking, swimming. Contact visitor centre near Rocky Harbour for guided boat tours (♿⊙open late Apr–early May Mon–Fri 9am–5pm; mid-May–mid-Oct daily 9am–5pm (til 9pm late Jun–Labour Day).* ☎709-458-2417. www.pc.gc.ca.

Bonne Bay Area★★

Take Rte. 431 from Wiltondale 50km/31mi to Trout River (food, fuel).

This is a beautiful drive along a deep fjord surrounded by the squat peaks of the Long Range Mountains. The road travels westward along the **South Arm** from Glenburnie, offering gorgeous **views★★** of the bay.

From Woody Point, as Route 431 ascends to the west, the red-brown rubble of a desertlike area known as the **Tablelands** is abruptly visible. These mountains consist of rock that was once part of the earth's mantle—a magnesium and iron layer surrounding the planet's core—and are evidence of **plate tec-**

tonics, the shifting of the plates within the earth's crust. For a closer look at the Tablelands, stop at the turnoff *(4.5km/2.8 mi from Woody Point),* where a **panel display** describes this unique natural feature.

This vantage point offers a striking **view** of the barren expanse. A footpath leads from the parking area into the heart of the Tablelands (⊛*for information on guided hikes, contact the Visitor Centre).* Beyond the little fishing village of Trout River is the long finger lake called **Trout River Pond** (♿⊙*tour boats depart Jul–Aug daily 10am, 11am, 12:30pm, 1:30pm, 3pm, 4pm; Jun & Sept 11:30am & 12:30pm; round-trip 2hrs 30mi; reservations required;* ⊛*$45-$62; for reservations* ☎709-458-2016, or 866-458-2016; www.bontours.ca). Ask about their new catamaran *Westbrook1.*

Dominating the return drive to Woody Point is the vast bulk of **Gros Morne Mountain** (806m/2,644ft) to the north, the park's highest point. Stop at Parks Canada's **Discovery Centre** (⊙*open late Jun–Labour Day daily 9am–6pm; mid-May–mid-Jun and rest of Sept–Oct daily 9am–5pm)* on the south side of Bonne Bay for a look at the geology and ecology of the area.

From Wiltondale Route 430 travels northeast along **East Arm,** a vantage point for lovely **views★★** of Bonne Bay, and along Deer Arm.

From Rocky Harbour to St. Pauls

40km/25mi by Rte. 430.
Overlooking Bonne Bay, the coastal community of **Rocky Harbour** functions as a service centre for park visitors.

On a promontory just north of Rocky Harbour, **Lobster Cove Head Lighthouse** (🕐 *open mid-May–mid-Oct daily 10am–5:30pm*) provides **views★★** of the town, Gros Morne Mountain, mouth of the bay and Gulf of St. Lawrence. Built on a narrow plain between the sea and the Long Range Mountains, the road affords a pretty drive past Sally's Cove, a little fishing community. Before the turnoff to Western Brook Pond's trailhead, the rusty remains of the **SS Ethie** shipwreck can be seen on the beach at Martin's Point. A small panel describes the fate of the ship's 1919 voyage.

Map:
PORT AU CHOIX NHS / L'ANSE AUX MEADOWS
GROS MORNE NATIONAL PARK
Shallow Bay
Cow Head
0 — 15 km
0 — 10 mi
Gulf of St. Lawrence
St. Pauls
St. Pauls Inlet
SS Ethie
Sally's Cove
Western Brook Pond ★★
★★ GROS MORNE NP
430
Rocky Harbour
△806 Gros Morne Mtn.
★★ Bonne Bay
Deer Arm
Trout River
Woody Point
Norris Point
East Arm
Tablelands
South Arm
Trout River Pond
431
430
Glenburnie
Wiltondale
LONG RANGE MOUNTAINS
N
DEER LAKE

Western Brook Pond★★

29km/18mi from Rocky Harbour.
Western Brook runs through a gorge in the Long Range Mountains before it crosses the narrow coastal plain and reaches the sea. A pond is flanked by vertical cliffs. The only way to see the interior of Western Brook Pond is to take the **boat trip** (*departs Jul–Aug daily 10am, 1pm & 4pm; Jun & Sept daily 1pm; round-trip 2hrs; ☞$58;* 🅿 *3km/1.8 mi walk from parking lot; park pass required; warm jacket recommended; reservations imperative; Bon Tours ✆709-458-2016 or 888-458-2016; www.bontours.ca*).

Tablelands Mountains, Gros Morne National Park

© Newfoundland and Labrador Tourism

Heart's Content Cable Station★

A little town founded about 1650 on Trinity Bay, Heart's Content is the site of the first successful landing, in 1866, of the **transatlantic telegraph cable**—the result of years of work by the New York, Newfoundland and London Telegraph Co., led by American financier Cyrus W. Field. After failed attempts in 1858 and 1865, Field in 1866 successfully used the ocean liner *Great Eastern* to lay the cable between Valencia, Ireland, and Heart's Content, where it joined a cable to New York. Messages initially cost $5 a word, and the station handled 3,000 messages a day. The station closed in 1965.

♖ **Michelin Map:** p 420.
≡ **Info:** Newfoundland and Laborador Tourism (◓*see Introduction*).
▷ **Location:** Heart's Content is located on Trinity Bay.

VISIT

58km/36mi north of Trans-Can Hwy. by Rte. 80, Avalon Peninsula. ◈*Open May-Oct daily 10am–5:30pm.* ∾*$6.* ₮*709-583-2160/800-563-6353. www.seethesites.ca.*
There is a **film** *(20min)* and a special section on the laying of the transatlantic cables. Costumed guides are on site for tours of the replica of the first cable office (1866) and operating room. A new exhibit (2004) describes the life of those who worked at the station.

L'Anse aux Meadows★★

On a grassy ledge facing Epaves Bay, the remains of the oldest authenticated European settlement in North America are preserved for posterity. This remote site, a National Historic Site of Parks Canada, has been included on UNESCO's World Heritage list as a property of universal value.

♖ **Michelin Map:** p 420.
≡ **Info:** Parks Canada. ₮709-623-2608. www.pc.gc.ca.
▷ **Location:** L'Anse aux Meadows is located on the Great Northern Penninsula, at the farthest northern tip of Newfoundland, opposite Labrador.
◈ **Timing:** Highway 430, the Viking Trail, leads here from Gros Morne. Services and accommodations are available in nearby St. Anthony.

A BIT OF HISTORY

In 1960, **Helge Ingstad**, a Norwegian explorer and writer, and his archae-ologist wife, **Anne Stine**, began a sys-tematic search of the coast from New England northward. Led to a group of overgrown mounds near L'Anse aux Meadows by a local resident, they exca-vated them from 1961 to 1968. Foundations of eight sod buildings of the type the Norse built in Iceland were uncovered and several artifacts unde-niably Norse in origin were found. Evi-dence of iron working—an art unknown to the North American Indians—was unearthed. Samples of bone, turf and charcoal were carbon-dated to around AD 1000.

Experts believe L'Anse aux Meadows was a base for further exploration in search of timber and trading goods. Occupied by about 100 men and women, the camp was probably deserted after five or ten years. Newfoundland's harsh condi-

Vinland

By AD 900 the Vikings (also known as the Norse) from present-day Scandinavia had settled in Iceland, and from there explored Greenland, Baffin Island and beyond. The account of a land sighting by a Greenland-destined ship blown off course inspired **Leif Ericsson,** then residing in Greenland, to go exploring. About AD 1000 Ericsson landed at a fertile spot and built a settlement for the winter.

He named the location "Vinland" for the wild grapes his crew is said to have found there. This story is preserved in two Norse tales: the *Saga of the Greenlanders* and the *Saga of Eric the Red,* which were communicated by word of mouth for hundreds of years before being recorded. Though many scholars have tried to find Vinland, its location is unknown. Once thought to be on the southeastern coast of the US because of the grapes, this location was determined to be too far for ships to have sailed in the time suggested by the sagas.

tions, coupled with the growing accessibility of southern European markets, most likely led to its abandonment.

Access

453km/281mi north of Trans-Can Hwy. by Rtes. 430 and 436.

VISIT

 🚻🅿🕐*Open Jun–early Oct daily 9am–6pm.* 🎟*$11.70.* 📞*709-623-2608. www.pc.gc.ca.*
In the **Visitor Centre** displays depict what a Norse settlement might have looked like, but the highlight is the collection of artifacts found on-site. A stirring **film** *(28min)* on the Ingstads' search introduces the visit.

Completely excavated, the site has been preserved as grassy borders that outline the foundations of the original structures. The layout of the dwellings, work buildings and a smithy can be clearly distinguished. Nearby, three **sod buildings**—a long house, a building and a work shed—have been reconstructed. Inside, wooden platforms that served as beds line the walls. Fire pits are placed at intervals in the middle of the earthen floors. Costumed staff demonstrate Viking skills.

At the end of "The Viking Trail," **St. Anthony**, a large service centre, is the nearest city *(food, accommodations and air service)* to L'Anse aux Meadows. At the turn of the 19C, a British doctor, Sir

L'Anse aux Meadows

Len Klingen/Michelin

Wilfred Grenfell (1865-1940), began his medical missionary work in the area, including Labrador. St. Anthony preserves his memory through the hospital he established, a cooperative craft shop and the house local residents built for him, now the **Grenfell House Museum** (&⏱ *open summer 8am–5pm, winter 9am–5pm;* ☞*$10;* ☎*709-454-4010; www. grenfell-properties.com.* Boat tours daily from late-May-mid-Sep 9am-4pm ($60, youth $32).

ADDRESSES

🛏 STAY

$ Tickle Inn – *RR#1. At Cape Onion, via Raleigh.* ☎*709-452-4321 (Jun–Sept), 709-452-4321 off season, or 866-814-8567. www.tickleinn.net. 4 rooms.* 🅿 ⛶*. This refurbished two-storey 1890s outport house is a retreat for travellers to this remote peninsula. Guests gather in the dining room for a meal of island favourites such as Newfoundland shrimp and scallops or poached Atlantic salmon, concluding with Northern berry flan. Rates include a deluxe buffet breakfast.*

St. John's★★★

One of the oldest cities in North America, this historic seaport owes its founding to a fine natural harbour that now services an international shipping trade.

A BIT OF HISTORY

Early Years – Throughout the 16C, ships from European countries used the harbour as a fishing base. Under charter from Elizabeth I of England, Sir **Humphrey Gilbert** (c.1537-83) arrived in St. John's harbour in 1583 to found a settlement. He is credited with claiming Newfoundland for England, but drowned near Sable Island before establishing the settlement. Determined to maintain their fishing monopolies, England's West Country merchants opposed settlement of Newfoundland; from 1675 to 1677 a formal ban on settlement was in effect.

The Anglo-French Wars – Fear of French expansion changed the attitude of the British government toward permanent settlement.
The French had established fortifications at Placentia in 1662 and attacked British harbours, especially St. John's. The city fell three times to the French, with the final battle in 1762 at the end of the Seven Years' War.

Devastating Fires – In the 19C the capital suffered five fires that virtually

- ▸ **Population:** 196,966.
- ⌖ **Michelin Map:** p 431.
- 🔢 **Info:** Tourist Office, 348 Water St. ☎709-576-8106. www.stjohns.ca.
- 🅿 **Parking:** Parking Meters in St. John's are in effect Mon–Fri 8am–6pm. Each digital meter will show the maximum time period a vehicle can park in the space on its display.
- 🧍 **Kids:** Signal Hill Tattoo and Johnson GEO Centre.

wiped out the entire community each time, the most extensive of all in 1892. Each time, the city was rebuilt, primarily in prevailing architectural styles such as Gothic Revival and, after the 1892 fire, Second Empire.

Confederation and Beyond – St. John's was a wealthy city in the early 20C and during World War II when it served as a base for North American convoys. After the war the Dominion of Newfoundland's decision to enter Confederation resulted in a decline in the city's economy, despite a substantial infusion of federal funds. Due to changes in the industry, St. John's importance as a fish-exporting centre declined. Finally, the 1992 collapse of

St. John's harbour viewed from Signal Hill, with The Rooms (left) and Basilica Cathedral of St. John the Baptist (right)

the commercial cod fishery dealt a blow to fish-processing plants.

In the 21C, however, the city has found prosperity underpinned by the province's vast mineral and hydroelectric wealth. The huge nickel mine at Voisey's Bay, Labrador, began production in 2005, three offshore oil fields are producing and the Lower Churchill Falls project is halfway to completion in 2017.

Harbour and Old City★★

The city's **site** borders a harbour almost landlocked except for a slim passage to the ocean known as **The Narrows,** which is flanked by cliffs rising on the north side to form Signal Hill.

Gradually the harbour widens to nearly 800m/.5mi, surrounded by the steep slopes on which the city is built. Parallel to the water, **Harbour Drive** skirts the busy dock where ships from around the world are often berthed. The main thoroughfares of the old city, **Water** and **Duckworth streets,** contain restaurants, shops and banks. Colourful **George Street** is home to a clutch of pubs and eateries.

The Rooms

9 Bonaventure Ave. ✕ & ⓒ *Open Jun–mid-Oct Mon–Sat 10am–5pm (Wed til 9pm), Sun & holidays noon–5pm. Rest of the year closed Monday.* ⓒ *Closed major*

Regatta Day

Each year **Quidi Vidi** [KID-dy VID-dy] **Lake** is the site of St. John's Regatta, the oldest continuously held sporting event in North America (since 1826). Held on the first Wednesday in August (or the first fine day thereafter), the regatta is probably the only civic holiday decided that morning. The local population waits for the cry, "The races are on!" and then crowds the lakeshore to watch competitors row the 2.6km/1.6mi course, the major event of the all-day carnival.

holidays. ⊜*$10.* ☎*709-757-8000. www.therooms.ca.*

This dramatic hillside museum is devoted to Newfoundland's history and prehistory. Its permanent collection numbers more than one million artifacts.

Cabot Tower on Signal Hill

© Marco Maccarini/iStockphoto.com

The Rooms (what compounds of fisheries buildings were once called) houses not only the provincial museum, but also the provincial archives and the provincial art gallery.

The basement holds an ongoing archaeological dig of a 1775 fort.

There are displays on native cultures, notably those of the Beothuk Indians and Labrador Inuit, and exhibits about the lives of fishing families.

Commissariat House★

King's Bridge Rd. ○*Open mid-May–early Oct daily 10am–5:30pm.* ⊜*$6.* ☎*709-729-6730. Off-season 709-729-0592. www.seethesites.ca.*

Dating from 1820, this clapboard house was one of the few buildings to escape the 19C fires. It was used for many years by the commissariat, which provisioned the military post of St. John's. After 1871 it became the rectory for the adjacent **Church of St. Thomas (A** on map**)**. A **coach house** lodges an exhibit on the commissariat's function.

Within walking distance *(Military Rd.)* stands the residence of the lieutenant-governor, **Government House** *(only the grounds can be visited without appointment;* ☞*for tours* ☎*709-729-4494; www.govhouse.nl.ca)* and the former seat of the provincial assembly, the **Colonial Building** *(o━ not open to the public)*, a limestone structure with a Neoclassical portico (1850).

Basilica Cathedral of St. John the Baptist (B *on map*)

200 Military Rd. ♿▣○*Open year-round Mon–Fri 8am–4pm, Sat 10am–after 5pm Mass, Sun 8am–12:30pm.* ○*Closed holidays except for mass.* ☎*709-754-2170. www.thebasilica.ca.*

This twin-towered 1850 Roman Catholic church is a landmark visible from the harbour and Signal Hill. The interior is ornate with statuary and altar carving.

Anglican Cathedral of St. John the Baptist (C *on map*)

9 Cathedral St. ○*Open early Jun–Sept. Mon–Fri 9am–5pm, Sat–Sun hours vary.* ☞*Guided tours daily in summer (entrance on Gower St).* ☎*709-726-5677. www.stjohnsanglicancathedral.org.*

This Gothic Revival stone structure was designed in 1843 by British architect Sir **George Gilbert Scott** (1811–78). Destroyed by fire in 1892, the church was reconstructed in the 20C.

The interior has wooden vaulted ceilings and **reredos,** an ornamental stone or wooden partition behind an altar. The **Crypt Tearoom** serves afternoon tea (○ *open Jul–Aug Mon–Fri 2:00pm–4:00pm;* ⊜*$10).*

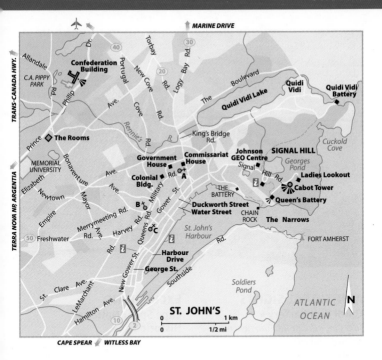

ST. JOHN'S

0   1 km
0   1/2 mi

CAPE SPEAR   WITLESS BAY

Signal Hill★★

Topped by Cabot Tower, Signal Hill rises steeply at the mouth of the harbour, permitting splendid views of the city.

In 1901 **Guglielmo Marconi** chose the site for an experiment to prove that radio signals could be transmitted long distances by electromagnetic waves. When he reputedly received the letter "S" in Morse code from Poldhu in Cornwall, England—a distance of 2,700km/1,700mi—he made history.

Visit

P⊙*Grounds open year-round daily. Visitor Centre open mid-May–mid-Oct daily 10am–6pm. Rest of the year Mon–Fri 10am-6pm. ⊙Closed mid-Oct-mid-May, Jan 1, Dec 25-26. ⊜$3.90. ☏709-772-5367. www.pc.gc.ca.*

Built in 1898, **Cabot Tower** (⊙*open Jun–Labour Day daily 8:30am–9pm; Apr–May & rest of Sept–mid-Jan daily 9am–5pm*) affords a **panorama★★★** of the city.

A path leads to **Ladies Lookout,** the crown of the hill (160m/525ft). From **Queen's Battery** (1833) there is a good **view★** of the harbour. On the other side of the Narrows stand the remains of Fort Amherst (1763), now housing a lighthouse.

In the summer, students in the 19C uniforms of the Royal Newfoundland Regiment perform a **military tattoo** ♟♟ *(early-Jun–mid-Aug Wed, Thu, Sat & Sun 11am & 3pm; ⊜$10)* consisting of fife-and-drum corps and military drills near the Visitor Centre.

♟♟ Johnson GEO Centre★★

175 Signal Hill Rd. ♿P⊙Open seven days per week 9:30am–5pm. ⊜$12 (youth $6). ☏709-737-7880 or 866-868-7625. www.geocentre.ca.

This modern, $12 million centre opened in 2002. It was built into Signal Hill, whose exposed rock, which is millions of years old, can be seen when visitors enter the centre.

On the ground level is a travelling space exhibit. The underground level displays the centre's permanent exhibits, many features of which are interactive. The Titanic Story gives an overview of the famous disaster off Newfoundland's coast. The second exhibit examines the province's oil and gas exploration.

Johnson GEO Centre on Signal Hill

© Sandra Phinney/Michelin

ADDITIONAL SIGHTS
Quidi Vidi Battery★

Take King's Bridge Rd. Turn right on Forest Rd. When road becomes Quidi Vidi Village Rd., drive 2km/1.2mi to Cuckhold's Cove Rd. and turn right. ○*Open mid-May–early Oct daily 10am–5:30pm.* ○*$3.* ○*800-563-6353.*
Built by the French during their occupation of St. John's in 1762, this emplacement was strengthened by the British in the early 19C. The house re-creates the living quarters of soldiers stationed there.
Below is the tiny fishing community of **Quidi Vidi,** which has a narrow channel connecting to the larger Quidi Vidi Lake, site of the annual St. John's Regatta.

Confederation Building

Prince Philip Dr. ○○○○*Open year-round Mon–Fri 8:30am–4pm.* ○*Closed major holidays. Guided tours when Assembly not in session; 9am, 10:30am, 2pm & 3pm.* ○*709-729-3630.*
Newfoundland's Parliament and some provincial government offices are housed in this building. Constructed in 1960 and expanded in 1985, the edifice provides a good **view** from its front entrance of the harbour and Signal Hill. When in session the **legislative assembly** can be observed *(sessions Feb–May Mon–Fri, third-floor visitors' gallery).*

EXCURSIONS
Cape Spear National Historic Site★

About 11km/7mi south; follow Water St. to Leslie St. Turn left at Leslie St. Go over bridge, continue straight after stop sign, following the road (Hwy. 11). ○*Grounds open year-round. Visitor centre & gift shop open late-May–late-Oct daily 10am–6pm.* ○*$3.90.* ○*709-772-5367. www.pc.gc.ca.* ○ *Wear warm clothing. It is colder here than in St. John's.*
At longitude 52°37′24″, Cape Spear is North America's most easterly point. On clear days there are **views★** of the coast. Whales are seen in the waters off the cape seasonally. Tea Room during summer.
The restored square **1836 lighthouse** (○ *open mid-May–mid-Oct daily 10am–6pm)* is the province's oldest. The return trip to St. John's *(30km/19mi)* can be made via the fishing villages of Maddox Cove and **Petty Harbour**.

Witless Bay Ecological Reserve★

Embarkation from town of Bay Bulls, 30km/19mi south of St. John's via Rte. 10. Then watch for directional signs of your chosen boat tour company to the dock. ○○○○*Departures May–Sept daily. Round-trip 2hrs. Reservations required.* ○*$57.50. For schedule, contact*

WALK ON THE WILD SIDE

On the  **East Coast Trail**, an intrepid hiker can trek south from downtown St. John's along the edge of the crashing surf for a total of some 450km/281mi.

The trail is well suited for day hikes, with parking at access points along the route, and superb options for walks among wildflowers and memorable vistas. Guidebooks and maps are available for purchase in many shops around the city *(East Coast Trail Assn., St. John's ℰ709-738-4453; www.eastcoasttrail.com).*

Looking for fresh, homemade goodies? **Rocket Bakery** at *272 Water Street*, has become the unofficial community hub, due partly because of the daily magic taking place on the second floor, where everything is baked from scratch. Dine in or take out, the choice is yours from a healthy menu of temptations such as savory stews, stocked soups, and daily main dishes, with an amazing list of possible desserts including fresh croissants, traditional scones, signature cakes, cookies, tarts and pies. *ℰ709-738-2011.rocketfood.ca.*

O'Brien's Whale & Bird Tours

ℰ709-753-4850 or 877-639-4253. www.obriensboattours.com. Departures May–late Oct daily. Round-trip 1hr 30min. ☏$57.50. For schedule, contact **Gatherall's Puffin and Whale Watch**. *ℰ709-334-2887 or 800-419-4253.www.gatheralls.com.*

The fish-filled waters and shore islands of Witless Bay *(disembarkation on the islands is not permitted)* attract thousands of sea birds annually. The **Atlantic puffin** colony here is reputedly the largest on the east coast of North America.

An additional highlight of the cruise is **whale watching★★** *(late spring and summer).*

Marine Drive★

12km/8mi north on Hwys. 30 and 20. Leave St. John's on Logy Bay Rd. (Rte. 30). After 5.5km/3mi, turn right to Marine Dr. The **view★** from **Outer Cove** is especially lovely. At **Middle Cove** there is an accessible beach, good for strolling along the shore.

Atlantic puffin flies over the waters of Witless Bay

ADDRESSES

🛏 STAY

$ Roses B&B – *9 Military Rd.* ☎*709-726-3336 or 877-767-3722. www.therosesnl.com. 21 rooms.* This bed-and-breakfast is within walking distance of downtown and Signal Hill. The Roses consists of four adjacent row houses that have been spruced up for guests. The rooms are bright and pleasantly furnished, some with antiques and original woodwork. Suites are spacious and have kitchens, perfect for families.

$$ McCoubrey Manor – *6-8 Ordnance St.* ☎*709-722-7577 or 888-753-7577. www.mccoubrey.com. 6 rooms.* 🖥. This pair of 1904 Queen Ann Revival town houses offers good value. Architectural details—such as the double oak mantel in the living room and plaster rosettes on the ceilings—end an historic air. The innkeepers offer wine and cheese in the afternoons, guest laundry facilities, and modern amenities. Four housekeeping apartments are nearby.

$$ The Narrows Bed & Breakfast – *146 Gower St.,* ☎*709-739-4850 or 866-739-4850. www.thenarrowsbb.com. 4 rooms.* 🅿 🆂🅿🅰 🖥. Short walk to everything, this location associated with O'Brien's Whale & Bird Tours is a perfect location at the heart of North America's oldest city. Private ensuite with colouyr TV, phone and radio, ceiling fans, top tier linens, harbour view and high-speed Internet. Eating area has a full kitchen with wood-burning stove, leather armchairs, regional art, music and info.

$$$ Murray Premises Hotel – *5 Becks Cove.* ☎*709-738-7773 or 866-738-7773. www.murraypremiseshotel.com. 28 rooms.* ♿🅿 🖥. This downtown boutique hotel occupies the third and fourth floors of a converted trading house (called "premises" throughout the province). While many of the beams are old, and some rooms are still tucked under eaves, the space has a modern gloss. Bathrooms have whirlpool tubs and heated towel racks. Boisterous weekends on George Street might take a toll on your sleep, however. Continental breakfast included.

$$$ The Ryan Mansion Boutique Hotel & Spa – *21 Rennies Mill Rd.* ☎*709-753-7926. www.ryanmansion.com. 6 rooms.* ♿🅿 🖥. This imposing Queen Anne Revival mansion was built by a prosperous family in 1911. Now an upscale boutique hotel and spa, it has the feel of an intimate inn. The main foyer features English white oak; staircase and mantels over the fireplaces were handmade by craftsmen who detailed the *Titanic*. Guest rooms, some with four-poster beds, have en suite bathrooms with heated marble floors. A gourmet breakfast is included.

🍴 EAT

$ Zachary's – *71 Duckworth St.* ☎*709-579-8050.* **Canadian**. Simple, tasty home-style fare with a regional bias served in relaxed surroundings rules the day here. Breakfast, served all day, is the best option, but lunch and dinner are also served. Fish is cooked perfectly, vegetables are served crunchy, and the partridgeberry cheesecake for dessert leaves patrons smiling.

$$ Blue on Water – *319 Water St.* ☎*709-7534-2583 or 877-431-2583. www.blueonwater.com.* **Canadian**. This downtown 7-room boutique **hotel ($$)** is considered an excellent place to eat as well as stay overnight. The weekend brunch is a great value: where else can you get banana pancakes with "Screech" (rum) roasted walnuts? The shrimp, scallops and mussels with tomato and green onion in white wine cream sauce is a dinner specialty.

$$ The Celtic Hearth – *300 Water St.* ☎*709-576-2880.* **British fare.** This is pub fare at its friendliest. The place is open year-round 24/7 and has a fireplace and lots of regulars. The Guinness steak pie is delicious, as are the codfish tongues. The top dining level has a higher-priced dinner menu.

$$$ The Duke of Duckworth – *325 Duckworth St.* ☎*709-739-6344. www.dukeofduckworth.com. Open daily for lunch, then until the wee hours.* For local colour, this classic pub and restaurant offers the largest draught selection in town, and more atmosphere per square inch than most addresses.Happy Hour menu includes fish & chips made with local cod.

Saint-Pierre and Miquelon★
(France)

These French islands, ceded to France by the 1763 Treaty of Paris, have a decidedly continental lifestyle. The two principal islands are Saint-Pierre and the larger Miquelon, connected by a long sandbar to what was once a third island, Langlade. Today, the only industries are tourism and fishing.

> ▶ **Population:** 6,287.
> ⚅ **Michelin Map:** p 420.
> ▤ **Info:** Comité Régional du Tourisme, Place du Général de Gaulle. ✆011-508-41-02 00. www.tourisme-saint-pierre-et-miquelon.com.
> ▶ **Location:** These tiny islands lie 48km/30mi southwest of Newfoundland's Burin Peninsula.
> ◷ **Timing:** The islands' time zone is 30min ahead of St. John's and 1hr ahead of Halifax.

VISIT
Saint-Pierre★
At the entrance to the harbour sits at **Ile-aux-Marins★** *(accessible from Saint-Pierre, in front of the tourist office, by 10min ferry ride)*, once a community of over 800 inhabitants. Centred in the old schoolhouse, the **museum** (👁open *May–Oct by guided tour; 3.50€; contact the tourist office*) contains a presenta-

PRACTICAL INFORMATION
GETTING THERE
BY BOAT – Passenger ferry from Fortune to Saint-Pierre island: *mid-Jul–Labour Day departs from Fortune daily 2:45pm; departs from Saint-Pierre daily 1:30pm. Jun & Sept–mid-Oct departs from Fortune Fri & Sun 2:45pm; departs from Saint-Pierre 1:30pm. 1hr–1hr 35min. Schedule may vary: call or go online to confirm. Winter service varies. Advance reservations required. Round-trip* 🚢*$93.* ▣*St.Pierre Ferry* ✆*709-832-3455 or 855-832-3455 (Canada/US). http://saintpierreferry.ca.* **Warning:** *the sea crossing can be rough.*

BY AIR – Air service from St.John's NL, Sydney and Halifax NS, and Montreal QC, provided by Air Saint-Pierre. *For information & reservations, contact Air Saint-Pierre* ✆*877-277-7765 (CanadaUS)* ✆*011-508-41-0000 in Saint-Pierre, or access www.airsaint pierre.com.*

CUSTOMS – European and US citizens must carry a valid passport, which is necessary to transit Canada. Canadian cizens must provide a valid passport. Other nationalities must have valid passport and in some cases a visa, which can be obtained from the nearest French embassy or consulate.

LANGUAGE – English is not commonly spoken on the islands. Telephone operators and tourist office staffs are bilingual, however.

ACCOMMODATIONS AND VISITOR INFORMATION
Contact in advance the Comité Régional du Tourisme, Place du Général De Gaulle, St-Pierre-et-Miquelon. ✆*011-508-41-02 00. www.st-pierre-et-miquelon.info (click "en" button in upper right-hand corner for English version).* There are several **restaurants** in St. Pierre that serve fine *cuisine française*, often as prix-fixe meals. Contact the tourist office for specific information.

tion of isle history. The treeless terrain permits **views** of Saint-Pierre and the remains of one of the more than 600 shipwrecks in the archipelago.

Miquelon and Langlade

Boat departures to Miquelon and Langlade available from Saint-Pierre. In summer, daily ferry to Langlade. Transportation by shuttle van to the village of Miquelon is available in summer or may be arranged off-season (contact the tourism office).

Except for the small working town of the same name, the northern island of Miquelon is untouched moorland. Seals might be seen lying on the sands of **Grand Barachois**. The road crosses the isthmus known as the Dune of Langlade, a sandbar formed in part by debris from shipwrecks. Situated at the southern end is the uninhabited "island" of Langlade.

Along the east side of the dune, a wide beach stretches out in the vicinity of Anse du Gouvernement.

Terra Nova National Park★

Scarred by glaciers of the past, this 396sq km/153sq mi area is a combination of rolling country and indented coastline. Deep fjords, or "sounds," reach inland, and in early summer these coastal waters are dotted with icebergs that float down with the Labrador Current.

Access

On Trans-Can Hwy. 58km/36mi east of Gander, or 210km/130mi northwest of St. John's.

VISIT

✕ ♿ ◷ *Open year-round.* ☞ *$5.80/ day use fee. Visitor Centre open mid-May–mid-Jun & Sept–mid-Oct daily 10am–4pm; late Jun–Sept daily 10am–6pm.* ℘*709-533-2801. www.pc.gc.ca.*

Bluehill Pond Lookout★★

7km/5mi from park's north entrance. Turn onto gravel road and continue approximately 2km/1mi to the observatory platform.

From the lookout platform there is a **panorama★★** of the whole park. To the south is Newman Sound and the ocean, scattered with icebergs (in season).

- ♿ **Michelin Map:** p 420.
- **Info:** ℘709-533-2801. www.pc.gc.ca.
- **Location:** Terra Nova National Park lies on the west side of Bonavista Bay. It is traversed by Trans-Canada Hwy 1.
- **Timing:** Ask at the visitor centre about boat tours of Newman Sound.

Newman Sound★

12km/8mi from park's north entrance. Take road to the Visitor Centre and Newman Sound. About 1.5km/1mi to the trail.

This deep inlet with a sandy beach can be appreciated by walking the trail along its wooded shore. Seasonal wildflowers and tiny seashells complement the setting.

Ochre Lookout

18km/11mi from park's north entrance. Take gravel road to the tower, about 3km/2mi. Observation deck.

From this lookout tower, another **panorama★** allows visitors to comprehend the vastness of the park. At this height, Clode and Newman sounds are clearly visible, weather permitting.

Trinity★★

This seaside community has a lovely **setting** and a small protected harbour. In 1615 the town became the site of the first Admiralty Court in Canada's history. Trinity's standing receded in in the 1850s when St. John's became the provincial capital.
Today it is a popular area for **whale watching** (*departures Jun–Labour Day weather permitting; 3hrs; ⌾$80; Sea of Whales Adventures ☎709-427-1217 or 709-464-2200; www.seaofwhales.com*).

Access

74km/46mi northeast of Trans-Can Hwy. by Rte. 230. Turn off Rte. 230 for 5km/3mi.

VISIT

Located in a restored house overlooking the harbour, the **Interpretation Centre** presents the community's history (*⌾open late-May–early Oct daily 10am–5:30pm; ⌾$20 admission to all 6 local historical sites, including Hiscock House; ☎709-464-2042 or 800-563-6353; www.tcr.gov.nl.ca/tcr*). Housed in a seven-room "salt box" dating to the 1880s, the **Trinity Museum** contains artifacts and historical documents (*⌾open May–Sept daily 10am–5:30pm; ☎709-464-3599; www.trinityhistorical-society.com*).
The 1881 **Hiscock House** has been restored to its early-1900s appearance and contains some original furnishings (*⌾open mid-May–early Oct daily 10am–5:30pm; ⌾$3; ☎709-464-2042 or 800-563-6353*).
St. Paul's Anglican Church (1892) stands as a village landmark. The 31m/102ft clock spire of this large wooden house of worship towers above the town. The **Holy Trinity Roman Catholic Church** has been In use for over 150 years.

▶ **Population:** 146.
⚲ **Michelin Map:** p 420.
▯ **Information:** Town of Trinity, 21 West St. ☎709-464-3836. www.townoftrinity.com.
👥 **Kids:** The whale-watching boat trip is only for older children.

Cape Bonavista Lighthouse
© Newfoundland and Labrador Tourism

EXCURSION TO CAPE BONAVISTA

From Trinity, Route 230 northbound continues inland and returns to the sea at Port Union and Catalina, two fishing communities set along the shore.
At Catalina, Route 237 crosses the peninsula, ending at Amherst Cove, where Route 235 continues northward to the cape town of Bonavista (*52km/31mi north of Trinity*).

ADDRESSES

⌖ STAY

$$ The Village Inn – *Taverner's Path (Rte. 239-10). ☎709-464-3269. 8 rooms, 1 apartment.* Early 1900s wooden structure offers charming rooms, brass beds and private baths. Serves home-cooked meals such as cod, halibut, shrimp, shepherd's pie, & nut roast. Breakfast, lunch and dinner are served. There's even an on-site pub.

A vast adventureland composing more than a tenth of Canada's size, the Northwest Territories embrace a varied landscape: mountains and forests, lakes and rivers, tundra and swamps. Two UNESCO World Heritage Sites, **Wood Buffalo National Park** and **Nahanni National Park Reserve**, lie partly or wholly within its boundaries. Except for the capital city of Yellowknife, few large settlements exist in this frontier wilderness. Although the size of the Northwest Territories was more than halved when Nunavut separated into an autonomous region in 1999, the Territories remains a diverse area suited for lovers of adventure, wilderness, wildlife and indigenous cultures.

Info: Northwest Territories Tourism, Yellowknife. ℘800-661-0788, international inquiries 867-873-7200 www.spectacularnwt.com.

Location: Comprising lands above the 60th parallel, the Territories stretch from the tundra above Saskatchewan to the Yukon. They include the extreme western parts of the Arctic Archipelago between the mainland and the North Pole.

Don't Miss: Yellowknife.

Timing: The drive from Edmonton to Yellowknife takes one very long day, or two shorter days.

Topography

Landscape – Two distinct landscapes border this vast region. In the east lies the giant plain between Hudson Bay and the Beaufort Sea. In the west rise the Mackenzie, Selwyn and Richardson mountain ranges. East of the Mackenzie Mountains is a broad river valley through which run the great Mackenzie River and its tributaries: the Slave and the Liard. East of the Mackenzie Lowlands lies the Canadian Shield, pitted with lakes, rivers and muskeg swamps left by glaciers that retreated 10,000 years ago.

Permafrost – Permafrost, where the ground remains at or below 0°C/32°F, generally starts about 0.3m/1ft or more below the surface. To prevent roadbeds and foundations from sinking, builders must avoid melting the frozen soil during construction work.

Vegetation – The treeline crosses the Territories diagonally northwest to southeast from the Mackenzie Delta to Hudson Bay at the Manitoba border. South and west of this line extends the **boreal forest** of spruce, poplar, tamarack (mascot tree of the Territories) and jack pine. To the north and east is the **tundra,** sometimes called "the Barrens" for its bleak look in winter and lack of trees. In summer dwarf shrubs, tiny flowers of all hues and lichens thrive in the surface ground above the permafrost. Known as **muskeg,** this surface ground is sometimes very wet and boggy because it cannot drain.

Climate – Annual precipitation over much of the Territories is so low (Yellowknife 254mm/10in, Inuvik 276mm/11in) that a great part of the region would be desert if the permafrost did not cradle what moisture there is on the surface. Generally the winters are long, cold and dark and the summers surprisingly warm and sunny, with long hours of daylight (and no real darkness in midsummer). The southern region has 20 hours of daylight, while north, in the Arctic Circle, daylight is continuous. The mean daily maximum temperatures for July are 21°C/70°F in Yellowknife and 19°C/66°F in Inuvik.

A Bit of History

Earliest Settlement – People who arrived from Asia some 15,000–20,000 years ago, across the land bridge now

Aurora Borealis in Yellowknife

© Northwest Territories Tourism

Aurora Borealis

Also known as the Northern Lights, this amazing phenomenon can usually best be viewed between December and March. The sky "dissolves" into folded curtains of elusive, dancing lights, sometimes multi-coloured, other times black and white. They seem to occur when electrically charged particles, emitted by the sun, collide with atoms and molecules in the earth's outer atmosphere, causing the latter to emit radiation, sometimes in the form of visible light. Research on these displays has been conducted at Churchill, Manitoba.

covered by the Bering Strait, settled south of the ice cap that covered the continent. Later, about 4,000 years ago, the ancestors of the Inuit crossed from Sibera into Alaska, eventually moving east. Today there are two distinct indigenous groups, the Dene and the Inuit, the latter of whom compose the majority of Nunavut's population.

The Dene – Of the 43,529 inhabitants in the Northwest Territories, slightly less than half claim First Nations origin. Of these, the majority are Dene, who make up roughly a quarter of the population. The Inuit (Inuvialuit) account for about 10 percent. The rest are Métis and nonaboriginal residents. The Athapaskan-speaking peoples of the subarctic hunted caribou and fished, constantly on the move to find food. Today some of these people have preserved a fairly traditional lifestyle, but many live on the fringe of contemporary society. Dene settlements have benefited economically from mineral

exploration. Dene peoples are known for their intricate beadwork.

Fur Traders – **Samuel Hearne** of the Hudson's Bay Company traversed much of the region, especially during his famous 1770-72 trip from Churchill to Great Slave Lake, seeking furs. Not long afterward, in 1789, **Alexander Mackenzie** of the rival North West Company travelled the river that bears his name. Some of the trading posts established after the two fur companies joined in 1821 remain to this day.

20C Development – In the late 19C and early 20C, the Geological Survey of Canada mounted expeditions under such men as **Joseph Burr Tyrrell,** Sir **William Logan** (after whom Mt. Logan is named), **George Mercer Dawson** (of Dawson City fame) and **Vilhjalmar Stefansson** to explore and map the Territories. By this time both Anglican and Roman Catholic missionaries were established in the region. In the 1930s major mineral finds encouraged more outsiders to come to the Territories.

Partitioning of the Territories – In 1992 the residents of the Northwest Territories voted to divide their land to create a new territory in the central and eastern portions. Named **Nunavut** (meaning "our land" in the native language, Inuktitut), this new territory became autonomous in 1999.

Resources and Industries

Mining – Since the 1930s the basis of the economy has been mining. Fur trapping, forestry, fishing, tourism and the sale of native arts and crafts also contribute, but to a much lesser extent. Deposits of pitchblende—a source of uranium—and silver were discovered on the shores of the Great Bear Lake in 1930. Subsequent gold discoveries at Yellowknife underpinned the economy for more than 50 years; the Con mine in Yellowknife closed in 2003, but other minerals are coming to the fore.

Diamonds were found in 1991 in the Lac de Gras area northeast of Yellowknife. One mine entered production in 1998; others, like Rio Tinto Diamonds, and De Beers, continue as of 2017. Snap Lake mine, northeast of Yellowknife, attained commercial production in 2008. Canada is the world's third-largest diamond producer by value, after Russia and Botswana.

Oil and Gas – Near Fort Liard, the largest natural gas well in Canada began production in 2000, and producing oil wells and a refinery at Norman Wells on the Mackenzie represent long-established fields. Two potentially rich areas for oil and gas are the Mackenzie Delta–Beaufort Sea region, and the high Arctic islands.

Handicrafts – Delicate carvings are fashioned from caribou antlers or mammoth tusks uncovered from beneath the tundra. Dene mukluks (waterproof boots, often made of sealskin), have become popular farther south. Fort Liard and Fort Simpson are good places to shop for beaded apparel.

PRACTICAL INFORMATION
GETTING THERE

BY AIR – Most flights to the Northwest Territories connect through Edmonton or Calgary, Alberta, to airports in Yellowknife and Inuvik. You can also connect through the Nunavut capital of Iqaluit. Within the Northwest Territories, scheduled and chartered flights are provided by **Canadian North** (℘800-661-1505, Canada/US: www.canadiannorth.com), **First Air** (℘800-267-1247; www.firstair.ca) and **Westjet**(℘ 888-937-8538; www.westjet.com). Air Canada and Westjet both connect Yellowknife and Edmonton (℘888-247-2262, Canada/US; www.aircanada.com, ℘888-937-8538; www.westjet.com).

GENERAL INFORMATION
ACCOMMODATIONS AND VISITOR INFORMATION

Every year Northwest Territories publishes the *Explorers' Guide*, which lists hotels, motels, lodges, camps and outfitters. There are also guides for campgrounds, hunting, fishing and for viewing the aurora borealis. Contact **NWT Tourism** (℘800-661-0788, Canada/US; www.spectacular nwt.com). You can download the guides from the website. Yellowknife, the provincial capital, has an extensive selection of hotels, motels and inns.

Driving in the North: While the Mackenzie Highway is paved all 1500km/938mi from Edmonton to Yellowknife, other highways are generally hard-packed gravel. Motorists are cautioned to pass other vehicles slowly to prevent flying rocks or skidding, and to pull to the right. Unless otherwise posted, the speed limit vary from 70km to 100km per hour (40-60mph) . **Seat belt** use is mandatory. Distances between gasoline stations can be great; it is advisable to fill up frequently. Most communities along highways have service stations; it is not necessary to carry extra fuel. However, full windshield-washer fluid reserves are essential. Drivers should be alert for **moose** and other large animals along roadways; collisions with wildlife can be disastrous. It is recommended that motorists carry at least one spare tire, jack, water, insect repellent, first-aid kit, emergency flares and in winter, snow shovel, sand or cat litter for traction, candles, matches, high-calorie snacks, gloves, parka, warm clothes, and a sleeping bag for each person in the vehicle. For highway conditions ☏*800-661-0750 (Canada only). www.dot.gov.nt.ca.* Government **ferry** service *(free)* is provided along the Mackenzie, Dempster and Liard highways *(for information ☏800-661-0750, Canada only; www.dot.gov.nt.ca)*. To access Yellowknife, Highway 3 crosses the river at Fort Providence. The **Dempster Highway** crosses the Mackenzie River at Arctic Red River (Tsiigehtchic) and the Peel River, near Fort McPherson, to reach Inuvik. Near Fort Simpson the **Mackenzie Highway** crosses the Liard River. There are ice bridges across these rivers in winter. During the three-to-six-week freeze-up and thaw periods *(Nov & May)*, the rivers cannot be crossed. The many cross-country winter roads and ice roads in the Northwest Territories are not advisable for use by passenger cars, and some privately published maps show roads that are not suitable for two-wheel-drive vehicles (4-wheel drive vehicles are recommended).

TIME ZONE – The Northwest Territories is in the Mountain Standard time zone. Daylight Saving Time is observed from the second Sunday in March to first Sunday in November.

TAXES – There is no provincial sales tax, but the 5% GST applies. Liquor Laws – The legal drinking age is 19. Liquor, wine and beer are sold in government liquor stores in the larger communities. Some communities have voted for restrictions on liquor, including prohibition of possession.

TERRITORIAL HOLIDAY
National Aboriginal Day: Jun 21

PRINCIPAL FESTIVALS

Jan	**Sunrise Festival:** *Inuvik*
Mar	**Caribou Carnival:** *Yellowknife*
Apr	**Beluga Jamboree:** *Tuktoyaktuk*
Jun	**Midnight Golf Classic:** *Yellowknife*
	Open Sky Festival: *Fort Simpson*
Jul	**Midnight Sun Float Plane Fly:** *Yellowknife*
	Great Northern Arts Festival: *Inuvik*
	Folk on the Rocks: *Yellowknife*
Aug	**Black Bear Jamboree:** *Norman Wells*
Sept	**Festival of Midnight Sun:** *Yellowknife*
Oct	**Delta Daze:** *Inuvik*

RECREATION
Outdoor Activities: Charter planes transport hikers, hunters, fishermen and **canoeists** (with their canoes) to remote regions. Outfitters organize and equip wilderness travel year-round. One of the world's great canoe trips is down the **South Nahanni River**. Opportunities

for hiking and mountain biking abound, including along the challenging **Canol Heritage Trail** through the Mackenzie Mountains from Norman Wells to the Yukon. All wilderness travellers (including boaters, canoeists, cyclists and hikers) are asked to register with the Royal Canadian Mounted Police detachment nearest their point of departure, and notify police when their trip is completed. Substantial wilderness equipment; warm clothing, sleeping bag, stove, fuel and GPS should be carried. Bear safety precautions are essential; travellers lacking wilderness experience are advised to hire local outfitters.

Wilderness lodges are scattered from Mackenzie Mountains to the Arctic coast, where **fishing** is superb (Arctic char, Arctic grayling, northern pike and lake trout). Licenses required; all nonresident hunters of big game must be accompanied by a licensed outfitter. For details and license information, contact Northwest Territories Tourism (🔆 see above).

Mackenzie Delta★★

The 100km/70mi-wide delta—one of the world's largest—is the estuary of the vast and fast-moving Mackenzie River, and the terminus of its 1,800km/1,100mi journey from the interior's Great Slave Lake. One of the most abundant areas for wildlife in Canada's Arctic, the delta supports innumerable muskrats, beavers, mink, marten, foxes, bears, moose, caribou and smaller mammals. Its channels and lakes abound with fish. Beluga whales calve in the warm waters, and migratory birds congregate here in the spring.

Access

The Dempster Highway from the Yukon (Dawson City to Inuvik 798km/496mi) is open year-round except during freeze-up and thaw periods. Few services on road. Motorists should be outfitted for emergencies. Also accessible by air from Edmonton via Yellowknife, and from Whitehorse, Yukon. The best way to appreciate the delta is to fly over it; charters can be arranged in Inuvik. For information contact NWT Tourism, Yellowknife 🖉 800-661-0788 (Canada/US). www.spectacularnwt.com.

🛈 **Info:** Northwest Territories Tourism. 🖉 800-661-0788. www.spectacularnwt.com.

▶ **Location:** The Mackenzie River Delta consists of a labyrinth of channels among thousands of lakes, 160km/100mi from the Beaufort Sea, at the northwest edge of the Territories' mainland.

👁 **Don't Miss:** Try to fly over the Mackenzie Delta to appreciate its complexity.

🕐 **Timing:** Tuktoyaktuk, although remote, does offer accommodations and services.

THE DELTA

Viewed from the air, this delta is an amazing place. The tangle of muddy arteries belonging to the Mackenzie and the Peel rivers, which join at this point, can be distinguished from the lakes by their colour. The western edge is clearly marked by the frequently snowcapped **Richardson Mountains**, the eastern edge by the low, humped **Caribou Hills**. Heading north, the land seemingly gives way as the areas of water become greater, until the vast Beaufort

Sea is reached, and the land disappears completely from view.

Except for areas of tundra along the coast, the land is covered with low scrubs (dwarf willow and juniper) that turn bright yellow with the first frost (usually late August), a most attractive sight. The tundra itself is full of lakes, and many colourful, multihued mosses, lichens and flowers bloom in the short but light (24 hours of daylight) Arctic summer.

THE COMMUNITIES

Many delta communities depend on trapping, hunting and fishing. However, huge reserves of oil and gas recently discovered under the Beaufort Sea have impacted the area.

Inuvik

On Dempster Hwy.; airport; lodgings.

Meaning "place of man" in Inuktitut, this outpost lies on a large stretch of flat land beside the east channel of the Mackenzie River. Inuvik is an administrative centre of the territorial government. In 1954 the government moved their administrative facilities here from Aklavik, which was frequently flooded. A model northern community was built and opened in 1959. Over the entire delta, the permafrost is only a few inches from the surface, causing problems for house building. The heat from a dwelling soon melts the ice, and residents find themselves living in a swamp. As

a result, houses are constructed on pilings, steamed into the permafrost before construction, so that heat from the house does not melt the permafrost underneath, causing the house to sink. Water, sewage and heating ducts are housed together in above-ground **utilidors**, or covered corridors, to keep them from freezing.

The **Our Lady of Victory Roman Catholic Church**, built in the shape of an igloo, features an expressive **interior★** with paintings of the Stations of the Cross done in 1960 by Mona Thrasher, then a young Inuit girl.

Tuktoyaktuk★

Daily flights from Inuvik; ice road in winter; accommodations.

A former centre for oil and gas exploration in the region, this pleasant little community on the shores of the Beaufort Sea is known simply as "Tuk" to northerners. It is best known for one of nature's most curious phenomena: **pingos**, or huge moss-and-turf-covered mounds of solid ice pushed out of the otherwise flat tundra by permafrost action. From the air, they resemble giant boils. Of the thousands in the Canadian North, the vast majority are located on the Tuktoyaktuk peninsula.

In the summer *(Jun–Aug)* Inuit women of the community can sometimes be seen making parkas and other items of clothing.

Mackenzie Delta

© T. Parker/Northwest Territories Tourism

Nahanni National Park Reserve★★★

A wild, remote and staggeringly beautiful place, this reserve in the southwest corner of the Northwest Territories was designated by UNESCO as a World Heritage Site in 1978. Unlike other national parks, it will probably never have roads and tourist facilities. But for those willing to make the effort, one of the world's great natural glories awaits.

A BIT OF HISTORY

Place of Mystery – Early in the 20C, tales of placer gold lured prospectors to the valley of the South Nahanni. In 1908 the headless bodies of two adventurers were found. Other men disappeared without a trace. Stories of fierce native inhabitants and of mythical mountain men were spread abroad, and the South Nahanni became known as a place to avoid. The mystery remains and the legends are recalled by names in the park such as Deadmen Valley, Headless Range, Broken Skull River and Funeral Range. The park's very inaccessibility is part of its beauty.

Expansion Plans – In June 2009 the Canadian government announced its intention, in collaboration with the Dehcho First Nations, to expand the boundaries of the reserve sixfold in 2014. The resulting 30,000 sq.km (18,000 sq.mi) is an area nearly as large as Vancouver Island. Places with exciting names and even more compelling features, such as **Hole-in-the-Wall Lake**, **Cirque of the Unclimbables**, **Death Lake** and the **Tlogotsho Plateau**, are protected forever.

Access by Road and Air

Overland routes are demanding. From British Columbia: take Alaska Highway to Fort Nelson, then Liard Highway to Fort Liard. From the Yukon: take Alaska Highway to Watson Lake (the road onward to Tungsten is frequently impassable). In the Northwest Territories: take Mackenzie Highway to Fort Simpson, or Liard Highway to Fort Liard. The vast majority of visitors arrive by chartered float plane. The only designated landing sites are Virginia Falls and Glacier Lake. Charter air transportation is available from several locations including Yellowknife, Fort Simpson, Fort Liard, Fort Nelson, Watson Lake, and Munco Lake. For chartered air companies, contact NWT Tourism or Parks Canada (&see above).

Access by Water

Outfitters offer trips descending the river by rubber raft or canoe (equipment is flown in first). Intermediate white-water specialists can descend the river in their own canoes; reservations must be made with the park first. Parks Canada has licensed only three outfitters to operate in the park; all guided trips must

Info: NWT Tourism ✆800 661-0788. www.spectacularnwt.com or Parks Canada, Fort Simpson ✆867-695-3151. www.pc.gc.ca.

Location: This park covers a large section of the South Nahanni River, which flows through the Selwyn, Mackenzie and Franklin mountains before joining the Liard River, a tributary of the mighty Mackenzie.

Don't Miss: A canoe trip down the South Nahanni River is one of the world's great wilderness trips.

Timing: A river trip takes 7–21 days, depending on where you start and end. This destination is popular, but access is limited, so book well in advance. Peak times are July and August.

Virginia Falls

by led by one of these outfitters. There is no hunting in any of Canada's national parks. (&see the Parks Canada, above).

VISIT

&*Open year-round. Peak is Jul–Aug. Overnighters must register with Parks Canada office in Fort Simpson or Nahanni Butte. Must de-register upon exit. Office hours are Jul–Sept daily 8:30am–noon & 1pm–5pm. Rest of the year Mon–Fri 8:30am–noon & 1pm–5pm (Nahanni Butte closed in winter). &$24.50/day-use fee ($147.20 annual). &867-695-7750.*

South Nahanni River

For more than 320km/198mi, this magnificent, serpentine waterway coils through the park, entering majestic canyons, cascading over a precipice twice the height of Niagara and passing a series of hot mineral springs that nourish vegetation unusual at this latitude (61°–62°N). Each year the river attracts countless canoeists and raft-riders to its adventurous waters and wilderness beauty.

The following describes highlights of a descent of the river. The 200km/125mi excursion downriver from Virginia Falls to Nahanni Butte is one of the world's great wilderness trips. Over this distance the river drops more than 120m/400ft

(which is why canoeists generally prefer to descend it, rather than canoe up).

The jewel of the park and one of the North's most spectacular sights is **Virginia Falls.** Parted by a central pointed rock at the precipice, volumes of water plunge 90m/294ft to the gorge below. The Albert Faille Portage can be followed around the falls *(1.6km/1mi)*. From it, a trail leads to the brink of the cataract where the river can be seen in spectacular rapids just before it cascades over the rocks.

Fourth Canyon is the first of four awesome canyons with immense cliffs and depths as great as 1,200m/3,900ft. Then come the surging waves of Figure of Eight Rapids. The river makes a 90-degree turn known as The Gate, guarded by mighty Pulpit Rock. Third Canyon is followed by the 34km/21mi stretch of Second Canyon. **Deadman Valley,** where headless bodies were found, separates Second Canyon from First Canyon, a twisting 27km/17mi channel.

The river passes close to a hot spring where pools of water, at nearly 37°C/98°F, have caused ferns, chokecherries, rose bushes and flowering parsnip plants to proliferate. Before reaching Nahanni Butte, the river divides into a series of channels known as the **Splits.**

Wood Buffalo National Park★★

Northwest Territories, Alberta

Designated a UNESCO World Heritage Site in 1983, Wood Buffalo is one of North America's most valuable wildlife preserves, containing two important features that are unique: one of the largest free-roaming **bison herds** on earth—5,000 strong; and the last natural nesting grounds for the endangered **whooping crane**. In 2014 it was also named one of the world's largest **Dark Sky Preserves**, with a Dark Sky Festival late in Aug. Accessible by car along all-weather gravel roads, the park offers visitors a subtle, tantalizing beauty highlighting the northern boreal plain, as well as an opportunity to view wild animals seldom seen elsewhere.

Peace/Athabasca Delta at the west end of Lake Athabasca is one of the largest inland deltas in the world and a vitally important wetland. Owing to four North American flyways that pass through the park, this delta is well known for its abundance of geese, duck and other wetland fowl. The surrounding plains are the northernmost fringe of the Great Plains that extend all the way to Mexico.

Info: NWT Tourism ℘800 661-0788. www.spectacularnwt.com or Parks Canada, Fort Smith ℘867-872-7960. www.pc.gc.ca.

Location: Canada's largest national park (44,807sq km/17,300sq mi) straddles the border dividing the province of Alberta from the Northwest Territories. About two-thirds of the parkland lies within Alberta, but park headquarters and principal access are located at Fort Smith in the Northwest Territories.

Don't Miss: The road between Fort Smith and Pine Lake is lovely; you can stop for short hikes.

Timing: Although there is road access to the park, it is a long way from anywhere: 748km/468mi from Yellowknife, 1310km/819mi from Edmonton. You may consider flying in and renting a car in Fort Smith.

VISIT

Open year-round. Hiking, camping, boating, fishing. Accommodations in Fort Smith. Park map and list of licensed guides and outfitters available at the

Access

Access by road 748km/464mi south of Yellowknife via Rte. 3, Mackenzie Hwy. and Rte. 5 (near Hay River) to the park entrance (Rte. 5 continues through the park to Fort Smith). From Fort Smith, an all-weather gravel road leads into Wood Buffalo's interior as far as Peace Point Reserve (119km/74mi). There is no all-weather road to Fort Chipewyan, although, for three months in the winter, a road is sometimes open linking Fort Smith, Fort Chipewyan and Fort McMurray.

Access by air *Westjet & Air Canada* operate scheduled flights from Edmonton & Yellowknife. ℘888-937-8538; www.westjet.com; ℘888-247-2262; www.aircanada.com. Charter flights to Fort Smith and Fort Chipewyan available. For information, contact NWT Tourism (above). Car rentals available in Fort Smith.

Wood Buffalo

© T. Parker/Northwest Territories Tourism

two park Visitor Centres: Fort Smith *(149 McDougal Rd. at Portage Ave;* 🕐 *open daily May 15–Sep 20 9am–8pm; Rest of the year Mon–Fri 9am–noon & 1pm–5pm; closed weekends;* 📞*867-872-7960) and* Fort Chipewyan *(MacKenzie Ave.;* 🕐*open year-round, but phone ahead. Mon–Fri 9am–noon & 1pm–5pm; in summer, open daily 9am-6pm;* 📞*867-872-7960).* 🚫*No entry or gate fees. Park administration* 📞*867-872-7900. www.pc.gc.ca.*

Route 5

The approach to the park from the vicinity of Hay River is a pretty **drive** through boreal spruce and aspen forest. Bison can often be seen grazing by the roadside closer to Fort Smith. At the Angus Fire Tower, a large **sinkhole** typifies the region's *karst* (limestone) topography. A short side road *(30km/19mi west of Fort Smith)* leads to the Salt River Plains **overlook★**, which provides an intriguing vista of a salt flat. This broad plain of the Salt River shimmers white in the summer sun, the river winding sinuously through scattered patches of forest and meadow, as well as beds of salt.

Fort Smith★

Once the major town in the Territories, Fort Smith is yet another of the historic fur-trading sites that dot Canada's North. At the park Visitor Centre *(for hours* ♿*see above),* a multimedia **presentation** *(18min)* offers an excellent grounding in the national park's history and ecology. Just a few blocks away, **Northern Life Museum & Cultural Centre** *(McDougal Rd. and King St.;* 🕐*call for hours;* 📞*867-872-2859; www. nlmcc.ca)* and **Fort Smith Mission**

Carver Extraordinaire

Fort Smith carver **Sonny MacDonald** is a self-taught native artist who began whittling toy boats and slingshots at age seven. Today his works, crafted from northern wood and bone, depict fish, wildlife and other denizens of the subarctic world. In addition to caribou and moose antlers, animal claws and teeth, the materials from which he fashions his creations include narwhal, and even fossilized mammoth, tusks. His pieces range from small amulets and earrings to large garden sculptures. Sonny was born in Fort Chipewyan, where he grew up; he now resides in Fort Smith and maintains a studio there. *To visit MacDonald's studio, contact him directly* 📞*867-872-5935.*

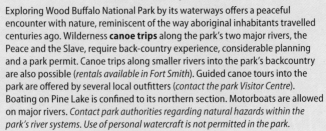

Wilderness by Water

Exploring Wood Buffalo National Park by its waterways offers a peaceful encounter with nature, reminiscent of the way aboriginal inhabitants travelled centuries ago. Wilderness **canoe trips** along the park's two major rivers, the Peace and the Slave, require back-country experience, considerable planning and a park permit. Canoe trips along smaller rivers into the park's backcountry are also possible (*rentals available in Fort Smith*). Guided canoe tours into the park are offered by several local outfitters (*contact the park Visitor Centre*). Boating on Pine Lake is confined to its northern section. Motorboats are allowed on major rivers. *Contact park authorities regarding natural hazards within the park's river systems. Use of personal watercraft is not permitted in the park.*

Historic Park★ offer insight into the area's history (*Breynat St. & Mercredi Ave;* ◷*open mid-May–mid-Sept daily;* ✆*867-875-5570*). The city's Slave River boardwalk *(end of Simpson St.)* affords a view of the **rapids,** where a party of early explorers perished. *For accommodations, contact Visitor Info-centre, Fort Smith;* ✆*867-872-3065; www. fortsmith.ca.*

Fort Smith to Pine Lake★★

The all-weather gravel road into the heart of the park affords access to several notable sights and the opportunity to see bison anywhere along the road. The Salt River day-use area *(25km/15.5mi south of Fort Smith)* provides a short hiking path, the **Karstland Trail**, through the park's unusual broken topography.

At 31km/19mi the South Loop trailhead initiates a pleasant *(4km/2.5mi)* hike through beautiful boreal forest down to **Grosbeak Lake**, an otherworldly salt flat dotted with boulders dropped by retreating glaciers. **Pine Lake Campground,** at 60km/37mi, is an attractive facility overlooking a turquoise lake with a sandy beach, a spot long used by natives as a summer retreat. The lake is a particularly good place for swimming.

Fort Chipewyan

Access by air or water only.
Situated on the shores of Lake Athabasca, "Fort Chip" is the gateway for boat or canoe trips into the Peace-Athabasca Delta and the site of the park's second Visitor Centre.

Wood buffalo on the salt plains

Yellowknife★

The administrative and economic capital of the Northwest Territories lies on a pretty site, which is set on pink, glacier-scarred granite topped by small trees and almost completely surrounded by the water of Great Slave Lake. A pleasant "old town" (c.1934) coexists with a modern "new town," where most of the population lives, shops and works.

A BIT OF HISTORY

Foundation of Gold – Named not for the colour of the gold underneath it, but for the copper knives traded by local First Nations Peoples, Yellowknife was visited by Samuel Hearne in 1771, Alexander Mackenzie on his epic journey to the mouth of the river that bears his name, and John Franklin, none of whom noticed the gold. Prospectors en route for the Klondike at the end of the 19C did record some sightings, but without pursuit. Not until the discovery of pitch-blende in 1930 on the shores of the Great Bear Lake was there interest in the rest of the region. In 1934 exposed gold was found beside the bay and a boomtown sprang up only to collapse until the next gold discoveries after 1945. Yellowknife became territorial capital in 1967 and is now a well-established community. The last gold mine closed in 2004, but a new find north of the city—diamonds—has fuelled continued growth.

The Diamond Boom – The first confirmed find of diamonds in 1991 kicked off the greatest mineral exploration rush since the Klondike gold stampede. Canada has now become a major player in the world gem diamond market. Production began in 1998 at the **Ekati** diamond mine about 322km/200mi northeast of Yellowknife; two other mines (**Diavik** and the **De Beers' Snap Lake** mine) in the same Lac de Gras area have followed. The **NWT Diamond Centre** at 5105 49th St. offers visitors chance to buy diamonds mined here by RioTinto Alcan. (open Mon–Fri 9am–5pm; 867-920-7108; **Midnight Twilight** –

▶ **Population:** 20,300.

Info: Northern Frontier Visitors Association, #4–4807-49th St. 867-873-4262 or 877-881-4262 (Canada/US). www.northernfrontier.com.

Location: Yellowknife lies beside Yellowknife Bay on the northern shore of the Great Slave Lake.

Parking: The downtown core has metered parking. There is one public lot, in Centre Square Mall.

Don't Miss: The Old Town.

Timing: During spring and fall, Yellowknife is accessible only by air.

Kids: Several trails around the city are easy, and you can rent canoes or kayaks for short excursions.

The city lies just north of latitude 62° and thus, in summer, experiences nearly 24 hours of daylight. Every year a golf tournament is held on the weekend closest to June 21, with tee-off at midnight.

Access

The route from Edmonton, comprising Mackenzie Hwy. (Hwy. 1) and the Yellowknife Hwy. (Hwy. 3), is paved for all 1,500km/938mi. To access the city, take the Mackenzie River ferry *(free)* in summer; an "ice road" bridges the river in winter. No road access during freeze-up and thaw periods. Also accessible by scheduled flights via Canadian North *(from Calgary, Edmonton and Ottawa;* 800-661-1505; www.canadiannorth.com*)*, First Air *(from Edmonton;* 800-267-1247; www.firstair.ca*)* and Air Canada Jazz *(from Calgary and Edmonton;* 888-247-2262; www.aircanada.com*)*.

Yellowknife is a major centre for boating, canoeing, fishing and camping. Its stores carry a fine selection of Dene and Inuit art and handicrafts. Its float plane base in Old Town is the departure point for numerous wilderness lodges and camps elsewhere in the Territories. The city itself has a thriving community of bed-and-breakfast inns as well as business hotels (for accommodations, contact Northern Frontier Visitors Assn. *see Introduction*).

SIGHTS
Prince of Wales Northern Heritage Centre★★
4750-48th St.
✕&☉*Open daily 10:30am–5pm, Thu unitl 9pm.* ☉*Closed major holidays.* ⊜*Contribution suggested.* ℘*867-767-9347. www.pwnhc.ca.*
Overlooking Frame Lake, this attractive museum and research centre houses displays on the history of settlement of the Territories and a fine collection of Inuit sculpture. The ways of life of Dene and Inuit peoples are described, as are the reasons European settlers came to the North. One room is devoted to bush pilot operations, and a small display explains the gold and diamond mining industries.

Legislative Assembly Building★★
Entrance off Ingraham Trail, in the capital park. ☛*Tours Jun–Sep Mon–Fri 10:30am, 1:30pm, 3:30pm and Sun 1:30pm. Rest of the year Mon–Fri 10:30am. Confirm hours at* ℘*800-661-0784. www.assembly.gov.nt.ca.*
Encircled by forest and edged with lakes, this striking, dome-topped building (1993) is sheathed in weather-hardy zinc panels; it was designed to make maximum use of available light and convey a sense of openness about territorial government.
Highlights include the **Great Hall,** with overhead banners depicting the subarctic seasons. Crafted by regional artists, the assembly's ceremonial **mace** is made of silver and bronze, with gold and diamond embellishments. A back gallery, accessible only during tours, contains a remarkable **quilt** created by residents of the Deline community.

Bush Pilots' Monument★
Steps from Ingraham Trail in Old Town.
Set on a rock that is the highest point in Yellowknife, this memorial honours the men who opened up the North. From this spot there is a splendid **panorama★** of the city, the surrounding waters and the rocky site. The red-topped tower of the former Cominco gold mine dominates the skyline. A hive of activity, the bay ripples with numerous float

Yellowknife's Old Town with Bush Pilots' Monument

© T. Parker/Northwest Territories Tourism

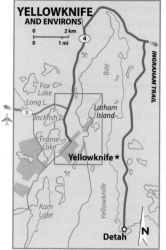

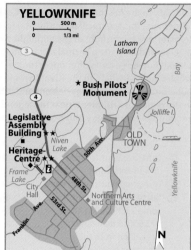

planes arriving from the mining camps or departing with supplies for exploration teams.

Below the monument, Old Town holds amazingly diverse houses stretching along famed Ragged Ass Road, whose street signs became such popular theft items they are now offered for sale.

From Old Town, a causeway crosses to **Latham Island**, where houses perch on rocks and stilts. Here, a Dogrib Indian settlement and views of the former Giant and Con gold mines can be seen.

Boat Trips

For cruises on the Mackenzie River and the Great Slave Lake, contact North Star Adventures ℘867-446-2900 or other operators listed with the Northern Frontier Visitors Assn. (www.northernfrontier.com).
These cruises enable visitors to see portions of the enormous lake (28,930sq km/11,170sq mi), which is part of the Mackenzie River system and an important fishing area.

EXCURSIONS
Detah and the Ingraham Trail

These excursions by vehicle in the vicinity of the capital allow the visitor to see the landscape in this transitional area of the Canadian Shield between boreal forest and tundra. The drive to Detah provides views of Yellowknife and its bay.

Detah
25km/16mi.
This Dogrib Indian settlement has a fine **site★** on flat rocks overlooking the Great Slave Lake.

Ingraham Trail★
64km/40mi to Reid Lake.
This all-weather road northwest of Yellowknife skirts five lakes—a paradise for campers and canoeists. Prelude Lake Territorial Park has a sandy beach and extensive campgrounds. Numerous other points along the trail offer access to more remote wilderness lakes and rivers. For canoe and kayak outfitting and area wilderness expertise, contact Narwal Adventures (℘867-873-6443; www.narwal.ca).

ADDRESSES

⊮/EAT

Don't miss the chance to eat at **Bullock's Bistro**, *3534 Weaver Dr., ℘867-873-3474. A must-do.*

Contrary to the misconception that the Canadian North is a frozen wilderness, this spectacular continental rooftop abounds in varied landscape, transformed by the light of the midnight sun. Canada's newest territory's diverse wildlife is the principal attraction for most visitors. In the **Baffin Island** region, floe-edge tours offer opportunities to see polar bears, bowhead whales, and narwhals. In the **Kivalliq** region, travellers come to view belugas, polar bears, snowy owls, gyrfalcons and other northern birds. Farther west, in the region of **Kitikmeot**, near the legendary **Northwest Passage**, human encounters with shaggy musk-oxen and caribou are real possibilities.

- **Info:** Nunavut Tourism 866-686-2888. www.nunavuttourism.com.
- **Location:** Stretching some 2,000,000sq km/ 772,000sq mi nearly to Greenland from the Manitoba border, Nunavut is, by far, Canada's biggest province or territory, making up one-fifth of the country's total landmass.
- **Don't Miss:** Opportunity to travel to one of the amazing Arctic adventure lodges for tour of a lifetime.
- **Timing:** Summer is easier for touring, but no matter what season: plan well ahead to reserve.
- **Kids:** Older kids will enjoy the same adventures as adults, including Inuit art, birdwatching, & wildlife.

Geography

Landscape – North of the 60th parallel, Nunavut lies west of Greenland, across Davis Strait. Its southern border in the west vaguely follows the tree line, then runs straight south to Manitoba's northern boundary and across Hudson Bay, wrapping around the southern end of Baffin Island. Nunavut includes most of the Arctic archipelago between the mainland and geographic North Pole, and the Hudson and James Bay islands south of the parallel, as well as Arctic mainland and major channels, straits and sounds. Of Canada's 26 largest islands, more than half are in Nunavut. The biggest—**Baffin Island**—is the size of

Spain. Rocky, treeless **tundra**, snow-covered most of the year, describes Nunavut's landscape. **Permafrost** can reach depths of 370m/1,220ft, as at Resolute on Cornwallis Island. Yet, from one end to the other there is diversity. While gulls and jaegers soar overhead, mosses and lichens carpet the land in the short spring and summer season. Hardy shrubs and flowers brighten the lowlands around Hudson Bay, and rolling hills elsewhere, with fluffy tufts of Arctic cotton, the tiny, fragile blossoms of white mountain avens or berries of purple and red. Glacial debris—huge boulders, piles of moraine, **eskers** (narrow ridges of sand and gravel) and **drumlins** (elliptical-shaped hills inclining in the direction of the glacier's retreat)— bear witness to the region's geological history. Sand eskers, basically leftover glacial river sediment, snake across the land like huge worm casts, some hundreds of kilometres long. These eskers provide perfect dens for wolves and foxes, and raised, windy "highways" for migrating caribou. Other phenomena common in the North are **polynyas** (open water in sea ice) and **shore leads** (channels of water through a field of ice). Lofty mountains with glacier-filled valleys, including 2,616m/8,633ft **Mount Barbeau**, Nunavut's highest peak, rise along eastern coasts of Baffin, Devon and Ellesmere islands.

Climate – Annual precipitation in Nunavut is sparse (Baker Lake 208mm/8in, Iqaluit 409mm/16in), less than half what a city in southern Canada receives. Generally winters are long, cold and dark, and summers (July and August) are surprisingly warm and sunny, with long hours of daylight. Towns near the

Dogsledding near Resolute

© Nunavut Tourism

coast or in the Baffin Island region are colder. In summer, the southern part of Nunavut has 20 hours of daylight, while farther north of the Arctic Circle, it never gets dark. Mean daily maximum temperatures for July are 15°C/59°F in Baker Lake and 12°C/53°F in Iqaluit.

A Bit of History

Early Settlement – Paleoeskimo people inhabited Canada's Arctic coasts and islands about 5,000 years ago. Though archaeologists disagree as to their origins, Paleoeskimos are believed to have crossed from Siberia over the Bering Strait into Alaska. They eventually moved eastward into the Canadian Arctic, where they lived in skin tents, travelled by foot or kayak and evolved into the **Dorset** culture (500 BC-AD 1500). New waves of migration brought families of **Thule** people (AD 1000-1600) into Nunavut and into contact with the Dorset. Over time, the Dorset were eventually driven off, or wiped out, by the Thule, who were different from the Dorset people—they travelled faster and farther on *qamutiit* (dogsleds) and in large *umiak* boats. Ancestors of today's Inuit, the Thule moved south into the interior to hunt caribou and along the Arctic coast and archipelago to find whales and other sea animals.

Although European explorers, traders and whalers journeyed to this area in the late 1500s (Norse explorers some 500 years earlier), their effect was minimal until the early 1800s, when whalers from both Europe and the Americas started coming to the Baffin Island region to hunt bowhead whale.

The Inuit – Nunavut is four times the size of France, yet is one of the least densely populated areas in the world: about one person per 100sq km/39 sq mi. Of the 37,315 Nunavummiut (inhabitants of Nunavut), 85 percent are Inuit. The rest, including people of the Dene Nation, are non-Inuit. Formerly known as Eskimo (an obsolete Cree word), the Canadian Inuit ("the people" in Inuktitut) make up part of a larger community of some 125,000 First Nations in polar regions of Russia, Alaska and Greenland. In Canada, Inuit live in 53 northern communities (more than half of which are in Nunavut), including those in Quebec's northern reaches and on Labrador's northern coast. A sizable number of Inuit inhabit their Quebec homeland of **Nunavik,** a region only formally recognized by government in 1988.

The life of the people of the Arctic Coast revolved largely around hunting sea mammals—especially seal and whale—as a source of food; blubber for heat and light; skins for clothing, shelter and boats; and bone or ivory for the blades of their harpoons or other tools. They hunted from one-man **kayaks**, while women, traditionally paddled cargo and passengers in larger **umiaks**, which held up to 12 people. The occasional excursion south was made by **dogsled** to hunt caribou, the skins of which were used for clothing or bedding. The hunters built stone markers, or rock cairns, called **inuksuks** in the shape of human figures to serve as landmarks or guides for hunting caribou; inuksuks can still be seen in Nunavut today.

Many Inuit are still seasonally nomadic—several families living and moving together. In winter they construct an **igloo** (iglu), a dome-shaped snow house made of blocks of ice, and enter by a tunnel; for insulation, the interior is lined with skins. In summer they live in tents made of skins. Time not spent hunting or making clothes is devoted to carving bone and stone, a craft for which they are famous.

The Inuit of Nunavut still hunt and fish for caribou, seal and char; however, many now work in tourism, government, transportation, and related supply and service companies.

The Northwest Passage – A sea route between the Atlantic and Pacific oceans across the north of the American continent was the quest of explorers for centuries. British sailor **Martin Frobisher** made the first attempt in 1576. His voyages were followed by those of John Davis, Henry Hudson and **William Baffin**. Their reports of ice-filled seas somewhat dampened enthusiasm for the passage. Except for exploration at the western end, no more attempts were made until the early 19C.

Naval Explorers – The 1789 voyage of Alexander Mackenzie sparked new interest in a northwest passage. **John Franklin** made two overland trips to the western end, sailing a third time in 1845. Years passed with no word from him. A series of 38 expeditions were sent to discover his fate. Dramatic dicoveries led by Parks Canada in 2014 & 2016 led to the discovery of both Franklin ships, HMS Erebus & HMS Terror, confirming Franklin and crew perished after being marooned in the frozen waters. One effect of this tragedy was the exploration by his would-be rescuers of a large part of the North. A passable route of the passage between the Canadian mainland and the Arctic islands was successfully navigated by Norwegian **Roald Amundsen** between 1903 and 1906. Since then many ships have followed the hazardous route which, with global warning, will likely become a major shipping route.

Nunavut Today – As with the Northwest Territories, mineral as well as oil exploration continue to attract investment. In 1964 vast zinc and lead deposits

Inuit girl

In Person

A trip to Nunavut is a discovery of another world, and of insights into Inuit ways. Heading out on the ocean in sturdy Lake Winnipeg boats, visitors find themselves enjoying the bobbing harp seals one minute, then wrapped up in the excitement of a hunting tradition that has fed and clothed these First Nations People for thousands of years. Next may come a chance meeting with a carver, sawing stone in his backyard and preparing to stock the active art markets worldwide. Or perhaps meeting a brilliant Inuit woman, working, taking a multiyear course, and destined for upper management; on weekends, she hunts seal with her husband and two sons. Or an encounter on the airplane with an Inuit singer, who, in this roadless land, flies five times more than the average Canadian, belittling the sissy pilot hesitant to land in a thick fog, then launching into some indescribable throat singing for the benefit of her seatmate.

were found at Pine Point on Great Slave Lake, in the Northwest Territories; these minerals are being mined at Nanisivik near Arctic Bay in the north of Baffin Island and on Little Cornwallis Island. Nunavut's first diamond mine began production in 2006.

Nunavut's tourism is rapidly developing—so far, without damaging consequences. The Territory has many territorial parks, heritage rivers, bird sanctuaries, game preserves and ecological sites, as well as polar bears, whales and more than five major caribou herds. To travel and discover this mythical land, prospective visitors should go to an adventure lodge, who will fly visitors in by charter floatplane. Good example s are Bathurst Inlet Lodge (www.bathurstarctic.com), and Arctic Watch Wilderness Lodge (www.arcticwatch.ca).

PRACTICAL INFORMATION
ART IN THE NORTH

For centuries, nomadic Inuit carved only small pieces to carry with them. Today, they transfer age-old artistic sensibilities to larger artforms, notably **sculpture**. Best-known forms are rounded human and animal shapes, created from black, grey or green stone. Bone, antlers or tusks are carved as sculpture or jewellery. Tapestries, stone-cut prints, and metalwork are popular, too, while some communities specialize in ceramics or miniature dolls. Listed here are selected shops offering arts and crafts of the North. Many artists sell from their homes, and keen shoppers should ask around town.

Few places in Nunavut have addresses; visitors must use town maps or ask for directions.

More information on art: **Nunavut Arts and Crafts Association** (✆867-979-7808, or 866-979-7808; *(www.nacaarts.org)*.

RANKING INLET – Ivalu Ltd. *(near Keewatin Meat and Fish building; ✆867-645-3400; www.ivalu.ca.* Retail outlet for arts & crafts from across Nunavut. **Matchbox Gallery** *(call for directions; ✆867-645-2674, daytime or 867-645-3117, evening; www.matchboxgallery.com)* sells carvings, drawings, paintings, prints & terra-cotta creations.

IQALUIT – Northern Collectables *(www.northernncollectables.com)*t 867-979-6495. Prints, watercolours, tapestries & sculpture. Prices range from a few hundred dollars to several thousand. **Rannva** *(located at 3102 Angel St., just off the Apex Road east of town; open daily 4pm–6pm;*

☎867-979-3183; www.rannva.com). This is the place for top quality Inuit clothing, kids items, gifts, and top quality souvenirs.

Carvings Nunavut (*Building 626, Tumiit Plaza, Suite 101; open Mon-Sat 10am–6pm, Sun by appoinment* ☎*888-828-0650, 867-979-0650; www. carvingsnunavut.com*). Find top drawer Inuit carvings by artists from across Nunavut. Good inventory of gift & souvenirs too. Order online.

Arctic Ventures 2000 (*Building 192 Radio Shack;* ☎*867-979-4233.* A grocery and department store, with excellent books on the Arctic.

Baffin Inuit Art Gallery (☎*416-931-3540; www.baffininuitart.com*) Established 15 years ago in Toronto, brings Inuit art of both Iqaluit & Cape Dorset to the global marketplace. All pieces delivered with authentication tag.

At **Iqaluit airport**, look at the arts and crafts displays featuring more than a dozen communities, such as the tapestries of Pangnirtung or the stone-cut prints or stone sculptures of **Cape Dorset,** a major centre for Inuit art. For that last-minute purchase, stop at **Coman Arctic Galleries** (*1127 Mivvik St. Coman Plaza;* ☎*867-979-6300*), right outside the airport doors. Coman features large pieces, plus also small, less costly items.

PANGNIRTUNG – For a wide array of native works, and to order online, visit **Uqqurmiut Centre for Arts and Crafts** (☎*867-473-8669; www. uqqurmiut.com*).

GETTING THERE

BY AIR – Flights are virtually the only way to access Nunavut; no roads enter Nunavut from the south and no roads connect the communities. The access cities from the south are Calgary, Edmonton, Winnipeg, Ottawa and Montreal, from which flights reach gateway cities in Nunavut: Cambridge Bay is the gateway city for the Kitikmeot region (via Yellowknife); Rankin Inlet for Kivalliq *(Keewatin);* and Iqaluit for Baffin. Airlines providing these connections, as well as scheduled service within Nunavut, are **Canadian North** (☎*800-661-1505; www.canadiannorth.com), **First Air** (☎*800-267-1247/Canada only; www. firstair.ca*) and **Calm Air** (☎*888-225-6247, or 800-839-2256 reservations; www.calmair.com*). Within Nunavut, scheduled and chartered service is provided by **Air Nunavut** (☎*867-979-4018), **Kenn Borek Air Ltd.** (☎*403-291-3300 in Calgary, 867-979-0040 in Iqaluit; www.borekair.com*) and **Air Inuit** (*based in Quebec;* ☎*800-361-2965; www.airinuit.com*).

GETTING AROUND

Although all-terrain vehicles (called bikes by the locals) and full-size cars and trucks are seen within communities, no roads connect the towns. Chartered float planes and scheduled commercial flights are the only means of transportation between communities, except for watercraft, or snowmobiles. Most settlements are small enough to cover on foot, but snowmobiles, ATVs or bicycles can sometimes be rented. Taxis service is available in some communities. Dogsleds are used mostly for tourist excursions.

GENERAL INFORMATION
ACCOMMODATIONS AND VISITOR INFORMATION

The free **Nunavut Travel Planner**, as well as guides for hunting, fishing, bird watching, whale watching and iceberg-viewing can be ordered online or downloaded from www.nunavuttourism.com. Iqaluit has several overnight accommodations, but most communities have only one or two places to stay. **Rankin Inlet** has four hotels and one B&B; Pangnirtung has one of each; in bad weather, guests may have to share a room with strangers. Homestays and overnighting in an igloo may be arranged with local guides.

For specific lodgings, go online to *www.nunavuttourism.com*.

LANGUAGE – The official languages of Nunavut are *Inuktitut*, the native tongue of the Inuit, English and French. In major communities such as Iqaluit and Ranklin Inlet, many Inuit speak English and Inuktitut. Tourist info is available in English. Signs are in English and Inuktitut. French is spoken by some in Iqaluit.

TIME ZONES – Nunavut uses three time zones and observes Daylight Saving Time.

TAXES – There is no territorial sales tax, but the 5% GST applies.

Liquor Laws: Determined by local vote, restrictions vary by community. Towns are designated dry, restricted or unrestricted. In dry communities, alcohol is not allowed to be brought in. In restricted communities, an approval form is required to bring liquor in. In **Rankin Inlet,** guests at the hotel may order a drink in the lounge when it opens in the evening. In **Iqaluit,** restaurants and hotels are licensed, and the much debated Iqaluit Beer & Wine Store is now open. In unrestricted communities, limits are set for the amount of alcohol that may be brought in. Contact the RCMP (*867-975-0123; www.rcmp-grc. gc.ca),* or the Liquor Commission in Rankin Inlet (*867-645-8475; www. gov.nu.ca)* for current regulations in each community. Trading alchohol for anything is illegal. Do not leave unused alchohol behind.

TERRITORIAL HOLIDAY
Nunavut Day: July 9

TOURS AND EXCURSIONS
OUTFITTER TOURS
Tourism in Nunavut continues to develop, with many spectacular sights and wildlife opportunities. Unforgetable memories of travelling here come from time on the land or water, chatting with hunters, fishermen, trappers, or carvers. Because of the need for safe, comfortable travel in this remote and often harsh land, many visitors book ahead with experienced outfitters. Most excursions operate from June to August. **Dogsledding** or ski trips run from April to June. Nunavut Tourism (*www.nunavuttourism. com*) provides information on outfitters. **Adventure Canada** (*905-271-4000 or 800-363-7566; www.adventurecanada.com)* organizes adventure trips and safaris in the high Arctic. **Frontiers North** (*204-949-2050, or 800-663-9832 in North America; www.frontiersnorth. com)* sponsors wildlife-watching tours. The Canadian Tourism Commission (*www.travelcanada.c*a) also has information.

SPECIAL EXCURSIONS
In the northern corner of **Ellesmere Island,** accessible from Resolute Bay, lies Quttinirpaaq National Park, the world's northernmost park (latitude 82°N) covering nearly 40,000sq km/15,000sq mi of mountains, glaciers, valleys and fjords. It also has 4,000-year-old archaeological remains (*867-975-4673; www.pc.gc.ca).*

PRINCIPAL FESTIVALS
April	**Toonik Tyme** *Iqaluit*
May	**Umingmak/Omingmak Frolics:** *Cambridge Bay*
Jun-Jul	**Alianait Festival:** *Iqaluit*
Aug	**Calm Air Cup Softball Tournament** *Rankin Inlet*

Baffin Island Region★★

Nunavut's largest, most inhabited area, **Baffin Island★★** receives the greatest number of visitors. Mountains rise to 2,100m/7,000ft with numerous glaciers, and coastlines are deeply indented with fjords. About two-thirds of Baffin Island lies north of the Arctic Circle (66.5°N); **Quttinirpaaq National Park**, on Ellesmere Island, is above 80°N. But it is the majestic and relatively accessible **Auyuittuq National Park** where visitors can best experience the high mountains of the Arctic ranges. Here, in the continuous daylight of summer, the tundra blooms with an infinite variety of tiny, colourful flowers, such as broad-leafed willow herb and Arctic poppies.

A BIT OF HISTORY

Although English seamen **William Baffin** and **Robert Bylot** mapped the south shore of Baffin's namesake island in 1616, others came before. Seeking the Northwest Passage, Sir **Martin Frobisher** discovered the island in a 1576 expedition. In 1585 **John Davis** explored Cumberland Sound. **Henry Hudson** followed what is now called Hudson Strait into Hudson Bay in 1610. For 200 years after Baffin's voyage, there was little outside interest in

Info: Nunavut Tourism. 866-686-2888. www.nunavuttourism.com.

Location: The Baffin region includes Ellesmere and Baffin islands, part of the Melville Peninsula, and the High Arctic islands of Cornwallis, Axel Heiberg and other parts.

Don't Miss: The boat trip to Auyuittuq National Park, organized through the Angmarlik Visitor Centre.

Timing: Parks Canada warns that you should take no risks with the weather; always leave time in your itinerary to wait out a bad stretch .

Kids: Children will enjoy exploring Iqaluit and taking the less rigorous boat trips, but don't overestimate their endurance.

exploring the region. Then, in a resurgence of the quest for the Northwest Passage, and coinciding with the onset of *qallunaat* (white people) whaling, came explorers John Ross (1818), William Edward Parry (1819), and Sir **John Franklin** (1845) on his famous, fateful expedition.

Searches for the Franklin party ensued over 12 years, the accounts of which

Pangnirtung residence

© Nunavut Tourism

prompted Charles Francis Hall to travel the terrain (1860-1862) using Inuit travel methods and native guides Tookoolito and Ebierbing.

By the early 1900s whaling had ended; trading and scientific exploration were on the increase; and missionaries, the Hudson's Bay Company and Royal Canadian Mounted Police (RCMP) were essentially "taking charge" of the Inuit. In the 1950s the presence of a Distant Early Warning (DEW) line meant **Iqaluit** [eh-CALL-oo-it]—formerly called Frobisher Bay—would become a regional supply centre. It is now the capital of Nunavut and its largest town. The 1960s introduced federal schools and housing, marking the end of traditional Inuit camp life.

Today most inhabitants of the region live either in Iqaluit or in a dozen small settlements along the coast of Baffin and Ellesmere islands. Inuit stone carvings, prints and lithographs, especially those from **Cape Dorset**, on Baffin Island's west coast, are internationally renowned.

PANGNIRTUNG★★

300km/186mi north of Iqaluit on Baffin Island's Pangnirtung Fjord, a northern finger of Cumberland Sound.

Dominated by the snowcapped mountains surrounding the **Penny Ice Cap** in Auyuittuq National Park—in particular, the steep face of **Mount Duval** to the southeast—this hamlet occupies a spectacular **site** on Pangnirtung fjord. Situated just south of the Arctic Circle, Pangnirtung is an ideal spot for viewing the midnight "light" in summer (there is no sun at midnight, but it never gets dark). It is also a good place to study the tundra landscape and wildlife (small mammals, and some large sea mammals in Cumberland Sound) and to purchase locally woven goods and soapstone carvings at the Inuit cooperative.

Although the Hudson's Bay Company established a trading post here in 1921, families did not begin to move off the land into Pangnirtung to any great extent until the early 1960s. Today dominant livelihoods include marine mammal harvesting, sculpture and handicrafts, and tourism.

Most visitors come here to hike the glacier-strewn landscape of Auyuittuq National Park *(accessible by boat; see box below).*

Angmarlik Interpretation Centre

 Open mid-Jun–mid-Sept Mon–Fri 9am–noon & 1pm–5pm. Rest of the year Mon–Fri 8:30am–5pm. 867-473-8737. Displays and artifacts tell the story of the Inuit of Cumberland Bay. Trips to Kekerten Territorial Historic Park, a whaling station in the late-19C, or boat rides to Mt. Overlord warden station (Auyuittuq Park entrance) can be arranged here. From inside the centre is a **view★★** of the steep, blue-layered fjord, where frigid water surges in some of the highest tides in the world.

Uqqurmiut Centre for Arts and Crafts★

 Open year-round. Call for hours. *867-473-8669. www.uqqurmiut.ca www.inuitoriginals.ca*

Housed in three distinctive circular buildings joined by boardwalks and designed to resemble a cluster of Inuit tents, this complex has an international reputation for its woven blankets, prints and tapestries.

⊠ Ikuvik and Ukama Trails★

Two splendid hiking trails that begin in town are well worth taking. Even with the brochure map provided by the Angmarlik Visitor Centre, the 13km/8mi Ikuvik Trail, which begins across from the campground and climbs the shoulder of 671m/2,214ft Mt. Duval, is difficult to follow. Nonetheless, a hike partway up the mountain presents a bird's-eye **view** of town and a clear **view★★** down the fjord. Far more trodden, the 6km/4mi Ukama Trail begins at the road past the arena and follows boulder-strewn Duval River along a steep slope, past pools and waterfalls, to a large boulder at a fork in the river. From here, an unmarked trail continues about 8km/5mi to a campsite and a group of small lakes.

Boat Trip★

Departs Jul–Sept. One-way 1hr 20min. ⬯more than $100; minimum 2 people required. Warm clothing essential. Reservations: Angmarlik Interpretive Centre ☎867-473-8737. Even if a visit to Auyuittuq National Park is not planned, the trip down the fjord to the park entrance by boat or by snowmobile is impressive. Small wooden boats (some with interior cabins for warmth) ply the waters through the high mountains of Pullosi Canyon to Mt. Overlord. From there, visitors may hike in for two or three hours to get a hint of the park's grandeur.

Auyuittuq National Park★★

🕑*Open daily. ⬯$24.50 day-use fee. Accessible by boat trip (☍ see box) or snowmobile. Parks Canada Visitor Centre located in Pangnirtung will provide a list of operators; park visitors must register there in advance (open daily Mon–Fri 8:30am–noon & 1pm–5pm, Wed-Sun summer til 8pm). ☎867-473-2500. www.pc.gc.ca.*
This remote, yet most accessible Arctic park on the southeastern edge of Baffin Island is a stark landscape of perpetual ice, jagged peaks of 2,100m/7,000ft and glacier-scarred valleys that become deep fjords along a coast of sheer cliffs (up to 900m/3,000ft high). *Auyuittuq* [ow-you-EE-took] means "land that never melts" in Inuktitut. Fully one quarter of its 21,470sq km/8,290sq mi is covered by the Penny Ice Cap.

The park draws climbers from all over the world to scale its rugged peaks, including Mt. Thor, the highest uninterrupted cliff face in the world, and Mt. Asgard. The most visited region is **Akshayuk (formerly Pangnirtung) Pass**, a huge U-shaped trench that stretches almost 100km/60mi across the peninsula and rises to 390m/1,280ft.

IQALUIT★

300km/186mi south of Pangnirtung, on Baffin Island
Set on the slightly pitched bank of lovely Koojesse Inlet on Frobisher Bay, Iqaluit is a community of brightly coloured houses, apartment units and newly erected government buildings. The Capital of Nunavut, Iqaluit is the "bright lights, big city" of the Territory, even with an estimated population of only 6,699.

While residents here hunt, fish and carve, they work in transportation, communications and other industries in the region as well. Tourism and government work resulting from Nunavut's birth in 1999 are on the increase. More than 40

Auyuittuq National Park

© Nunavut Tourism

Hiking the Pass

Backpackers come to Akshayuk Pass for the challenge of hiking in this remote, yet breathtakingly grand landscape. Properly equipped and experienced hikers prepared to ford icy streams of glacial meltwater can hike the pass north to south in about 10 days. Most hikers, however, hire a boat from Pangnirtung to the Mt. Overlord warden station, then traverse 20km/12mi to the height of land along the pass at Summit Lake before returning to Pangnirtung. In addition to the cold-water crossings (pack neoprene socks), the trail offers plenty of moraine climbing, day scrambles, an Arctic Circle crossing and, always, stunning views of glaciers creeping down a valley flanked by peaks 1,200m/3,960ft and higher in five hues of blue. By early July the pass is usually free of snow and ice at the south entrance of Pangnirtung Fjord, and by late July, at North Pangnirtung Fjord. There is constant wind, little shelter, and much of the route is over glacial moraine (ridges of boulders). However, this is a spectacular trip for those willing to make the effort on their own, or with an organized tour.

percent of the residents here are non-Inuit and of those, 400 speak French as a first language.

For tourists, Iqaluit is a jumping-off point for destinations farther north, or for the **Itijjagiaq Trail**, which traverses the Meta Incognita Peninsula to Kimmirut, a 10-day hike. Yet, plenty of one- to three-day trips can be arranged here, including boat cruises, snowmobile or ski trips to Kimmirut, and floe-edge wildlife tours.

The town itself also warrants a visit of at least two days. A drive from the centre of town climbs up the bank through suburbs, each higher—and newer— than the previous one and offering more spectacular **views**★★ over the ruddy rock coastline. Tours of Iqaluit are available from Polynya Adventure and Coordination Ltd. (*867-979-6260 or 866-366-6784; www.polynya.ca*).

Unikkaarvik Centre★

Open Jun–Sept Mon–Fri9am6pm, Sat–Sun 1pm–4pm. Rest of the year Mon–Fri 9am–5pm, Sat 1pm–4pm. 866-686-2888.

Inside this helpful, friendly complex, among other things, is a list of things to do in town. The central theme of the exhibits is "Man on the Land", focusing on all three regions of Nunavut, the life of the Inuit, and dioramas of wildlife. The centre also houses the offices of Nunavut Tourism (*866-686-2888.*

www.nunavuttourism.com), which distributes a list of licensed tour operators. To the right is the Iqaluit Centennial Library, where the **Thomas Manning Collection**★ of northern books can be handled with gloves *(provided)*.

Nunatta Sunakkutaangit Museum★

Next to Unikkaarvik Centre in Bldg.#12. Open Jun–Sept daily 1pm–5pm. Rest of the year Tue–Sun 1pm–5pm. Contribution requested. 867-979-5537.

This small museum is housed in a renovated Hudson's Bay Company warehouse. Displays include Inuit clothing, tools, toys and carvings, pottery, sculptures and a changing collection of prints.

Qaummaarviit Territorial Park★★

12km/7mi west of Iqaluit across Peterhead Inlet. To visit the park by dog team, snowmobile, or boat ride (30min) in summer, contact Unikkaarvik Centre, 867-979-4636. For information, Nunavuk Parks 867-975-7700. www.nunavutparks.com.

Guides anchor their freighter canoes and Lake Winnipeg boats so visitors can follow a boardwalked trail past the sod houses to the island's other end, where meat caches (2ft-high circular rock fences) and graves with human ribs and skulls testify to the harsh environment.

Kitikmeot Region

The biggest centres in this region are Cambridge Bay (also known as Iqaluktuuttiaq) on the southeast end of Victoria Island, and Kugluktuk on the Coppermine River. More than 300km/186mi to the east of Kugluktuk lies the community of Bathurst Inlet, also known as Kitikmeot (summer population 20-25), on an inlet of the same name.

BATHURST INLET

48km/30mi north of the Arctic Circle.
This area of Nunavut is an especially good place to experience a mid-Arctic blend of wildlife and traditional culture plus the thrills of char fishing, rafting and canoeing on Arctic rivers.

Thought to be the oldest ecotourism lodge in Canada, the people at **Bathurst Inlet Lodge** have been devoted to interpreting the Arctic world for outdoor enthusiasts. In summer, knowledgeable Inuit/non-Inuit staff provide guided hikes and natural history interpretations of the barrens and river gorges of this part of the mainland.

Outpost camps for fishing or wildlife watching are also available, and activities from cross-country skiing to dogsledding can be arranged. Seven-day all-inclusive packages include air transportation from Yellowknife, accommodations, meals and guided excursions. *For information, access and reservations, contact Bathurst Inlet Lodge and Bathurst Arctic Services based in Yellowknife, NT:* ℘*867-873-2595. bathurstarctic.com.*

CAMBRIDGE BAY

On southeast coast of Victoria Island.
Canada's second-biggest island (after Baffin) is **Victoria Island**, located across the Queen Maud Gulf from the Arctic mainland. Kitikmeot's regional centre, Cambridge Bay is also its most populous community at 1300.

▤ **Info:** Nunavut Tourism.
℘866-686-2888.
www.nunavuttourism.com.

▶ **Location:** This region comprises the central Arctic, including a swath covering almost the entire northern coastline of mainland Canada up to the Gulf of Boothia, as well as King William Island, the southern section of Prince of Wales Island, and the eastern and southern parts of Victoria Island.

👁 **Don't Miss:** A trip out onto the land, hiking or skiing.

🕐 **Timing:** Recourse to outfitters is the best way to ensure your time is well-spent.

👥 **Kids:** These strenuous tours are for older children only.

Cambridge Bay is situated along the Northwest Passage; in fact, Roald Amundsen's ship, which sank after it was acquired by the Hudson's Bay Company, is still visible in the bay.

Arctic Coast Visitor Centre (℘*867-983-2842; www.nunavutparks.com/english/visitor-information/visitor-centres.html)*, across from the Elders' Centre, visitors can learn about Amundsen and other explorers who risked their lives searching for an easier route between Europe and Asia. In 2016 the first luxury cruise ship plied the waters of the Northwest Passage signalling a new epoch for this region.Staff will help arrange a local tour and provide a guidebook and information for Ovayok (Mount Pelly) Territorial Park. Char fishing and musk-ox viewing are also popular activities here. The Inuit name for Cambridge Bay, Iqaluktuuttiaq, means "good place with lots of fish."

Kivalliq Region★

The community of **Rankin Inlet**, one of the string-of-pearl hamlets along the northwest coast of Hudson Bay, serves as the main regional transportation and communications centre. Miles offshore, lovely **Marble Island** sits, surrounded by the waters of the bay. To the northwest, the town of Baker Lake occupies a fine site on its namesake body of water, the departure point for Sila Lodge, a popular spot for wildlife viewing on Wager Bay.

RANKIN INLET★ (KANGIQTINIQ)

1,560km/975mi north of Winnipeg, and about midway between Yellowknife and Iqaluit, Rankin Inlet is on the west coast of Hudson Bay, and on the north side of an inlet extending 27km/16m inland.

The centre of transporation and communications for the region, Rankin Inlet (population 2,577) is also a major hub for commercial airline flights. In summer, purple fireweed adds colour to an otherwise rocky, dusty place.

The community was established when the North Rankin Nickel Mine opened in the 1950s. Although the mine closed in 1962, the federal government set up a school and housing. People found work in construction, transportation, government services or their own business enterprises.

A walk on Deadman Island (part of **Marble Island★★**) reveals rock graves, some with crosses and whalebones, as well as spectacular **views** past the low cliffs of Marble Island and the bay.

Iqalugaarjuup Nunanga Territorial Park★

On east side of Iqalugaarjuk (Meliadine) River, 10km/6mi northeast of Rankin Inlet via road by arena, the only road out of town.
To hire a guide, contact the Kivalliq Regional Visitor Centre at the Rankin Inlet airport ☎867-645-3838.

Info: Nunavut Tourism. ☎866-686-2888. www.nunavuttourism.com; Kivalliq Regional Visitor Centre, located at Rankin Inlet airport. ☎867-645-3838.

Location: This region includes the west coast of Hudson Bay and the mainland west to the border of the Northwest Territories near Dubawnt Lake and the Thelon Wildlife Sanctuary, as well as Southampton Island and Coats Island.

Don't Miss: The trail in the Territorial Park.

Timing: Rankin Inlet, a major transport hub, will be your headquarters for excursions.

A foot-wide circular interpretive **trail** (*about 1km; to access, turn right at the fork to a parking lot with outhouse*) set in the flat, treeless valley, leads past more than two dozen 15C and 16C tent rings—circles of stones used to hold the skins down in the wind—at this major archaeological site. Another 100 are located on the other side of the Iqalugaarjuk River, where the Thule people channelled Arctic char into stone weirs in order to spear them in shallow water. Food caches, burial cairns and other indicators of a Thule hunting and fishing camp can be seen. Five sunken areas near the riverbank are Thule winter houses—once large and subterranean, covered with skin and sod—that these people lived in as far back as 800 years ago.

Local elders have constructed a sod house at the site, and cultural performances are often held here, with drum-dancing, throat-singing, games and story-telling. The park guidebook (*download at www.nunavutparks.com, or pick up at the airport Visitor Centre*) provides a key for numbers printed on the rocks, to explain various structures.

Thelon Wildlife Sanctuary★★

Nunavut, Northwest Territories

The Thelon is a remote, Denmark-size refuge of rolling, rocky tundra, threaded with meandering **sand eskers** so large, pilots navigate by them (eskers are ridges composed of the sedimentary remains of glacial rivers). The 1,000km/620mi-long **Thelon River**, designated a heritage waterway for its forest oasis along one stretch and for its rich Inuit history, flows through the sanctuary from its headwaters in Whitefish Lake to Baker Lake, west of Hudson Bay.

A BIT OF HISTORY

In 1900 young surveyor James Tyrrell—brother of Joseph Burr Tyrrell, for whom the Tyrrell Museum in Alberta is named—travelled through what is now the sanctuary. He was conducting a Dominion Lands Survey of the Keewatin (now Kivalliq) Region. His half-year journey by dogsled, canoe and on foot covered more than 7,000km/4,340mi. In 1927 the game preserve was formally established by the government to protect resident herds of musk-oxen. Today the Thelon expanse falls under Nunavut's jurisdiction.

VISIT

The contrast of high spruce groves in a sinuous oasis among the treeless, see-forever tundra is stunning, but it is primarily the resident animals that epitomize the Arctic context. The sanctuary and the land for miles around it attract white tundra wolves, hairy musk-oxen,

- **Info:** Nunavut Parks, Iqaluit, Nunavut. ☎867-975-7700. www.nunavutparks.com.
- **Location:** This colossal game preserve—Canada's largest—straddles both Nunavut and the Northwest Territories.
- **Timing:** An expedition here must be organized months ahead.

☺ Access by Air ☺

Access by chartered aircraft from Baker Lake, Fort Smith or Yellowknife or by canoe via lakes and the Thelon River. Nunavut Parks offers a list of licensed outfitters who organize trips and provide guides. The jumping-off point for canoe trips is Baker Lake.

barren-land grizzly, caribou, raptors and even moose (unusual this far north of the tree line). A 30m/99ft-high esker skirts Whitefish Lake. Though not within the borders of the sanctuary, the esker falls along the migratory path of the Beverly herd of caribou, once Canada's biggest, estimated at 275,000, and now extinct as of 2016. The Qamanirjuaq herd estimated at half a million, is now half that number. both these catastophes blamed on climate change, human encroachment and other factors.These are two of four of the once major herds of **barren-ground caribou** in the North. The caribou often use the eskers as highways. Wolves, bears and foxes may den in the eskers and often prey on the herd's young.

Canada's Newest Wilderness Lodge Offers Arctic Caribou Tour

Breathtaking caribou Spring migration tour departs from Yellowknife. Details through North America's last in-tact wilderness (The Barrens), contact Arctic Haven Wilderness Lodge (*☎819-923-0932 or 855-459-1794; www.arctichaven.ca*). Advance reservations and deposit are required.

© Nunavut Tourism

Caribou Viewing at Close Range

Near the headwaters of the Thelon River, I held my arms over my head like antlers, moving from one scrub spruce to the next, inching to within 10m/30ft of 10,000-plus snorting, bleating, grunting caribou. Spotted from the air minutes earlier, the herd was so massive it made the ground shake. Yet this conclave composed a mere fraction of the entire Beverly herd. We had come to see the annual caribou migration that occurs each summer after the flooding of the calving grounds. The thrill of watching wildlife at close range out in the wilds is an experience like no other. (Staying at an isolated fly-in camp in relative luxury elevates the experience even more!) During the remainder of the 14-day wildlife photo tour at Whitefish Lake's north camp, I stalked a solitary musk-ox, watched an abandoned wolf pup wail plaintively to the pack, and enjoyed the escapades of the camp *siksik* (Arctic ground squirrel) as it foraged around the cookhouse.

Set up to afford close access to the 100km/62ft Boomerang esker, our comfortable camp, complete with GPS (Global Positioning System) receiver, satellite phone, airplanes, motorboats, canoes, first-aid kits, pepper spray (bear repellent), great cooks, skilled pilots and top-notch wilderness guides, was *the* place to enjoy a fascinating wilderness experience. We slept in individual expedition tents with wooden floors, foam-cushioned beds, heaters and easy-to-use propane lanterns. A hot-shower hut and pit toilets stood nearby. The cookhouse was a cozy space with a well-stocked pantry, two propane stoves, an oil heater and a common room/library for guests.

One day, while heading out on Whitefish Lake for trout fishing, we were buzzed by one of the airplanes. Upon landing, the lead guide poked his head out the door, "We have a musk-ox—let's go." Back at camp, we grabbed our cameras and jumped into the float planes, flying to the site where the lone ox had been spotted. So far, our ox was oblivious to us and our whirring cameras. But, it was a hot, buggy day for this 400-pound beast—a perfect day to be aggravated. We crept closer until he started grazing toward us. Directly facing our small group, he started pawing the ground—not a good sign. Suddenly, the musk-ox simply turned and walked away, his shiny black skirt swaying in the wake. Gliding onto a nameless lake, we scrambled ashore. When our guide crouched, we did, and stalked quietly when he motioned to do so. I felt an ambitious flow of adrenaline. Biologists will tell you a solitary male ox is unpredictable: he can easily be intimidated and charge, but fortunately that didn't happen.

INDEX

INDEX

INDEX

INDEX

INDEX

🛏STAY

🍴EAT

MAPS AND PLANS

THEMATIC MAPS

MAPS AND PLANS

British Columbia/Rockies/Yukon

Prairie Provinces

Ontario

Quebec

Atlantic Provinces

Northwest Territories

MAP LEGEND

★★★ **Highly recommended**
★★ **Recommended**
★ **Interesting**

Sight symbols

Recommended itineraries with departure point

Church, chapel – Synagogue		Building described
Town described		Other building
Map co-ordinates locating sights		Small building, statue
Other points of interest		Fountain – Ruins
Mine – Cave		Visitor information
Windmill – Lighthouse		Ship – Shipwreck
Fort – Mission		Panorama – View

Other symbols

Interstate highway (USA)   US highway   Other route

Trans-Canada highway   Canadian highway   Mexican federal highway

Highway, bridge	Major city thoroughfare
Toll highway, interchange	City street with median
Divided highway	One-way street
Major, minor route	Pedestrian Street
15 (21) Distance in miles (kilometers)	Tunnel
2149/655 Pass, elevation (feet/meters)	Steps – Gate
△6288(1917) Mtn. peak, elevation (feet/meters)	Drawbridge - Water tower
Airport – Airfield	Parking – Main post office
Ferry: Cars and passengers	University – Hospital
Ferry: Passengers only	Train station – Bus station
Waterfall – Lock – Dam	Subway station
International boundary	Digressions – Observatory
State boundary, provincial boundary	Cemetery – Swamp
Winery	Long lines

Recreation

Gondola, chairlift	Stadium – Golf course
Tourist or steam railway	Park, garden
Harbor, lake cruise – Marina	Wildlife reserve
Surfing – Windsurfing	Wildlife/Safari park, zoo
Diving – Kayaking	Walking path, trail
Ski area – Cross-country skiing	Hiking trail

Sight of special interest for children

Abbreviations and special symbols

MP Marine Park	NP National Park	NF National Forest
NHS National Historic Site		PP Provincial Park

Visitor centre: Local -   Provincial -

16 Yellowhead Highway   Subway station (Montreal)

All maps are oriented north, unless otherwise indicated by a directional arrow

COMPANION PUBLICATIONS

MAPS OF CANADA

North America Road Atlas
♦ A geographically organized atlas with extensive detailed coverage of the USA, Canada and Mexico. Includes 246 city maps, distance chart, state and provincial driving requirements and a climate chart
♦ Comprehensive city and town index
♦ Easy to follow "Go-to" pointers

Map 585 Western USA and Western Canada
♦ Large-format map providing detailed road systems; includes driving distances, interstate rest stops, border crossings and interchanges.
♦ Comprehensive city and town index
♦ Scale 1:2,400,000 (1 inch = approx. 38 miles)

Map 583 Northeastern USA and Eastern Canada
♦ Large-format map providing detailed road systems; includes driving distances, interstate rest stops, border crossings and interchanges
♦ Comprehensive city and town index
♦ Scale 1:2,400,000 (1 inch = approx. 38 miles)

Château Frontenac, Quebec City
© F. Klingen/Michelin

INTERNET

Michelin is pleased to offer a route-
planning service on the Internet:
travelguide.michelin.com
www.viamichelin.com
Choose the shortest route,
a route without tolls, or the Michelin
recommended route to your destination.

**MICHELIN
IS CONTINUALLY
INNOVATING
FOR SAFER, CLEANER,
MORE ECONOMICAL,
MORE CONNECTED...
BETTER ALL-ROUND
MOBILITY.**

Tyres wear more quickly on short urban journeys.

? TRUE!

You tend to accelerate and brake more often when driving around town so your tyres work harder!
If you are stuck in traffic, keep calm and drive slowly.

Tyre pressure only affects your car's safety.

? FALSE!

Driving with underinflated tyres (0.5 bar below recommended pressure) doesn't just impact handling and fuel consumption, it will shave 8,000 km off tyre lifespan.
Make sure you check tyre pressure about once a month and before you go on holiday or a long journey.

If you only encounter **winter weather from time to time** - sudden showers, snowfall or black ice - **one type of tyre** will do the job.

TRUE!

The revolutionary **MICHELIN CrossClimate** - the very first summer tyre with winter certification - is a practical solution to keep you on the road whatever the weather.

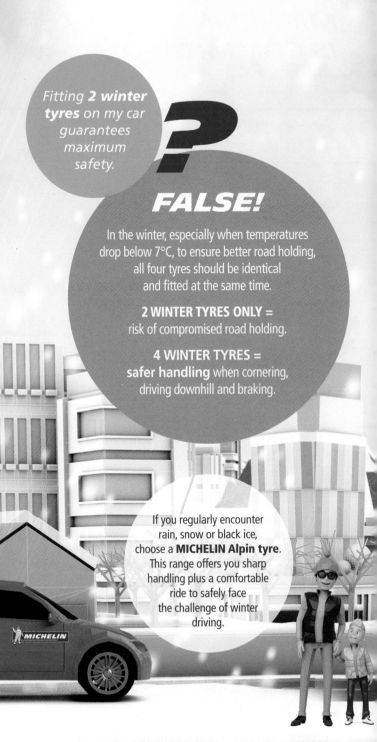

MICHELIN IS COMMITTED

▶ MICHELIN IS **GLOBAL LEADER IN FUEL-EFFICIENT TYRES** FOR LIGHT VEHICLES.

▶ **EDUCATING OF YOUNGSTERS IN ROAD SAFETY,**
NOT FORGETTING TWO-WHEELERS
LOCAL ROAD SAFETY CAMPAIGNS
WERE RUN IN **16 COUNTRIES**
IN 2015.

QUIZ

1 TYRES ARE BLACK SO WHY IS THE MICHELIN MAN WHITE?

Back in 1898 when the Michelin Man was first created from a stack of tyres, they were made of natural rubber, cotton and sulphur and were therefore light-coloured. The composition of tyres did not change until after the First World War when carbon black was introduced. But the Michelin Man kept his colour!

2 FOR HOW LONG HAS MICHELIN BEEN GUIDING TRAVELLERS?

Since 1900. When the MICHELIN guide was published at the turn of the century, it was claimed that it would last for a hundred years. It's still around today and remains a reference with new editions and online restaurant listings in a number of countries.

3 WHEN WAS THE "BIB GOURMAND" INTRODUCED IN THE MICHELIN GUIDE?

The symbol was created in 1997 but as early as 1954 the MICHELIN guide was recommending "exceptional good food at moderate prices". Today, it features on the MICHELIN Restaurants website and app.

If you want to enjoy a fun day out and find out more about Michelin, why not visit the l'Aventure Michelin museum and shop in Clermont-Ferrand, France:
www.laventuremichelin.com

A better way forward

NOTES